MODERN CHINA
Continuity and Change 1644 to the Present

BRUCE A. ELLEMAN
S. C. M. PAINE

Prentice Hall

Boston   Columbus   Indianapolis   New York   San Francisco   Upper Saddle River   Amsterdam   Cape Town   Dubai
London   Madrid   Milan   Munich   Paris   Montréal   Toronto   Delhi   Mexico City   São Paulo   Sydney
Hong Kong   Seoul   Singapore   Taipei   Tokyo

Editorial Director: Craig Campanella
Editorial Assistant: Lauren Aylward
Director of Marketing: Brandy Dawson
Senior Marketing Manager: Maureen Prado Roberts
Marketing Assistant: Marissa O'Brien
Senior Managing Editor: Ann Marie McCarthy
Production Project Manager: Debra Wechsler
Senior Operations Supervisor: Nick Sklitsis
Operations Specialist: Christina Amato
Senior Art Director: Maria Lange
AV Project Manager: Mirella Signoretto

Cover Designer: Suzanne Duda
Manager, Visual Research: Beth Brenzel
Manager, Rights and Permissions: Zina Arabia
Image Permission Coordinator: Vicki Menanteaux
Manager, Cover Visual Research & Permissions: Karen Sanatar
Cover Art: Bruce A. Elleman Private Photograph Collection
Full-Service Project Management: Kelly Ricci
Composition: Aptara®, Inc.
Printer/Binder: Hamilton Printing Co.
Cover Printer: Coral Graphics
Text Font: AGaramond

Credits and acknowledgments borrowed from other sources and reproduced, with permission, in this textbook appear on the appropriate page within the text or on page C-1.

Library of Congress Cataloging-in-Publication Data

Elleman, Bruce A.
    Modern China: continuity and change, 1644 to the present / Bruce A. Elleman & S. C. M. Paine.
        p. cm.
    Includes bibliographical references and index.
    ISBN-13: 978-0-13-600060-0
    ISBN-10: 0-13-600060-6
    1. China—History.
    2. China—Civilization.   I. Paine, S. C. M.   II. Title.
    DS735.E47 2009
    951—dc22   2009038203

10 9 8 7 6 5 4 3 2 1

Prentice Hall
is an imprint of

ISBN 13: 978-0-13-600060-0
ISBN 10:   0-13-600060-6

To Charlotte Ann and Thomas Smith Elleman

with love, respect, and gratitude.

Contents

List of Maps

List of Features

List of Tables

Preface

Why another text on China? Four reasons: This textbook places special emphasis on China's culture, warfare, and immediate neighbors, while its organization provides structural convenience not found in other surveys of modern Chinese history.

First, this textbook uses a comparative approach to bridge the cultural divide separating Chinese history from Western readers trying to understand it. It compares the embedded assumptions, patterns of analysis, and primary values that distinguish these two great civilizations, not to suggest the superiority of either but rather to reach a Western audience, who may be unaware that many of their core assumptions and values are not shared by others. This is not an attempt to understand China in its own terms, but in comparison to the West so as to bridge the cultural divide. Everyone gives lip service to culture: "It is important." There is an entire field devoted to its study: anthropology. Yet, there has been little attempt among historians to explain to a general audience, in broad terms, what distinguishes Chinese culture from that of the West and what has been the essential impact of such differences on the course of Chinese history. All generalizations are simplifications. Every Chinese is different. Yet, no one can keep straight the individuals making up a population exceeding 1 billion. The human mind requires generalizations in order to comprehend. The Introduction lays out an analytical framework for understanding the basic differences separating Chinese and Western culture.

Such an attempt is inherently controversial. Although all may agree that fundamental differences distinguish cultures, there is little consensus on any one list of essential differences. Because such features are unquantifiable—meaning that they are virtually impossible to measure with any accuracy—they are subject to dispute. Intangibles, however difficult to measure, cannot be removed from discussion simply on the grounds that reasonable people, who have carefully considered the evidence, do not always agree. Philosophical, moral, and religious values all are intangible, controversial, and yet of the utmost importance in people's lives.

For those in the West who reject the idea that there is an overarching shared Western culture, we have a question, a quotation, and a comment. Question: Have you mastered a non-Western foreign language and lived where it is generally spoken for several years in order to test your belief? If not, find acquaintances who—even if they cannot speak a non-European language—have lived abroad for a number of years. Question them. Contrasting a non-Western culture to that of the West places in sharp relief the overarching similarities among Western nations. We reached this realization while spending seven of the last twenty-five years conducting research in China, Japan, Taiwan, and Russia.

Quotation: Long ago in graduate school, a classmate complained about the inequities of the foreign language requirement that accorded Chinese the same weight as a Western language: "Western languages shouldn't count; they are mere dialects." She realized that her language studies of Chinese had required not only a linguistic but also a cultural leap unimaginable to her fellow Westerners studying Indo-European languages.

Comment: Americans, particularly of the Vietnam War generation, have bemoaned the general ignorance in the United States of foreign cultures and often point to an insensitivity to foreign values. At universities, they have promoted the increase in non-Western-history and area-studies requirements. They remember that America went into Vietnam ignorant of Vietnamese culture and paid an enormous price. China is the rising power of the twenty-first century. Americans are ill-advised to remain equally ignorant of a country whose population includes one out of every five people on earth, whose arsenals have nuclear weapons, and whose history has been one of enormous regional influence. However controversial the undertaking, it is essential for more Americans to understand the cultural assumptions separating them from their counterparts in China. This textbook does not pretend to provide the last word on this subject, but for many it may be the first word. The issue of culture should be raised and discussed in university classrooms.

Second, this textbook emphasizes the tragic role of warfare in Chinese history. Far more so than in most other countries, warfare has wracked Chinese society for the last two centuries: A cascade of internal rebellions, secession movements, and civil and foreign wars continued with only short interruptions from 1800 until the death of Mao Zedong in 1976. These include the White Lotus Rebellion on the eve of the nineteenth century, followed by the succession of civil and foreign wars and secession movements of the nineteenth century. After the fall of the Qing dynasty in the early twentieth century, endemic civil war broke out among China's many provincial warlords until this instability culminated in the Japanese invasion and the greatest of all civil wars that brought the Communists to power in 1949. Within a year of their victory, China was at war again, this time in Korea, but the Korean armistice did not bring internal peace. In the ensuing political campaigns of the Communist period—the Great Leap Forward and the Cultural Revolution—millions more Chinese perished. Chinese history cannot be understood without examining why so many tens of millions of Chinese have come to violent ends. On a human level, it is incumbent on this and succeeding generations not to forget the holocaust that has been a hallmark of modern Chinese history.

It is hard for a Western audience to grasp the magnitude and scope of this tragedy. The total European casualties for World War II have been estimated to be between 45 and 55 million people.[1] The total Chinese deaths from the Great Leap Forward and the ensuing Great Famine (1959–61) have been estimated to be in the 30-million range. (See Chapter 24, Section III.) This was just one political campaign—a campaign of ideas that had the human consequences of a military campaign. The total for all of the internal and foreign wars in the last two centuries of Chinese history may exceed 100 million. By comparison, as many Americans died in the American Civil War (1861–5) as in all other American wars combined: 615,000

Americans perished in that conflict.[2] It took another century before the full emancipation of African-Americans became law with the 1964 Civil Rights Act and the 1965 Voting Rights Act. Some would argue that the United States has yet to recover entirely from a civil war that took place a century and a half ago.

In contrast to the American Civil War, in China warfare was not confined to a single region, the central government did not weather the storm, the entire economy—both North and South—was ravaged, and the warfare continued not for years but for decades. Too many textbooks have given short shrift to warfare. Yet, no one in China has escaped war's catastrophic effects. To this day, they are felt by the generation whose families and formal education were torn asunder during the internal warfare of the Cultural Revolution (1966–76), who must deal with the environmental degradation accruing from decades of internal upheaval, and in whose minds the contours of China's tragic modern history are indelibly etched. Constant warfare and internal upheavals help explain the high value attached to social order by the Chinese government and people.

Third, all too often, the study of China has been done in semi-isolation from its neighbors. The authors of this textbook have spent years living not only in China and Taiwan, but also in Russia, Japan, Britain, and Australia, and have visited South Korea, Vietnam, Indonesia, Malaysia, the Philippines, Singapore, and Thailand. Modern Chinese history cannot be understood without a deep appreciation of the foreign influences that have bombarded China from all sides. Western textbooks generally give due attention to the Western European powers and to the United States. Some devote time to discussing the Japanese influence. None gives adequate attention to the activities of Russia. Most Western Sinologists do not read Russian, nor do most Chinese secondary sources emphasize Russia's extensive influence because Russian diplomats from the nineteenth century on consistently succeeded in promoting their country's national interests at Chinese expense. On a human level, this is not a story many Chinese want to tell. On a national level, Sino-Russian relations are so central to China's national security that the topic is generally classified. The authors learned about Russo-Chinese relations from years of research in the archives of Russia, China, Taiwan, Japan, and the United States, reading materials covering Russo-Chinese diplomatic relations from the eighteenth through the twentieth centuries.[3]

[1]Mortimer Chambers, Theodore K. Robb, Isser Woloch, Barbara Hanawalt, and Raymond Grew. *The Western Experience*, 7th ed., special edition (New York: McGraw-Hill, 1999), 1064.
[2]The United States Civil War Center, "Statistical Summary of America's Major Wars," http://www.cwc.lsu.edu/cwc/other/stats/warcost.htm; George Brown Tindall and David E. Shi, *America: A Narrative History*, 4th ed., vol. 2 (New York: W. W. Norton, 1996), 751.
[3]See Bruce A. Elleman, *Diplomacy and Deception: The Secret History of Sino-Soviet Diplomatic Relations, 1917–1924* (Armonk, NY: M. E. Sharpe, 1997) and *Wilson and China: A Revised History of the Shandong Question* (Armonk, NY: M. E. Sharpe, 2002); S. C. M. Paine, *Imperial Rivals: China, Russia, and Their Disputed Frontier: 1858–1924* (Armonk, NY: M. E. Sharpe, 1996).

For Americans, who tend to look at the world either in terms of bilateral U.S. relations or in terms of Western-Chinese relations, it is particularly important to consider China's relations with the non-Western great powers. We do not live in a bilateral but rather in a multilateral world. All important events and ideas do not emanate from the West, let alone from Washington, DC. It is critical for students to understand this and have the data to back up their understanding. China faces many strategic issues; its relationship with the United States is but one in a long list. Where appropriate, we intersperse information on China's relations with its most powerful and influential neighbors, Russia and Japan.

Fourth, this textbook has been specifically geared to the teaching requirements of the semester system. It is divided into four parts and a total of twenty-eight chapters. This corresponds either to two chapters per week in a fourteen-week semester or to one chapter per week in a two-semester course. The four parts can be broken in half for a midterm in a one-semester course or into quarters for midterms and finals in a two-semester course. Similarly, each chapter is divided into five sections so that students can read one section per day of the week if they so desire.

Teaching aids provided in Chinese textbooks have not matched the quality taken for granted in the commonly used textbooks for European and American history. We have attempted to integrate some of these learning aids into the current volume. While the narrative of the text focuses on political, diplomatic, military, and economic history, each chapter has highlighted sections that feature ethnic and social groups, economic sectors, influential books, festivals, and practices. In addition, there are numerous maps and tables to present information visually and statistically. Each chapter also provides a chronological table summarizing the events covered, and each of the four parts of the book provides an overarching thematic chronological table covering the economy, politics, society, culture, and diplomacy. For general bibliographic references, there is a section entitled "Teaching References" that lists key reference works, literature in translation, movies, and Web sites potentially useful for teachers and paper writers alike. Each chapter also provides a separate bibliography of the key sources for further reading or paper writing. In addition, the introductions to the four parts, as well as the introductions and conclusions to the individual chapters, are intended to be comprehensive in order to reinforce the most important points of that chapter or part.

The text has been designed to give maximum flexibility to teachers, accommodating courses with different time-period coverage, sub-field focuses, and reading assignments. Key ideas are referenced where relevant in each chapter so that skipping a section, a chapter, or even a part will not undermine the thematic unity. The text can comprise the entire reading list for a course or be one of numerous readings. Since the length of additional readings may vary from week to week, the clear subdivisions of the textbook chapters enable teachers to eliminate specific topics to make way for other readings and to tailor the textbook to highlight their particular interests. For instance, those wishing to emphasize cultural history should assign the Introduction comparing Chinese and Western culture. Those wishing to emphasize social history should consult the final section, "Teaching References," which provides extensive annotated references for anthologies of short stories, poetry, interviews, and short biographies, as well as currently available movies. Those wishing to emphasize politics and primary sources will find annotated references to document collections. The "Teaching References" also lists single-volume surveys on culture, Asian philosophy, Sino-U.S. relations, economic history, and more. For graduate students, the concluding chapter provides an analytical overview of overarching themes in Chinese history.

Finally, we have tried to make this textbook a good read. Chinese civilization is among the world's great civilizations. Chinese achievements have captivated the West from the moment literate travelers first came into contact with China over a millennium ago. Today China is rapidly restoring its former status as a great power whose influence is increasingly felt across the international stage. It is already a major trading partner of the United States, and there are fears that it may soon become a strategic competitor, with unknown but potentially momentous consequences. For these reasons alone, Chinese history is both important and fascinating. It has been the focus of our research for the last two and half decades. We hope that this textbook will help students to understand China better and become an introduction, not a conclusion, to their studies of it.

Bruce A. Elleman and S. C. M. Paine
Portsmouth, Rhode Island

Acknowledgments

This text has benefited from the insights offered by many. In alphabetical order they are Samuel Chu, The Ohio State University; Benjamin A. Elman, Princeton University; John F. Garofano, U.S. Naval War College; Marc A. Genest, U.S. Naval War College, Gertraude Roth Li, University of Hawai'i; Margarete Prüch, Internatssule Schloss Hansenberg, Geisenheim-Johannisberg, Germany; Joshua R. Rovner, U.S. Naval War College; Robert E. Schnare, U.S. Naval War College; Arthur Waldron, University of Pennsylvania; Karl F. Walling, U.S. Naval War College; and Miin-ling Yu, Academic Sinica, Taipei, Taiwan. It has also benefited from the comments provided by numerous readers arranged by Pearson: James M. Carter, Drew University; Edward Dreyer, University of Miami; David Kenley, Elizabethtown College; Colin Mackerras, Griffith University, Nathan, Australia; Wing Chung Ng, University of Texas at San Antonio; Juanjuan Peng, Georgia Southern University; Jackie Sheehan, University of Nottingham, Nottingham, United Kingdom; Michael Sheng, Missouri State University; Peter Worthing, Texas Christian University; and Pei-yi Wu, Queens College. We are especially grateful to our department chairmen, John B. Hattendorf and John H. Maurer, and former department chairman George W. Baer, who arranged for two year-long leaves of absence to conduct research. Bradford A. Lee's framework concerning "nested" wars has been invaluable for understanding China. Our other colleagues in the Strategy and Policy Department and the Maritime History Department at the U.S. Naval War College have also educated us about the influence of war on politics and the interrelationship of civil and military institutions.

At the Henry E. Eccles Library at the United States Naval War College, we are grateful for the generous help of Heidi Garcia, Alice K. Juda, and Robin A. Lima, who tracked down a wide variety of obscure sources. Likewise, we are grateful to the library staffs of the Australian National University, Harvard University, the National Library of Australia, Princeton University, and the University of Hokkaido. At Prentice Hall, we are indebted to Charles Cavaliere for transforming our manuscript and map fragments into a publication and to Lauren Alyward for locating all the photographs, George Chakvetadze and Mirella Signoretto for creating such wonderful maps, Charles Morris for obtaining copyrights, Debra Wechsler for production, Helen Greenberg for copyediting, and Kelly Ricci for formatting. We would like to express special thanks to Heather McCallum, who ten years ago was looking for someone interested in writing a new textbook on Chinese history. It has been a far larger project than we ever imagined, but we have become better educated in the process. Finally, we give our deepest thanks to our children, Anna and Steven, who have assisted us at every stage of this endeavor, our parents, who have always been so supportive, and the author's brother, Thomas M. Paine for his suggestions—artistic and grammatical. In an undertaking of this breadth, inevitably there are errors, which, alas, are ours alone. It is important to emphasize that the thoughts and opinions expressed in this textbook are those of the authors and are not necessarily those of the U.S. government, the U.S. Navy Department, the U.S. Department of Defense, or the U.S. Naval War College.

Technical Note

The Romanizations for Chinese names and words have been rendered in *pinyin*. The Name Index and Subject Index also provide cross references to the Wade-Giles system commonly used during much of the twentieth century. The only exceptions are Sun Yat-sen; Wellington Koo; Chiang Kai-shek; Chiang's son, Chiang Ching-kuo; and their Nationalist Party successors, Lee Teng-hui and Ma Ying-jeou. In *pinyin* they are known, respectively, as Sun Zhongshan or Sun Wen, Gu Weijun, Jiang Jieshi, Jiang Jingguo, Li Denghui, and Ma Yingjiu. In the Name Index and Subject Index, other common transliterations are given in parentheses after the *pinyin* version: Guangzhou (Canton) or Li Hongzhang (Li Hung-chang). Place names on Taiwan are rendered in English according to Taiwanese conventions, hence Taipei (not Taibei), Kaohsiung (not Gaoxiong) and Keelung (not Jilong). Certain Chinese words have also entered into the English language, such as kungfu (not gongfu) and Tai Chi (not taiji).

The terms "Chinese" and "China" are ambiguous. In English, "Chinese" can mean either a specific ethnic group or the citizens of a country. In this textbook, "Chinese" refers to the citizens of the state called China, while "Han" refers to the Han Chinese ethnic group constituting over 90 percent of Chinese citizens. Thus, unless specifically stated, "Han" does not refer to the Han dynasty (206 BC–220 AD). Likewise, the terms "Qing empire" or "lands of the former Qing empire" refer to the territories under Manchu rule by the late nineteenth century. In addition to the eighteen core provinces of China, this includes Tibet, Xinjiang, Mongolia, Manchuria, and Taiwan. "China proper," "intramural China," and "the core provinces of China" refer to the provinces south of the Great Wall (intramural) that have long been populated by a Han majority. In the north and west, these lands also approximate the maximum extent of settled agriculture. Beyond lay

the lands of the nomads. From 1911 to 1949, "China" and "Chinese" refer to the government, nation, empire, and general population of the Republic of China and, after 1949, to those of the People's Republic of China (PRC). "Taiwan" and "Taiwanese" refer to the inhabitants of Taiwan, with no racial implications, while "Republic of China" (ROC) after 1949 refers to Taiwan's government up to the present.

English-language sources often refer to the Chinese Nationalist Party as the Kuomintang (KMT) or the Guomindang (GMD). For simplicity, this textbook refers to the party as the "Nationalist Party" and its members as the "Nationalists." Lowercase "nationalist" is used according to the dictionary meaning of the term. "Communist" refers to a member of the Chinese Communist Party (CCP).

The word "peasant" has been used to describe farmers, agricultural laborers, and pastoralists for both the Qing and later periods. There is no precise uncumbersome translation for the Chinese word *nong*, which traditionally had no class implications and could therefore apply equally to the rural rich and rural poor. The word *guanxi* has been used to describe human networks both in the Qing dynasty and in modern times. The term is not of Japanese origin, as some believe, but dates to the Ming dynasty.

This textbook has used "modernization" to refer to the ability to use, produce, and create state-of-the-art technologies. Over time, what is state-of-the-art changes so that "modernization" is a relative term. "Westernization" refers to the use of westernized institutions, including political, judicial, economic, military, educational, and other institutions, although there is much variation. "The West" includes Western Europe, the United States, Canada, Australia, and New Zealand. As a result of World War I and the ensuing Great Depression, two powerful Western critiques of the West developed—fascism and communism—which are treated separately from the liberal-democratic West.

Finally, this book is intended as a textbook, not as a scholarly monograph. Therefore, with few exceptions, it has no endnotes. The relevant sources for the information in each chapter can be found in the bibliography at the end of the chapter. We realize that information concerning Russia and Japan may be unfamiliar to many China specialists and that statistics on China remain sketchy even in the current period. The purpose of the textbook is not to bog down in details but to present a framework for understanding Chinese history and, by extension, modern China.

About the Authors

Bruce A. Elleman is a Research Professor in the Maritime History Department, Center for Naval Warfare Studies, at the U.S. Naval War College, and author of *Diplomacy and Deception: The Secret History of Sino-Soviet Diplomatic Relations, 1917–1927* (Armonk, NY: M. E. Sharpe, 1997); *Modern Chinese Warfare, 1795–1989* (London: Routledge, 2001, translated into Chinese); *Wilson and China: A Revised History of the Shandong Question* (Armonk, NY: M. E. Sharpe, 2002); *Japanese-American Civilian Prisoner Exchanges and Detention Camps, 1941–45* (London: Routledge, 2006); and *Moscow and the Emergence of Communist Power in China, 1925–30: The Nanchang Uprising and the Birth of the Red Army* (London: Routledge, 2009).

S. C. M. Paine is a Professor in the Strategy and Policy Department at the U.S. Naval War College and author of *Imperial Rivals: China, Russia and Their Disputed Frontiers* (Armonk, NY: M. E. Sharpe, 1996), winner of the Jelavich Book Prize, and *The Sino-Japanese War of 1894–1895: Perceptions, Power and Primacy* (Cambridge: Cambridge University Press, 2002); and co-editor with Bruce A. Elleman of *Naval Blockades and Seapower; Strategies and Counter-strategies, 1805–2005* (London: Routledge, 2006) and *Naval Coalition Warfare: From the Napoleonic War to Operation Iraqi Freedom* (London: Routledge, 2008).

Introduction

A Cultural Framework for Understanding China

Only when a man invites insult will others insult him.
Only when a family invites destruction will others destroy it.
Only when a state invites invasion will others invade it.

The Taijia says,

When Heaven sends down calamities,
There is hope of weathering them;
When man brings them upon himself,
There is no hope of escape.[1]

Confucius (551–479 BC)

Where armies have dwelt thistles and thorns grow.
Behind battles follow years of hunger.[2]

Laozi (604?–531 BC)

This textbook provides an overview of modern Chinese history from the creation of the Qing dynasty in 1644 to the retirement of President and Party General-Secretary Jiang Zemin in 2004 and the early years of the new Chinese leader Hu Jintao. It is aimed at a Western audience. Historically, Chinese and Westerners have perceived, analyzed, and understood the world and humankind in fundamentally different ways. Crossing the boundary separating these two venerable civilizations requires an understanding of cultural differences. This chapter will attempt to bridge this divide by presenting a framework for understanding Chinese culture's and society's enduring features. It will construct a cultural bridge out of generalizations, contrasting contemporary Western mind sets with those of the traditional Chinese cultural world. These generalizations will help clarify why the Chinese have made the choices that have channeled their history in particular directions.

To construct a cultural bridge, this text will use Western civilization as a counterpoint to Chinese civilization. By "West" is meant the civilization of Europe, North America, Australia, and New Zealand. While there is much variation among these areas, there is also much in common. It is important to note that any civilization is a moving target. It evolves over time; Western civilization in the twenty-first century is not identical to Western civilization in the nineteenth century, nor is Chinese civilization a fixed entity.

In the case of China, the name for the civilization, the empire, the nation, the citizens, and the race all derive from one linguistic root. There is no equally comprehensive term for the West. Western civilization does not define itself in terms of a succession of empires or dynasties. Unlike China, European empires have never occupied the same territories nor, since the Roman Empire at least, have they endured for long. Every empire has a distinct name, such as the Roman, Napoleonic, or Nazi, whose different names indicate discontinuities, not continuities. The core lands of Western civilization are mainly in Europe, but these lands are populated by peoples speaking diverse languages and belonging to distinct nations. Thus, language and nationality do not define the West either, nor do race or ethnicity. In fact, the English language has distinct words to express these differences: "the West" for the civilization; "Europe" for its geographic core; "England," "France," and so on for its political parts; "Caucasian," "Slav," and so on for its ethnic groups and races.

The term "China," however, has encompassed all of these things and continues to be used with different meanings, depending on the preoccupations of the moment. When this book refers to "Chinese civilization," it means the civilization of the dominant ethnic group, the Han, who comprise the overwhelming majority of the Chinese population and who speak one of the many dialects of Chinese that are all written in Chinese characters. Although the Yellow River Basin constituted the original center of Chinese civilization and the home of the earliest recorded dynasties, the Han migrated north, south, and later west into those lands suitable for settled agriculture that comprise the core territories of China proper. The name "Han" comes from the Han dynasty (206 BC–220 AD), whose long rule helped create a unified civilization. While Chinese culture is primarily Han culture, China's minority peoples, in particular the Manchus, have exerted great influence. Conversely, over the millennia, many other ethnic groups gradually adopted the Chinese language and Han customs, so they were considered Han.

For thousands of years, the Han thought of their homeland as an empire and took great pride in its territorial extent. Only the advent of Marxism-Leninism transformed "empire" from a laudatory into a pejorative term in Chinese thinking. Much of Classical Chinese philosophy has focused on the problems of empire and the exercise of power. How should the empire be maintained? How should the sovereign rule? How should his subjects be organized? What obligations should they have to each other? Traditionally, the Chinese have sought to answer these questions by examining their own history, their classical literature from the humanities, and a golden age of dynastic rule on the very fringes of human memory and imagination. Historically, their answers have emphasized social relations, proper decorum, and obligations between superiors and inferiors.

This approach to knowledge and to the problems of governance contrasts to that of the West, which has not focused specifically on the humanities or on the proper ordering of social relations. Rather, the Western turn of mind has emphasized a combination of Greek analytical reasoning employing analysis, synthesis, and inductive and deductive reasoning; a Roman primary emphasis on law and institutions to organize society; and a preoccupation with natural rights originating from the Christian belief that every individual possessed a soul and, therefore, had certain rights both inherent in that person's very humanity and superseding those recognized by any government.

The discussion so far has been very general. The remainder of this chapter will flesh out this framework by focusing on specific cultural characteristics defining traditional China. They have been categorized in spatial and temporal terms: top-down, radial, bottom-up, cyclical, and retrospective. Time and space have been chosen as organizing principles to provide as value-neutral an analytical framework as possible

and thereby minimize the imposition of categories drawn from Western civilization on Chinese civilization. The rationale is that all humans live in time and space.

The first set of elements can be conceptualized as the vertical exercise of power from the top down. The second set of cultural elements can be thought of as radial in nature, meaning that they emanate from a common conceptual point like spokes branching out from the hub of a wheel. The third set of cultural elements is bottom-up in constitution, that is, they are not orchestrated by the top ranks of society but rather permeate that society as a whole. These first three sets of cultural elements—top-down, radial, and bottom-up—are spatial. They concern the allocation of power among humans. The last two sets are temporal. They concern the laws governing the natural world in which humans live. The fourth set of cultural elements is cyclical, while the fifth and final category of cultural elements is retrospective in nature.

These five sets of elements—top-down, radial, bottom-up, cyclical, and retrospective—will be discussed at length below. Taken together, they help provide a framework for understanding China, just as the study of Greco-Roman and Judeo-Christian beliefs is essential for understanding the West. The specific terms and ideas introduced in this chapter will be referred to throughout the book as a shorthand to explain how and why many important events in modern Chinese history took place.

I. Top-down Characteristics: Confucianism, Militarism, Legalism, and Sinification

This section will examine four important top-down vertical elements defining traditional Chinese culture. The top controlled the rest by means of this top-down flow of power. Chronologically, the ideas started with Confucius, but they continued to develop with the innovations of Mencius and the Legalists, whose views merged into State Confucianism by the time of the early Han dynasty to create a powerful ideology of civil rule. (See Table I.1.) The military doctrine underpinning civil power came from Sunzi, while Sinification became the means to transmit this civil-military ideology to others.

Confucianism has constituted the bedrock of Chinese thinking for the last two millennia. Confucius lived during the middle period of the Eastern Zhou dynasty known as the Spring and Autumn period (771–484 BC). This was a time of small feuding states, forever striving to find new ways to organize their governments both to fend off attack and to extend their influence over others. The relatively large number of independent states allowed for a wide range of competing ideas, like the many city-states that brought ancient Greek

Table 1.1   Chinese Dynasties and Philosophers

Dynasty	Duration	Schools of Thought
Xia dynasty	2205–1766 BC	Neolithic, preliterate
Shang dynasty	1766–1122 BC	Bronze Age, literate
Zhou dynasty	1122–222 BC	
Western Zhou period	1122–771 BC	
Eastern Zhou period	770–222 BC	Golden age of Confucianism
Spring and Autumn period	771–484 BC	Laozi (604?–531 BC), Daoism Confucius (551–479 BC)
Warring States period	484–221 BC	Period of dynastic decline Mozi (480–397 BC) Sunzi (440–381 BC), *Art of War* Mencius (371–289? BC) Zhuangzi (360–280 BC) Xunzi (298–238 BC) Han Fei (280?–233 BC), Legalism
Qin dynasty	221–206 BC	Unification of China under Legalism
Han dynasty	206 BC–220 AD	Classic period in Chinese history Buddhism spreads to China
Three Kingdoms period	220–280	
Western Jin dynasty	265–316	
Eastern Jin dynasty and Sixteen States	317–420	Faxian (c. 337–c. 422) brings Buddhist texts to China
Southern and Northern dynasties	386–581	Damo (470–543), Zen Buddhism
Sui dynasty	581–618	
Tang dynasty	618–907	Tang poetry and painting Zenith of Buddhism in China
Five dynasties and Ten Kingdoms period	907–960	
Song dynasty	960–1279	Zhu Xi (1130–1200),
Northern Song	960–1126	Neo-Confucianism
Southern Song	1127–1279	Song poetry and painting Development of printing
Yuan dynasty	1279–1368	Mongol conquest
Ming dynasty	1368–1644	Return to Han Chinese rule
Qing dynasty	1644–1911	Manchu conquest Sun Yat-sen (1866–1925)

Note: Shaded areas indicate eras of unified rule under one dynasty. Unshaded areas indicate periods with multiple dynasties and/or kingdoms. Dating especially prior to the Qin dynasty is subject to dispute. The dates used come from Hugh B. O'Neill, *Companion to Chinese History* (New York: Facts on File Publications, 1987), and Zhang Dainian, *Key Concepts in Chinese Philosophy*, Edmund Ryden, trans. (New Haven, CT: Yale University Press, 2002), 487. The periods for unification come from Joseph Needham, *Science and Civilisation in China*, vol. 1 (Cambridge: Cambridge University Press, 1965), Table 5, "Chinese Dynasties."

civilization and, much later, the Renaissance to their height. Much of what we think of as Chinese culture today was established at this time. This period differed from the long succession of unitary dynasties, which later made State Confucianism orthodoxy and discouraged what were condemned as heterodox beliefs.

According to the teachings of Confucius (551–479 BC), a classical scholar and itinerant political adviser, the sovereign, like the father in a traditional family, was the focus of political and moral authority. Just as the senior male dominated each Chinese family, the sovereign stood at the pinnacle of the Chinese social hierarchy. While those from below might offer advice, only those above made decisions and issued orders. Mencius, the Legalists, and the Mohists then branched out from this basic idea. Even Mozi, the father of Mohism, who espoused a doctrine of universal love and whose ideas did not form a part of State Confucianism, emphasized social hierarchy.

Although Confucius was not very successful during his own lifetime, the subsequent and evolving interpretation of his work as embodied in State Confucianism exerted an enormous influence over the rest of Chinese history. Confucian thinking focused on two general areas: (1) the organization of society and (2) the training of scholar-officials to govern that society. With these, Confucius provided both the ends (a proper organization of society) and the means (a lettered bureaucratic elite) to achieve those ends. This meant that government leaders and aspiring officials alike latched on to his ideas.

Confucius viewed human society as organized from the top down. Government officials, whom Confucius called "gentlemen," constituted the lettered elite qualified to execute the king's orders and administer China. These scholar-officials mastered history, classical literature, and state rituals to gain the privilege of serving their sovereign. Just as a tree has its roots, society's roots were the common man, whom Confucius called the "small man." In a predominantly agrarian society, years of study and preparation to take the demanding civil service examination to become a scholar-official was one of the only sanctioned methods for social mobility. Peasants, who occasionally acquired great wealth and a high station through hard work, pushed their children to study to become part of the scholar elite. Chinese students turned to Confucius to chart their path to earthly success.

Using the family as a model, Confucius described a whole series of interlocking social obligations binding all into the overarching power structure of vertical authority. Inferiors had the obligation of obedience to their superiors, while superiors had the obligation of benevolence to inferiors. Children should be filial to their parents, especially to their father and male ancestors. Adults should, in turn, be respectful to local authority figures, who should be obedient to local

officials, and so on up the vertical hierarchy, with the sovereign at its summit. Confucianism focused on harmonizing human relations through the inculcation of shared rules of etiquette and the performance of rituals. It sought to prescribe the appropriate behavior for individuals to create social harmony. Rituals served the spirit world in order to bring good fortune to the human world.

The ruler at the top of the social pyramid acquired his authority directly from heaven through the mandate of heaven. According to Confucian beliefs, if the sovereign conducted all of the necessary rituals, remained benevolent to his subjects, and fulfilled his duties, heaven would favor him with its mandate. As long as the sovereign retained the mandate of heaven, all members of society were expected to conform to this hierarchical model and remain in their respective sphere. Mencius radicalized the theory to argue that rulers retained their mandate to the extent that they ruled for the benefit of the people. He implied that rulers without righteousness or benevolence should be deposed. "Revolution" is the word for a change in the mandate of heaven. Many Chinese interpreted dynastic continuity and dynastic change in terms of heaven approving virtuous rulers while withdrawing approval from the unjust. Ever since, governmental legitimacy in China has rested in part on an ethical foundation. These Confucian views concerning the mandate of heaven have not disappeared in China.[3]

Absent from this discussion were notions of individual rights and liberty that so preoccupied Western philosophical debates. People had obligations, not rights. By the eighteenth century, the Anglophone West (in this period meaning Britain and its colonies, including those in North America) had largely rejected both the divine origin of social obligations and an unquestioning deference to seniority, relying more on reason to guide action. The Anglophone West also gravitated toward competition, emphasizing the benefits from competing interests. Doctrines on the separation of state power and laissez-faire economics assumed that competition rather than harmony yielded justice in politics and prosperity in economics. Individuals acted according to their own interests but within an overarching legal system setting universalistic rules. In China the reverse was the case: The web of particularistic relations created the overarching but opaque framework under which the general Confucian principles applied, each according to its category.

Whereas traditional China revered hierarchy and assumed inequality, the West increasingly emphasized social equality, although the elimination of glaring violations like slavery took centuries. In the universalistic Western schema, all possessed basic underlying equality affording greater freedom to express individuality. Humans were assumed to share certain traits taking precedence over any subsequent social or legal inequalities. This meant limitations on exercising power over others. In the particularistic Chinese schema, differences distinguishing individuals took precedence. At birth, fate, family, and birth order shunted individuals into prescribed paths of life, while the power of superiors over inferiors was close to absolute. This meant less leeway for individual expression, particularly at the expense of the group. Instead of equality, the Chinese stressed equity. Equitable treatment took into account seniority, kinship, gender, and other status determinants and also demanded reciprocity. Relationships flowed in both directions so that reciprocity softened the hierarchy. (See Table I.2.)

The Spring and Autumn period in which Confucius lived was followed by an increasingly unstable era known as the Warring States period in which Sunzi (Sun-tzu), China's preeminent military strategist, lived. Whereas Confucius focused on the moral foundations of authority, Sunzi emphasized the military underpinnings of power. Although the Chinese emphasize their venerable tradition of civil rule as embodied in Confucianism, the reality has included warfare of breathtaking scale and frequency. Only with the Napoleonic wars of the early nineteenth century and the rise of the modern nation-state did the soldiers deployed in European battles number in the hundreds of thousands, whereas huge numbers have characterized Chinese warfare for many centuries.

Sunzi wrote *The Art of War* in order to instruct kings how best to take and retain power. For Sunzi, politics, diplomacy, and warfare constituted an unbroken continuum. Warfare was but one point along the broad spectrum of conflict, whose optimal resolution avoided bloodshed altogether. He emphasized diplomacy, deception, intelligence, spies, assassins, psychological warfare, and other methods short of fighting. According to Sunzi, a successful general could come from any station in life. Periodically, ambitious Chinese youths and failed imperial-examination candidates dreamed of becoming great generals in order to take power by force. The Chinese Classic *The Water Margin* (also translated as *All Men Are Brothers*) is a romantic tale about a group of young men who reject society for banditry in the pursuit of personal power. Young Chinese, like the leader of the Taiping rebellion, Hong Xiuquan, or the Communist leader, Mao Zedong, were raised with the belief that military means could catapult them to power.

Under normal circumstances, the state monopolized the exercise of military power to keep the ruling sovereign on the throne. In periods of instability, Sunzi's teachings had revolutionary implications because he argued that military leaders should ignore misguided orders from the emperor. Mutinies played critical roles in the Manchu conquest, the Manchu overthrow, the warlord period, and the Chinese civil war, when China was ruled by its generals or their equivalent. Sunzi's *The Art of War* has also influenced the West, where it has become a basic text on military and business strategy.

Table I.2   Comparison of Traditional Western and Chinese Values

	Ancient Greek Values and Mode of Analysis	Ancient Chinese Values and Mode of Analysis
Field of Focus	part	whole
Method of Analysis	categorization of the part	relationship of the part to the whole
View of the Natural World	simplicity and isolation	complexity and interrelation
Intellectual Goal	truth	the Way (*Dao*)
Intellectual Focus	search for abstract principles	search for concrete application
Basic Social Unit	the individual	the group
Motive Force	personal agency	collective agency
Social Priority	individual choice	social harmony
Method of Social Control	rights	obligations
View of Social Relations	low context*	high context*
Goal of Law	fairness, universal principle	social harmony, high context*

*Low and high context concern the number of factors needed to be taken into account to understand a situation.

Note: This table and Table I.6 summarize the key differences pointed out by Richard E. Nisbett in his book *The Geography of Thought: How Asians and Westerners Think Differently . . . and Why* (New York: Free Press, 2003). Dr. Nisbett, a psychologist, bases his findings on numerous psychological studies done in both the United States and the People's Republic of China, as well as in other Asian countries, on subjects from the United States, Hong Kong, the People's Republic of China, Korea, and Japan. In the case of the United States, the studies included Americans of both Chinese and non-Chinese descent.

While Sunzi emphasized coercion against foreign states, the Legalists emphasized coercion at home through laws maximizing state power. Unlike the Confucianists, they assumed human nature to be evil, which required strict education and harsh laws. The Confucian disciple Xunzi (Hsün-tzu; 310–220 BC) recommended state-sponsored education focusing on mastery of the Classics and the performance of rituals to mold the human character to shun evil and to support the social hierarchy. Without hierarchy, he believed there would be chaos. Nevertheless, his focus on education and ethical rule meant a corresponding emphasis on righteousness over coercion. Effective rulership meant ethical rulership, which in turn required the rectification of names. Like Confucius, Xunzi believed that concepts and meanings should match: "[I]f the names and the realities to which they apply are made fixed and clear, so that he [the sovereign] can carry out the Way . . . then he may guide the people with circumspection and unify them."[4]

Xunzi's disciple Han Fei transformed some of these ideas into a more coercive philosophy. Han Fei and the Legalists rejected the Confucian emphasis on the ritual and moral basis of power. Because they considered human nature to be evil, they believed the Confucian ideal of virtue in government to be unattainable and, therefore, dangerous to attempt. Like Sunzi, they stressed secrecy, deception, and manipulation. Effective kings were keen judges of character. They monopolized information, rewards, and punishments to manipulate their subordinates into obedience. "If the ruler lends even a little of his power to others, then superior and inferior will change places."[5]

This system required clear laws, hence the name Legalism. Kings ruled through compulsion in a system of punitive accountability. Expediency guided power. Even the most loyal retainers were expendable. The ruthless enforcement of laws, the requirement of unquestioning loyalty, and the demand for the fulfillment of promises guaranteed effective rule. Because mercy undermined blind obedience, it threatened effective rule. People obeyed their sovereign not out of mutual interests but out of fear of retribution. All were suspect, even one's own children. In this bleak world, Han Fei believed: "Prepare as you may against those who hate you, calamity will come to you from those you love."[6]

Although Han Fei's system is called Legalism, he actually provided the means to rule in a personalistic, not an institutional, system where the key to power lay in the prevention of cliques and coups and in an effective chain of command. Sovereigns kept their subordinates divided in order to rule. They ruthlessly suppressed unorthodox ideas

and eliminated those who overstepped their office. The aristocracy found such ideas highly threatening, since they became the primary targets of coercive rule. Nevertheless, elements of Legalism merged into State Confucianism. In addition to the ethical foundations of rule emphasized by Confucius and Mencius, governance in China has been characterized by harsh punishments and brutal treatment of dissent. In the Qing dynasty harsh punishments were evident in the suppression of rebellions, which entailed the slaughter of men, women, and children even after their capitulation. Chiang Kai-shek and Mao Zedong used a broader reading of Legalism to eliminate followers whose loyalty they suspected.

Although different elements of State Confucianism received different emphasis at different times, the ideology had enormous influence in China and beyond, because China exported it and many neighbors emulated it. "Sinification" (or "Sinicization") derives from the ancient Greek word for the Chinese, *sinai*. It means the process or intent of making others more like the Chinese through gradual adoption of Han ways of thought, government, education, religion, dress, and food. The Chinese faith in the superiority of their own civilization led them to extend its bounds to the surrounding minority peoples.

In traditional China, when barbarian peoples were considered at all, it was assumed that they would eventually adopt Chinese ways or remain marginalized by their cultural backwardness. Sinification presupposed Chinese superiority. Historically, this superiority was considered to be not just cultural but also political, economic, military, technological, educational, moral, and even racial. For centuries Han Chinese never doubted their own superiority, given their overwhelming cultural dominance over all of their neighbors. Like the peoples of other great civilizations, they assumed that their own belief system was correct, while those of others were fundamentally flawed; others would either have to accept Chinese ways or remain benighted "barbarians," a pejorative term designating un-Sinified outsiders and used in Chinese writing well into the twentieth century. Chinese applied their notion of top-down exercise of power to the surrounding barbarian peoples. Confucius described all non-Han peoples as barbarians in *The Analects*. The Chinese have distinguished civilized China from all other uncivilized cultures ever since.

Like westernization and globalization, Sinification was a gradual process that included such nonviolent means as trade. Non-Han people either within the empire or on the periphery acquired technology and fine goods from China. In the process, some adopted Chinese ways. Intermarriage also became a means for Sinification. Often, Chinese emperors sent Han women as gifts to tributary leaders as a way of Sinifying them. Some of the children of such unions grew up speaking a Chinese dialect as well as the local language. Sinification has been so successful in China that well over 90 percent of the people enter "Han Chinese" on official census forms, even though there are fifty-five recognized national minorities with their own distinct languages and seven largely mutually unintelligible families of Chinese dialects.

The Chinese written language, based on thousands of distinct ideographs, became another element of Sinification. As in medieval Europe, where there were hundreds of different spoken languages but the unifying written language was Latin, Chinese characters have been used throughout China and formed the foundation of the traditional writing systems of Korea, Japan, and Vietnam. (See the feature below.) The Classical Chinese language, like Latin, provided the means of communication for educated persons throughout much of East Asia, regardless of their native language. The Chinese classics, written in the Classical language, were the texts used to acquire proficiency. Through these texts, students also acquired a Chinese education and exposure to Chinese ways of governance. Elite education became another vital avenue for Sinification as China's Sinified neighbors adopted Chinese political institutions, laws, tax system, religions, painting, calligraphy, high culture, and Confucianism.

CALLIGRAPHY

Calligraphy is one of the oldest Chinese art forms. The *Kangxi Dictionary* listed over 47,000 distinct characters. These characters have been rendered on bone, stone, or paper for over 3,000 years. For the Confucian scholar, calligraphy was one of the four essential arts, which also included music, painting, and chess or *Go.* Because calligraphy was thought to reveal a person's character, penmanship was one basis for the selection of state officials. Since false strokes could not be erased, fine calligraphers were thought to be careful planners and confident executors, valued qualities in officials.

There were five types of calligraphy. Upon the unification of China, the Qin dynasty (221–207 BC) made an official index of just over 3,000 characters written in seal script, or *zhuanshu.* This style was patterned on oracle bone inscriptions and is still used today to make seals bearing a person's name called "chops." People use their chop to sign official documents. The creator of this script, Prime Minister Li Si, is said to have engraved a stele that still stands over 2,200 years later in a temple on Taishan Mountain in Confucius's home province of Shandong.

Characters written in the clerical script, or *lishu,* are straighter than those for seal script and therefore are easier to read and write. Official scribes wrote in clerical script. Regular script, or *kaishu,* produced even more angular characters making use of only eight distinct brush stroke types: the dot, horizontal, vertical, hook, rising, left falling (short and long), and right falling strokes. These three types of calligraphy are printed scripts. Running hand, or *xingshu,* calligraphy falls between printed and cursive script. Grass writing, or *caoshu,* is the equivalent of cursive script. It can be written in two ways: *zhangcao,* where the characters remain separate and the dots are unlinked, and *jincao,* where the characters and dots run together. Such characters are extremely difficult for foreigners to read.

Calligraphers require four tools: ink, an ink stone to prepare the ink, a brush, and various types of paper. Although the basic structure of each character remains the same, calligraphers can express their individuality by varying the concentration of ink, the thickness and absorption of the paper, the size and flexibility of the brush, and the pressure and speed of the brush stroke. The basic form, brush strokes, and style were thought to convey the calligrapher's character, emotions, and aesthetic sense. Chinese calligraphy had an enormous impact on such modern Western artists as Picasso and Matisse.

After 1949, calligraphy changed rapidly in the People's Republic of China with the simplification of about 2,000 of the most commonly used characters in an effort to eradicate illiteracy. Meanwhile, Taiwan, Singapore, and Hong Kong prior to its return to China in 1997 all continued to use traditional characters, which were written in vertical columns and were read from top to bottom and right to left. The reforms in the People's Republic of China included following the Western practice of writing in rows read from left to right. Such language reforms have had a political impact since it is easier for someone educated in complicated characters to read simplified texts than the reverse. This creates a barrier for citizens of the People's Republic of China wishing to read Taiwanese and pre-1949 materials.

Sinification remained unquestioned until the nineteenth century, when China's repeated defeats in foreign wars cast doubt on the superiority of its civilization. A gradual appreciation of Western technological superiority struck a blow at Sinification but did not destroy it. The Chinese educational system continued to emphasize Han cultural achievements. In the twentieth century, the radio and public education became important avenues of Sinification under Mao when, for the first time in Chinese history, Mandarin (the primary northern dialect of China) became widely used among the general population throughout the country. Television has since magnified this trend.

II. Radial Characteristics: Sinocentrism, Barbarian Management, and the Provincial System

Radial characteristics of Chinese civilization refer to those elements that the center projected outward, either like numerous spokes from a central hub on a wheel or like concentric circles radiating out from a center. Sinocentrism means literally "China at the center," while barbarian management and the provincial system entail the projection of power from the center outward to the periphery and to the provinces.

The most important of the three was the Han Sinocentric view of the world, with China at the center and other nations surrounding it in concentric rings of diminishing importance and cultural sophistication. Like the early Christians, who believed that the planets orbited the earth, the Chinese made China the sun of the international solar system, expecting others to succumb to its gravitational pull. Sinification, gravitating to the Han cultural center, was assumed to be a one-way process. According to Mencius, "I have heard of the Chinese converting barbarians to their ways, but not of their being converted to barbarian ways."[7] Although barbarians had periodically conquered China, like the Manchus of the Qing dynasty, the Chinese portrayed their neighbors and conquerors as adopting Chinese ways, never the reverse.

Until the nineteenth century, when China became actively engaged with the West, the Chinese believed that the earth had but one civilization ruled by one emperor. According to Mencius, "There is one Way and one only."[8] The Chinese referred to their land not only as "the Central Kingdom," *Zhongguo,* but also as *Tianxia,* meaning "all under heaven." The West also fixated on its own centrality: The Greeks considered non-Greeks barbarians, and the word "barbarian" is of Greek origin. Later, the Romans thought of all roads as leading to Rome; the word "Mediterranean" means "the center of the lands." In the eighteenth century, France was widely accepted as the cultural center of Europe and, by extension, of the Christian world until it was supplanted by the British Empire. Europeans used the terms "Middle East," "Far East," "East Indies," and "West Indies" in reference to their own centrality. During the twentieth century, the United States assumed this position by standing at the forefront of globalization. Until the carnage of World War I, many in the West believed that all other nations would ultimately follow Western ways. The bloodshed of the war, however, called into question Western assumptions concerning their superiority.

"Barbarian management" was a strategic concept subsidiary to Sinocentrism. It presupposed not only that China had the authority to rule over and regulate the trade and military affairs of the "barbarians," meaning the inferiors living along China's frontiers, but also that intelligent barbarians would actively seek to emulate Chinese customs and in so doing become Sinified. Sinification was one method to mitigate threats to China. Over time, the Chinese government developed the tributary system in order to keep the various barbarian groups divided and sated so that they would not join forces against China. The tributary system both linked the ethnic minority populations on the Chinese frontiers to the Han center via regular barbarian tribute missions to the imperial capital and insulated China from outside cultural influence by channeling the interaction within culturally acceptable Chinese norms. Its purpose was to trade goods for peace on the frontier. Those who presented such local products as horses and furs as tribute to the emperor in Beijing generally received far more valuable gifts in return—silks, teas, gold, and silver.

The tributary system has often been schematized as a set of concentric circles, with the Han at the center and ever more barbaric peoples inhabiting the more distant concentric rings surrounding China proper. The near barbarians were Sinified, meaning that they accepted many Han ways, while the more distant barbarians partook of Chinese culture in ever-lessening degrees to the extreme of total barbarity and total ignorance. In the Chinese solar system, the latter were the planets in eternal darkness. China's Sinified tributaries included the Koreans, Mongols, Tibetans, Burmese, Thais, Vietnamese, and such island cultures as Taiwan and Okinawa (the Liuqiu or Ryukyu Islands). Unsinified tributaries included Tungus peoples of Manchuria and the Uighurs and other Muslim peoples of Central Asia. Later, select European countries, such as Russia, were included in this system and were duly registered as Chinese tributaries.

Prior to the Industrial Revolution, the Han regarded the un-Sinified peoples as particularly dangerous because they did not share Chinese norms of conduct or accept Chinese authority. Many were nomadic peoples who desired Chinese

The Great Wall, which was started in the third century BC., remains a potent symbol of Sinocentrism and barbarian management, since it was built primarily to keep unwelcome nomads from entering China.

goods such as silks and porcelains, the hi-tech products of this earlier era. But nomadic ways directly threatened settled Chinese agriculture along the frontiers. The Chinese tried to prevent these peoples from invading or otherwise interfering in Chinese affairs. The Great Wall provides enduring evidence of the tremendous resources expended on this task.

The tributary system abounded in symbolism demonstrating barbarian acceptance of Chinese hegemony. The most important symbols were the presentation of tribute and the kowtow to the emperor. The act of sending a tribute mission to the Chinese capital and representatives to perform the kowtow—three sets of three total prostrations before the emperor—signified the tributary states' political and cultural subservience to the Han. The Chinese used the kowtow to indicate deference in numerous social settings: Children kowtowed to parents, the living kowtowed to their ancestors, ministers kowtowed to the emperor, and the emperor kowtowed to heaven.

In order to strengthen tributary ties, the emperor granted official titles to tributary leaders and occasionally married off a daughter by a minor concubine. This Han princess would be sacrificed in the interest of state policy in the hope that she would raise her sons and daughters to respect China and further the long-range goal of Sinifying the leadership of the trib-

utary state. For similar reasons, the Chinese encouraged leaders of barbarian states to send a son to study in China. He would learn Chinese and become Sinified, and would also serve as a hostage should relations between the two states sour.

Fundamentally, the tributary relationship was financial and coercive, its primary positive and negative incentives. Those who cooperated received lucrative gifts and trade. Those who did not risked wars of annihilation obliterating whole frontier peoples, as occurred during the Qianlong emperor's conquest of Central Asia in the eighteenth century. Periodically, neighboring barbarian states rebelled against Han domination, sometimes to the point of attacking China proper and occasionally even overthrowing the dynasty. The Mongols and the Manchus created China's most territorially extensive empires, those of the Yuan (1279–1368) and Qing (1644–1911) dynasties, respectively; the Turkic Northern Wei dynasty (386–534) was an earlier example. Just as the astute use of military power could take a Han peasant up the vertical ladder to become emperor, so too could tributary peoples seize the throne. The tributary system was meant to prevent this.

China employed a strategy of "barbarian management" to deal with its uncooperative neighbors. This strategy for empire entailed employing bilateral diplomacy and war to keep neighbors weak and divided so that they could not unite against China. The Chinese encapsulated some of their key barbarian management strategies in a variety of four-character idioms: *Zong heng bai he* referred to political manipulation to unite and divide others, which meant alternating the carrot and the stick. *Yuan jiao jin gong* entailed maintaining good relations with the far threat while attacking the near threat. *Yi yi zhi yi* meant using one barbarian to control another, often pitting a more distant group against a closer group. In keeping with these traditions, down to the end of the Maoist era, the Chinese emphasized bilateral over multilateral relations.

A third radial element of Chinese civilization concerned the delegation of power from the center to officials in charge of provincial and local administration. China's autocracy required officials to live throughout the country in order to extend imperial rule to the localities. The emperor sent Confucian officials, often referred to as "Mandarins," throughout the country on government business. Power radiated from the emperor to his provincial governors and from his governors to their subordinates at the district level. Through this network of officials, the emperor could exert power from the top down to the provincial and then to the district level. The emperor delegated his power not to institutions, but to the individuals whom he appointed to provincial posts.

Taxation and flood control constituted two of the most important functions of local government. Tax collection was important not only to the central government but also to local officials since they received inadequate funding from the central budget. Any surplus became their income. Such a system guaranteed what in the West would be considered corruption because there was no clear segregation of public and private funds. With these taxes, local officials were expected to pay for public services, such as roads, flood control, famine relief, and local militia. Government officials were responsible for building dikes to prevent floods and for digging networks of irrigation ditches to water crops. The Yellow River was particularly dangerous. Over the last two millennia, it has changed course over 20 times and broken through dikes over 1,500 times, killing millions in its wake. Because the Chinese widely interpreted natural disasters as signs of a dynasty's imminent demise, the central government considered the prevention of flooding, famine, and other local disasters to be essential for its survival.

Although provincial officials derived their position from the emperor, their power was based on a complex network of connections, or *guanxi*, with local gentry and other government officials. Acting unobserved and generally unchecked by the center, these officials wielded enormous power within their personal fiefdoms. To ensure that officials would not abuse their power on behalf of family and friends, the central government, in addition to emphasizing Confucian norms of conduct, prohibited them from serving in their home provinces. This meant that new officials arrived in assigned provinces without prior connections. To get anything done, they had to rely on locally recruited minor officials and clerks. This division of power helped promote cooperation between central and local officials. Although individual emperors and dynasties might come and go, the local officials and the government structure remained. Together they preserved the autocratic nature of the state despite the many periods of crisis and dynastic upheaval.

The term *guanxi* will be used throughout this book and requires a detailed explanation. The term was coined during the Ming dynasty (1368–1644) and refers to the actual exercise of power in the past and present. Each person had a *guanxi* network of family, friends, and associates that could be summoned in a time of need. Favors entailed reciprocity, meaning the future obligation to return the favor. The favors necessary to create a strong *guanxi* network were thought of as both an investment in the present to secure future rewards and an insurance policy to provide protection from future troubles. They could be cashed in at will. *Guanxi* was transitive, meaning that it had the mathematical property of transferring through interlocking *guanxi* networks, so that if C was in the *guanxi* network of B and B was in the *guanxi* network of A, then C was obligated to help not only B but also A.

The extent of a person's *guanxi* with every other person in a *guanxi* network depended in large measure on "face," or the public perception of a person's worth. While *guanxi* was the conduit of power, face was the currency of power. Those with face stood far above those without it in Chinese society's steep hierarchy. Face could be maintained, lost, or given. To "have face" meant to acquire public tokens of respect from others. Only those with face could call on others for favors and expect a positive response. In addition, only those with face could occupy positions of authority. Maintaining and augmenting face became a key goal for many Chinese because, without it, they had no social position.

Face could be lost through public displays of incompetence, corruption, or meanness. So long as these faults remained private, there was no loss of face because face accrued only in the public arena. When dominance was asserted to force another to lose face, face became a zero-sum game. Losing face was something to be feared and avoided because, as a part of the public record, any loss became permanent—hence the imperative to cover up rather than to admit guilt. In some ways, those at the top of the social pyramid could less afford to lose face than those at the bottom. A major loss of face could topple elites from their high position. Emperors were no more immune to the loss of face than commoners. The Chinese were well aware of this and therefore did not unintentionally cause others to lose face but paid scrupulous attention to matters of etiquette. If everyone adhered to the same rules of etiquette or social interaction, this minimized the chances of any unintended losses of face.

Face could also be given. This entailed giving someone the public tokens of respect regardless of whether or not they were deserved. Merit, truth, and reality were all irrelevant. Face reflected not reality, but public interpretations of reality. Gift giving played a central role. What might be considered corruption in the West was an integral part of proper decorum in China. Gifts showed gratitude for services rendered, provided evidence of humble respect, and indicated loyalty to seniors. Hence, Chinese traditions have emphasized lavish gift giving, sumptuous banquets, spectacular weddings, and ornate funerals. Those who put on a good show demonstrated to others their wealth, decorum, and worthiness of respect, enhancing both their face and *guanxi*. Appropriately placed gifts created an obligation of reciprocity from the receiver: Inferiors used gifts to cultivate connections with superiors. Alternatively, superiors could use gifts to cement loyalty with inferiors. Either way, astute gift giving strengthened and expanded *guanxi* networks. In the *guanxi* scheme of things, face had a multiplier effect. Gaining face strengthened *guanxi* ties, whereas a major loss could cause the *guanxi* network to implode. Power was brittle in a face culture like China's.

III. Bottom-up Characteristics: Daoism, Buddhism, and Poetry

Bottom-up characteristics were also connected to power. They refer to vertical elements that did not usually percolate from the top down but more often bubbled up from the bottom. Although the philosophical system of Daoism and the religion of Buddhism each had some degree of hierarchy, both were widely dispersed throughout China and had extensive, albeit informal, communications networks linking religious centers. Confucianism, Buddhism, and Daoism constituted the three primary belief systems in China. In contrast to Confucianism—which did not have a metaphysical basis, but was secular and modeled on the family—Daoism and Buddhism emphasized such metaphysical issues as creation, life and death, and the nature of the universe.

The most important Daoist text was *Laozi* (*Daodejing* or *Tao Te Ching*). China's most eminent Daoist philosopher, Laozi (Lao Tzu or Old Master), who was roughly a contemporary of Confucius, focused on the mystery of life, the need to harmonize with nature, and that which cannot be ex-

pressed. A person, like water, which flows along the path of least resistance, could likewise effortlessly follow the Way and attain harmony with nature and inner serenity. Laozi rejected catering to one's desires and relying on one's senses for enlightenment. The pursuit of goals or knowledge was an illusion that strayed ever further from the Way. Goals created human desires. This brought people into conflict, which generated evil. The solution was emancipation from desires. Instead of reason, action, or the pursuit of goals, Laozi recommended passivity: "He does the non-doing, / and thus everything falls into place." He continued, "Being without desire makes still, / and the world rights itself."[9] *Wuwei*, meaning "to do nothing," was a central concept of Daoism.

Laozi also stressed the complementarity of opposites, which were always present but whose proportions remained in a state of constant flux. The one never obliterated the other. This implied no beginnings and no endings, but instead the continuousness of change. In the political realm, Daoists believed that a wise ruler was in harmony with his people and so ruled effortlessly; indeed, he need hardly rule at all. This contrasted with the active and interventionist sovereign of Confucian teachings or Western-style leadership. Unlike Confucius, Laozi attached no special importance to the perpetuation of culture or the protection of state institutions. The Daoist emphasis on inaction appeared to some Westerners as a fatalistic acceptance of the status quo.

Laozi's most famous disciple, Zhuangzi, was a contemporary of Mencius and one of China's finest writers. He also emphasized passivity and rejected reason as the pathway to understanding. He advised: "Do not hanker for fame. / Do not make plans. / Do not try to do things. / Do not try to master knowledge . . . Just be empty."[10] Zhuangzi took a more hostile stance than Laozi toward Confucianism by rejecting order, control, and political hierarchy. For him, rulers did not resolve but instead caused social and political problems.

The Daoists recommended a retreat from the political world to an inner world of reflection and solitude. Daoist masters passed on their knowledge directly to disciples. This body of knowledge soon included Daoist medicinal uses for herbs, a practice that spurred the development of traditional Chinese medicine, as well as such breathing exercises as *qigong* and empty-hand boxing, known as Tai Chi (*taijiquan* or *t'ai-chi-ch'uan*), that form a basis for Chinese martial arts. (See the feature on page 212.) Eventually, the Daoist canon grew to over 1,400 texts. The most important deities were the Three Clarities, who each reigned in a separate heaven. There were numerous branches of Daoism that worshiped a wide variety of additional deities.

Traditional Daoist views contrasted with the Western belief, of Renaissance origin, that reason and rationality allowed humans to understand the natural and human worlds. For Westerners, analysis, synthesis, induction, deduction, logic, and empiricism were not the illusions criticized by Daoists, but rather the means not only to understand the world, but ultimately to bend it to human objectives. Far from considering goals pointless, people in the West organized their populations and governments around the pursuit and attainment of objectives. Whereas Daoists stressed the limitations of human understanding and rationality, the West considered them to be the foundations of wealth and power.

Buddhism originated in India at about the time of Confucius, spread to China during the first century AD, and reached its maximum influence during the Sui and Tang dynasties (581–907), when it overshadowed both Confucianism and Daoism. When Buddhism first came to China, Daoists helped translate and spread its message. Not only did the two philosophies not conflict, but many Chinese considered themselves to be both Buddhists and Daoists. Buddhism had an enormous impact on Chinese art and architecture, such as the pagodas the Chinese built based on Indian stupas to hold Buddhist texts called "sutras." Major surviving Buddhist cultural artifacts in China include cave paintings in Dunhuang, Gansu, at Yungang in Datong, Shanxi, and the giant Buddhist sculpture at Dazu, Sichuan.

Buddhists believed that a life of spiritual devotion and ethical conduct would break the otherwise endless cycle of life, death, and rebirth to transform the believer into a Buddha, or "enlightened one." (See Table I.3.) Core Buddhist beliefs included the Four Noble Truths: (1) existence is suffering, (2) craving and attachment cause suffering, (3) nirvana ends suffering, and (4) proper conduct provides the way to nirvana. Whereas Theravada Buddhism, also known as Hinayana or the "Lesser Vehicle," had a greater impact on Southeast Asia, Mahayana or the "Greater Vehicle" school spread to China, Korea, and Japan. According to Mahayana Buddhism, anyone could attain enlightenment, not just monks and nuns. Chinese Buddhists included among their primary saints not only the bodhisattvas (those who forego nirvana to save others) like Guanyin (Kuan-yin), the Goddess of Mercy, but also Amitabha (in Chinese *Amituofo*, in Japanese *Amida*, or "Immeasurable Light"). The two main Buddhist sects in China, the Pure Land Sect and Zen Buddhism, stressed faith rather than right conduct as the path to nirvana. According to the Pure Land Sect, the temporal world had already entered the third and final age when Buddhist teachings had so decayed that right conduct no longer sufficed to reach nirvana. Because of increasing corruption in the human world, pure faith alone offered salvation.

This sculpture, from the Dazu caves in Sichuan province, dates to the Song dynasty (960–1279), when southwestern China became a major center for the worship and teaching of Buddhism.

Table I.3   Buddhism's Twelve-link Chain of Causal Conditions*

Ignorance	causes the appearance of	Manifestations of the Will
Manifestations of the Will	cause the appearance of	Consciousness
Consciousness	causes the appearance of	Mind and Body
Mind and Body	cause the appearance of	the Six Sense Organs
the Six Sense Organs	cause the appearance of	Contact
Contact	causes the appearance of	Sensation
Sensation	causes the appearance of	Craving
Craving	causes the appearance of	Grasping
Grasping	causes the appearance of	Coming into Existence
Coming into Existence	causes the appearance of	Birth
Birth	causes the appearance of	Old Age, Sickness, Death, and All Miseries
Old Age	causes the appearance of	Ignorance, etc.

*This table shows the cycle of life, causation, and reincarnation according to Buddhism. Note that the final stage, Old Age, then causes the return to the initial step, Ignorance.

Source: Joseph Needham, *Science and Civilisation in China,* vol. 2, *History of Scientific Thought* (Cambridge: Cambridge University Press, 1962), 400. Reprinted with permission of Cambridge University Press.

In 520 AD, a Buddhist monk named Bodhidharma (Damo in Chinese and Daruma in Japanese) came from India to China. His philosophy of Zen Buddhism did not depend on written texts but emphasized a highly personal relationship between master and disciple. Thus, it survived the mid-ninth-century anti-Buddhist purge during the Tang dynasty. In the twelfth century it gradually spread to Japan, where it became even more influential, so that the English term comes from the Japanese, Zen, not the Chinese, *chan.* Bodhidharma is said to have stayed nine years at the Shaolin Temple in central China, where he taught the monks self-defense. The Shaolin Temple remains the most famous kungfu (*gongfu*) center in China today, so Buddhism, like Daoism, has made a major contribution to the development of the martial arts in China. Zen Buddhism also stressed meditation as the path to sudden enlightenment.

Both the Pure Land Sect and Zen were pessimistic about the human condition: Each saw life as a process of unremitting decline and suffering. To live was to suffer. Yet, they were optimistic about the afterlife. They believed that some could break the cycle of birth, decay, death, and reincarnation in order to enter nirvana. Other than forms of right conduct to enter nirvana, all other human goals were illusory since all living beings eventually succumbed to death. Therefore, the focus of Buddhism, like that of Daoism, was not on ends but on means, not on goals but on right conduct. What mattered was not what an individual achieved in life, since human achievement was an illusion; what mattered was how that individual lived.

Unlike the highly regimented vertical Confucian hierarchy, Buddhism and especially the Pure Land Sect preached

that anyone could attain salvation. Buddhists emphasized religious practices and faith, not social status. Similarly, Daoism was intended for all, not only for a religious or ethical elite. According to Daoist beliefs, following the inward-looking Way liberated humanity from want, inner turmoil, and external conflict. Emperors and commoners had an equal ability to follow the Way and to reach heaven. This egalitarianism sharply contrasted with Confucianism.

Both Buddhism and Daoism had an enormous core of believers whose faith spread from the bottom up throughout China and included many non-Han peoples in the Chinese empire. The Tibetans and Mongols practiced their own interpretation of Buddhism, called Lamaism. It was much more hierarchical and put greater emphasis on ritual. Such Mongol rulers as Khubilai Khan practiced Buddhism. The Turkic Northern Wei dynasty acquired some of the greatest collections of Buddhist sculptures—at Datong and Luoyang. Thus, Buddhism and Daoism helped create horizontal links from below between the Han Chinese and non-Han peoples. Buddhism and Daoism remain influential in China to the present day. Such contemporary movements as Falun Gong are rooted in these traditions.

The Confucian rulers of China tolerated Buddhism and Daoism because both encouraged the dissatisfied to seek internal peace, not to foment revolution. These religions either did not question or actively supported a society that was hierarchical, a government that was absolutist, a history that was considered cyclical (see Section IV), and a population that was submissive to established authority. Buddhists and Daoists generally focused on their own private behavior, not on upsetting the ruling social or political order. In the event of dissent, they usually recommended withdrawal from worldly cares. Their emphasis on the passive endurance of earthly pain did not threaten imperial claims to power. While there were exceptions, such as the White Lotus Rebellion (see Chapter 6, Section III), these groups were classified as heterodox sects. Unlike in the West, religious differences did not usually lead to conflict in China. Indeed, quite often emperors and the faithful claimed simultaneous adherence to Buddhism, Daoism, and Confucianism. There is nothing comparable in China to the religious wars of the Reformation, in which Protestants and Catholics butchered each other for a century over differing interpretations of Christianity.

As in Buddhism and Daoism, there is also a very pessimistic strain in Western thinking concerning life on earth. Christianity, particularly its Calvinist variant, emphasized original sin and damnation of the unrepentant sinner. But Christians did not conceptualize the world as an endless cycle of decay and ephemeral renewal; rather, they took a more linear and goal-oriented approach to the entry into heaven. They baptized children to immunize them from original sin. During their lives, Catholics confessed their sins to atone, while certain Protestant groups atoned through good works. Other Protestant groups tried to correlate earthly wealth with heavenly intent, interpreting achievements in this life as a reflection of the everlasting life to come.

After the Scientific Revolution of the seventeenth century, and particularly with the advent of the Industrial Revolution in the late eighteenth century that greatly accelerated economic and social change, those in the West increasingly conceptualized history in terms of progress. Rather than eternal damnation, Westerners increasingly viewed life as the triumph of progress and the pursuit of happiness, the latter concept highlighted in the U.S. Declaration of Independence, an eighteenth-century document. In Buddhist and Daoist thinking, such ideas were but seductive illusions. No human could break the cycle of life or trump the *Dao*. In contrast to the increasingly goal-oriented approach of the West, both Buddhism and Daoism emphasized a detachment from worldly cravings and a strong inner life in harmony with nature.

The Chinese have used poetry to express dissent since the appearance of the *Book of Odes*. While the educated have written such poetry for an immediate audience of the literate, when the ideas embedded in the poetry have reached a mass audience, the ideas have sometimes taken on a life of their own. Because China's hierarchical autocratic society did not tolerate free expression, political criticism had to be couched ambiguously. Confucianism stressed obedience and deference to superiors, Sunzi emphasized coercion to suppress enemies, and Legalism recommended the swift punishment of dissent. For those who did not choose the Daoist or Buddhist route of isolated meditation and internal search for perfection, and who had not abandoned the hope of directly influencing the political order, poetry became a powerful outlet for dissent.

On the surface, political criticism disguised as poetry appeared benign. One of China's most famous poets, Li Bo (Li Po), of the Tang dynasty, wrote poems critical of the dynasty after his exile to a frontier province for participation in a failed uprising. In one poem he described an imperial concubine looking up at the "autumn moon," despairing of her fading youth. It was a symbol of her impending demise. Although harmless on the surface, the term "autumn moon" applied equally to the ruling dynasty, whose heavenly mandate was likewise fading. Later poets, including Mao Zedong, used the phrase "autumn moon" with the same meaning in reference to their political adversaries. Mao's life demonstrated that embers of political criticism could ignite peasant dissatisfaction and break out in open warfare, with the dispossessed attempting to take power. Poetry, harmless on the surface, occasionally produced lethal effects: Criticism of China's rulers, when combined with other factors such as rural poverty, pervasive corruption, or a powerful new ideology, could have devastating consequences. Both social critics and China's rulers have often used poetry to reach a larger audience. Each chapter of this book begins with a poem commenting on political issues. Unlike in the West, poetry in China remains an important form of communication and a mark of intellectual accomplishment, not simply among Chinese intellectuals but also among its highest leaders.

IV. Cyclical Elements: *Yin* and *Yang*, the Dynastic Cycle, and Historical Continuity

The first three categories defining traditional Chinese culture concern power and have been described in spatial terms: top-down, radial, and bottom-up. The last two will be described in terms of time. The first of these temporal categories is composed of the cyclical elements that the Chinese traditionally have used to explain change within an overarching framework of continuity. They have expressed this in the conceptual framework of *yin* and *yang* drawn in an interlocking S pattern bounded within a circle.

At the most abstract level, the Chinese looked at time, natural forces, and dominant trends in terms of the opposites, *yin* and *yang*. *Yin* represented femininity, passivity, softness, darkness, coolness, and dampness, while *yang* represented masculinity, activity, hardness, light, warmth, and dryness. (See Table I.4.) Human history could be explained in terms of the balance between these two forces. Deciphering this bal-

Table I.4   *Yin* and *Yang* Correlations*

Yang	Yin
heaven	earth
spring	autumn
summer	winter
day	night
big states	small states
important states	unimportant states
action	inaction
stretching	contracting
ruler	minister
above	below
man	woman
father	child
elder brother	younger brother
older	younger
noble	base
getting on in the world	being stuck
taking a wife, begetting a child	mourning
controlling others	being controlled
guest	host
soldiers	laborers
speech	silence
giving	receiving

*This table has been included to illustrate the different analytic framework used in traditional China to understand the natural and human worlds.

Source: Richard J. Smith, *China's Cultural Heritage: The Qing Dynasty 1644–1912,* 2nd ed. (Boulder, CO: Westview Press, 1994), 132.

ance was very complicated and was connected with traditional Chinese doctrines concerning the Five Elements: metal, wood, water, fire, and earth. (See Table I.5.) Interaction among the elements and between *yin* and *yang* accounted for

change within the universe and also for its essential continuity. Varying balances explained changes, but the dominant element of each era followed in a prescribed succession, explaining the endlessly repeating cycles in history. Deciphering such balances gave rise to highly elaborate theories of divination. These had their own sets of extremely complicated rules, such as those pertaining to the eight trigrams and the sixty-four hexagrams explained in the *Book of Changes,* the classic of Chinese divination and also one of the Five Classics that formed the core of a Classical Chinese education.

Just like *yin* and *yang,* every concept had its opposite: such as big (*da*) and small (*xiao*), which together in Chinese form the word *daxiao,* meaning "size." These paired concepts were considered complementary and their simultaneous existence necessary for the overarching reality that encompassed the two, size in the case of *daxiao.* The Greeks, in contrast, fixated on the law of noncontradiction to reason that opposites could not simultaneously exist; if one was true, the other was false. The Greeks emphasized a second element of logic, the law of identity, meaning that A is A regardless of its context. Whereas the Greeks focused on the nature of A, the Chinese focused on its context to conclude that A was actually a function of its context and therefore changed accordingly. These differences in principle had profound implications.

The Greeks set the West on a path toward logical consistency, analysis, and empiricism. In contrast to analysis, meaning the examination of the parts in isolation from the whole, the Chinese believed that profound understanding came only from taking into consideration the whole. Their holistic understanding of the natural world did not require logical consistency or unity of thought among Confucianism, Daoism, and Buddhism. The Chinese thought it natural to enjoy simultaneously the best elements of each, while Westerners felt compelled to choose. In the Middle Ages, Europeans went on Crusades to kill the infidel; during the Reformation they butchered each other in religious wars, believing that only one religion could be right and the others should be expunged. The Chinese did not fight wars over the rule of noncontradiction because they believed that religions and modes of thinking ebbed and flowed over the ages.

The dynastic cycle and its motor, the mandate of heaven, together were the second cyclical element in the Chinese understanding of the world. Traditionally, the Chinese have explained their country's many periods of internal turmoil in terms of the strength, weakness, or absence of the government's mandate of heaven. In keeping with the *yin-yang* framework and Buddhist beliefs concerning the life cycles of all living organisms, the Chinese believed that dynasties, like all living things, rose and fell, flourished for a time and then declined as they aged until a virtuous new dynasty replaced its

Table I.5   The Five Elements*

Elements	Wood	Fire	Earth	Metal	Water
Seasons	spring	summer	—	autumn	winter
Cardinal points	east	south	center	west	north
Tastes	sour	bitter	sweet	acrid	salt
Smells	goatish	burning	fragrant	rank	rotten
Numbers	8	7	5	9	6
Heavenly bodies	stars	sun	earth	constellations	moon
Planets	Jupiter	Mars	Saturn	Venus	Mercury
Weather	wind	heat	thunder	cold	rain
Yin-Yang	lesser Yang	greater Yang	equal balance	lesser Yin	greater Yin
Human capacities	demeanor	vision	thought	speech	hearing
Governance	relaxed	enlightened	careful	energetic	quiet
Ministries	Agriculture	War	the Capital	Justice	Works
Colors	green	red	yellow	white	black
Animal types	scaly (fishes)	feathered (birds)	naked (man)	hairy (mammals)	shelled (invertebrates)
Domestic animals	sheep	fowl	ox	dog	pig
Internal organs	spleen	lungs	heart	kidney	liver
Body parts	muscles	pulse (blood)	flesh	skin, hair	bones (marrow)
Sensory organs	eye	tongue	mouth	nose	ear
Affective states	anger	joy	desire	sorrow	fear

*To a Westerner such a table appears to be incomprehensible. It has been included to illustrate the different analytic framework used in traditional China to understand the natural and human worlds.

Source: Joseph Needham, *Science and Civilisation in China,* vol. 2, *History of Scientific Thought* (Cambridge: Cambridge University Press, 1962), 262–6. Reprinted with permission of Cambridge University Press.

decaying predecessor. After a period of moral ascendancy, the new dynasty would succumb to a gradual decline, or its "autumn" period, until it was replaced by yet another virtuous rising dynasty. Like the seasons of the year, dynasties followed each other in an unending and predictable succession.

The term "dynastic cycle" presupposed that the mandate of the sovereign to rule and, by extension, the authority of his dynasty to retain power changed over time. The dynastic cycle expressed the fluctuating mandate of heaven, which was the measure of the virtue of the ruling dynasty. If a sovereign lost his mandate, then the Chinese believed he would lose the throne. Either a new sovereign or new dynasty would replace him. To delay this eventuality, emperors strove to balance the opposing forces of *yin* and *yang* and thereby ensure cosmic harmony. For those who failed, the mandate passed on to the succeeding dynasty. Thus, dynasties rose and fell in relation to their mandate to rule.

This cycle repeated itself throughout Chinese history, with an ascendant dynasty replacing a declining one, often through military force. Military victory demonstrated the mandate to rule. Might indicated right and victory the proof of virtue.

Might did not make right; rather, the dynastic cycle assumed the triumph of right, so military victory was a strong indicator of dynastic virtue. The fortunes of individuals and families, like those of dynasties, rose and fell. Heaven could accelerate this process through its changing favor that affected the fortunes of all. A rich man today could easily become a poor man tomorrow. Luck and fate tended to reinforce the workings of the dynastic cycle; ill-fated or luckless rulers lost their mandate to rule.

The origins of the concepts of the dynastic cycle and the mandate of heaven go back to the Eastern Zhou dynasty (770–222 BC), which together with the Western Zhou (1122–771 BC) constitutes the longest enduring Chinese dynasty. The Eastern Zhou comprised the Spring and Autumn period (771–484 BC), the time of Confucius and Laozi, and the Warring States period (484–221 BC) the time of Mozi, Mencius, Zhuangzi, and Xunzi. The Xia dynasty immediately preceded the Shang, the dynasty overthrown by the Western Zhou. The dynastic cycle enabled the Zhou to portray its victory over the Shang as a "rebirth" of the original founding dynasty. This not only gave the Zhou political legitimacy, but also played on Chinese beliefs in a past golden age whose virtues new dynasties should attempt to restore. Emperors or family patriarchs should match, but never supersede, the achievements of illustrious ancestors. Not to aspire to restore the golden age or the family name indicated a lack of respect for the past, while to outdo illustrious ancestors would be unfilial.

Under the mandate of heaven, sovereigns derived their power directly from heaven in accordance with the correctness of their behavior and with their ability to maintain order in the empire. If either faltered, so would their mandate to rule. Emperors carried out the proper rituals at the prescribed times lest heaven deliver a succession of natural disasters presaging the impending fall of the dynasty. Disasters included natural calamities, such as earthquakes, floods, and famines; political upheavals, such as domestic rebellions or barbarian incursions; physical disabilities, such as sickness; or bad omens, such as comets or eclipses. Natural disasters often became the catalyst for rebellion, while rebellion often was the precursor to dynastic change—hence the close association in traditional China between the mandate of heaven, on the one hand, and natural and man-made calamity, on the other. Chinese rulers were sensitive to any action or event that could cast doubt on their mandate.

Effective rule required a strong mandate. Signs of this included the defeat of the ruler's political rivals, the absence of internal rebellions, strong central control over the provinces, and especially domestic prosperity. In order to minimize the scope of natural disasters, Chinese rulers made enormous efforts to control floods by building massive dikes and to prevent famine by establishing state-controlled granaries and irrigation projects. Emperors also emphasized the study of the movements of the heavenly bodies that were thought to presage disaster. In order to understand celestial changes such as eclipses, the Qing emperors turned to European Jesuits in the seventeenth century to improve their royal astronomical institute.

As long as the mandate appeared strong, the vast majority of Chinese accepted their fate and went along with the status quo. If, however, the government's mandate of heaven seemed questionable, then a new leader might be tempted to claim the mandate for himself, while the military could

The Imperial Dragon (*Long*), symbolizing wisdom and power, is the highest of four benevolent spiritual animals, which also include the phoenix, unicorn, and tortoise. Emperors of China were thought to be descended from dragons and so sat on a dragon throne, rode in a dragon boat, and slept in a dragon bed. Only the Chinese dragon has five claws—representing the five basic elements of metal, wood, water, fire, and earth—while Korean dragons have four claws and the Japanese dragon has only three claws. This photograph was taken in Huhehaote (Hohhot), the capital of Inner Mongolia Autonomous Region, so the dragon has four claws.

suddenly change sides in an internal rebellion to abandon the ruling government in favor of its challenger. When the ruler no longer appeared to fit Confucian norms of benevolent or ethical rule, challengers might employ the strategies of Sunzi to topple the dynasty. In such cases, the Han officials of a deposed dynasty would often shift their loyalties laterally and serve the new and ascendant dynasty. This was true of the Qing dynasty, the Nationalist government, the Japanese puppet governments of both Manchuria and mainland China in the 1930s and 1940s, and the Communist government, in which elements of defeated predecessors served the victorious new regimes and entire armies defected.

The third cyclical element is history. The concepts of *yin* and *yang* and the dynastic cycle together gave the Chinese a cyclical conception of history, stressing historical continuity and analogies to understand the present. A cyclical view of time reinforced this view. Unlike Westerners, who typically visualize time as progressing along a straight line, the Chinese traditionally understood time in terms of cycles. They combined the Ten Celestial Stems with the Twelve Terrestrial Branches to create a sixty-year cycle. This was composed of the sixty possible two-character combinations made by simultaneously cycling six times through the single characters for the Ten Celestial Stems and five times through the single characters for the Twelve Terrestrial Branches. The dynastic cycle overlaid this system. The Ming and Qing dynasties measured time in terms of the year of the ruling emperor's reign. For example, Qianlong 3 meant the third year of the reign of the Qianlong emperor, or 1738 by Western calculations. The dating cycle began anew with the accession of the next monarch. Earlier dynasties often changed the era names within reigns, suggesting multiple cycles per reign.

Traditionally, Chinese have represented time graphically as vertical, with the past above and the future below. This is reflected in their characters for "up" (*shang*) and "down" (*xia*) when used as prefixes meaning "preceding" (past) and "following" (future) in such word combinations as "yesterday," "tomorrow," "last month," "next month," "last year," "next year," and so on. The past appeared to bear down on the individual from above, while the future was below. The combination of a vertical representation of time with a cyclical view of historical change created not the progressive forward march of the Western imagination, but instead a downward, uncontrolled spiraling fall into the future. Conversely, the joss sticks burned as incense in temples sent smoke spiraling back upward along a vertical path showing respect for the dead.

The Christian West used the birth of Christ as the permanent reference point to mark time; from that point, time either marched forward to AD or backward to BC. The Western conception placed the past behind so that the passage of time be-

came a march into the future. These timelines progressed from a known past into an unknown future. Note the English word "progression," which means both "to move forward" and "to improve." In the Western mind, history was open-ended. The past might suggest future possibilities but, ultimately, it did not bound the future. The view of history as progress and the future as open-ended has deep roots in the Western tradition. In contrast, the Chinese assumed that they knew the broad outlines of the future because it would be a combination of the known elements of the past that ebbed and flowed over the ages.

Westerners, particularly since the Industrial Revolution, have tended to think of time and historical change in terms of horizontal linear relationships in which certain factors could improve or strengthen indefinitely. They have tended to look forward into the future, to view change as positive and progress as highly desirable, if not inevitable. In contrast, the Chinese have tended to think in terms of cycles, repetition, and historical continuity, where at some point trends, like the tides, reverse. Modern Western economic thinking has often been discussed in the popular arena in terms of a growing economic pie providing ever larger slices for all or in terms of a rising tide lifting all ships. This faith in the benefits of economic growth contains an embedded worldview not of a zero-sum game in which some must lose for others to win, but of numerous win-win scenarios. The cyclical view of history and the bounded forces of *yin* and *yang*, in contrast, imply a more zero-sum approach where one opposite grows in force at the expense of its pair until the tide reverses yet again. Thus, where Westerners may see win-win scenarios, the Chinese may see win-lose ones.

V. Retrospective Elements: Fate and the Sources of Knowledge

The final category of cultural elements is retrospective, meaning those factors emphasizing the past versus the future. In traditional Chinese thinking, heaven determined the fate of each individual, family, and dynasty. Fate was unalterable and inescapable. It determined the general course of the present and future. The Chinese believed that the future of a dynasty, like the future of a family, depended on the independent yet interwoven factors of fate and luck. Although heaven determined fate at birth and that fate was inescapable, luck was random. For example, if a dynasty collapsed through corruption and decay, the Chinese might say that it was the dynasty's fate. However, if it collapsed because of the outcome of one battle, due perhaps to a poor decision on the part of a general, this premature death might be ascribed to bad luck. Bad luck hastened a bad fate, while good luck could delay it. The exact relationship between fate and luck depended on circumstances.

In Chinese, the ideographs for life and fate, *ming*, are the same because, traditionally, the two were inseparable and, indeed, synonymous. Fate determined life and life was fate. The Chinese have encapsulated these views in such terms as *ming zhong zhu ding*, meaning "predestined"; *ming bu gai jue*, meaning "not destined to die" (used to describe a narrow escape); *ming bo ru hua*, meaning "fated to the rapid demise of a flower" (said of a woman's beauty); *ming gai ru ci*, meaning "it is predestined" (literally, "fate should be thus"); and *ming bo xiang qiong*, meaning "ill-fated and poor"; as well as in such words as *mingding*, meaning "destined" (literally, "fate has been decided"), and *mingyun*, meaning "destiny" (literally, "life cycle").

A belief in fate entailed fatalism, a sense that human intervention had only limited influence over events. Traditional Chinese thinking emphasized the powerlessness of the individual in the vast scheme of things. With birth came fate, family, and obligations. Fate determined the basic contours of a person's future; family determined his or her status and related social obligations; and birth order fixed his or her rank and obligations within the family. There was also the random influence of luck that operated outside of human control. This left very little latitude for autonomous action. The family, not the individual, was the basic social unit. People were born not with inherent rights but with social obligations.

Westerners and Chinese alike believe that luck, meaning random events, also affects people's lives and fatalism has also characterized certain strands of Western thinking, but the dominant trend in the West has been in the direction of free will and willpower. In English, the term "fatalism" is used to describe an atypical and generally negative outlook. The dominant outlook is contained in such expressions as "Where there's a will, there's a way," "God helps those who help themselves," "Seek and ye shall find," "It is up to you," and so on. Embedded in these expressions are the assumptions that individuals can make a difference, that hard work determines success, and that individuals have the freedom to make the choices that set the course of their lives. In contrast to the Western focus on personal freedoms, traditional Chinese thinking emphasizes duties to others. From the Chinese point of view, the Western focus on the individual is both selfish and narcissistic.

Such views were expressed in art. Western artwork from the time of the ancient Greeks has emphasized the human form and the centrality of the individual. By contrast, Chinese art has rarely separated individuals from the greater social or environmental context. More often, it has depicted vast landscapes that overwhelm any small human forms. From the Chinese point of view, they have examined the whole, while the West has narrowly considered the part. This is in keeping with Chinese analytical thinking, which focuses on the interconnection of the many parts of the whole, whereas Western analytical thinking more often focuses on categorizing parts in isolation from the whole.

Although the Chinese did not believe that they could alter their fate, they wanted to understand it to anticipate the future. In imperial times, Chinese scholars studied *The Book of Changes*, the classical text on divination, to sort out the ebb and flow of *yin* and *yang* and to attempt to understand what fate would bring. Fate had been set. The trick was to decipher and perhaps delay it. Westerners took the opposite approach. They sought to understand the natural world so that they could bend it to their will. Westerners sought to control nature, a ludicrous presumption from the Chinese point of view.

This divergent outlook was connected to the second retrospective element in Chinese thinking: their approach to knowledge. Traditionally, the Chinese explicitly sought knowledge in the past in contrast to the empirical approach increasingly favored in the West. They understood the present through the prism of the past. They sought wisdom in ancient texts, pursued knowledge through the study of their history, and determined right action through historical analogies. This approach to knowledge was backward-looking. In the West, "backward" has a pejorative connotation in addition to its basic directional meaning. In English the term contains the embedded assumption that the past is inferior to the present. Traditionally, the Chinese have made the opposite assumption. They have assumed that an ideal golden age existed on the fringes of human memory and that it was incumbent upon governments and individuals to strive to emulate this golden age.

The Western interest in the past has often focused on causality, hence the preoccupation with origins: the origins of Western civilization, of wars, of intellectual movements, and so on. Western interest in the past has been primarily to explain the present: How did the past cause the present? This interest has been causal, linear, and often with a future purpose. If one can plot trends, can they not, by extrapolation, be plotted into the future to help guide planning? This is a routine form of analysis for governments and corporations. Westerners do not generally wish to return to the past. Rather, they focus on learning from the past to understand natural and human events in order to harness them to the human will. In contrast, the Chinese sought to learn about such events to put humans in conformity with nature lest nature wreak revenge on humankind. Whereas Westerners have focused on the past to explain the present and improve planning for the future, the Chinese have used the past to mold the present.

Traditionally, the Chinese applied their knowledge of the past to the present through the analytical framework of historical analogies. They scoured classical texts to provide parallels and, thereby, answers to current problems. Students spent much of their education memorizing classical texts so that appropriate analogies readily came to mind. Because they believed life and history to be cyclical, knowledge was a closed system: The past contained everything necessary to understand the present, including a model for the present in the form of an ancient golden age. The Chinese proverb "Know the future by examining the past" (*jian wang zhi lai*) encapsulates this belief.

In the West, the Reformation entailed a century of constant and bitter wars fought in large part over the issue of the sources of knowledge: the church, the Bible, or a person's understanding of the Bible. With the Scientific Revolution, the West gravitated toward an open system of knowledge, not limited to Scripture or the humanities but branching far afield into the many disciplines of the natural and social sciences. Western thinking drew a dichotomy between faith and reason. Matters of reason were subject to rules of logic. The Greeks had already divided the universe between humans and culture on the one hand, and nature on the other, to distinguish the subjective from the objective. This permitted a comprehensive study of the objective world. Westerners sought knowledge through empirical observation, inductive and deductive reasoning, and synthesis and analysis. Historical analogy was a minor analytical tool, not the fundamental tool that it was for the Chinese. Westerners primarily sought knowledge not in the past, but in the surrounding empirical world, where they applied this knowledge not to re-create an idealized past but to chart an unknown future that, it was

East Asia has long had a thriving maritime trade and China maintained active ties with Southeast Asia, which has large overseas Chinese communities. Chinese inventions included many navigational instruments, including the compass.

hoped, would prove to be better than the past. China also has a venerable scientific tradition and an impressive list of discoveries and inventions, but in imperial times its focus was on the concrete application of knowledge rather than the discovery and study of abstract principles.

Thus, while the West placed its hopes in "progress," China focused on continuity and stability. Since history was cyclical, the Chinese anticipated no expansion in human understanding. Their closed system had no place for the unprecedented because to be without precedent was a clear impossibility in a cyclical world. The Chinese looked to the past and to the humanities for guidance to understand the natural world and to determine proper courses of action in it. Until the final years of the last Chinese dynasty, education was based on the memorization of a limited number of classical works from the humanities; reasoning was often by historical analogy; and good governance entailed making current institutions approximate those of an idealized past.

The terms "universalistic" and "particularistic," and "elemental" and "holistic," help get at the heart of the cultural differences between China and the West. Whereas the West has long emphasized universalistic laws—whether scientific or legal—that applied to all like cases equally, China, by contrast, has gravitated toward particularistic rules dependent on the particular social context among particular people of different statuses. Laws and institutions with jurisdictions defined by law have created the social glue binding the West. The social glue in China has been *guanxi*. Traditional Chinese thinking focused on defining the proper behavior among people in a vertical society, where no two ever held precisely the same status and where degrees of inequality always defined relationships.

The Chinese took a particularistic view of laws because they had a holistic approach to knowledge. Whereas Western scientific thought from the time of ancient Greece broke things down into their constituent parts, or elements, and then examined these parts in isolation from the others, the Chinese believed that understanding, particularly concerning people, required consideration of the entire situation, hence their focus on relationships. (See Table I.6.)

Table I.6 Modern Reflection of Traditional Values

West	East
The Individual in Society	
individualistic social system	collectivist social system
individual as one among equals	individual as part of and subordinate to the whole
independence	interdependence
success for oneself	success for the group
individual action	collective action
individual distinctiveness	harmonious blending
self-esteem	self-improvement
transmitter orientation	receiver orientation
egalitarianism	hierarchy
achieved status	ascribed status
universal rules of behavior	particularistic rules dependent on the social context
control the situation	adjust to the situation
control of the environment	self-control
The Analytical Approach to Understanding Society	
formal logic	common sense
reason	reasonableness
logic	dialectic
right/wrong, forcing a choice	both/and, allowing a melding (*yin* and *yang*)
law of noncontradiction	harmonizing of opposites to find a middle way
law of identity: cross-situational consistency	pointless to discuss the thing without its context

Source: Richard E. Nisbett, *The Geography of Thought: How Asians and Westerners Think Differently . . . and Why* (New York: Free Press, 2003), *passim*.

Conclusions

These five sets of top-down, radial, bottom-up, cyclical, and retrospective cultural elements provide a framework for understanding the distinguishing features of Chinese culture. In the twenty-first century, China has been undergoing enormous change and these characteristics are also changing, but they are not necessarily disappearing. Rather, these traits should be understood as dynamic elements of Chinese history.

The top-down elements of Confucianism, military strategy, Legalism, and Sinification all presupposed a vertical hierarchy, assigning each to his or her proper station with obligations to superiors and inferiors. There were no equals in the traditional Chinese world. The emperor sat at the apex of the civilized world, meaning the part of the universe that counted. Peoples became relevant to the degree that they became Sinified. Individuals became important to the degree that they became educated and ascended the social hierarchy. Place in this steep hierarchy determined expected treatment of and by others. *Guanxi* and face then reinforced these behavioral expectations and amplified the ramifications of any perceived deviations from the accepted norms of conduct. Lack of due deference to superiors not only insulted but also, if unpunished, threatened a potential loss of face and injury to the superior's *guanxi* system. This made dealing with foreigners who did not adhere to Chinese beliefs particularly troublesome.

The Chinese attempted to solve this problem through their radial cultural elements. Sinocentrism put China at the center and barbarians at increasing degrees of inferiority in proportion to their lack of Sinification. But China still had relations with the barbarian world. It insulated its citizenry from these contacts through a system of barbarian management that attempted to keep trade and punitive military action on the frontiers. To administer China proper, the Chinese employed another radial system: the delegation of power from the center to the provinces through an extensive bureaucracy staffed by Confucian scholars.

Although authority radiated down from the top, popular sentiments still bubbled up from the bottom. Daoist and Buddhist beliefs permeated all strata of Chinese society. Often, those out of power expressed their discontent through Daoist or Buddhist withdrawal from the temporal to the spiritual world. Poetry could also be used to criticize injustice.

The cyclical elements of *yin* and *yang*, the dynastic cycle, and historical continuity explained both change and continuity in human affairs. While events were eternally in flux, they changed within prescribed cycles. A system of cycles implied that all knowledge could be found within the cycle and, in this sense, constituted a closed system. The cycles were predetermined. This fit with the Chinese emphasis on fate. Belief in a closed system had profound implications for the pursuit of knowledge.

Fate and the sources of knowledge were the two retrospective elements of Chinese culture. Just as the cycles of history kept returning to points in the past, the quest for knowledge was a journey into the past. Individuals looked to their own fate as an explanation for their present circumstances, while scholars mined the past for analogies to understand the present. The Chinese sought to understand the human and natural worlds in order to bring the human world in conformity with the laws of heaven. Only by doing so could humans avert disaster in the otherwise tragic cycle of life that brought decay to all beings. Humans should strive to re-create the golden age in the present. But in the manner of all things, the attempt would be temporary, since history, in conformity with Buddhist views, moved in its endless cycle of decay and rejuvenation.

To survive in this natural world, the Chinese created a particularistic social system emphasizing an intricate hierarchy of social relations and the ethical rules governing these relations. Rules applied not universally to all individuals, but specifically to a particular situation involving individuals with a particular absolute social status as well as a particular social status relative to each other. This system emphasized prescribed rules of conduct, and social relations were conceived in terms of obligations. In contrast, the West gravitated toward universalistic social *and* intellectual constructs where laws applied universally to all, with comparatively little attention to differences in status. Laws were more often proscriptive than prescriptive. Individuals had rights and freedom of action, with little or no emphasis on obligations. In the intellectual world, laws tended to be even more universal as scientists sought ever more overarching generalizations to explain the natural world. On the other hand, Westerners preferred to analyze the world a piece at a time, while Chinese took a holistic approach to knowledge.

Chinese and Western civilizations embraced fundamentally different views of the world, of a person's place in it, and of a person's ability to understand and manipulate it. These views were not only different but largely incompatible. Each civilization assumed its own superiority. The universalism of the West implied conformity of the rest, just as China's Sinocentric view of the world assumed cultural assimilation with China. Both China and the West used education to shape others. The Chinese educational system focused on shaping proper conduct, which they found severely wanting in most Westerners. Chinese demanded that foreigners wishing to interact with China conform to its norms of social conduct. But the Chinese did not, as a rule, travel far afield in order to impose their customs. Rather, the Chinese model for dealing with outsiders assumed a gradual and largely passive assimilation of Chinese culture by others.

The Western emphasis on logical consistency made the Western intellectual tradition far more intrusive than that of China. Logical consistency entailed an active corrosion of the traditions of others. When Westerners encountered different civilizations, they set about analyzing them. When they found inconsistent philosophical principles, they endeavored to discover, through the rules of logic and evidence, which was correct. More often than not, they found themselves correct, whereupon they set about educating others concerning their errors. Their rules of logic were not tolerant of other belief systems that did not put a primacy on logical consistency. They did not allow for the layered belief system of the Chinese, which could accommodate inconsistent belief systems.

Westerners also had a truly grand agenda, not only for themselves, but for everyone else. Whereas the Chinese sought to conform to natural forces, Westerners worked to rewrite the rules of the game. They coined a term for it, "the conquest of nature." Westerners used their analytical framework to understand the natural world. With this understanding, they created technological inventions that increased labor productivity. This, in turn, produced a dramatic increase in the standard of living. By creating economic growth—on an unprecedented scale from the Industrial Revolution on—the West irrevocably altered standards of living, life expectancies, the international balance of power, and the very face of the planet now etched with the transportation and metropolises of an industrial world. For better or worse, the West fundamentally altered not just its own future but the world's, including China's.

It is important for Westerners to understand that the industrial world in which they live and that many take for granted is a product, in huge measure, of Western ways of thinking. They need to understand it as a product that others often view as a Western export and, in many cases, as an objectionable one. Other civilizations have not necessarily welcomed the Industrial Revolution or the intellectual and social traditions at its root. In fact, these traditions have been highly destabilizing to traditional societies. It is also important to understand that an emphasis on individual rights and intellectual freedom is likewise a product of Western conventions, dearly won over a period of centuries.

It is incorrect to assume that most Chinese desire to import this Western world. Throughout their history, China's leaders have repeatedly made it clear that they, at least, reject Western civilization. In the modern era, these leaders have often coveted the technological creativity and high standard of living of the West but have generally tried to eschew the rest of Western civilization. This desire for modernization—the technological products of an industrial society—without westernization—the institutions characterizing today's most economically developed societies—may well be unattainable. It remains to be proven that self-sustaining modernization is possible without an underlying westernized institutional base. In other words, the fruits and much of the garden may turn out to be a package deal.

Differences between civilizations and their underlying assumptions remain a source of tensions and misunderstandings. While the Chinese have often fumed at what they have considered reprehensible Western conduct rooted in a breathtaking ignorance of the most elementary rules of human conduct, Westerners have fumed at what they have considered to be Chinese logical inconsistency and consequently "irrational" behavior. Westerners have tried to understand these tensions in terms of form versus content, pigeonholing the Chinese preoccupation with proper conduct as an obsession with form instead of a proper (and rational) focus on content. Irritation over these two issues—Chinese views of proper conduct versus Western notions of rational conduct—has not disappeared but remains very much a part of the present. To understand China, one must look to its history and cultural traditions.

BIBLIOGRAPHY

Cai, Deborah A. "Looking Below the Surface: Cultural Subtleties in U.S. and Chinese Negotiations." In *Tigers' Roar: Asia's Recovery and Its Impact,* edited by Julian Weiss, 213–221. Armonk, NY: M. E. Sharpe, 2001.

Chan, Wing-tsit, trans. and comp. *A Source Book in Chinese Philosophy.* Princeton, NJ: Princeton University Press, 1963.

Ch'ü, T'ung-tsu. *Law and Society in Traditional China.* Paris: Mouton, 1961.

Confucius. *The Analects.* Translated by Raymond Dawson. Oxford: Oxford University Press, 1993.

de Bary, William Theodore. *Eastern Canons: Approaches to the Asian Classics.* New York: Columbia University Press, 1990.

———. *East Asian Civilizations: A Dialogue in Five Stages.* Cambridge, MA: Harvard University Press, 1988.

Eberhard, Wolfram. *Guilt and Sin in Traditional China.* Berkeley: University of California Press, 1967.

Elman, Benjamin A. *A Cultural History of Civil Examinations in Late Imperial China.* Berkeley: University of California Press, 2000.

Fairbank, John K., ed. *Chinese Thought and Institutions.* Chicago: University of Chicago Press, 1957.

———*The Chinese World Order: Traditional China's Foreign Relations.* Cambridge, MA: Harvard University Press, 1968.

Fung, Yu-lan. *A History of Chinese Philosophy.* Translated by Derk Bodde, 2 vols. Princeton, NJ: Princeton University Press, 1952.

Gold, Thomas, Doug Guthrie, and David Wank, eds. *Social Connections in China: Institutions, Culture, and the Changing Nature of Guanxi.* Cambridge: Cambridge University Press, 2002.

Han Fei. *Han Fei Tzu: Basic Writings.* Translated by Burton Watson. New York: Columbia University Press, 1964.

Hu, Hsien Chin. "The Chinese Concepts of 'Face.'" *American Anthropologist* 46 (1944): 45–64.

Huang, Philip C. C. *Code, Custom, and Legal Practice in China: The Qing and the Republic Compared.* Stanford, CA: Stanford University Press, 2001.

Jullien, François. *A Treatise on Efficacy: Between Western and Chinese Thinking.* Translated by Janet Lloyd. Honolulu: University of Hawai'i Press, 2004.

Koller, John M. *Asian Philosophies.* 4th ed. Upper Saddle River, NJ: Prentice Hall, 1998.

Lao Tzu. *Tao Te Ching.* Translated by Richard Wilhelm and H. G. Oswald. London: Penguin, 1985.

Lattimore, Owen. *Inner Asian Frontiers of China.* New York: American Geographical Society, 1940.

Lee-Wong, Song Mei. *Politeness and Face in Chinese Culture.* Frankfurt am Main: Peter Lang, 2000.

The Lotus Sutra, translated by Burton Watson. New York: Columbia University Press, 1993.

Mair, Victor H. "Classical Chinese Thought and Culture in Early Chinese History." *Newsletter of the Foreign Policy Research Institute.* http://www.fpri.org/footnotes/123.200702.mair.classicalchinesethought.html.

Mencius, *Mencius.* Translated by D. C. Lau. London: Penguin, 1970.

Mozi. *Mozi: Basic Writing,.* Translated by Burton Watson. New York: Columbia University Press, 2003.

Needham, Joseph. *Science and Civilisation in China.* Vols. 1, 2. Cambridge: Cambridge University Press, 1962–5.

Ng On-cho and Q. Edward Wang. *Mirroring the Past: The Writing and Use of History in Imperial China.* Honolulu: University of Hawai'i Press, 2005.

Nisbett, Richard E. *The Geography of Thought: How Asians and Westerners Think Differently . . . and Why.* New York: Free Press, 2003.

Nylan, Michael. *The Five "Confucian" Classics.* New Haven, CT: Yale University Press, 2001.

Schwartz, Benjamin I. *The World of Thought in Ancient China.* Cambridge, MA: Harvard University Press, 1985.

Smith, Richard J. *Fortune-tellers and Philosophers: Divination in Traditional Chinese Society.* Boulder, CO: Westview, 1991.

——— *China's Cultural Heritage: The Qing Dynasty, 1644–1912.* 2nd ed. Boulder, CO: Westview, 1994.

So, Ying Lun and Anthony Walker. *Explaining Guanxi: The Chinese Business Network.* London: Routledge, 2006.

Sun Tzu. *Sun Tzu: The Art of War.* Translated by Ralph D. Sawyer. Boulder, CO: Westview, 1994.

van der Sprenkel, Sybille. *Legal Institutions in Manchu China: A Sociological Analysis.* London: Athlone Press, 1962.

Wilson, Thomas A., ed. *On Sacred Grounds: Culture, Politics, and the Formation of the Cult of Confucius.* Cambridge, MA: Harvard University Press, 2002.

Xunzi. *Hsün Tzu: Basic Writings.* Translated by Burton Watson. New York: Columbia University Press, 1963.

Yan, Yunxiang. *The Flow of Gifts: Reciprocity and Social Networks in a Chinese Village.* Stanford, CA: Stanford University Press, 1996.

Yang, Mayfair Mei-hui. *Gifts, Favors & Banquets: The Art of Social Relationships in China.* Ithaca, NY: Cornell University Press, 1994.

Zhang, Dainian. *Key Concepts in Chinese Philosophy.* Translated and edited by Edmund Ryden. New Haven, CT: Yale University Press, 2002.

Zhuangzi. *The Book of Chuang Tzu.* Translated by Martin Palmer and Elizabeth Breuilly, London: Penguin, 1996.

Zito, Angela. *Of Body & Brush: Grand Sacrifice as Text/Performance in Eighteenth-Century China.* Chicago: University of Chicago Press, 1997.

NOTES

1. Taijia was the son and successor of the founder of the Shang dynasty (1766–1122 BC). Mencius citing Confucius in *Mencius,* D. C. Lau, trans. (London: Penguin, 1970), 121.

2. Lao Tzu, *Tao Te Ching,* Richard Wilhelm and H. G. Ostwald, trans. (London: Penguin, 1989), 40.

3. Orville Schell, *Mandate of Heaven* (New York: Simon & Schuster, 1994).
4. Hsün Tzu, *Hsün Tzu: Basic Writings,* Burton Watson, trans. (New York: Columbia University Press, 1963), 140.
5. Han Fei, *Han Fei Tzu: Basic Writings,* Burton Watson, trans. (New York: Columbia University Press, 1964), 89.
6. Ibid., 86.
7. Mencius, *Mencius,* D. C. Lau, trans. (London: Penguin, 1970), 103.
8. Ibid., 95.
9. Lao Tzu, *Tao Te Ching,* Richard Wilhelm and H. G. Ostwald, trans. (London: Penguin, 1989), 28, 43.
10. Zhuangzi, *The Book of Zhuang Tzu*, Martin Palmer and Elizabeth Breuilly, trans. (London: Penguin, 1996), 64.

Thematic Chronology (1644–1842)

Decade	Politics	Economy	Diplomacy	Society	Culture
1620s	Nurgaci (r. 1616–26)		Korea recognizes Qing suzerainty (1637)		
1640s	Shunzhi (r. 1644–61)		Fall of Ming (1644)		
1660s	Kangxi (r. 1662–1722)	Economic recovery			First Qing emperor to master Han culture
1680s			Revolt of the Three Feudatories (1673–81) Border treaty with Russia (1689)		
1700s					Completion of *Kangxi Dictionary* (1716)
1720s	Yongzheng (r. 1723–35) Creation of Grand Council (1729) Qianlong (r. 1736–95)	First law restricting opium (1729)	Trade treaty with Russia (1727)		Completion of official history of Ming (1739)
1740s			Zunghar Campaigns (1755–7) Western ships limited to Guangzhou (1757)	Jinchuan Uprising (1747–9)	Cultural flowering under Qianlong
1760s		Population growth outstripping productivity	Burma Campaign (1766–70)	Publication of laws of Qing Dynasty (1766) Jinchuan Uprising (1771–6)	Compilation of *Complete Library in Four Branches of Literature*, (1773–85), 36,358 volumes
1780s	Jiaqing (r. 1796–1820) Death of Qianlong (1799)		Annam Campaign (1788–9) Macartney Mission (1793)	Miao Uprising (1795–1805) White Lotus Rebellion (1796–1805)	
1800s		Ban on opium consumption (1813)		Eight Trigrams Rebellion (1813)	Ban on Western books and contacts (1805)
1820s	Daoguang (r. 1821–50)	Ban on opium production (1830)	Defeat of Jahangir (1820–8) Opium War (1839–42)		

Part I

The Creation and Maturation of an Empire, 1644–1842

Part I of this book will focus on the creation and maturation of the Qing empire, when the Manchus consolidated their rule over China, grafted Manchu ways onto Han institutions and practices, and made many of their own institutional innovations. In keeping with the Chinese method of periodizing their own history—a dating system based on the reign year of the ruling emperor, not on the open-ended continuum of consecutive years used in the West—these changes will be discussed in rough accordance with the reigns of the main emperors. Part II will discuss the decline and collapse of the Qing Dynasty, followed by an analysis of the Republican interregnum in Part III, and Part IV will focus on the Communist period in Chinese history. These four parts correspond to the dynastic cycle of rise, fall, interregnum, and back to rise. The features presented in the introductions to these parts concern the celebrations taking place during the cycle of the calendar year.

CHINESE NEW YEAR AND LANTERN FESTIVAL

Unlike the Western New Year celebration, Chinese New Year falls on a different date every year because the traditional calendar was lunar, not solar, meaning that it followed the cycles of the moon. Like the Western solar calendar, the traditional Chinese calendar generally had twelve months per year. Also like the solar calendar, which every fourth or leap year adds an extra day to February, periodically the lunar calendar added a thirteenth month to keep up with the phases of the moon. Although China adopted the Western or civil calendar beginning in 1911 with the fall of the Qing dynasty, holidays still follow the lunar or farmers' calendar.

New Year's is the most important festival of the year. It focuses on family, feasting, and prosperity. The Chinese New Year starts with the new moon on the first day of the lunar year and ends with the full moon fifteen days later with special events in between. People display paper scrolls, called "spring couplets," featuring auspicious words such as "good fortune," "wealth," "longevity," and "springtime." Often people display the scroll upside down because the Mandarin word for "upside down" is a homophone for "arrival" (*dao*), meaning the arrival of the good fortune prophesied on the scrolls. Family members do their best to return home for massive family get-togethers and a New Year's Eve feast that often includes seafood and dumplings. Prawns symbolize liveliness and happiness, raw fish bring good luck, angel hair (an edible seaweed) brings prosperity, and dumplings signify wealth. Family members and friends exchange bags of oranges and tangerines, symbolizing happiness. Tangerines with their leaves still attached symbolize secure friendship and, for newlyweds, a wish for fertility.

There are many superstitions associated with the holiday. While it is lucky to see or hear songbirds, red-colored birds, or swallows, it is unlucky to greet someone in a bedroom. Using knives or scissors on New Year's Day is taboo, since they may cut off good fortune. The color red and fireworks are thought to ward off evil spirits. According to legend, when a god dared *Nian,* the man-eating beast, to eat all unwanted predators, the monster did so, only to be taken

Continued

China's New Year is determined by the lunar calendar and is usually celebrated during late January or early February. The Lantern Festival is celebrated on the fifteenth day of the first lunar month, which falls on the first full moon. On this day, bright lanterns are hung to symbolize good luck and children play with firecrackers.

away by the god. Since *Nian* is a homophone for the Mandarin word for "year," *guonian* means both "to survive the *Nian* monster" and "to celebrate the New Year." For the festivities, people often festoon windows and doors with red decorations, wear red clothing, and set off firecrackers, all to make sure that the *Nian* never returns. Likewise, lion and dragon dance performances are intended to scare away evil spirits.

The Lantern Festival occurs on the fifteenth and final day, with people celebrating at night with songs, dances, and lantern displays. According to legend, the Jade Emperor in heaven intended to burn down a village responsible for killing his favorite goose, but a good-hearted fairy warned the villagers to light lanterns so that from heaven the lights made the Jade Emperor think that the town had already been destroyed.

According to traditional age calculations, all children became one year old at birth and a year older with each passing New Year's Day. This can become quite confusing if a child is born immediately before New Year's, since a newborn could suddenly be two years old. More and more Chinese now use the Western calendar to calculate ages and to celebrate individual birthdays on the date of birth, particularly in Taiwan and increasingly in the PRC.

Chapter 1 begins with an examination of the decline of the Ming dynasty and the founding of the Qing empire by Nurgaci, the leader of the Manchus. It then evaluates the contributions to the empire of his first three successors. The Shunzhi emperor successfully grafted Manchu institutions onto the preexisting Han administrative structure; the Kangxi emperor helped extend and consolidate Manchu power throughout the empire; and the Yongzheng emperor made important institutional innovations. The structural, territorial, and institutional reforms put in place by these three Manchu rulers prepared China for the flowering of the Qing dynasty discussed in Chapters 2 through 4.

Chapter 2 focuses on the territorial, military, political, and economic changes during the reign of the Qianlong emperor, who ruled at the height of Qing power. His conquests in Mongolia, central Asia, and Tibet brought the Qing empire to its maximum territorial extent. To make conquests, to incorporate new territories, and to administer a much-expanded empire, he instituted military, administrative, and commercial reforms.

Chapter 3 describes Chinese society at the height of Qing power. It shows how the Manchus maintained their minority rule over Han China by relying on Han social structures and ideology. Traditional Han notions of social organization divided society into a four-part ascending hierarchy of merchants, artisans, peasants, and scholars, with scholars staffing the imperial bureaucracy. Confucianism provided the ideology to justify their rule. The Qing allowed traditional Chinese religions, Han culture, and Confucian government to flourish both to disguise their alien origins and to legitimate their rule.

The inculcation of the imperial ideology is the subject of Chapter 4. Manchu dominance over Han China and civil administration of an empire required the acquiescence, if not cooperation, of a vast Han administrative apparatus and of a far more vast Han population. The Manchus, like their Han predecessors, acquired this cooperation, in part, through the educational system that promoted an ideology to justify and facilitate imperial rule. The imperial examination system determined the content and standards for this educational system emphasizing the Chinese Classics, analysis by historical analogy, and a cyclical understanding of history and human affairs.

The focus of Chapter 5 turns from events within the Qing empire to China's relations with its neighbors. From the late Ming dynasty forward, China had increasing contacts with Europeans. The first Westerners to maintain extensive contacts with the Chinese were explorers and missionaries.

By the eighteenth and nineteenth centuries there was a two-pronged European advance on China: the maritime advance from Portugal, Spain, Holland, and England and the continental advance from Russia. With these expanding contacts came increasing friction over legal, social, and religious differences.

Growing contacts with the West coincided with internal decline, which is the focus of Chapter 6. Over the years, the Chinese government had become increasingly corrupt and the Manchus had become ever more decadent administrators of their empire. Simultaneously, population growth had begun to outstrip agricultural productivity. This led to growing poverty, which, in turn, exacerbated the ethnic and anti-Manchu tensions that fed rebellion. The Miao, White Lotus, and Eight Trigrams rebellions indicated serious and widespread grievances within the Qing empire. As these internal tensions worsened, so did the friction with the growing number of European traders.

Chapter 7 examines this foreign trade, the institutions regulating it, and the economic implications of the widening trade imbalance. Initially, the West coveted Chinese tea, silks, and porcelains, while China had no equivalent desire for any Western products. Then the British discovered the Chinese appetite for opium. As the Europeans increasingly rejected Chinese institutions for barbarian management and the Chinese pressure for Sinification, war soon supplanted negotiations. The Treaty of Nanjing settled the First Opium War by opening so-called treaty ports to Western commerce, setting tariffs on Chinese trade, and granting Western expatriates extraterritoriality in China. This concludes Part I on the creation and maturation of the Qing empire.

Chronology

1616	Founding of the Jin dynasty by Nurgaci
1620	Death of the Wanli emperor
1622	Nurgaci's conquest of the Manchurian cities of Shenyang and Liaoyang
1624	Establishment of a Dutch fortress on Taiwan
1636	Change of dynasty name to Qing by Hong Taiji; Qing occupation of the Korean capital
1637	Korean recognition of the Qing suzerainty
1644	Establishment of the Shun dynasty and conquest of Beijing by Li Zicheng
	Suicide of the last Ming emperor; fall of the Ming dynasty; fall of Beijing to the Qing army
	Shunzhi emperor assumes the throne
1645	Qing occupation of Nanjing, the capital of the Southern Ming dynasty
	Qing execution of Li Zicheng
1650	Fall of Xiamen (Amoy) and the island of Jinmen (Quemoy) to Zheng Chenggong
	Death of Dorgon
1651	Shunzhi emperor assumes majority and rules
1661	Death of Shunzhi emperor; Kangxi emperor assumes the throne
	Zheng Chenggong attacks Taiwan and expels the Dutch
	Wu Sangui attacks Burma to eliminate the last Ming pretender
1662	Death of Zheng Chenggong in Taiwan
1667	Kangxi assumes majority and rules
1673–81	Revolt of the Three Feudatories
1683	Qing conquest of Taiwan
1689	Sino-Russian Treaty of Nerchinsk
1690s	Campaigns against the Zunghars
1716	Completion of the *Kangxi Dictionary*
1722	Death of Kangxi emperor; Yongzheng emperor assumes the throne
1724	Pacification of Qinghai
1727	Sino-Russian Treaties of Bura and Kiakhta
1729	Creation of the Grand Council
1735	Death of Yongzheng emperor; Qianlong emperor assumes the throne

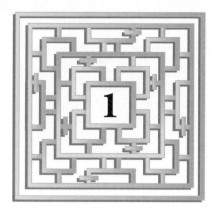

The Creation of
the Qing Dynasty

As Yü the Great treasured each moment,
So must you value time in its passing.
Learn from the Ancients in each book you open,
Seek inner meanings of every occurrence.
Slowly your heart will grow joyful,
And the beauty of sacrificial foods be yours.[1]

Kangxi emperor (1654–1722)
to the heir apparent, 1684

The Qing dynasty (1644–1911) supplanted the declining Ming dynasty (1368–1644) and continued to prosper and expand until about 1795. At its height, the Qing state was one of the largest, wealthiest, and most powerful empires in world history. Qing rule extended in the northeast into the Amur River Basin in Siberia, in the north beyond the Gobi Desert of Outer Mongolia, in the northwest through much of Central Asia, in the southwest to the Himalayas, in the south to Hainan Island, and in the southeast across the Taiwan Strait. The extended empire included China's tributary states of Korea, Mongolia, Tibet, Burma, Thailand, Laos, Vietnam, and Okinawa, as well as numerous peoples living in southeast, central, and northeast Asia. Only the thirteenth-century Mongol Yuan empire exceeded Qing China in geographic extent and population.

I. The Ming Dynasty

Like most Chinese dynasties, the Ming ultimately gained and lost power through military force. (See Table 1.1.) With the famine of the 1340s and the peasant revolts of the 1350s, the Han founder of the Ming, the future Hongwu emperor, led his army to victory against the Mongol, or Yuan, dynasty (1279–1368). By 1363,

he defeated his internal rivals. His army then consolidated control over the Yangzi River valley. On 23 January 1368, the Hongwu emperor (1328–98) proclaimed his new dynasty the "Ming," meaning "brilliance," while his reign title, "Hongwu," meant "vast and martial." By 1372, he consolidated Ming rule as far north as the Great Wall and as far south and southwest as Guangxi and Yunnan provinces. For over twenty years, the Ming dynasty also unsuccessfully tried to make central Vietnam a province, but withdrew in 1427.

The Hongwu emperor made many important structural changes to consolidate his rule: He divided the military into five separate but equal commissions to reduce the possibility of coups; he promulgated the *Great Ming Code* to rule his subjects; and he issued a separate set of *Ancestral Injunctions* to govern the imperial clan. These parallel legal systems provided the Han Ming emperors imperial authority similar to that of the Mongol khans. Later the Manchu emperors took such powers for granted from their own non-Han heritage.

After the Hongwu emperor died in 1398, his grandson, the Jianwen emperor (1377–1402?), succeeded him. Infighting quickly erupted when the Hongwu emperor's son, the Yongle emperor (1360–1424), seized power in 1402. Although the new emperor's father founded the Ming dynasty in Nanjing, a city in central China whose name translates to "southern capital," in 1420 the Yongle emperor moved the capital to the northern city of Beiping, meaning "northern peace," renaming it Beijing or "northern capital." This position allowed the Yongle emperor to defend China's vulnerable northern and northeastern borders and provided a suitable base from which to extend the empire.

The Yongle emperor also enacted extensive government reforms, completing the subordination of Nanjing

Table 1.1   Ming Dynasty Emperors (1368–1644)

Reign Title	Year of Birth	Age at Accession	Reign*
Hongwu	1328	40	1368–98
Jianwen	1377	22	1399–1402?
Yongle	1360	43	1403–24
Hongxi	1378	47	1425
Xuande	1399	27	1426–35
Zhengtong†	1427	9	1436–49
Jingtai†	1428	22	1450–7
Tianshun†	1427	30	1457–64
Chenghua	1447	18	1465–87
Hongzhi	1470	18	1488–1505
Zhengde	1491	15	1506–21
Jiajing	1507	15	1522–67
Longqing	1537	30	1567–72
Wanli	1563	10	1573–1620
Taichang	1582	38	1620
Tianqi	1605	16	1621–7
Chongzhen	1611	17	1628–44

*The reign ends with the monarch's death, although the reign title was sometimes used into the following year.

†The Zhengtong and Tianshun emperors were the same person. The Mongols held the Zhengtong emperor hostage from September 1449 to September 1450. He was not restored to the throne until 1457, the year of the Jingtai emperor's death.

Source: L. Carrington Goodrich, ed., *Dictionary of Ming Biography 1368–1644,* vol. 1 (New York: Columbia University Press, 1976), xxi. Copyright © 1985, Columbia University Press. Reprinted with permission of the publisher.

to the new offices in Beijing. Although after his death the capital nominally reverted to Nanjing from 1425 to 1441, his successors remained in Beijing. Except for the 1928–49 hiatus, when the Nationalist government once again called the city Beiping in deference to their Yangzi River capitals, Beijing has remained the accepted capital of China ever since 1441.

The Ming move to the north affected the military, the economy, and domestic transport. Protecting the northern borders became the army's primary responsibility. The Yongle emperor himself led several military campaigns into Mongolia to subordinate rebellious tribes to the tributary system. Likewise, the Ming court expended much effort to bring the Jurchen tribes in Manchuria into the tributary system. Although it failed in Japan, it succeeded in Korea, which remained China's closest tributary until Japan supplanted China in Korea in 1895. To this day, many Koreans consider China to have been an exemplary suzerain. The transformation of Beijing into the imperial capital also had important economic consequences. Tax revenues from throughout the empire converged on the new capital. These were often paid in grain, entailing a massive transfer of wealth from South to North China and an efficient transportation system to get it there.

By 1415 the Ming had rebuilt the Grand Canal and constructed a fleet of 3,000 flat-bottomed boats to keep the grain tribute flowing. Following the move from Nanjing to Beijing, the Yongle emperor commissioned such famous Beijing sites as a new palace complex called the Forbidden City, a bell tower, and the Altar to Heaven and had the massive city walls repaired. These buildings remain potent symbols in China, which, with the exception of the city walls taken down during the Cultural Revolution, continue to grace Beijing.

The Ming dynasty also supported an unprecedented policy of naval exploration. In a series of voyages under the command of the palace eunuch Zheng He (1371–1433), an enormous fleet numbering about 250 ships and manned by over 27,000 military personnel sailed as far south as Siam, Java, and India and as far west as the Maldives, the Persian Gulf, the Red Sea, and Africa. Although the Ming expeditions linked China with fully one half of the known world and created dozens of new tributary relationships with kingdoms in Southeast Asia, India, and eastern Africa, the costs of the voyages did not provide comparable benefits to the state. About a decade after Yongle's death in 1424, Ming bureaucrats canceled the expeditions by successfully arguing that overseas trade had little purpose in

The Forbidden City in Beijing was built from 1406 to 1420. At its height, it included almost 1,000 buildings with 9,000 rooms and occupied close to 8 million square feet of space. It was the home of the emperor for almost five centuries, until 1925, when it was turned into the Palace Museum. In 1625, the Manchus built their own palace modeled on the Forbidden City in Shenyang, Manchuria, but moved to Beijing's Forbidden City in 1644.

agrarian China. It is unclear whether or not the voyages had any long-term impact on the thriving private trade with Southeast Asia or on the Chinese diaspora, visible in the large overseas Chinese communities throughout the region.

The Ming decision proved fateful, since it halted an era of exploration that, had it continued, might have brought China into contact with Europe prior to the Industrial Revolution that shifted the international balance of power so decisively in Europe's favor. Since Zheng He's voyages preceded, by over half a century, Europe's so-called age of exploration and by over three centuries the beginnings of the Industrial Revolution, China might well have been technologically superior, not inferior, to the Europeans. If early Sino–European links had been forged, then China might have been able to retain its technological lead. Instead, in 1517, it was ships

from the small but vibrant European nation of Portugal that first arrived in the South China city of Guangzhou (Canton).

The cancellation of China's naval expeditions had an especially negative impact on Chinese technological development. China did not become aware until the late nineteenth century of Western European theoretical advances in chemistry, physics, and metallurgy. In particular, the European technology for warfare changed rapidly during the intervening years, and this asymmetry allowed Europe to dominate China militarily in the nineteenth century. By the sixteenth century the Chinese became eager to purchase technologically superior European-made muskets, but they missed the theoretical advances at the root of the improved technology.

Another important European import was religion. In 1580 the Italian Jesuit Matteo Ricci (1552–1610) arrived in Macao. After mastering both vernacular and written Chinese, Ricci finally obtained permission in 1602 to reside permanently in Beijing. By dressing and behaving like a Confucian scholar, Ricci and other Jesuits were able to form cordial relations with the Ming Court. Although they made few religious converts, they introduced Western scientific learning to the Ming Confucian elite, who were particularly interested in Western advances in astronomy. They wanted the most accurate astronomical calculations possible in order to determine appropriate times to conduct Court rituals. Thus, there was a convergence of the Chinese preoccupation with ritual and the Western scientific expertise in measuring time.

Ming society was diverse and dynamic. At Court, over 50,000 eunuchs served as functionaries in the palace, the government bureaucracy, and the military. Other officials came from those members of China's gentry class who performed well on the civil service examination. The government administration was divided into the Six Boards of the Outer Court (Personnel, Revenue, Rites, War, Justice, and Public Works) and the Six Halls of the Inner Court (composed of imperial palace residents and the emperor's closest advisers). The Ming concentrated civil and military power in the hands of the emperor by abolishing the traditional executive posts in the Six Boards and splitting the military.

Although the Ming government functioned reasonably well even without a strong emperor, by the late sixteenth century there were signs of decline associated with the final stages of the dynastic cycle. The Wanli emperor (r. 1573–1620), in particular, generally ignored his imperial responsibilities despite virtually constant warfare. Chinese troops successfully quelled a Mongol rebellion in northwest China, fought the Japanese to a draw in Korea, and extended Ming power southwest into Sichuan and Guizhou provinces.

Although Wanli's troops invariably won his frequent battles, the financial drain weakened the state, while his enemies gathered strength. Ming troops were already fighting the Manchus during the final years of his rule. Following his death, the final three Ming emperors became increasingly weak. As anticipated by the dynastic cycle, the end of the Ming proved to be similar to its rise: Widespread rural unrest destabilized the government and heralded a new dynamic dynasty to replace the now decadent Ming.

II. The Qing Conquest of Ming China: Nurgaci and His Successors

In 1583, during the reign of the Wanli emperor, Nurgaci (Nurhaci, 1559–1626) began to combine the Jurchen tribes to create the Jurchen dynasty (referred to as "Manchu" only after 1635) through a combination of warfare, intermarriage among the major Jurchen tribes, and the cultivation of Ming rulers. In 1619 his 50,000-man cavalry defeated a larger Ming army, and by early 1620 he ruled Manchuria unopposed. The Wanli emperor died that summer amid fears that the Ming dynasty was at an end.

Nurgaci, from 1620 until his death from battle wounds in 1626, continued to consolidate his rule from his capital at Shenyang (Mukden) in south Manchuria's Liaoning province. Many Han members of Nurgaci's civil and military elite, who were essential for the Manchu conquest of China, came from Manchuria. Nurgaci's eighth son, Hong Taiji (1592–1643, also known as Abahai), ruled the Jurchen until 1643, the year prior to the establishment of Qing rule in Beijing. During Hong Taiji's seventeen-year reign, he focused on conquering Beijing, which almost fell in 1630.

Hong Taiji faced an ill-prepared opponent, the Chongzhen emperor (r. 1628–44), who was only seventeen years old when he ascended the Ming throne. During the 1630s, Hong Taiji's power grew, while Chongzhen's gradually declined. Hong Taiji carefully cultivated Han Chinese support by trying to treat the Han with respect and punishing Manchu officers who allowed their troops to pillage Han villages. By practicing the Confucian virtue of benevolence, Hong Taiji hoped to demonstrate that the Manchus had the mandate of heaven. Hong Taiji also accepted and richly rewarded defecting Ming officers. With their assistance, he was able to seize Lüshun (later called Port Arthur), a major harbor on the tip of the Liaodong Peninsula on the sea approaches to Beijing. To secure his flank, he invaded Korea in 1636 and forced it to shift allegiance, a shift that many Koreans regretted for the duration of Manchu rule over China. That same year, in a direct challenge to Ming dynastic authority, Hong Taiji proclaimed himself emperor of the Qing dynasty, meaning "pure and unsullied," but the Ming dynasty remained in power.

Meanwhile, the Chongzhen emperor's cruelty undermined his military support; he executed numerous military commanders who failed to defeat the Qing. Even the dead were not safe. On occasion he had remains exhumed for public humiliation, to the horror of his subjects who followed Confucian prescriptions for ancestor worship. Simultaneous with the outer war against the Manchus was an inner war in the capital among competing Court factions that would ultimately allow the Qing to pick off Ming factions in detail, which means using a large force to defeat a number of smaller enemy units one after the other. Finally, the refusal of the Court to use treasury funds to suppress the Manchus resulted in huge increases in local taxes. This sparked the White Lotus Rebellion in 1622 and almost continuous peasant rebellions during the 1630s, creating a third layer of conflict in the countryside. The rapid turnover of grand secretaries indicated the precarious Ming hold on power; between 1634 and 1638 no fewer than nineteen court officials served in this position.

Political infighting in the capital, internal rebellion in the countryside, and foreign invasion on the periphery combined to undermine the Ming dynasty. Hong Taiji died the year before the collapse of the Ming dynasty. Peasant rebels, not Manchu forces, first surrounded Beijing and precipitated Chongzhen's suicide on 25 April 1644. While the bulk of the Ming army was north of the capital repelling Manchu invaders, Li Zicheng (1605?–1645) led a Xi'an-based peasant insurgency. With the Chongzhen emperor's death, Li's rebel forces entered the capital unopposed. (See Map 1.1.)

Li, who lacked funds to pay his troops, approved a reign of terror to extract money from Court officials and wealthy Beijing merchants. This so outraged the remaining Ming supporters that they allied with the Manchus to defeat Li. Included among the defectors was the pivotal military commander Wu Sangui (1612–78), who controlled the strategic pass at Shanhai, where the Great Wall meets the sea. In Shenyang, Prince Dorgon (1612–50), the fourteenth son of Nurgaci and the half-brother of Hong Taiji, became the new Manchu leader during the minority of Hong Taiji's son. With the assistance of Wu Sangui, who allowed Prince Dorgon and his troops through the Shanhai pass, the Manchus for the first time deployed large forces in China proper. Wu allegedly promised the Manchus gold and territory if they would help rid China of Li Zicheng, presumably leaving Wu as the new emperor.

On 5 June 1644, just two days after Li Zicheng declared himself emperor of the Shun dynasty, Dorgon took Beijing to proclaim a Qing emperor of China. This marked the transition from the Ming to the Qing dynasty. Although Ming loyalists in the South hoped to persuade Dorgon to accept a yearly stipend of 100,000 taels and any high title short of emperor, Dorgon instead installed his nephew, Hong

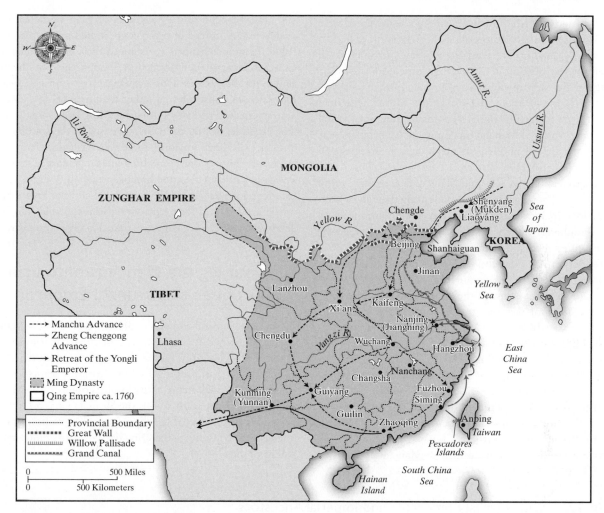

Map 1.1 Manchu Conquest

Taiji's six-year-old son, Fulin (1638–61), on the throne as the Shunzhi emperor. In October 1644, the Manchu Court moved to Beijing. The two major successor governments to the Qing, the Republican and Communist governments, also established themselves through military victory.

Qing power was based on the banner system created by Nurgaci. It constituted a military, not a civil, tradition of government authority. The banner system provided not only an army but also the means to administer conquered territories. Originally, Nurgaci divided his troops into four banners—yellow, white, red, and blue. During wartime, only a certain proportion of the men were called up at the same time. During peacetime, the banners, which included the family members of the bannermen, operated as military administrative district leaders, governing the territories under their jurisdiction and

performing such key administrative tasks as registration, taxation, and mobilization. This system proved so successful that in 1615 Nurgaci added another four Manchu banners, while in 1635 Hong Taiji added eight Mongol banners and two Han banners in 1637 and six more Han banners by 1642, making an equal division among the three ethnic groups, although the Manchu banners remained superior in status to the others. This totaled twenty-four banners or eight segregated banners each of Manchu, Han, and Mongol troops. Most bannermen were Han; in 1648 less than 16 percent were Manchu.[2]

The Manchus maintained a system of segregation for the duration of their dynasty. They distinguished between Han who had helped them conquer Ming China and who were part of the "conquering elite" and the vast majority who constituted the subject population. The Manchus drew firm lines between themselves and the latter.[3] Included among the privileged were Han and also Mongol bannermen. Segregation applied to many areas: Manchu intermarriage was not permitted until 1902; only Manchus could live in Manchuria until late in the dynasty; senior administrative appointments were paired— that is, a Manchu and usually a Han Chinese held dual appointments to each of the Six Boards forming the central government, with the Manchu predominant; Manchu banners protected the capital; and China's major cities were segregated into Manchu and Han districts. These rules allowed the Manchus to retain a safe haven in Manchuria and firm control over the central government while preventing their absorption into the Han majority through marriage or combined military forces. Simultaneously, the system cemented Han loyalties by allowing gifted scholars to achieve high appointment.

To perpetuate Manchu dominance, the twenty-four banners remained largely separate from the primarily Han infantry, known as the Army of the Green Standard. The command structure of the infantry remained weak as officers rotated constantly from post to post, precluding coup attempts. High-ranking military officers obtained their posts not necessarily for their military expertise, but often for their loyalty. Midway through the Qing period, the bannermen were estimated to total only 250,000. In contrast, by 1764, the Army of the Green Standard had grown to over 600,000 soldiers. This force was primarily deployed in the northwest, along the coast, and in southern China—that is, on the periphery, not in the areas most central to Manchu power.

The Manchu and Mongol cavalry, in particular, were widely feared. Instead of being concentrated in one place, after 1644 the various banners were spread throughout China, with especially large garrisons located in frontier regions in the north and in the major cities along the Yangzi River. They focused on the defense against internal rather than external foes. Internal unrest remained endemic during the Ming and Qing dynasties. For example, during the Ming dynasty in the southwestern province of Guizhou alone, there were at least seventy-seven Miao rebellions, or one every three and a half years.[4] Despite the image of China as a natural homogeneous unit, central control was repeatedly contested. Banner forces and the Han infantry made up one lever for perpetuating Manchu rule. The other lever was control over China's Confucian civil administration.

III. Grafting the Manchus onto Han China under the Shunzhi Emperor

During the Shunzhi emperor's reign (r. 1644–61), the Manchu court confirmed its claim to the mandate of heaven. (See Table 1.2.) Not only had it removed the decadent Ming Court, but it had preserved China from the atrocities of Li Zicheng. Although many Ming loyalists opposed the Manchu usurpation, by the early 1660s the Shunzhi emperor, through a combination of artifice, diplomacy, and military power, managed to consolidate the Qing dynasty throughout most of Ming China.

Table 1.2   Qing Dynasty Emperors and Imperial Ancestors

Reign Title	Year of Birth	Age at Accession	Reign
Nurgaci*	1559	57	1616–26
Hong Taiji*	1592	35	1627–43
Shunzhi	1638	6	1644–61
Kangxi	1654	8	1662–1722
Yongzheng	1678	45	1723–35
Qianlong†	1711	25	1736–95
Jiaqing	1760	36	1796–1820
Daoguang	1782	39	1820–50
Xianfeng	1831	20	1850–61
Tongzhi	1856	6	1861–75
Guangxu	1871	4	1875–1908
Xuantong‡	1906	2	1908–12

*In 1636, the later Jin dynasty changed its name to the Qing. It did not conquer China until 1644, the official beginning of the Qing dynasty.

†The Qianlong emperor abdicated in 1795 but died in 1799.

‡The former Xuantong emperor died in 1967.

The Shunzhi emperor began to rule directly in 1651, when he turned thirteen. His first task was to consolidate control, which entailed using the banner system to dominate the Han army. He also placed Manchus in high positions to oversee the day-to-day workings of the government. The most important challenge remained Ming loyalists, known as the Southern Ming. The Shunzhi emperor spent his entire reign trying to suppress them, but the collapse of the final resistance in Taiwan did not occur until 1683, many years after his death. The Southern Ming were based first in Nanjing under the authority of Zhu Yousong (1607–46), a first cousin of the Chongzhen emperor, formally enthroned in 1645 as the Hongguang emperor. His contemporaries described him as avaricious, licentious, unfilial, and cruel. Therefore, his Han court in Nanjing did not offer Confucian Ming loyalists a clearly superior alternative to the Manchu court in Beijing.

It is an open question whether the Manchus originally intended to take all of China. Suppression of the Ming and of peasant rebellions culminated in massive campaigns into Central and South China. By 1645, they defeated the peasant rebel Li Zicheng. In 1647 they executed Zhang Xianzhong (1606–47), another rebel leader, who had established a kingdom in Sichuan. Dorgon also focused his energy on the Ming loyalists. In late 1644, a massive army of 250,000 Manchu, Mongolian, and Han troops moved south toward the Yangzi River, surrounding and destroying the Ming base of operation in Yangzhou by late May 1645. The ensuing ten-day massacre was meant to eradicate Ming sympathizers and to terrorize anyone from questioning Qing rule.

The Manchu troops then crossed the Yangzi River to take the Southern Ming capital of Nanjing on 8 June 1645. The Hongguang emperor fled, only to be caught and delivered to Beijing for execution. Meanwhile, the Manchu army drove into Zhejiang province near modern-day Shanghai. Dorgon ordered a turncoat Ming official, Hong Chengchou (1593–1665), to head the Office for Pacification South of the River. In this way, Dorgon combined Manchu military supremacy with accepted practices from the Ming to consolidate Manchu rule. From 1646 to 1648, Hong largely succeeded in consolidating Qing power from the Yangzi River valley southward toward Guangzhou.

Flush with their success in June 1645, the Qing rulers unwittingly fed Han resistance by ordering all Han males to shave their foreheads and grow a long queue in the back. This not only conformed to Manchu customs but also made it easier to distinguish Ming from Qing loyalists. However, the order violated Confucian proscriptions against altering the skin or hair as a mark of filial piety. Han Chinese resisted; some committed suicide rather than submit. Throughout the rest of the Qing dynasty there was constant dissent.

Traditionally, the Manchus were nomads and were well known for their skill with the bow and arrows. Their long hair was braided into a long pigtail—called a "queue." During the early twentieth century, revolutionaries and many students in Japan and Europe expressed defiance by cutting off their queue, an act still punishable by death in China, and upon returning would wear a fake one (see Sun Yat-sen's 1910 photograph on page 227).

With the Manchu capture of Nanjing and the Hongguang emperor, the Southern Ming dynasty was leaderless. Two noble princes vied for the throne. On 18 August 1645, the followers of Zhu Yujian (1602–46) acted first; Zhu declared himself to be the Longwu emperor. Although his reign was short, ending the very next year, his promotion to general of the twenty-two-year-old Zheng Chenggong (1624–62) had long-term repercussions.

By the mid-1650s, Zheng Chenggong, better known in the West as Koxinga, gathered a large number of Ming loyalists in the coastal province of Fujian. In 1660, a large Qing army forced him to defend his base on the island of Jinmen (Quemoy). Although the Dutch fortified the southwestern corner of the island of Taiwan (Formosa) in 1624, in 1661 Zheng Chenggong attacked and forced the Dutch out of their fortress. Zheng surprised the Qing by promoting Han Chinese immigration to Taiwan. In just a couple of years over 100,000 Chinese emigrated, mainly from Fujian province. Over time, they gradually pushed the indigenous people into the foothills of Taiwan's central mountain range, formed their own distinctive culture, and spoke the southern Fujian Min dialect, also known today as Taiwanese. After Zheng Chenggong's death in 1662, his followers gradually fell into disarray. In 1683 the Qing attacked Taiwan, defeated Zheng's grandson, and turned the island into a prefecture of Fujian province. (Taiwan did not become a province until 1885.) Nevertheless, Zheng Chenggong established a precedent. Just as the last Ming loyalists fled to Taiwan, so would the defeated Republicans in the mid-twentieth century.

The last of the Ming military opposition ended when forces under Wu Sangui entered Burma to hunt down and dispatch the last Ming pretender, the Yongli emperor (1623–62). The Shunzhi emperor did not live to see the full reunification of China under Manchu rule but died in 1661 at the age of twenty-two. In his short life, he became thoroughly versed in Han traditions. The year before his death, he reportedly wished to shave his head to become a Buddhist monk until dissuaded by his advisers. As he lay dying of smallpox, the Shunzhi emperor unexpectedly designated his third son as his successor. Just shy of seven years old, the Kangxi emperor appears to have been chosen mainly because he survived the disease. This choice proved to be especially fortuitous. The Kangxi emperor would become one of the two greatest Qing rulers.

IV. Territorial Consolidation under the Kangxi Emperor

The Kangxi emperor (r. 1662–1722) began to rule directly when he turned fifteen in 1669. His reign title means "Glorious Peace," in anticipation of the final suppression of the Ming loyalists and projection of Manchu rule throughout the former Ming empire. At thirteen he fathered his first son and was already deeply involved in the Court intrigues to consolidate his rule against the wishes of competing regents. This culminated in his palace coup and the execution or imprisonment of these rivals in 1669. His ability to control such political intrigue allowed him to prevent the breakup of the newly created Qing empire and instead to solidify Manchu minority rule. His reign was the longest of that of all Qing emperors because his grandson, in an act of filial piety, abdicated on Chinese New Year's Day following his own sixtieth year so as not to exceed Kangxi's sixty-one-year reign. The grandson, the Qianlong emperor (r. 1736–95), is considered to be the dynasty's other great monarch.

Kangxi's ethnic heritage was mixed. He inherited Mongol blood from both his paternal grandfather, Hong Taiji, who was of Manchu-Mongol descent, and his paternal grandmother, who was fully Mongol. He was also one-quarter Han Chinese, since his mother, the Empress Xiaokang (1640–63), was born of a Manchu-Han union. Thus, less than one-half of his ancestry was Manchu. Although he grew up at the Manchu Court, he learned to speak and read both Manchu and Chinese, and he enjoyed reading works on history, government, and Confucianism. He usually dressed in traditional Chinese clothing, meticulously followed the many ancient Han customs, and brought many Han into his government.

The Kangxi emperor took seriously his position as the protector of Han culture. He promoted a variety of massive literary projects in order to help secure the loyalty of the Han literati, the Confucian scholar-administrators necessary to run the vast Qing empire. He commissioned a compilation of the history of the Ming dynasty, many major collections of literature and art, a complete anthology of Tang dynasty poetry, a comprehensive Chinese language dictionary, the *Kangxi Dictionary* (1710–16), and a massive encyclopedia, *A Collection of Books and Illustrations of Ancient and Modern Times* (1700–25), which became the longest encyclopedia in history. In deference to Han traditions, he visited the family shrine of Confucius located in Qufu, Shandong, and climbed the nearby Daoist sacred mountain, Mount Tai (Taishan).

Kangxi was also forward-looking. In 1668, when he was only fourteen, he became involved in creating an official state calendar. Jesuits working in the service first of the Ming and then of the Qing Court calculated the calendar differently from the Imperial Board of Astronomy. Because the Jesuits made use of new scientific discoveries in Europe, their calculations proved more accurate. Recognizing the superiority of these Western methods, the Kangxi emperor named the Jesuit Ferdinand Verbiest (1623–88) vice-director of the Board of Astronomy. In 1692, he decreed that Christianity could be practiced by Chinese if converts continued to carry out their ancestral rites, but later he expelled any Europeans who refused to comply with this decree.

Literary and intellectual achievements were not the only focus of the Kangxi emperor's reign. Far more important to the emperor were the consolidation of Manchu control over Han China and the expansion of the empire. He demonstrated his independence and daring by overthrowing the regency of his youth, arresting the most powerful regent in 1669, and, four years later, against the advice of most of his high officials, consolidated his control over South China. In 1649 Dorgon had rewarded certain Ming generals instrumental in the Qing conquest with large fiefdoms in the southern provinces of Guangdong, Fujian, and Yunnan. In 1673, the Kangxi emperor abolished the so-called Three Feudatories (*sanfan*) in South China. The most powerful of the three was the Yunnan feudatory headed by Wu Sangui, whom the Manchus rewarded by giving him control of the provinces of Yunnan in 1659 and Guizhou in 1663, where he exercised complete military and civilian authority.

Tensions escalated when the emperor disbanded the Yunnan-Guizhou feudatory on 16 September 1673 and Wu rebelled, rallying all remaining Ming loyalists. Although there was temporary panic in Beijing, with many Manchus even preparing to evacuate the capital and return north, the Kangxi emperor did not flinch. Instead, he ordered Wu's son, Wu Yingxiong, who was being held hostage in Beijing, to commit suicide. From Beijing, the Kangxi emperor then directed the ensuing military campaign. Wu Sangui responded by establishing a new dynasty, the Zhou, south of the Yangzi River. Although the fighting would last for eight years, the tide turned in Kangxi's favor beginning in 1677. With Wu's death in 1678, Kangxi's troops gradually encircled Wu's grandson, the second Zhou emperor. Surrounded and pushed back into Yunnan province, the grandson committed suicide rather than be taken alive. By 1683, the Kangxi emperor destroyed the final organized Ming loyalists, both in southern China and on Taiwan.

The Kangxi emperor involved himself in the day-to-day workings of his empire. He exerted control through his six inspection tours to southern China. In these he stressed conservancy projects such as maintaining the dikes on the Yellow River system. Flood control was one of the Confucian hallmarks of good governance. He also personally led a number of military expeditions to the north and northwest, extending his rule deep into Mongolia. His grandson, the Qianlong emperor, completed the conquest of Mongolia. (These Mongolian campaigns will be discussed together in Chapter 2, Section I.) In South China, the Kangxi emperor compelled the Miao tribes to submit to his rule, while in Southeast Asia, central Vietnam and Burma once again became tributaries. Thus, he not only firmly established Qing rule throughout the former Ming empire, but also restored China's traditional tributary relations with its immediate neighbors.

Diplomatically, one of the most important events during his reign was the arrival of the Russians. They moved in to fill the vacuum caused by the collapse of Mongol power in the fifteenth and sixteenth centuries. By the 1660s isolated groups of Cossacks appeared on the Amur River, the waterway that forms the modern boundary between Russia and China. Diplomatic contacts ensued in 1669, with the Kangxi emperor exchanging several letters with the tsar in the 1670s. Beginning in the early 1680s, however, the Kangxi emperor demanded that the Russians either withdraw from their set-tlements along the Amur River at Albazin and Nerchinsk or submit to Chinese suzerainty. A number of Russian settlers subsequently decided to do so and were organized into their own company under the yellow banner. After fighting erupting at Albazin in 1685 and 1686, Chinese military superiority along the Amur forced a Russian withdrawal, confirmed by the Treaty of Nerchinsk in 1689. (See Map 5.2.)

This was China's first treaty with a European power. It began the long process of establishing the borders between the rapidly expanding Qing and Russian empires. The treaty set the border across the mountains separating the Lena and Amur River valleys all the way to the Sea of Okhotsk. This meant that all of the Amur River lay within Chinese domains, not to mention the coastal territories across from Sakhalin Island that later formed the Russian Maritime Province. At the end of the Kangxi emperor's reign, his empire bordered on Russia, Mongolia, and Tibet.

V. Institutional Consolidation under the Yongzheng Emperor

What the Kangxi emperor did for the physical territory of the Qing empire, his fourth son, the Yongzheng emperor (r. 1723–35), did for its governmental institutions. The Yongzheng emperor created an extensive apparatus to enhance his personal control over the Qing state and to transform himself into a religious leader of Lama Buddhism, the dominant faith of Mongolia and Tibet. His administrative reforms helped eliminate the more collegial rule of his predecessors and consolidate Manchu control over China and the surrounding tributary states. The Yongzheng emperor received a Classical Chinese education and was particularly knowledgeable about Chinese and Buddhist literature. Throughout his reign he maintained a keen interest in Buddhism and Daoism. Although a follower of Zen Buddhism, he had the palace of his youth transformed into a Lama Buddhist temple, the *Yonghe Gong,* located in Beijing. It is one of the few religious sites in China to have escaped destruction during the Cultural Revolution of Mao Zedong.

The Yongzheng emperor was already middle-aged when he ascended the throne. At the time of his father's death, there were twenty surviving sons but no designated heir apparent. The Kangxi emperor favored a younger son, Yinti (1688–1755), during his final decade on the throne. Yinti led an army in the campaign to suppress the Zunghar Mongols, who invaded Tibet. Yinti's army occupied Lhasa, the capital of Tibet, in 1719, meaning that he was far away from the Court during his father's final years. Rumors circulated that the Kangxi emperor from his deathbed designated Yinti as his successor. The fifteen older brothers divided into factions. When the Yongzheng emperor emerged victorious, he imprisoned seven of them, five of whom subsequently died, and initiated a purge of both his immediate family and his extended family. He had dozens of relatives executed and created an enormous secret police network to watch over the government and potential political rivals. Despite his destruction of numerous records pertaining to his father's reign, he was never able to dispel the rumor that he had usurped the throne. (See Table 1.3.)

The Yongzheng emperor's accession to the throne marked a departure from Manchu traditions. With the exception of the Shunzhi emperor, who had suffered poor health and died young, the previous Manchu rulers had been both civil and military leaders. They both administered their empire and personally commanded their armies. Yinti would have fit this tradition. From the time of the Yongzheng emperor on, however, no Manchu emperor ever led an army again. Indeed, the Yongzheng emperor distrusted his generals to the point of persecution. The succession of the Yongzheng emperor marked the beginning of the long and gradual decline of Qing martial traditions.

While the Kangxi emperor focused on expanding the geographic extent of the Qing empire, the Yongzheng em-

Table 1.3   Succession Struggle at the Death of the Kangxi Emperor
Sons of the Kangxi Emperor (r. 1662–1722)

†1. Yinti (1672–1734). Originally allied with 8 (Yinsi) vs. 2 (Yinreng).

†2. Yinreng (1674–1725). Heir apparent until 1708; mentally ill.

†3. Yinzhi (1677–1732). Originally allied with 2 (Yinreng).

4. **Yinzhen, Yongzheng Emperor (r. 1723–35)**, present at Kangxi's death.

5. Yinqi (1679–1732) Not imprisoned but had strained relations with Yongzheng.

7. Yinyou (1680–1730)

†8. Yinsi (1681–1726)

†9. Yintang (1683–1726)

*10. Yin'e (1683–1741). Imprisoned, 1735; rehabilitated by Qianlong.

12. Yintao (1685–1763). Not imprisoned but had strained relations with Yongzheng.

13. Yinxiang (1686–1730)

*14. Yinti (1688–1755). Rumored heir apparent; away fighting Zunghars at Kangxi's death; imprisoned, 1735' rehabilitated by Qianlong.

15. Yinwu (1693–1731)

16. Yinlu (1696–1767). Present at Kangxi's death.

17. Yinli (1697–1738)

20. Yinyi (1706–55)

21. Yinxi (1711–58)

22. Yinhu (1711–43)

23. Yinqi (1713–85)

24. Yinmi (1716–73)

Notes: This table indicates the complexity of Qing successions. At the time of the Kangxi emperor's death, five of his sons were age seventeen or younger. Nine of the remaining fifteen sons died during the reign of the Yongzheng emperor. The Yongzheng emperor's political reforms focused on depriving the Manchu princes of political power.

*Sons who survived imprisonment.

†Sons who died in prison.

Names enclosed in boxes indicate supporters of the Yongzheng emperor.

Names in shaded areas indicate supporters of other contenders for the throne.

Because many of the records pertaining to the succession seem to have been destroyed, the sympathies of many of the sons are not known.

Numbers refer to the birth order of sons. Only sons surviving early childhood and alive at the time of the succession are listed. Fifteen others had already died.

Source: Arthur W. Hummel, ed., *Eminent Chinese of the Ch'ing Period (1644–1912)* (Washington, DC: U.S. Government Printing Office, 1943), passim; Jin Songqiao et al., comps., *Aixinjueluo zong pu* (Fengtian: Aixinjueluo Xiupuchu, 1938), 49–53.

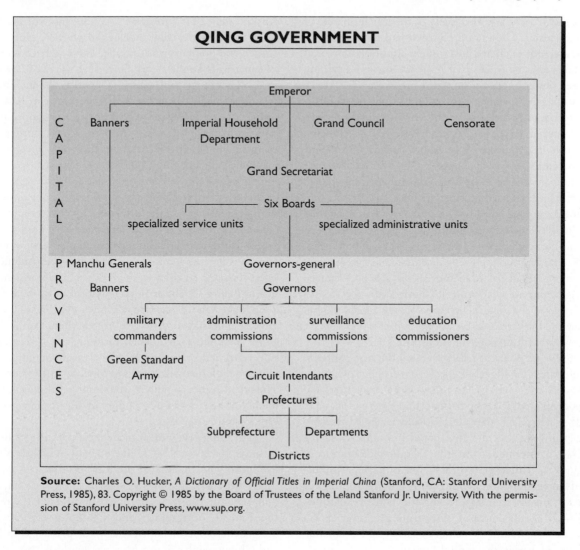

QING GOVERNMENT

Source: Charles O. Hucker, *A Dictionary of Official Titles in Imperial China* (Stanford, CA: Stanford University Press, 1985), 83. Copyright © 1985 by the Board of Trustees of the Leland Stanford Jr. University. With the permission of Stanford University Press, www.sup.org.

peror focused on extending the effective reach of Qing authority. He sought to control the government through the centralization of power. To avoid a succession crisis, he wrote the name of his successor on a piece of paper but instructed that this decision should be kept secret until his death. This method kept the competing clans at bay, since no one knew who might become a future enemy or ally. His own hazardous rise to power probably spurred him to eliminate the collegial rule of his predecessors. Nurgaci ruled jointly with his sons and nephews, who commanded the banner forces. Collective rule remained the norm during the minorities of the Shunzhi and Kangxi emperors. While the Kangxi emperor initiated the centralization of authority within the imperial house, the Yongzheng emperor completed the process by putting all of the banners under bureaucratic, not princely, control. By severing the connections

among the different banners and removing their control from specific Manchu princes, he created a military system both more hierarchical and more firmly under his authority. In modern parlance, he destroyed his potential rivals' *guanxi* connections to the military.

The Yongzheng emperor also created the predecessor institution of the Grand Council or Office of Military Strategy. (See the feature above.) This would be his most important institutional innovation. Previously, the Grand Secretariat transmitted both memorials to the throne and imperial edicts to the field, but the system proved inefficient during the Mongol campaigns. The Yongzheng emperor staffed the Grand Council with six to ten of his most trusted advisers—half Manchus and half Han—and sidelined the Grand Secretariat to routine government business. This undercut the power of the grand secretary, who, during the declining years of the Ming dynasty, assumed many of the responsibilities of a prime minister. The Grand Council had daily meetings with the emperor to discuss government administration, military affairs, and the issuance of imperial edicts. Its creation centralized power in the person of the emperor.

The Yongzheng emperor also weakened the power of the Censorate, the main investigatory institution, and expanded a system of palace memorials set up by the Kangxi emperor. Henceforth, palace memorials could be opened and read only by the emperor, thereby bypassing the Grand Council and the Grand Secretariat. The Yongzheng emperor used this system to communicate directly and secretly with government officials throughout the empire. The memorial system allowed him to intervene directly even in local affairs and became an important means to confirm the loyalty of his subordinates. Because of the enormous power concentrated in the emperor's hands, the system of palace memorials has also been blamed for strengthening autocratic rule in China. The new memorial system reflected the Yongzheng emperor's distrust of the bureaucracy and the literati. Its long-term impact was to slow the development of strong government institutions.

Yongzheng's political reforms ended the first period of Qing rule, when the Manchus exercised a dual line of authority through the civil Ming bureaucratic structure and through the martial Manchu banners under the command of imperial princes. The Manchus gradually extended their influence southward over the Han population, first by allying with Han bannermen from the Liaodong Peninsula of Manchuria; then, during Shunzhi's reign, by allying with successful Han examination candidates primarily from North China; and finally, after suppressing the Three Feudatories, by securing the allegiance of elites from the lower Yangzi River region, the traditional center of successful examination candidates. However, the central bureaucracy and the banners remained rife with factional politics.

The Yongzheng emperor implemented other changes: To root out government corruption and promote fiscal stability, he initiated extensive economic reforms to fund all levels of government. He promoted new water projects to reduce flooding along the Yellow River. To pay for these public works, he instituted a new system of public levies that replaced the former Ming system of taxes and fees. He also decreed the end of hereditary groups, which greatly expanded the possibilities for social mobility. These institutional reforms helped make possible the achievements of his successor, the Qianlong emperor, who ruled at the height of the Qing dynasty.

The Yongzheng emperor also strengthened the Qing empire, especially with regard to Russia. In 1727, the two countries signed treaties continuing the demarcation of their frontier and the formalization of trade relations. The Treaty

of Bura, signed on 20 August 1727, set more of the border, while the Treaty of Kiakhta, signed on 21 October 1727, opened two border towns to trade. These were the continental precursors to the treaty ports that the Western powers established in coastal China a century later. This new arrangement greatly simplified trade between Russia and China. After 1755 there were no more Russian caravans to Beijing; rather, trade was conducted in the border towns. From the mid-eighteenth through the mid-nineteenth century, when the opening of the Suez Canal greatly shortened shipping routes from Europe to China, Russia served as one of the primary intermediaries for Sino–European trade, although it was gradually undercut by Western traders at Guangzhou and by Chinese junk trade with Southeast Asia.

In addition to establishing continental versions of treaty ports, the treaties granted the Russians other unique privileges. Russians, in contrast to all other Europeans, could reside in Beijing, establish an ecclesiastical mission, and found a language school to learn Chinese. As a result, Russian traders could stay at their own hostel when visiting Beijing, and a small ten-man Russian Orthodox Ecclesiastical Mission remained permanently. The Yongzheng emperor also sent two diplomatic embassies to Moscow in 1731 and 1732. The other European powers would not gain equivalent treatment for over a century as part of the settlement of the Opium and Arrow Wars.

The Qing government made these concessions to Russia in order to ensure that it did not ally with the Zunghar Mongols, who challenged the Kangxi emperor's authority over Tibet and neighboring Qinghai. The Qing campaign to dominate the Mongols continued throughout the reigns of the Kangxi, Yongzheng, and Qianlong emperors. The Yongzheng emperor hoped that trade privileges in Beijing and Chinese embassies to Moscow would both mollify the Russians and make it unnecessary for them to penetrate Mongolia or Xinjiang in search of trade. This strategy was in keeping with traditional Han barbarian management techniques of playing off the far barbarian against the nearer foe. In the late 1720s, the Yongzheng emperor ordered a new series of campaigns against the Zunghars, inhabitants originally from north of the Tianshan Range. He expelled them from Lhasa in 1720 and soon detached Qinghai from Tibet.

The Yongzheng emperor also undertook a major military "pacification" campaign in the south in 1726, which resulted in the incorporation of many of the minority peoples of Yunnan, Guizhou, and Guangxi provinces directly into the Qing empire. By 1731, the Qing eliminated half of the native chieftainships to solidify its control over these areas and began the process of Sinifying these non-Han minority peoples. This included opening Confucian schools, regularizing tax collection, and appointing local officials in order to bring these areas administratively and fiscally under Qing rule. As a result, many tribal peoples in South China became gradually Sinified. It is interesting that a non-Han Chinese dynasty turned to Sinification as the most reliable means to increase its own power. The governments of the succeeding Nationalist interregnum and the ensuing People's Republic of China likewise used Sinification to maintain the lands of the Qing empire.

Conclusions

The Manchus had firmly established their dynasty by the time of the Yongzheng emperor's death in 1735. Under Nurgaci, Hong Taiji, and Dorgon, they took advantage of the weakening Ming dynasty and the support of defecting Han Chinese to breach the Great Wall and take power in Beijing. Dorgon's nephew became the first emperor of the Qing dynasty. The Shunzhi emperor assimilated Han practices to begin consolidating minority Manchu rule over Han China. His son, the Kangxi emperor, extended the physical size of the empire, while his grandson, the Yongzheng emperor, adopted institutional reforms.

The reigns of the Shunzhi, Kangxi, and Yongzheng emperors comprise the rise of the Qing dynasty. Their enormous political, economic, and military achievements conformed to the cyclical Han understanding of history expressed in the dynastic cycle. These were the years of a vibrant new dynasty whose achievements, it was believed, reflected a period of moral ascendancy. To a great extent, the Qing ruled in the manner of their Han predecessors. On the empire's periphery, they employed traditional techniques of barbarian management— a combination of commercial inducements and military punishments—to subjugate the foreign policies of their neighbors to Chinese interests. Within the empire, they employed Sinification to force minorities to conform to Chinese norms. In the manner of virtuous Confucian monarchs, they attempted to rejuvenate the provincial and tax administration to extend effective rule throughout the empire.

But Qing rule posed special problems. The Manchus were a tiny ethnic minority in a vast and diverse empire. The core was inhabited overwhelmingly by the Han, but the extensive periphery was inhabited by a variety of other non-Han and non-Manchu peoples. The Manchu ability to enforce their minority rule was remarkable. They did so through a combination of institutional reforms, control over the instruments of coercion, and cultivation of the loyalties of the Han literati. This combination eliminated the ability and the will of the Han to contest Manchu rule. Institutional reforms centralized government administration under the

emperor; control over an effective military and a secret police network gave the emperor a monopoly over coercive power; and securing the loyalties of the Han literati enabled the Qing to administer their vast empire.

The ability to secure Han literati loyalties indicates the deftness of Manchu rule. The Manchu emperors succeeded by appearing to be more Han than the Han themselves in stressing traditional Confucian norms for governance and behavior. Notable exceptions were their demands that males conform to Manchu hair styling and that officials conform to Manchu dress codes, which were visible signs of Han allegiance to the dynasty. In addition, royal succession followed Manchu, not Han, norms, meaning even less emphasis on enthroning the eldest son by the empress. Nevertheless, in keeping with Confucian models, the early Manchu emperors performed expected Court rituals, lowered taxes, reduced corruption, promoted conservancy projects, and reformed local administration in order to promote prosperity throughout the empire. The Manchus also emphasized Classical Chinese education as the mark of status and the route to social mobility.

The examination system continued to test traditional subjects, while the Manchu emperors immersed themselves in Classical Chinese literature, philosophy, and calligraphy and mastered Mandarin Chinese so that they could communicate directly with their subjects. They reinvigorated the Hanlin Academy in Beijing as the coveted appointment for the most talented degree winners and the sorting house for rising officials. Hanlin members advised emperors, taught princes, administered the provincial and capital examinations, and engaged in official scholarly activities. The Qing also maintained the outward Ming structure by retaining the Six Boards—Personnel, Revenue, Rites, War, Punishments, and Public Works—and an oversight and enforcement agency, the Censorate. Finally, they promoted Daoism and practiced Buddhism, even using Tibetan Lama Buddhism to smooth their relations with the peoples of Central Asia.

The Qing rewarded loyal non-Manchu subjects who excelled in the civil service examinations. The dyarchical pairing of Han and Manchu ministers at the highest level of government helped disguise the Manchus' ultimate control. Because the Manchus restored stability, many Han Chinese were grateful for peace and renewed prosperity. The Manchus' effective administration and competent economic management made continuance of their rule in the general interests of their Han subjects. Ultimately, the legitimacy of the Qing dynasty depended on a broadly shared perception that the emperor held the heavenly mandate to rule. His ritual responsibilities were considered critical to maintaining harmony among the human, natural, and supernatural worlds. To maintain cosmic harmony, Qing

The "Imperial Vault of Heaven" was part of a larger templex in Beijing called the Temple of Heaven. It was built by the Ming dynasty in 1420. Chinese emperors would pray to heaven twice a year for a good harvest. Since the emperor was considered the "son of heaven," offering sacrifices to heaven showed his filial piety toward heaven.

emperors performed state rituals at the Altar of Heaven, the Altar of Earth, the Temple of Ancestors, and the Altar of Land and Harvest.

Simultaneously, the Manchus prevented their own absorption into the vast Han population by establishing rules prohibiting intermarriage, preserving Manchuria for themselves, and segregating their elite military units, the banner forces. Manchu rulership over Han China entailed an extremely delicate balance between Manchu dominance and Han allegiance. The Qing was among the most prosperous dynasties in Chinese history. In size, it was second only to the Mongol dynasty, which was as short as it was brutal. It was also among the longest in duration of the post-Qin dynasties. The first three Qing emperors—Shunzhi, Kangxi, Yongzheng—and the reforms that they promoted made possible the flowering of the dynasty under the Qianlong emperor. During his reign, China may have become the richest country in human history.

BIBLIOGRAPHY

Chan, Hok-lam. "The Chieng-wen, Yung-lo, Hung-hsi, and Hsuan-te Reigns, 1399–1435." In *The Cambridge History of China*, edited by Denis Switchett and John K. Fairbanks, 182–304. Vol. 7, part 1. New York: Cambridge University Press, 1988.

Crossley, Pamela Kyle. *The Manchus.* Cambridge, MA: Blackwell, 1997.

Elliott, Mark C. *The Manchu Way: The Eight Banners and Ethnic Identity in Late Imperial China.* Stanford, CA: Stanford University Press, 2001.

Hucker, Charles O. "Introduction: Governmental Organization Era by Era." In *A Dictionary of Official Titles in Imperial China.* Stanford, CA: Stanford University Press, 1985.

Hummel, Arthur W. *Eminent Chinese of the Ch'ing Period (1644–1912).* Washington, DC: U.S. Government Printing Office, 1943.

Mancall, Mark. *Russia and China: Their Diplomatic Relations to 1728.* Cambridge, MA: Harvard University Press, 1971.

Michael, Franz. *The Origin of Manchu Rule in China.* 1942. Reprint, New York: Octagon Books, 1979.

Mote, F. W. *China 900–1800.* Cambridge, MA: Harvard University Press, 1999.

Naquin, Susan and Evelyn S. Rawski. *Chinese Society in the Eighteenth Century.* New Haven, CT: Yale University Press, 1987.

Oxnam, Robert B. *Ruling from Horseback: Manchu Politics in the Oboi Regency, 1661–1669.* Chicago: University of Chicago Press, 1975.

Powell, Ralph L. *The Rise of Chinese Military Power, 1895–1912.* Princeton, NJ: Princeton University Press, 1955.

Rawski, Evelyn S. *The Last Emperors: A Social History of Qing Imperial Institutions.* Berkeley: University of California Press, 1998.

Rhoades, Edward J. M. *Manchus & Han: Ethnic Relations and Political Power in Late Qing and Early Republican China, 1861–1928.* Seattle: University of Washington Press, 2000.

Spence, Jonathan D. *Ts'ao Yin and the K'ang-hsi Emperor, Bondservant and Master.* New Haven, CT: Yale University Press, 1966.

———*Treason by the Book.* New York: Viking, 2001.

———"The K'ang-hsi Reign." In *The Cambridge History of China,* vol. 9, edited by Willard J. Peterson, 120–82. Cambridge: Cambridge University Press, 2002.

Struve, Lynn A. *Southern Ming, 1644–1662.* New Haven, CT: Yale University Press, 1984.

———ed. and trans. *Voices from the Ming-Qing Cataclysm: China in the Tigers' Jaws.* New Haven, CT: Yale University Press, 1993.

Twitchett, Denis and John K. Fairbank, eds. *The Cambridge History of China.* Vol. 10. Cambridge: Cambridge University Press, 1978.

Wakeman, Frederick, Jr. *The Great Enterprise: The Manchu Reconstruction of Imperial Order in Seventeenth Century China.* 2 vols. Berkeley: University of California Press, 1985.

Zelin, Madeleine. *The Magistrate's Tael: Rationalizing Fiscal Reform in Eighteenth-Century Ch'ing China.* Berkeley: University of California Press, 1984.

———"The Yung-cheng Reign." In *The Cambridge History of China,* vol. 9, edited by Willard J. Peterson, 183–229. Cambridge: Cambridge University Press, 2002.

NOTES

1. Yü the Great was the founder of the Xia dynasty (2205–1766 BC), who is said to have ended a period of great floods to inherit the empire. *Emperor of China: Self-portrait of K'ang-hsi,* Jonathan D. Spence, trans. (New York: Alfred A. Knopf, 1974), 117.

2. Susan Naquin and Evelyn S. Rawski, *Chinese Society in the Eighteenth Century* (New Haven, CT: Yale University Press, 1987), 4, 141.

3. Evelyn S. Rawski makes this distinction between the "conquest elite" and the "conquered population." See Rawski, *The Last Emperors: A Social History of Qing Imperial Institutions* (Berkeley: University of California Press, 1998), 59.

4. Robert Darrah Jenks, "The Miao rebellion, 1854–1872: Insurgency and Social Disorder in Kweichow During the Taiping Era" (Ph.D. diss., Harvard University, 1965), 90.

Chronology

1644	Implementation of the *baojia* population-control system
1648	Implementation of the *lijia* tax-collection system
1691	Kalkha (Outer Mongolian) leaders swear allegiance to Qing
1697	Kangxi emperor's defeat of the Zunghars
1717	Zunghar occupation of Tibet
1720	Qing expulsion of the Zunghars from Tibet
1721	Failed revolt in Taiwan
1724	Pacification of Qinghai
1731	Truce in the campaign to subjugate the Zunghars
1736	Qianlong emperor assumes the throne
1747–9	Jinchuan uprising
1755	First Zunghar campaign; Qing occupation of the Ili Valley
1756–7	Second Zunghar campaign
1758–9	Subjugation of the Muslim rebellion in the Tarim Basin
1766–70	Unsuccessful Burma campaign
1771–6	Jinchuan uprising followed by Qing campaign of annihilation
1781	Suppression of the Muslim uprising in Gansu
1787–8	Taiwan uprising
1788–9	Unsuccessful central Vietnam (Annam) campaign
1790–2	Qing deployment of troops to Tibet
1792	Qing invasion of Nepal in a punitive expedition against the Gurkhas
1795–1806	Miao Uprising in Guizhou and Hunan
1796	Retirement of Qianlong emperor; Jiaqing emperor assumes the throne
1796–1804	White Lotus Rebellion
1799	Death of the Qianlong emperor

2

The Maximization of Empire under the Qianlong Emperor

After the Troops Have Withdrawn en Route to Nan-yang

The woods are empty—only setting sun;
the place remote—few signs of lingering spring.
I want to find out how to reach Nan-yang,
But in the next village, nobody is left.[1]

Wu Li (1632–1718),
painter, poet, Catholic priest

The Qianlong emperor (r. 1736–95) vastly expanded China's boundaries, firmly ruled over the Qing empire, and presided over its golden age. The Qing dynasty reached its maximum territorial extent, internal power, and cultural flowering during his sixty-year reign. As a result of his military victories, Xinjiang, or the "New Territories," were permanently added to the Qing empire, central control was reasserted over Tibet, and rebellions were suppressed within China proper and on Taiwan. Military expertise, administrative competence, and the wealth to fund expensive campaigns made possible this vast expansion of the empire far beyond the boundaries of Ming China, and the Qianlong emperor frequently traveled throughout his domains in order to ascertain the execution of his orders. Finally, he provided the symbolic trappings of power by initiating a lavish building program in Beijing.

The Qianlong emperor presided over the world's most highly bureaucratized and populous country, with a Chinese population estimated to be at least 300 million in 1800, dwarfing the Russian population of 40 million and the Japanese population of 30 million, let alone the English population of 11 million.[2] His China was an empire second to none, ranking supreme in both territorial extent and wealth, which together meant power. This was a China prior to the advent of the Industrial Revolu-

tion. This image of China in the age of Qianlong has captivated Han Chinese ever since. During the Qianlong emperor's time, China was indeed the Central Kingdom designated by the characters of its name, *Zhongguo*. As a human being, the Qianlong emperor combined breathtaking self-assurance with profound insecurity. Like his father and grandfather, he skillfully managed the political intrigues fracturing both the Manchu ruling house and the Han literati to maintain peace in the core provinces and keep wars on the periphery. Yet, he exhibited rage and extreme reactions when he felt slighted, such as his punishment of over one hundred high officials for failing adequately to mourn the death of his consort in 1748 or his brutality toward unsuccessful generals.

I. The Conquest of the Zunghar Mongols

The Qianlong emperor expanded his domains in ten military campaigns, which he himself used to characterize his reign, when as an old man he named himself the "Venerable One of the Ten Glorious Campaigns" (*shiquan laoren*). (See Map 2.1.) These included two to suppress the Zunghar Mongols in the far northwest in the Ili Valley separating the Poluokenu Mountains from the Tianshan Range (1755 and 1756–7), the suppression of the Turkic Muslims in the Tarim Basin to the south, two campaigns (1747–9, 1771–6) to repress uprisings of the Jinchuan minority in Sichuan province, unsuccessful attempts to subjugate the Burmese (1766–70) and the Vietnamese (1788–9), the suppression of a rebellion on Taiwan (1787–8), and two campaigns to expel the Nepalese (Gurkhas) from Tibet (1790–2). While generally successful militarily, these campaigns proved very

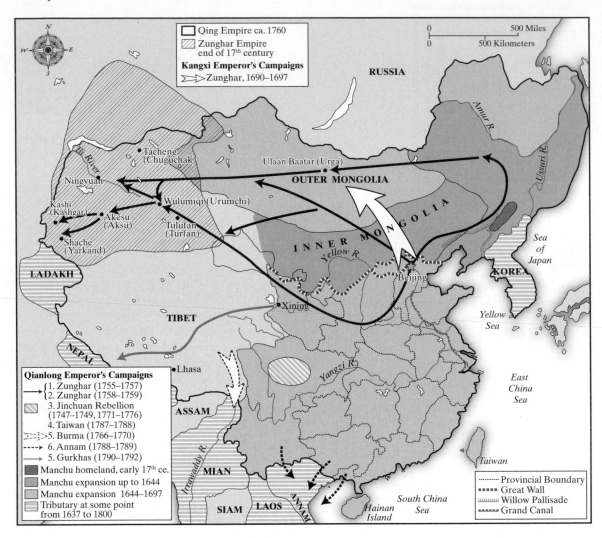

Map 2.1   Campaigns of the Kangxi and Qianlong Emperors

costly to the treasury. This section will focus on the Qing conquest of the Mongols that ended with the Qianlong emperor's final campaign from 1755 to 1757, while the following section will describe the defeat of the Turkic Muslims in the Tarim Basin from 1758 to 1759. These combined campaigns extended Qing control over the vast areas composed of the Tarim and Junggar basins, whereas the other military campaigns brought comparatively little new territory.

China's interaction with the peoples of Central Asia has been long and contentious. Modern-day Xinjiang is a desert region of some 635,000 square miles known for its sparse rainfall and sharp extremes in continental weather. It is divided along its east-west axis by the Tianshan Mountain Range and the comparatively fertile Ili Valley. To the north

lies the Junggar Basin, the world's largest land basin. To the south lies the Tarim Basin. Beginning in 100 BC, Han Wudi (154–87 BC), the greatest emperor of the Han dynasty (206 B–C–220 AD), defeated the Xiongnu barbarians to dominate this region. He is also credited with initiating trade between China and the Mediterranean world. Thereafter, camel caravans traversed this desert region by way of the Silk Route.

This lucrative Western trade in silk, tea, and porcelains soon led to the founding of rich Central Asian trading centers, such as Urumqi (Urumchi), Tulufan (Turfan), and Kashgar (Kashi). Western imports and also, in all probability, early Christians, Jews, Buddhists, and Muslims made their way to China by this route. Buddhism had an especially strong impact on the Chinese with its cyclical views of life and death that also underlay the Chinese conceptions of time, history, and a dynastic cycle. Beginning in the third and fourth centuries, Buddhists constructed shrines in caves to both the east and northeast of Turpan. Some have survived intact to the present.

Beginning in the 1630s, before the Qing conquest of Beijing, the Manchus began to conquer the Eastern Mongols of Inner Mongolia. (Inner Mongolia refers to Mongolia south of the Gobi Desert, and Outer Mongolia includes lands north of the desert.) While still in Shenyang (Mukden), the Manchus created the Court of Colonial Affairs (*Lifanyuan*) to regulate relations with the Mongols. Intermarriage between the Manchus and the Mongols helped ease tensions. The Manchus allowed cooperative Mongol leaders to retain power over their tribes, which they structured as autonomous principalities. In contrast, when the Inner Mongolian Chahar, who lived northwest of Beijing, refused to ally with the Manchus, they were defeated and deprived of their tribal autonomy.

The next Mongol group conquered by the Qing was the Khalkhas of Outer Mongolia. Pressured from the north by the Russians and from the west by the Zunghars, the Khalkha Mongols desperately sought allies against the Qing. During this uneasy period, the Qing carefully cultivated the Russians in order to avoid a combined Russian–Mongol war. This explains the relatively generous treatment of the Russians in the Treaty of Nerchinsk of 1689 (discussed in Chapter 1, Section IV). The Russians remained neutral, thus allowing the Qing to defeat the various Khalkha Mongol tribes in detail, replace their leaders with Qing loyalists, and incorporate the Mongol military forces into the banner structure. In 1691, the Khalkha princes and their religious leader, the Living Buddha (the Jebtsundamba), took a formal oath of allegiance to the Qing throne.

The final and most dangerous independent Mongol group was the Zunghars (the Oirat or Western Mongols). They originally came from the Junggar Basin north of the Tianshan Range, but they quickly spread both to the east as far as Outer Mongolia and to the south as far as Tibet. During the late seventeenth century, the Zunghar khan, Galdan, received religious training in Lamaism in Lhasa. He soon claimed equal status with the Qing emperor by insisting that he was the emperor of a Zunghar federation.

In 1688 a dispute originally over pasture land culminated in war between the Zunghars and the Khalkha Mongols of Outer Mongolia. When the Khalkhas gave their allegiance to the Qing in 1691, the Kangxi emperor personally led one of the three Qing armies that defeated Galdan in 1696. In 1697, the Kangxi emperor brought the war to the Junggar Basin, the Zunghar homeland. Galdan committed suicide in May, resulting in the temporary defeat of his forces. During these years, the Russians again remained neutral, still satisfied with the lucrative trading privileges in Beijing granted in the Treaty of Nerchinsk. In 1717, the Zunghars rose again, attempting to expand south into Tibet.

Although the Qing emperors did not administer Tibet directly, they did play an important role in choosing the Dalai Lama, who exerted both religious and secular control throughout much of the region. From 1652 to 1653, the Fifth Dalai Lama (1617–82) visited Beijing, where the Qing Court treated him with great deference. In 1706, the Kangxi emperor orchestrated the assassination of the uncooperative Sixth Dalai Lama (1683–1706) and replaced him with the pro-Manchu Seventh Dalai Lama (1708–57). The Kangxi emperor carefully monitored the new Dalai Lama's upbringing and education before Manchu troops escorted him to Lhasa in 1720 to put him on the throne.

Beginning in 1716, the Zunghars, led by Galdan's nephew, attacked Xining, the main city of Qinghai, the eastern part of Tibet. Control of this strategic city would have cut the main lines of communication between Beijing and Lhasa, which the Zunghars captured in 1717. Kangxi's fourteenth son, Prince Yinti (1688–1755), however, retook the city in 1720. Fighting continued under the sons of Galdan and the Kangxi emperor, Galdan Tseren (r. 1727–50) and the Yongzheng emperor, respectively. A major Zunghar victory in 1731 led to a long truce lasting from 1732 to 1755.

In 1750, the Qianlong emperor decreed the Dalai Lama to be the sole ruler of Tibet and sent Qing ministers to assist in his rule. In 1755, the Qianlong emperor decided to ensure that the Zunghars could never again threaten Tibet. He organized an enormous army to drive them out of the Tarim Basin and into the Ili Valley, where he defeated them in a campaign lasting from 1755 to 1757. The Qing armies employed a strategy of annihilation applied equally to soldiers and civilians: The Qing deliberately tried to eliminate the Zunghars as a race and resettled other loyal ethnic groups in the formerly Zunghar lands. The strategy was largely successful. After taking the strategic Ili Valley passes, the Qing forces were in a strong position to attack southward in order to consolidate control over the Tarim Basin. These annihilation campaigns, however, have left lasting tensions between the local population of Xinjiang and those ruling from Beijing.

II. The Conquest of the Tarim Basin and Tibet

After the destruction of the Zunghars, the Qianlong emperor focused on consolidating his control south of the Tianshan Range over the Tarim Basin, which became a permanent part of the empire by 1759. This success allowed him to tighten his control over Tibet. The annexation of the territories comprising modern-day Xinjiang and closer ties with Tibet expanded Qing territories by nearly one-third.

Following the defeat of the Zunghars, the Qing officials settled in the former Zunghar capital of Ningyuan (Kulja), located in the Ili Valley. The area constituted a strategic enclave vital for the control of the Junggar Basin to the north and the Tarim Basin to the south. The Tarim Basin had six main cities—at times virtual city-states—giving rise to an oasis culture. These included Kashgar, Yarkand (Shache), Turfan, Akesu (Aksu), Khotan, and Kucha. Whereas the Junggar Basin was settled mainly by Mongols, the Tarim Basin was populated by a Turkish-speaking people, the Uighurs, who were Sunni Muslims.

The Manchu general, Zhaohui, who conducted the final campaign to defeat the Zunghars in 1757, also commanded the campaign to subjugate the Tarim Basin. He sent envoys to demand the submission of Yarkand and Kashgar. When the leader of Yarkand killed the envoy, General Zhaohui took both cities and completed the conquest of the Tarim Basin by chasing enemy remnants into the forbidding Pamir Mountains. Following his success, a Manchu governor-general was posted in the Ili Valley stronghold of Ningyuan, while lieutenant-governors were placed in Urumqi and Yarkand to govern the north and south, respectively. Because so few Zunghars survived the conquest, the Qing encouraged Uighurs to immigrate north to populate the Junggar Basin. The Qing gave the Uighurs wide autonomy in return for cooperation on matters of border security and revenue collection. The Qing respected the Uighurs' Islamic faith and left rule in the hands of the local leaders, who collected taxes for the central government.

The consolidation of Qing control both north and south of the Tianshan Range made possible greater influence over Tibet. In 1792, the Qianlong emperor used a military campaign against the Gurkhas as a pretext to limit Tibetan religious autonomy. Beginning in the 1760s, the Hindu Gurkhas invaded Buddhist Nepal. Then, in 1788, they invaded southern Tibet in response to disputes over currency valuations and control over Sikkim, the tiny kingdom lying on the easternmost boundary of Nepal. This gave the Qing court a pretext to send troops to Tibet in 1790. In 1791 the conflict reignited when the Gurkhas renewed their attack on Tibet in retribution for its failure to pay the agreed-upon tribute. Qing forces defeated the Gurkhas in one of the most amazing military campaigns in Chinese history: The Qing deployed troops 3,000 miles from Beijing to fight on one of the world's highest plateaus. As a war settlement, the Gurkhas had to pay tribute to Beijing. Gurkha tribute payments to China gave rise to later Chinese claims of sovereignty over Nepal, a claim that was disputed when the British arrived in India.

The campaign against the Gurkhas allowed the Qing to consolidate territorial control over Tibet. The Qianlong emperor also expanded his administrative powers by modifying the previous administration established under the Yuan or Mongol dynasty (1279–1368). That system granted the Tibetans broad religious and political autonomy. The Qianlong emperor decreed that the Dalai and Panchen lamas could not address the Qing throne directly, but only through the senior Qing officials assigned to Tibet known as "ambans," giving them authority over the Tibetan court, army, currency, trade, and travel. Most importantly, the ambans supervised the selection of final candidates for the new incarnations of lamas, including the Panchen and Dalai lamas.

In doing so, the Qianlong emperor employed barbarian management by dividing barbarians among themselves (*yi yi zhi yi*). He sought to weaken the independence of the Tibetan religious hierarchy and its bonds with the Mongolian elite by creating a parallel Tibetan Buddhist hierarchy under Qing control. To break the virtual monopoly of certain powerful noble clans over the positions of Dalai Lama and Panchen Lama, he introduced the Golden Urn method of selection whereby Beijing forwarded an urn containing the names of all possible candidates to Lhasa for final selection by the lamas and the amban. In effect, the Dalai Lama retained his religious authority but lost his secular powers, now exercised by Qing-appointed ambans. For a time, the Qing interfered vigorously in the selection of the lamas; later, the right became mainly symbolic.[3]

The Qianlong emperor's successful campaigns in Central Asia and Tibet brought the Qing empire to its maximum territorial extent. He forbade such Tibetan customs as the "sky burial," in which corpses were fed to mountain birds. But Sinification was not successful in Tibet. The ambans and other local Qing officials were too few and too far removed from the sources of Qing power to interfere much beyond the realm of high politics. Therefore, Tibet—and to a lesser degree the Tarim and Junggar basins and Mongolia—remained impervious to Sinification. What the Manchus perhaps saw as sovereignty was later interpreted by Britain and Russia as suzerainty, whereby Beijing influenced their foreign, military, and trade relations but had little day-to-day control over their social system or domestic affairs. Unless the Manchus sent an army, it was difficult to impose their will. The Qing succeeded in keeping Tibet isolated from British and later Russian influence, leaving it to the mercy of the Chinese army.

In contrast to the conquest of the Junggar and Tarim basins, the campaigns against the Jinchuan minority in Western

Sichuan, the rebellion in Taiwan, and the autonomy of Burma and Vietnam (Annam) added little to the empire. Twice the Jinchuan minority, who lived in remote and mountainous Western Sichuan, rebelled against Qing rule. They proved extremely difficult to dislodge because of the readily defensible terrain and their system of stone fortresses. The Qing achieved a temporary settlement after the campaign from 1747 to 1749, but two decades later the Jinchuan rebelled again. The second campaign, from 1771 to 1776, proved extremely costly and succeeded only with the aid of Portuguese missionaries who helped the Qing construct cannon to destroy the stone fortresses. The Qing conquest of Western Sichuan cost more than 70 million silver taels, or more than twice the cost of conquering the Junggar and Tarim basins, whose area was twenty times greater.[4] But their annihilation strategy was similar. Afterward, they garrisoned and repopulated Western Sichuan with loyalists.

The Qing also tried to pressure the Burmese and Vietnamese into maintaining regular tributary relations. The Qing campaign into Burma (1766–70) failed. Tropical diseases decimated their forces. Likewise, the Qing attempt to interfere in Vietnam's civil war from 1788 to 1789 did not restore the deposed central Vietnamese dynasty, while the rebel Vietnamese forces destroyed the Qing army. The Qing successfully intervened in Taiwan to put down a rebellion (1787–8). The Manchus, not known for their maritime prowess, staged an amphibious landing to eliminate the unrest. Although they retained control over Taiwan, it remained a remote backwater with little economic or strategic significance. It did not become particularly prosperous until the Japanese colonized it from 1895 to 1945 or strategically significant until the advent of modern navies and global trade.

The cost of conquering and maintaining many parts of the periphery of the Qing empire exceeded any economic benefits from holding these areas. The campaigns constituted a massive redistribution of wealth away from central China, where taxes were levied to field the armies, and also away from civil to military projects. Money spent on armies was money not spent on the maintenance of such key infrastructure as dikes, irrigation canals, and roadways.

III. Qing Imperial Administration: The Tributary System

By modern standards the Qing empire was a loose construct, with the emperor ruling over Han provinces, Han and non-Han colonies, and a wide range of tributary states. Because the Qing ruled over a continental empire composed of contiguous lands—unlike, for example, the maritime British empire, with seas clearly separating the imperial center from the empire—the geographic boundaries among provinces, colonies, and tributary states were extremely fluid and ill-defined.

The tributary system was China's attempt to institutionalize relations with neighbors in order to protect its own security. Rather than the balance-of-power system practiced in the West, China's rulers attempted to maintain a web of discrete bilateral relations that extended outward like spokes from a Chinese hub. Unlike the extractive Western system of empire of the sixteenth through twentieth centuries that focused on economics and specifically on channeling trade between the colonies and the imperial center, the Chinese system was fundamentally military and defensive. Its goal was to prevent disruptive barbarian incursions or, worse yet, the conquest of China. Once the periphery of China was secure, Chinese cared little about what lay beyond. In contrast, Europe's restless pursuit of wealth led to global exploration and global maritime empires.

The tributary system can be traced back at least to the first century BC during the Han dynasty, when the barbarian Xiongnu tribes in Central Asia became Chinese vassals. The barbarians recognized Chinese suzerainty by sending periodic tribute missions to the Chinese capital with envoys bearing gifts for the emperor and willing to kowtow before him. The kowtow was a highly symbolic act of submission whereby the supplicant knelt to make three sets of three full prostrations with arms outstretched and forehead scraping the floor. Often, a son of the vassal ruler resided in China as a hostage to guarantee cooperative behavior. In return, the Chinese gave extravagant gifts of silk and silk floss, which were rare and in great demand throughout the border regions.

Although this system sponsored some trade, it represented a resource drain for China; as much as ten percent of state revenues were expended on tributary gifts. Trade was not an end, but a means. It was a vehicle to stabilize the frontiers. These exchanges were intended to buy China security from invasion, a far more costly proposition than any number of tributary gifts. The system also reduced the long-term barbarian threat through gradual Sinification. Central Asian hostages were educated in Chinese language and customs, and Central Asian rulers often married daughters of the reigning Chinese monarch. But Sinification could backfire. The Mongols in the thirteenth century and the Manchus in the seventeenth century used this knowledge to establish their own dynasties.

The Qing dynasty differentiated institutionally between its more docile and more dangerous tributaries. Whereas the Ming dynasty handled all Sinicized barbarians through the Bureau of Receptions of the Board of Rites, the Manchus established the Court of Colonial Affairs (*Lifanyuan*) to deal with their Inner Asian neighbors. They brought this institution with them when they conquered Ming China. Under the Qing, the Bureau of Receptions retained jurisdiction over the Sinicized tributaries of Korea, Japan, Annam (central Vietnam), Siam (Thailand), the Liuqiu (Okinawa) Kingdom, and Burma, while the Court of Colonial Affairs oversaw Tibet, Mongolia, the Tarim and Junggar basins, and eventually Russia. Inner Asians traditionally posed a far greater security threat. As an indication of the importance that the Manchus ascribed to their Inner Asian neighbors, they staffed the Court of Colonial Affairs exclusively with Manchus. There was not even an illusion of equal Han rule in this vital institution.

The Qing were most concerned with the Mongols, the closest neighbors to Manchuria and former conquerors of China during the Yuan dynasty. They differentiated sharply between the Inner and Outer Mongolians. Many Inner Mongolian tribes had been organized into banners and were part of the conquest elite. Qing sovereigns and royal siblings routinely intermarried with them but not with the other Mongols. By blood, the Qing royal house was equally Manchu and Inner Mongolian. The Gobi Desert had formerly insulated the Outer Mongolians from Qing influence. Now the Qing organized Outer Mongolia's clans into banners and promoted Tibetan Lamaist Buddhism as levers. The Qing also used religion to secure loyalty by presenting an image of universal rulership (see Chapter 3, Section V).

Thus, the Qing extended their territorial control outward by transforming former tributaries in Inner Asia into directly administered colonies. Whereas tributary relations had been fluid, waxing and waning over time, direct administration implied permanence. This Manchu innovation produced an empire of vast size and long duration. However, central administration was a far more expensive proposition than tributary relations. Direct administration included expensive military garrisoning of areas generally poorer than China's core provinces. While the tributary system minimized security costs, garrisoning multiplied them; the advantage was stability, but the trade-off was expense.

IV. Domestic Administration: Central and Local Government

Institutional changes promoted by Yongzheng, in particular his creation of the Grand Council and the development of the palace memorial system, reached maturity under the Qianlong emperor (see Chapter 1, Section V, for a discussion

In 1703, the Kangxi emperor began to build a new Summer Palace about 150 miles northeast of Beijing outside Chengde, Hebei province (not to be confused with the much larger city of Chengdu, Sichuan). Many of the buildings in the Manchu Summer Palace reflected a mixed Sino-Tibetan style, which shows the influence of Tibetan Buddhism on the Manchu court through the tributary system.

of the memorial system). Whereas the first Manchu leaders—Nurgaci, Hong Taiji, and Dorgon—presided over such key military innovations as the banner system that had made possible the conquest of an empire, the subsequent early Qing leaders—Shunzhi, Kangxi, Yongzheng, and Qianlong—introduced and perfected innovations in civilian governance making possible the effective administration of that vast empire.

The Qing created a government capable of extending its reach to enforce order and to extract revenue from all parts of the empire. Although the empire was multiethnic, the overwhelming majority of the population was Han. Therefore, the Qing had to cultivate Han loyalties by basing their legitimacy on orthodox Han views of governance. Qing emperors ruled from the Ming Forbidden City, which the Qianlong emperor refurbished as part of lavish building projects throughout the capital. But he segregated Beijing into a Manchu inner city and a Han outer city, both enclosed by imposing walls. With few exceptions, these walls banned Han from the Forbidden City, the seat of the Qing empire, while the Qianlong emperor drew his closest advisers from the Inner Court of Manchu nobility. It is therefore a misnomer to say "Chinese empire," meaning the empire of the Han people, for they were largely treated as a subjugated population.

In the way of Han dynasties, the Qing posed as guardians of Han traditions. They sponsored massive literary anthologies to establish their cultural credentials among the Han literati. Administratively, they retained the outward form of Ming governmental structures, which consisted of several interlocking essential parts: The emperor and his Court set policy, while the Qianlong emperor implemented his will though the Six Boards, or ministries inherited from the Tang dynasty (618–907). The boards of Personnel, Taxation, Rites, Military, Punishment, and Public Works oversaw all government activities. The Qing emperors asserted their control over these boards by appointing to each dual ministers, one bannerman and usually one Han. Again, the form remained Han, but the control was Manchu. In the early years of the Qing, the Manchu minister strictly controlled his Han deputy minister, but as the dynasty declined, Han officials exerted greater control.

On the provincial level, nine bannerman governors-general each presided over a pair of provinces, with each of the eighteen provinces under the authority of a Han governor. The Manchu governor-general and his two Han governors shared administrative power and would normally jointly memorialize to the emperor. Military forces in their jurisdiction were under divided command. A Manchu general commanded any banner forces, while most Green Standard troops were under a provincial commander in chief for constabulary duties. Small contingents of Green Standard troops were under the separate command of the governor-general and the governor. While civilian administrators controlled the de facto police force (the Green Standard army), the Manchus retained control over the real military (the banner forces).

Below the provincial government were circuits that consisted of two or more prefectures. Each prefecture was in turn composed of two or more counties. All told, there were approximately 200 prefectures and some 1,500 county-level administrations. The local administration was based in offices known as "yamen." Typically, officials known as "magistrates" drawn from the pool of successful Han examination candidates administered each yamen. Assisting them were half a

dozen or more lesser officials, who had also passed lower-level imperial examinations and had special skills in such fields as law or taxation. The magistrate's staff included a number of uneducated officers, such as the police captain or menial clerks, which extended Qing rule down to the local level.

The Qing never solved the Ming problem of funding local government, an enduring problem throughout Chinese history. Although local administrators were obliged to collect taxes, they did not automatically receive a portion of the proceeds to finance local government. Therefore, they imposed many surcharges, which easily blurred into corruption. As administrative responsibilities grew over the course of the dynasty, local officials scrambled to find ever more creative sources of revenue, so that taxation merged into extortion. The gift giving inherent in the *guanxi* system exacerbated the problem of corruption. Lower officials were expected to give gifts to more senior officials, particularly to those one level higher on the scale. This pyramid scheme funneled resources to senior local officials. Over time, Qing control over local administrators weakened and corruption spiraled out of control. The Yongzheng emperor attempted to regularize local financing through established surcharges. Although this reform worked for a time, it did not eliminate the proliferation of illegal surcharges and gratuities. After the Yongzheng emperor's death, corruption continued to increase.

The Qing also tried to overcome local corruption and eliminate the development of rival centers of power through strict enforcement of the rule of avoidance. This rule barred successful examination candidates from serving in high positions in their province of origin. It helped neutralize the *guanxi* networks of the local elites by severing the connection between the local economic and social elite, on the one hand, and the political elite, on the other hand. In doing so, it prevented the intellectual elite from setting up fiefdoms in their province of origin. This proscription was essential in a clan-oriented social structure like that of China. Without it, the Qing empire might have broken into competing factions long before it did. The rule of avoidance also served to homogenize the empire, throwing into contact people from diverse provinces and then requiring them to work together. Magistrates had little choice but to rely on their lower officials, clerks, and police, who were usually locals with wide-ranging connections.

In addition to the system of central, provincial, and local government administration, the Qing maintained a mutual responsibility system called the *baojia*. It was based on units of 10 groups of 10 households then grouped into units of 1,000 households. Because of the multigenerational nature of Chinese families, these units of 1,000 households could easily number over 10,000 people. The local magistrate had the responsibility of designating the leaders of the larger units, which ensured a separate line of governmental control outside the hands of the local gentry or village elders. The *baojia* system maintained records on population movements and crime, the latter reported to the district magistrate. Failure to report and prosecute criminals brought collective punishment. Although the effectiveness of the *baojia* system varied from county to county, in theory it gave the emperor, working through the offices of the local magistrate, a potentially powerful mechanism for law enforcement.

The Qing and their Ming predecessors were aware that provincial and local government administrators were corrupt. Therefore, the Qing retained the Censorate, another key Ming institution. The Censorate enforced the will of the emperor by rooting out those who sought personal gain at the expense of the autocrat's will. It helped prevent the rise of rival powers to the central government and the tendency for power to degenerate and disperse. Located in autonomous agencies that paralleled to a large degree the structure of the central government, officials in the Censorate reported their findings both to the central government and directly to the emperor. The Qing made the system more effective (and intrusive) by superimposing the palace memorial system on the Censorate. The Yongzheng emperor consolidated the operations of the Censorate and diverted some of its functions to the palace memorial system, which bypassed the Censorate entirely. Together the Censorate and the palace memorial system provided oversight to ensure the proper execution of government policies.

An extensive imperial examination system and the Confucian ideology it tested credentialed the people who served in these governmental institutions. By the time of the Tang dynasty, the imperial examination system had evolved into a civil service merit system, making it the first of its kind anywhere in the world in both extent and efficacy. The West would not widely introduce standardized civil service examinations until the nineteenth century. Again, the Manchus kept the outward institutional form but altered the internal workings. They created three separate examination systems: One for the aspiring conquered Han population (the Han literati), one for the conquest elite (mainly for bannermen), and one for the constabulary force (the Green Standard army).

The examinations for the conquered Han population were the most rigorous in order to ensure their loyalty as well as a high level of competence. The examinations for bannermen were not nearly as exacting since their loyalty was known and the services of loyal administrators were essential for the perpetuation of Manchu rule; these examinations helped eliminate the incompetent loyal. The examinations

given to the constabulary force were less demanding still. In the earlier years of the dynasty, it was essential to confirm the loyalties of any armed subjects. The examination system helped do this for all three populations. It also provided three set routes to social mobility, and the rewards to those in high office tended to reinforce loyalty to the regime.

Success in the examinations depended on memorizing the Classics. This became an important channel for Sinification since the examination system left a deep imprint on the entire Chinese educational system. The literate all read the same Classical texts and studied the same Confucian ideology. Confucianism provided both the content of the examinations and the ideology undergirding the Chinese imperial system of government. It justified the steeply hierarchical Chinese world. Confucius preached deference to superiors, loyal service to the emperor, and hard work. In times of dynastic unrest, Confucius required the scholar elite to withhold service from corrupt rulers and to offer their fealty instead to a virtuous ruler. The Qing had proven their superior virtue over the Ming through military conquest and the restoration of order and prosperity. Confucius admonished his followers to serve such rulers. He preached rule by a civilian scholar elite and held the military in contempt. He emphasized upright moral conduct, leadership by example, and persuasion, not coercion. Confucianism was an ideology of civilian rule.

The great military strategist Sunzi provided the source book for the military side of imperial rule. He described the means to conquer and then retain an empire and also to depose an emperor. His teachings were as valuable as they were potentially subversive. The original Manchu monarchs were first and foremost military leaders; their successors made the transition to civilian rule. The Kangxi emperor and some of his sons went to the front to take command of major military campaigns. Potentially, this entailed a lack of supervision in the capital. Upon the sudden death of the Kangxi emperor, the future Yongzheng emperor took advantage of the absence on a military campaign of his more talented brother, Yinti, to assume the throne. Perhaps to avoid such usurpation, never again would a Qing emperor personally lead his armies into battle.

The monopoly on coercive tools remained critical to effective minority rule. This would be demonstrated in a negative way when the Qing lost its monopoly in the great nineteenth-century internal rebellions. The military had the crucial task of keeping the peace and enforcing the emperor's will in the central provinces, among China's contiguous colonies, and, when necessary, in the surrounding tributary states. Although the emperor appointed and

Manchu men and women dressed almost identically in long gowns and wore black skull caps trimmed with fur. Note, in particular, the Manchu woman's feet. Manchu women, unlike Han Chinese women, did not bind their feet (see the feature on page 182), so they could walk, run, ride horses, and generally interact as equals with Manchu men. The "*qipao*" (banner gown) was a special Manchu dress for women with slits up both sides to allow for easy movement while horseback riding. While it was originally loose and baggy, a tighter-fitting version of the *qipao* was developed in Shanghai during the 1920s and soon became associated with high-class courtesans. It was this more modern version of the *qipao* that was featured during the 2008 Olympics.

removed military leaders at will, in times of war their power could prove difficult to control. Therefore, the generals who commanded the Chinese army were both the emperor's most necessary supporters and also potentially his greatest adversaries.

The top-down elements of Chinese culture—Confucianism, Sunzi, and Sinification—made the Chinese autocratic system extremely strong. Sinification allowed the government to extend its influence deep into the non-Han frontier lands and provided a common cultural ground for interaction with diverse peoples. In China, the civilian and military sides of government and the Confucian ideology of imperial rule all reinforced the power of the emperor. There were indeed checks and balances within the Qing government, such as the Censorate and overlapping jurisdictions of imperial institutions, but these were all intended to ensure

the implementation of imperial edicts, not in any way to check the power of the emperor.

V. The Economy of an Empire: Agriculture, Commerce, and Taxation

According to Confucian ideology, agriculture provided the economic foundation of the empire. Upon the conquest of Ming China, the restoration of agriculture became a top priority. Much formerly cultivated land had been abandoned, decreasing food output and the tax base. The Manchus reduced taxes on the regions devastated by the fighting. The Yongzheng emperor's public works projects helped restore the agricultural infrastructure. Its essential parts included dikes to prevent flooding, irrigation canals for rice cultivation, and granaries to tide over the population during inadequate harvests. The Qing emperors devoted ten percent of their total revenues to flood control projects on the Yellow River. The cultivation of new crops and double-cropping increased productivity. Peace and land reclamation restored agricultural prosperity. This permitted a remarkable increase in population. Between 1650 and 1850, the population may have more than tripled, but the cultivated land probably only doubled. (See Table 6.1.)

The rapid increase in agricultural productivity and rural prosperity of the early Qing period resulted from an unusual confluence of favorable circumstances: The new dynasty ended the civil wars of the late Ming period; there was an abundance of arable land relative to the population; the early Qing emperors removed the crushing tax burden of the late Ming emperors and kept taxes low; cultivation of the New World crops increased harvests; and ever-earlier-ripening rice strains were introduced. Faster-yielding rice strains permitted more double- and even triple-cropping in certain areas.

Such New World crops as peanuts, sweet potatoes, corn, and white potatoes significantly increased the amount of arable land because they could be planted in drier, sandier, and hillier areas where rice would not grow. Prior to 1700, the arid hill and mountain country surrounding the Yangzi Basin had not been cultivated. In the eighteenth century, it became an important producer of corn and sweet potatoes. The North and South both profited, since corn prospered in the dry soil of the North, while sweet potatoes, peanuts, and tobacco all flourished in the sandy soils of the South. Peanuts provided nitrogen-fixing properties that enhanced soil fertility. New World crops became staples of China's poor and, in the case of peanuts, key to crop rotation systems. Thus, even before the arrival of great numbers of Europeans in the nineteenth century, the Chinese economy had been decisively—and positively—influenced by relations with the West.

Cities also flourished during the rising years of the Qing dynasty through the spread of market towns integrating the agricultural and urban economies, facilitating brisk interregional trade. A growing "sojourner," or guest worker, population engaged in this trade made urban populations more cosmopolitan. These guest workers sponsored a variety of guildhalls or local origin clubs (*huiguan* in Chinese) for others from their place of origin in the cities along their commercial routes. A heterogeneous mix of merchants, officials, and literati constituted the urban elite. Tourism, the theater, service trades, handicrafts, textile production, prostitution, and philanthropic organizations such as orphanages and poorhouses all flourished to varying degrees in different locales. Increasingly, urban residents acquired a social identity distinct from that of the rural population.

Despite the Confucian emphasis on agriculture, commerce was extremely important. In the Confucian social hierarchy, however, merchants sat at the bottom, below artisans. Yet, commerce brought the grain to market and vital goods, such as salt, to the countryside. The same transportation routes also brought local tax revenues to government coffers. But the Qing used foreign trade to buy security, not to seek profit, a concept demeaned by Confucian norms of morality. Thus, foreign trade was used primarily to promote peace on the imperial periphery, not wealth within China proper, and included monopoly export goods such as tea, silk, and porcelain, versus goods for domestic consumption, such as grain, cotton, tobacco, soybeans, and the salt monopoly.

Prior to about 1800, the average per capita standard of living in China was among the highest in the world. China's strong commercial base provided the social underpinnings for a fiscally solvent government. A system of almost universal taxation of the peasantry allowed the state to tap a relatively large proportion of China's wealth. Although the effective tax rate was perhaps only 5 to 6 percent of the total annual harvest, this rate was significantly higher than that of many other countries at that time. New crops and commerce led to a population explosion in Qing China. Under the Ming dynasty, the population exploded from 60 million to about 150 million, and by some accounts to as many as 200 million. By the mid-1800s, the population grew to over 400 million. As a result of this enormous increase, a network of market towns quickly developed throughout rural China. Regional trade increased dramatically, including traditional commodities such as grain and cotton, as well as cash crops like sugar cane.

Specialization also increased during the early Qing: Raw cotton was transported from the North via the Grand Canal to Shanghai, where yarn was spun for the textile firms even farther south in Guangzhou. Ceramic manufacturing centered in Jiangxi, where the Jingdezhen kilns became famous for their porcelain exports to Europe. (See the feature on the next page.) Farther up the Yangzi Valley, Hankou became a major center for the trade of rice, spices, and, later, domestically produced opium. In this environment, trade guilds proliferated. Banks in Ningbo began to experiment with letters of credit for large sums instead of insisting on transactions in bullion, while small-denomination government-issued paper money had circulated throughout China since the twelfth century. Commerce and trade in Qing China reached unprecedented levels, far surpassing those of European nations.

Since the Roman era, the sale of tea, silk, and porcelain had made China famous throughout Eurasia. The Chinese government maintained a close monopoly over most foreign trade. This system worked well when the East–West trade was conducted along the lengthy and precarious Silk Route

PORCELAIN PRODUCTION

In the third century, Chinese potters invented porcelain. Unlike earthenware pottery, porcelain is fired at a very high temperature to fuse a fine-textured pure clay and an exterior glaze. The Chinese mixed their special clay, called "kaolin," and their glazes with feldspar-rich porcelain stone. Firing then transformed this combination into a thin-walled, highly translucent, watertight material. By the late sixth century porcelain was produced throughout China, and by the ninth century it was being exported overland along the Silk Route and also overseas on the Porcelain Road. By the time of the Tang dynasty (681–907), there were about twenty types of kilns. Improvements in kiln design and developments in glazing techniques continued over the succeeding dynasties. By the time of the Ming dynasty (1368–1643), the Jingdezhen porcelain works in the Fuliang district of Jiangxi province produced more porcelain than all other kilns combined. The dominance of the Jingdezhen kilns became even more pronounced during the early and middle Qing periods.

Qing dynasty potters created some of the finest ceramics in Chinese history during the reigns of the Kangxi, Yongzheng, and Qianlong emperors, mainly in the period from 1683 to 1756, when particularly creative supervisors ran the imperial porcelain works at Jingdezhen. After the Qing conquest, the Manchus had reorganized the imperial factories in 1680. They soon employed about 300 painters, calligraphers, kiln loaders, and other specialists and craftspeople, who produced over fifty different types of wares, including copies of the many pre-Qing ceramic types, especially those popular in the Song and Ming dynasties. The copies were so authentic that dating Chinese porcelains can be extremely difficult. Qing dynasty porcelain makers also created the famille rose (rose family) and famille verte (green family) enamel colors that made designs appear three-dimensional.

No other product in preindustrial China required the number of specialized skills necessary for porcelain production. There were three types of workshops: clay workshops, ornamentation workshops, and kilns. Each relied on a wide variety of specialists: some to build the workshop, others to provide and work the raw materials of the workshop, and still others to sell the manufactures. The specialized skills required by clay workshops included clay preparation, pigment grinding, glaze mixing, mold making,

Porcelain became so closely associated with China that in most countries the terms "Chinaware" or "China" are often used. Pictured is a Qing dynasty piece of export porcelain dating to the period of the Qianlong emperor.

Continued

pot throwing, painting of unfired pots, pattern painting, outline painting, color painting, calligraphy, glaze dipping, glaze blowing, and unfired pot trimming. Each was a full-time profession. Ornamentation workshops also required many specialists. The workshops themselves also specialized by type of ornamentation: black-and-white wares, red-and-white wares, celadon wares, and so on.

Porcelain production required kilns capable of maintaining the temperature of 1450°C necessary for porcelain stone to become glasslike (to vitrify) as the clay solidified to maintain the shape of the article. There were many types and sizes of kilns, depending on the quantity, size, and quality of the output. Some kilns were large, capable of firing thousands of items per batch, while items of very high quality were often fired in small batches. Firing also required a wide array of specialists, including the makers of small clay containers for firing pots, kiln loaders, those specializing in fast firing, those specializing in slower firing, those specializing in maintaining even kiln temperatures, and kiln unloaders.

Much of the production was for export, originally for the tribute trade and eventually for the trade with the West, where, by 1715, it had become widespread in aristocratic homes. At the end of the seventeenth century, Western firms sent representatives to Jingdezhen to special order items created specifically for the European market, although most porcelain exports to Europe and Southeast Asia left via Guangzhou. Europeans were not able to produce porcelain until the beginning of the eighteenth century and high-quality porcelain only after 1750. Until recently, Westerners have been more familiar with the multicolored export ware than the more subdued pieces intended for Court use.

Porcelain production at Jingdezhen probably peaked during the Qianlong reign. The industry never recovered from the decline in imperial patronage and the rebellions of the nineteenth century. Although the Communist government restored many of the country's famous porcelain works, including the one at Jingdezhen, which again is the country's primary porcelain producer, the industry has never matched the artistic standards of the early Qing dynasty.

through Central Asia, the Black Sea, and to the Mediterranean. However, beginning in the sixteenth century, the Spanish and Portuguese opened up maritime trade routes that significantly reduced transport costs between China and Europe. This soon led to an explosion in foreign trade, conducted mainly through the southern city of Guangzhou (Canton). During the eighteenth century, the Dutch gradually dominated this trade; during the late Ming and early Qing periods, the Dutch East India company alone imported about 12 million pieces of Chinese porcelain to Europe.

By the eighteenth century, however, the British gradually took control of the bulk of the China trade through the joint-stock company the British East India Company. Under English administration, the tea trade quickly outpaced both silk and porcelain. Whereas in 1684 England imported only five chests of tea, this number rose quickly to 400,000 pounds per annum by 1720. Later in the eighteenth century, the British tea trade increased to 23 million pounds per year. The maritime trade essentially wiped out the overland trade, effectively cutting Russia out of the China trade.

The caffeine content of tea made it a potent stimulant. It was a greatly sought-after beverage during the early years of the Industrial Revolution, when twelve- to fourteen-hour workdays were common. By contrast, in China, the first brew from new tea leaves was usually discarded, thereby eliminating over 90 percent of the caffeine. As will be discussed in greater detail in Chapter 7, one of the only profit-making products the British traders could offer to Chinese buyers was another

well-known and popular drug, opium. Unlike caffeine, which is a stimulant, opium is a depressant. Thus, opium's impact on economic productivity was the opposite of that of tea.

The most important consequence of Confucian prejudices against commerce was the failure to tax it. The Qing, by retaining the traditional Han focus on extracting tax revenues from agriculture, forfeited an important source of revenue and inadvertently promoted the eventual shift in the balance of economic power from China's agricultural to its commercial elite. The Qing tax collection apparatus, the *lijia* system, structurally resembled the *baojia* system but focused instead on tax collection. In order to collect the land and poll taxes, it maintained registers of both arable land and population. The *lijia* and *baojia* systems remained separate through the eighteenth century.

Under the Ming and early Qing dynasties, central taxes were paid in grain and in labor, despite a failed Ming attempt to combine the two into a "single whip" tax. The Qing dynasty maintained separate registers for land and adult males until the Yongzheng emperor consolidated the tax system into one tax. This combined the land and head taxes along with the duties on salt, tea, and imported goods and provided more of the revenues to the central government. While these monies helped fund the Qing conquest of Inner Asia, they deprived local government of its primary source of revenues. As a result, there was a proliferation of additional fees that increasingly burdened the local economy.

The Qianlong emperor took the tax reforms one step further in 1740 when he ordered that the grain and labor taxes be merged. He ordered the *baojia* administration to take a census to determine the size of each household. In 1772 he made the labor tax a percentage of the land tax, eliminating the need to keep a registry of adult males. Despite these reforms, the gentry bore a relatively light tax burden because consumption taxes on such items as salt fell on the whole population. This perceived inequity fueled rural tensions. The government's failure to tax commerce only compounded the failure to extract more tax revenues from the prosperous rather than from the poor.

Conclusions

The Qianlong emperor ruled premodern China at its geographical, administrative, and economic peak. Geographically, he extended his rule to Mongolia, the Junggar and Tarim basins, Tibet, and Western Sichuan. In doing so, he transformed China into a vast Inner Asian empire. Previously, "China" had meant the eighteen core provinces bounded on the north by the Great Wall; now it included these Inner Asian conquests as well. Thus, the alien Manchu dynasty transformed what the Han population defined as China, a transformation that has endured to the present day. But these conquests came at a high price. Some minorities, such as the Zunghars, suffered annihilation, while others endured the devastation of war. Much of the extended empire generated few revenues but required high occupation costs. This forced a reallocation of resources from central China to the periphery, which hurt growth.

The Qing astutely cultivated Han loyalties by relying on the institutional framework of Ming China. They retained the Forbidden City as the residence of the imperial clan, and they kept the Six Boards, the Censorate, the structure of provincial administration, the examination system, and the Confucian ideology. But they also embedded Manchu control in these institutions by pairing Manchu and Han senior appointments; putting Manchus in control of military and national security institutions, the banners, and the Court of Colonial Affairs; and introducing the palace memorial system, creating the Grand Council, and having separate Han and Manchu examinations.

The Qing presided over a long period of stability and internal prosperity. The reform of the tax system, the expansion of land under cultivation, and the introduction of New World crops all contributed to the prosperity of the Qianlong period. Administratively, the Grand Council and the secret palace memorial system were at their greatest efficiency. Economically, the empire benefited from administrative and economic reforms combined with a prolonged period of stability, so economic growth and per capita standards of living probably peaked during the latter part of the Qianlong emperor's long rule. Although there was war on the periphery, there was peace in China's core provinces.

In the late eighteenth century, China became the wealthiest country the world had ever known. The achievements of the Qianlong period became the standard of Chinese achievement for future generations of Han who lived in far less fortunate times. Qianlong's China would be the China they aspired to re-create, a China that held the world in its thrall and whose boundaries were those of the Qing empire. In keeping with the Confucian tradition of looking backward to a remote golden age, the Qianlong period became a more modern golden age for subsequent Chinese generations. The Confucian belief system, however, reinforced the imperative for empire: Each emperor, out of filial piety, had to maintain the lands accumulated by his ancestors. These were the patrimony of China. This imperial legacy proved to be extremely difficult to shed.

BIBLIOGRAPHY

Barfield, Thomas J. *The Perilous Frontier: Nomadic Empires and China 221 BC to AD 1757.* Cambridge, MA: Blackwell, 1989.

Bartlett, Beatrice S. *Monarchs and Ministers: The Grand Council in Mid-Ch'ing China, 1723–1820.* Berkeley: University of California Press, 1991.

Bergholz, Fred W. *The Partition of the Steppe: The Struggle of the Russians, Manchus, and the Zunghar Mongols for Empire in Central Asia, 1619–1715: A Study in Power Politics.* New York: Peter Lang, 1993.

Ch'u, T'ung-tsu. *Local Government in China under the Ch'ing.* Stanford, CA: Stanford University Press, 1962.

Crossley, Pamela Kyle. *The Manchus.* Cambridge, MA: Blackwell, 1997.

———*A Translucent Mirror: History and Identity in Qing Imperial Ideology.* Berkeley: University of California Press, 1999.

Deal, David. M. and Laura Hostetler, trans. *The Art of Ethnography: A Chinese "Miao Album."* Seattle: University of Washington Press, 2006.

Elliott, Mark Christopher. *The Manchu Way: The Eight Banners and Ethnic Identity in Later Imperial China.* Stanford, CA: Stanford University Press, 2001.

Elman, Benjamin J. *A Cultural History of Civil Examinations in Late Imperial China.* Berkeley: University of California Press, 2000.

Elvin, Mark. *The Pattern of the Chinese Past.* London: Eyre Methuen, 1973.

———*Retreat of the Elephants: An Environmental History of China.* New Haven, CT: Yale University Press, 2004.

Fairbank, John K., ed. *The Chinese World Order: Traditional China's Foreign Relations.* Cambridge, MA: Harvard University Press, 1968.

Fang Zhuofen, Hu Tiewu, Jian Rui, and Fang Xing. "The Porcelain Industry of Jingdeshen." In *Chinese Capitalism, 1522–1840,* edited by Xu Dixin and Wu Chengming, translated by Li Zhengde, et al., 308–26. New York: St. Martin's Press, 2000.

Fletcher, Joseph. "Ch'ing Inner Asia c. 1800." In *The Cambridge History of China*, vol. 10, edited by Denis Twitchett and John K. Fairbank, 35–106. Cambridge: Cambridge University Press, 1978.

———"The Heyday of the Ch'ing Order in Mongolia, Sinkiang and Tibet." Ibid., 351–408.

Grunfeld, A. Tom. *The Making of Modern Tibet.* Rev. ed. Armonk, NY: M. E. Sharpe, 1996.

Ho, Ping-ti. *Studies on the Population of China, 1368–1953.* Cambridge, MA: Harvard University Press, 1959.

Hummel, Arthur W. ed. *Eminent Chinese of the Ch'ing Period (1644–1912).* Washington, DC: U.S. Government Printing Offices, 1943.

Kessler, Lawrence D. *K'ang-hsi and the Consolidation of Ch'ing Rule, 1661–1684.* Chicago: University of Chicago Press, 1976.

Kierman, Frank A., Jr. and John K. Fairbank, eds. *Chinese Ways in Warfare.* Cambridge, MA: Harvard University Press, 1974.

Kim, Hodong. *Holy War in China: The Muslim Rebellion and State in Chinese Central Asia, 1864–1877.* Stanford, CA: Stanford University Press, 2004.

Lattimore, Owen. *Inner Asian Frontiers of China.* 1934. Reprint, New York: Oxford University Press, 1988.

Lin, Man-houng. *China Upside Down: Currency, Society, and Ideologies, 1808–1856.* Cambridge, MA: Harvard University Press, 2006.

Liu, Adam Yuen-chung. *The Hanlin Academy: Training Ground for the Ambitious, 1644–1850.* Hamden, CT: Archon Books, 1981.

Millward, James A. *Beyond the Pass: Economy, Ethnicity, and Empire in Qing Central Asia, 1759–1864.* Stanford, CA: Stanford University Press, 1998.

———and Peter C. Perdue. "Political and Cultural History of the Xinjiang Region through the Late Nineteenth Century." In *Xinjiang: China's Muslim Borderland,* 27–62. Edited by S. Frederick Starr. Armonk, NY: M. E. Sharpe, 2004.

Metzger, Thomas A. *The Internal Organization of Ch'ing Bureaucracy: Legal, Normative and Communication Aspects.* Cambridge, MA: Harvard University Press, 1973.

Perdue, Peter C. "Fate and Fortune in Central Eurasian Warfare: Three Qing Emperors and their Mongol Rivals." In *Warfare in Inner Asian History (500–1800),* edited by Nicola Di Cosmo, 369–404. Leiden: Brill, 2002.

———*China Marches West: The Qing Conquest of Central Eurasia.* Cambridge, MA: Harvard University Press, 2005.

Rossabi, Morris. *China and Inner Asia from 1368 to the Present Day.* New York: Pica, 1975.

Rowe, William T. "Social Stability and Social Change." In *The Cambridge History of China*, vol. 9, edited by Willard J. Peterson, 473–562. Cambridge: Cambridge University Press, 2002.

Smith, Warren W., Jr. *Tibetan Nation: A History of Tibetan Nationalism and Sino-Tibetan Relations.* Boulder, CO: Westview Press, 1996.

Watt, John R. *The District Magistrate in Late Imperial China.* New York: Columbia University Press, 1972.

Woodside, Alexander. "The Ch'ien-lung Reign." In *The Cambridge History of China*, vol. 9, edited by Willard J. Peterson, 230–309. Cambridge: Cambridge University Press, 2002.

Wu, Silas H. L. *Communication and Imperial Control in China: Evolution of the Palace Memorial System, 1693–1735.* Cambridge, MA: Harvard University Press, 1970.

Xu Dixin et al., eds. *Chinese Capitalism, 1522–1840.* Translated by Li Zhengde et al. New York: St. Martin's Press, 2000.

NOTES

1. Jonathan Chaves, *Singing of the Source: Nature and God in the Poetry of the Chinese Painter Wu Li* (Honolulu: University of Hawai'i Press, 1993), 98.
2. Susan Naquin and Evelyn S. Rawski, *Chinese Society in the Eighteenth Century* (New Haven, CT: Yale University Press, 1987), 8–9, 107.
3. As recently as 1995, the appropriate method of selection for the Dalai and Panchen lamas was disputed. Beijing has claimed the authority of the Golden Urn method, while the current Dalai Lama has argued that Tibetans have rarely employed that method and then only under duress.
4. Arthur W. Hummel, ed., *Eminent Chinese of the Ch'ing Period (1644–1912)* (Washington, DC: U.S. Government Printing Office, 1943), 7–8.

Chronology

1115–1234	Jin Dynasty
1599	Manchus adopt Mongol alphabet
1616	Nurgaci names the dynasty the Jin (gold)
1635	The term "Manchu" comes into existence
1636	Hong Taiji changes dynasty name to the Qing
1644	Shunzhi emperor assumes the throne in Beijing

Chinese Society at the Zenith of the Qing Dynasty

Ethnicity and status were extremely important during the Qing dynasty. The Manchus dominated the imperial Court, filled the highest government and military positions, and retained inviolate possession of their Manchurian homeland. However, they were a tiny fraction of China's total population, which remained overwhelmingly Han in the central eighteen provinces. On the periphery of the empire there were hundreds of other ethnic minorities, including Mongols, Tibetans, and Uighurs, using mutually unintelligible spoken and written languages. The four main social divisions of traditional China—scholars, peasants, artisans, and merchants—cut across these ethnic lines, with scholars at the top serving the government and merchants at the bottom educating their sons to pass imperial examinations and acquire official status commensurate with their wealth. Unlike people in the West, who aspired—often successfully—to social or legal equality, Chinese sought social harmony, with lower levels of society obliged to honor and obey the higher levels. Like a Chinese family, where a father could punish his children, the Chinese emperor remained above reproach, but was required to treat inferiors with benevolence and guide them with ethical rule. Such reciprocal behavior would create social harmony. The Qing creatively manipulated Han and other traditions to facilitate their control over the Manchu tribes, their conquest of Han China, and their expansion into Inner Asia. They used shamanism, Confucianism, and Tibetan Buddhism as vehicles to power in Manchuria, Ming China, and Mongolia and Tibet, respectively.

I. Manchu and Han Society

The Manchus were the titular rulers of imperial China, but Han were the motive force behind the empire. The Chinese took their ethnic name from what was considered the most humane dynasty, the Han dynasty (206 BC–220 AD), which followed China's warlike founding dynasty, the Qin (221–206 BC), whose name—formerly spelled Ch'in—provides the Western term "China." Activities in Beijing were remote to most Han, who focused on immediate economic concerns, not on capital intrigues. As long as the imperial mandate of heaven appeared secure, people went about their business.

The Manchus were descended from the Jurchen, a tribe that inhabited Manchuria, now part of northeastern China, as well as much of the land currently comprising Russia's maritime province in eastern Siberia. The Jurchen defeated the Liao in northern China to establish the Jin dynasty (1115–1234), which ruled in the North, while the Southern Song dominated the South. Both dynasties were, in turn, ousted by the Mongols, who founded the Yuan dynasty in the thirteenth century. During the Ming dynasty, numerous Manchu tribes paid tribute. Even though out of power, the Jin dynasty gave the Manchus claims to the throne, and the Manchus recalled these claims in 1616, when they officially named their dynasty the Jin. The Manchus were composed of many tribes bearing their own individual names and the term "Manchu" actually dates only to 1635.

The Manchus were originally nomadic tribesmen who spoke an Altaic language. After arriving in northeast

China, they also became farmers in the cold but fertile valleys and plains of the Amur and Ussuri River basins. Like most Mongol tribes farther to the west, they converted to Tibetan Buddhism (also known as Lamaism) but they also maintained their own shamanistic traditions. Their language was originally exclusively a spoken language, but in 1599 they adopted the Mongolian alphabet. During this early period, the Manchus differed significantly in appearance from both the Han and the Mongols, although a combination of "Hanification" of the Manchus and "Manchuification" of the Han gradually blurred these racial differences. But differences remained, such as the Manchu women's unbound feet and the Han dress used by Han men and women, save imperial officials who donned Manchu robes. The requirement that all men adopt the queue obscured the visual differences between Manchu and Han males.

In 1644, when the Manchus took control of China, their total population probably did not exceed 1 million. By contrast, the Han population was perhaps closer to 200 million. The Manchus could not hope to rule Han China without securing Han allegiance. Conversely, the huge disparity in the two populations demonstrates the enormity of the Manchu achievement to conquer, let alone to rule Han China, much less to expand that empire over vast non-Han lands. Although the Qing forbade intermarriage between Manchus and Han, and imperial consorts were usually chosen from a select group of Mongol and Manchu banner clans, intermarriage was actually quite common. Not only was the Kangxi emperor's mother half Han, the mothers of the Kangxi, Qianlong, and Jiaqing emperors were all bondservants who probably entered the palace originally as maids. These children of mixed blood became emperor because the Manchus chose successors not on the basis of seniority or descent, but on merit.

The Han population originated in the fertile valleys of the Yellow and Yangzi rivers. In contrast to their primarily nomadic neighbors, whom they referred to as "barbarians," the Han settled in villages and raised crops. In the South, rice was the staple; in the North, wheat. (See the feature below.) The Han adopted a single written language, Classical Chinese, but their spoken language was never standardized. In addition to Mandarin, important dialects include Shanghaiese and Cantonese. The letters or characters may be the same, but their combination, their grammatical forms, and especially their pronunciations vary as widely in China as they do in Europe. Linguistically, China was like medieval Europe, where Latin was a common written language, for the highly educated, but where locals used many mutually unintelligible spoken languages. The Europeans have always called their particular spoken forms "languages," while the Chinese have classified theirs as "dialects." Yet, spoken vernacular Cantonese is as different from Mandarin as French is from German.

RICE CULTIVATION

Rice is the staple food, particularly of South and Central China, where the climate is mild and the rainfall abundant. There are many varieties of rice, with different rates of maturity, yields, and taste. By the eighteenth century, rice strains maturing in forty days had been introduced, permitting the harvest of three crops per year in some areas. Earlier improvements in rice strains had produced two harvests per year. Most rice varieties require flooded fields, but some lower-yield varieties can also be grown in dry fields. Until recent times, rice production was extremely labor intensive. Most types were first planted in seedbeds. After twenty-five to fifty days, the seedlings were transplanted to well-tilled fields submerged in two to four inches of water.

This meant that the fields had to be level and the water supply reliable and carefully controlled, which in turn required complicated irrigation systems based on dikes and dams. Low-lying coastal areas required extensive land reclamation projects and dikes to keep out salt water. In some cases this entailed moated dikes encircling an interior system of dikes separating cultivated fields. The water level within the fields remained lower than that in the surrounding moat. Sluice gates provided well-watered fields. Irrigation in higher elevations depended on dams, catchments, and lateral irrigation channels to water fields at a particular elevation. Regular water supplies required catchments at higher elevations and linked sluiceways.

When gravity would not suffice, redistributing water for irrigation or drainage required various pumping and water transfer devices powered by the water current itself or by oxen, wind power, and, in many cases, strenuous human labor. The Chinese developed a variety of devices for this purpose: the noria, the well-sweep, the square-pallet chain pump, and the water shuttle, to name the most common.

This complicated irrigation system transformed the face of China into a patchwork of rice paddies sharply delineated by dikes and water channels. Complex irrigation systems required canal networks that also became transportation arteries. The Grand Canal

Continued

provides the most notable example. Rice was so important to the Chinese economy that in imperial times many taxes were paid in rice. Another key purpose of the Grand Canal was to deliver the rice tribute to the capital. Rice also played a key role in famine control. It stocked the state granaries maintained to tide over the population in times of crop failures.

After the harvest, the rice had to be threshed in order to remove the husks. The Chinese preferred to eat well-milled white rice, which could be stored longer than brown rice. This entailed the loss of many nutrients, however, with the removal of the germ and the outer layers. Because rice produces the highest number of calories per acre of any grain, it has allowed China to support a very large population for a very long time. The Chinese divide food into two groups, *fan* and *cai*. Carbohydrates fall into the first category, while meats and vegetables fall into the second. Most of their daily calories come from *fan* in general and rice in particular.

Rice culture created an interlocking set of livestock and produce. The separation of fields into rice paddies required dirt embankments where farmers often grew mulberry bushes to produce the leaves to feed silkworms. Wet fields made a good environment for raising ducks, while pigs could be raised in close quarters.

Learning to read and write Chinese is difficult even for Han Chinese. Because of the enormous amount of time required to memorize thousands of characters, universal literacy has been difficult to achieve. In imperial China, only scholars, aristocrats, and affluent merchants could pay for tutors to teach them to read; peasants often could recognize only a limited number of basic characters and could not write at all. Instead of signing documents by hand, most Chinese used carved rock or wooden blocks, called "chops," which had the characters making up their name engraved in reverse so that they appeared properly oriented when inked and applied to paper.

"China" is a concept with multiple elements. Language is one of them. Race is another. Civilization is yet another. Those in control of the capital have often exaggerated the degree of linguistic, racial, and cultural conformity to present the image of a homogeneous polity that China, and certainly the Qing empire, never actually was. But as an imperial ideology, the image was highly effective in holding the empire together. Initially, the Chinese written and spoken languages distinguished the Han from the Manchus, as well as from the other so-called barbarian tribes on the periphery of the Ming empire. The Manchus eliminated this distinction by mastering Mandarin soon after the conquest. However, they took great pains to preserve their own traditions and ethnic identity among themselves in order to maintain the necessary cohesion to continue to dominate China. They used Manchu for communications concerning military matters and other security issues such as relations with Mongolia, Russia, and Tibet.

The Shunzhi emperor assiduously studied Chinese until he could read books, write edicts, grade official examinations, and comment on Court documents. Fluency in Mandarin Chinese, the dialect spoken in Beijing and throughout much of North China, meant that the Shunzhi emperor could communicate directly with his Han bureaucrats. He enjoyed Chinese literature and followed Zen Buddhist practices. Later, he learned about the world outside China through contact with Johann Adam Schall von Bell (1591–1666), who cured his mother of a serious illness. Schall ran the Jesuit mission in

Chinese cities have changed with the disappearance of the large wooden arches, called "*paifang*," built to commemorate a family's achievements or to honor ancestors. Since widows were not allowed to remarry without losing their virtue, a *paifang* often celebrated virtuous widows. During the Cultural Revolution (see Chapter 25), many *paifang* were destroyed as symbols of China's imperial past, while the modernization and widening of many modern city streets has led to the removal of virtually all the rest.

Beijing and served on the Imperial Board of Astronomy. As the Shunzhi emperor came to rely increasingly on Court eunuchs to implement his orders, he established thirteen eunuch-staffed palace offices with the authority to issue edicts and appoint officials. His immediate successors adopted reforms to slow this growing influence of Han eunuchs.

To many Han, the Manchus remained usurper barbarians, not the rightful heirs to the throne. The consolidation of Manchu rule required the new dynasty to remove both the will and the ability of the Han Chinese to rebel. To remove the will, the Manchus carried out a delicate public relations campaign demonstrating their legitimacy by retaining Han bureaucrats who served the Ming; they reinstituted the imperial examination system; they followed Han etiquette; and they studied the Chinese language. They also followed Confucian prescriptions for model rulers, such as lowering taxes. Of particular importance was their meticulous observance of Confucian rites and rituals, since proper etiquette to ancestors lay at the heart of the heavenly mandate to rule.

The problem for later rulers changed from the mastery of Han civilization to the retention of traditional Manchu practices. For his Manchu subjects, the Qianlong emperor emphasized mastery of the Manchu language and traditional Manchu skills such as horsemanship and archery. Manchuria, the ancestral homeland of the dynasty, remained the oasis of Manchu culture essential to its preservation in a vast Han world. When the Manchus relaxed the prohibition on Han immigration to Manchuria late in the dynasty, the Han population rapidly overwhelmed the region. Today it is difficult to distinguish between the Han and Manchus, although they have different census categories.

II. The Four Social Groups: Scholars, Peasants, Artisans, and Merchants

Confucian traditions divided Han society into four groups: scholars, peasants, artisans, and merchants. This ranking was not accidental, but reflected the long-held view that the tiny elite who could read and write alone possessed the educational and moral authority to serve as government officials. Second in stature came peasants, the bulk of China's population, who produced the staples necessary for life. Third in line were artisans, who built houses, crafted porcelain, and made everyday necessities. Last came merchants, disdained for gaining wealth by trading in commodities produced by others. Although these groups were not castes, as in India, upward mobility was not easy, but required years of hard work and luck, and there was downward mobility as well. Land could be freely bought and sold; all except Manchus could engage in trade; and the

examination system was open to all, with relatively few exceptions such as slaves and actors, providing economic and educational paths for social mobility.

Throughout Chinese history, not only literacy but also training put scholars at the top of the social pyramid. Since the time of the Qin dynasty, serving the government was a scholar's prime duty. A Classical education trained youth to excel on examinations, which funneled the most talented into government service. While merchants might accrue great wealth, only government service conferred the highest status, while status within clans reflected seniority. Competition for public office was fierce. Passing the imperial examinations to enter government service was widely seen as key to rapid social mobility. The famous novel *Dream of the Red Chamber* describes the rise and decline of a scholar family. For Manchus, becoming scholar-officials and bannermen were the two main avenues of employment. By law, bannermen were forbidden to accept gainful private employment, but instead were assigned to a banner and received state subsidies. This meant that as the martial skills of the banner forces gradually declined, in some regions more quickly than in others, the Manchus became increasingly parasitic wards of the state.

The second most important group, the peasantry, constituted 80 percent or more of the population. They tilled the land, produced all staples, raised livestock, and were also the main labor source. During virtually any season, the village headman or the local magistrate could order them to build public works with little or no pay. The peasantry also paid the bulk of taxes in the form of the head tax. For these reasons, even though individual peasants were virtually powerless, the peasantry as a group was seen as the economic foundation of the state. Within the peasantry, however, there were enormous divisions, beginning with day laborers or lease holders, poor farmers who did not own the land that they cultivated, versus those who owned land and usually earned enough to survive and pay their taxes. Higher still were more prosperous peasants with larger plots of land, perhaps even enough to lease some to a poorer neighbor. At the highest level were rich peasants, who obtained income by leasing their holdings rather than working the land themselves. These divisions were not rigid; rather, the peasantry constituted a broad continuum. Those who were more affluent could have their daughter's feet bound. The richest land-owning peasants became gentry and could move to provincial cities, while overseers tended their lands. They had money to educate their sons to take the imperial exams. The scholar elite of China, the so-called literati, came primarily from the Han gentry, which created tight bonds between the government and gentry.

Next were artisans, who produced fine porcelain, lacquerware, silk fabric, and the myriad handicrafts that made China

Even today, 60 percent of China's population works the land. Although Communist propaganda made it seem that most peasants were poor and were forced to pay huge rents to local landlords, Pearl Buck's 1931 novel *The Good Earth* showed that most peasant families underwent a gradual process of gathering more land, becoming landlords themselves, and then losing their holdings and becoming peasants again.

so famous in the West. Although not as respected as peasants, who produced food, artisans made many items that were necessary for civilized life, and porcelain and silk were especially important for China's export market. Chinese artisans also acquired a reputation for carving jade and other semiprecious stones. With the beginning of industrialization during the late nineteenth century, many artisans turned to industrial work, especially in such industries as spinning and weaving.

The fourth and final social class was the merchantry. Merchants transported and exchanged goods, a crucial role in an empire as large as China. Many acquired great wealth. Confucian traditions, however, denigrated merchants because they produced nothing tangible. A lust for profit was a hallmark of a "small man" (*xiaoren*) in Confucian terminology, the antithesis of the scholar-gentleman (*shi*). Although many merchants purchased land to become country gentlemen and provided their sons with the expensive Classical educations necessary to become scholars and government officials, Confucian traditions did not emphasize such

social mobility. Likewise, they overlooked what would become known in modern terminology as the "service economy." Confucian analysis did not recognize the important economic function of those who organized the distribution of goods, the financial systems for investing money, the mechanisms for providing credit, or the means for spreading risk.

In imperial China, the ownership of private property was not a legal right, as in the West, whose legal system emphasized contract law. Even members of the imperial clan lived in their residences at the discretion of the emperor. Because underfunded local officials were tempted to tap visible wealth, profits from trade were generally used for money lending, especially in rural areas, and not put back into industrial development. Chinese merchants did not have the opportunity, seized by their Western counterparts, to demand political influence commensurate with their economic power. In China, the emperor ruled supreme and his powers remained untrammeled. Since Chinese merchants had no input into government policy, such policies did not reflect their interests.

In Western Europe and especially in England, where the Industrial Revolution began, merchants invested their capital in labor-saving technologies and new factories, in the process destabilizing traditional urban–rural relations and putting pressure on farmers to move to the cities and become part of the working class. In China, where land-based scholar-officials and peasants controlled the accepted sources of wealth and power, there was widespread and effective opposition to changing these traditional relationships. Moreover, ambitious merchants often spent large sums to provide their sons with a Confucian education in order to compete in the imperial examination to become government officials, not to expand the family business.

III. The Legal System

The Qing dynasty had a highly developed legal tradition, including a complex legal code of 436 primary statutes and over 1,900 substatutes, listing over 4,000 specific crimes and punishments. This legal code emphasized penal and public law, not commercial and administrative law or the constitutional law that so preoccupied the West, where the division into secular and canon law eventually led to clear separation of church and state. Many matters that Westerners resolved through the courts the Chinese resolved through intermediaries. Because Chinese values put primacy on social harmony and abhorred social conflict, courts were often a last, not a first, resort.

The Qing legal code focused on lawbreakers and on the financial ramifications of marriage and inheritance. In most commercial and economic disputes, informal mediation by families, clans, commercial guilds, or other nongovernment groups was considered sufficient for an equitable solution. That is, personal relations or *guanxi* rather than universal laws regulated these situations. Matters that the West regulated with commercial law China settled through guilds, which could trade *guanxi* to create a informal system of customary arrangements. Rather than using impersonal laws, the Chinese settled such issues with face-to-face contacts.

When a case came before the magistrate, it was taken seriously. Criminal cases required a confession before the criminal could be punished. It was common to use torture to gain confessions. Widespread methods included flogging, face slapping, and ankle, leg, or finger presses. Magistrates who did not obtain confessions could themselves be punished for their apparent dereliction of duty.

China's legal structure was vertical, starting from the county level at the very bottom and extending all the way to the emperor at the top. A case appealed at the county level went up to one of the 180 prefectures. Appeals at that level went on to one of the eighteen provinces and from there to the Board of Punishments in Beijing. Three high courts constituted a fifth level. Above that was the emperor, who had the power either to accept or to overturn court decisions. Unlike the system of judicial precedent originating in Britain, previous cases and court decisions could be cited in trials only as examples and were not legally binding. Jury trials were unknown. Instead, written laws, unwritten cultural norms, and specific local customs, which were not considered to be contradictory but rather mutually reinforcing, determined judicial outcomes. This was in keeping with the emphasis on harmony not only in society, but in the cosmos and in the law.

Westerners have been preoccupied with the punitive aspects of the Qing legal system, disregarding the emphasis placed on social harmony. Once a decision was made, an appropriate punishment was chosen from five levels. From light to harsh, these were a light bamboo caning, a heavy bamboo caning, servitude, banishment to an inhospitable corner of the empire—sometimes combined with military service—and finally the death penalty. The code mandated light or heavy bamboo canings for about one-quarter of the listed infractions, servitude or banishment for about one-half, and the death penalty for fully one-fifth of all crimes. Capital punishment was widespread. Its form depended on the severity of the crime. In ascending order it included suicide on command, strangulation, decapitation, exposing the corpse, and slicing. Death by "a thousand cuts" entailed slow dismemberment. Other penalties, not capital in theory, became capital in practice: Canings were mandated by the number of strokes and so could result in death.

The penalty depended on the relative status of the accused and the victim and on their respective *guanxi* networks. In keeping with the Confucian view of the natural hierarchy that existed in families and in society, a parent who killed his own child—whether deliberately or by mistake—was rarely punished, while a son who killed a parent, even by accident, invariably faced the death penalty. Similar Confucian relationships between older and younger brothers, nephews and uncles, husband and wife, and seniors and juniors in all categories had an equally important impact on the outcome of a trial. For a peasant to criticize a government official could be considered a crime, since it proved his lack of proper Confucian respect for the social hierarchy. Without high status or disposable income, ordinary peasants and others without connections or money could be arrested and imprisoned indefinitely. Guilt was assumed, confessions were extracted by torture, justice was severe, and punishments were excruciating. Conversely, the emperor stood above the law altogether. He was under no formal requirement to make his edicts consistent with existing laws. For the Chinese, ethical behavior required close attention to status. Without appropriate deference there would be social chaos.

Since the time of the Warring States period, there existed a legalistic body of thought that provided an alternate model of governance to Confucianism. This was the Legalism of Han Fei, who based legality and morality exclusively on the will of the emperor. What the emperor desired was right; what he abhorred was wrong. Mutual responsibility was a Legalist concept making neighbors responsible—and accountable—for each other's conduct. The concept was at the root of the *baojia* system for local administration. The Legalists developed a harsh system of punishment in order to mobilize all subjects for food production and for military conquest, thought to be the prerequisites for a durable peace. They rejected Confucianism's implied dual loyalty to the family and to the state, replacing it with exclusive loyalty to the emperor. The Qin dynasty followed the advice of Legalists in 213 BC to destroy most books on competing schools of thought. Although Confucianism dominated Chinese thinking thereafter, the criminal law retained elements of Legalism. The Confucian emphasis on social harmony and the Legalist emphasis on social order have been mutually reinforcing in the area of criminal law.

Just as there was no concept of social equality, there was no discussion of rights. In the West, there has been great attention both in law and in philosophy to the topics of natural rights and, later, human rights, giving rise to the concepts of inalienable rights, equality before the law, and civil rights. All of these were unknown in traditional China, where

Before the arrival of Europeans by sea, most of China's foreign trade was conducted by caravan. Camels on the Western Silk Route usually had only one hump and were often called "Arabian" camels, while the two-humped Bactrian camel, still found wild in the Gobi desert, predominated along the Eastern Silk Route.

children were the chattel of their parents and so could not possess natural or inalienable rights and where equality did not exist as a social category. Even identical twins had a birth order. Western legal codes and constitutions reflected Western social values. In traditional China, the thought of creating a constitution in order to limit a sovereign's power was antithetical to the view of the emperor as harmonizer of the universe. The interests of ruler and ruled were thought to be identical, thus maintaining cosmic harmony.

The arrival of Western traders initiated a legal conflict that is still with us today. One of the main ideological struggles in China throughout the nineteenth and twentieth centuries has been between universalistic Western conceptions of a "rule of law"—laws that apply to all, regardless of wealth, power, or social position—and particularistic Chinese traditions emphasizing social harmony, social order, and hierarchy. Chinese harmonize particular factors making up any social situation, if possible, through the particularistic human network of *guanxi* rather than through the impersonal framework of law.

IV. Confucianism as an Ideology

Confucianism focused on the preservation of the state. Because of its utility, dynasty after dynasty relied on it as the ideology of imperial rule. For the Han, the nightmare scenario consisted of civil wars, instability, and economic hardship that characterized periods of dynastic decline and change. In Mandarin, this was known as "chaos" or *luan,* a term also synonymous with "rebellion" and "confusion." Periods of dynastic fall have been so horrendous and their human toll so enormous that Chinese have long prized the antithesis of chaos–order. Confucianism provided the state with a framework to maintain order and, by extension, prosperity. According to Confucianism, its prescriptions provided the *only* way to maintain order. Rejection of the Confucian framework resulted in chaos.

Section I of the Introduction presented Confucianism as a belief system based on social hierarchy. This section will elaborate on Confucianism as a state ideology. Most Confucian scholars hoped to work for the government; this was the avowed purpose of their education. According to Confucius, the role of the gentleman—the scholar—in Chinese society was to influence the little men—the people—through a superior example. Since the acquisition of personal wealth was disdained, a Confucian scholar would instead use his training in the Classics, reading and writing skills, and organizational abilities for the benefit of the government, which meant serving the emperor. Virtuous rule guaranteed order in the cosmos, which guaranteed prosperity for China's peasantry.

The common Western image of Confucius is that of an elderly sage scholar wandering through China's many small states during the tumultuous Spring and Autumn period advising kings on effective rule. Yet, Confucius was still a young man when he entered government service and started thinking about how to create order from chaos. Confucius emphasized training ambitious students for career success. Not surprisingly, ambitious youths considered a Confucian education as the primary path to rapid social mobility.

As a teacher, Confucius inspired his disciples to study Chinese history, songs, and poetry in order better to serve their ruler. He provided detailed norms for the behavior necessary to gain the respect not only of rulers but also of the people to be governed. In *The Analects,* he instructed his followers to leave behind the common everyday cares of small men in order to strive to become a gentleman. Being a true gentleman meant more than scholastic achievement: It included such social obligations as the proper performance of rituals, appropriate attire for each occasion, meticulous adherence to court etiquette, and appropriate behavior both in public and in private settings. A man who could do this was virtuous, and his virtue would command respect and inspire emulation by others.

Ritual was important for Confucian scholars. To survive in a Han-dominated China, the Manchus relied on ritual to legitimate their rule. They did so in no small measure by appropriating Confucian, Buddhist, and Daoist rituals to cement their role as protectors of Chinese civilization. For the Han, Confucian rituals were the most important. Not only did public rituals have to display the proper respect for family—both living and dead—but their proper performance was an important element of humaneness, or *ren,* one of the cardinal Confucian virtues. Due respect for parents and elders—filial piety—and for fellow men—fraternal duty—was the foundation of humaneness, which in turn showed the Way, or *Dao,* for both individuals and governments.

The Confucian scholar's proper observance of ritual both reconfirmed and strengthened the hierarchical nature of society, with the emperor and, by extension, the emperor's officials, at the top of the pyramid. For a gentleman, the proper observance of rituals helped to stabilize Chinese society; rituals helped to educate the small man concerning his proper

social station. In *The Analects,* Confucius described the obligations of the gentleman to the small man: "If you lead them by means of government and keep order among them by means of punishments, the people are without conscience in evading them. If you lead them by means of virtue and keep order among them by means of ritual, they have a conscience and moreover will submit."[2]

While proper behavior and observance of ritual were key to forming a gentleman's intellect, Confucius did not ignore his external appearance. Fine clothing showed proper respect. In *The Analects* Confucius described the appropriate dress for different occasions: "The gentleman . . . [d]uring hot weather . . . wears an unlined garment of fine or coarse material. . . . With a black robe he wears lambskin, with an undyed robe he wears fawnskin, and with a yellow robe he wears fox fur. . . . Lambskin garments and black caps are not used for visits of condolence. On the first day of the month he always puts on court dress and goes to court. When he is purifying himself, he always wears a spirit robe made of cotton."[3] Etiquette was also important. Confucius discussed table manners, elocution, and public appearance. His advice was intended to enable disciples to impress the kings and princes they served and also the people whom they were charged to rule. The sage's advice extended to their private lives, even recommending "not to talk in bed," meaning not to discuss state secrets with lovers.[4]

In China, proper decorum for gentlemen included appropriate dress, performance of rituals, and appropriate behavior in accordance with their station in life, the station in life of those they were with, and the occasion at hand. In a highly hierarchical system, behavior at the top mattered the most. Emperors who flaunted Confucian ethics or neglected their ritual duties risked losing their mandate to rule. Conversely, adherence to Confucian norms would bring stability to the empire. According to Confucius: "If their superior is fond of ritual, then none of the people will dare not to behave with reverence; if their superior is fond of what is right, then none of the people will dare not to be obedient; if their superior is fond of good faith, then none of the people will dare not to go by the true circumstances."[5] The Confucian scholar advised the emperor and implemented his will. This relationship benefited both the state and those fortunate enough to pass the imperial examinations and enter government service. Government service was the only respected path to personal success, and officials could amass vast fortunes through their positions.

But this system had a number of negative implications. Because Confucius and his disciples looked to the past for guidance, this philosophy was ill-equipped to deal with unprecedented situations for which the past could provide no guidance. When national security issues required institutional changes, Confucian traditions constrained the Manchus' ability to respond in a timely and effective manner. It was unthinkable for Confucians to look to the barbarian West for alternate models of governance or for any other important human activity. China's emphasis on static norms of behavior and the unquestioning respect for both seniority and established authority discouraged reform and unorthodox thinking, which together could make original thinking a career-threatening activity.

China's model for governance was based on long-gone dynasties. History was cyclical, which suggested boundaries to human action. Yet, the Manchus were both innovators and upholders of China's Confucian traditions. After taking power, they disguised their institutional innovations under the umbrella of Ming institutions.

V. Shamanism, Confucianism, and Buddhism as Instruments of Manchu Rule

The Qing dynasty used the belief systems of its subjects in order to extend its rule over them and to cement their loyalties to the dynasty and create an image of universal rulership. It used shamanism, Confucianism, and Buddhism to win over the main constituencies: the Manchus, the Han, and the Mongols and Tibetans, respectively. Thus, it ruled with many distinct audiences in mind in order to maintain its multiethnic empire.

For the Manchus, the Qing emperors became protectors of the shamanistic religious practices uniting the peoples of Manchuria with the leaders of their banners; for the Han, they assumed the role of Confucian emperors and protectors of Chinese civilization; for their Mongol subjects, they became the Mongol khans and promoters of Lamaist Buddhism; and for their Tibetan subjects, they became reincarnated Buddhas. The requirements of empire and Manchu ethnic preservation demanded that the Qing reject the total Sinification assumed by Confucianism, and accept and even promote the cultural differences among their subjects. Although the Qing emperors attempted to become the universal symbol of rulership, they did so by projecting distinct, culturally specific images to each of their varied subject populations. Rather than Sinify their non-Han subjects, which would have eventually entailed the Manchus' own disappearance, Qing emperors sought to project the image of rulership required to maintain the loyalty of each group.

The Qing used shamanism to unify the many tribes and create a new ethnic group named the Manchus. According to shamanism, humans inhabited the intermediary world between the realm of deities in the skies and the subterranean realm of the dead, and shamans could summon deities into this world. To strengthen the Qing imperial clan's legitimacy, Nurgaci sought secular as well as religious symbols of power. Hearkening back to the Jin or "Gold" dynasty (1115–1234), he assumed the clan names *aisin,* meaning "gold," and *gioro,* meaning "clan," so his imperial lineage became known as the Aisin Gioro. Subsequent Manchu emperors promoted descendants of this elite clan, at the expense of other clans, in order to glorify the beginnings of Manchu rule. Manchu emperors ruthlessly limited the subsidies given to royal princes so that the Qing empire survived with a small aristocracy and avoided the financial drain usually associated with aristocracies.

The Qing used this same pattern to extend their rule over the peoples of Han China and Inner Asia: They appropriated the religious symbols of these peoples in order to enhance the legitimacy of Qing rule over them. Manchu emperors communicated in their subjects' own languages. Emperors studied Manchu, Chinese, and Mongolian, while the Qianlong emperor, who subjugated Tibet and the Tarim Basin, also learned Tibetan and Uighur. Despite prohibitions against intermarriage, the Qing used imperial marriages to cement alliances with the royalty of Inner Asia, particularly that of Inner Mongolia. Whereas Han Chinese dynasties rarely used imperial marriages to strengthen foreign alliances, when dealing with Inner Asians the Manchus honored their own traditions.

By far the largest ethnic group was the Han. The Manchus deftly manipulated Confucianism both to justify their mandate to rule and to cement Han loyalties. Upon entry into Beijing, they ordered proper funerary rites for the last Ming emperor. Before long, the Manchus created an imperial ancestral cult in conformity with Han traditions; sponsored a Confucian educational system; relied on a civilian Ming-structured bureaucracy; adopted Han rituals of filial piety, marriage, and burial; patronized the visual and literary arts; and even awarded the descendants of Confucius a dukedom. To overawe those who came to the capital, the Qianlong emperor engaged in a massive building program. This included repairing Beijing's infrastructure and palaces, as well as building numerous temples representing the religions of the subject peoples, thereby providing symbolic trappings of power. Until the very end of the dynasty, the Manchus retained the loyalty of their Han officials and Han troops, the two pillars of imperial rule.

After the Han, the most important group for the initial success of the Qing dynasty was the Mongols. During the seventeenth century, the Mongols occupied not only Inner and Outer Mongolia, but also parts of the Tarim and Junggar basins, half of Manchuria, and beyond. Their influence extended to Tibet, where they had earlier undermined Ming dynasty ties with Lhasa. At the time of the Qing conquest, they constituted the main rival to Manchu control of Inner Asia.

Historically, Buddhism had long been popular among non-Han Inner Asian rulers. It served as an alternative to Han cultural hegemony, while Tibet provided an alternate cultural center. Many weak Mongol leaders sought confirmation from Lhasa to legitimate royal successions. The Han had also been attracted to Buddhism. Previous Han Chinese dynasties had been drawn to its theories of rulership, specifically to its concept of *cakravartin* or "world conqueror." The Tibetan Buddhist variant of this belief entailed reincarnated lines of descent, meaning that each imperial successor was the reincarnation not just of his immediate predecessor but of all of them and, as such, was a deity. The Dalai Lama in Lhasa had long served as mediator of Mongol feuds and dispenser of Mongol seals of royal office. The Manchus soon appropriated this role from the Tibetans. Their military occupation of Tibet and the absence of an effective Tibetan army allowed them to do so.

The Qing employed a variety of strategies to subjugate the Mongols: They took advantage of their many tribes to divide and rule and to conquer in detail one by one. Those, like the Zunghars, who repeatedly rebelled suffered annihilation. To the loyal, they married off imperial princesses and awarded noble titles. Mongol tribes that came over to the Manchus were incorporated into the banner system and served as guards on the frontiers with Russia, as well as provided the forces to subjugate other Mongol tribes.

The Qing also astutely promoted Tibetan Buddhism in order to consolidate their rule over the Mongols. The Manchus patronized Tibetan Buddhism by constructing numerous temples in Beijing and throughout Inner Asia, by funding multivolume translations and compilations of sacred texts, and by transforming Beijing into a center of Buddhist learning. Their promotion of Tibetan Buddhism was highly effective. At least one-third of all males in Outer Mongolia and an even greater percentage in Inner Mongolia became lamas and resided in monasteries. This neutralized the Mongols as a potential military or economic threat.

The combination of military occupation and the projection of culturally appropriate norms of rulership transformed Han China, Mongol Inner Asia, and the Tibetan highlands into submissive parts of the Qing empire. The Manchus were not as successful with the Muslim population of Central Asia. Although their military conquest was equally complete, they were unable to project culturally acceptable rulership to their Muslim subjects because Islam rejects rule by unbelievers and Manchu monarchs did not convert to Islam. Thus, Islam was not susceptible to the Qing strategy for empire and Muslims constantly desired to secede from China. Military

superiority, however, held this desire at bay. To this day, there are strong undercurrents of ethnic separatism in Xinjiang.

Conclusions

The Confucian framework for understanding society included four social groups arranged in a hierarchy, with scholars at the top, followed in descending order by peasants, artisans, and merchants. It defined people in terms of occupation and yet was silent on the two groups that combined, dynasty after dynasty, to rule China, namely, soldiers and aristocrats. The Confucian social framework applied to the subjects, not the rulers of China. Confucius was also silent on matters of ethnicity. He did not go beyond the dichotomy of barbarian and Chinese but instead focused on the Chinese world, meaning the civilized world. For Confucians, civilization was a concept with a singular but not a plural form. There were no competing civilizations, just one, which alone provided the means for man to live an orderly and prosperous life. Its alternative was barbarism and chaos.

The Manchus did not fit neatly into this framework. In their case, ethnicity, meaning differences in race, culture, and religion, was of the utmost importance. To state the obvious, the Manchus were not Han. Their mother tongue was a non-Sinitic language, meaning that it belonged to an entirely different language group from Mandarin. They came from the barbarian world outside of the Ming empire. The Manchu tradition was a warrior tradition of military, not civilian, rule. In contrast to Confucianism, the Manchus honored, not denigrated, martial traditions. They governed themselves with collegial, not autocratic, rule. Their rulers came from within the imperial clan, but the eldest brother did not necessarily or even usually inherit the throne. Rule was based more on merit than on seniority. The imperial family intermarried with the royalty of neighboring tribes, particularly with Mongols. Whereas the Han routinely crippled their daughters through footbinding, Manchu women not only could walk normally, but also appeared in public, rode horses, and even hunted. Manchu religious and philosophical traditions were not Buddhist, Daoist, or Confucian, but shamanistic. None of this fit Han traditions.

In order to rule as a tiny minority over the vast Han population of post-Ming China and over the even more vast territories populated by other ethnic groups, the Manchus could not emphasize these differences and hope to rule for long. Yet, among themselves, they needed to preserve a separate identity to prevent being engulfed by the surrounding Han population. This problem posed a dilemma for the Manchus that they solved by skillfully manipulating the religious traditions and norms for rulership of their subject peoples in order to present themselves as protectors and sponsors of these traditions. This mode of empire also might account for their ability to extend the borders of China far beyond those of any Han Chinese dynasty.

Modern China can be traced back to the Qing's imperial history. In particular, ethnic divisions along the frontiers, social distinctions emphasizing hierarchy, the high respect for education, education as a route to social mobility, inequality before the law, the importance of state ideology, the pervasiveness of *guanxi,* and the Confucian primacy on family loyalties have had a continuing impact on China. Although foregoing Sinification might have promoted imperial expansion in Inner Asia, it did nothing to lessen the ethnic differences there. In modern times, this spelled trouble for Han rulership, as ethnic minorities sought independence after the fall of the Qing dynasty and secession after the reunification of much of the old Qing empire under the Communists.

BIBLIOGRAPHY

Bernhardt, Kathryn and Philip C. C. Huang, eds. *Civil Law in Qing and Republican China.* Stanford, CA: Stanford University Press, 1994.

Bodde, Derk and Clarence Morris. *Law in Imperial China.* Philadelphia: University of Pennsylvania Press, 1973.

Chan, Wing-tsit, trans. and comp. *A Source Book in Chinese Philosophy.* Princeton, NJ: Princeton University Press, 1963.

Crossley, Pamela Kyle. *The Manchus.* Cambridge, MA: Blackwell, 1997.

Eastman, Lloyd E. *Family, Field, and Ancestors: Constancy and Change in China's Social and Economic History, 1550–1949.* New York: Oxford University Press, 1988.

Fung, Yu-lan. *A History of Chinese Philosophy.* 2nd ed. 2 vols. Translated by Derk Bodde. Princeton, NJ: Princeton University Press, 1952.

Guy, R. Kent. *The Emperor's Four Treasuries: Scholars and the State in the Late Ch'ien-lung Era.* Cambridge, MA: Harvard University Press, 1987.

Huang, Philip C. C. *Code, Custom, and Legal Practice: The Qing and the Republic Compared.* Stanford, CA: Stanford University Press, 2001.

Koller, John M. *Asian Philosophies.* 4th ed. Upper Saddle River, NJ: Prentice Hall, 2002.

Naquin, Susan and Evelyn S. Rawski, *Chinese Society in the Eighteenth Century.* New Haven, CT: Yale University Press, 1987.

Rawski, Evelyn S. *The Last Emperors: A Social History of Qing Imperial Institutions.* Berkeley: University of California Press, 1998.

Rhoads, Edward J. M. *Manchus & Han: Ethnic Relations and Political Power in Late Qing and Early Republican China, 1861–1928.* Seattle: University of Washington Press, 2000.

Smith, Richard J. *China's Cultural Heritage: The Qing Dynasty, 1644–1912.* 2nd ed. Boulder, CO: Westview Press, 1994.

NOTES

1. According to Stephen Owen, the Hua-xu dream refers to "the Yellow Emperor's dream of a primordial world of innocence"; Zhao Yi, "Local Song," in Owen, *An Anthology of Chinese Literature: Beginnings to 1911* (New York: W. W. Norton, 1996), 1142. From AN ANTHOLOGY OF CHINESE LITERATURE: BEGINNINGS TO 1911 edited and translated by Stephen Owen. Copyright © 1996 by Stephen Owen and The Council for Cultural Planning and Development of the Executive Yuan of the Republic of China. Used by permission of W. W. Norton & Company, Inc.

2. Confucius, *The Analects,* book 2, no. 3. Raymond Dawson, trans. (Oxford: Oxford University Press, 1998) 6.

3. Confucius, *The Analects,* book 10, no. 5, 36.

4. Ibid., 36.

5. Ibid., 49–50.

Chronology

2205–1766 BC	Xia dynasty
1766–1122 BC	Shang dynasty
770–222 BC	Eastern Zhou dynasty, Five Classics
771–484 BC	Spring and Autumn Period
403–221 BC	Warring States Period (latter period of the Eastern Zhou)
551–479 BC	Confucius
400–200 BC	Four Books
371–289? BC	Mencius
221–206 BC	Qin dynasty
206 BC–220 AD	Introduction of the imperial examination system (Han dynasty)
145–85? BC	Sima Qian
1368–1644 AD	Ming dynasty
	Zhu Xi interpretation of Confucianism used
1487	Eight-legged essay becomes the format of imperial examinations
1613–1662	Gu Yanwu
1644–1911	Qing dynasty
1679	Examinations to identify scholars to write the official history of the Ming dynasty
1724–77	Dai Zhen
1739	Publication of the official history of the Ming dynasty
1851–64	Taiping Rebellion

The Foundations of Knowledge

If one opens a book, one meets the men of old;
If one goes into the street, one meets the people of today.
The men of old! Their bones are turned to dust;
It can only be with their feelings that one makes friends.
The people of today are of one's own kind,
But to hear their talk is like chewing a candle!
I had far rather live with stocks and stones
Than spend my time with ordinary people.
Fortunately one need not belong to one's own time;
One's real date is the date of the books one reads!.[1]

Yuan Mei (1716–98),
most popular Chinese poet
of the eighteenth century

From the late Ming dynasty until the Taiping Rebellion, there was a major critical reexamination of Neo-Confucianism, a synthesis of Buddhism and Confucianism that had been the dominant philosophical school since the Song dynasty, when the scholar Zhu Xi wrote his long-definitive commentaries on the Confucian classics. Because the civil service examinations of the Yuan through Qing dynasties tested Zhu Xi's Neo-Confucian interpretations, the philosophical debate during the Qing dynasty had both academic and political implications. Both Neo-Confucianism and the new philosophical school, called *Kaozheng* Scholarship (meaning "evidential scholarship"), revered the Classics but disagreed over what should be their orthodox interpretation, their relative importance, and their definitive published editions. *Kaozheng* Scholarship differed from Neo-Confucianism in its emphasis on the Five Classics over the Four Books, inductive over deductive reasoning, and evidential over intuitive analysis.

I. Fidelity to the Past

Followers of both Neo-Confucianism and *Kaozheng* Scholarship made ancient models the standard for contemporary human organizations and achievements. Despite their differences, they shared an emphasis on historical continuity and the glorification of China's ancient past. Their philosophical differences emerged within a very different intellectual and political landscape than that of the West.

The constant improvements over time assumed in the West violated Han principles of filial piety, seniority, and historical and cultural continuity that all emphasized stability. Many Chinese associated change and discontinuity with the devastating warfare accompanying dynastic change, whereas many in the West glossed over the terrible human costs of change. On one level, the Han emphasis on continuity reflected their understanding of the natural world and the cyclical operation of time in it. On other levels, it reflected the traditions of clan organizations, bureaucratization, and education; Han pride of place; the mandate of heaven; and later the requirements for minority Manchu rule over Han China. For the Han, continuity was not a choice but a fact. Time was an endless cycle. The dynastic cycle reflected this reality. Continuity was an a priori condition of life and so was an article of faith. Finding the *Dao* or Way entailed keeping the human world in conformity with the natural world, so the Han elaborated a variety of systems to imitate the sages. Confucius stated: "Do not look at what is contrary to ritual, do not speak what is contrary to ritual, and make no movement which is contrary to ritual."[2] In short, follow established practices. Traditional Han values put a primacy on continuity.

Ancestor worship constituted perhaps the main impetus for the Chinese emphasis on continuity. Filial piety enjoined the young to honor the old and the living to heed the dead. It required the upright to preserve or restore, but not exceed, the achievements of illustrious ancestors. Reverence of ancestors and respect for seniors was a core belief of Confucianism, and its rituals were in large part rituals of filial piety. A family altar served as the focus for prayers and sacrifices to ancestors. Offerings could include prepared food, fruit, and drink, as well as lit incense. Ancestors might reward a filial son, who conducted all the appropriate rituals, with long life, numerous offspring, wealth, and the respect of his community. Neglect of ancestor worship might entail official sanctions.

Large clans often had kinship or descent groups governed by elaborate rules. Wealthy clans established lineage organizations in control of ancestral halls. Although these descent groups provided economic and social support in times of need, failure to cooperate and abide by the rules could lead to expulsion from both clan and family. Thus, clans provided a strong enforcement mechanism for conformity.

Confucianism also stressed hierarchy and seniority in government service, while the vast size of China required a commensurately large bureaucracy, where honors, remuneration, and authority were allocated by seniority, ability, and loyalty. In China, disloyalty was severely punished, while the balance between seniority and ability was skewed heavily in favor of seniority. The young and middle-aged had little influence over decision making in any sphere of life; rather, they obeyed the dictates of their elders. Men did not usually achieve positions of authority until well past the prime of life, when they became the senior men in control of groups and organizations, ranging from the family to the government administration. The seniority system served to preserve tradition and slow change. Unlike in the West, which sought efficiency, seniority came before competence because the supposed virtue of seniority trumped efficiency.

Social mobility and personal success within a Confucian bureaucracy required support of the status quo. Examination candidates memorized the Classics in order to succeed. Because the successful examination candidates who ran the Qing government were among the primary beneficiaries of the status quo, there was no direct incentive for them to change. During the Qing dynasty, the Han literati, not the Manchus, were among the most conservative forces. They demanded that Han civilization be preserved in its entirety. As the Qing dynasty matured, even its hybrid model for empire tended to grow brittle with age. Nevertheless, government officials generally supported the status quo.

Han pride of place also constituted an important source of continuity. The Chinese have long emphasized China's historical continuity stretching back 5,000 years. The records actually go back 3,000 years, while earlier periods remain quite speculative, which means that the Chinese civilization is not as old as the Sumerian or Egyptian civilizations, but is roughly on par with that of ancient Greece. The enormous Han sense of their own history, deep pride in the numerous achievements of Chinese civilization, and awareness of its great success over the millennia provided a strong sense of self-confidence, although the historic continuity was actually more illusory than real. Dynasties ruled over areas of widely different extent. Periods of dynastic change were often long and bloody. There were lengthy periods when China was divided among two or more competing northern and southern dynasties and other long periods when the Han were under barbarian rule—as during the Qing dynasty. Nevertheless, the Han perception of historical continuity became a powerful impetus for actual continuity.

Ethnic differences between the Manchus and the Han, which constituted a major discontinuity from Han rule, made the Manchus vulnerable to charges of illegitimacy as the usurpers of Han China. Only those dynasties with the mandate of heaven could continue to rule any dynasty. In particular, non-Han like the Qing risked losing their mandate to rule if they tampered with the hallowed traditions of China. Qing emperors therefore derived legitimacy as protectors of these traditions, and Manchus used the meticulous observance of Han traditions to cement their rule. Changes could only be made either at the fringe and out of sight, or with the intent to restore righteous past practices. Thus, the late Qing reform period became known as the Tongzhi Restoration to create the appearance of restoring hallowed traditions, not tinkering with them. Real reform entailed deviations from accepted precedents, which would have weakened the Manchu hold on legitimacy. Therefore, once they solidified their rule over Han China, highly visible radical reform became very unlikely. When the Manchus finally resorted to sweeping reforms in the early twentieth century, they lost power within a decade.

II. The Confucian Classics

Throughout much of Chinese history, a traditional education focused on the Classics. Originally, there were thought to be only the so-called Five Classics, but over time others were added. The Five Classics were the *Book of Changes*, the *Book of Odes*, the *Book of History*, the *Book of Rites*, and the *Spring and Autumn Annals*. These books or early versions of them formed the basis for Confucius's own education and date to the Eastern Zhou dynasty (770–222 BC). The so-called Four Books comprised the key works of Confucianism codified by the Song dynasty philosopher Zhu Xi (1130–1200) and then made orthodox under the Yuan dynasty as the standard for the imperial examinations. Neo-Confucians considered Zhu Xi's commentaries to be authoritative and emphasized the Four Books, whereas scholars of the *Kaozheng* School rejected Zhu Xi to give greater weight to the Five Classics as older works than the Four Books (let alone Zhu Xi's commentaries) and therefore less corrupted by later additions.

The first and greatest of the Five Classics was the *Book of Changes* (*Yijing*, or *I Ching*). Intended to help divine the will of heaven, this book presents a total of 4,096 interpretations of sixty-four hexagrams, which constituted all the possible combinations of the six lines made from combining two trigrams. A trigram was a set of three parallel lines, each of which was either continuous or consisted of two dashes. The eight trigrams consisted of all their possible combinations. The legendary scholar-emperor Fuxi was said to have created this system in 2852 BC to enable diviners to answer questions. If one repeatedly threw sticks of the yarrow or milfoil plant to divine a number, the corresponding number in the *Book of Changes* indicated the correct passage from which to derive an answer.

The *Book of Changes* referred to many key Han concepts, such as the *Dao*, meaning the Way, and *yin* and *yang*, or the duality of the attracting and opposing female–male forces. Divination was also closely connected with the Han emphasis on fate. It presupposed the future to be preordained and, therefore, knowable in advance. Such views contrasted to the Western emphasis on free will and the assumption that individuals could alter outcomes through preemptive action. The *Book of Changes* remained in use through the end of the Qing dynasty; in 1900, the Boxer rebels, who attempted to expel foreigners from China, took the hexagram called "the abyss" for their flag.

The second of the original Five Classics, the *Book of History*, was also known as the *Book of Documents* (*Shujing* or *Shu Ching*). It is an anthology of documents, speeches, and other primary sources from 2000 to 700 BC. It provides descriptions of the foundation of the Chinese state and empire during the golden age of Chinese history. This was the distant era that Confucians hoped to emulate in subsequent dynasties. The *Book of History* also illustrates such core Han values as filial piety. In one story the Duke of Zhou, upon hearing that his brother, the king, was ill, dutifully prayed to their family ancestors begging to have his own life taken instead. Future generations of Confucian scholars studied these stories for lessons in proper behavior and model government. The *Book of History* also describes the dynastic cycle from the decline of the Xia dynasty (2205–1766 BC), its overthrow by the rising Shang dynasty (1766–1122 BC), the decline of the Shang, and its overthrow by the then-ruling Western Zhou dynasty.

Perhaps the Xia dynasty was contrived so that the Zhou would not be accused of overthrowing China's founding dynasty, but instead would be lauded for restoring the exemplary rule of its predecessor. The book shows how the abuse of power by the Shang rulers cost them their mandate of heaven and legitimated their overthrow by the Zhou dynasty.

The third classic, the *Book of Odes*, is also known as the *Book of Poetry* or the *Book of Songs* (*Shijing* or *Shih Ching*). It contains some 300 songs dating from the tenth to the sixth centuries BC describing everyday events, such as courtship and marriage, and matters of state, such as sacrifices to imperial ancestors. Most of these songs were written as four-syllable rhymes and so were also poems. Generations of aspiring Confucian scholars memorized the verses and used them as a literary shorthand. Given the proper context, many could even be construed as critical of the government, so that poetry became a means to circumvent censorship. One poem bemoans the fate of ordinary soldiers: "Which plant is not brown? / Which man is not sad? / Have pity on us soldiers. / Treated as though we were not men!"[3] Another describes the horrors of dynastic change: "Heaven has let down a drag-net of ill-doing; / the locusts have gnawed us with word-work, / they have hollowed our speech, / Perverse alliances and continuing crookedness have divided us, / evil men are set above us, in ease."[4] Perhaps as a result of the *Book of Odes*, poetry has played a special role in Chinese politics, with great statesmen portrayed as accomplished poets and with social critics disguising their political barbs in poetry.

The odes, in addition to setting the literary standard for subsequent poetry, presented a moral framework for future generations. In one ode describing a ceremony honoring ancestors, the ancestors granted long life to their faithful descendants who performed the required rites in an exemplary manner. Other odes were treated as allegorical tales with ascribed moral meanings. In another description of ancestor worship, a grandson dressed as his grandfather in order to become a medium for the grandfather's spirit. The story demonstrated the close spiritual link between grandfather and grandson, just as a new dynasty often had special links to its grandfather dynasty two governments before, like the Western Zhou and Xia dynasties, the alien Manchu and Mongol dynasties, the Han Republic of China and the Ming dynasty, or perhaps even the Soviet-backed Communists and the Qing dynasty, both from the north.

The fourth classic, the *Book of Rites* (*Liji* or *Li Chi*), is composed of three collections on official rituals, the history of Zhou dynasty rituals, and various treatises discussing rituals from the early Han dynasty. Recompiled during the Han dynasty from fragments of the original *Book of Rites* and more contemporary sources, this compilation originally included the *Spring and Autumn Annals,* which later became a separate classic. Confucius was thought to have written parts of the *Book of*

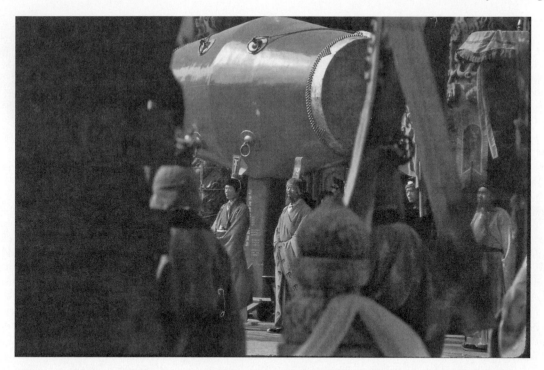

Every year, Confucius is honored in his birthplace in Qufu, Shandong province, on 1 October, the day of his death, while in Taiwan the celebration is held on 28 September, the day of his birth. Kong Fuzi, or "Master Kong," was a Chinese philosopher who helped to establish the basic structure of Chinese society.

Rites. Such early Confucian texts as the *Great Learning* (*Da Xue* or *Da Hsueh*) and the *Doctrine of the Mean* (*Zhongyong* or *Chung Yung*) were taken from the *Book of Rites*. These works describe how scholars must study the way of the world around them and of their own inner world before they can correct either their own mistakes or the deficiencies of society by creating a properly organized society and a just government.

The fifth Classic, the *Spring and Autumn Annals* (*Chunqiu* or *Ch'un Ch'iu*), was also thought to have been partially written or compiled by Confucius himself. Focusing on the period from 722 to 481 BC, it describes historical events in the state of Lu, in modern-day Shandong province. These highly didactic accounts provide the underlying Confucian analytical framework of using history as a moral lesson to teach correct behavior. The use of the terms "Spring" and "Autumn," referring to the seasons of the year, was in keeping with the cyclical Han view that governments, like the seasons, rise and fall in an unending cycle. This book, along with the other four Classics described above and a later historical work by Sima Qian (c. 145–90 BC) called the *Historical Records* (*Shiji* or *Shih Chi*), helped set the pattern for historical writing in China. In these moral and historical accounts, the Han set themselves apart from their immediate neighbors—referred to collectively as "barbarians"—and praised China for its unique language, culture, and complex political and social organization.

Over time, other classics were added to the original five. The Four Books consisted of three works attributed to Confucius (551–479 BC) and one attributed to his most famous disciple, Mencius (371–289? BC). These were the teachings of Confucius removed from the *Book of Rites* and made into two separate volumes, the *Great Learning* and the *Doctrine of the Mean*, as well as the *Analects* (*Lunyu* or *Lun Yü*), and the *Book of Mencius* (*Mengzi* or *Meng Tzu*). The *Analects* is a collection of anecdotes about Confucius and teachings by him and his immediate disciples. An additional Classic, the *Canon of Filial Piety* (*Xiaojing* or *Hsiao Ching*), exhorted Chinese to be respectful of their elders and ancestors. The Classics, after growing to a total of thirteen in the Song dynasty (960–1279), were later reduced to the Four Books, the core teachings of Confucianism. These books played a major role in Chinese society until the end of the Qing dynasty, and their impact on China remains strong down to the present. China also had a rich tradition of fiction, but these books did not gain official sanction. (See the feature on the next page.)

DREAM OF THE RED CHAMBER

Cao Xueqin's (1716?–1763?) novel *Dream of the Red Chamber* (*Honglou meng*) is often counted among China's greatest novels, which include *Romance of the Three Kingdoms* (late Yuan or early Ming dynasty), *Journey to the West* (Ming dynasty), and *Tale of the Water Margin* (1644 revision of a Yuan dynasty work). The novel first appeared in print in 1792 at the height of the Qianlong emperor's reign.

Cao was a member of the Bond Servant Division of the Imperial Household of the Manchu Plain White Banner. The novel portrays the tragic love story of Jia Baoyu and Lin Daiyu against the backdrop of the rise and fall of the Jia family. Critics have interpreted it as an allegory of the cyclical fortunes both of the Qing dynasty and of Cao's own family. The Yongzheng emperor's removal of Cao's father from the superintendancy of the Imperial Textile Factory at Nanjing reduced the family to poverty when Cao was a boy.

Some critics have suggested that the hero, Baoyu, represents the youthful Qianlong emperor, who reportedly, like Baoyu, licked the rouge off the lips of young women. According to this interpretation, Baoyu's stern father represents the Yongzheng emperor. Others believe the novel to be semiautobiographical. Both the author and the protagonist were raised in aristocratic families but died in poverty. The story of the once rich and famous Jia family is long, intricate, and replete with Buddhist and Daoist imagery. In discussing the Jia family's declining fortunes, the novel covers the interaction between the family's two main branches and many long-lost cousins. It also discusses many aspects of Chinese culture and society, including marriage, religion, education, politics, law, food, entertainment, poetry, holidays, funerals, women, etiquette, social hierarchy, relationships, and even the taboo subject of homosexuality.

When still a child, Baoyu receives a stone amulet from a passing monk. Baoyu's family expects him to study hard to pass the imperial examinations. Instead, he prefers to cavort with his female cousins and servants. After falling in love with the orphaned Daiyu (Black Jade), who is sickly and temperamental, Baoyu is tricked into marrying another. On his wedding night, Daiyu dies, thinking Baoyu has betrayed her. Heartbroken, Baoyu fulfills his duty to pass the imperial examinations, and his calligraphy is so good that the emperor grants an amnesty to the entire family, restoring them to good fortune. However, instead of taking up a position as a government official, Baoyu suddenly disappears with the monk who gave him the amulet as an infant. Life, according to the novel, is just a dream.

In addition to the hero and heroine, there are fifty or sixty other important characters. Unlike Western novels that tend to follow in detail the fortunes of a few individuals, Cao's novel follows the fortunes of an entire family. This is in keeping with Chinese traditions, where the family, not the individual, is the basic social unit, and the whole not the part is the focus of analysis. The rising and falling fortunes of the Jia family reflect a cyclical view of time and a conception of *yin* and *yang* in which good fortune merges into bad and bad into good in an endless cycle.

Early Chinese Marxists took inspiration from the novel's message of life as an illusion. Mao Zedong belonged to a study group called Dream of the Red Chamber. During the Cultural Revolution, readers emphasized the novel's sympathetic portrayal of servants and peasants. During the 1990s, the People's Republic of China released a popular television series based on the novel as well as opened a theme park in Beijing called the Grand Prospect Garden.

III. Thinking by Historical Analogy

Neo-Confucianism emphasized not empiricism and inductive thinking, but deductive analysis and especially historical analogies. Analogy was ingrained in the traditional Chinese educational system, a by-product of the intensive study of a small number of Classical texts. The standardization of the curriculum pushed students along accepted lines of analysis. This clearly defined band of knowledge provided the educated elite with a deeply felt common ground. Sinified non-Han also shared the Classical Chinese educational experience and, therefore, had strong common bonds and a common written language with Han Chinese. This accounts for the generally harmonious relations within the Sinified tributary world and the historically cordial relations with Korea and Japan, which intensively studied and emulated Chinese religious, philosophical, governmental, social, economic, legal, institutional, and artistic models.

In traditional China, writing also relied on analogy and its structure was highly regulated. After 1487, most candidates for the imperial examinations were expected to structure their answers in the form of the so-called eight-legged essay, which reinforced thinking by analogy, since the starting point was the Confucian classics. In Table 4.1, note the analogy in the section entitled "Beginning Discussion," which refers to Book 12, passage 9 of *The Analects* concerning

Table 4.1   Eight-Legged Essay Format

Break Open the Topic	When the people are prosperous, the ruler above will be prosperous.
Receiving the Topic	The wealth of the ruler is stored among the people. If the people are prosperous, why should the ruler alone be poor?
Beginning Discussion	In giving advice to Duke Ai, You Ruo said profoundly that the people and the ruler were one. He implied that the Duke had increased taxation because he lacked resources. To ensure his resources, the Duke should have first satisfied his people.

Initial Leg	If one can honestly
	    tithe one hundred *mou** with a mind to stay frugal and love the people,
	    and the one-tenth tax is not levied so the people provide his livelihood,
	then
	    what the people would produce would not be for tax levies,
	    what resources they have would not all be for tax collection,
	    there would be accumulation and surplus in village households,
	        and no worries in caring for parents or raising children,
	    there would be abundant grain and millet in the fields,
	        and no anxiety about nurturing the living or seeing off the dead.

Transition Leg	If the people have enough, how can the ruler alone be poor?

Middle Leg	I know that
	    The ruler could have everything if it were stored in village households,
	        with no need to hoard it in his treasury as his goods.
	    The ruler could use everything if it were placed in the fields,
	        with no need to accumulate it in his vaults as his possessions.
	With unlimited access, why worry that requests would not be honored?
	With unlimited resources, why fret over unpreparedness in an emergency?

Later Leg	Sacrificial animals and ritual grains would be sufficient for religious offerings; jades and silks would be abundant as gifts for tribute and audiences.
	    Even if insufficient, the people would supply what they have, so what shortages would there be?
	Foods and delicacies, beef and drinks would be sufficient for the needs of official guests; carriages and horses, weapons and armor would be sufficient for wartime preparations.
	    Even if insufficient, the people would respond with what they have so what shortage would there be?

Conclusion	Oh! Tithing originally was for the benefit of the people, and the sufficiency of the dynasty's resources arose in this way. Why should one raise taxes to seek prosperity?

*A *mou* was a unit to measure land, the equivalent to about 0.16 of an acre.

Source: Benjamin A. Elman, *A Cultural History of Civil Examinations in Late Imperial China.* (Berkeley: University of California Press, 2000), 389–90. © 2000 Regents of the University of California. Elman has translated an eight-legged essay by Wang Ao, written in the fifteenth century and cited in Qing collections as a model essay.

Duke Ai. Essay topics emphasized the enduring relevance of the Confucian texts for contemporary issues of state, and their structure followed a prescribed formula. By the end of the Qing dynasty, the eight-legged essay became a focus of attack for educational reformers. (See Table 4.1.)

In the contemporary language, proverbs, usually four-character idioms, sometimes served as analogies and at other times as a literary shorthand. Many proverbs consisted of lines from a famous poem. For example, a literal translation of the phrase *shenzhai dayuan* would be "large house, big yard," while

Chinese culture has long emphasized education. Early Manchu emperors were fluent in numerous languages. Pictured here are young Manchu students.

the actual meaning is more specific: "the house of a wealthy man." Another idiom, *yizhe sanyou,* literally means "there are three kinds of beneficial friends"; again, the real meaning is more specific: "honest friends, understanding friends, and learned friends." In the case of couplets, it is common to state just the first line, since it is assumed that the listener knows the second line. Such a system assumes a common educational background, extending to a host of specific idioms. While English has proverbs, their number, frequency, and complexity do not compare to those of the vast collection of proverbs in

common usage in China, with entire dictionaries devoted to the subject. This reliance on set phrases has led to miscommunication between Chinese and foreigners.

The reliance of the Chinese language on characters created a barrier to the introduction of foreign ideas not present in alphabetic languages. To introduce foreign words, the Chinese searched for analogous concepts within their own vocabulary. When Buddhism entered China, it appropriated preexisting Daoist terminology, such as the use of the word for the "Way" to translate the Buddhist term *dharma* or the term *wuwei* ("to do nothing") to translate "nirvana." Much later, the Jesuits borrowed from this Sinified Buddhist vocabulary to introduce the Christian notions of heaven and hell, translated as *tiantang* and *diyu*, respectively. *Tiantang* literally means "heavenly hall," while *diyu* means "earthly prison," and both translations bring associations with their Buddhist origins, which are totally alien to the Christian concepts. Later still, word combinations, often invented by the Japanese, were used to translate alien Western philosophical concepts and technological innovations. For instance, *gexing* stands for "individualism" but literally means "this nature," while the combination of the characters for "concealed" and "selfish," *yinsi*, stands for "privacy." *Diannao* or "lightning brain" is the translation for "computer." None of these translations provides the full meaning of the imported concept; instead, each carries the baggage of the Chinese characters chosen for the translation. Foreign place names and surnames are translated even more laboriously by inconsistently using cumbersome phonetic sound-alike characters.

History and historical analogies had enormous political implications in China. Because the Han considered history to be cyclical, they looked to the past to understand the present. History constituted the database not only to understand contemporary issues but also to legitimate current policy making, which meant that it was essential for policymakers to control this database. For this reason, the official history of the preceding dynasty was a critical issue of state. The new ruling dynasty compiled the history of the preceding dynasty and then often destroyed the relevant records. These histories glorified the early achievements of the previous dynasty in order to glorify the concept that was China. But they also emphasized the predecessors' eventual decline to legitimate the new dynasty and suggest a rebirth of lost virtue. To this day, the Chinese define themselves in terms of their long history and its presumed continuity from dynasty to dynasty, often finding similarities where they did not exist.

The Chinese reliance on the past both to model and to understand the present did not easily accommodate the unprecedented, which by definition had no apt analogy from the past. The Han repertoire of analogies provided few insights concerning the industrialized powers that barged into China in the nineteenth century, bringing with them the precedent-shattering Industrial Revolution.

IV. Understanding the Natural World

Even earlier, the precedent-jarring Ming-Qing transition and the advent of Manchu minority rule so shocked the surviving Han literati that some blamed the debacle on the limitations of Neo-Confucianism. This inspired a new mode of analysis that, unlike Neo-Confucianism, emphasized inductive, not deductive, analysis and evidential, not intuitive, reasoning. Ironically, a Ming loyalist, Gu Yanwu (1613–82), was the inspiration for the *Kaozheng* Scholarship that became the dominant critique of Neo-Confucianism during the Qing dynasty prior to the Taiping Rebellion.

Gu came from a family that for generations served as Ming dynasty officials and scholars. On his flight south ahead of the invading Manchu armies, he unsuccessfully organized the defense of his native city, where his foster mother starved herself to death rather than see the Manchus rule. He honored her final wish never to cooperate with the Manchus and blamed their success on the flaws of Neo-Confucianism. Rather than using the speculation and intuition favored by Neo-Confucianism, Gu sought wide-ranging evidence and original source material. Rather than relying on the Song scholar Zhu Xi, he demanded a return to much earlier Han dynasty commentaries.

Initially, *Kaozheng* Scholars applied these Han sources to the study of the Chinese language in the fields of phonetics and etymology. By using inductive analysis for the study of ancient poems, they determined the original pronunciation of Chinese characters by rediscovering ancient rhyming systems. They used this evidence from poetry to correct widespread mistakes in pronunciation. Gu Yanwu also studied geography by turning to local gazetteers as well as dynastic histories. He then began applying his methodology to historical texts by supplementing them with archaeological evidence from ancient bronze and stone inscriptions.

Later followers, such as Dai Zhen (1724–77), perhaps the greatest philosopher of the Qing dynasty, continued Gu's work on phonetics but did not limit their interests to the humanities. Dai also loved mathematics and rediscovered and preserved numerous rare mathematical treatises. Over time, he applied Gu's methodology to the study of history. He assembled evidence from a wide variety of sources not only to reinterpret ancient historical texts but also to determine which parts of the Classics were authentic and which were later additions. This had implications for the imperial examinations, which tested these texts.

Dai Zhen's philosophy attacked Neo-Confucianism for amalgamating numerous Buddhist and Daoist ideas with Confucianism. These corruptions included the core framework of Neo-Confucian metaphysics that analyzed the world through the dual concepts of *li* and *qi*, meaning "abstract principle" and "material force," respectively. The former meant the principles under which the universe operated, while the latter meant the dynamic physical matter composing the universe. While heaven-sent principles, or *li*, propelled humans toward the good, passions, or *qi*, disrupted this course. Education, however, could contain the passions and bring out the innate human goodness. Like Buddhists, Neo-Confucians stressed meditation, and like both Buddhists and Daoists, they recommended minimizing desires.

Dai Zhen attacked this dualistic framework by using historical, linguistic, and literary evidence to show that the Song dynasty's Neo-Confucian texts were not based exclusively on ancient texts after all, but on much later Buddhist and Daoist additions. Dai discarded *li* to argue that the study of *qi* alone could explain the universe. He also rejected meditation, arguing that enlightenment came from the examination of evidence, not from isolated reflection or personal inspiration. The Neo-Confucian emphasis on the latter allowed the powerful, the persuasive, and the corrupt to dominate society, and this accounted for the fall of the Ming dynasty. Human reason applied to evidence could discern the principles explaining the universe. Only the reliance on proofs based on evidence open for all to scrutinize could undermine the pernicious influence of the powerful, the persuasive, and the corrupt that Neo-Confucianism allowed to flourish.

V. The Examination System

The *Kaozheng* Scholarship indictment of Neo-Confucianism had major implications for the content of the imperial examination system that determined government appointments and thus for the allocation of power within China. Imperial rule required the loyalty of the many officials scattered throughout the empire. Loyal officials reflected the virtue of their rulers. Both were essential for the perpetuation of the mandate of heaven. For the continuation of Manchu minority rule, bureaucratic loyalty became even more important. For the ambitious, the examination system offered a respected route to social mobility for themselves and, given China's clan organization, for their entire clan. The imperial civil service examination system tested knowledge of the Chinese civilization and loyalty to the autocratic system of governance. It did so by focusing on the Classical literature and by emphasizing Classical modes of analysis. The Confucian educational system, which prepared candidates for these examinations, emphasized memorization and emulation and abhorred unorthodox thought.

A system of tests intended to base government service on merit, rather than on rank or birth, dates back to the Han dynasty (206 BC–220 AD). The Sui dynasty (581–618) used written examinations to test knowledge of the Confucian Classics, while the Tang dynasty (618–907) established schools, published authorized versions of the Five Classics and Four Books, and made available to students appropriate commentaries to guide their interpretation. During the Tang dynasty, only twenty to thirty candidates passed the highest level of exams each time. The Song dynasty (960–1229), and especially the Southern Song dynasty (1127–1279), greatly expanded the examination system from 30,000 successful candidates early in the second millennium to almost 400,000 by the end of the dynasty.

The Mongol Yuan dynasty (1279–1368) canceled the examinations for almost forty years. Even after their reinstatement, strict quotas kept the number of successful Han candidates low. The Yuan preferred to hire foreigners, like the Italian Marco Polo, to conduct government business, since they owed allegiance only to the Mongols. The numbers of successful exam candidates rebounded during the Ming dynasty (1368–1644), when the Han once again ruled. There were three levels of degrees, at the prefectural, provincial, and metropolitan levels, the last being the highest.

In 1487 the Ming government instituted the eight-legged essay as the only acceptable format for writing the exam essays. From the fifteenth to the early twentieth century, this essay structure predominated. The Manchus retained the examination system. Initially, they held special exams for Manchu candidates, allowing answers in both Chinese and Manchu, but they soon phased out the special Manchu-language exams. Separate examinations remained for bannermen and many Manchus without the highest degree acquired high posts anyway, reflecting the primacy placed on loyalty.

In 1679, the Qing dynasty held a special examination in the capital to identify scholars to write the official history of the Ming dynasty. The act of writing the *Ming History* signified that dynasty's extinction. It was intended to convince Ming loyalists to accept their fate and to justify the succession of the new dynasty. To many Han scholars in South China, this duty seemed particularly onerous since their version of Ming history would have to be approved by their Qing overlords. The *Ming History* emphasized the virtue of the rising Ming dynasty, followed by a period of decline when the Ming lost the mandate of heaven to the rising Qing dynasty, which, in turn, restored sacred Chinese traditions.

The Manchus did not publish the *Ming History* until 1739, almost a century after they came to power. In contrast, Ming scholars produced an official history of the Yuan dynasty within months of its overthrow in 1368. The long delay in publishing the *Ming History* reflected the problems of minority rule. The task of writing Chinese history was far more contentious for an alien ruling dynasty. The Qing needed to go to greater lengths to justify their rule than did the Han Chinese Ming dynasty.

Imperial examination halls. Doing well on the imperial examinations was the most common method of rising up through Chinese society. The Chinese examination system lasted for 1,300 years, from its beginning in the Sui dynasty in 605 to the final Qing exam given in 1905. Only about 5 percent of students passed these exams. The examination halls pictured here were located in Guangzhou. Conditions were harsh, with students locked up in small cubicles for several days at a time. While those who passed the exams were in theory elevated on the basis of merit, cheating was common.

Despite the persuasiveness of *Kaozheng* Scholarship, their demand to test the Five Classics rather than the Four Books was never implemented. Although *Kaozheng* Scholarship made an enormous contribution to the study of language and history, the Taiping Rebellion of the mid-nineteenth century cut short its progress and left *Kaozheng* Scholarship to be rediscovered in the late nineteenth century. The Taiping rebels sacked the Yangzi River cities where most *Kaozheng* Scholars resided, torched their libraries painstakingly accumulated over generations, lost much of their writings forever, and left them without the financial means to continue their work. (See Chapter 8, Sections II and III, for a discussion of the Taiping Rebellion.) *Kaozheng* Scholarship never recovered. The Neo-Confucians staged a comeback and remained dominant until the final decade of the dynasty. Tragically, just as the European powers posed a major security threat, those Chinese most capable of analyzing the threat had already been neutralized by their countrymen.

Conclusions

The Han believed that the Classics set the bounds for human knowledge and achievement. Therefore, they put in place an examination system that tested this knowledge. They made memorization and emulation the basis for social status and political power. Education, political power, and the status quo were all mutually reinforcing. Like the social structure of traditional Chinese society, discussed in Chapter 3, the Chinese educational system had a conservative influence, making China both resistant to change and ill-prepared to cope with unprecedented external challenges. To be without precedent was impossible under the Han cyclical understanding of history.

Even some of the preoccupations of the *Kaozheng* Scholars, who engaged in a highly rational mode of analysis, seem irrational to the modern Western mind. For instance, the *Book of Changes*, which they made one of their central texts, is a reference book for interpreting hexagrams for divination. It was believed that the correct interpretation of the hexagrams representing the current situation could help foretell the future. The *Book of Changes* served as a spiritual link with heaven so that individuals could "establish fate," meaning that they could set an appropriate moral course of action for the given environment and thus potentially improve their own fate.

Likewise, although the Chinese very early assimilated the mathematics and astronomy brought by the Jesuits, they desired accurate calculations of the calendar in order to determine auspicious and inauspicious days. On any given day there was a list of proscribed and prescribed activities such as the performance of rituals; the issuance of edicts; the granting of favors such as amnesties or titles; the appointment of personnel; and the scheduling of affairs of state, banquets, births, marriages, baths, house cleaning, moving, traveling, construction, and planting. Chinese from all walks of life heeded these injunctions, some of which have endured to the present. In 1644, in order to ensure the auspicious beginning of the Qing dynasty, the Shunzhi emperor delayed his accession to the throne until the first day of the new sixty-year cycle of celestial stems and terrestrial branches. (See the Introduction, Section IV.) This indicated that the dynastic cycle had begun anew.

Geomancy, or the proper siting of structures, was thought to provide the capability to alter fate. The modern term is *fengshui*, meaning "wind and water." The Han emphasized *fengshui* to choose auspicious locations for tombs, homes, and other buildings. The purpose was to harmonize the structures for the living and the dead with the natural environment, and thereby with the cosmic environment, in order to bring good fortune. In other words, proper siting could manipulate the cosmic forces to one's future advantage, whereas poor siting could bring ill fortune. These principles are still often used today. In addition to geomancy, many Han studied physiognomy, numerology, astrology, and dream interpretation and looked for omens and portents of impending events. *Kaozheng* Scholars did not reject these traditions.

Chinese civilization became the victim of its own success. It had so dominated all areas of human achievement for so many millennia that there was little reason for the Han to question their approach to security, domestic peace, social hierarchy, or education, let alone their approach to understanding the world by historical analogy. Although the Manchu conquest stirred doubts among *Kaozheng* Scholars, the Taiping Rebellion cut short their impact. Most Han remained complacent in the belief that the Han had always Sinified their conquerors.

In reality, the changes these periods of invasion wrought in China were far more mutual and reciprocal than the Han were willing to admit. The Manchus made numerous innovations in Han civilian and military institutions and developed a distinctive approach to empire in Inner Asia, yet the myth of Sinification endured. The arrival of the Westerners and the rise of Japan, however, stirred irrepres-sible doubts that would eventually shatter the Confucian educational system. Even then, the function traditionally played by the Classics endured in a new incarnation. The Chinese Communists soon replaced the Confucian core texts with their own triumvirate of sages—Marx, Lenin, and Mao—whose teachings would be memorized and tested in Communist examinations in keeping with traditional educational practices. To the present day, political education remains one of the six mandatory fields for anyone in China seeking higher education in the humanities or social sciences. Only those studying the natural sciences have escaped the imperial examination tradition of testing political orthodoxy.

BIBLIOGRAPHY

Chan, Wing-tsit, trans. and comp. *A Source Book in Chinese Philosophy.* Princeton, NJ: Princeton University Press, 1963.

de Bary, William Theodore. *East Asian Civilizations: A Dialogue in Five Stages.* Cambridge, MA: Harvard University Press, 1988.

Elman, Benjamin A. *From Philosophy to Philology: Intellectual and Social Aspects of Change in Later Imperial China.* Cambridge, MA: Harvard University Press, 1990.

———*A Cultural History of Civil Examinations in Late Imperial China.* Berkeley: University of California Press, 2000.

———*On Their Own Terms: Science in China, 1550–1900.* Cambridge, MA: Harvard University Press, 2005.

———*A Cultural History of Modern Science in China.* Cambridge, MA: Harvard University Press, 2006.

Fairbank, John K., ed. *Chinese Thought and Institutions.* Chicago: University of Chicago Press, 1957.

Fung, Yu-lan. *A History of Chinese Philosophy.* 2nd ed. 2 vols. Translated by Derk Bodde. Princeton, NJ: Princeton University Press, 1952.

Needham, Joseph. *Science and Civilisation in China.* Vols. 1, 2. Cambridge: Cambridge University Press, 1962–5.

Ng, On-cho and Q. Edward Wang. *Mirroring the Past: The Writing and Use of History in Imperial China.* Honolulu: University of Hawai'i Press, 2005.

Schwartz, Benjamin I. *The World of Thought in Ancient China.* Cambridge, MA: Harvard University Press, 1985.

Smith, Richard J. *Fortune-tellers and Philosophers: Divination in Traditional Chinese Society.* Boulder, CO: Westview Press, 1991.

———*China's Cultural Heritage: The Qing Dynasty, 1644–1912.* 2nd ed. Boulder, CO: Westview Press, 1994.

Xu Dixin and Wu Chengming, eds. *Chinese Capitalism, 1522–1840.* Translated by Li Zhengde et al. New York: St. Martin's Press, 2000.

NOTES

1. Yuan Mei, "On Books," in *Anthology of Chinese Literature from the Fourteenth Century to the Present Day*, Cyril Birch, ed. (New York: Grove Press, 1972), 196. "On Books, I" from *Anthology of Chinese Literature*, Vol. 2 edited by Cyril Birch, copyright © 1972 by Grove Press, Inc. Used by permission of Grove/Atlantic, Inc.

2. Confucius. *The Analects*, Book 12, no. 1. Raymond Dawson, trans. (Oxford: Oxford University Press, 1993), 44.

3. Cited in Patricia Buckley Ebrey, *The Cambridge Illustrated History of China* (Cambridge: Cambridge University Press, 1996), 34. Reprinted with permission of Cambridge University Press.

4. Ezra Pound, trans., *Shih-ching: The Classic Anthology Defined by Confucius* (Cambridge, MA: Harvard University Press, 1954), 195. Reprinted by permission of the publisher from THE CONFUCIAN ODES: THE CLASSIC ANTHOLOGY DEFINED BY CONFUCIUS by Ezra Pound, pp. 194–195. Cambridge, Mass.: Harvard University Press, Copyright © 1954, 1982 by the President and Fellows of Harvard College.

Chronology

1254?–1324?	Marco Polo
1514	Portuguese discover the maritime route to China
1517	Portuguese send the first embassy to China
1521	Portuguese and Spanish divide up Asia in the Treaty of Saragossa
1542	Portuguese open trade with Japan
1557	Portuguese settlement in Macao, colony (1557–1999)
1584	Russian empire extends to Siberia
1588	Britain defeat the Spanish Armada, ending Spanish naval supremacy
1600	Creation of the East India Company
1618	Russian trade delegation arrives in Beijing
1624	Holland founds the town of Zeelandia on Taiwan
1648	Peace of Westphalia
1650	Russians establish a fort at Albazin in the Amur River basin
1652–89	Intermittent Russian-Chinese clashes on the frontier
1662	Ming loyalists expel the Dutch from Taiwan
1683	Qing expel Ming loyalists from Taiwan
1689	Russo-Chinese Treaty of Nerchinsk
1699	East India Company establishes a trading post in Guangzhou
1727	Russo-Chinese Treaty of Kiakhta
1757	British establish rule over India
	Western commercial ships limited to Guangzhou
1765	Invention of the cotton-spinning jenny
1769	Invention of the waterframe spinning machine
1780s	Invention of the steam engine
1793	Macartney Mission arrives in Beijing
1815	Congress of Vienna ends the Napoleonic Wars

The Arrival of the West

Formerly Portugal presented tribute
Now England is paying homage.
They have out-traveled Shuhai and Hengzhang;
My Ancestors' merit and virtue must have reached their
distant shores.
Though their tribute is commonplace, my heart approves
sincerely.
Curios and the boasted ingenuity of their devices I prize not.
Though what they bring is meagre, yet,
In my kindness to men from afar I make generous return,
Wanting to preserve my good health and power.[1]

Qianlong emperor (1711–99)
on the Macartney mission, 1793

Beginning in the late seventeenth and continuing through the nineteenth century, the rise of Western maritime and continental powers presented a growing challenge to the Qing empire. In particular, the maritime powers, Portugal, Spain, Holland, and Britain had a significant impact on coastal China, while Russia's land influence was both Western and Asian. Chinese and Western civilizations clashed over differences in legal systems, social mores, religious beliefs, and foreign relations. The relentless onslaught from the West called into question the Qing dynasty's mandate of heaven, but until very late in the dynasty the Manchus upheld Confucian methods of governance and strove to defend Chinese civilization against the latest round of barbarian incursions. Effective policies to deal with the West required a departure from Confucian traditions that the Han and Manchus, for different reasons, both abhorred. The preservation of Manchu rule also required a vibrant economy based on the maintenance of modcrate tax rates; a stable currency; commerce; and infrastructure such as dikes, canals, roads, and granaries. Commerce

was not exclusively domestic but included foreign trade, especially of Chinese luxury goods. In South China, commerce became increasingly international with the arrival of European merchants. The Manchus were torn by the crosscutting demands of retaining control while maximizing profits, a problem that remains with China even today.

I. Early Explorers

Trade between China and the Mediterranean world probably goes back thousands of years. As early as the fifth and fourth centuries BC, Greek historians like Herodotus described these trade routes. Alexander the Great, in 334 BC, began an eight-year-long journey of conquest that ended as far east as India. Although Alexander did not continue on to China, Chinese goods still found their way to European markets, and at the height of the Roman Empire, Chinese silks were highly prized. During the first century AD, Arab ships dominated the maritime trade from India to the Mediterranean via the Red Sea.

Meanwhile, Chinese expeditions reached Central Asia during the Han dynasty and perhaps got as far as the Caspian Sea. In 97 AD a Chinese envoy left for but did not reach Rome. Other Chinese envoys traveled to modern-day Iran and India. During the fourth and fifth centuries AD, the monk Faxian (Fa-hsien, c.337–c.422) traveled to India, while in the seventh century AD, the monk Xuanzang (Hsuan-tsang, 602–64) went to India and came back carrying Buddhists texts. The emperor honored him upon his return in 645 AD and built the Big Wild Goose Pagoda in Xi'an to house 657 manuscripts. In the sixteenth century, the novel *Journey to the West* (*Xiyouji* or *Hsi-yu Chi*) by Wu Cheng'en chronicled

Xuanzang's travels. During the Middle Ages, contact between Europe and China languished, although Christianity was an accepted religion in China during the eighth and ninth centuries. Christians continued to practice despite an official ban during the ninth century, and Marco Polo mentioned Christian communities in the thirteenth century.

Two events spurred increased contacts between Europe and China. The first was the Crusades. Thousands of Europeans journeyed to Palestine to fight the Muslims. Beginning in 1095, at the instigation of Pope Urban II, European knights prepared to fight the Saracens to take Jerusalem, which they stormed in 1099. For the next 200 years, Europeans tried and ultimately failed to retain Christian control over the Holy Land. The second major event was the Mongol conquest of Eurasia. Chinggis Khan (1167?–1227) unified the various Mongol tribes. His grandson, Khubilai Khan (1215–94), proclaimed the Yuan dynasty (1279-1368) in 1271, overran the Song capital at Hangzhou in 1276, and killed the last Song pretender in 1279. Mongol rule extended far beyond China to encompass Central Asia, most of Russia, and Hungary, creating the largest land empire in human history. Although the captive populations widely portrayed the Mongols as cruel and uncultivated, their rule created the so-called *Pax Mongolica,* meaning "the Peace of the Mongols," which provided the necessary stability for trade to flourish.

The early decades of the Yuan dynasty coincided with the Crusades, which allowed the Venetian merchant Marco Polo (1254?–1324?) to travel to China. During this period the Mongol khan and his armies protected overland trade between Europe and East Asia. After a three-year journey, Marco Polo reached China, where he remained for seventeen years. He served as an official in the Mongol Court, which commonly hired non-Han servitors. The published account of his travels inspired generations of Europeans to attempt the trip in search of the vast wealth and lands of Asia. To many Europeans, the very thought of Chinese cities with hundreds of thousands of inhabitants, let alone the description of the khan's palace adorned with gold and silver, seemed both improbable and tantalizing. Just after Marco Polo left, the Franciscan priest Giovanni di Montecorvina established the first Roman Catholic mission in China.

A generation later, the Morrocan jurist Abu 'Abdallah ibn Battuta (1304–68) traveled to China. Previously, he had toured much of North Africa and the Middle East, and served for many years as a judge for the sultan of Delhi in India. Like Marco Polo, ibn Battuta returned home impressed by Yuan China, which he described as "the safest and most agreeable country in the world for the traveler." [2] Under the preceding Song dynasty, a flourishing trade had developed between China and India and the Muslim world beyond. While the

Song could and did regulate Chinese merchants, the dynasty had far less control over the Muslim merchants it encouraged to establish trading bases in South Chinese cities. Many Chinese engaged in this trade converted to Islam. When the Yuan tried to impose stricter controls over Chinese merchants, even more of the trade fell into Muslim hands. Perhaps the most famous Chinese explorer was Zheng He (1371–1433), the Hui eunuch in command of the vast Ming fleet that made seven naval expeditions between 1405 and 1433 throughout Southeast Asia and as far afield as India, Sri Lanka, Arabia, and Africa. (See Chapter 1, Section I.)

European traders did not arrive until much later. The first to come in significant numbers were the Portuguese in the late sixteenth century. Soon afterward came the Spanish, the Dutch, and, later still, the English. Before trade became firmly established in the nineteenth century, explorers and missionaries, most notably the Jesuits, established the first Western presence. (For a discussion of the Jesuits, see Chapter 1, Sections I and IV, and Chapter 3, Section I.)

It is important to point out that until modern times this East–West trade was carried out primarily because of foreign demand for Chinese luxury goods, not because of Chinese demand for Western goods. Until the industrial era, China possessed the finest luxury goods available anywhere. China's primary imports were livestock from Central Asia, coinage from Japan and the New World, and furs from Siberia. Foreigners, however, desired increasing quantities of Chinese silks, porcelains, and, later, tea. The Chinese government regarded this trade as a means to promote frontier security under the institutional umbrella of the tributary system—in other words, trade was a means to forestall barbarian invasions. The Chinese government demanded, with the exception of tribute missions to the capital, that all such commercial exchanges took place at the frontier. The long-standing trade among Asian countries conformed to these preferences in that it was conducted on the maritime frontiers, and the Chinese and Asian merchants involved did not attempt to alter Chinese economic or political institutions.

The combination of Marco Polo's tales of faraway China and the spread of the Ottoman Empire, including the fall of Constantinople in 1453 and the invasion of Egypt in 1517, gave an urgency to the Western European quest to find a direct trade route to East Asia that bypassed the dangerous Ottoman lands. During much of the fifteenth and sixteenth centuries, Venice and Genoa dominated the eastern trade. However, Portugal took the lead in the search for a sea route to China, bypassing both the Italian monopoly over Mediterranean trade and the Ottoman dominance of the overland trade. Prince Henrique (1394–1460) actively supported the

One aspect of Western thinking that interested the Chinese emperors was astronomy, since more accurate calendars aided agriculture. Based on examples brought to China by Jesuit missionaries, the Chinese learned how to use Western astronomical instruments.

the maritime route via India to East Asia, however, did this trade become both regular and affordable. This quickly led to competition among the European powers to exploit the expanding commercial opportunities.

II. The Maritime Advance: Portugal, Spain, Holland, and England

The Portuguese and Spanish, urged on by stories of the riches of China, took the lead in pioneering new maritime routes to Asia and dominated the trade during the sixteenth century. (See Map 5.1.) However, in the seventeenth century, the Dutch took the lead for a time, only to be supplanted by the British from the end of the seventeenth century on. Following the success of Vasco da Gama's explorations in the Indian Ocean, the Portuguese created the maritime trade route along the coast of India and on to Southeast Asia and China. Profits inspired redoubled efforts to dominate the pepper trade, and they defeated Arab Muslims, Hindus, and Egyptian Muslims to establish bases on the Indian coast.

Following this military success, Portugal explored the Strait of Malacca, the vital sea lane through Southeast Asia to China, seizing the Indian city of Goa in 1510 and consolidating control over Malacca in 1511. Goa was located on the Western coast of India, while Malacca was located on the Western tip of the Malay Peninsula. The Portuguese soon took Hormuz and Aden to form a trade monopoly. These successes opened the way to China. The Portuguese sent an embassy to China in 1517, and by 1557 they convinced the Ming dynasty to allow them to occupy Macao, the first European settlement in China; they would not return Macao to China until 1999. In 1542, Portugal also became the first European country to open trade relations with Japan.

In 1494, the Spanish and the Portuguese had divided their global spoils in the Treaty of Tordesillas by drawing a line 370 leagues west of the Cape Verde Islands located off the western coast of Africa. This put Spain in control of most of the Americas and Portugal in control of the sea routes around Africa to Asia. When Ferdinand Magellan, a Portuguese in the service of Spain, rounded South America in 1520, however, and then landed in the Philippines in 1521, it became necessary to divide up Asia as well. In 1521, the Treaty of Saragossa divided virtually all of East Asia into Spanish and Portuguese colonies.

Meanwhile, the British tried to break the Spanish and Portuguese East Asian trade monopoly by sailing across the Atlantic to Asia. Although the British believed that they had discovered the sea route to Asia, they had actually landed in Nova Scotia and Maine. In 1578, Francis Drake passed

exploration of almost the entire coast of West Africa. In competition, the Spanish monarch employed Christopher Columbus to find a new route to China, but instead he discovered a sea route to the New World in 1492. Meanwhile, in 1498, the Portuguese explorer Vasco da Gama first reached the Indian Ocean and later sailed all the way to India. By 1514, the first Portuguese trade mission reached China. Thus, tiny Portugal opened the maritime trade routes to Asia.

The East and West had long-standing though intermittent contacts. At times trade was brisk, and during periods of empire, such as under the Mongols, it was even possible for merchants to travel from one end of Eurasia to the other along the Silk Route. Only after the Portuguese discovered

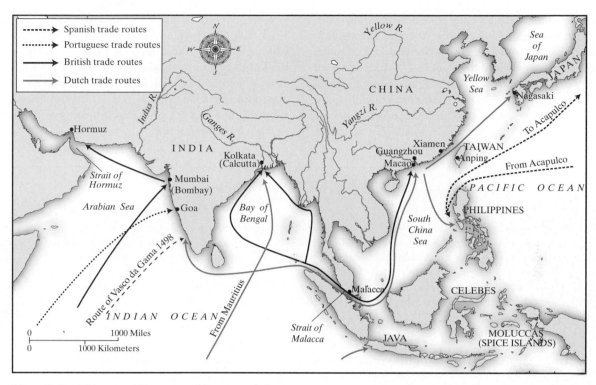

Map 5.1   Western European Maritime Advance

through the Strait of Magellan at the southern tip of South America to reach the Pacific Ocean. When he reached the Moluccas or Spice Islands and Java, he took a load of precious spices and returned safely to England in 1580. This exacerbated Anglo-Spanish tensions, and in 1588 the English fleet destroyed the Spanish Armada, ending Spanish naval dominance. Through World War I, England's domination of the world's oceans became the foundation of the British Empire.

The interregnum between Spanish and British naval dominance allowed a small European power, Holland, to obtain a toehold in Asia. By the dawn of the seventeenth century, the Dutch reached Japan and in 1601 succeeded in circumnavigating the globe. After the Dutch occupied the East Indies (Indonesia), they moved northward to establish a base on the island of Taiwan, named "Formosa" or "beautiful island" by the Portuguese. In 1624, the Dutch built the fort Zeelandia in Anping (Tainan) in central Taiwan. They urged Chinese merchants and traders to immigrate to Taiwan. From this base the Dutch dominated much of the coastal trade in southeast China. Perhaps because of the small size of their empire, the Dutch became early proponents of free trade, a position Britain later adopted. The Dutch lost their hold on Taiwan in February 1662, when Zheng Chenggong (Koxinga) besieged Zeelandia. Zheng used the Penghu—

Pescadores—Islands as stepping stones to cross the Taiwan Strait. These offshore islands remain strategically important for the defense or invasion of Taiwan. Zheng forced the Dutch to retreat to their colony Batavia in the East Indies. Ming loyalists retained control over Taiwan through 1683.

After the destruction of the Spanish Armada, England contested Spanish and Portuguese domination over the Asian trade. In 1600, Queen Elizabeth I granted a charter to the "Governor and Merchants of London Trading into the East Indies," better known as the East India Company. The next year, five English ships reached India and returned with rich cargoes of spices. Although the Portuguese and the Dutch initially restricted the East India Company to trade only in India, eventually a triangular exchange developed whereby English merchants purchased cotton and, later, opium in India, transported it to China, and then returned to Europe with tea, spices, silks, and porcelains. This triangular trade became one of the most profitable sources of income for the British Empire.

Beginning in 1699, the East India Company established a trading post, or "factory," in the southern Chinese port city of Guangzhou (Canton). English merchants worked with the local trading monopoly, known as the Cohong or simply Hong. The Cohong was the local Chinese guild licensed to conduct foreign trade. The Qing government required that all foreign maritime commerce be funneled through the Cohong. This was consistent with the standard tributary practice of keeping trade and un-Sinified barbarians on the periphery of the empire. Soon, English trade began to exceed that of the Portuguese and Dutch. An extraordinarily lucrative trade in tea developed (see the feature below). Following the establishment of British rule over India in 1757, the Crown took an even greater interest in the East India Company. In 1793, King George III sent Lord Macartney to open up other Chinese cities to trade. Although the mission failed, the British made absolutely clear their intention to dominate Europe's trade with China. Great Britain would be primarily responsible for deflecting China from its continental preoccupations to confront an unprecedented maritime, technological, and cultural threat.

TEA CULTIVATION

The Chinese have been exporting tea for over 2,000 years. According to legend, the mythical emperor Shen Nong not only introduced agriculture and herbal medicine to China, but also tea cultivation. Europeans did not discover the drink until the sixteenth century by way of Venice and it did not become popular until the eighteenth century, particularly in Britain via the British East India Company.

The tea plant, *Camellia sinensis,* is an evergreen that grows up to thirty feet tall in the wild but, when cultivated, is usually cut back to no more than five feet. It flourishes in the tropical and subtropical climates of South China that have heavy rainfall and grows at elevations of up to 6,000 feet. In China it has usually been cultivated in the fertile soil of mountainous regions in small plots right next to farmers' homes.

Tea is propagated from seeds, which, in about six months, produce seedlings ready for permanent transplant in rows several feet apart. The plants begin producing crops in their third year, reach maturity in their tenth year, and continue to produce for up to fifty years. Full-grown tea leaves vary from two to five inches in length.

The cultivation of tea in China may date back 4,000 years. According to legend, an early Chinese ruler named Shen Nong was trying different herbs to determine their medical value when he was saved from poison by drinking tea. From that time on, tea was used as a medicine. Tea shops, like the one pictured here, first became popular 1,000 years ago during the Tang dynasty. Tea is considered one of the seven necessities of Chinese life, along with firewood, rice, oil, salt, soy sauce, and vinegar.

Continued

The hundreds of varieties of tea fall into three general color/processing classifications: unfermented or green tea, fermented or black tea, and semifermented or oolong tea. The last is also referred to as "red tea." Oolong teas are produced mainly in Taiwan and Fujian province, while both black and green teas are produced more generally in South China. For all types, the harvested leaves are dried for up to two days so that they wither but remain pliable. The leaves are then rolled for several hours to release the enzymes and juices that make the flavor distinctive. Afterward they are completely dried.

To produce black tea, the leaves are fermented for several hours under a damp cloth and then redried. Green tea leaves, however, are not fermented but steamed or warmed so that they keep some of their color, gently rolled again, and redried, while oolong teas are only partially fermented. At this point, the leaves can be divided into two more general categories: broken and whole leaves, with the former providing the stronger drink.

Teas are graded from the most tender to the most coarse leaves. Leaf quality depends on the maturity of the leaf, the time of the harvest, the climate, the soil, the processing of the leaf, and the variety of the plant. The highest-quality teas come from leaf buds as opposed to mature and particularly old leaves. The highest-quality leaves produce a light yellow-colored brew without any bitterness. From best to worst, the grades range from orange pekoe, pekoe, pekou souchong, and congou to pekoe dust. Flavor additives include jasmine blossoms, chrysanthemum flowers, orange buds, rose petals, ginger, and tangerine rind. Tea connoisseurs focus on the aroma, appearance, and origin of teas and are very careful to store tea in airtight containers and to use good water for brewing.

Usually the Chinese pour boiling water over tea leaves in a ceramic teapot to steep for up to ten minutes. Often the first brew is discarded and boiling water poured over the leaves a second time to produce a richer flavor, losing most of the caffeine content in the process. The Chinese believe that tea benefits the mind, the nerves, and the digestion.

III. The Continental Advance: Russia

While the maritime advance of the Europeans was an unprecedented event in Chinese history, another European nation, Russia, had a long history of direct overland contact with China. For over 800 years Russia had interacted with Asia, ever since the first Mongol hordes swept across the steppes, dominated Moscow, and were only halted by the swamplands bordering the Baltic. The brutal Mongol treatment of Russians not only created an undying fear of Asian invasion, often described by them as a "Yellow Peril," but also, once the Mongol empire fell, the resultant power vacuum in the east lured Russian expansion. The Russians took the first steps eastward under Ivan the Terrible, who made Russia a Eurasian power in 1584 by extending his realm from the White Sea all the way to Siberia. During the early 1600s, Russians settled Western Siberia. In the late 1630s, they founded the settlement of Udsk on the Sea of Okhotsk. (See Map 5.2.) This rapid Russian expansion soon led to friction with Qing China, which had long assumed that these territories were either theirs outright or were tributaries.

Russia occupied a unique position as both a European power and a former Mongol tributary, meaning that it had long-standing links with both the West and the East. The Mongol legacy included autocracy, subjects as servitors of the state, the destruction of Russia's cities and urban wealth, and the corresponding rise of landed estates as the basis for wealth. Like other Eastern European countries, Russia did not fully participate in such key Western European movements as the Reformation that led to the separation of church and state in the West and did not eliminate serfdom until centuries after Western European countries had done so. The enserfment of nearly half of its population until the mid-nineteenth century had enormous social implications. Although European, Russia was not fully Western.

The first official contacts between the Ming dynasty and Russia occurred in 1618, when a Russian trade expedition reached Beijing. During the mid-1600s, Russian explorers moved into the strategic Amur River valley, which two centuries later became the modern Russo–Chinese boundary. This valley had the only arable land in the eastern Siberian interior, and the river offered the only major east–west transportation route in northeast Asia. In 1650, one of these explorers, Erofei Pavlovich Khabarov, built a fort at Albazin. From this base of operations he and his men moved far down the Amur River, fighting with the natives on the way. Khabarov ordered a second fortress, Achansk, built near the mouth of the Songhua River (Sungari), which flows into the Amur. The Russian Cossacks spent the winter of 1651–2 in Achansk. These actions quickly drew the attention of the Qing Court. Manchu forces attacked Achansk on 24 March 1652. Although outnumbered, the Russians fought bravely and routed the Manchus. The

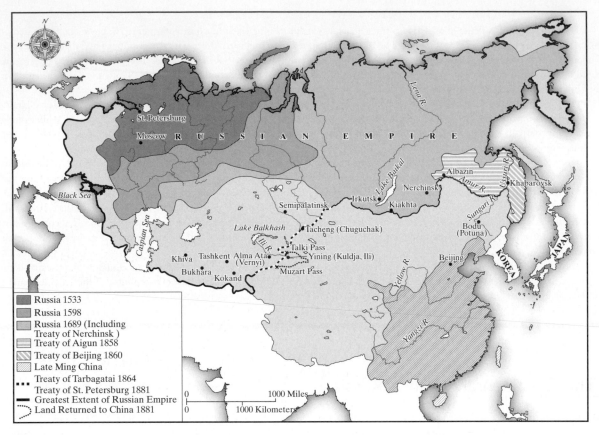

Map 5.2   Russian Continental Advance

Russian position remained tenuous and clashes continued between 1655 and 1658, when a Manchu fleet defeated the Russians. Nevertheless, Russian settlers continued to move into the Amur Valley.

In the 1670s, the Russian government actively supported expansion into the Amur Valley, creating a protectorate over Albazin in 1672. The first official Russian delegation, under Nikolai Milescu-Spafarii (Spathari), reached Beijing in 1676 but failed to open diplomatic relations. Faced with ever-growing Russian immigration, the Manchus sent an expedition in the early 1680s to expel them from the Amur Valley. Although they managed to retake Albazin, the Russians soon returned in even greater numbers.

Border talks opened at Nerchinsk in 1689 between Fedor Golovin and two members of the Qing imperial household, Songgotu and Tong Guogang. The talks resulted in the Treaty of Nerchinsk, China's first treaty with a European power. It remained in effect for the next 170 years. Russia failed to gain control over the Amur River but acquired all of the vast lands

west and north of the Argun River, located inland of the headwaters of the Amur. The treaty provided Russia with valuable trading privileges, particularly for sable and black fox pelts, which Russia monopolized. In 1727, the Treaty of Kiakhta established continental treaty ports, subject to special trade regulations. These would become the model for the maritime treaty ports established a century later.

Because Russia was a continental power, China treated it differently from the Western maritime powers. Administratively, Russians were categorized with the other un-Sinicized barbarians populating the northern frontiers. This status, in combination with the treaties of Nerchinsk and Kiakhta, gave Russia diplomatic privileges not shared by the other European powers. In addition to gaining the right to send emissaries directly to Beijing, Russia maintained a permanent ecclesiastical mission that served as a quasi-embassy and language school. The other powers would not gain equal diplomatic privileges in the capital until 1860, after fighting and winning two wars against China.

In the late seventeenth and early eighteenth centuries, when China signed its first treaties with Russia, the military

In addition to using the Silk Route, China conducted extensive trade with its land neighbors. In this picture, horse-drawn carriages are transporting people and a wide range of goods in Beijing.

balance of power overwhelmingly favored the Qing empire. The Manchus had highly competent military forces, demonstrated by the ongoing conquest of a vast empire, while Russia could deploy very few forces in theater. The Industrial Revolution had reversed this military balance by the time Russia signed its next round of treaties with China. Unique among the European powers, Russia bordered on China. Unlike the maritime powers, whose interests focused on commerce, Russian interests remained territorial. This basic divergence has endured to the present. Although Russia no longer seeks territorial expansion, it has great concerns about the security along their long mutual border where 6 million Russians in Siberia face 150 million Chinese.

IV. The Legal and Religious Sources of Cultural Conflict

The Western European powers had very different cultural roots from China, although the problem was less extreme for Russia because of the shared experience of the Mongol con-

quest. European civilization was based on Greco-Roman and Judeo-Christian foundations, whereas that of China was based on a combination of Confucian, Legalist, Buddhist, and Daoist traditions. China had not shared the Western path from ancient Greece and Rome to the Renaissance, Reformation, Scientific Revolution, and Enlightenment. Nor had it shared in the evolution of the Western nation-state system that developed a growing body of international law. There was no cultural overlap; rather, the traditions of East and West originated and developed separately.

The Chinese and the Western Europeans both had highly developed legal systems, but their priorities, sanctions, and underlying values differed. The Chinese legal system focused on maintaining social harmony on the basis of hierarchy. In Europe, the competition between secular and canon law resulted in legal limits on the exercise of both church and state power. But this division came at the price of the horrendous wars of the Reformation. There were no such limitations on the authority of the Chinese emperor. The 1648 Peace of Westphalia, the diplomatic settlement of the Thirty Years War, established a new framework for international relations, which entailed juridically equal nation-states interacting in conformity with international law. China knew no law but its own, recognized no other civilization, and considered outsiders as existing in varying degrees of barbarity. The Confucian hierarchy could not easily accommodate the concept of equality, since superiors and inferiors were the basis for social relations. The act of shaking hands in the West suggested equality, while in the East the act of bowing implied a degree of submission and the kowtow indicated total submission.

In China, all those allowed into the Forbidden City had to adhere to prescribed rituals because the emperor's ability to harmonize the cosmos depended on the proper performance of rituals. The Western insistence on its understanding of international law and its refusal to comply with even key Chinese rituals such as the kowtow directly threatened the mandate of heaven. Under the Confucian order, the Chinese emperor stood above all law and was the ruler of all who crossed his doorstep. Obey or be punished. The Manchus, as resident aliens, could not easily compromise on the issue of the kowtow, whereas the Europeans could not fathom why they clung to this dated ritual.

As distant un-Sinified barbarians, the Europeans sat at the bottom of the Chinese social hierarchy. Therefore, they could expect few protections under Chinese law. Their lack of connections, or *guanxi,* reinforced their subordinate position in China, which did not have a comprehensive commercial and administrative legal code precisely because such matters were resolved through *guanxi.* For a Sinocentric familial society, un-Sinified foreigners were excluded from the *guanxi* networks and quite naturally occupied an inferior position in any Chinese legal proceedings. From the Han point of view, those who expected better treatment needed to adopt Han ways.

There were also different views on punishment. While the Europeans had increasingly restricted the use of torture since the Middle Ages, the Chinese legal system still regularly employed torture to extract confessions and prescribe elaborate variations of capital punishment. Historically in China, obstreperous barbarians who refused either to go away or to convert to Han ways had been annihilated. The Chinese term was *zhengjiao,* meaning "a righteous army of extermination."[3] The Zunghars were a case in point. The Qianlong emperor had made sure that they disappeared from the ethnic map.

The Chinese spurned international law and insisted that the Europeans accommodate themselves to the tributary system (and vice versa). Combined European and Chinese intransigence on this matter led to conflict almost from the very start. At issue was whose norms should regulate foreign relations, meaning the interface of their two civilizations. In their long historical experience, Chinese rulers had always set these norms for others. Russia accepted this process.[4] But Western Europeans saw no valid reason to grant China an exceptional status above that of all other nations. To this day, there is a strain in Chinese thinking that rejects international law as a Western creation to dominate others.

Religious differences exacerbated the legal and social tensions between Westerners and Chinese. In the West, Roman law and Judaism provided a legalistic foundation to Christianity. Whereas Christians had a tendency to make blanket judgments, Chinese favored contingencies dependent on the status of those involved. The Ten Commandments applied to all, regardless of their status, whereas Confucian rules were conditional: Although lying to a parent would be unfilial, Confucius demanded that family members lie to strangers in order to protect relatives. The contrary Judeo-Christian commandment was: "Thou shalt not bear false witness against thy neighbor."

Such differences had little impact when only a handful of foreign merchants were involved, but beginning in the eighteenth and nineteenth centuries, large numbers of Christian missionaries came to China emphasizing salvation and conversion of the heathen. Since man lived but once, the failure to convert resulted in eternal damnation. According to Chinese beliefs, there were repeated opportunities for salvation. Buddhism emphasized reincarnation and multiple chances to find the path to righteousness, while Confucian beliefs prescribed ancestor worship to keep the spirits of the dead at peace. The Han did not seek out others for conversion, in part, because there was no alternative to China's unitary civilization. Time was on their side. Eventually, the barbarian would absorb Han ways or remain irrelevant. Whereas the Han dealt with those barbarians who entered their lands, Westerners scoured the world for religious converts. When missionaries arrived in China, some Chinese converted, but they usually also retained their preexisting Buddhist, Daoist, and Confucian beliefs. The Han cyclical view of history and understanding of the opposing forces of *yin* and *yang* did not require the reconciliation of contradictory belief systems. Belief systems, like opposing forces in nature, were expected to coexist and wax and wane in force.

In contrast, the Christian imperative to convert the heathen gave missionaries a divine mission to impose their culture on others. In addition to building churches, they often established schools, orphanages, and hospitals and advocated social reforms, notably concerning the treatment of women. The Chinese state, in particular, rejected the Christian claim of a moral law that was separate from secular law. The Chinese government quite rightly considered this concept of legal duality as potentially threatening to its own authority and power.

Most subversive of all was the Western approach to knowledge embedded in both Christian teachings and the

Western educational system. The missionaries who came to China were children of the Scientific Revolution and, in the eighteenth century, of the Enlightenment. They divided issues into the spheres of faith and reason. From the Middle Ages on, the sphere of reason had grown relative to the sphere of faith, with politics and political theory fully in the sphere of reason. Westerners approached knowledge as a quest for the truth to be discovered by logic applied to evidence. They considered human knowledge to be expanding. As people better understood the natural world, they could build on this knowledge to extend it further. By the time of the Industrial Revolution, the West emphasized efficiency over tradition and change over social harmony.

Missionaries brought with them this subversive way of understanding and ordering the world, a way that contradicted the very premises of Chinese civilization. The Chinese government met European attempts to missionize with great suspicion and often with animosity because they saw missionizing for what it was: a frontal attack on Chinese civilization. Even had the Europeans not focused on spreading their religious beliefs, the evident power of their governments and their technology would have eventually threatened the bedrock assumptions of Chinese society, in particular the assumption concerning the comprehensive superiority of all aspects of Chinese civilization. As long as there was contact, a clash between East and West was highly likely, given that conflicting practices extended all the way to the most basic principles of foreign relations.

By the nineteenth century, differences in legal, social, and religious traditions between East and West produced competing sets of interests, especially in commercial matters: The Manchus focused on security of the empire and their hold on the throne, and therefore wished to limit interaction with the West and any deterioration in the balance of power between themselves and the Han that trade might bring; Han merchants sought to enrich themselves by trading with the West and cared little for their Manchu overlords. British merchants also desired to enrich themselves, could not understand why the Chinese would not want to engage in this mutually beneficial trade, and wished to change Chinese laws constraining trade. The maritime Europeans remained focused primarily on the mechanisms of trade, whereas the Manchus feared trade's impact on the maintenance of their minority rule over Han China.

V. The Technological Revolution

If legal, social, and religious differences were the tinder for conflict between the East and the West, the Industrial Revolution lit the match by creating a technological asymmetry that undermined Chinese power, pretensions, and, ulti-

mately, many key aspects of its civilization. In the past, the Chinese had consistently maintained technological superiority over their neighbors and retained unchallenged hegemony over the East; it was the Chinese, for example, who invented gunpowder, rockets, and the compass. Real technological superiority, in combination with China's many other political, philosophical, and economic accomplishments, formed the basis for Sinocentrism and the Chinese assurance of their own superiority. Prior to the Industrial Revolution, the Chinese had no reason to doubt this assumption.

China had its own long history of technological innovation. The Han had been centuries ahead of Europeans in many areas. For instance, Europeans did not cultivate plants in rows until the eighteenth century, whereas the Chinese had been doing so since the sixth century BC. China's lead diminished with the Renaissance and the Scientific Revolution in the West and disappeared with the Industrial Revolution. The reign of the Qianlong emperor occurred before the Industrial Revolution had taken off in Europe. Steam power was still in its infancy in England, while the Napoleonic Wars preoccupied Britain and delayed the spread of industrialization until after 1815.

Technological changes outside China were to have a profound and irrevocable impact. In about 1765, James Hargreaves of England invented the cotton-spinning jenny. In 1769 Richard Arkwright, also of England, patented the waterframe spinning machine. These two inventions combined dramatically increased productivity for textiles, making possible the rapid and cheap manufacture of thread. As a result, international prices for cotton goods plummeted, which made Chinese silks correspondingly more dear.

Early steam engines became commercially viable in England by the 1780s and provided the basis for the Industrial Revolution by supplying a widely available and cheap source of energy that revolutionized production. Steam engines meant that Britain no longer required a large class of artisans and laborers, something China had in abundance. The steam engine dramatically decreased the price and increased the availability of energy previously supplied by men and animals. Its use spread to textiles, mining, milling, and metallurgy, where it transformed iron from a rare and expensive commodity into the backbone of industrial economies. By the early nineteenth century, primitive railways appeared, and with their rapid development, land transport costs plummeted.

British industry, which had grown at a rate of 0.7 percent per annum prior to the Industrial Revolution, began in the second half of the eighteenth century to grow at a 3 percent rate, a very modest figure by contemporary standards. The consequences, however, were revolutionary. A 3 percent growth rate meant that a country with a stable population would double its per capita standard of living in one generation. After several generations of compounded growth rates, industrializing countries achieved standards of living, national wealth, and technological capabilities that turned the international balance of power in their favor. Although this created the impression of an implosion of living standards outside of the West, in reality the Industrial Revolution produced an explosion in living standards within the West. Traditional societies, even those that suffered no internal decline, suddenly found themselves in a position of ever greater relative material and military inferiority vis-à-vis the industrializing West.

On the civilian side, the Industrial Revolution made the comparatively small British population breathtakingly wealthy by world standards. On the military side, industrial developments in armaments made the British fabulously powerful as well. The invention of flintlocks and rifled barrels improved the range, accuracy, and rapidity of fire of small firearms. Artillery changed even more rapidly. In the eighteenth century, artillery was classified by use—field, siege, and coast defense—and each was developed separately for its intended purpose. In the nineteenth century, advances in chemistry, mechanics, metallurgy, and optics culminated in the production of a rifled cannon firing elongated projectiles, whose more streamlined shape and greater weight than the traditional spherical cannon ball gave them far greater range and more accurate flight. Improvements in powder also contributed to the greater range. Soon, British guns and artillery were the envy of the world.

Britain projected its global power through its navy, the preeminent fleet during the entire nineteenth century. The Royal Navy was composed of ships of the line, frigates, and sloops. The seventy-four-gun ship of the line, thirty-eight- and thirty-six-gun frigates, and sloops usually with no fewer than twenty guns apiece became standard. Metal did not replace wood for navy hulls until after the mid-nineteenth century, but early on, metal plates were added to wooden hulls for protection. Chinese junks could provide nothing to compare with the Royal Navy's offensive firepower or defensive shielding and so could not avoid defeat.

The Industrial Revolution broke many precedents: It radically altered the international balance of power. Even today, levels of industrialization still define the international power structure and per capita gross national prod-

Chinese have used boats for thousands of years, but mainly on the country's extensive river and canal systems. Many Chinese families lived and worked on their boats, earning a living by transporting goods and passengers between various towns.

ucts. For better or worse, the Industrial Revolution transformed the West into the dominant civilization of the world. Western powers remapped the globe, defined and imposed international law, became wealthy beyond imagination, and set the standard for what was meant by modernity and progress. The desirability of these changes can be disputed, but not the reality of the revolution that gradually enveloped the globe.

Conclusions

The European powers progressively challenged China from the late seventeenth century on. The Portuguese, Spanish, Dutch, and English had a significant impact on the coast, while the Russians advanced overland. For the first time in history, this put China in close contact with Europeans, the standard bearers of another great civilization.

The Chinese would have preferred that Westerners would simply go away, since they had comparatively little interest in the outside world. They maintained tributary relations not out of interest in barbarian lands but to prevent the invasion of and interference within China. The Chinese largely ignored European knowledge developing from the Scientific Revolution on, the notable exception being astronomy, which the Manchus put to use, not to further scientific discovery, but to make a more accurate calendar to predict their dynasty's fortunes. War with the West later created a Chinese interest in Western armaments, but their curiosity did not extend to other subjects until the final decade of the Qing dynasty.

Europeans were far more curious about China than the reverse. During the seventeenth century, collecting Chinese luxury goods became a fad throughout Europe. This trend sponsored a new art form, "chinoiserie," the Western decorative style of incorporating intricate Chinese patterns into Western arts and crafts. Similarly, philosophes on the eve of the French Revolution displayed an intense interest in Chinese philosophy and government. Whereas Europeans desired to go to China, study its practices, and imitate its art forms, the Chinese had no comparable curiosity about Europe.

While the Europeans were eager to trade for the many high-quality goods produced by China, the Chinese took great pride in their own self-sufficiency. Frictions also multiplied as a result of incompatible legal systems, social mores, and religious beliefs. The mutual lack of deep knowledge and understanding of the other culture exacerbated the growing tensions. Philosophical differences between East and West were so extreme that they inhabited radically different mental worlds. At a very basic level, both the Chinese and the Europeans were baffled by the goals, strategies, and likely responses of the other. It would take generations for each side more fully to understand the other. To each, the other seemed "inscrutable." Such basic cultural misunderstandings were to have enormous political repercussions.

The technological changes caused by the Industrial Revolution overturned the international balance of power. Europe had both the wealth and the technology to support a much more aggressive foreign policy in Asia. The growing Western pressure made ever more precarious the Manchus' balancing act, which rested on their effectiveness as custodians of Han culture and guardians of Chinese supremacy. Failure to do so would open them up to charges of usurpation of Han rule. Because the Manchus constituted a tiny minority, they had to divide in order to rule: They had to keep their subjects separated regionally, administratively, and militarily to prevent a coup d'état. Promoting Han culture required continuity in institutions, rituals, and laws, while retaining their supremacy demanded a no-nonsense foreign policy.

Just as the Qing dynasty appeared to have brought China to the pinnacle of its success—the long-sought-after "golden age"—European ideas, practices, and technology threatened to overturn the international balance of power on which the Qing mandate depended. Soon, foreign technology and obstreperous Western behavior called Qing rule into question. From the Manchu point of view, trade with the West was becoming increasingly subversive. In response, they sought to roll back European influence by limiting trade. This strategy ended in a war that China was ill-equipped to win.

BIBLIOGRAPHY

Cipolla, Carlo M. *Guns, Sails, and Empires: Technological Innovation and the Early Phases of European Expansion, 1400–1700.* New York: Minerva, 1965.
Dunn, Ross E. *The Adventures of Ibn Battuta: A Muslim Traveler of the 14th Century,* rev. ed. Berkeley: University of California Press, 2005.

Fang Xing, Shi Qi, Jian Rui, and Wang Shixin. "Tea, Tobacco, Distilling and Oil Pressing." In *Chinese Capitalism, 1522–1840*, edited by Xu Dixin and Wu Chengming, translated by Li Zhengde, et al., 184–94. New York: St. Martin's Press, 2000.

LeDonne, John P. *The Grand Strategy of the Russian Empire: 1650–1831*. Oxford: Oxford University Press, 2003.

Mancall, Mark. *Russia and China: Their Diplomatic Relations to 1728*. Cambridge, MA: Harvard University Press, 1971.

Needham, Joseph. *Science and Civilisation in China*. Vols. 1, 2. Cambridge: Cambridge University Press, 1962–5.

Parry, John Horace. *The Age of Reconnaissance: Discovery, Exploration and Settlement, 1450–1650*. New York: Praeger, 1963.

Penrose, Boies. *Travel and Discovery in the Age of the Renaissance, 1420–1620*. New York: Atheneum, 1952.

Peyrefitte, Alain. *The Immobile Empire*. Translated by Jon Rothschild. New York: Alfred A. Knopf, 1992.

Pritchard Earl H. *The Crucial Years of Early Anglo-Chinese Relations, 1750–1800*. New York: Octagon Books, 1970.

Scammell, Geoffrey Vaughn. *The World Encompassed: The First European Maritime Empires, c. 800–1650*. Berkeley: University of California Press, 1981.

Sebes, Joseph S. *The Jesuits and the Sino-Russian Treaty of Nerchinsk (1689): The Diary of Thomas Pereira*. Rome: Institutum Historicum, 1961.

Sykes, Sir Percy. *The Quest for Cathay*. London: A. & C. Black, 1936.

Temple, Robert. *The Genius of China: 3,000 Years of Science, Discovery and Invention*. London: Prion, 1998.

Vernadsky, George. *A History of Russia*. Vol. 3, *The Mongols of Russia*. New Haven, CT: Yale University Press, 1953.

Widmer, Eric. *The Russian Ecclesiastical Mission in Peking during the 18th Century*. Cambridge, MA: Harvard University Press, 1976.

Wills, John. *Pepper, Guns and Parleys: The Dutch East India Company and China, 1662–1681*. Cambridge, MA: Harvard University Press, 1974.

NOTES

1. According to Hsü, Shuhai and Hengzhang were mythical travelers. Cited in Immanuel C. Y. Hsü, *The Rise of Modern China*, 6th ed. (New York: Oxford University Press, 2000), 159.

2. Ross E. Dunn, *The Adventures of Ibn Battuta: A Muslim Traveler of the 14th Century*, rev. ed. (Berkeley: University of California Press, 2005), 258.

3. Peter C. Perdue, "Fate and Fortune in Central Eurasian Warfare: Three Qing Emperors and Their Mongol Rivals," in *Warfare in Inner Asian History (500–1800)*, edited by Nicola Di Cosmo (Leiden: Brill, 2002), 378.

4. In contrast with the other European powers, Russia shared certain important historical experiences with China. Both were vast continental empires that had suffered Mongol rule. The Russian tsar, like the Chinese emperor, was an autocrat whose fiat ruled the land. In Russia, there was no real separation of secular and canon law, as in the West, because tsars dominated the Russian Orthodox Church. Russia had been at the periphery of the Renaissance, the Reformation, and the Scientific Revolution. The Russian legal code continued to rely heavily on torture, enforced confessions, and summary capital punishment well into the nineteenth century. But Russia, unlike China, accepted the notion of juridically equal nation-states and so was willing to operate within the channels of international law.

Chronology

1793	Macartney Mission arrives in Beijing
1795–1806	Miao Uprising
1796	Qianlong emperor retires; Jiaqing emperor assumes the throne
1796–1804	White Lotus Rebellion
1799	Death of the Qianlong emperor
	Jiaqing emperor orders suicide of Heshen
1813	Eight Trigrams Revolt
1817	End of imperial subsidies to the khan of Kokand
1820	Jiaqing emperor dies; Daoguang emperor assumes the throne
1820–8	*Jihad* led by Jahangir; last important banner force military victory

6

Systemic Crisis and Dynastic Decline

The addicts' lamps are ranged in groups,
scattered autumn fireflies,
a registrar, fallen on hard times,
his tear-filled eyes aglow.

Why not go govern a city
in some county of poppy flowers,
and sleep through spring never waking
in the Gold Food Festival?[1]

Gong Zizhen
(1792–1841), official

If Qianlong's reign was a golden age, it was also a turning point. Harbingers of a systemic crisis appeared in its latter years. The Qianlong emperor's impressive conquests came at the cost of great treasure. The extent of these lands ultimately exceeded the capacity of the Qing to maintain order, while rapid population growth undermined their ability to open new lands or improve the productivity of those already under cultivation. Unwittingly, the Qianlong emperor may have overextended the Qing empire and, in doing so, helped push the Qing past the period of ascendance and into the period of gradual decline anticipated by the dynastic cycle. Immediately upon the retirement of the Qianlong emperor, the first of the great internal rebellions of the Qing period, the White Lotus Rebellion, began, calling into question the Qing mandate of heaven; this occurred at the end of the eighteenth century, after over 150 years of Manchu rule but prior to the large-scale arrival of Westerners in China. The West and the Industrial Revolution not only did not cause this decline, but eventually helped keep the Manchus in power by providing military assistance during the Taiping Rebellion and by creating an efficient Customs Inspectorate to tax foreign trade and deliver these moneys directly to the central treasury. The West's arrival did, however, greatly complicate and undermine the Qing's ability to address internal problems.

I. Government Corruption and Manchu Decadence

In China, government corruption, meaning the imposition of extralegal surcharges and the distribution of gifts with the expectation of future favors, was not the exception but the rule. Insufficient funding for local officials, powerful *guanxi* networks, and unscrupulous imperial favorites combined with growing Manchu incompetence to create the pervasive corruption in the late Qing period observed by Chinese and Westerners alike.

Much of what most Westerners today would pejoratively label as government corruption was part of the normal functioning of government in China. Unlike in the West, gift giving and special fees were not considered corrupt by Chinese. Because local officials did not have a separate source of income to fund their official responsibilities, it was assumed that they would levy surcharges. Government salaries were nominal, so officials had to supplement them with "melting charges" for those who paid their taxes in silver. During the early eighteenth century, the Yongzheng emperor tried to limit surtaxes by granting "honesty-nourishing allowances" for fiscal officers, but by the end of the century the allowance was insufficient and corruption was again on the rise.

Under the Chinese tax system, the land tax constituted the government's main source of income. During the eighteenth century, the land tax equaled about three-quarters of the total tax revenue. In 1712 the Kangxi emperor fixed these rates in perpetuity, so land taxes rose through the end of the nineteenth century only as new land came under cultivation. Beijing's total income was 36,106,483 taels in 1725 and only 38,600,750 taels in 1841, more than a century later.[2] Yet, during this time, the Chinese population and economy grew rapidly. This meant that the Manchus' ability to extract revenue through mandated taxes declined in per capita terms. Tax reforms by the Yongzheng and Qianlong emperors diverted more revenue to Beijing but away from local governments.

While local governments' responsibilities grew in tandem with the population, their revenues declined. This fostered corruption even in good times, let alone in times of crisis. It is hard to estimate the percentage of local taxes taken by corrupt officials. Virtually all government expenses for the provincial governments, including those for water projects and disaster relief, came directly from local tax collectors, who took an ever-increasing share of the total tax revenues. The tax system was incapable of shifting moneys among the provinces. In times of flooding, famine, or war, this proved disastrous, as afflicted provinces were left to their own devices. Local loyalties reinforced such provincial divisions and impeded the development of a sense of nation or of a greater common good above the local level.

A second element of corruption was connected with *guanxi*. Outside the family and in public office, this system of mutual obligation was maintained, in significant part, by gift giving. Inferiors gave gifts to superiors with the expectation of future benefits. This was not considered unethical. On the contrary, not to exhibit due respect through gifts showed deplorable impropriety. Since personal relations, not laws, constituted the bedrock of the Chinese body politic, their cultivation was essential for career success and, on occasion, for physical survival. In times of growing economic hardship, *guanxi* networks became essential for the maintenance or improvement of personal status, and giving gifts and doing favors increased. For those without strong *guanxi* networks, such as the poor, who had little to offer others, this system reinforced their inferior status.

Such gift giving goes back literally millennia in Han culture. According to *The Book of Rites,* one of the Five Classics: "In the highest antiquity they prized (simply conferring) good; in the time next to this, giving and repaying was the thing attended to. And what the rules of propriety value is that of reciprocity. If I give a gift and

nothing comes in return, that is contrary to propriety; if the thing comes to me, and I give nothing in return, that is also contrary to propriety."[3] By the late Qing period, such gift giving no longer reinforced a system of rule based on merit. Instead, it increasingly concentrated wealth and power in the hands of those who, through their official positions, controlled access to scarce opportunities, which they allocated on the basis not of merit but of personal gain.

A third source of corruption was the emperor's heavy reliance on eunuchs and favorites in order to conduct imperial business. (See the feature on the next page.) These people had personal access to the emperor and, to the degree that they were favored, could manipulate his will. At the beginning of the Qing dynasty, eunuchs were shunned and abused. Over time, they were taught to read and write, and so gradually became important as secretarial staff within the palace bureaucracy. These contacts provided the opportunity to amass wealth and political power. Over the course of the Qing dynasty, eunuchs became ever more entrenched. After the time of the Kangxi emperor, when the ruling monarchs no longer had battlefield experience, and after that of the Qianlong emperor, when they became ever more the products of the sheltered life within the Forbidden City, Qing emperors became increasingly unable to constrain their ambitious retainers. In the nineteenth century, a succession of child emperors under the supervision of empress dowagers gave eunuchs and other retainers greater opportunity to amass power.

This problem became evident in the waning years of the Qianlong emperor's life. Although he lived until the age of eighty-eight, it remains unclear how long he retained his full faculties. At age sixty-five, he became enamored of a twenty-five-year-old Manchu bodyguard, Heshen (1750–99), whom within a decade he put in charge of the Boards of Appointments and Revenue, giving him a virtual stranglehold on government hiring and finance. For the final fifteen years of Qianlong's reign, Heshen used these offices, and many others in which he also served, to appoint his own associates throughout the empire, creating a *guanxi* network of stupendous proportions and also to enrich himself. Although Heshen's activities were notorious, nothing could be done as long as he enjoyed the protection of the declining emperor. After the Qianlong emperor's death in 1799, his son, the Jiaqing emperor, ordered Heshen to commit suicide, thereby decapitating and destroying the latter's *guanxi* network. Heshen's property upon his death was assessed at 800 million ounces of silver, equal to billions of dollars.

CONCUBINES AND EUNUCHS

From the earliest dynasties on, Han imperial courts had tried to eliminate outside influence by relying on eunuchs, the castrated servants of emperors. It was hoped that the absence of children would limit their *guanxi* networks and focus their loyalties on the throne. Although the practice did limit nepotism, it did not constrain personal ambitions. Originally, eunuchs were intended to guard the imperial harem, but in fact, they served in innumerable responsible official capacities. Regardless of their government positions, when favored by the emperor, they could exert enormous power within the Forbidden City and throughout the realm. During the Ming dynasty, the number of palace eunuchs rose from fewer than 100 to perhaps as many as 100,000. Initially, the Manchus looked down on eunuchs, although eunuchs remained in charge of the imperial palace, where they gradually increased in number over the course of the dynasty.

The institutions of concubinage and eunuchs were complementary: Concubines were so numerous that the most efficient means of surveillance was to prevent their contact with fertile males; so, sexually impotent men guarded the chastity of the imperial concubines to guarantee royal bloodlines. Males in potential contact with imperial concubines were rendered sexually impotent either by mutilation or by the surgical removal not just of the testes, but of all external genitalia. Because of incontinence problems, some Chinese referred to such men as "stinking eunuchs." For most, this operation took place before adolescence and the scars eventually healed. However, grown men, who hoped to advance their careers by gaining access to palace offices, often did not survive the operation but bled to death.

Eunuchs filled all major positions within the Forbidden City, acting as palace officials, harem guards, and spies. Unlike the well-educated literati who had to pass the imperial examinations to serve in office, eunuchs were often poorly educated, but they gained power through their contacts with the emperor. Government officials repeatedly memorialized to the throne demanding the curtailment of

It was common in China for a wealthy man to have more than one wife. Usually, his first wife was considered the only true wife, while the rest were concubines. A concubine could be favored by her husband by producing sons, and so might displace the first wife. In Hong Kong, this practice was particularly common until the Qing Code was replaced by the Marriage Act of 1971. While polygamy is outlawed in China today, it is not uncommon for Taiwanese businessmen to leave their families in Taiwan and to start a second family in the People's Republic of China, a practice that has been equated with concubinage.

Continued

eunuch interference in state affairs, but emperors found eunuchs useful. Because eunuchs had no children, they could be particularly loyal supporters of the dynasty. Their lack of progeny also put them outside the pale of Chinese society, since castration rendered a man unfit to worship his ancestors; the failure to produce offspring was considered the ultimate unfilial act.

Official histories often associated undue eunuch influence with dynastic decline and attributed the fall of the Han, Tang, and Ming dynasties to such "eunuch disasters." Sometimes eunuchs allied with concubines. If the empress failed to bear a son, which often happened, sons of concubines competed to have their son succeed to the throne. The Qing were even less inclined to practice primogeniture than Han Chinese dynasties, causing a potential free-for-all during successions. This could lead to plotting and assassinations directed at the children of competing concubines. Eunuchs could obtain great personal power and wealth by ensuring the succession of a later grateful emperor. Similarly, the mothers of potential heirs could exert enormous influence before their sons reached maturity and sometimes even longer. In the Qing period, the Empress Dowager Cixi, originally a low-ranking concubine, became notorious for her influence over her son and his successor and ruled through her eunuchs. Weak emperors could become the captive of their eunuchs, while astute emperors could capitalize on their loyalties. Other eunuchs excelled in their chosen fields: Zheng He, a Muslim eunuch, commanded the Ming dynasty's naval explorations.

During the Qing dynasty, in addition to the hundreds of eunuchs serving the emperor, each prince and married princess could have thirty eunuchs at his or her private residence, while imperial nephews and younger unmarried princes could have twenty and grandsons only ten. When the Qing dynasty collapsed in 1911, there were over 2,000 eunuchs in Beijing. With the loss of their livelihood, they lived in poverty.

Although eunuchs disappeared with the Qing dynasty, concubinage remained quite common after the 1911 Revolution and continued in Taiwan into the late twentieth century. In April 2001, the People's Republic of China attempted to prevent wealthy citizens from taking concubines by proscribing married Chinese from living with someone other than their spouse. According to the Xinhua News Agency, "Bigamy and keeping concubines by the country's new rich are eroding social morality."

Traditional Chinese law did not distinguish between the children of the main wife and those of concubines. Families actively sought the honor of having their daughters become imperial concubines with the chance of a descendant becoming emperor. In the case of commoners, although the main wife had to be from the same social background as her husband, the concubines did not. Concubines were usually purchased from tenant farmers or merchants desiring to establish connections with their more wealthy contacts. Patrons also sometimes bought sing-song girls or prostitutes and entertainers to make them concubines. Maids also sometimes became concubines. In other cases, concubines could be received as a gift. Once accepted into a household, concubines remained until their death. Expulsions were rare because of the incurred disgrace to the family honor.

Not only did the Court display growing incompetence, but so did the banner system that had brought the Manchus to power. During the reign of the Qianlong emperor, opium made the transition from a medicine, generally used in limited quantities to treat specific ailments, to a recreational drug and aphrodisiac widely used in the Court by the Manchu elite and among Chinese officials. Opium addiction increased dramatically among both rich and poor. The domestic production of opium, especially in Sichuan, grew to meet this demand, while Europeans soon augmented these supplies with Indian opium, helping to reduce the price and thus making possible a truly mass market. Growing civilian and military incapacity translated into an increasing inability of the dynasty to protect China either from internal or external threats.

By the late nineteenth century, the banner forces were considered a laughingstock by Western military personnel, who commented on their antiquated armaments, their negligible military capabilities, and their widespread opium addiction. The gradual decline of the banner forces, in turn, made the dynasty vulnerable both to internal and external threats, as domestic rebellion and foreign war ensued in rapid succession.

II. Population Growth, Ethnic Tensions, and the Miao Revolt

In the third quarter of the eighteenth century, the population of the Qing empire reached its optimal size given its level of technology. But China's prosperity meant that the population rose from about 140 million in 1700 to 270 million in 1770. However, it kept on growing to 340 million in 1780 and to 410 million by 1850, when it peaked on the eve of China's great civil wars of the mid-nineteenth century. (See Table 6.1.) By the last quarter of the eighteenth century, declines in rural living standards started to alarm officials. The balance between a rapidly growing population and a much more static land supply concerned the Qianlong emperor from the beginning of his reign. He realized the inaccuracy of the existent population surveys when a crop failure in 1775 in Hubei province indicated 100,000 more people in need of aid than were on the registers, demonstrating gross undercounting. Thereafter, he made population registration a central function of the *baojia* system. The maintenance of accurate records,

Table 6.1   Population Changes during the Qing Dynasty

Year	Recorded Total Population	% Change in Recorded Population	Adjusted Total Population	% Change in Adjusted Total Population
1651	10,633,326		(1650)123,000,000	
1660	19,087,572	79.5	152,000,000	23.6
1670	19,396,453	1.6	148,000,000	(2.6)
1680	17,094,637	(11.9)	126,000,000	(14.9)
1690	20,363,568	19.1	144,000,000	14.3
1700	20,410,963	0.2	138,000,000	(4.2)
1710	23,312,236	14.2	149,000,000	8.0
1720	25,029,949	7.4	154,000,000	3.4
1730	26,332,457	5.2	151,000,000	(1.9)
1741	143,411,559	444.6	219,000,000	45.0
1750	179,538,540	25.2	260,000,000	18.7
1760	196,837,977	9.6	268,000,000	3.1
1770	213,613,163	8.5	272,000,000	1.5
1780	277,554,431	29.9	342,000,000	25.7
1790	301,487,115	8.6	359,000,000	5.0
1800	295,237,311	(2.1)	340,000,000	(5.3)
1810	345,717,214	17.1	385,000,000	13.2
1820	353,377,694	2.2	381,000,000	(1.0)
1830	394,784,681	11.7	409,000,000	7.3
1840	412,814,828	4.6	412,000,000	0.7
1850	414,493,899	0.4	412,000,000	0.0
1860	260,924,675	(37.0)	377,000,000	(8.5)
1870	268,040,023	2.7	358,000,000	(5.0)
1880			369,000,000	3.1
1887	377,636,000		(1890) 380,000,000	3.0
1901	426,447,325	12.9	(1900)400,000,000	5.3
1911	341,423,867	(19.9)	(1910) 423,000,000	5.8

Note: Percentages in parentheses indicate negative numbers. The shaded area indicates the period of rapid population growth. The boxed area indicates the height of nineteenth-century civil wars.

Source: Gabe T. Wang, *China's Population: Problems, Thoughts and Policies* (Aldershot: Ashgate, 1999), 38. Wang bases his recorded population statistics on S. Y. Wu, *The Draft of Population Thought in China* (Beijing: Chinese Social Science Academy Press, 1986), and his adjusted total population on P. K. C. Liu and K. W. Hwang, *Modern Chinese Economic History* (Taipei: 1979).

while crucial to govern effectively, was close to impossible in a preindustrial empire of such vast extent.

The size of the growing population exceeded the ability of the Qing to administer it effectively, since the number of bureaucrats necessary to govern exceeded the capacity of the imperial examination system to vet competent administrators. The sheer number of examination candidates dwarfed the ability of the exam administrators to read the examinations carefully and promote the most talented entrants. Many students who passed the examinations were labeled "waiting for appointment," but often grew old and frail before receiving their first appointment. Finally, the size of the examination apparatus and an ever larger pool of aspiring applicants meant increasing opportunities for cheating. The Qianlong emperor made repeated attempts to reform the examination system, but irregularities persisted. Bribery of examiners and the purchase of degrees eroded the legitimacy of the examination system until such irregularities became endemic by the first half of the nineteenth century. This meant that the examination process was no longer regarded as fair and that the Manchus no longer had firm control over their civil service. The emperor's closest servitors were increasingly regarded as suspect.

A shortage of arable land greatly exacerbated the consequences of population growth. Together these problems put increasing pressure on the natural environment. Upstream deforestation to make way for agriculture caused not only permanent soil erosion but also downstream silting and, with silting, increasingly lethal flooding, particularly on the Yellow River. China's heavy reliance on irrigation entailed restructuring the rural landscape, leaving little room for undomesticated animals and birds. Indeed, the original animals populating much of China included tigers, elephants, and rhinoceroses. In ancient times, rhinoceroses were so numerous that for more than 1,000 years their hides armored China's huge armies. They became extinct in China in the late nineteenth century, but the erosion of their habitat had begun centuries before on the Yangzi River and gradually spread south in tandem with the southward migration of the Han population and the accompanying deforestation. Over three-quarters of the Qing empire was unsuitable for agriculture.

As the population grew, peasant holdings became smaller. This required more intensive cultivation and greater reliance on new irrigation systems and fertilizers, which increased deforestation, soil erosion, desertification, silting, and flooding. Population pressure and environmental degradation greatly magnified the effects of natural disasters. North China rainfall is erratic, meaning frequent droughts, while the Yellow and Yangzi rivers have always been prone to flooding. By the mid-nineteenth century, famines had become massive, with 15 million people perishing in 1849 alone. The mid-nineteenth-century rebellions then ravaged good farmland so that famine spread into normally prosperous areas. (See Table 24.1.) Farmers adopted a variety of cottage industries to supplement their incomes, including spinning and weaving; but these cottage industries soon become vulnerable to international competition when the Industrial Revolution sent many prices tumbling.

Even with changes in crops, improved irrigation, and additional fertilizers, the need for new land became acute. This led to the gradual Han settlement of wilderness areas and cultivation of marginal lands that could not sustain rice but could grow the New World crops, like peanuts. Much of this land was originally inhabited by non-Han minorities. Today there are fifty-five recognized minority groups in China, but there were many more in the eighteenth century.

Population growth and a shift to frontier areas brought Han migrants into direct competition with the many minority peoples of the Qing empire, such as the Miao.

During the eighteenth and nineteenth centuries, the Miao minority (also known as the Hmong) rebelled repeatedly against Qing rule. The Miao followed Daoist practices but, unlike the Han, had no written tradition. During the Zhou dynasty they lived on the middle and lower reaches of the Yangzi River, but the Han gradually forced them southward so that they became scattered into separate but related tribes inhabiting central and Western China and modern-day Vietnam, Laos, and Thailand. They were especially numerous in Guizhou (Kweichow) province, where they made up 40–60 percent of the population. Ethnic tensions had led to large-scale uprisings in the past, such as the Miao and Yao rebellions in Guangxi, Guangdong, Sichuan, Hunan, and Guizhou provinces from 1464 to 1466.

The Qing government pursued a policy of accommodation on its own terms: Native leaders retained their rule as long as they tolerated the spread of the Han settlers; gave nominal respect to the emperor and Confucian values; and ceded control of their foreign policy to the Qing dynasty. In return, they continued to administer many local issues and were allowed to retain their languages, customs, and religions. As the number of Han settlers increased, so did the government's interest in tightening control over the Miao. This policy included drawing local Miao leaders directly into the Qing bureaucracy as petty officials, but this in no way stemmed the tide of Han settlers into Miao lands. In 1795, an enormous Miao revolt broke out along the Hunan–Guizhou border in response to the huge influx of Han immigrants. The government immediately deployed troops not only to put down the rebels but also to confiscate Miao lands, assimilate the Miao people into Han society, build military garrisons, and segregate the Han and Miao populations by constructing a long, fortified wall. The policy of land confiscation merely heightened tensions, especially since the new government rents were extremely high.

The Qing army defeated the Miao again in 1806. After the Manchu banners' initial victory, they attempted to implement a policy of military occupation and cultural annihilation. Their first order established agricultural colonies to keep the Miao under strict military control. In an attempt to Sinify them, they banned all traditional Miao religious practices and mandated the introduction of Chinese education. Incomplete and coerced Sinification became a source of future unrest. During the 1850s, when the Qing authorities were preoccupied with quelling the Taiping Rebellion, the Miao rebelled again. Although the Qing dynasty successfully defeated the Miao revolts, ethnic rebellions came with increasing frequency and magnitude during the nineteenth century, leaving a swath of economic devastation in their wake.

III. The White Lotus Rebellion and the Eight Trigrams Revolt

Unlike the Miao, who wanted to secede from the empire, most of the members of the White Lotus Society were Han, who wanted to overthrow the dynasty. (See Map 6.1.) This was not unrest on the imperial periphery but a far more dangerous attempt to decapitate the imperial center. There had been previous White Lotus rebellions in Shandong province in 1622 and earlier outbreaks centered in Hubei, Sichuan, and Shaanxi provinces. This time, the Miao revolt indirectly contributed to the outbreak in 1796, since the militias in rebellion had originally been created to suppress the Miao but then turned on the Qing dynasty.

Religion, not ethnicity, unified the White Lotus followers. Their religious beliefs were a mixture of Daoism, Buddhism, and Manicheism. The last viewed the world in terms of an epic struggle between good and evil, with humanity as its ambiguous product. According to its core beliefs, the dual deities, Buddha and the Manichean "Prince of Light," would establish an earthly paradise of health and prosperity for the devout in this life and happiness in the next life. This included the restoration of the last Han dynasty, the Ming, a promise that attracted many Han followers from among the peasantry.

The peasantry was receptive to White Lotus beliefs because of the growing economic hardship of the late Qianlong period. The area bordering on Hubei, Sichuan, and Shaanxi was mountainous and inhospitable. Many of the Han settlers were recent immigrants, in varying degrees of conflict with the local population. White Lotus members included not only poor farmers, but also lower-level officials and yamen clerks. The military wing was composed mainly of mercenaries, who practiced martial arts, including boxing techniques. They formed loose alliances with salt smugglers, who took advantage of the chaos during the Miao and ensuing White Lotus rebellions. These alliances meant that by 1800, only about one-tenth of the White Lotus troops were religious followers.

As in most insurgencies, the Qing commanders sent to quell the rebellion had difficulty distinguishing rebels from noncombatants. As one Qing official complained: "The rebels are all our own subjects. They are not like some external tribe . . . that can be demarcated by a territorial boundary and identified

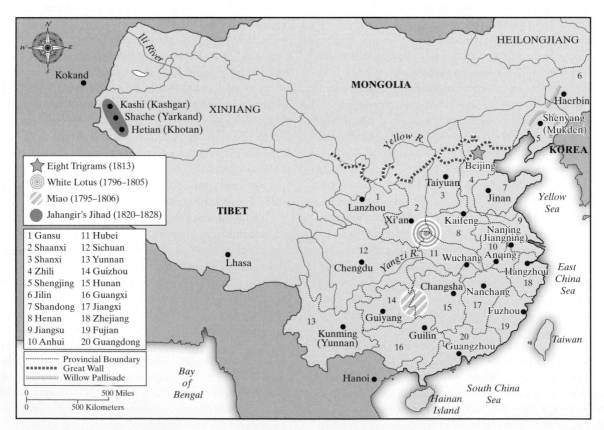

Map 6.1   Late-Eighteenth- and Early-Nineteenth-Century Rebellions

by its distinctive clothing and language. . . . When they congregate and oppose the government, they are rebels; when they disperse and depart, they are civilians once more."[4] Without a clear enemy, Qing military forces soon acquired the name "Red Lotus Society" for all the blood they shed.

Brutality did not quell but fueled the spreading rebellion. Only after 1800 did the Qing forces adopt new tactics. Most importantly, they began to organize village militias to help surround and destroy the White Lotus forces. The Qing dynasty largely suppressed the rebellion in 1804 with a combination of military and social policies. An estimated 7,000 banner troops from Manchuria; dependable Green Standard battalions from Guizhou and Yunnan; and tens of thousands of local mercenaries combined forces to drive the White Lotus from their strongholds and defeat a movement that had once numbered an estimated 100,000. This victory cost Beijing 120 million taels, which not only eliminated the budget surplus accumulated under the Qianlong emperor but also emptied the imperial treasury. Upon the restoration of order, the Qing dynasty disbanded the local Han militias in an attempt to restore central control and prevent more mutinies.

White Lotus rebels, however, continued to be active. Rebellion broke out anew in 1813, this time in Shandong, Henan, and Zhili (Hebei) provinces under the name of the Eight Trigrams Sect. It divided followers into eight groups, or trigrams, and collected contributions with promises of future benefits. Advance sales of land became a main source of income—the land would be delivered after the seizure of power. The Eight Trigrams Revolt resembled more an attempted coup d'état than a widespread rebellion. Although its Han leaders proclaimed their intent to revive the Ming dynasty, they seemed more focused on regicide and usurpation. Unlike ethnic separatists, fighting for the independence of their homeland, or domestic rebels, fighting for regional and then national control, the Eight Trigrams focused on the Forbidden City in Beijing.

The founder of the Eight Trigrams Sect, Lin Qing, at one point declared himself the future Buddha. As an illustration of the importance attached to divination and fate, the appearance of a bright comet in 1811 allegedly inspired him to overthrow the Qing dynasty. Droughts, floods, and the soaring price of wheat not only added to the hardships of the population, but also indicated an ebbing mandate of heaven for the ruling dynasty. Although Beijing claimed that the comet glorified the dynasty, the rebels took its appearance as an auspicious blessing foretelling the success of their rebellion. The Eight Trigram leaders chose 15 September 1813 as an auspicious date to begin because it came right after the harvest and coincided with the Jiaqing emperor's (r. 1796/9–1820) absence from Beijing, meaning that the Forbidden City would be lightly guarded.

About eighty rebels made it within the gates before they were closed. Prince Mianning, the future Daoguang emperor

(r. 1820–1850), was in the Forbidden City and joined the battle. With the advantage of surprise lost, the rebels turned and fled, while members of the royal family, officers of the imperial household, and eunuchs killed a total of thirty-one rebels, captured forty-four alive, and suffered over one hundred casualties within the Forbidden City. Meanwhile, the Jiaqing emperor was less than fifty miles from the city.

By the time the revolt was suppressed, more than 20,000 Eight Trigram members had been killed in battle or executed. In response, the Jiaqing emperor tried to suppress internal dissent, but he was not equal to the task. His reign was not considered particularly auspicious. In addition to rebellions by the Miao and the White Lotus Society, the army mutinied, pirates roamed the southern coast, the Yellow River flooded at least seventeen times, and a deranged servant nearly assassinated him. The rebellions made imperial finances even worse, which became the Daoguang emperor's burden in 1821.

IV. Imperial Overextension

In accordance with the cyclical understandings of *yin* and *yang* and of Buddhist views of regeneration and decay, the very success of the Manchu empire contained within it the seeds of decay. The Manchu conquests changed the way the Han defined China. The end of the Great Wall at Jiayuguan in central Gansu province marked the reach of Han settled agriculture. Beyond it lay nomad lands. In the past, Han conquests had focused on areas suitable for settled agriculture and with economies similar to China's. The Manchus, however, were northern nomads who felt a close kinship to their neighbors, the Mongols. The Manchu approach to empire brought control of vast, sparsely populated lands in Mongolia, Xinjiang, and Tibet that were not suitable for Han modes of agriculture. These territorial conquests created an economic burden because these areas generated little tax revenue but created enormous administrative and military costs.

The Manchus offered their neighbors a choice of accommodation or extermination. Agricultural productivity in the core provinces of China financed the ambitious conquest of Xinjiang, while horses provided by the Mongols made force projection and long logistical lines sustainable. Together these new factors made the conquest of Xinjiang possible. But this military adventurism constituted a massive transfer of resources from the settled agricultural economies of the core provinces to the remote and hostile imperial periphery, with no commensurate economic benefits to offset the costs of conquests, let alone of permanent garrisoning.

Whereas the Manchus were quite successful in reaching an accommodation with the Mongols and the Tibetans, in part through a shared interest in Buddhism, the Muslim faith did not permit alien rule. Force, not accommodation, would be necessary to maintain control over the vast spaces of Xinjiang. Muslim resistance at its root was not connected with Qing strategy but with core cultural values of the Muslim population, which rejected Qing overlordship outright in a way that neither Mongol nor Tibetan culture did. Like Christianity, Islam rejected the layered belief system of the Chinese and required believers to choose one belief system, one religion, one God. These difficulties of cultural accommodation meant that the inclusion and retention of Xinjiang in the Qing empire would be extraordinarily expensive, and peace and prosperity in Xinjiang would be unlikely. Prosperity required the stability that an ongoing insurgency would preclude.

To occupy Xinjiang, the Qing encouraged Manchu and particularly Han migration. But even this was not cheap. It did not represent a spontaneous migration but rather a heavily subsidized state program. Xinjiang's economy never became self-sustaining even in times of peace. Unrest in Xinjiang affected both Qing internal administration and finances immediately after its occupation. The Yongzheng emperor created his palace memorial system and Grand Council in part to ensure rapid communication with his commanders in the field. By the 1770s, the Qing already had difficulty ensuring honest and competent administration of Xinjiang. Its remoteness meant that Beijing was even less capable of controlling corruption there. Widespread embezzlement of grain from the land tax and the granaries, of funds intended to build new granaries, and of funds to purchase examination degrees fed the local unrest that became endemic in Gansu and Xinjiang in the second half of the eighteenth century. The late-nineteenth-century rebellions simply occurred on a greater regional scale. At that time, the cost of reasserting central control constituted the main drain on late Qing finances.

In contrast to the Ming dynasty that occupied overwhelmingly Han lands, most of the territories of the Qing empire lay in non-Han areas. This changed the definition of "China" from the core provinces within the Great Wall into a vast multiethnic empire. Unlike the Han provinces that shared a cultural affinity, the Qing imperial frontiers did not. Nor were these non-Han peoples content with Chinese rule. The post-1911 Han successors to the Manchu dynasty maintained this new and expanded definition of the integral lands of China only through the liberal use of force.

V. Qing Attempts to Restore Governmental Efficacy

The Jiaqing emperor initiated reforms to stem the corruption and declining imperial finances of his father's later years. They included purging the bureaucracy, halting imperial tours of the South, ending the distribution of tributary gifts to non-Han border states, and protecting rice shipments on the Grand Canal. These reforms did help shore up the faltering Qing dynasty, but they also increased tensions between the Manchus and both their subjects and their neighbors. These decisions also exacerbated the dynasty's new problems with the Europeans arriving in South China to trade.

The Jiaqing emperor did not simply execute his father's corrupt favorite, Heshen, he also tried to eliminate Heshen's entire *guanxi* network. This purge entailed the replacement of many high officials, including eight of the eleven highest officials in the central government. Anticorruption reforms affected the provinces as well. Reviving a method pioneered by his grandfather, the Yongzheng emperor, the Jiaqing emperor urged officials to memorialize to the throne secretly with their complaints. This led to the impeachment and replacement of large numbers of provincial officials.

The Jiaqing emperor seems to have understood the economic predicament of the empire in terms of an impending budget deficit. His solution focused on reducing expenses by halting imperial tours of the South, not on increasing revenues or improving productivity. His father, the Qianlong emperor, had emulated his grandfather, the Kangxi emperor, by making a total of six extended tours of South China and over one hundred shorter trips to other parts of the empire. Tour preparations entailed the construction of lavish palaces and gardens and the repair of roadways, with the local population bearing the expenses. The expenditures, although enormous, improved the infrastructure and provided more up-to-date information about the distant South, while the Qianlong emperor's presence helped solidify northern control over the South. Finally, the Qianlong emperor—in the manner of Louis XIV, who induced the French aristocracy to maintain a costly presence at the Versailles palace—might have used his trips to drain excess money from potential rivals, including the wealthy officials in South China.

Although the Jiaqing emperor saved money, this reform actually might have loosened northern control over South China. The Manchus soon lost touch with the South at a time of rapidly increasing European influence there. The Daoguang emperor likewise did not make tours of the South. By the end of his reign in 1850, the Taiping Rebellion began in the South and soon almost unseated his successor.

In the early nineteenth century, a dispute raged over whether rice tribute from the South should be transported along the Grand Canal or by sea. The Jiaqing emperor and his successor, the Daoguang emperor, both sided with those wishing to use the Grand Canal. The sea route was more direct, more reliable, and therefore cheaper, but the grain tribute administration preferred the canal because the livelihoods of so many government officials depended on the canal fees paid by the tribute ships. From 1824 to 1827, the sea route temporarily predominated because of extensive silting in the canal. But the Daoguang emperor, reluctant to alienate an important faction within the government, supported repairs to reopen the canal. To encourage use of the Grand Canal, the government enforced strict limits on the sea trade. While oceangoing ships could deliver northern goods, such as salt, to the South, they could not legally bring back southern goods, like rice. As a result, many seagoing ships returned north empty. The decision to subsidize the Grand Canal trade undercut China's seagoing trade, a situation foreigners soon exploited.

The Jiaqing emperor also tried to save funds by halting the annual missions from Central Asian tributaries and provincial officials living in remote provinces like Xinjiang. In 1800 the central government spent an estimated 1.2 million silver taels per year to support the Xinjiang garrison. In 1817, the Jiaqing emperor ended the annual subsidies to the khan of Kokand, valued at as much as 50,000 taels of silver, plus valu-

able shipments of tea, and ceased allowing the khan to send embassies to Beijing to trade. This decision not to send gifts to China's border states contributed to unanticipated military problems. Canceling these gifts made the emperor and his court less aware of frontier security and suggested a failure to appreciate the rationale for the tributary system: Cost-effective barbarian management relied as much as possible on gift giving to buy off potentially restive frontier peoples rather than using the far more expensive military alternative.

In 1820 the khan of Kokand reacted to the end of these subsidies by supporting Jahangir, a descendant of the Kashgar Muslims, who had fled to Kokand during the Qianlong emperor's conquest of Xinjiang. Jahangir declared a *jihad,* collected several hundred followers, and raided Altishahr. Qing troops soon expelled Jahangir, but in 1826 he took Kashgar, Yingeshar, Yarkand, and Khotan in Western Xinjiang. The Qing dynasty responded by deploying a 20,000-man banner force that relieved the cities in 1827. Qing troops captured Jahangir alive in 1828, brought him to Beijing for the rituals

In traditional China, the punishment of criminals was harsh. Torture to extract confessions was common. The capital punishment known as *lingchi* (meaning "slow slicing" or "death by a thousand cuts") was used in China from roughly 900 until it was finally abolished in 1905.

of presenting and receiving captives, and then executed him by slicing. According to Han burial practices, the body should remain whole at death; therefore, slicing constituted the most ignominious as well as the most painful form of death.

Never again would these ceremonies be performed, because the Qing banner forces would never have another untarnished victory over frontier peoples. Han provincial forces, not banners, put down the great rebellions of the mid-nineteenth century. The 1828 victory marked the end of the military competence of the Manchu banner forces.

In this nineteenth-century photograph, note the number of laborers carrying water up the stairs. Until recently, many Chinese—especially those in rural areas—did not have access to running water or indoor plumbing.

The mid-nineteenth-century rebellions decimated the Manchu garrisons in their path, while the Russian invasion of Manchuria in 1900 during the Boxer Uprising destroyed the remaining Manchu banner strongholds in their ancestral homeland. The Boxer Uprising also entailed the destruction of the Manchu palace guards in Beijing. Thus, 1900 marked the end of a very long and gradual process of Manchu military decline that began with the Yongzheng emperor's seizure of the throne while his brother Yinti was off at war.

The Jiaqing emperor misidentified the problem. Where he saw the need to economize, the actual problem concerned inadequate growth of the money supply. The Qing dynasty unknowingly allowed foreign markets to determine China's money supply. After 1775, China relied almost exclusively on Latin America for silver imports. Silver was crucial because tax payments, large transactions, and transactions between provinces were all calculated in silver. Although most people used copper coins for ordinary transactions, they had to convert these coins into silver to pay their taxes, and the rate of exchange fluctuated, depending on foreign silver supplies. These supplies collapsed with the Napoleonic Wars (1796–1815) and the ensuing independence movements in Latin America (1810s–1830s). This meant that the copper–silver exchange ratio started to increase in the late Qianlong period, which in effect constituted a tax increase for Chinese peasants, who had to scrounge up increasing amounts of copper coins to pay their taxes in silver. People from all walks of life felt the impact of the resulting dampening of economic growth.

Conclusions

At the end of the eighteenth century and the beginning of the nineteenth century, increasing governmental corruption and decadence, rapid population growth, growing competition for scarce arable land, and increasing impoverishment combined to create an environment conducive to rebellion. The Manchu empire suffered a series of ethnic and antidynastic uprisings at this time: The Miao, White Lotus, Eight Trigrams, and Muslim rebellions all threatened the empire, while their suppression further burdened the poor and further strained government finances. Each of these many problems exacerbated the others. Collectively, they typified periods of dynastic change. Faltering dynasties generally exhibited blatant corruption, falling rural living standards, and growing domestic unrest. The Eight Trigrams rebels, in particular, breached the imperial palace in the empire's own capital. Han beliefs in the dynastic cycle reinforced these negative trends.

After the failed Eight Trigrams Rebellion, the Qing attempted to reassert central control over the empire, but on the cheap by eliminating corruption and curtailing outlays. This produced savings in the short run but false economies in the long run. Unintended consequences included increasing isolation of the emperor from his empire and a weakening Manchu hold over both South China and the imperial periphery. Laxness on the frontiers allowed the restive to foment rebellions whose suppression proved far more costly than any initial savings from canceled tribute missions or imperial tours. Over the long run, the Qing conquest of Xinjiang constituted a growing drain on the empire's weakening finances. Because the Muslim population never accepted Qing rule, rebellion remained endemic from the time of the conquest on, entailing enormously expensive garrisoning and periodic suppression.

Not only were China's Manchu emperors increasingly separated from their empire, but they were also increasingly isolated from their original source of power: their military. After the reign of the Kangxi emperor, banner forces gradually atrophied since emperors and princes no longer led them. As the Manchus were a tiny ethnic minority, this further isolated them and made the emperor ever more a captive of his Han civilian bureaucracy. The weakening Manchu military base became progressively more incapable of counteracting this process. By 1900 there were no effective banner forces left.

Finally, the government's decision not to placate the khan in Kokand also set a precedent for the future treatment of European merchants, as did the strict limitations on seagoing trade. Just when the Qing leadership decided to curtail interaction along the frontiers and to funnel trade along the Grand Canal, the Europeans demanded a greater share of the ocean-going coastal trade. Ultimately, the Jiaqing and Daoguang emperors' reforms, instead of consolidating Manchu control, actually heightened tensions. These soon erupted along China's lengthy maritime frontiers just at the time when the Manchus were most ill-prepared to deal with them.

Thus, prior to the escalating European aggression of the mid-nineteenth century, the Qing empire became overextended both territorially and economically. The problems of imperial overextension, corruption, overpopulation, environmental stress, impoverishment, and domestic unrest were systemic in scope and internal in origin, meaning that the European powers had nothing to do with these early indicators of dynastic decline. Prior to the Congress of Vienna in 1815, the European powers remained preoccupied with a competition for empire in North America and a desperate fight to win the Napoleonic Wars. Only afterward did England turn its attention eastward beyond India.

BIBLIOGRAPHY

Dreyer, June Teufel. *China's Forty Millions: Minority Nationalities and National Integration in the People's Republic of China* Cambridge, MA: Harvard University Press, 1976.

Elman, Benjamin A. *A Cultural History of Civil Examinations in Late Imperial China.* Berkeley: University of California Press, 2000.

Feuerwerker, Albert. "Economic Trends in the late Ch'ing Empire, 1870–1911." In *The Cambridge History of China*, vol. 11, edited by John K. Fairbank and Kwang-ching Liu, 1–69. New York: Cambridge University Press, 1980.

Ho, Ping-t'i. *Studies on the Population of China, 1368–1953.* Cambridge, MA: Harvard University Press, 1959.

Jones, Susan Mann and Philip A. Kuhn. "Dynastic Decline and the Roots of Rebellion." In *The Cambridge History of China*, vol. 10, edited by Denis Twitchett and John K. Fairbank, 107–162. New York: Cambridge University Press, 1978.

Kim, Hodong, *Holy War in China: The Muslim Rebellion and State in Chinese Central Asia, 1864–1877.* Stanford, CA: Stanford University Press, 2004.

Kuhn, Philip A. *Rebellion and Its Enemies in Late Imperial China: Militarization and Social Structure, 1796–1864.* Cambridge, MA: Harvard University Press, 1970.

Lipman, Jonathan N. *Familiar Strangers: A History of Muslims in Northwest China.* Seattle: University of Washington Press, 1997.

Naquin, Susan. *Millenarian Rebellion in China: The Eight Trigrams Uprising of 1813.* West Haven, CT: Yale University Press, 1976.

Perdue, Peter C. "Culture, History, and Imperial Chinese Strategy: Legacies of the Qing Conquests." In *Warfare in Chinese History*, edited by Hans van de Ven, 212–87. Leiden: Brill, 2000.

Perkins, Dwight H. *Agricultural Development in China, 1368–1969.* Chicago: Aldine, 1969.

Powell, Ralph L. *The Rise of Chinese Military Power, 1895–1912.* Princeton, NJ: Princeton University Press, 1955.

Wang Yeh-chien. *Land Taxation in Imperial China, 1750–1911.* Cambridge, MA: Harvard University Press, 1973.

Will, Pierre-Etienne. *Bureaucracy and Famine in Eighteenth-Century China.* Translated by Elborg Forster. Stanford, CA: Stanford University Press, 1990.

Zelin, Madeleine. *The Magistrate's Tael: Rationalizing Fiscal Reform in Eighteenth-Century Ch'ing China.* Berkeley: University of California Press, 1984.

NOTES

1. Cited in Stephen Owen, *An Anthology of Chinese Literature: Beginnings to 1911.* (New York: W. W. Norton, 1996), 1147. From AN ANTHOLOGY OF CHINESE LITERATURE: BEGINNINGS TO 1911 edited and translated by Stephen Owen. Copyright © 1996 by Stephen Owen and The Council for Cultural Planning and Development of the executive Yuan of the Republic of China. Used by permission of W. W. Norton & Company, Inc.

2. Albert Feuerwerker, "Economic Trends in the late Ch'ing empire, 1870–1911," in *The Cambridge History of China,* vol. 11, edited by John K. Fairbank and Kwang-ching Liu (New York: Cambridge University Press, 1980), 61.

3. Cited in Mayfair Mei-hui Yang, *Gifts, Favors, and Banquets: The Art of Social Relationships in China* (Ithaca, NY: Cornell University Press, 1994), x. Yang is quoting James Legge's translation in his volume entitled *The Sacred Books of the East,* vols. 27, 28 (Oxford: Oxford University Press, 1885).

4. Quoted in Philip A. Kuhn, *Rebellion and Its Enemies in Late Imperial China: Militarization and Social Structure, 1796–1864* (Cambridge, MA: Harvard University Press, 1970), 40–1.

Chronology

1600	Establishment of the East India Company
1635	East India Company starts trading with China
1729	First Chinese anti-opium law; bans coastal smuggling
1735	Yongzheng emperor dies; Qianlong emperor assumes the throne
1757	Western commerce
1784	Commutation Act lowers the British duty on trade; imports surge
1793	Macartney Mission arrives in Beijing
1796	Qianlong emperor retires; Jiaqing emperor assumes the throne
1799	Death of Qianlong emperor
1805	Western books and contact with Westerners forbidden
1811	Westerners forbidden to live in the interior or to missionize
1813	Eight Trigrams Revolt
	Ban on private sales of opium targets consumers
	British East India Company loses its Indian trade monopoly
1820	Jiaqing emperor dies; Daoguang emperor assumes the throne
1830	Empirewide prohibition against poppy cultivation and opium production
1831	Opium investigations of yamen personnel
1834	End of East India Company monopoly on China trade
	Trading offices set up in Guangzhou
1838	Lin Zexu named imperial envoy to Guangzhou
1839–42	Opium War
1839	Lin Zexu confiscates and destroys opium
	Battle of Kowloon
	Battle of Chuanbi
1840	British blockade southern coast and mouths of Yangzi and Yellow rivers
	Qishan replaces Lin Zexu
1841	British reduce forts at Guangzhou
	Convention of Chuanbi
	Sanyuanli Incident
	British expeditionary forces sail north up the Chinese coast
1842	Manchu banner forces fight fiercely at the Battle of Zhapu
	Zhenjiang falls, cutting Yangzi River and Grand Canal trade
	Treaty of Nanjing
	Hong Kong ceded to Britain
	Five treaty ports opened

7

Expanding Commercial Relations with the West

The long walls of the Bogue forts,
So strong, so thick;
The great general's confident air,
So full of pride.
But the black barbarians came from afar,
Invaded this land of peace,
Nightly belched their cannon-fire
Before our towered gates.

Admiral Guan falls and dies in bitter battle,
Sitting, looking, none to save,
Who can pity him?

The women of Guangdong weep to the gods above.
White bones lie across fields,
Flocks of sheep asleep.[1]

Sun Yiyan (1815–95),
official and scholar

During the seventeenth and eighteenth centuries, the Manchus demonstrated great competence at creating and managing a vast empire and dealing with foreigners. During the nineteenth century, their surprising inability to deal with obstreperous Western traders highlighted an unexpected military incapacity, bringing into the open the underlying systemic crisis. Ever since, generations of Chinese and Westerners have disputed the nature of the problem, its underlying causes, and the necessary remedies. The rising European powers of the nineteenth century constituted the greatest security threat to China since the Mongol conquest in 1279. Until the 1830s, China held unchallenged the balance of power in East Asia, but the Industrial Revolution irrevocably changed this world. The Chinese, whose long and venerable educational tradition had been based on precedent and historical analogy, found such changes difficult to fathom, as indicated by

their many references to Westerners in official documents as "unfathomable." China, which had always sought to deal with barbarian threats bilaterally and sequentially, suddenly faced simultaneous threats from numerous directions. Worse still, unlike past barbarians, the new set coordinated with each other, neutralizing the traditional Han method of barbarian management. Westerners were eagerly seeking foreign markets and products for trade, resulting in an ever-increasing number of European merchants bent on commerce with China. The British, in particular, saw unencumbered free trade as mutually beneficial for themselves and their trading partners. They created a navy and a merchant marine second to none to protect and transport this global trade. China's weakness, Europe's strength, and the growing importance of trade produced a combustible mix. In the Opium War (1839–42), China's first war with a Western European power, the internal weakness of the Qing dynasty became evident for all to see. This put the Qing dynasty, in the minds of many Han Chinese at least, in the declining phase of the dynastic cycle, which encouraged domestic revolt, thus reinforcing the downward trend. Western influence did not precipitate China's decline, but it did accelerate that decline.

I. The Tea Trade and the Silver Inflow

The root cause of the Opium War was trade. On the British side, an imperial-licensed corporate monopoly, the East India Company, dominated the China trade, while on the Chinese side, there was a state-sponsored monopoly, the Cohong or more simply Hong. Initially, Britain's insatiable demand for tea fueled this trade, but beginning in the late eighteenth century, the Chinese demand for opium became increasingly important. (See the feature below.) By the 1830s, the Chinese believed that their purchase of opium, mainly imported from British India, was causing a large outflow of silver currency that was distorting the copper-to-silver exchange rate. This silver drain and, by extension, the opium trade at its root greatly concerned the Qing.

OPIUM CULTIVATION AND CONSUMPTION

The first written record of opium consumption in China dates to the Han dynasty (206 BC–220 AD), while its cultivation in China began over 1,000 years ago during the Tang dynasty (618–907 AD). The tributary states of Siam (Thailand), Java (Indonesia), and Bengal (India) included opium as part of their tribute. Before the Qing dynasty, the Chinese ingested opium to treat diarrhea, coughing, asthma, aching, and malaria and other illnesses, but in the final years of the Ming dynasty, when traders from Portugal, Spain, and Holland brought tobacco, recently introduced from the Americas, the Chinese soon followed the Dutch practice of smoking a combination of tobacco and opium. Even before the Qing conquest, the Manchus had become tobacco smokers, so that, by the early Qing, opium was no longer consumed primarily as a medicine but instead as a luxury item by the elite.

Opium consumption fit Chinese cultural patterns of a highly elaborated cuisine and a ritual of tea consumption, both of which emphasized careful preparation and cooking and required specialized utensils. Like opium, food and tea were also closely associated with the treatment and prevention of illnesses. Opium sets, like tea sets and fine dinnerware, became objets d'art, including beautifully crafted pipes. Opium consumption also fit Chinese norms of behavior in that unlike alcohol, which created drunkards, opium did not produce addicts who became obstreperous. In the eighteenth century, opium increasingly became a recreational drug and popular aphrodisiac.

Taiwan had a flourishing opium culture, so the Qing conquest of the island in 1683 helped spread the habit among Qing solders and administrators. Until the early eighteenth century, recreational opium consumption remained confined to the Chinese coast. In the late eighteenth century, the British East India Company became increasingly involved with the trade, and during the reign of the Qianlong emperor (r. 1736–95) the habit became widespread among the wealthy living in cities and along the coast. This spread of opium consumption throughout the elite became a powerful harbinger of imperial decline since it set the stage for other social groups to emulate the practices of the elite.

From the imperial Court, the habit spread inland and down the economic scale during the early nineteenth century. This was the reign of the Qianlong emperor's son, the Jiaqing emperor (r. 1796–1820). In the following generation, the Daoguang emperor (r. 1820–50) became an opium addict. This was confirmed in the 1950s, when the Communist government exhumed his body to find pervasive evidence of opium in his bones, documenting opium use at the Court, where its consumption spread through the staff of eunuchs who prepared the opium for Manchu aristocrats. The Empress Dowager (1835–1908) also smoked opium, but allegedly in moderation.

As opium became an increasingly valued product, commercial guilds, seafarers, and significant numbers of Hakka entered into the opium trade. It remained extremely expensive for many years, which effectively limited its market to the rich and those engaged in the trade. The foreigners saw the opportunity to mass market it. Extensive domestic cultivation probably began around 1800 and had become large enough to compete with smuggling by 1830, causing prices to tumble and making the drug accessible to the poor. The foreigners, however, delivered their opium to Guangzhou, and from there, Chinese merchants marketed it throughout China. Commercial guilds emerged specializing in the opium trade. Domestically produced opium would increase from perhaps 10 percent of the value of imported varieties in the 1850s to 30 percent by the 1870s and perhaps 50 percent by the 1880s. The value of the trade was staggering. Each opium chest sold for $700 Mexican dollars (a large silver coin), so that the 60,000 chests imported in 1847 brought an unbelievable profit of $42 million.

By the time of the Daoguang emperor's reign, opium had become an essential product for the leisure class and part of social occasions, where good meals ended with an opium pipe instead of an aperitif. Opium-smoking literati spread the habit throughout the provincial administration. Opium consumption infiltrated markets, shops, guildhalls, tea houses, theaters, brothels, and, of course, opium dens. During the 1830s, opium consumption spread throughout the urban population, greatly increasing imports and, in the process, creating a silver drain problem. As many as 10–20 percent of central government officials, 20–30 percent of local officials, and 50–60 percent of private secretaries (very-low-level officials) consumed opium. Opium consumption had also become widespread in the military, making the army and banners far less effective forces. By the time of the Opium Wars, opium

Continued

By 1905, an estimated one-quarter of all male Chinese were addicted to opium. In 1906, the "Ten Year Agreement" stated that by 1917, both imported and domestic opium sales would be phased out. Customs officials worked hard to stop illegal smuggling of opium, and all captured stocks, like these in Nanjing taken during 1919, were destroyed. However, China's domestic turmoil precluded efficient enforcement. Only following the 1949 creation of the People's Republic of China was the opium ban effective.

had become an item of mass consumption. In 1869, for example, Beijing consumption rates were estimated at 40–60 percent of the general population and 30–40 percent of bannermen. Opium use was particularly prevalent among merchants, officials, and prostitutes, with estimated consumption rates of 80, 90, and 95 percent, respectively. Opium consumption became closely associated with gambling houses and brothels. For the poor employed in hard physical labor, like rickshaw coolies, whose consumption rate approached 100 percent, opium relieved their exhaustion and muscular pain.

Opium would create its own economic regime. The *lijin* tax was introduced in 1853 and soon became a transit tax, which meant that *lijin* revenues depended increasingly on the opium trade. The opium trade largely financed the Huai and Xiang armies, the Self-strengthener armies that put down the mid-nineteenth-century rebellions. Even though Britain moved out of the opium trade by the early twentieth century, Japan moved right in. The late-Qing effort to eradicate opium cultivation was highly successful, resulting in vastly reduced poppy fields from 1906 to 1917, but opium soon became a major source of warlord revenue, so that in the 1920s China accounted for four-fifths of the world's opium production. At that time, farmers cultivated opium nationwide. The most productive provinces were Yunnan, Guizhou, and Sichuan; other major producers included Gansu, Shaanxi, Henan, Anhui, Fujian, and Manchuria. The highest-quality domestic opium came from Yunnan, Guizhou, Sichuan, and Gansu. Indian opium, however, was still preferred and sold at a much higher price than the locally grown product.

In the Republican period, warlords and revolutionaries alike used opium to finance their armies, while opium merchants expanded the banking system to finance the trade. Opium was also a major source of income for Sun Yat-sen's third Guangzhou government and the Nationalist Party. The Nationalist suppression of opium production actually constituted an opium monopoly that maximized their cut of the drug income. The opium monopoly soon became closely associated with tax farming and licensing agreements. Opium was also a source of income for the Communists in Yan'an, the heart of the poppy-growing country. The Nationalists could not eradicate opium because of the dependence of their warlord coalition and themselves personally on the income. There is evidence that the People's Republic of China continued to export opium into the 1950s. Today opium cultivation helps fund Muslim separatists in Xinjiang.

Apart from the silver drain in the Qing period that skewed the internal silver-to-copper money exchange rate and wreaked economic havoc as a result, poppy cultivation exacerbated famines since poppies tended to be planted instead of grains, resulting in smaller food harvests in bad years. In the 1930s it cost over $100 per year to sustain an opium addict, while all other living expenses could be met for $50 per year and a low-paying job might provide $50 per annum. Thus, one incapacitated addict, who failed to bring in the $50 but cost $150 to sustain, could absorb the incomes produced by three other family members. Worse still, opium promoted a culture of lawlessness and strengthened the underworld. The huge sums involved meant lavish bribes that undermined the rule of law.

Opium smoking took time, and the greater the addiction, the more time it took. Because opium changed the biochemical balance in the body, addicts required increasing doses to compensate for their reduced endorphin production while producing the desired high. When deprived of opium, addicts faced intense withdrawal symptoms not simply from the lack of the high, but more fundamentally because opium consumption had undermined their ability to produce endorphins, the body's internal painkillers. Therefore, withdrawal produced agony. The physical effects of withdrawal set in eight to ten hours after the last dose of opium, starting with dizziness and progressing to intense sweating, drooling, and eye-watering. Within twenty-four hours, vomiting, diarrhea, terrible abdominal pains and headaches, persistent sneezing, and yawning set in that prevented sleep and produced hallucinations. There was no cure for opium addiction, only treatment, so that former addicts remain vulnerable to readdiction. Over time addicts lost weight, strength, and attention span, although they could live to old age.

The Qing government closely regulated foreign trade. The trade was a South Chinese phenomenon, centered in the city of Guangzhou (Canton), located in Guangdong province. Many Han Chinese were eager to engage in this lucrative trade. The Manchus, however, saw the matter not only in economic but also in political terms. Beyond the economic ramifications of a growing trade imbalance, there was also the issue of political control over the Han of South China. The imperial Court exerted its control through the governor-general—also known as the "viceroy"—of Guangdong and neighboring Guangxi provinces, and through the governor of Guangdong province. Under these officials was an imperial appointed superintendent of maritime customs, known to foreigners as the "Hoppo." Beneath the Hoppo were Chinese merchants licensed to trade with foreigners, collectively called the "Cohong" from the Chinese *gonghang*, meaning "combined merchant companies," and later just called the "Hong." At the bottom of the pyramid were the foreign merchants, who could only deal with the Hong merchants.

Until 1834 the British trade was also a monopoly. The East India Company had been founded in 1600, began trading with China in 1635, and monopolized that trade for the next two centuries. Although silk was originally the most important Chinese export, tea soon dominated Sino–British trade. Between 1700 and 1751, the East India Company's yearly shipments of tea to London increased from 92,000 pounds to

well over 2,700,000 pounds, a 3,000 percent rise. Britain also exported large quantities of tea to its colonies, where the tea tax was used to finance the colonial government and ultimately became a pretext for rebellion. As a consequence of the Boston Tea Party and the ensuing American Revolution, American merchants began to trade directly with China in 1784.

Throughout the early 1780s, the value of British imports and exports remained roughly balanced, although usually in China's favor. With the passage of the Commutation Act on 20 August 1784, however, the British duty on tea dropped from 119 percent to only about 12–13 percent to compete with the recently independent Americans. In this way, the Opium War and the American Revolution were linked. Within the space of a year, British tea imports doubled, and then tripled within the decade. This surge outstripped British exports, so that the trade deficit quickly reached almost 500,000 pounds sterling per year. Since the trade was conducted in silver, the British trade deficit resulted in a significant outflow of British silver to China. This coincided with the Qianlong emperor's frequent trips to South China and also helped defray the costs associated with garrisoning the expanded empire in the Junggar and Tarim basins.

The trade imbalance caught the attention of the British government, which sent Lord Macartney to China in 1793 to negotiate changes in the trading system. The British desired an end of the Hong system, a less arbitrary tariff system, additional ports opened to trade, and permission to station a British representative in Beijing. These British commercial intentions did not fit the five-category framework of Qing rites defining the emperor's public life. Trade negotiations did not naturally fall into the Qing categories of auspicious rites entailing lunar sacrifices to heaven and earth, felicitous rites when the emperor addressed his civil servitors, martial rites when he addressed his warriors, guest rites when he interacted with other sovereigns, or funerary rites for imperial relatives. The closest category of guest rites focused on the choreography of the meetings of sovereigns, not on negotiations between imperial representatives on behalf of their subjects.

While the Qing tried to adjust their ceremonies to fit the odd commercial preoccupations of the British, this did not overcome the fundamental disconnect between the two systems for managing the interaction with outsiders, what the West categorized under foreign relations and the Chinese under ritual. The Qianlong emperor granted two audiences to Macartney, who presented gifts, but refused to kowtow. He would only kneel on one knee in keeping with the British custom to kneel before kings. To the Manchus, whose high officials customarily referred to themselves as "slaves" and prostrated themselves before their emperor, this British break with ritual constituted a gross affront. It demonstrated the British rejection of the emperor's ritual responsibilities to maintain harmony in the cosmos.

The Qianlong emperor demonstrated his benevolence by allowing Macartney to live to tell the tale, but he dismissed British trade demands. He famously wrote back to King George III of England that the items offered by his "tribute envoys" had been accepted, but he explained that "we have never valued ingenious articles, nor do we have the slightest need of your country's manufactures."[2] In the manner of all tributary missions, the emperor heaped sufficient gifts on Macartney to expect him to return home in gratitude. But Macartney represented not simply himself or the household of his sovereign, but also the commercial interests of a much broader cross section of British subjects, whose interests were not in the least bit advanced by the Qianlong emperor's generous gifts. When the Chinese closed the door to negotiations for an ameliorated trading regime, the British looked for solutions elsewhere. To reverse the trade deficit, they sought a product that was in high demand in China. Opium, which was produced in India, seemed to be the answer. Opium was widely available in China, but was relatively expensive and poor in quality because most of it was either produced locally or transported overland from India and Southeast Asia.

The Chinese valued opium as a medicine to treat diarrhea and other conditions, to a reduce fevers, and to use as an aphrodisiac. In 1729, the Yongzheng emperor promulgated the first law in Chinese history to ban opium, but it limited the ban to coastal smuggling. It did not apply to either the cultivation or consumption of opium, but focused solely on the maritime trade. The Jiaqing emperor became concerned when he discovered opium addiction among the palace guards and eunuchs at the time of the Eight Trigrams Rebellion. That year, 1813, he promulgated statutes for the first time targeting consumers. The problem continued to worsen. In 1830, his successor, the Daoguang emperor, broadened the focus of the prohibition to include domestic production, banning both the opium trade and opium poppy cultivation. In 1831 a probe targeted yamen personnel for opium consumption. Increasingly, opium was cultivated by minority peoples on China's periphery, particularly the Yi, Dai, and Miao minorities in the South and Southwest and the Muslims of Xinjiang.

By 1832, opium addiction among growing numbers of soldiers had undermined their military effectiveness. Despite the increasing legal penalties for opium use, distribution, and production, there remained a lively opium trade in China, including both domestic and imported varieties. Beijing directed penalties more against smokers and dealers than against cultivators. Local governments soon saw opium as a way out of their financial distress. Taxes on opium later became a major percentage of *lijin* collections, first implemented in the early 1850s, and Chinese farmers became major opium producers. This created powerful interest groups backing opium cultivation.

As long as opium addiction remained confined to the Han population, in a way it contributed to Manchu minority rule by inducing passivity. However, key addict populations included the imperial court and banner forces, which undermined the ability of the dynasty to rule. By the 1870s, the opium addiction rate was estimated at 10 percent of the total population. Opium had become an essential source of local revenue that funded both the provincial armies raised to put down the midcentury rebellions and the modernization projects of the Han innovators of the late Qing period, the so-called Self-strengtheners (see Chapter 10). This range of vested interests made eliminating opium cultivation and smoking very difficult.

II. The Opium Trade and the Silver Outflow

After the British realized that there was a huge market for Indian opium, a triangular trade soon developed: Britain traded manufactured goods for Indian opium and then

Table 7.1 The Opium Trade

Year	Yearly Average of Chinese Opium Imports for the Decade
1800s	3,921 chests
1810s	4,568 chests
1820s	10,361 chests
1830s	26,003 chests
1840s	40,484 chests
1850s	68,607 chests
1860s	63,900 piculs
1870s	68,600 piculs
1880s	72,300 piculs
1890s	59,700 piculs
1900s	50,500 piculs
1910s*	13,333 piculs

Note: One chest ≈ 140 pounds; 1 picul = 133$\frac{1}{3}$ pounds.
*Data for the 1910s run only from 1911 to 1916.

Source: Man-houng Lin, *China Upside Down: Currency, Society, and Ideologies, 1808–1856* (Cambridge, MA: Harvard University Press, 2006), 89.

traded the opium for Chinese tea. (See Tables 7.1 and 7.2.) Prior to the Macartney mission, during the period from 1775 to 1800, raw cotton from India accounted for about one-half of British sales to China, while opium came in a poor second, constituting only 15 percent of the trade. After the failure of Macartney's mission and, in particular, after the death of the Qianlong emperor in 1799, the opium trade took off.

It is unclear why opium was in such demand in China. It had not been previously, nor was it in particular demand in either Japan or the West, where it was both available and legal but not generally coveted. Only in 1868 did Britain require that products containing opium be labeled as poisons, but there were still no restrictions on its sale. The increasing British opium trade coincided with the collapse of China's Latin American silver supplies, so perhaps the Chinese associated their economic distress with the opium trade, not with the actual problem, the disruption of their money supply.

The halt of Latin American silver exports skewed the copper-silver ratio in China, thereby imposing a major tax increase on a population already experiencing a declining standard of living from overpopulation relative to a static arable land supply. It also severely eroded the incomes of officials and soldiers. From 1808 to 1856, silver-to-copper coinage appreciated by 250 percent, and the total silver outflow constituted about one-fifth of the coinage previously in circulation. Supplies did not start to recover until 1850. In the meantime, as the economy suffered, so did the Qing mandate of heaven. These economic distortions fueled both corruption by those on top and rebellion by those below. The disruption in the silver trade also affected the British, who could no longer acquire enough silver to finance their taste for tea and so relied on opium instead.

The de facto tax increase threatened many poorer peasants with the loss of their small holdings. The inability to pay taxes became such a serious problem in the lower Yangzi River region that government officials, such as the soon-to-be-famous Lin Zexu, reported fictitious natural disasters to qualify for debt relief. Lin, like many others, saw the opium trade not primarily as a moral or public

Table 7.2 British Imports from China and British Possessions (1854–7) (£ Million Sterling)

Country	1854	1855	1856	1857
British East Indies	10.67	12.67	17.26	18.65
China	9.13	8.75	9.42	11.45
British North America	7.19	4.69	6.85	6.34
Australia	4.26	4.47	5.64	5.77
British West Indies	3.98	3.98	4.57	5.22
British South Africa	0.69	0.95	1.50	1.79
New Zealand	0.04	0.03	0.10	0.16

Source: J. Y. Wong, *Deadly Dreams: Opium, Imperialism, and the Arrow War (1856–1860) in China* (Cambridge: Cambridge University Press, 1998), 342. Reprinted with permission of Cambridge University Press.

health problem of opium consumption, but as a balance-of-payments problem producing a disastrous silver outflow. He recommended in 1833: "We must grow opium to keep silver home."[3]

The silver shortage became acute in the 1830s, coinciding with the military campaigns in Xinjiang. For a time, the Manchus considered legalizing opium imports but taxing them at the high rate levied on foreign medicines. If the trade continued to thrive, in the long run this would have increased the wealth of southern Han merchants and could have possibly weakened North China's control over South China. The government had a more immediate problem: Opium consumption had infiltrated military units in South China, which were also involved in opium distribution, raising the specter of compromised defenses in the South. Ultimately, the Daoguang emperor decided not to legalize opium, but instead to enforce stringent controls on the opium trade. In September 1836, he ordered the governor-general who oversaw the Guangzhou trade to eliminate all opium imports. When this official proved ineffective, in 1838 the emperor appointed a minister plenipotentiary to enforce the opium ban in Guangzhou. He chose Lin Zexu (Lin Tse-hsü) (1785–1850), an advocate of opium suppression and governor-general of Hubei and Hunan provinces. The result was war with Britain.

Lin Zexu was a Han loyal to the Manchu dynasty and intent upon clamping down on the Han merchants of Guangzhou, who over time had become increasingly independent of Manchu rule. Southern merchants resented the trading regime imposed by the North that diverted all foreign trade to the southern extremity of the Manchu empire in Guangzhou. They had to bear the costs of shipping their tea, silk, and other items hundreds of miles from where they were produced in Fujian, Anhui, and Jiangxi to Guangzhou, the only place where they could legally be sold to foreign merchants. They also resented the short trading season from October to January and the need to work through the Cohong, which undoubtedly took its cut from the profits. Therefore, both Han and Western merchants shared similar grievances over trade restrictions.

Lin, in addition to civil authority, had military authority as commander in chief of the Guangdong navy. He soon realized the superiority of the foreign ships and tried to avoid a direct military conflict. When this proved impossible, he claimed victories regardless of the actual outcomes. Initially, he tried to control the foreign traders by alternately suspending and restoring trade. In February 1839, the execution of a Chinese opium smuggler in front of the foreign-run factories in Guangzhou increased Sino–British tensions. In mid-March, Lin ordered foreign merchants to hand over their opium stocks and sign a pledge never to resume the opium trade. When they delayed, Lin blockaded the foreign factories. Captain Charles Elliot, the British chief superintendent, ordered the British merchants to hand over their opium chests to him, thereby making them British property. This meant that instead of facing individual British merchants, Lin was now dealing with the British Crown. Elliot turned over the chests to Lin, but the British sought compensation for the confiscated opium by sending an expeditionary force to China.

Han and Manchu officials were uninformed about Europe. They ignored the admonition of their greatest military strategist, Sunzi: "Thus it is said that one who knows the enemy and knows himself will not be endangered in a hundred engagements."[4] Chinese officials believed that Elliot's decision to give up the opium chests constituted a retreat, so they proclaimed victory. Under Lin's supervision, they confiscated and destroyed over 20,000 chests of opium, while the foreign factories in Guangzhou remained surrounded. Blockaded and unable to carry on business, the British merchants retreated from Guangzhou to British ships anchored off Hong Kong Island.

In midsummer, the situation became even more tense when British sailors on shore leave killed a local islander. The British refused Chinese demands to turn over the accused, citing the common practice in China of torturing prisoners to force confessions. Until the British delivered the guilty party, Lin forbade Chinese merchants from selling supplies to them. He further ordered that all local springs near Hong Kong be poisoned to deprive the British of potable water. This precipitated the first battle of the Opium War on 4 September 1839, when the British forced their way to Kowloon in search of supplies. It was a minor skirmish resulting in fewer than twenty deaths. Nevertheless, Chinese officials proclaimed this battle the first victory of what would later be referred to in Chinese histories as the "Six Smashing Blows" against the British navy.

This official misrepresentation of events set the pattern for the many foreign wars of the late Qing dynasty. The Qing Court declared the Opium War won. Soon after it backed down and agreed to Britain's peace conditions in August 1842. Because Chinese reports proclaimed victory despite the reality of defeat, the Chinese government and military learned few political or military lessons. This set in motion a pattern of defeat, denial, and complacency followed by yet another cycle of defeat. Alternate strategies could not be developed if past failures were not recognized, let alone analyzed. The importance of maintaining face made the appraisal of failure particularly difficult for the Chinese. The appraisal of failure was more difficult still for the Manchus from their tenuous position of minority rule during the declining years of the dynastic cycle.

III. The British Rejection of Sinification

Commissioner Lin Zexu's optimistic reports helped lull the Manchus into a false sense of security. The Daoguang emperor assumed that his forces were successfully repelling the British, so he made none of the much-needed military preparations that could have taken advantage of China's vast size and huge population and Britain's long sea lines of communication and limited naval assets. The Chinese analytical framework emphasizing historical analogies to explain current events left them poorly prepared. British behavior was not analogous to that of traditional barbarians, most of whom controlled land, not naval, forces and desired territory, not trade in mass-market consumer goods. Nor, like former barbarian invaders, were the British technologically and organizationally weaker than the Chinese. False analogies in combination with a reluctance to examine the reasons for China's inability to defeat the British left the Manchus unprepared to parry the threat.

Tensions remained high throughout September and October 1839. The British still refused to turn over the accused or sign the required Chinese bond pledging not to trade in opium. The bond stated that should opium subsequently be discovered aboard a ship, all cargo would be confiscated and the perpetrators executed. Elliot argued that not only did the bond interfere with free trade, but signing it constituted acceptance of the Chinese court system and its brutal punishments.

In late October 1839, a British ship defied the blockade. On 3 November a second ship also tried, but Elliot ordered one of his ships to fire a warning shot across its bow. Chinese war junks moved in to protect the foreign merchant ship. The ensuing Battle of Chuanbi (Ch'uan-pi or Chuenbi) involved Han junks fighting to protect a foreign ship, which had signed the Manchu's anti-opium bond, from other foreign ships trying to stop it from entering port. The Battle of Chuanbi was short and one-sided. Only a single British sailor was wounded, while the Chinese reported fifteen deaths and many more wounded. But official Chinese reports greatly exaggerated the British losses, giving the impression to the Court of another Chinese victory. The Chinese military strategy of delay falsely assumed that the British would remain in the South, but the British could leverage their maritime strength to attack directly the North.

This photo shows a steam paddle-wheel ship being loaded at a Chinese port. While Westerners were eager to buy Chinese goods, including tea, silk, and porcelain, the Chinese were restricted in what they could buy from the West. Western labor-saving devices—for example, steam power—were less desirable and necessary in a country like China, which had such a large population. The one foreign commodity that the Chinese were eager to buy turned out to be opium.

In the early 1840, tensions between Britain and China continued unabated. Commissioner Lin, having failed to force the foreign ships to halt their end of the opium trade, set his sights on the Chinese end. He now targeted Chinese smugglers, traders, and smokers. The British also had a policy aimed at their own nationals. In April, British warships blockaded Guangzhou, Xiamen (Amoy), the Ningbo coastline, and the mouths of the Yangzi and Yellow rivers. They focused on keeping foreign ships from entering Chinese ports, but in the process they also commandeered large Chinese ships, such as salt junks. By early July, they had impounded seven or eight such ships near Guangzhou.

The British realized that from South China they had little leverage over Beijing. Therefore, they designed a strategy to put pressure directly on the Manchu Court by deploying their navy northward up the Chinese coast. The Chinese had taken no countermeasures. By the early summer of 1840, a British expeditionary fleet was ready to move north.

The British force included twenty-two warships, twenty-seven transports, and 3,600 Scottish, Irish, and Indian infantry. On 4 July, it arrived at Zhoushan Island (Chusan), located to the south of Shanghai, and the next day occupied the island port of Dinghai, which, many years later, would become a major naval base for the People's Republic of China.

A smaller British force then moved farther north and on 9 August 1840 arrived at the mouth of the Beihe River, the waterway leading to the port of Tianjin (Tientsin) and from there on to Beijing. The Dagu (Taku) fortress guarded the river approach to Tianjin. Although the Daoguang emperor supported Lin's policies, the arrival of British troops in the vicinity of Beijing forced him to reconsider. There was a tentative agreement for talks, although the Manchus insisted that all negotiations take place in South China in an attempt to force the British back to China's frontiers. On 17 September 1840, the emperor replaced Lin Zexu with a Manchu official, Qishan. The emperor's strategy seemed successful, for on 25 September 1840 the British left Tianjin. Far from planning to meet British demands, the Daoguang emperor called up reinforcements, apparently believing that time was on his side, so that if he waited long enough, the British would either leave or become more compliant.

Meanwhile, in Guangzhou, Lin had already issued an edict offering the equivalent of $100 per corpse for British sailors, just $20 for the head, and as much as $5,000 for a live British ship's captain. The Chinese captured several unlucky foreigners and refused British and Portuguese demands for their release. (Some had fallen prisoner near the Portuguese settlement at Macao.) The Chinese deployed troops in the direction of Macao, but the British struck first on 19 August 1840, destroying Chinese stores and magazines before retreating back to their base. Although the British gained their objective and retreated in good order, Lin reported another "smashing blow" victory, only to learn in October 1840 that the emperor had summoned him to Beijing for trial. By the summer of 1841, he had been exiled to remote Ili in the far Western province of Xinjiang.

IV. Chinese Strategy and the First Opium War

The number of combatants involved in these first battles of the Opium War was tiny. Even the number of modern ships was small compared to the vast Chinese coastline. Yet, the consequences for the Manchus were enormous, because they showed their weakness. Lin Zexu's Manchu replace-ment, Qishan, initially took a more conciliatory approach to the British in keeping with the traditional barbarian management practice of alternating severe with more conciliatory treatment expressed in the idiom *en wei bing yong*, meaning "the proper combination of kindness and intimidation when dealing with subordinates." When the British took the two supposedly impregnable forts guarding Guangzhou's harbor in an hour and a half, Qishan negotiated and signed the Convention of Chuanbi (Chuenpi) on 20 January 1841. By this convention, Britain received possession of Hong Kong, compensation of $6 million for the destroyed opium, and the right to communicate directly with Chinese officials in Guangzhou. From the British point of view, this solved their problems and trade could return to normal.

Qishan's acceptance, however, was probably a delaying tactic, and Beijing later rejected the terms outright. Chinese officials in this period did not consider treaties to have the sanctity of law that they had for Western officials. In the Chinese legal system, the emperor's writ always ruled supreme and could supersede any legal instrument. Therefore, the Chinese did not consider legal agreements with foreigners to be binding. It took the Chinese several decades to appreciate the rigid Western understanding of treaties and international law. Differing interpretations of the role and flexibility of law continue to divide China and the West even today.

When the British realized that the emperor had no intention of implementing the Convention of Chuanbi, they took the Chinese forts along the sea approaches to Guangzhou in February 1841 and occupied the foreign factories in March. (See Map 7.1.) When the Chinese tried to retaliate in May, the British responded by sinking some seventy junks, destroying Guangzhou's shore batteries, and burning the waterfront. To save Guangzhou from an imminent British attack, the Chinese officials agreed on 27 May to pay the $6 million indemnity. The British appeared to have secured a complete victory. Only two days later, however, a relatively small incident at the nearby village of Sanyuanli convinced many Chinese that they would win the war. This incident entered Chinese lore as another great antiforeign victory, later glorified by the Chinese Communists as a victory of a citizens' militia against a foreign army. In fact, the Sanyuanli incident resulted in the death of one British private and the injury of an officer and fourteen men. The British threatened to attack if the Chinese failed to disband the militia, estimated at 10,000 to 12,000 men. Tensions eased as the militia dispersed, and on 1 June 1841 the British troops evacuated to their ships and departed.

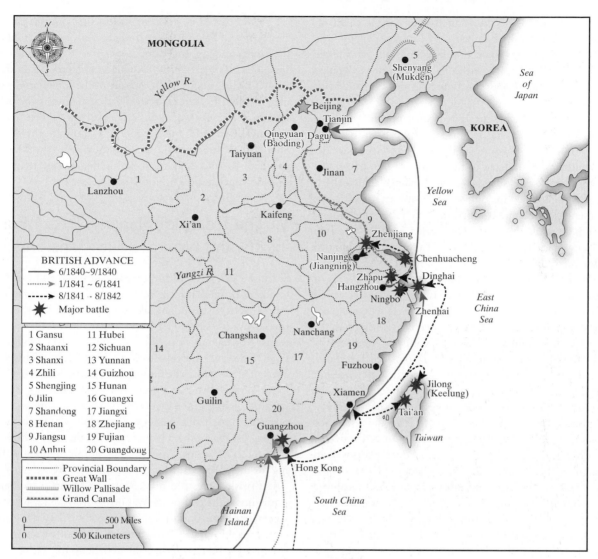

Map 7.1   First Opium War (1839–42)

To the Chinese, the British departure after the Sanyuanli incident seemed to demonstrate the efficacy of using local militias. This conclusion obscured the more accurate lesson, namely, the ability of superior Western firepower in combination with well-trained troops to repel a force ten times its size halfway around the globe. Instead, the Chinese drew the false lesson that willpower and moral superiority by themselves could defeat the forces of the industrializing West. Over the following months, as news of this incident spread, officials in neighboring provinces, such as the governor-general of Fujian and Zhejiang, implored the emperor to organize similar militias throughout China. In addition to relying on outdated weapons, the Chinese employed question-

able military tactics. Earlier, Lin had even tried to recruit "water devils," swimmers reputed to be able to remain at the bottom of the sea for hours at a time, from among the fishermen of Guangzhou.

Sinocentrism produced ignorance of the West and an assumption of cultural superiority that hindered the Chinese from responding creatively to the new military challenge. They actually had numerous policy alternatives. Instead of halting trade with Britain, they could have channeled it to sponsor their own internal development. Alternatively, the Manchus could have designed a military strategy to take the conflict inland in order to force the British to fight on Manchu terms, far away from their ships and supplies.

There was no need for the Manchus to engage them on the coast, where the British had an advantage. Finally, the Chinese failed to appreciate the deep divisions within the West and neglected to ally with one Western power against another. This was the way the European powers dealt with one another.

The traditional Chinese strategy presupposed a technologically inferior foe, who would succumb to Sinification. With the Industrial Revolution, this was no longer the case. Chinese officials floundered to fit Westerners into traditional but inappropriate categories. Historical analogy as an analytical framework entailed making apt comparisons between past and present. While some comparisons might be enlightening, the search for analogous situations created a tendency to find similarities where they did not exist. False analogies blinded the Chinese to the magnitude of the problem.

When Chinese officials rifled through their stores of analogies from their Classical educations, the closest would have been the Japanese marauders of the mid-sixteenth century or the Taiwan-based Zheng Chenggong (Koxinga) of the late seventeenth century, who had both unsystematically raided China's coastline until Chinese intransigence and passive resistance made the raids unprofitable. In the eighteenth century, many Chinese considered British activities to be analogous to the Japanese predations of the sixteenth century. Both groups came by sea bent on trade. The Chinese called the Japanese *wokou*, or "midget pirates," and continued to use this highly derogatory term in official documents well after the fall of the Qing dynasty. The analogy between Britain of the nineteenth century and Japan of the sixteenth proved to be singularly unhelpful during the Opium War, when Chinese officials assumed that China would have just as much leverage over the industrial British as over the preindustrial Japanese of the earlier era. This Chinese condescension backfired against a country armed with the equipment of the industrial age, and the West responded to Chinese intransigence not with compliance or remorse but with escalating aggression.

Lin Zexu and other Qing officials disregarded Sunzi's imperative to understand the enemy. They grossly underestimated the enemy's capabilities and failed to understand their enemy's real goal, which was to open China to free trade. Once Chinese officials made the crucial mistake of pigeonholing the British with pirates, the need to organize large-scale resistance disappeared. Pirates would have no capacity to threaten vital areas of China, so it would be more economical to outlast them by fighting on the remote maritime frontiers of China. Lin Zexu focused his attentions on fortifying the Guangdong coast with what he considered to be state-of-the-art defenses.

It did not seem to occur to Lin that the British might choose not to fight on his preferred terms, but to avoid these preparations by going directly for the jugular in Beijing. Imagine the shock of the Daoguang emperor when the arrival of British troops in the vicinity of the capital in the summer of 1840 indicated not only that Commissioner Lin's reports of victories were nonsense, but that the British might conceivably intend and be able to decapitate the dynasty. Such a dire threat cast a deep shadow over the Manchus' mandate to rule, and they capitulated rather than risk a showdown with such an unpredictable enemy.

V. The Treaty of Nanjing: Treaty Ports, Tariffs, and North–South Tensions

Since the 1840 expedition clearly had failed to force China to accept Britain's trading regime, the following summer the British sent a second naval expedition, which they reinforced by the summer of 1842. British military strategy focused on taking control of the Yangzi River, stopping all river trade, and thereby cutting China in two. This would also cut trade along the Grand Canal, which intersected the lower Yangzi River, and prevent crucial food supplies from reaching Beijing, thereby exerting direct pressure on the dynasty. Although this strategy succeeded, victory came at a higher cost than any previous battles of the war. Whereas the Han forces of South China seemed ambivalent about fighting for the Manchus, Manchu bannermen were determined. The British forces did not encounter Manchu bannermen until almost the end of the war on 14 May 1842, when they stormed Zhapu (Cha-p'u), in Hangzhou Bay close to the mouth of the Yangzi River, and on 21 July 1842 during the final major battle of the war at Zhenjiang (Chinkiang), which overlooked the Yangzi River at the intersection of the Grand Canal.

In all, British forces sustained over 1,500 casualties out of a total expeditionary force of 9,000. Although the British sent reinforcements from India, compared to the immensity of China, the force was tiny. If the Chinese had continued to exact casualties at that rate, they could have compelled the British to withdraw. But these banner forces seem to have been the exception, not the rule. Most Chinese forces in the Opium War fought poorly. The Han Chinese inhabitants of Zhenjiang displayed little determination to fight on behalf of the Manchus. Perhaps they saw the foreign invasion as one barbarian, the British, fighting against another, the Manchus. One account of this battle written by a Han observer displayed much more hostility to the Manchus than to the British.[5]

The Daoguang emperor, faced with the immediate loss of grain and other necessary foodstuffs and commodities for the capital, as well as the gradual erosion of Manchu power in South China, agreed to reopen negotiations. Once talks got underway, Qiying, the Manchu negotiator, warned the Court that failure to grant the British free trade might result in the loss of all of China south of the Yangzi River. Confronted with this possibility, the Manchus accepted most of the British demands.

The Treaty of Nanjing, signed on 29 August 1842 and ending the Opium War, abolished the Cohong trading system in Guangzhou, set tariffs, regulated the opium trade by banning smuggling, ceded Hong Kong Island to the British in perpetuity, and opened the port cities of Guangzhou, Xiamen (Amoy), Fuzhou, Ningbo, and Shanghai to foreign trade. Britain promised to make Hong Kong a free and open port for ships of all countries. The agreement stipulated that any future privileges and immunities granted by China to other foreign powers would likewise accrue to England. By means of this so-called most-favored-nation clause, Britain sought to ensure that no other nation gained an advantage in China, as Russia had previously. France and the United States used the Treaty of Nanjing as the model for their treaties signed with China in 1844.

Most-favored-nation clauses meant that the demands extracted by one power accrued to all. Such clauses, which proliferated in China's many nineteenth-century treaties, undermined Beijing's traditional method of barbarian management. In the past, China had maintained bilateral relations with its neighbors in order to prevent them from combining forces, which allowed China to defeat enemies sequentially. The European powers, however, since the Treaty of Westphalia, increasingly used international law to regulate interstate relations. This system was inherently multilateral and inclusive. It denied any one power the grand-puppeteer role that China had long assumed in its tributary system. Table 7.3 shows the rapidly increasing number of treaty ports opened under these agreements.

Later generations of Chinese used the term "unequal treaties" to describe the treaties defining the emerging treaty port system because these documents granted privileges to foreigners in China that were not reciprocated by foreign governments to visiting Chinese delegations and merchants. Later generations of Chinese considered the treaties unequal because the European powers imposed them by force. However, many treaties between European powers were also imposed by force, often as a result of war.

While much attention has focused on Western imperialism in China, the Chinese have skirted the issue of the Manchu occupation of Han China and the lands of surrounding frontier peoples. The primary Chinese beneficiaries of the European trading regime were Han Chinese, not Manchus. The concentration of great wealth in Han Chinese hands in South China, far from the seat of Manchu control in Beijing, constituted a growing threat to the Manchu hold on power. Thus, the Opium War actually comprised a nesting set of conflicts: the Sino–British conflict over trade, the struggle of localities to escape central control, the North China struggle to retain control over South China, and the Manchu struggle to dominate the Han and frontier peoples. This complexity worked to the advantage of the British, who never had to fight a unified China. In fact, there would be no unified China in the form of a nation-state until after the Communist Revolution in 1949.

The tension between North and South China is longstanding. North and South China have not always been united, nor have they historically spoken the same language. Although the Qin dynasty (221–206 BC) incorporated parts of Guangdong into the Chinese empire, the South remained largely autonomous. A three-and-a-half-century period of disunity followed the Han dynasty (206 BC–220 AD), during which there was a variety of northern and southern dynasties. The Sui and Tang dynasties then reunited a Chinese empire for over three centuries before their territories again fragmented. Between 909 and 971 AD, the provinces of Guangdong and Guangxi were independent, forming the separate kingdom of Nanhan. The Song dynasty (960–1279) never fully reacquired all of the northern territories of the Han empire up to the Great Wall.

The last three dynasties, under the Mongols (Yuan), Han (Ming), and Manchus (Qing), respectively, reunited North and South China, but underlying divisions were reflected in linguistic differences. Mandarin was the language of North China and of rulership from Beijing, whereas the South was the home of numerous other languages, such as Cantonese, Shanghaiese, and Taiwanese. Han have called these languages "dialects" to suggest that they are variations on a theme, but linguistically they are as distinct from each other as are the languages of Western European. Calling them "dialects" is a political statement intended to bolster the case for Chinese unity and for the historical continuity of the Chinese polity. Alternatively, calling them "languages" indicates a Han Chinese empire centered in the North, which has long dominated the South.

In many ways, the merchants of Guangzhou had more interests in common with the British than with their Manchu overlords. According to the Qing government, China had no need to trade with the West. It considered foreign trade as a means to mollify barbarians, not to enrich the

Table 7.3   Opening of Treaty Ports (1843–94)

Date Opened	City (*Pinyin*)	City (traditional spelling)	Treaty	Signatories (in addition to China)
1843	Guangzhou	Canton	1842 Treaty of Nanjing	Britain
1843	Xiamen	Amoy	1842 Treaty of Nanjing	Britain
1843	Shanghai	Shanghai	1842 Treaty of Nanjing	Britain
1844	Ningbo	Ningpo	1842 Treaty of Nanjing	Britain
1844	Fuzhou	Foochow	1842 Treaty of Nanjing	Britain
1852	Yili	Kuldja	1851 Ili-Tarbagatai Trade Agreement	Russia
1852	Tacheng	Tarbagatai	1851 Ili-Tarbagatai Trade Agreement	Russia
1860	Shantou	Swatow	1858 Treaty of Tianjin	Britain, France, United States
1861	Tianjin	Tientsin	1860 Treaty of Beijing	Britain, France
1861	Yingkou	Newchwang	1858 Treaty of Tianjin	Britain
1861	Kashi	Kashgar	1860 Treaty of Beijing	Russia
1861	Zhenjiang	Chinkiang	1858 Treaty of Tianjin	Britain
1861	Kulun*	Urga	1860 Treaty of Beijing	Russia
1862	Hankou	Hankow	1858 Treaty of Tianjin	Britain
1862	Yantai	Chefoo	1858 Treaty of Tianjin	Britain, France
1862	Jiujiang	Kiukiang	1858 Treaty of Tianjin	Britain
1862	Danshiu	Tamsui	1858 Treaty of Tianjin	France
1863	Tainan	Tainan	1858 Treaty of Tianjin	Britain
1876	Qiongzhou	Kiungchow	1858 Treaty of Tianjin	Britain, France, Russia
1877	Wenzhou	Wenchow	1876 Yantai Convention	Britain
1877	Wuhu	Wuhu	1876 Yantai Convention	Britain
1877	Yichang	Ichang	1876 Yantai Convention	Britain
1877	Beihai	Pakhoi	1876 Yantai Convention	Britain
1881	Jiayuguan	Suchow	1881 Treaty of St. Petersburg	Russia
1881	Tulufan	Turfan	1881 Treaty of St. Petersburg	Russia
1881	Hami	Hami	1881 Treaty of St. Petersburg	Russia
1881	Wulumuqi	Urumchi	1881 Treaty of St. Petersburg	Russia
1881	Gucheng	Kucheng	1881 Treaty of St. Petersburg	Russia
1881	Wuliyasutai†	Uliassutai	1881 Treaty of St. Petersburg	Russia
	Kebuduo‡	Kobdo	1881 Treaty of St. Petersburg	Russia
1887	Gongbei		1887 Draft Treaty with Portugal	Portugal
1889	Longzhou	Lungchow	1887 Commercial Agreement	France
1889	Mengzi	Mengtze	1887 Commercial Agreement	France
1891	Chongqing	Chungking	1876 Yantai Convention	Britain
1894	Yadong	Yatung	1893 Tibet Treaty	Britain

*Ulaanbaatar, Mongolia. For a continuation of this table, see Table 12.1.

†Ulyasutay, Mongolia.

‡Hovd, Mongolia.

Source: Zhang, Haipeng, ed. *Zhongguo jindai shigao dituji* (Shanghai: Dituchubanshe, 1984), 83.

Chinese and particularly not the Han merchants of South China, whose interests the Manchus considered expendable. Expanding trade potentially set the economic development of North and South China on different paths. The Han merchant Wu Bingjian (Howqua) amassed a fortune so vast that he was reputed to have been the richest man in the world during the early nineteenth century. Such wealth implied power and autonomy that the Manchus regarded as dangerous.

Merchants, outcasts of the traditional Confucian hierarchy, had no input into policy making, while the Manchus regarded South China separatism as a far more deadly threat than British commerce. Many of the so-called unequal provisions of the Treaty of Nanjing, such as opening other port cities in South China, actually furthered Han interests, especially of those engaged in foreign trade. In particular, the elimination of smuggling and the orderly collection of tariffs meant that profits from this trade suddenly became available to provincial governments instead of to corrupt functionaries, who had formerly accumulated great wealth by allowing the smuggling to continue unopposed. By means of the Sino-British treaty, therefore, the Han of South China regained a degree of autonomy that they had lost following the Qing conquest of China. There was now a British counterbalance to the Manchu occupation. Over time, this new situation exacerbated the preexisting North–South split; seventy years later, it would be the southern regions of China that led the rebellion that finally overthrew the Manchus.

Conclusions

The collapse of the international silver trade, China's growing weakness, Europe's gathering strength, and the increasing importance of trade culminated in conflict. During the 1830s, the Chinese government became particularly concerned about the impact of the opium trade, not so much out of anxiety about addiction, but because of the destabilizing consequences of the silver outflow associated with the growing trade deficit. The domestic scarcity of silver had an inflationary impact on the land tax, so the trade imbalance in effect raised taxes. The growing tax burden eroded rural prosperity, causing unrest, and eventually threatened Qing rule. Unrest then increased the government's requirements for silver to pay for the troops to put down domestic rebellion, sending China on a downward trajectory.

China's misidentification of the underlying economic problem, a skewed money supply, with the opium trade had tragic consequences. The solution to economic distortions caused by hemorrhaging international silver supplies lay in adjusting tax rates to accommodate the reduced money supply or reintroducing one of China's greatest inventions: paper money. Foreign war at a time of increasing internal distress only made matters worse.

Basic philosophical and cultural differences over trade lay at the heart of Sino-British conflict. For the Chinese, trade was an instrument to prevent barbarian incursions, not a way to economic prosperity. For Europeans, trade was an end in itself. It produced wealth. The British stood behind free trade and rejected state interference beyond the assessment of modest tariffs. With the development of increasingly complex trading webs, such as the triangular trade among Britain, India, and China, state interference by any one country threatened the interlocking system.

A primary goal for the British was to trade with the Chinese not as a subordinate but an equal in status, as presupposed by international law. For the Chinese, this constituted a frontal attack on their conception of foreign relations and proper social relations as expressed by the tributary system, with the emperor in charge of mediating the cosmic order. Equality threatened not simply the Qing dynasty but the entire dynastic system. The mandate of heaven required the emperor to maintain ritual continuity in order to harmonize the cosmos. British demands shattered the ritual continuity for dealing with barbarians and, in doing so, threatened the legitimacy not only of Manchu rule, but of the entire Confucian imperial system. The Chinese and European systems for ordering international relations were mutually exclusive. This meant that increasing contact would bring increasing conflict until one system won or some new hybrid emerged.

The issue of equality remained highly contentious, poisoning Sino–Western relations. Since the Qing system did not accommodate equality, diplomatic negotiations quickly broke down, and the Europeans responded with superior force. Military defeat could not be disguised for long. During the Opium War, the Qing dynasty's internal weakness suddenly became clear for all to see. But Britain did not win the Opium War; rather, China lost it. Even with Britain's technological superiority, given the vastness of China's territory, population, and distances, China should have won.

The Japanese carefully studied these events. A decade after China's defeat, the United States put Japan in an identical position when Commodore Matthew Calbraith Perry arrived in Tokyo Bay with his "Black Ships." When the West insisted that Japan too open up to trade, the Japanese chose a radically different strategy of accommodation and careful study of the West. Unlike the Qing, who clung to power, the last Tokugawa shogun stepped down, accepting the shame for defeat by the West and opening the way for others to engage in creative reforms. The Manchus, however, could not assume their population's loyalty. On the contrary, they very carefully kept their population divided to make minority rule possible. Given this precarious situation, the Manchus maintained their mandate to rule to the extent that they remained faithful caretakers of a civilization. Ethnicity prevented the Manchus from adopting the role of radical reformers, the path followed in the late nineteenth century by Japan's highly successful Meiji reformers.

During the Qing dynasty, the retrospective view of knowledge as emanating from antiquity hamstrung China, especially once the Scientific Revolution rolled into the Industrial Revolution of the nineteenth century. The emphasis of the imperial examinations on a static body of knowledge, an exclusively literary focus, and rote memorization as the measure of ability could not effectively counter the national security challenges spawned by the Industrial Revolution. The traditional Chinese educational system taught that Han civilization in the end always triumphed. Either the Han conquered the barbarian directly through military force or they conquered indirectly through Sinification, transforming the barbarian into a Chinese. Sinification was a one-way street so that time would always be on China's side. While dynasties came and went, China remained eternal and invincible. In reality, Sinification was not necessarily a complete process. The Manchus functioned within Han institutions and manipulated Han culture in order the rule the Han, but they retained their separate ethnic identity.

The Opium War came at a time when Manchu military prowess had already been in large measure compromised from a century of neglect and when more and more Han anticipated the end of the dynasty. While the West did not create the Qing's problems, it exposed them for all to see. If the Manchus had dared to give a Han George Washington unified command over Han and Manchu forces, such a general would have made the Forbidden City his first target. The Manchus divided in order to rule. This worked when they were facing technologically inferior foreign foes, but it was disastrous against an industrializing West. Far from moderating Western demands, resistance only increased them. Thus, the Qing policy of halfhearted and chaotic resistance delivered the worst possible outcome.

BIBLIOGRAPHY

Bello, David Anthony. "The Venomous Course of Southwestern Opium: Qing Prohibition in Yunnan, Sichuan, and Guizhou in the Early Nineteenth Century." *Journal of Asian Studies* 62, no. 4 (November 2003): 1109–42.

———*Opium and the Limits of Empire: Drug Prohibition and the Chinese Interior, 1729–1850.* Cambridge, MA: Harvard University Press, 2005.

———*Opium and the Limits of Empire: Drug Prohibition and the Chinese Interior, 1729–1850.* Cambridge, MA: Harvard University Press, 2005.

Chang Hsin-pao. *Commissioner Lin and the Opium War.* New York: W. W. Norton, 1970.

Elleman, Bruce A. *Modern Chinese Warfare, 1795–1989.* London: Routledge, 2001.

Fairbank, John K. *Trade and Diplomacy on the China Coast: The Opening of the Treaty Ports, 1842–1858.* 2 vols. Cambridge, MA: Harvard University Press, 1953.

———"The Creation of the Treaty System." In *The Cambridge History of China,* vol. 10, edited by Denis Twitchett and John K. Fairbank, 213–65. Cambridge: Cambridge University Press, 1978.

Fay, Peter Ward. *The Opium War 1840–1842.* Chapel Hill: University of North Carolina Press, 1975.

Graham, Gerald S. *The China Station: War and Diplomacy 1830–1860.* Oxford: Clarendon Press, 1978.

Hevia, James L. *Cherishing Men from Afar: Qing Guest Ritual and the Macartney Embassy of 1793.* Durham, NC: Duke University Press, 1995.

Inglis, Brian. *The Opium War.* London: Hodder and Stoughton, 1976.

Morse, Hosea Ballou. *The International Relations of the Chinese Empire.* Vol. 1. Shanghai: Kelly and Walsh, 1918.

Polachek, James M. *The Inner Opium War.* Cambridge, MA: Council on East Asian Studies, 1992.

Slack, Edward R., Jr. *Opium, State, and Society: China's Narco-Economy and the Guomindang, 1924–1937.* Honolulu: University of Hawai'i Press, 2001.

Spence, Jonathan. "Opium Smoking in Ch'ing China." In *Conflict and Control in Late Imperial China,* edited by Frederic Wakeman, Jr., and Carolyn Grant, 143–73. Berkeley: University of California Press, 1975.

Wakeman, Frederick, Jr. *Strangers at the Gate: Social Disorder in South China 1839–1861.* Berkeley: University of California Press, 1966.

———"The Canton Trade and the Opium War." In *The Cambridge History of China,* vol. 10, edited by Denis Twitchett and John K. Fairbank, 163–212. Cambridge: Cambridge University Press, 1978.

Waley, Arthur. *The Opium War through Chinese Eyes.* London: George Allen & Unwin, 1958.

Zheng Yangwen. *The Social Life of Opium in China.* Cambridge: Cambridge University Press, 2005.

NOTES

1. The Bogue is the nineteenth-century English name for Humen (literally, the Tiger's Mouth Strait) or the Bocca Tigris located in Guangdong province. Geographically, it refers to the mouth of the Zhu or Pearl River. Qing forts located at the Bogue defended the river approach to Guangzhou (Canton). Admiral Guan Tianpei had been in charge of defending these approaches during the first Opium War but was killed in battle along with over 400 of his men. Cited in Frederick Wakeman, Jr., *Strangers at the Gate: Social Disorder in South China 1839–1861* (Berkeley: University of California Press, 1966), 11. Copyright © 2000, The Regents of the University of California.

2. Alain Peyrefitte, *The Immobile Empire,* Jon Rothschild, trans. (New York: Alfred A. Knopf, 1992), 291.

3. Quoted in Man-houng Lin, *China Upside Down: Currency, Society, and Ideologies, 1808–1856* (Cambridge, MA: Harvard University Press, 2006), 288–9.

4. Sun Tzu, *Art of War,* Ralph D. Sawyer, trans. (Boulder, CO: Westview Press, 1994), 179.

5. Athur Waley, *The Opium War Through Chinese Eyes* (London: George Allen & Unwin, 1958), 209.

Thematic Chronology (1842–1911)					
Decade	**Politics**	**Economy**	**Diplomacy**	**Society**	**Culture**
1840s	Daoguang (r. 1820–50) Xianfeng (r. 1850–61) Creations of provincial armies (1852, 1854, 1862)	Yellow River changes course, massive flooding (1855)	Opium War (1839–42) Commercial treaty with Russia (1851) Arrow War (1856–60) Border treaty with Russia (1858)	Taiping Rebellion (1851–64) Nian Rebellion (1851–68) Panthay Rebellion (1855–73)	Spread of Christianity
1860s	Establishment of Zongli Yamen (1861) Tongzhi (r. 1861–75) Establishment of College of Foreign Languages (1862) Guangxu (r. 1875–1908) First official embassy to Europe (1876)	Manufacture of first Chinese steamship (1865) Self-strengthening Movement (1860s–95)	Border treaty with Russia (1864) Russian occupation of Ili (1871–81) Japanese annexation of Ryukyu Islands (1879)	Donggan Rebellion (1862–73) Xinjiang Rebellion (1862–78)	British burn Summer Palace (1860) Tongzhi Restoration First students sent abroad to study go to the United States (1872)
1880s	Xinjiang (1884) and Taiwan (1885) become provinces Hundred Days' Reform (1898)	First railway (1881)	Sino-French War (1883–5) Sino-Japanese War (1894–5) Scramble for Concessions (1895–8)		First students sent to Japan (1896)
1900s	Late Qing reforms (1901–11) Death of Cixi (1908) Xuantong (r. 1908–11) Wuchang Uprising (1911)	Plan to nationalize railways	Russian occupation of Manchuria (1900–5) Russo-Japanese War (1904–5)	Boxer Uprising (1899–1900)	

Part II

Dynastic Decline and Collapse, 1842–1911

Part II focuses on the years of decline between the mid-nineteenth century and the fall of the dynasty. Civil wars and foreign wars, in combination with increasing overpopulation and corruption, sent the Qing dynasty into a steep decline. Chapter 8 describes the Taiping Rebellion, a Han attempt to overthrow the Manchus that almost succeeded. This upheaval caused the deaths of over 20 million Chinese and ravaged the central provinces. Simultaneously, Britain and France fought a second Opium War, the Arrow War, to enforce the Treaty of Nanjing. The Qing used the Western barbarians to help suppress the internal rebellions, offering the Europeans a favorable settlement to the Opium War in return for military aid against the Taipings.

Chapter 9 examines secondary rebellions, primarily secession movements by minorities who fought along the periphery of the Qing empire. These coincided with the Taiping Rebellion and included three Muslim rebellions—the Panthay, the Donggan, and Xinjiang Rebellions—and a Han attempt in eastern China to overthrow the Manchus—the Nian Rebellion. Once the Manchus overthrew the Taipings, they defeated the other rebellions sequentially. Had the rebels coordinated, the Qing dynasty would have fallen.

Chapter 10 examines the reform efforts of loyal Han provincial officials to save the dynasty. The so-called Self-strengthening Movement led to the adoption of Western military technology and organization and a westernized institution for conducting foreign affairs. In this period, China sent its first embassy to the maritime powers. But the reforms were highly selective and primarily intended to preserve traditional values. The Chinese looked to tradition to save the dynasty. This period was known as the Tongzhi Restoration in reference to the Manchu attempt to restore virtuous Confucian rule.

Chapter 11 describes tensions with the West as a series of crises in the 1870s and 1880s further undermined the dynasty. They include Western outrage over the murders of their subjects in China and the Chinese rivalry with Japan over Taiwan, with Russia over Xinjiang, and with France over Vietnam. Qing success in pressuring the Russians to withdraw from Xinjiang led to misplaced self-confidence when dealing with France, whose victory in the Sino-French War ended China's tributary relationship with Vietnam.

Worse was to follow. Chapter 12 focuses on the First Sino-Japanese War, which effectively ended the tributary system by depriving China of its most important tributary, Korea. The war also overturned the traditional balance of power when Japan, much to the surprise of the world and to the utter shock and dismay of China, defeated China. The great powers responded to Qing incapacity with the so-called scramble for concessions, in which each sought to carve out spheres of influence at the expense of the others.

Chapter 13 discusses the Han resistance to the growing foreign presence in China. The Boxers led an uncoordinated uprising of poorly armed throngs that small numbers of well-equipped Western, Russian, and Japanese troops rapidly defeated. As in the Opium Wars, Chinese resistance led to even more onerous foreign intrusions, this time including a huge indemnity both to cover the damage and to serve as punishment. With the Boxers' failure, the faltering Qing dynasty had exhausted all traditional national security strategies. Attempts at modernization without westernization had failed.

After the Boxer Uprising, the Qing attempted to follow the Japanese path to modernity by pursuing some degree of westernization. This is the topic of Chapter 14.

In the early twentieth century, the Manchus initiated far-reaching and very un-Confucian reforms. They westernized their educational, their military, and, to a lesser degree, their governmental institutions. It turns out that they had been correct in their reluctance to adopt such changes: The newly created Han military overthrew the Manchus within the decade. The fall of the dynasty in the 1911 Revolution concludes Part II.

DRAGON BOAT FESTIVAL

The Duanwu Festival is held on the fifth day of the fifth month of the lunar calendar. This usually corresponds with the summer solstice, or the longest day of the year in the Northern Hemisphere. Special teams race boats bearing dragon heads. While long celebrated in Hong Kong, Taiwan, and prerevolutionary China, Duanwu was celebrated in the PRC for the first time as a public holiday only in 2008.

The Dragon Boat Festival (*Duanwujie*) is one of the three most important festivals in China, which include the Chinese New Year and the Autumn Moon Festival. Held in late May or early June, this is perhaps China's most well-known festival in the West, mainly because of the colorful teakwood boats sporting a hand-painted dragon's head at the prow and dragon's tail on the stern.

    The festival honors the scholar-official Qu Yuan (340–278 BC). Although the accounts vary, most agree that Qu Yuan served King Huai (329–299 BC) of the Chu during the Warring States Period. Prime Minister Qu enjoyed the full confidence of his sovereign until Qu objected to extending the state by force. King Huai banished him. Qu then wandered the Hunan countryside collecting legends and writing poetry. During these wanderings, he wrote one of the greatest poems in Chinese history, entitled "The

Continued

Lament," which describes his search for a prince willing to follow wise counsel: "I marvel at the folly of the king, / So heedless of his people's suffering." The poem foreshadowed his own suicide: "Since in that kingdom all my virtue spurn, / Why should I for the royal city yearn? / Wide though the world, no wisdom can be found. / I'll seek the stream where once the sage was drowned."[1]

According to legend, Qu Yuan never regained the king's favor. On the fifth day of the fifth moon, clasping a stone to his chest, he plunged into Hunan's Miluo River. In a vain attempt to save him, a local fisherman furiously paddled from the shore, creating the historical basis for the dragon boat race. The fisherman then scattered rice dumplings in the water to prevent the river dragons from eating Qu Yuan's body. Later, the local people threw cooked rice into the water as a sacrifice for Qu Yuan, but fearful that fish would eat it instead, they stuffed the rice into a long section of bamboo. This gradually evolved into the custom of wrapping rice in bamboo leaves stuffed with bean paste, nuts, and vegetables.

The modern-day festival focuses on the boat races. Each dragon boat has a crew of eighteen paddlers, a steersman, and a drummer to keep pace. Competing teams race along a straight course varying from 250 to 1,000 meters in length. If all twenty team members work in unison, the dragon boat can ride above the water on the crest of the wave created by its bow. A seasoned dragon boat crew rows at a rate of seventy to eighty strokes per minute and can travel at speeds of up to ten miles per hour.

NOTES

1. Qu Yuan, "Li Sao (The Lament)," Yang Hsien-yi and Gladys Yang, trans., http://www.cs.uiowa.edu/~yefeihe/poetry/chin_poems.html, 4, 10.

Chronology

1839–42	First Opium War
1842	Treaty of Nanjing; five ports opened to foreign commerce
1850	Death of the Daoguang emperor; Xianfeng emperor assumes the throne
1851	Ili Commercial Treaty with Russia
	Taiping Rebellion
	Taipings proclaim a new dynasty
1852	Zeng Guofan organizes the Xiang Army in Hunan
1853	Wuchang falls to the Taipings
	Anqing falls to the Taipings
	Nanjing falls, becomes Taiping capital of Tianjing
	Northern Expedition threatens Beijing
	Western Expedition retakes Hankou, Hanyang, and Wuchang
1854	Northern Expedition in retreat
	Zeng Guofan retakes Wuchang
1855	Defeat of the Northern Expedition
1856	Internal fighting in the Taiping capital
	Defeat of the Western Expedition
	Arrow incident
1856–60	Arrow War
1857	British and French take Guangzhou
1857–63	Taiping Sichuan Expedition
1858	British and French take Dagu and Tianjin
	Treaty of Aigun (Russia)
	Treaties of Tianjin (United Kingdom, France, United States, Russia)
	Xiang Army retakes Jiujiang
1859	Dagu Repulse
1860	Taipings take Suzhou and threaten Shanghai
	Anglo–French force retakes Dagu and Tianjin and approaches Beijing
	Xianfeng emperor flees to Chengde
	British and French troops reach Beijing and burn Yuanming Yuan
	Treaties of Beijing (United Kingdom, France, United States, Russia)
1861	Death of Xianfeng emperor; Tongzhi emperor assumes the throne
	Xiang Army retakes Anqing
	Ningbo and Hangzhou fall to Taipings
1862	Taiping attack on Shanghai
	Li Hongzhang organizes Huai Army
	Xiang Army and Ever-Victorious Army clear Shanghai environs
1863	Taipings lose Suzhou
1864	Taipings lose Hangzhou
	Hong Xiuquan commits suicide
	Taipings lose Nanjing
	Execution of remaining Taiping leaders
	Treaty of Tarbagatai (Russia), trade and boundary

Civil War and Foreign Intervention

8

My hand grasps the killing power
in Heaven and earth;
To behead the evil ones, spare the just
and ease the people's sorrows[1]

Hong Xiuquan (1813–64),
leader of the Taipings

The Taiping Rebellion (1851–64) attempted to replace the Manchus with the Taipings' own religious and social system. It ravaged the central provinces of China, killing an estimated 20 million. Simultaneously, the second Opium War, known as the Arrow War (1856–60), broke out with Britain and France. As in the first Opium War, the Manchus lost, but following their defeat they combined forces with the Westerners against their far more dangerous enemy, the Taipings. To do so, China created its first foreign-officered modern land force, known as the Ever-Victorious Army, while Han provincial governors created semiautonomous forces that proved highly effective against the Taipings. These were Zeng Guofan's Xiang Army and Li Hongzhang's Huai Army. Such Han-led armies gradually shifted the balance of force within China away from the Manchus to the Han Chinese and from the capital to the provinces.

I. North–South Tensions and the Origins of the Taiping Rebellion

By the mid-nineteenth century, China's population growth meant increasing competition for arable land between the dominant Han majority and the empire's minority groups. Simultaneously, the Manchus were becoming ever more incapable of maintaining order within their own tribe, as indicated by the declining military capabilities of the banner forces. Without credible coercive powers, the Qing could not maintain order in the empire. Secession movements on the imperial periphery and Han agitation within the imperial core areas threatened Manchu rule. This chapter will focus on the Taiping Rebellion (1851–64), the greatest of the nineteenth-century upheavals.

Unlike the brief period of unrest under the Jiaqing emperor, these civil wars lasted for almost thirty years. Their human toll was staggering even by modern standards of carnage. Tens of millions of Chinese noncombatants died, crops were ruined, and famine spread. The devastation in China occurred prior to development of the means of mass slaughter after the Industrial Revolution. Together these civil wars ravaged large sections of the heavily agricultural and commercial South as well as lands on the imperial periphery.

The Taiping Rebellion was a South China attempt to overthrow North China rule. Tensions between North and South China were long-standing. (See Table 8.1.) South China had been the last bastion of Ming loyalties. Secret societies such as the Triads had long opposed Manchu rule. In terms of banner forces, the South was the least well garrisoned at a time when banner forces everywhere were in decline. It was far from Beijing, so that the South had more opportunity to revolt than areas closer to the capital. The Taiping Rebellion began among the poor of Guangdong and Guangxi provinces and particularly among the Hakka (*kejia*) minority. (See the feature on the next page.)

Over the years other Han groups had pushed the Hakka, like the Miao, ever farther south. As more and more Han migrated south, they continued to push the local inhabitants, such as the Zhuang, Miao, Hakka, Yao, and Li tribes, onto marginal lands. In response, these original inhabitants periodically rose up against

Table 8.1   Differences between North China and South China

	North China	**South China**
Population	ancient population center core area of Han culture comparatively uniform ethnicity language: Mandarin	populated by southward migration from the Han core area numerous ethnic groups language: many different dialects
Agriculture	four- to six-month growing season one to two crops per year erratic rainfall, often inadequate comparatively poor soil relatively low yields key crops: gaoliang, millet, wheat	nine- to twelve-month growing season two to three crops per year adequate year-round rainfall fertile soil high yields key crops: rice and beans
Housing	mud-walled housing heated by brick beds (*kang*) wide city streets	woven bamboo-walled, thatched-roof housing narrow city streets
Seaboard	smooth coastline, poor harbors little fishing	rough coastline, many harbors abundant fishing
Trade	foreign trade by land	foreign trade by sea
Wealth	frequent droughts and famines	prosperous

Source: Based on Richard J. Smith, *China's Cultural Heritage: The Qing Dynasty 1644–1912* (Boulder, CO: Westview Press, 1994), 18. Smith divides North and South China along the thirty-third parallel to correspond with the course of the Huai River, bifurcating Jiangsu province and extending to the Qinling Mountains in southern Shaanxi province.

the central government, and so were particularly receptive to anti-Qing movements. South China had also borne the brunt of Western influence, since the maritime trade centered in the southern cities of Macao and Guangzhou. Missionaries had long been active in South China. Judging from the receptivity of South Chinese to the Christian-based teachings of the Taipings, they were influential. In the nineteenth century, many Hakka converted to Christianity, and the leader of the Taiping Rebellion was a Hakka Christian convert.

HAKKA MINORITY

"Hakka" is the Cantonese reading of *kejia*, meaning "guest people" or "strangers," indicating people from afar. Most Hakka now live primarily in the South China provinces of Guangdong and Fujian, Hong Kong, Taiwan, Singapore, Malaysia, Thailand, and Indonesia. Originally, they inhabited the Yellow River Valley straddling Shandong's borders with Anhui and Henan provinces. Although Han by ethnicity, they have a distinctive cuisine, language, and customs. They left North China due to severe persecution, particularly during periods of dynastic decline or foreign invasion. Major southward migrations occurred as a result of the expansion of the Western and Eastern Jin dynasties (265–420), the declining period of the Tang dynasty (618–907), the Jurchen invasion of the Northern Song dynasty (960–1126), the Mongol conquest of the Southern Song dynasty (1127–1279), and the Manchu conquest of the Ming dynasty (1368–1644). Each time, they fled farther south through the coastal provinces of China into increasingly marginal hill country.

In the final period of the Qing conquest of China during the late seventeenth century, the Manchus ordered the depopulation of the Fujian and Guangdong coast in order to defeat Zheng Chenggong, who had set up his base in Taiwan. This resulted in the deaths of many Punti, the local inhabitants ordered to move. To restore the population after the defeat of the Ming loyalists, the Qing encouraged not only the original Cantonese-speaking Punti inhabitants but also the Hakka to move to the coast. Tensions between the groups arose over a century later when dramatic population growth had created extreme land scarcity, culminating in bloody clan wars in Guangdong between 1855 and 1867 that devastated Hakka communities. Many Latin Americans of Chinese descent trace their ancestry to the losing side of these clan wars. Many converted to Christianity in the nineteenth century.

The Hakka survived repeated periods of persecution and forced migrations by relying on strong communal bonds. Lack of fertile land meant that Hakka men sought nonagricultural occupations, such as government or military service, leaving Hakka women to tend the fields. This meant an emphasis on education for men to pass the imperial examinations and unbound feet for women to engage in farm labor. In imperial times, Hakka women had more freedom than other Han women. The traditional dress of rural women included a crownless wide-brimmed hat with a cloth curtain shading the neck and face and a thigh-length jacket. They prepared the cuisine for which the Hakka are famous. Because of their inland and hilly location, fresh produce was not always available, and seafood was a rarity. Instead, their cuisine relies on such preserved foods as fermented bean curd and on easily stored items such as onions or pork—particularly fatty bacon—and stews. Their dialect betrays their origins, for it most closely resembles Mandarin, the dominant North China dialect, not Cantonese, the primary language of the South. Today Hakka comprise nearly two-thirds of the population of Guangdong province and a tenth of the population of Taiwan.

Hakka leaders figure disproportionately in Chinese history. Famous Hakka include Hong Xiuquan, the leader of the Taiping Rebellion; Sun Yat-sen, the founding father of the Republic of China; the Song family, which provided wives for Sun Yat-sen and Chiang Kai-shek; Deng Xiaoping, the leader of the Communist Restoration; Taiwan's first native-born president, Lee Teng-hui; and the founding leader of Singapore, Lee Kuan Yew. In the twentieth century, the only Han of equal influence in Chinese history were Mao Zedong and Chiang Kai-shek. Other Hakka mentioned in this textbook include Marshal Zhu De, whose leadership was vital for the Communist victory in the civil war; General Secretary of the Chinese Communist Party Hu Yaobang, who helped inspire the democracy movement of the 1980s; and Premier Li Peng, who was instrumental in crushing the movement.

The British victory over the Manchus in 1842 gave the Han of South China and many ethnic minorities hope that the Qing dynasty had finally lost the mandate of heaven and that a new dynasty would soon replace it. Belief in a dynastic cycle became a self-fulfilling prophecy as more and more Chinese perceived the Qing to be in decline. The Opium War not only increased tension between the Manchus and the British, but also widened fissures between the Manchus and the Han and between North and South China.

In addition to political tensions dividing North and South China, there were trade tensions. From ancient times, North China had been the center of political control, while South China remained the agricultural breadbasket. From the time of the Sui dynasty (581–618) on, the Grand Canal had been used to transport rice and grain from South to North China. As many as 12,000 barges were constantly in motion, providing Beijing with foodstuffs and wealth. Raw cotton and various manufactured goods were shipped south in return, but the flow of tax revenues was always north. During the Qing dynasty, the southern trade in effect funded South China's occupation by the North.

In keeping with the Treaty of Nanjing, foreign merchants opened five treaty ports along China's coast. The Daoguang emperor attempted to protect the internal canal system, so instead of a gradual transition from the canals to the cheaper sea routes, Qing resistance propped up the canal system until the Opium War settlements suddenly legalized sea trade. This meant that almost overnight the many day laborers who worked on the canals found themselves unemployed. These disgruntled workers were receptive to the Taiping message. The peasants in South China also had serious grievances. During the mid-nineteenth century, floods and droughts caused widespread famine. Beijing, with its creeping decadence and corruption, did not respond adequately. It failed to maintain the granaries necessary to prevent starvation. This meant more frequent famines. Many peasants interpreted the growing list of natural disasters as a sign that the Manchus had lost the mandate of heaven. Peasants initially flocked to the Taipings in search of food and shelter, but they soon adopted its anti-Manchu goals as well.

The Taipings cultivated this large constituency by promising the abolition of private property. They classified land by its productivity and apportioned it equally among the adult population, with children receiving half-allotments. The land allocation was subject to population changes and therefore was temporary, while any surplus production reverted to the state. The Taipings promised to create one vast commune. The Communists later made much of this land reform program, which was never widely implemented by the Taipings because of the constant fighting.

The merchants in South China were also disaffected with Manchu rule. Wealth accumulated through commerce was an unofficial and unsanctioned route to social mobility. Guangdong had long been a center of maritime trade with Southeast Asia and India. With the appearance of European traders in the sixteenth century, first the Portuguese city of Macao and later the Chinese city of Guangzhou became the center of China's ever-growing maritime trade with the West. Given the value of this trade, some southern Han Chinese supported Britain against their own Manchu-dominated government. The combination of ethnic minorities, Christian converts, unemployed laborers, disaffected peasants, and wealthy merchants made the Taiping Rebellion dangerous to the dynasty.

II. The Taiping Movement

The leader of the Taipings, Hong Xiuquan (Hung Hsiu-ch'üan, 1813–64), was born in Guangdong province into a Hakka family. As a young man, he studied calligraphy and the Classics in preparation for the imperial examinations, which he failed three times. In 1837, after his third failure, he fell ill and allegedly remained in a trance for forty days until God awakened him to appoint him supreme ruler of the world—a remarkable turnaround for a failed examination candidate. This divine illness became a face-saving explanation for his inability to pass the examinations, his subsequent shift in loyalties, and his rapid promotion to emperor elect.

Hong did not immediately act on these visions. For six years he worked as a teacher, continued his studies, and took and failed the imperial examination for a fourth and final time in 1843, the year after the first Opium War. This time he focused his frustrations on the dynasty. He believed that God had empowered him to overthrow the alien Qing and create a heavenly kingdom on earth. Those who failed the examinations had few legitimate outlets for their aspirations, and militant movements offered an alternative to frustration and submission. After the Opium War, Hong chose rebellion.

Hong's ideology was a mixture of Confucian and Christian ideas acquired from preparation for the imperial examinations and his exposure to European influence. He converted to Christianity in June 1843. Since he was unable to read English, his main source of information on Christianity was a series of nine Chinese-language pamphlets by the Protestant convert Liang Afa. Although the pamphlets presented a simplified version of Christianity, Hong concluded that heaven had sent them to reaffirm his earlier religious visions. Eventually, he claimed the exalted position of younger brother to Jesus Christ. Perhaps Hong believed that Christianity was an essential underpinning to European military power; this was certainly the prevailing European view.

Following his conversion, Hong immediately began to proselytize and quickly converted two of his cousins, Feng Yunshan and Hong Ren'gan (Hung Jen-kan). Like Hong Xiuquan, both were Hakka who had failed the imperial examinations and sought a new path to social mobility. Feng founded the religious organization that would grow into the Taipings and served as its military leader. Meanwhile, Hong Ren'gan remained in Guangdong until the late 1850s, but in 1859 he became active politically in the Taiping capital of Nanjing, renamed Tianjing or Heavenly Capital.

In 1846 Feng Yunshan organized the Society of God Worshipers, but Hong Xiuquan soon took charge of it. During 1847, he spent several months in a Guangzhou Baptist church studying with an American Protestant missionary, but they soon quarreled. Although the Taiping leaders often cited the Bible, Hong claimed that he alone had the authority to direct religious affairs on earth. The Taipings recognized Christ as their savior, made the Ten Commandments their central teachings, underwent baptism, and claimed to worship the Christian God, but they rejected the Trinity. Instead, they placed God the father at the pinnacle of a Confucian hierarchy, with Jesus Christ the son, second, and Hong the younger brother, third. After Hong's first son was born, in traditional Chinese fashion he made the boy the adopted son of the childless Jesus Christ. The boy called Jesus his "Heavenly Father" and Hong simply "Father."

Hong denounced the Confucian respect for the emperor because it usurped God to make the emperor an idol for worship. Although Hong's Christian ethics incorporated many Confucian traits, such as the Five Relationships (*wulun*)—between ruler and ruled, father and son, husband and wife, elder brother and younger brother, and between friends—he rejected Confucianism. This set the Taipings apart from previous antidynastic movements, which simply wanted to put themselves on the throne, and foreshadowed the revolutionary movements of the twentieth century.

A unique aspect of the Taiping ideology was their more equal treatment of women. In part, this reflected Hakka practices, which accorded women greater freedom. For the first time in Chinese history, women could take the civil service examination, hold government office, serve in the military, and obtain noble ranks. In the early days of the movement, women made up a large part of the armed forces. Although the Taipings promulgated puritanical laws, prohibiting gambling, prostitution, adultery, footbinding, slavery, concubinage, and opium, tobacco, and alcohol consumption, the senior leaders had harems and exhibited increasingly questionable morals. In the case of polygamy, Taiping leaders claimed to be following biblical sanctions. Unlike Han custom, they granted additional wives full social status as religious sisters of the primary wife.

In 1849 the Society of God Worshipers, based in Guangxi province, was rapidly evolving into an insurgency. The Taipings merged civil and military institutions to create an armed citizenry under the guidance of an emerging theocracy. By 1851, it evolved into an anti-Manchu revolution when Hong proclaimed himself Heavenly King, becoming a rival to the emperor in Beijing. Beginning in 1853, the Taipings established their own system of examinations at the district, provincial, and capital levels as well as separate military examinations. They tested an amalgam of Christian and Taiping teachings and opened the examinations to all. Their respect for education appealed to southern scholars and artisans, who often served in high positions within the movement.

Following Confucian traditions, the Taipings sought historical models. They based their social organization on that of the Qin dynasty, which first unified China in 221 BC, when they adopted a variation of the *baojia* system. Local officials were responsible for the actions of families, grouped into a hierarchy of combined units of 5, 26, 105, 526, 2,631, and 13,156 members. The Taipings organized a church for every unit of 26 families. It was hoped, though never fully implemented, that the churches would be used for public worship on Sundays and public education during the rest of the week.

Their land tenure system resembled a hybrid of the Well-Field System of the Zhou dynasty—in which the state distributed land equitably among families who collectively cultivated certain communal lands—and its successor system, the Equal Field System—in which the state owned all land and distributed it equitably for life tenure, reclaiming it upon the death of the cultivator. Later generations of Chinese Communists lauded the Taiping economic system as a forerunner of communism for its state ownership and distribution of property, as well as its state allocation of income and land on the basis of need without distinction based on sex. The Taiping economic and land distribution program was very popular because it gave impoverished people the use of land, the expectation of an income, and a greatly improved social status in a society based on equality.

Once the Taipings established their capital in Nanjing, where the Qing government had signed its treaty of submission to the British, they opened trade with Shanghai, located downriver at the mouth of the Yangzi. In return for tea and silk, foreign merchants provided basic necessities, luxury goods, and black market products such as weapons and ammunition. The Taipings coined their own money and collected customs on the river trade, but after Britain signed the Treaty of Tianjin with Beijing in 1858, the British claimed exemption from the Taiping customs. The Taiping government also made opium smoking a capital offense, but opium remained the most important Western trade commodity in China during the 1850s. When the Manchus legalized the opium trade as part of the settlement of the second Opium War (the Arrow War), foreigners began to support the Manchu suppression of the Taiping movement.

III. The Taiping Capital in Nanjing

Unlike the British, who had the limited goal of improving trade, the Taipings had the unlimited goal of overthrowing the Qing dynasty. While Beijing could negotiate a treaty with the British, there was no negotiating with the Taipings. Hong Xiuquan and his cousin, Feng Yushan, focused on creating a strong military to overthrow the Manchus. As early as 1844, they traveled to Guangxi province in search of a suitable base for their future

army. In the manner of Confucian scholars, Feng looked retrospectively through Chinese history in search of an ancient model for his military. Again he found one in China's founding dynasty. He subdivided armies of 13,155 men into divisions, brigades, companies, platoons, and squads; enforced discipline through corporal punishment, public shaming, beating, or loss of rank; and imposed a strict military code, emphasizing loyalty to the movement and to the supreme leaders. Even enemies, such as General Zeng Guofan (Tseng Kuo-fan), came to admire the Taiping determination and military structure and modeled their own armies on those of the Taipings.

An initial position of weakness forced the Taipings to innovate: They allowed Hakka women to fight alongside men and appealed to disaffected Han to join them. They focused on the capture of the three sister cities of Hankou, Wuchang, and Hanyang, located on the Yangzi River at the confluence of its most important tributary. (See Map 8.1.) They took Hanyang and Hankou in December 1852 and Wuchang in January 1853. This put them in control of the upper Yangzi River and its trade, cutting off China's interior from the coastal regions.

Although the Taipings considered heading straight for Beijing, reports of a large imperial force blocking the way persuaded them to turn to the east. Since Wuchang was a good strategic base from which to attack downriver, the Taipings struck at China's traditional southern capital (the former Ming capital) of Nanjing, in the heart of the Yangzi River valley. On 8 February 1853, an estimated force of 500,000 left Wuchang. Virtually unopposed, the Taipings easily took Anqing, the capital of Anhui. After reprovisioning from the abandoned imperial storehouses, the Taipings moved on to Nanjing, the capital of Jiangsu province. By the time they arrived on 6 March 1853, their numbers had swelled to 750,000. They tunneled under the massive city walls, set explosions, breached the city's defenses, and annihilated the Qing forces within. After the Taipings made Nanjing their capital, it became a focus of Manchu military operations, which eventually retook the Yangzi River cities of Wuchang, Hankou, and Anqing. Over the next eleven years, the Taipings survived three imperial sieges of Nanjing.

The Taipings established a theocratic government under Hong Xiuquan, who ruled religious and temporal affairs as the Heavenly King and effectively administered through five subordinate kings, but with the capture of Nanjing, the kings turned from allies to rivals. The unsuccessful attempt by a subordinate king to overthrow Hong began a bloodbath that took the lives of three of the five subordinate kings and 20,000 to 30,000 of their followers, including men, women, and children. This as much as any Qing military successes weakened the movement. Afterward, the Taiping leadership never reclaimed the moral high ground but gradually devolved into a life of personal extravagance and debauchery,

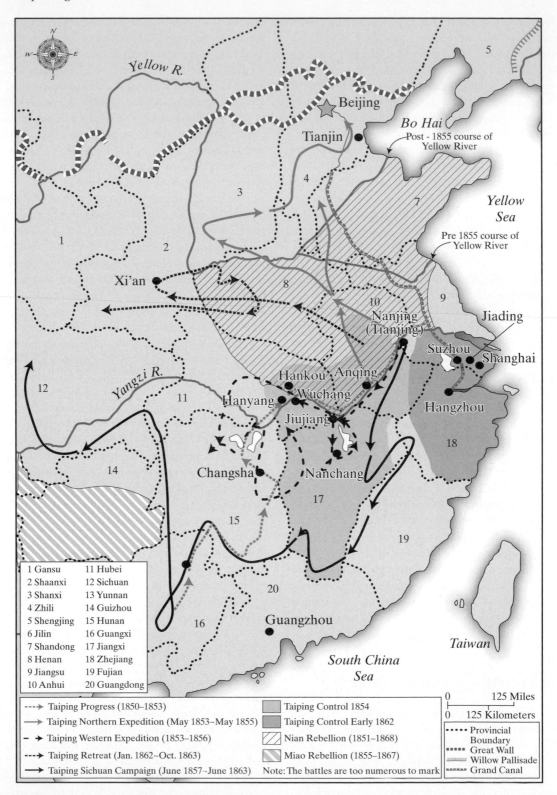

Map 8.1   Taiping Rebellion (1851–64)

Legend from map:

1 Gansu
2 Shaanxi
3 Shanxi
4 Zhili
5 Shengjing
6 Jilin
7 Shandong
8 Henan
9 Jiangsu
10 Anhui
11 Hubei
12 Sichuan
13 Yunnan
14 Guizhou
15 Hunan
16 Guangxi
17 Jiangxi
18 Zhejiang
19 Fujian
20 Guangdong

- - ▶ Taiping Progress (1850–1853)
→ Taiping Northern Expedition (May 1853~May 1855)
- ▶ Taiping Western Expedition (1853–1856)
⋯▶ Taiping Retreat (Jan. 1862~Oct. 1863)
→ Taiping Sichuan Campaign (June 1857~June 1863)

Taiping Control 1854
Taiping Control Early 1862
Nian Rebellion (1851–1868)
Miao Rebellion (1855–1867)
Note: The battles are too numerous to mark

⋯ Provincial Boundary
▦ Great Wall
▥ Willow Pallisade
▨ Grand Canal

0   125 Miles
0   125 Kilometers

with Hong presiding over a large harem of wives rumored to number from 30 to 300.

Despite the vicious internal fighting, the Taipings pursued an aggressive military program. The long-range Taiping military strategy entailed the consolidation of control over the Yangzi River valley, the dispatch of a Northern Expedition (1853–5) to take Beijing, and a Western Expedition (1853–6) to recapture Wuchang and then extend control westward up the Yangzi River valley. In 1853, the Northern Expedition of 70,000–80,000 men crossed the Yangzi River and headed northwest through Henan province. The Manchus panicked as it approached, ordering that all future taxes be sent to their ancestral retreat at Chengde, north of Beijing. In a last-ditch effort, the Manchus called in bannermen and cavalry from Manchuria and Mongolia to fortify the capital. By 30 October 1853 the Taiping force had moved to within three miles of Tianjin, the port city for Beijing, and only seventy miles from the capital. But they became overextended. They were too far

from their South China base of support and were not accustomed to North China winters. By February 1854, the Northern Expedition was in retreat. During the next year, it was unable to join up with reinforcements, while imperial forces remained in hot pursuit. Qing forces captured the commanders of the Northern Expedition on 31 May 1855 and brought them back to Beijing for torture and execution.

Although the Western Expedition endured longer, it fared no better than the Northern Expedition. A 50,000-man force went up the Yangzi River by boat and quickly retook control of Anqing. The well-defended city of Nanchang did not fall, however, and after a ninety-day siege the Taipings gave up and moved on upstream to capture Jiujiang on 29 September 1853 and the cities of Hankou, Hanyang, and Wuchang; the first two fell on 20 October, but Wuchang fell only after a four-month siege on 26 June 1854.

New conquests brought responsibilities to defend them. As in the Northern Expedition, the Taipings became overex-

During the Taipings' Northern Expedition, the Manchus prepared to evacuate the capital and ordered future taxes to be delivered to their Summer Palace at Chengde (pictured here), the capital of Rehe (Jehol) province, north of Beijing. In October 1853, the Taipings were only seventy miles away. But on 31 May 1855, the Qing forces defeated the Taipings; this date was later to embody North-over-South significance.

tended. Throughout 1854–5, they successfully opposed separate imperial advances from the north, west, and south. Imperial forces under Zeng Guofan, a reform-minded Han official who helped organize the Xiang Army (the provincial army of Hunan), attacked Wuchang. Although the Xiang Army had only 20,000 troops, ample funding from Hunan provided new ships, new cannons, and modern armaments. With these advantages, the Xiang Army succeeded in taking control over all of the territory west of Wuchang, as well as over the Yangzi River. On 14 October 1854 the Xiang Army took Wuchang and pursued the Taipings downstream.

The Xiang Army was composed of Han Chinese since the Taipings wiped out any Manchu garrisons in their path; most notably, they slaughtered the lower Yangzi River banner forces based in Nanjing and Hangzhou. This meant that the victorious Qing forces would be Han, not Manchu. The destruction of these garrisons marked the withdrawal of Qing banner influence from central China. It indicated a continuing decline in Qing military effectiveness, while the new Han provincial armies demonstrated increasing military skills. In the long run, this would be dangerous both to the dynasty and to central rule in general, constituting an early phase in the evolution of Han warlords.

By 1856, Qing forces had stopped both the Northern and Western Expeditions, but the Taipings still occupied the heart of the Yangzi River valley, putting them in control over central China's trade. This threatened the interests of both Beijing and Western commerce. In particular, the ongoing turmoil and piracy adversely affected British trade and led to a renewal of the fighting between China and Britain.

IV. The Arrow War

The British and French governments were displeased that China had not fully implemented the treaty terms from the first Opium War. The Taiping Rebellion disrupted trade, aggravating tensions between the British and the Manchus even more. The British demanded Chinese protection for their ships from Taiping piracy along the Yangzi River. Britain, now in cooperation with France, believed that an amelioration of trade conditions required treaty revision. The Manchus resisted these demands. A squabble over the Chinese impoundment of a treaty-port boat escalated into the second Opium War, also known as the Arrow War (1856–60). (See Map 8.2.)

On 8 October 1856, Guangzhou police boarded a Chinese-owned and crewed but Hong Kong–registered and British-captained ship called *Arrow*. The police hauled down the British flag and arrested twelve crew members. Although

the viceroy of Guangdong and Guangxi provinces, Ye Mingchen (Yeh Ming-ch'en), soon released the crew, he refused to apologize for violating the British flag. In a face culture such as China, no official could apologize to the British and hope to retain his position. Power depended on *guanxi*, which depended on face, which required competence on the job, whereas an apology would be construed to indicate incompetence. A spat over an apology escalated into war.

In response to the viceroy's refusal to apologize, the British besieged Guangzhou but lacked sufficient forces to go further. In the spring of 1857, the British government appointed James Bruce, the eighth Earl of Elgin, as minister plenipotentiary to China to lead Britain's military and diplomatic effort. In December 1857, a joint Anglo–French force of 5,000 troops and thirty ships took Guangzhou. Compared to the vast Taiping forces, the foreign contingent was tiny. Thereafter, the Anglo–French force moved north, taking the Dagu forts protecting the capital on 20 May 1858. On 26 May 1858, foreign ships docked at Tianjin for the first time. The path to Beijing lay open.

The twenty-seven-year-old Xianfeng emperor (Hsienfeng), who had assumed the throne upon his father's death in 1850, reconsidered his refusal to negotiate. On 26 June 1858, imperial commissioners signed the Treaty of Tianjin with Great Britain. Immediately thereafter, France, Russia, and the United States signed separate but parallel treaties. The treaty indemnified Britain with more than 1 million pounds' compensation for its losses in Guangzhou, made tariff revisions, opened Beijing to foreign representation, dispensed with the kowtow, and opened ten additional treaty ports, including the Yangzi River as far inland as Hankou, which the Taiping controlled at the time. The British did not yet insist on the legalization of opium, although the illegal opium trade continued as usual. Most-favored-nation clauses in the treaties meant that the privileges negotiated by any one power accrued to them all. Thus, Russia obtained the same treaty port privileges as the maritime powers; previously, Russians had been categorized with the peoples of Inner Asia and denied access to the treaty ports. Conversely, the British and French now acquired the privilege, long ago granted to the Russians, of sending envoys to Beijing.

Following what appeared to be a diplomatic victory, the British fleet withdrew to the South. As before, once the immediate threat to Beijing passed, the emperor ignored the treaty, this time ordering the main bannermen negotiators to commit suicide. Predictably, the hostilities resumed. Over the summer of 1860, Lord Elgin was redeployed for further negotiations with a reinforced second expedition. On 13 October 1860 the Anglo–French forces reached the walls of Beijing. In retaliation for the torture and death of British prisoners, Lord Elgin ordered the destruction of the Yuanming Yuan, the

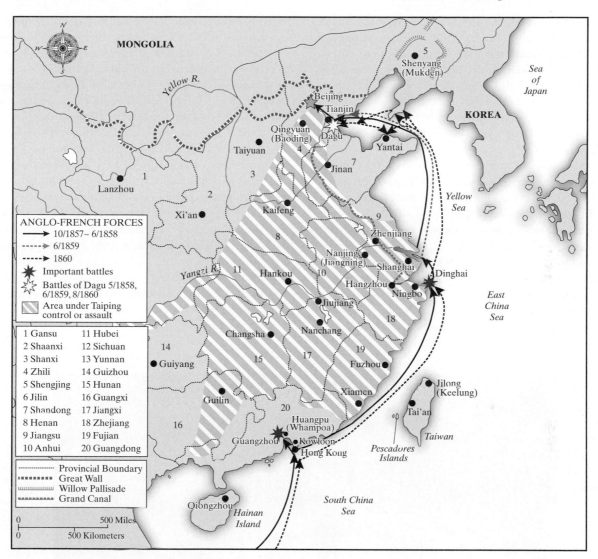

Map 8.2   Arrow War (1856–60)

Qing Summer Palace funded with Western loans and based on Greek architectural styles, to bring the war home to the emperor. The Arrow War ended in a flurry of treaties that achieved the British objectives of establishing a treaty port system to facilitate trade in China. The British and French signed separate Treaties of Beijing on 24 October and 25 October 1860, respectively, followed shortly by Russia and the United States. The provisions for foreign diplomatic representation in Beijing signaled an end to the tributary system vis-à-vis the European powers and the United States.

During the Opium Wars on China's coast, Russia was active in its interior. In 1849, Russian exploration of Siberia revealed that the Amur River was the only major transportation artery flowing from west to east. Without the Amur, Russia could not effectively access Siberia, while the only arable land in eastern Siberia lay on its banks and on the coastline between the Ussuri River and the sea. These were Qing territories inhabited by either Manchus or Manchu tributaries. The Crimean War (1853–6) with Britain and France deflected Russia's attention, although it sent flotillas down the Amur in 1855, 1856, and 1857 despite Chinese objections, and in 1856 it annexed the region between the Amur and Ussuri rivers and set up a Siberian Pacific Fleet to defend it.

At the height of the Arrow War, there was a chance encounter between Nikolai N. Murav'ev, the Russian governor-general of eastern Siberia, and Yishan, the Manchu military governor of the Manchurian province of Heilongjiang. In less than a week, they negotiated the Treaty of Aigun setting the Russo–Chinese border along the Amur and Ussuri Rivers. Yishan did not consider the document to be permanent, but he hoped to placate Russia on the frontier while China restored order in the central provinces. Unknown to Yishan, Russia would soon sign its own Treaty of Tianjin. As with the various Treaties of Tianjin, the Manchu Court also refused to ratify the Treaty of Aigun.

As the Arrow War went from bad to worse for China, a Russian negotiator operating out of the Russian Ecclesiastical Mission in Beijing offered his services to the Qing Court to intercede with the British and the French. Nikolai P. Ignat'ev was a virtually unfunded one-man-show in Beijing. Initially, the Court wanted nothing to do with him, but when the Anglo–French forces reached Beijing and the emperor fled the city, the skeleton team left behind sought Ignat'ev's services. Ignat'ev actually had nothing to offer, since the British and French did not intend to overthrow the Manchus, making mediation unnecessary. In fact, the Russian Treaty of Beijing looked like the British and French Treaties of Beijing also negotiated in 1860, with one key difference. The Russian treaty set the Xinjiang border. The Manchus did not realize the extent of the ceded territory until the subsequent negotiations to survey the border for the 1864 Treaty of Tarbagatai, but by then it was too late. They lost as much as 350,000 square miles of territory—the equivalent of France and Germany combined. With a growing Muslim rebellion in Xinjiang, the Manchus were in no position to contest the survey.

The Treaties of Beijing reflected a long Han tradition of using trade to defuse military threats in line with *yi yi zhi yi*, meaning to play one barbarian off another. As in the past, it worked in the short term, appeasing the minor threat to parry the major threat. Once the Qing dynasty agreed to adopt a westernized trading regime, the Western powers, the minor threat, had a vested interest in Qing survival and rallied to its defense against the Taipings. While the treaties constituted a de facto legalization of opium, the Taipings, the major threat, stuck to their opium ban and their goal of dynastic overthrow.

In China, one of the most remembered events about the Arrow War was the 18 October 1860 destruction of the Yuanming Yuan Summer Palace, just north of Beijing, by British and French forces, in retaliation for the torture and death of almost twenty foreign prisoners of war (including a journalist working for the *London Times*). Since only Manchus and their trusted Han officials could enter the Summer Palace, it was chosen specifically to punish just the Manchu Court. Later, Chinese nationalists blamed foreigners for destroying a national treasure.

Meanwhile, Russia focused not on trade but on territory, which it got in abundance by acting as the free rider of the Opium Wars. Russia acquired 665,000 square miles of territory under the Treaties of Aigun, Beijing, and Tarbagatai, or almost five times the total area of Japan. This did not sate its appetite, however, and soon it tried to expand into Mongolia and Manchuria. Murav'ev enunciated Russian goals quite clearly: "The political and commercial interest of Russia, even the security of our extensive land frontier, compel us to hope that these regions will return to their former independence . . . in the event of the fall of the Empire of the Manchus our activities must be so aimed as to enable the formation of an independent domain . . . in Mongolia and Manchuria."[2] Unlike the defunct Western treaty-port system, Russia remains in possession of Siberian land gained in the mid-nineteenth century, while former parts of the USSR retain territories in Central Asia. Some Chinese would like to redress these losses.[3]

V. Manchu–Western Cooperation to Destroy the Taipings

The Taiping Rebellion continued unabated through the 1850s. With Nanjing's capture, Taipings controlled the Yangzi River trade and threatened Western trading interests in Shanghai. While the Taipings' adoption of Christianity might normally have garnered Western support, over time the foreigners became increasingly disillusioned with the Taipings' strange mixture of Christian and Chinese beliefs. In addition, the Taiping denunciation of opium, tobacco, alcohol, and prostitution alienated Western merchants. In 1860, Taiping forces committed a crucial strategic error when they converged on Shanghai, thus threatening European interests. By doing so, they triggered a third-party intervention before they defeated their main adversary, the Manchus.

As the Taipings suffered defeats, divisions within the movement mounted. Yang Xiuqing (Yang Hsiu-ch'ing) became very influential because of his abilities as a military commander, his purportedly miraculous curative powers, and his many visions direct from God (in contrast to those of Hong Xiuquan, which came only from Jesus). Yang, as commander in chief of the armed forces, had ordered the Northern and Western Expeditions. By 1856 he was competing with Hong for leadership of the Taipings until Hong arranged for his assassination. When the assassins went overboard to wipe out numerous family members and officials associated with Yang, Hong had the assassins killed, causing further waves of infighting that decimated the Taiping leadership.

Afterward, Shi Dakai, the Hakka Taiping general, unified the five Taiping armies into a single army under his command. Accused by Hong's brothers of plotting to take full power, Shi left Nanjing in May 1857 and led his army of 200,000 men to the west to conquer Sichuan province. Although Shi continued to profess loyalty to Hong, he refused to return to Nanjing. Shi's six-year expedition reached as far west as Sichuan and Yunnan provinces, where Manchu supporters finally captured and executed him on 6 August 1863.

In the central territories of the Taiping empire, fighting continued uninterrupted during 1856–9. In 1859, with the arrival in Nanjing of Hong Ren'gan, Hong Xiuquan's Western-educated cousin, the Taipings changed strategy to undermine the Qing dynasty economically by disrupting South China trade to Beijing. Previously, the Taiping armies had tried unsuccessfully to conquer the North and the West, areas devoid of any Western presence. The eastward shift put the Taipings in conflict with the foreign communities in Shanghai, whose countries had just secured new trade privileges with the Manchus.

The Taipings' eastern movement began in February 1860. Taipings mustered 100,000 troops to break the seven-year siege of Nanjing. This made possible an eastern expedition into Jiangsu to take Suzhou and Shanghai to expel Manchu forces from South China. Over the summer of 1860, however, foreign troops under the American commander, Frederick Townsend Ward, prevented the Taipings from taking Shanghai, while Zeng Guofan's Xiang Army surrounded the Taiping-held territory. On 5 September 1861, after a fourteen-month siege, Zeng's forces finally took Anqing, a stepping stone to Nanjing. Again foreigners played a role in this outcome: After July 1861, British ships blockaded the ships of other foreign merchants, preventing them from supplying Anqing. Its fall corresponded with the death of the Xianfeng emperor and the enthronement of the five-year-old Tongzhi (T'ung-chih) emperor under the regency of his mother, now titled Empress Dowager Cixi (Tz'u-hsi), and his father's brother, Prince Gong (Kung), a special title making him second in rank to the emperor.

British and French forces and Ward's foreign-officered Chinese force deflected a second attack on Shanghai in January 1862. The Manchu Court promoted Ward and renamed his troops the Ever-Victorious Army. Upon Ward's death from combat wounds in September, the British commander, Charles G. Gordon, replaced him. From early April to May 1862, the foreign troops cleared out the most important Taiping strongholds within thirty miles of Shanghai. British steamships also transported from Anqing to Shanghai the Huai (Anhui) Army, a new imperial army, commanded by the Han Chinese Li Hongzhang (Li Hung-chang), to defend Shanghai. Over the summer of 1862 the combined forces of the Huai Army, the Ever-Victorious Army, and Anglo–French forces successfully defended Shanghai and forced

During the Taiping Rebellion, Chinese troops for the first time began to be trained in Western ways of warfare. An American, Frederick Townsend Ward, created the Ever-Victorious Army, while the Han Chinese official Li Hongzhang commanded the Huai (Anhui) Army, a new imperial army equipped with Western weapons. Because these military forces were loyal primarily to their commanding officer, not to the Manchus, over time they became the nucleus of warlord armies in China.

the Taipings into retreat. In October 1862, the Anglo–French forces participated in their last major engagement at Jiading.

While the Huai Army attacked the Taipings on the coast, the Xiang Army besieged their capital in Nanjing. Although the Taipings launched a final, and ultimately futile, second Northern Expedition to take Beijing, their hold over the Yangzi River valley became ever more tenuous. With their losses in Zhejiang province during 1864 and the death of Hong Xiuquan on 1 June 1864, the Taiping movement fragmented. Imperial forces breached Nanjing's walls on 19 July 1864, taking the city. Isolated groups of Taipings continued to resist for the next year and a half until 9 February 1866, when imperial forces defeated the final Taiping detachment.

Imperial forces waged a war of annihilation. They butchered any captured Taipings. The rebellion ravaged the central provinces of China, destroying crops, farmland, homes, and entire cities. Some of the most prosperous regions of China lay devastated. The Taiping Rebellion lasted for over fifteen years, and 20 million died. These deaths dwarfed the casualties of the Opium and Arrow wars, which numbered in the thousands. Although the Taipings failed, their attempt captivated future generations of revolutionaries. A century later, Mao Zedong, the leader of the Communists, drew inspiration from them. Mao carefully studied the Taiping military lessons when crafting his own revolutionary strategy to overcome a weak central government propped up by Western military aid. His archenemy, Chiang Kai-shek, the leader of the Nationalists, tried to duplicate the highly unusual conquest of China from the south in his own Northern Expedition of the 1920s. Paralleling the Taiping Rebellion, the Nationalists and Communists fought the final major battles of the Chinese civil war over control of Nanjing and Shanghai.

Conclusions

Although the Taiping and Arrow conflicts began independently, they became interlinked. Both grew out of the first Opium War. For the Taipings, China's defeat cast doubt on the Qing mandate of heaven, offering them the opportunity to claim the mandate for themselves by introducing a unique hybrid of Western and Chinese thinking. For Britain and France, when the trade agreements negotiated as a result of the first Opium War proved unsatisfactory to all parties, they again resorted to force. The settlements of the two conflicts were even more directly linked when the Manchus negotiating the end to the Arrow War on Western terms in order to concentrate on the far more lethal internal foe. Once the Qing dynasty agreed to the treaty port system, Western interests required the survival of the dynasty, lest the hard-fought treaties become dead letters with its demise, whereas the Taipings were bent on dynastic overthrow.

The Manchus struggled to keep their enemies divided and eventually pitted them against each other, contributing to the Taipings' defeat. China also formed a new modus vivendi with the West based on free trade, which the United States replicated in Japan soon afterward. The so-called treaty port system endured in China until the middle of World War II. It had four salient features: Foreign concession areas in designated treaty ports, tariffs on this trade set by the Western powers but paid to the host government, extraterritoriality for Westerners in Asia, and most-favored-nation clauses guaranteeing equal privileges for all the Western powers.

The system was unreciprocal in that Asian countries received no corresponding privileges in the West. In the twentieth century, Asians referred to these agreements as the "unequal treaties" because they were imposed by force; allowed Europeans, Americans, and, later, Japanese to live under their respective legal systems while in China; carved out concession areas under foreign, not Chinese, jurisdiction; and put foreigners in control of the tariffs levied in China. Although China's central government received the customs on the trade, which was a major and dependable source of government revenue, this benefit did not compensate for the other infringements on Chinese sovereignty. Chinese historians consider this period as the beginning of an era of humiliations extending until the Communist victory in 1949. The burning of the Yuanming Yuan remains a potent symbol of imperialism.[4]

While China's strategy of keeping enemies divided worked well against the maritime powers, it proved disastrous against Russia, resulting in a loss of huge territories on the Sino–Russian frontier. Russia carefully conducted these negotiations in secret lest the other powers interfere. Had China made the other powers aware of the proceedings, they would have had a common interest with China in limiting Russian expansion and Russia's transformation into a Pacific Ocean power.

The Taiping Rebellion and the Opium Wars differed in magnitude. Casualties in the Opium Wars were small. Battles were short, few, and far between. The Europeans targeted combat forces, not the civilian population, while both the Qing and the Taipings exterminated civilians. The Taiping conflict entailed hideous losses. In some cases, populations did not recover for generations. Likewise, the economic impact of the Taiping Rebellion was devastating. The Chinese economy had never centered on the seaboard that so preoccupied the Europeans, but in inland areas like the Yangzi River valley that the rebellion ravaged. In comparison to the destruction from the Taiping Rebellion, the Opium and Arrow Wars were minor sideshows. Yet, for political and cultural reasons, the Chinese collective memory of these antiforeign wars is far greater.

BIBLIOGRAPHY

Boardman, Eugene Powers. *Christian Influence upon the Ideology of the Taiping Rebellion.* New York: Octagon, 1972.
Cheng, J. C. *Chinese Sources for the Taiping Rebellion, 1850–1864.* Hong Kong: Oxford University Press, 1963.
Curwen, C. A. "Taiping Relations with Secret Societies and with Other Rebels." In *Popular Movements and Secret Societies in China, 1840–1950,* edited by Jean Chesneaux, 65–84. Stanford, CA: Stanford University Press, 1972.
———*Taiping Rebel, The Deposition of Li Hsiu-ch'eng.* London: Cambridge University Press, 1977.
Elleman, Bruce A. *Modern Chinese Warfare, 1795–1989.* London: Routledge, 2001.

Erbaugh, Mary S. "The Hakka Paradox in the People's Republic of China: Exile, Eminence, and Public Silence." In *Guest People: Hakka Identity in China and Abroad,* edited by Nichole Constable, 196–231. Seattle: University of Washington Press, 1996.

Fairbank, John K. *Trade and Diplomacy on the China Coast: The Opening of the Treaty Ports, 1842–1858.* 2 vols. Cambridge, MA: Harvard University Press, 1953.

———"The Creation of the Treaty System." In *The Cambridge History of China,* vol. 10, edited by Denis Twitchett and John K. Fairbank, 213–265. Cambridge: Cambridge University Press, 1978.

Graham, Gerald S. *The China Station: War and Diplomacy 1830–1860.* Oxford: Clarendon Press, 1978.

Hurd, Douglas. *The Arrow War: An Anglo-Chinese Confusion, 1856–1860.* New York: Macmillan, 1967.

Jen, Yuwen. *The Taiping Revolutionary Movement.* New Haven, CT: Yale University Press, 1973.

Kuhn, Philip. *Rebellion and Its Enemies in Late Imperial China: Militarization and Social Structure, 1796–1864.* Cambridge, MA: Harvard University Press, 1970.

———"The Taiping Rebellion." In *The Cambridge History of China,* vol. 10, edited by Denis Twitchett and John K. Fairbank, 264–317. Cambridge: Cambridge University Press, 1978.

Michael, Franz and Chang Chung-li, eds. *The Taiping Rebellion.* 3 vols. Seattle: University of Washington Press, 1965.

Morse, Hosea Ballou. *The International Relations of the Chinese Empire.* Vol. 1. Shanghai: Kelly and Walsh, 1918.

Paine, S. C. M. *Imperial Rivals: China, Russia, and Their Disputed Frontier.* Armonk, NY: M. E. Sharpe, 1996.

Perdue, Peter C. *Exhausting the Earth: State and Peasant in Hunan, 1500–1850.* Cambridge, MA: Harvard University Press, 1987.

Quested, Rosemary K. I. *The Expansion of Russia in Asia, 1857–1860.* Kuala Lumpur: University of Malaya Press, 1968.

Reilly, Thomas H. *The Taiping Heavenly Kingdom: Rebellion and the Blasphemy of Empire.* Seattle: University of Washington Press, 2004.

Rhoads, Edward J. M. *Manchus & Han: Ethnic Relations and Political Power in Late Qing and Early Republican China, 1861–1928.* Seattle: University of Washington Press, 2000.

Shih Yu-cheng. *The Taiping Ideology: Its Sources, Interpretations, and Influences.* Seattle: University of Washington Press, 1967.

Smith, Richard J. *Mercenaries and Mandarins: The Ever-Victorious Army in Nineteenth Century China.* Millwood, NY: KTO Press, 1978.

Spence, Jonathan D. *God's Chinese Son: The Taiping Heavenly Kingdom of Hong Xiuquan.* New York: W. W. Norton, 1996.

Teng, Ssu-yü. *The Taiping Rebellion and the Western Powers.* Oxford: Clarendon Press, 1971.

Wong, J. Y. *Yeh Ming-ch'en, Viceroy of Liang Kuang, 1852–8.* London: Cambridge University Press, 1976.

———*Deadly Dreams: Opium, Imperialism, and the Arrow War (1856–1860) in China.* London: Cambridge University Press, 1998.

NOTES

1. Jonathan D. Spence, *God's Chinese Son: The Taiping Heavenly Kingdom of Hong Xiuquan* (New York: W. W. Norton, 1996), front jacket. From GOD'S CHINESE SON: THE TAIPING HEAVENLY KINGDOM OF HONG XIUQUAN by Jonathan D. Spence. Copyright © 1996 by Jonathan D. Spence. Used by permission of W. W. Norton & Company, Inc.

2. Cited in Thomas Ewing, *Between the Hammer and the Anvil? Chinese and Russian Policies in Outer Mongolia 1911–1921* (Bloomington: University of Indiana Press, 1980), 19.

3. In 1989, Deng Xiaoping, the leader of the People's Republic of China, stated that "Russia, with the aid of these [Qing dynasty–era] treaties, usurped territory of China exceeding one and a half million square kilometers, and the time has now come to pay that account." Aleksey Khazbiyev, "China Takes a Swing at the Sacred," *Moscow Ekspert,* 24 May 2004, translated by *FBIS.* For a similar quotation by Mao, see Dennis J. Doolin, *Territorial Claims in the Sino–Soviet Conflict: Documents and Analysis.* (Stanford, CA: Stanford University Press, 1965), 43–4.

4. In contrast, few Americans realize that the British burned the central buildings of Washington, D.C., to the ground in the War of 1812.

Chronology

1851–64	Taiping Rebellion
1851–68	Nian Rebellion
1852	Zeng Guofan organizes the Xiang Army in Hunan
1855	Yellow River changes course; massive flooding
1855–73	Panthay Rebellion
1856–60	Arrow War
1858	Treaty of Aigun
1858	Treaties of Tianjin (United Kingdom, France, United States, Russia)
1860	Treaties of Beijing (United Kingdom, France, United States, Russia)
1861	Establishment of the Zongli Yamen
	Death of Xianfeng emperor; Tongzhi emperor assumes the throne
	Prince Gong and Empress Dowager Cixi stage coup d'état
1861–5	U.S. Civil War
1862	Li Hongzhang forms the Huai Army
1862–73	Donggan Rebellion
1862–78	Xinjiang Rebellion
1864	Treaty of Tarbagatai (Russia), trade and boundary
1865	Li Hongzhang establishes the Jiangnan Arsenal near Shanghai
1866	Birth of father of the Republic, Sun Yat-sen
	Zuo Zongtang establishes the Fuzhou Shipyard
1868–1912	Meiji Restoration
1871	Russian occupation of the Ili Valley
1872	Yakub Beg negotiates treaties with Russia
1874	Yakub Beg negotiates treaty with Britain
1875	Tongzhi emperor dies; Guangxu emperor assumes the throne

9

Quelling Domestic Rebellions

How painful to think that, since the uprisings,
Troops have been killing the people everywhere;
They consider that killing the people is like killing thieves,
And this poisonous attitude has spread across the land.[1]

Jin He (1818–85), poet

From 1840 to 1850 alone, there were over one hundred armed insurrections in China. Although the Taiping Rebellion was by far the largest, there were other local civil wars. In particular, China's long restive Muslim population on the imperial periphery took advantage of the Qing preoccupation with the Taipings to launch a variety of secessionist movements. (See Table 9.1.) After defeating the Taipings, the Qing quelled the Nian (Nien) Rebellion (1851–68) in the central part of eastern China, the Panthay Rebellion (1855–73) in Yunnan province, the Donggan Rebellion (1862–73) in Shaanxi and Gansu, and the Muslim Rebellion in Xinjiang (1862–78). Although the Manchu suppression of these rebellions promised a restoration of imperial rule, Beijing had been forced to rely on provincial militias under Han command, such as the Xiang Army under Zeng Guofan and the Huai Army under Li Hongzhang. For the remainder of their rule, the Qing were unable to assert full control over these semiautonomous armies. Impeding the restoration of order was a power struggle triggered by the 1861 death of the Xianfeng emperor that left the throne occupied by a five-year-old child and power in the hands of an unstable regency composed of eight regents and two empresses dowager. Xianfeng's only consort to bear him a son, Cixi, soon orchestrated a palace coup, allying first with Prince Gong, a brother of the deceased Xianfeng emperor, and later with his even younger brother, Prince Chun (Ch'un), whose son became the Guangxu emperor in 1875. For forty-seven years, the Empress Dowager Cixi was the power behind a throne held by child emperors.

I. The Rise of the Empress Dowager Cixi

The Manchu dynasty survived the Taiping Rebellion, but with an enormous loss of prestige, or face. The very existence, tenacity, and geographic extent of the uprising provided strong evidence that the Qing had entered the final phase of their dynastic cycle. With the impending demise of Qing rule, infighting broke out among the competing Manchu factions. Turmoil within the Manchu Court became critical in 1861, with the death of the Xianfeng emperor after only a decade of rule. One of the strongest leaders to emerge from this period was Cixi (1835–1908), originally a minor concubine but greatly elevated in status when she gave birth in 1856 to his only surviving male heir, the future Tongzhi emperor (1856–75). Following a palace coup in 1861, Cixi became a co-regent for her son but in fact concentrated power in her own hands.

The future Empress Dowager Cixi became a Manchu concubine to the Xianfeng emperor at the age of sixteen. Upon the death of her father, a minor official assigned to Anhui province, her mother took their two daughters to live in Beijing. Described as charming and magnetic, the future empress dowager was also ambitious. She learned to read and write Chinese, essential skills for governing China. She also became an accomplished calligrapher and painter. In 1852, she was one of the dozen or so Manchu maidens summoned to meet with the Xianfeng emperor, whose first consort had died before bearing children. She was a third-rank concubine,

Table 9.1   Civil Wars during the Qing Dynasty

Duration	Name	Goal	Location
1747–9	Jinchuan uprising	Jinchuan secession	Western Sichuan
1771–6	Jinchuan uprising	Jinchuan secession	Western Sichuan
1787–8	Heaven-Earth Society uprising	Taiwan secession	Taiwan
1795–1806	Miao uprising	Miao secession	Guizhou, Hunan
1796–1805	White Lotus Rebellion	Overthrow dynasty	Sichuan, Hubei, Shaanxi
1813	Eight Trigrams Rebellion	Overthrow dynasty	Zhili, Shandong, Henan
1817–21	Yi uprising	Yi secession	Yunnan
1820–8	Muslim uprising	Muslim secession	Xinjiang
1822	Ethnic uprising	Secession	Qinghai
1826	Blue Lotus Sect		Taiwan
1831	Li uprising	Li secession	Guangdong
1832	Yao uprising	Yao secession	Hunan, Guangdong, Guangxi
1832–3	Heaven-Earth Society uprising	Taiwan secession	Taiwan
1835	Prebirth Sect uprising		Shanxi
1836	Yao uprising	Yao secession	Hunan
1837	Yi uprising	Yi secession	Sichuan
1845	Muslim uprising	Muslim secession	Gansu
1846	Muslim uprising	Muslim secession	Yunnan
1847	Muslim uprising	Muslim secession	Xinjiang
1847	Yao uprising	Yao secession	Hunan
1851–64	Taiping Rebellion	Overthrow dynasty	Guangxi, Guangdong, Hunan, Jiangxi, Hubei, Anhui, Jiangsu, Henan, Zhili, Zhejiang, Shandong, Shanxi, Shaanxi, Guizhou, Yunnan, Sichuan, Gansu, Fujian
1851–68	Nian Rebellion	Overthrow dynasty	Anhui, Henan, Shandong, Jiangsu, Zhili, Hebei, Shanxi, Shaanxi, Gansu
1853–65	Heaven-Earth Society uprising	Overthrow dynasty	Guangdong, Hunan, Jiangsu, Fujian
1853–5	Small Knife Society uprising	Overthrow dynasty	Shanghai (Jiangsu)
1855–72	Miao uprising	Miao secession	Guizhou
1855–73	Panthay Rebellion	Muslim secession	Yunnan
1862–4	Heaven-Earth Society uprising	Taiwan secession	Taiwan
1862–73	Donggan Rebellion	Muslim secession	Gansu, Shaanxi
1862–78	Xinjiang Rebellion	Muslim secession	Xinjiang
1887	Li uprising	Li secession	Guangxi
1888–9	Aboriginal uprising	Aboriginal secession	Taiwan
1891	Jindan Sect uprising		Zhili, Inner Mongolia
1895	Muslim uprising	Muslim secession	Gansu
1899–1900	Boxer Uprising	Overthrow dynasty	Zhili, Shandong, Shanxi, Heilongjiang, Shaanxi, Fengtian, Jilin, Gansu, Hunan
1908	Tibetan Uprising	Tibetan secession	Tibet

Note: The shaded area denotes the period of most intense rebellions. The Li, Yi, Miao, and Yao are different ethnic groups.

Source: C. K. Yang, "Some Preliminary Statistical Patterns of Mass Actions in Nineteenth-Century China," in *Conflict and Control in Later Imperial China*, edited by Frederic Wakeman, Jr., and Carolyn Grant (Berkeley: University of California Press, 1975), 209–10.

promoted to the second rank when she conceived, and, after giving birth to a son, became a first-rank concubine but still not the imperial consort. Although it was rumored that the child's father was not the emperor, who was ill and semiparalyzed at the time, the boy nevertheless became heir to the throne. This solidified the future empress dowager's position.

Intelligent, a quick learner, and a natural politician, Cixi soon began to read the emperor's confidential memorials and listen to his audiences from behind a silk curtain near the Dragon Throne. As the Xianfeng emperor became increasingly ill, she became one of his most trusted advisers. A firm supporter of the empire and the prerogatives of the throne, she was one of the few influential Manchus in 1860 to advise the Xianfeng emperor not to flee the capital in the midst of the Arrow War. He did so anyway. In prepa-

Empress Dowager Cixi was the real ruler of China from 1861 until her death in 1908. During her almost half century in power, Cixi attempted to balance the demands of foreigners with those of her Han Chinese subjects, often pitting them against each other so that the Manchu minority could remain in control. This photograph was taken in 1903 by an American artist, Katherine Carl, while painting an official portrait of Cixi.

ration for the power struggle that would follow the emperor's impending death, she began to extend her own *guanxi* network among the palace eunuchs, the key civilian servants within the Forbidden City, and the Imperial Guard.

In the autumn of 1861, the Xianfeng emperor died in exile in Chengde, the Qing retreat in Manchuria. Qing domestic policy was in disarray. Although the 1860s treaties had mollified the foreigners, the Taiping Rebellion remained active, while other major rebellions were spreading along the imperial periphery and a second antidynastic rebellion, the Nian, broke out in the Chinese core area. The composition of the regency to govern during the minority of the five-year-old child emperor was a critical issue of state. Initially, there were eight co-regents, nominally under Chief Regent Zaiyuan (Tsai Yuan) and Prince Zheng (Cheng) but really under the control of Sushun, the ambitious foster brother of Prince Zheng. They hoped to relegate the two dowager empresses to a ceremonial status, whereas Manchu traditions gave joint veto power over imperial edicts issued by the regency to the surviving imperial consort, Ci'an (Tzu-an), a cousin of Cixi, and Cixi, the mother of the child emperor.

Cixi, the more active of the two, allied with two younger brothers of the deceased emperor, Princes Gong and Chun, although in this period Prince Gong played the dominant role. They used their connections within the Imperial Guard to arrest the co-regents, executing the three principals. With the backing of Prince Gong and the Imperial Guard, the dowager empresses, Cixi and Ci'an, became co-regents. The Empress Dowager Cixi consolidated partial control in 1865, with the first demotion of Prince Gong, and complete control after the sudden death of Ci'an in 1881 and the permanent demotion of Prince Gong in 1884. Cixi was the power behind the throne during the reign of her son, who died at age eighteen in 1875, and until her own death in 1908.

The Tongzhi emperor's reign was one of internal turmoil and the suppression of the Taiping, Nian, Panthay, Donggan, and Xinjiang rebellions. It was also a period of superficial westernization of the Qing institutions for conducting foreign policy. As part of the settlement of the Opium and Arrow Wars, the British demanded that China westernize its conduct of diplomacy. This entailed not only adherence to treaties and Western norms concerning diplomatic representation, but also the creation of a quasi-foreign office to regularize diplomatic channels. In 1861, Prince Gong oversaw the establishment of the Zongli Yamen (Tsungli Yamen) to administer China's foreign relations with Europe and the United States. This, along with the Imperial Customs Inspectorate to collect the tariffs levied on the maritime trade, were the only westernized governmental institutions adopted by the Qing dynasty until after the Boxer Uprising in 1900. Only those political institutions directly in charge of dealing with Westerners were westernized.[2] In the 1870s, there was an attempt to westernize certain aspects of the military but not the banner forces so central to the Qing rise to power. To this day, many Chinese institutions and laws sharply diverge from Western norms.

II. The Nian Rebellion (1851–68)

Once the Manchus suppressed the Taipings, they turned their attention to the second most threatening rebellion, which shared the Taiping goal of dynastic overthrow. Like Taipings, the Nian rebelled in core territories and were mainly impoverished farmers. Some had turned to banditry and salt smuggling to supplement their meager incomes, while others were members of various secret societies. They studied martial arts and forged periodic alliances with the White Lotus Sect. This heterogeneous group gradually coalesced around a common desire to restore native Han rule to China. The rebellion centered in Anhui province, where a tragedy unfolded with the shifting course of the Yellow River from the southern to the northern side of Shandong Peninsula. (See Map 8.1.)

With growing corruption in the Qing bureaucracy and the Taiping threat, essential infrastructure maintenance had been neglected. The Yellow River has been a source of disastrous flooding for generations. With extensive silting, the river even in normal times partially ran above ground level so that there were no river banks, just dikes separating the local population from disaster. The flooding began in 1851 and climaxed in 1855 with a catastrophic collapse of the dikes, enabling the river radically to change course, from one side of the Shandong Peninsula to the other, wiping out the densely populated and once fertile plains in between. Failure of the levies indicated governmental corruption, while corruption and natural disasters were associated with a faltering mandate to rule and dynastic change.

Rural devastation aggravated tensions between prosperous landlords and the growing throngs of dispossessed. The arrival of the Taiping Northern Expedition in 1853 catalyzed the ground swell of discontent into an antidynastic movement, although the leaders of the two rebellions never overcame the geographic dispersion that made coordination difficult. They retained separate armies, which the Qing tried to keep apart and defeat independently. The Nian military accomplishments were notable. Women played an important role in the movement and fought alongside men. Zhang Luoxing (Chang Lo-hsing) organized the rural population into armed bands that spent the spring and summer tending their fields and the

fall and winter engaging in highly profitable salt smuggling. After local Qing officials declared him an outlaw, the Nian bands became the Nian League and Zhang remained its leader until his capture and execution in 1863.

It is difficult to separate the early history of the Nian from that of the Taipings. In 1854, when the Taipings took northern Anhui during their Northern Expedition, many Nian joined them. (See Map 9.1.) In 1855 the Nian Army adopted the title *Da Han*, meaning "Great Han," which was in line with the Taipings' anti-Manchu ideology. By 1856, when the Nian had an estimated 1 million followers in northern Anhui alone, they formally allied with the Taipings. This alliance allowed the Taipings to rely on northern Anhui for supplies. Taiping and Nian forces soon launched a combined attack to the northwest on neighboring Henan province from 1856 to 1857. Although this campaign initially met with great success, it ground to a halt when Beijing rushed in reinforcements.

The Nian also participated in defending the Taiping capital at Nanjing, but in mid-1858 the Nian commander, Li Zhaoshou, defected to the imperial army with his 18,000 men. Beijing quickly conferred on him the rank of lieutenant general. The Nian leader Miao Peilin also betrayed the Taipings. The resulting tensions allowed the Qing to concentrate their forces against the remaining Nian troops under the command of Zhang. Although the Taipings and the Nian remained allies in name, with the fall of Anqing in the autumn of 1861 the rest of the Nian army had to return to northern Anhui to protect its base area. In late 1861 and early 1862, when the Taipings started the second Northern Expedition, Zhang participated, but the Taiping defeat effectively split the Nian army away from the Taipings, gravely weakening both.

Beginning in 1863, the Nian situation in northern Anhui became dire with the arrival of a new imperial commissioner, the Inner Mongolian Prince Senggerinchin (Sengko-lin-ch'in). In mid-March 1863, a group of Nian chiefs betrayed Zhang and his son for a reward. Senggerinchin ordered not only their immediate execution, but also that of their betrayers. Zhang Luoxing's nephew, Zhang Zongyu, led the Nian survivors of this debacle, but in this period the Nian forces had no choice but to become a full-time army because they no longer could return home to farm.

With Senggerinchin's death in early 1865 at the hands of a former Taiping soldier, the Manchus put a Han Chinese general, Zeng Guofan (Tseng Kuo-fan), not a bannerman, in charge. A year later, Zeng was replaced by his Han Chinese protégé, Li Hongzhang. Both Zeng and Li gained Manchu trust for their effective suppression of the Taipings, yet both modeled their own armies on the Taiping forces. Although Zeng recognized the bravery, horsemanship, tactics, and mobility of the Nian, they lacked the modern weaponry that he used to destroy

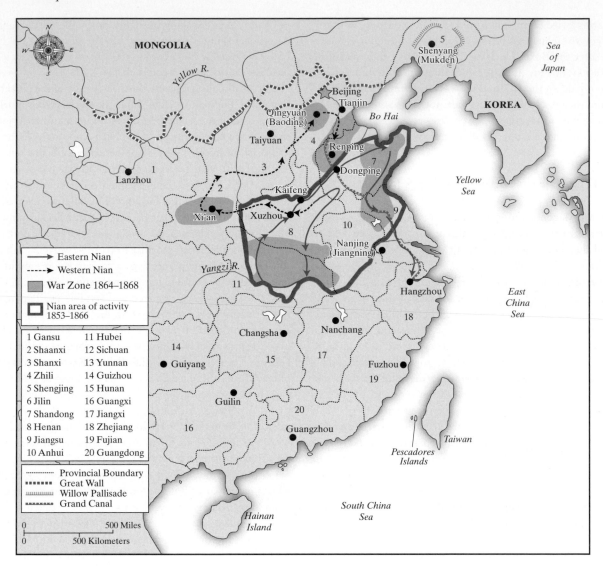

Map 9.1   Nian Rebellion (1851–68)

them. Zeng devoted an entire year to organize a force of 50,000 men capable of surrounding and defeating the mobile Nian forces and in 1861 established China's first modern arsenal at Anqing. Thereafter, China began to produce an ever larger proportion of its modern weapons and ammunition.

Although the Taiping Rebellion ended in February 1864 the Nian fought for two more years. When Zhang returned to Shandong with a new army in late October 1866, the Qing forces managed to split his forces so that thereafter they were divided into the Eastern Nian and the Western Nian. A former Taiping king, Lai Wenguang, led the Eastern Nian, while Zhang continued to lead the Western Nian. In 1867, Li Hongzhang led the Huai Army to victory over the Eastern Nian, capturing

Lai on 5 January 1868. Zuo Zongtang, the third of the great Han generals of the Taiping conflict, was the imperial commissioner in Shaanxi and Gansu. In 1868 he helped orchestrate a blockade that trapped the Western Nian. On 16 August 1868, Zhang Zongyu disappeared after fleeing across a river in Shandong province to avoid capture and execution.

While only negligible foreign forces participated in the suppression of the Nian and Taiping Rebellions, the Qing employed modern weaponry, purchased from the West, which contributed to their victory. This was China's first attempt at modernization, meaning the adoption of superior foreign technology, but the Manchus continued to reject westernization, meaning the adoption of westernized institutions.

III. The Panthay Rebellion (1855–73)

The Panthay Rebellion centered in Yunnan province in southwest China, where Muslims constituted between 10 and 30 percent of a population composed of the Hui (Muslims), Yi (or Lolo), and Han ethnic groups. In addition, there were many other smaller groups. Even today, Yunnan accounts for about 40 percent of all non-Han in China.

With growing overpopulation in China's central provinces, the government encouraged Han immigration to Yunnan, where the population increased from 4 to 10 million between 1775 and 1850. These new Han immigrants competed aggressively with the local population for land and focused increasingly on the relatively prosperous Hui. (See the feature below.) The Hui bore the onus of their cooperation with the Mongol conquest of China that also eliminated 500 years of independent Yunnan rule under the Nanzhao (738–902) and Dali (937–1253) kingdoms. The new Han immigrants sought to reorient Yunnan from its traditionally close relations with Tibet and Southeast Asia toward China, and the Yunnan population divided over this issue.

Growing tensions between Yunnan's new and old populations resulted in numerous clashes that the Qing increasingly attributed to the Hui even though they were more Sinified than the other ethnic minorities of Yunnan. The provincial government of Yunnan was complicit in the Han massacres of Hui residents in 1839, 1845, and 1849, with 1,700 and 8,000 men, women, and children slaughtered in the first two, respectively. These escalating clashes culminated in the Kunming Massacre of 1856 when the Manchu judicial commissioner in the provincial capital of Kunming, in combination with Han gentry–organized local militias, instigated a massacre of several more thousand Hui.

The Hui responded by combining with other long-time Han and Yi inhabitants of Yunnan, who also opposed the growing control of the new Han immigrants. Like the Nian, the long-term residents of Yunnan were eager to take advantage of the ongoing Taiping Rebellion. In September 1856, the leader of the Panthay Rebellion, the Hui leader Du Wenxui (1828–72) and his followers occupied the prefectural capital of Dali, declaring an independent Dali sultanate with Du as sultan. Perhaps influenced by the Taipings, whose name translates as "Great Peace," they proclaimed their kingdom Pingnan, which meant "Peaceful South." By 1858 they controlled almost half of Yunnan, including over thirty prefectural and county capitals, and claimed a military force of 350,000.

HUI AND UIGHUR MINORITIES

There are many Muslim minorities in China, including the Hui scattered throughout Western and central China, Inner Mongolia, and Manchuria; the Uighurs, Kazakhs, Dongxiang, Kirghiz, Tajiks, Uzbeks, and Tatars of Xinjiang; the Salar of Qinghai; and the Bonan of Gansu. Most Muslims in Xinjiang speak Turkic languages, including the Uighurs, Uzbeks, Kazakhs, and Kirghiz as well as the Salars of Qinghai. The so-called Quran (Koran) Belt of China comprises the provinces of Gansu, Ningxia, Qinghai, and Xinjiang. The closest language to Uighur is Uzbek. The Dongxiang are Mongol Muslims, while the Tajik are non-Arab Persian-speaking Muslims. Most Chinese Muslims follow Suni practices. The only Shiites are the Bonan and the Tajiks. About 2 million Hui follow Sufi practices. Today, by far the most numerous Muslim groups in China are the Hui followed by the Uighurs, numbering nearly 10 million and over 8 million, respectively. Most other Muslim groups number less than half a million.

Islam came to China during the Tang dynasty via Persian and Arab traders, who conducted both overland and overseas trade. Many of those engaged in the overland trade settled in Xi'an, Shaanxi, while those engaged in the maritime trade settled in Guangzhou, Guangdong, and Quanzhou, Fujian. Xi'an has some of China's most famous mosques, including the Great Mosque, established in 742. The overland trade goes back to the Silk Route, which had long connected the Chinese and Islamic worlds. A Southwestern Silk Route developed linking Central China via Yunnan with the maritime trade route over the Indian Ocean. During the Song and Yuan dynasties, Quanzhou flourished with an influx of Muslims. The Muslims of Yunnan were instrumental in that province's conquest by the Yuan dynasty, which rewarded them with high positions in the provincial bureaucracy. Islam rapidly spread throughout Yunnan but was later virtually eradicated during the failed Panthay Rebellion (1855–73). In the eighteenth century, the Qing incorporated many Turkic Muslims into the Chinese empire with the conquest of Xinjiang.

Uighurs traditionally earned their living as traders, farmers, and artisans, residing in the scattered oases of Xinjiang. Eighty percent of Uighurs live in the area bordering on Pakistan and Afghanistan, a center of nationalist sentiment. They consider Xinjiang to be their homeland, and there has been a persistent separatist movement, with repeated rebellions during the Qing dynasty and an underground separatist movement in the Communist era. When the Great Leap Forward (1958–60) pushed China's nomadic Muslims onto collective farms, many Kazakhs fled to the Soviet Union (now Kazakhstan). Kazakhs and Uighurs continued

Continued

Muslim minorities in China include the Hui, Uighurs, Kazakhs, Dongxiang, Kirghiz, Tajiks, Uzbeks, Tatars, Salar, and Bonan. Muslims in Xinjiang speak a variety of Turkic languages and usually follow Suni practice. The country's 8 million Uighurs, in particular, have long supported a separatist movement, and historically, many antigovernment rebellions have occurred in Xinjiang. Pictured here are Muslim men studying at the Great Mosque in Xining, Qinghai.

to flee across the border following the Sino–Soviet split in 1960. Significant numbers have emigrated to Kazakhstan, Turkey, and Western Europe. During the Cultural Revolution (1966–76), the Chinese government closed all mosques except the main mosque in Lanzhou, Gansu. With the liberalization under Deng Xiaoping in the 1980s, many mosques damaged in the Cultural Revolution were restored. Although the Chinese introduced a Romanization system for Uighur in 1958 to replace an earlier system relying on the Russian Cyrillic alphabet, since 1980 the government has permitted the Uighurs to publish in their preferred traditional writing system based on a Persian-Arabic script. This has strengthened their ties with the Muslim community outside of China.

In contrast to the Uighurs, most Hui dress like the Han and speak Chinese. Today Gansu, Qinghai, Xinjiang, and Ningxia are the home of most Hui. The Hui of Xinjiang are also called the Donggan (e.g., Donggan Rebellion). The cities of Guangzhou and Xi'an also have significant Hui populations. They constitute the second largest minority group in China after the Zhuang. (See the feature in Chapter 21, page 346.) They are descended from Arab traders and soldiers, who took Chinese wives, and from other Chinese converts to Islam. During the Tang dynasty, Arab soldiers had helped prevent the overthrow of the dynasty during the An Lushan Rebellion (703–57). In recompense, they received Chinese wives and lands in northwestern China.

The Qing found Muslims to be the most challenging minority population because their monotheistic beliefs rejected the Qing approach to empire that sought to amalgamate different belief systems under the universal rulership of the emperor. Commonly used terminology reflects these tensions. The Qing divided the Hui into "barbarian" and "subject" Hui. During the Republic period the terminology was updated to "turbaned" and "Chinese" Hui.

The Hui, like the other Muslim minorities, follow the religious and dietary rules prescribed by Islam. Muslims adhere to a monotheistic religion that does not permit the layered belief system of *yin* and *yang*, whereby some Chinese adhere simultaneously to a variety of belief systems, often a combination of Buddhism, Daoism, and Confucianism. Muslims worship one god, Allah, in mosques under the authority of their religious leaders, and follow the teaching of the prophet Mohammed as revealed to him by Allah in the sacred book called the Quran. The five duties of Muslims are belief in one God and His prophet Mohammed, prayer five times daily at prescribed intervals, alms giving, fasting at Ramadan in commemoration of the first revelation of the Quran, and a pilgrimage to Mecca, Saudi Arabia. Unlike the Chinese diet, which is based on pork and pork fat for frying, pork consumption is taboo for Muslims.

For ten years the rebellion remained centered in Dali, where Du Wenxiu unified his heterogeneous followers under a program based on freedom of religion and authority legitimized by the corruption of the Qing. While the Qing hoped to use rival Hui groups to defeat Du, in what proved to be an unsuccessful attempt to use one barbarian faction against another, Du hoped to join with the Taipings to overthrow the dynasty. When the Taiping Western Expedition entered Sichuan province, Du assigned two commanders to combine forces with it. Imperial troops, however, prevented this by expelling the Taipings from Sichuan.

After the total defeat of the Taiping Rebellion in 1864 brought fears that the Qing would focus their resources on Yunnan, Du tried to act preemptively in the spring of 1867 by launching highly successful offensives southward and

The average Chinese soldier was equipped with a sword and often carried a "gingal," a large single-shot musket. This type of firearm was sufficient to defeat a premodern foe, but it proved woefully inadequate when facing a modern force armed with breech-loaded rifles using percussion bullets, military developments that quickly became standard worldwide.

eastward, and besieging Kunming in the hopes of expelling the remaining Qing presence in Yunnan. In the 1860s, the attention of the Qing forces based in Kunming remained divided between the escalating Panthay Rebellion and the decade-long Miao Rebellion in neighboring Guizhou province. Unfortunately for Du and his followers after the 1867 suppression of the Miao Rebellion, Cen Yuying was able to turn his attention to the Miao Rebellion. Indicative of these divided attentions was government funding, which increased by nearly 65 percent after phase one in the suppression of the Miao in 1867 and more than tripled in 1872.

Cen Yuying came from Guangxi province, where his military experience grew out of his personal militia initially formed to suppress unrest in his home village. In 1871, when he became the provincial governor of Yunnan, he had been fighting the Panthay Rebellion off and on for fourteen years. He organized an army with modern weapons and trained by French military advisers. By late 1872, sufficient imperial troops gathered to retake Du's capital of Dali. By early 1873 they surrounded Du, who took a fatal dose of opium before delivering himself to his enemies with the request that they spare the civilian population. Cen appeared to honor this request by accepting the surrender of Du's generals and posting notices banning looting and killing. This gave him time to deploy his troops around Dali and arrange a banquet for Du's seventeen defeated generals, who, when seated around the banquet table, were beheaded, marking the beginning of a three-day massacre that left some roads ankle deep in blood and at least 10,000 men, women, and children dead. Twenty-four baskets of severed ears from these victims, along with the heads of the generals, were then shipped to Beijing as proof of a mission accomplished. Many Hui fled to Burma, Laos, and Thailand. The Muslim population of Yunnan never recovered. The combination of the rebellion, massacre, and ensuing epidemics and famine reduced the provincial population by half, entailing the death or flight of 5 million people.

IV. The Donggan Rebellion (1862–73)

Just as the Muslims in South China rebelled, so did the Muslims of the North. (See Map 9.2.) Those in the North also opposed the increasing Han immigration into their lands and hoped to take advantage of the unrest caused by the Taiping Rebellion to secede. In 1862, the Taiping invasion of neighboring Shaanxi province likewise provided the spark to ignite a rebellion of the Donggan minority.

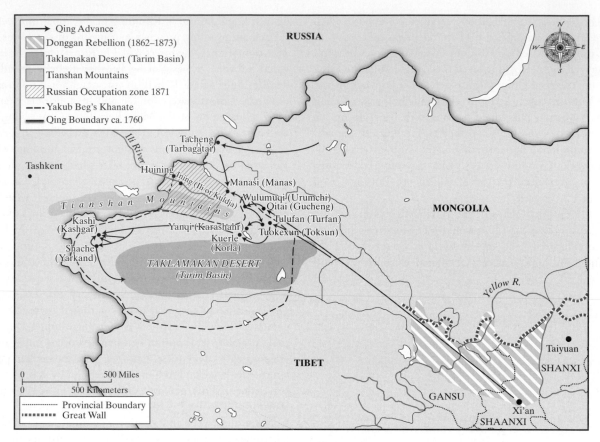

Map 9.2   Donggan and Xinjiang Rebellions (1862–78)

The Donggan were Sufi Muslims, who in speech and dress resembled the Chinese. Previously, they had used their role as a bridge between the Muslim and Chinese worlds to promote trade with both groups. The Han, however, looked down on them. Starting in the early nineteenth century, Chinese officials attempted to Sinicize them further by decreeing queues for men and bound feet for women. In order to intermix the two groups, various administrative rules pressured the Donggan to marry their daughters to non-Muslim Chinese, a practice that the Donggans found particularly offensive. In addition, they found the growing imperial tax burden onerous.

In April 1862, one wing of the final Taiping Northern Expedition moved into Shaanxi province, where it was opposed by the Han. Although the Taipings soon moved eastward into Henan province, local Muslims responded by creating their own armed forces for fear that the Han forces would eventually turn on them. By late May 1862, Han–Muslim tensions escalated following the Han burning of a Muslim town and the Donggan murder of the imperial commissioner for local defense. The Manchus, beset by the

Taiping Rebellion, left the suppression of the Donggan Rebellion in the hands of poorly equipped and often corrupt local officials, many of whom soon fled their posts. In the absence of firm central policies, the uprising spread rapidly westward from Shaanxi to neighboring Gansu province and then, in the second half of 1864, into southern Xinjiang. The fighting was vicious on both sides, with widespread civilian casualties.

The unrest threatened to cut the Gansu corridor, the peninsula of arable land extending deep into the deserts of Central Asia that controls the main transportation artery connecting Central China with Xinjiang and the Central Asian khanates. This was the ancient Silk Route caravan route. Although the rebellion began among the Donggan, it eventually spread to other Muslim peoples throughout Xinjiang and into Mongolia.

Ma Hualong led the rebellion centering on Shaanxi and Gansu provinces. He was the descendant of Ma Mingxin, the founder of the New Sect, a particularly militant Muslim group. Although the Donggan Muslims spoke Chinese and had intermarried with the Han for centuries, their community centered on an activist interpretation of Islam. Religious leaders had long claimed a special link with God, allowing them to perform such miracles as curing disease and forecasting future events. The Sufi practice of "vocal recollection" was central to the New Sect's teachings, and Ma Hualong became a major leader of this school. His followers believed that Ma could use vocal recollection to eliminate all thoughts except those of God to predict the future and also cure such medical problems as infertility.

The Donggan originally divided their forces into eighteen "great battalions," which roughly corresponded to the Qing banner system. They deployed them throughout Shaanxi, where they besieged Xi'an for a year until the new imperial commissioner, the Manchu, Dolonga, relieved the town in 1863 and forced the defeated Donggan to retreat to neighboring Gansu province. The Donggan Rebellion in northern Gansu took Lingzhou in December 1863, only fifty miles from Ma Hualong's hometown, reportedly killing 100,000 Han inhabitants. From this base they spread to the rest of Gansu province. Many Muslims did not agree with Ma's New Sect teachings, causing continuous internecine strife. In May 1866, Ma switched sides to support the Qing in return for arms to suppress his Muslim rivals. Beijing exonerated Ma, proclaiming him a loyalist, yet the rebellion continued unabated and spread west into Xinjiang.

Manchu suppression of the Donggan began in earnest only after the defeat of the Taiping and Nian Rebellions. In 1867, Zuo Zongtang and his Hunan Army entered the fray. Imperial forces from Sichuan, Anhui, and Henan also arrived, creating a total force of almost 100,000 men, partially armed with Western weaponry. Zuo then organized an enormous supply train and goaded his troops with promises of pillage from captured areas. Even with these incentives, however, Zuo's troops repeatedly mutinied during the campaign.

Despite Ma Hualong's arrangement with the Qing, Ma continued to strengthen his position in northern Gansu. After Zuo methodically recaptured Shaanxi, in early 1869, he moved into Gansu. By fall 1870, he surrounded and executed Ma Hualong and his followers. This victory crushed the main base of the New Sect, but a grueling three-year campaign ensued to recapture the rest of Gansu. On 24 October 1873, the final stronghold at Jiayuguan, the westernmost gate of the Great Wall, fell and Zuo executed the 7,000 surviving Muslim troops. Zuo was to write that this victory, which ended the Donggan Rebellion, was the "most perfect feat of my military career over decades."[3]

To fund the seven-year campaign, Zuo received government and provincial money from a special Western Expedition fund. In addition, he took out loans from foreign firms, securing these funds with the custom revenues from the treaty ports. These loans bore the seals of the relevant provincial governors. A Qing victory was of great interest both to the foreign companies, since repayment could begin only after the reconquest of northwest China, and to the provincial governors, since their only means of repaying the money would be tax receipts from trade with those provinces. Once again, the Manchus were trying to use barbarians, this time foreign firms, and the Han to defeat another barbarian, the Muslims, and once again, the Western powers provided key aid while the Han did most of the fighting. The Qing used modern military equipment and elements of modern finance, a spillover effect of the Industrial Revolution, to tip the precarious balance of power in their favor.

V. The Muslim Rebellion in Xinjiang (1862–78)

News of the 1862 Donggan Rebellion in Shaanxi and Gansu provoked sympathetic uprisings in Xinjiang. These began in the strategic Ili Valley during March 1863 but were quickly defeated by Qing troops. Although the Qing quelled smaller revolts throughout Xinjiang during 1863, in mid-1864 they lost control. Instead of facing one opponent, the Qing faced three separate revolts: the first in eastern Xinjiang, near Urumchi, the second in Western Xinjiang, near Ili, and the third in southern Xinjiang, near Kashgar. These three movements coalesced during the late 1860s under Yakub Beg (c. 1820–77), a former general in the neighboring Kokand Khanate Army.

The Qianlong emperor had incorporated Xinjiang into the Qing empire only in 1759. Afterward it did not become a Chinese province but remained under the direct authority of a military governor in Ili, backed by three assistant military governors stationed in Ili, Tarbagatai, and Yarkand, respectively. Under the assistant military governors were twelve military commanders stationed in the main cities of the region. All of these top Qing officials were either Manchus or bannermen, that is, persons of unquestionable loyalty to the Qing, while the civil administration was in the hands of local chiefs given the official title of "beg." In reality, Xinjiang was under military occupation because the local population continued to resist Qing rule. Discontent with Qing rule in Xinjiang had a long and continuous history, with uprisings in 1765, 1815, 1817–26, 1830–5, 1847, 1852, 1854, and 1857.

By the mid-nineteenth century, the ethnic mix of Xinjiang included Uigurs (Muslim agriculturalists), various Mongol tribes (herdsmen), Kazakhs (Turkic-speaking Muslim steppe nomads), and Kirghiz (Turkic-speaking Muslim Alpine nomads). Although many groups were mutually hostile, most shared a common overriding animosity toward the Manchus and Han Chinese. The latest round of rebellions stemmed from a combination of long-standing ethnic tensions between Qing officials and the local Muslim population; administrative corruption; and the spreading unrest elsewhere in the empire.

Donggan Muslims in eastern Xinjiang struck first during July 1864. Their leader, Tuo Ming, was originally from Gansu province and a follower of Ma Hualong's New Sect movement. He gained the military support of Suo Huanzhang (So Huan-chang), an officer of the Green Standard Army, whose Han Chinese garrison revolted and killed the commanding officer, a Manchu general. Backed by the garrison, Tuo Ming easily took control over the Muslim portion of the city of Urumchi and was proclaimed a Muslim king. By October, the Manchu section of Urumchi fell and the revolt spread to several neighboring cities, including Turfan.

The second focus of the Muslim revolts was in the Ili Valley, where rebels under the Uighur, Mu'azzam Khan, besieged the Manchu cities of Huining and Huiyuan for eighteen months. During this time, the local Qing officials repeatedly requested military assistance from neighboring Russia. With no help forthcoming, the two cities fell in March 1866. A month later, the far Western Sino-Russian border area near Tarbagatai also fell to Muslim rebels.

The third focus of the rebellion was in southern Xinjiang, close to Kashgar. Two groups competed for control. In 1865 one group requested help from the neighboring Central Asian khanate of Kokand, and Buzurg Khan led a small force into southern Xinjiang to unify the warring factions. General Yakub Beg led the military force of Buzurg Khan, the son of Jahangir, whom the Qing had ritually executed for a failed rebellion in the 1820s. By 1867 Yakub Beg succeeded in forcing Buzurg Khan out of Xinjiang and, in taking power himself, declaring that all of the Muslim rebels in Xinjiang should submit to Kashgar's rule.

From 1867 to 1870, Yakub Beg consolidated his rule throughout Xinjiang. Leading a force of 20,000 men, he took the cities of Khotan, Aksu, and Kucha in the Tarim Basin. Attacking eastward, he took Korla in 1869, and in 1870 captured Karashahr and Turfan. Finally, in December 1870, Tuo Ming, the Donggan leader, fled Urumchi, which fell to Yakub Beg. During the next seven years, until his death, Yakub Beg ruled much of Xinjiang, combining religious authority with military and political power. The emir of Bukhara granted him a religious title, strict Islamic law was followed, and many religious schools were opened.

During this period of the Muslim Rebellion, Xinjiang also played an important international role as the buffer zone with the Qing empire to the east, the Russian empire to the north, and the British empire to the south. Yakub Beg sent envoys simultaneously to British India and Russia in 1868, offering trade in return for their diplomatic recognition. He also solicited friendly relations with the Ottoman empire. This bore fruit on 9 April 1872, when he negotiated a commercial treaty with Russia, which tacitly recognized the independence of Xinjiang. In competition with Russia, England also sent a mission to Xinjiang. In the resultant commercial treaty, Britain recognized Yakub Beg's government and sold him modern weapons in return for preferential trade rights. Finally, diplomacy with the Ottoman sultan resulted in the arrival of military aid and advisers. Yakub Beg's diplomacy ensured the survival of his government through 1875, when the Qing victory over the Donggan Rebellion permitted a massive Qing troop redeployment to Xinjiang.

The Han general Zuo Zongtang, who had so successfully put down the Donggan Rebellion in Shaanxi and Gansu provinces, took charge of retaking Xinjiang. His 90,000 men faced approximately 45,000 troops under Yakub Beg. As in the defeat of the Donggan Rebellion, Zuo maintained massive logistical trains to ensure adequate supplies in the inhospitable wastelands of Xinjiang. The central government provided him with vast sums supplemented by additional foreign loans. This time Zuo made even better use of European weaponry, as a new Chinese arsenal at Lanzhou now manufactured European ammunition and shells, and by 1875 also began to produce weapons. Zuo's Xinjiang expedition set out in April 1876. Turmoil in the rebel leadership facilitated his task. When Yakub Beg died suddenly in 1877, perhaps poisoned by one of his followers, his sons fought over the throne. A combination of internal disarray of the rebels and concerted Qing military pressure defeated the uprising by December 1877 and restored Qing control over Xinjiang, with the notable exception of the Russian-occupied Ili Valley.

Because the Russians feared that the rebellion might spill over into their territory, they occupied the strategic Ili Valley in 1871. They also began formally integrating the area into the Russian provincial system on the assumption that the Qing dynasty could never reassert control over Xinjiang. When Zuo Zongtang proved them wrong, acrimonious negotiations for a Russian withdrawal ensued. This event is known as the Ili Crisis (see Chapter 11, Section IV).

Conclusions

The Taiping Rebellion provided an opportunity for numerous other dissatisfied ethnic groups to rebel against Qing rule. These included Han desiring the restoration of Han rule and Muslims desiring independence from the Qing empire. As the Qing focused virtually all their forces on suppressing the Taipings, rebellions spread in central China with the Nian and among the Muslims populating the imperial periphery. The final collapse of the Taipings freed Qing forces to concentrate on these other rebellions and defeat them sequentially. By 1878, the Qing had reasserted control over the vast empire.

Although these Qing efforts to reassert control were successful, they came at a high cost; Muslim dissatisfaction with Chinese rule continued and, indeed, has persisted to the present day. The rebellions devastated the civilian populations and economies where they took place. Collectively, they affected most provinces and regions of the empire, with the notable exception of Manchuria, the loyalist stronghold of the dynasty. In the absence of reliable census data, casualty estimates can only be speculative. Estimates for deaths in the Taiping Rebellion range from 20 to 30 million,[4] while the combined Muslim Rebellions' death toll has been estimated at 30 million.[5] According to another estimate, the population of Gansu province fell from 15 to 1 million inhabitants,[6] while the Ili Valley lost two-thirds of its population and still had not recovered over a generation later in 1910.[7] In the east-central provinces most affected by the Taiping Rebellion (Hubei, Jiangxi, Anhui, and Zhejiang), the population still had not recovered to prerebellion levels in 1933, while that of Jiangsu recovered only because of the expansion of Nanjing and Shanghai.[8] Whatever the death toll, it was staggering, and certainly well over 60 million. It is difficult for Westerners to grasp the magnitude of such losses. Those who travel to China today are usually struck by the widespread environmental degradation. Arguably, China has yet to recover from these internal rebellions and the warlord period that they spawned. These rebellions were a human tragedy of stupendous proportions.

It is equally difficult for Westerners to grasp the extent of the economic dislocations and infrastructure losses. These rebellions and the campaigns to suppress them were wars of annihilation. Cities were surrounded and reduced to rubble. Armies on both sides gave no quarter to civilians. Massacre and scorched earth were widely employed tactics. Victory meant obliteration of the other side, including the destruction of property, on the one hand, and children and women, on the other. In the absence of accurate data on such infrastructure losses in China, it is possible to make only generalizations. The Nian and Taiping rebellions wiped out major parts of the infrastructure in such key regions as the Yangzi River Valley and northward through central and eastern China. This occurred at a time when China was already becoming increasingly impoverished, making it ill-equipped to reconstruct.

Certainly the Qing dynasty never recovered from the effects of this almost thirty-year period of civil war. Although the Manchus remained in power for another forty years, they were never able fully to restore their mandate to rule. Instead, to prevent a repeat of the unrest, they relied increasingly on customs revenues collected and delivered to the imperial coffers by foreigners. With a treaty system in place and signed by the dynasty, the Western powers had a vested interest in the continuation of Manchu rule. The *lijin* tax was also essential for suppressing the mid-nineteenth-century rebellions since it funded the Han provincial armies that defeated the rebels on the field of battle.

Although the Manchus removed the immediate threat to their rule, they created a dangerous long-term threat: Taking a calculated risk, they permitted the Han generals primarily responsible for suppressing these rebellions to form, fund, and train their own armies. These troops were loyal to their commanding officers, usually Han Chinese, and to their provinces of origin, usually in Central or South China, not to the Manchu dynasty or to Manchuria.

So long as the fighting remained on the imperial periphery, the Qing military proved to be very effective at defeating various rebels. However, the destruction of Manchu banner forces during the rebellions and the creation of more effective Han forces tipped the future internal balance of power from Manchu to Han and from the central government to the provinces. The Xiang Army under Zeng Guofan and the Huai Army under Li Hongzhang were the first indigenous modern armies in China. They spawned a Self-strengthening Movement intent on westernizing institutions directly connected with military power. After the suppression of the rebellions, not all the new provincial forces were disbanded. Some became the nuclei of future warlord armies. After the fall of the Qing dynasty, Li Hongzhang's Huai Army fragmented into competing warlord armies. Thus, the time of troubles during the 1850s, 1860s, and 1870s saw the establishment of the regional armies and incipient warlordism that would wreak havoc throughout China in the early twentieth century. These regional forces also became instrumental in the final overthrow of the dynasty in 1911 and in the formation of the Republic of China under Sun Yat-sen.

The Manchus have long been vilified for their misrule of China. They were actually extremely clever at retaining power. They deftly played off the Han against the Western barbarians to eliminate their far more dangerous internal foes. If the Manchus' objective was to cling to power, they succeeded, an amazing feat considering the tiny size of their population in comparison to the vast empire they ruled and the enormity of the empire's problems. Despite these escalating internal and external threats, the Han bureaucracy remained loyal to the dynasty until the bitter end, when the military, not the bureaucrats, mutinied. Because the rebellions coincided with the Opium Wars, it has been difficult to disaggregate the suffering and dislocations caused by foreigners and those brought by the Chinese on themselves. In terms of numbers dead, most of the killing in China in these horrific years was done by Han killing one another or killing Muslims. Deaths at the hands of Westerners in the two Opium Wars were comparatively minor in comparison. Nevertheless, Chinese bitterness over the foreign aggression during the Opium Wars remains intense.

BIBLIOGRAPHY

Atwill, David G. *The Chinese Sultanate: Islam, Ethnicity, and the Panthay Rebellion in Southwest China, 1856–1873.* Stanford, CA: Stanford University Press, 2005.

Berlie, Jean A. *Islam in China: Hui and Uyghurs between Modernization and Sinicization.* Bangkok: White Lotus Press, 2004.

Chiang, Siangtseh. *The Nien Rebellion.* Seattle: University of Washington Press, 1967.

Chu, Wen-Djang. *The Moslem Rebellion in Northwest China 1862–1878.* The Hague: Mouton, 1966.

Dillon, Michael. *Xinjiang—China's Muslim Far Northwest.* London: Routledge, 2004.

Elleman, Bruce A. *Modern Chinese Warfare, 1795–1989.* London: Routledge, 2001.

Feuerwerker, Albert. *Rebellion in Nineteenth-Century China.* Ann Arbor: University of Michigan Press, 1975.

Kim, Hodong, *Holy War in China: The Muslim Rebellion and State in Chinese Central Asia, 1864–1877.* Stanford, CA: Stanford University Press, 2004.

Kuhn, Philip A. *Rebellion and Its Enemies in Late Imperial China: Militarization and Social Structure, 1796–1864.* Cambridge, MA: Harvard University Press, 1970.

Lipman, Jonathan N. *Familiar Strangers: A History of Muslims in Northwest China.* Seattle: University of Washington Press, 1997.

Liu, Kwang-ching. "The Ch'ing Restoration." In *The Cambridge History of China,* vol. 10, edited by Denis Twitchett and John K Fairbank, 409–90. Cambridge: Cambridge University Press, 1978.

———"The Military Challenge: The North-west and the Coast." In *The Cambridge History of China,* vol 11, edited by Denis Twitchett and John K Fairbank, 202–73. Cambridge: Cambridge University Press, 1980.

Liu, Xiaoyuan. *Frontier Passages: Ethnopolitics and the Rise of Chinese Communism, 1921–1945.* Stanford, CA: Stanford University Press, 2004).

Overmeyer, Daniel L. *Folk Buddhist Religion: Dissenting Sects in Late Imperial China.* Cambridge, MA: Harvard University Press, 1976.

Paine, S. C. M. *Imperial Rivals: China, Russia, and Their Disputed Frontier.* Armonk, NY: M. E. Sharpe, 1996.

Perry, Elizabeth J. *Rebels and Revolutionaries in North China, 1845–1945.* Stanford, CA: Stanford University Press, 1980.

———*Chinese Perspectives on the Nien Rebellion.* Armonk, NY: M. E. Sharpe, 1981.

Rawski, Evelyn S. *The Last Emperors: A Social History of Qing Imperial Institutions.* Berkeley: University of California Press, 1998.

Richardson, Philip. *Economic Change in China, c. 1800–1950.* Cambridge: Cambridge University Press, 1999.

Spector, Stanley. *Li Hung-chang and the Huai Army: A Study in Nineteenth-Century Chinese Regionalism.* Seattle: University of Washington Press, 1964.

Teng, S. Y. *The Nien Army and Their Guerrilla Warfare, 1851–1868.* Paris: Mouton, 1961.

Wakeman, Frederic, Jr. and Carolyn Grant, eds. *Conflict and Control in Late Imperial China.* Berkeley: University of California Press, 1975.

NOTES

1. The poem describes the chaos of the Taiping Rebellion. Chin Ho, "Ballad of the Maiden of Lan-ling." In *The Columbia Anthology of Traditional Chinese Literature,* edited by Victor Mair (New York: Columbia University Press, 1994), 501. From *The Columbia Anthology of Traditional Chinese Literature,* by Victor Mair, Copyright © 1994, Columbia University Press. Reprinted with permission of the publisher.

2. Japanese reformers, by contrast, concluded that the only effective way to parry the Western threat was to westernize their country's political, legal, military, economic, and educational institutions. These reforms, collectively known as the Meiji Reforms in honor of the reigning Japanese emperor, Meiji (r. 1868–1912), started in 1868 and were largely in place by 1890.

3. Cited in Kwang-ching Liu, "The Military Challenge: The North-west and the Coast." In *The Cambridge History of China*, edited by Denis Twitchett and John K Fairbank, vol. 11 (Cambridge: Cambridge University Press, 1980), 235.

4. Hosea Ballou Morse, *The International Relations of the Chinese Empire*, vol. 2 (Shanghai: Kelly and Walsh, 1918), 111; Pamela Kyle Crossley, *Orphan Warriors: Three Manchu Generals and the End of the Qing World* (Princeton, NJ: Princeton University Press, 1990), 137.

5. Ivan Fedorovich Babkov, *Vospominaniia o moei sluzhbe v Zapadnoi Sibiri, 1859–1875 gg* (*Memoirs of My Tour of Service in Western Siberia, 1859–1875*) (St. Petersburg: Tipografiia V. F. Kirshbauma, 1912), 301.

6. Wen-Djang Chu, *The Moslem Rebellion in Northwest China 1862–1878*, Central Asiatic Studies, no. 5 (The Hague: Mouton, 1966), vii.

7. Key-Hiuk Kim, "The Aims of Li Hung-chang's Policies toward Japan and Korea, 1870–1882," in *Li Hung-chang and China's Early Modernization*, edited by Samuel C. Chu and Kwang-ching Liu (Armonk, NY: M. E. Sharpe, 1994), 144.

8. Philip Richardson, *Economic Change in China, c. 1800–1950* (Cambridge: Cambridge University Press, 1999), 74.

Chronology

1854	Establishment of Imperial Maritime Customs
1861	Establishment of the Zongli Yamen
	Death of Xianfeng emperor; Tongzhi emperor assumes the throne
1861–75	Tongzhi Restoration
1862	Establishment of the College of Foreign Languages
	Li Hongzhang organizes the Huai Army
1865	Establishment of the Jiangnan Arsenal in Shanghai
	Manufacture of first Chinese steamship
	First telegraph line laid
1866	Zuo Zongtang establishes the Fuzhou Shipyard
	First informal diplomatic mission to Europe
1868–1912	Meiji Restoration
1870	Li Hongzhang made governor-general of Zhili
1872	China sends first students abroad to study in the United States
	Chinese Merchants Steam Navigation Company founded
1875	Tongzhi emperor dies; Guangxu emperor assumes the throne
1876	First official embassy to Europe
1878	Kaiping Mines opened
1881	China builds its first railway
1885	Establishment of the Tianjin Military Academy
1894–5	Sino-Japanese War marking the end of the Self-strengthening Movement

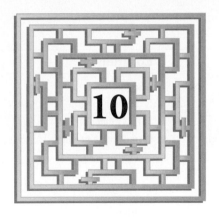

The Self-strengthening Movement and Central Government Reforms

10

Act sincerely and carefully when you are alone and your heart will be at peace
Order yourself in reverence and your conduct will be firm.
Seek benevolence and men will delight in you.
Labour industriously and the gods will respect you.[1]

Zeng Guofan (1811–72),
Self-strengthener, general, scholar

Foreign war and domestic rebellion made apparent to key members of the Han leadership, particularly at the provincial level, the pressing need to reform. In 1861, the concept of self-strengthening *ziqiang* came under discussion for the first time. Those engaged in the recent fighting were keenly aware of the power of Western armaments, and Western participation and funding helped quell the Taipings, the Nian, and the various Muslim uprisings. Some Han officials now began to argue that China had to change in order to parry the threat represented by the European nations. The reform movement emanating from the provinces became known as the Self-strengthening Movement. The Manchus could not fail to recognize the precariousness of their situation. The disasters that had befallen the dynasty—barbarian invasion, internal rebellion, massive flooding, and exploding poverty—were hallmarks of a dynasty on the verge of collapse. The traditional remedy was imperial restoration, meaning the return to model Confucian rule to restore the dynasty's virtue and, thereby, its mandate to rule. The brief reign of Cixi's son, who died at age eighteen, became known as the Tongzhi Restoration. The Han and Manchu elite followed a two-track strategy: Han Self-strengtheners looked to the West for technological guidance to parry what they construed to be primarily a military threat, while Manchus, concerned about dynastic restoration,

defined the fundamental problem in moral terms and sought inspiration from Confucian values. In practice, many high officials shared both concerns and tried to combine the two remedies.

I. Military Reform: Xiang and Huai Armies, Beiyang and Nanyang Navies

The Self-strengthening Movement focused on modernizing China's army and navy. It sought the creation of Chinese military forces equal to those of the European powers. The Chinese saw this mainly in terms of acquiring and then learning how to produce modern armaments, not in terms of understanding and then adopting the institutional underpinnings of Western power. The most famous Self-strengtheners were Han officials put in charge of raising provincial armies to defeat the mid-nineteenth-century rebellions. (See Table 10.1.)

Zeng Guofan came to fame for his role in quelling the Taiping and Nian Rebellions. He had been born into a poor peasant family, but a high score on the imperial examinations earned him a coveted appointment in the Hanlin Academy. In 1850–1, when the Court realized that local militias were more effective than regular troops at fighting the Taipings, Zeng was appointed to organize a new military force in Hunan. This became the Xiang Army. Zeng also tried to create the infrastructure necessary for a modern army by establishing the Jiangnan Arsenal in Shanghai with its complementary shipyards and iron works. He also sent promising young men abroad to study, promoting the career of Li Hongzhang, who became China's most famous Self-strengthener.

Table 10.1   Self-strengthening Projects

Year	Self-strengthener	Project	Location
1862	Zeng Guofan	armory	Anqing, Anhui
	Li Hongzhang	cannon factory	Shanghai, Jiangsu
1863	Li Hongzhang	cannon bureau	Suzhou, Jiangsu
1864	Zuo Zongtang	steamship construction	Hangzhou, Zhejiang
1865	Zeng Guofan and Li Hongzhang	Jiangnan Arsenal	Shanghai, Jiangsu
1866	Zuo Zongtang	Fuzhou Shipyard	Mawei, Fujian
1867	Chonghou	Tianjin Machinery Bureau	Tianjin, Hebei
1871	Zuo Zongtang	Lanzhou Machinery Bureau	Lanzhou, Gansu
1872	Li Hongzhang	China Merchant's Steam Navigation Company	Shanghai, Jiangsu
1874	Cen Yuying	copper mine	Yunnan
1875		coal mine	Jilong (Keelung), Taiwan
1876	Li Hongzhang	coal mine	Guangji, Hubei
1877	Li Hongzhang	mining bureau	Kaiping, Hebei
		coal mine	Chizhou, Anhui
1880	Li Hongzhang	coal mine	Yixian, Shandong
	Zuo Zongtang	woolen textile mill	Lanzhou, Gansu
		coal mine	Hexian, Guangxi
1881	Li Hongzhang	copper mine	Chengde, Hebei
		machine bureau	Jilin, Jilin
		merchant shipping company	Guangzhou, Guangdong
1882	Li Hongzhang	textile mill	Shanghai, Jiangsu
		coal mine	Likuoyi, Jiangsu
		mining bureau	Licheng, Hebei
1886	Zhang Zhitong	silk bureau	Guangzhou, Guangdong
		iron foundry	Qingxixian, Guangdong
1887	Li Hongzhang	lead mine	Zichuan, Shandong
	Zhang Zhitong	purchases machinery for mint	Guangzhou, Guangdong
	Zhang Zhitong	munitions factory	Shijingxu, Guangdong
1888	Li Hongzhang	gold mine	Mohe, Heilongjiang
1889	Zhang Zhitong	gun and cannon factory	Hanyang, Hubei
1890	Zhang Zhitong	steel mill	Hanyang, Hubei
	Zhang Zhitong	textile mill	Wuchang, Hubei
1891	Zhang Zhitong	iron mine	Dazhi, Hubei
	Zhang Zhitong	coal mine	Dazhi, Hubei
	Zhang Zhitong	coal mine	Jiangxiaxian, Hubei
1894	Zhang Zhitong	cotton spinning bureau	Wuchang, Hubei
	Zhang Zhitong	silk bureau	Wuchang, Hubei
	Zhang Zhitong	hemp bureau	Wuchang, Hubei

Note: Where the column "Self-strengthener" is blank, the project was run by a secondary figure.
Source: Qian Dongxian and Tan Songshou, comps., *Zhongguo lishi dituji* (Taipei: Tianweiwenhua, 1995)

Li Hongzhang came from a family of great scholarly achievement and, like Zeng Guofan, did brilliantly on the imperial examinations, likewise earning an appointment at the Hanlin Academy. Li established arsenals in Suzhou, Shanghai, and Nanjing; a merchant marine; China's first modern mines, first railway, first telegraph, and first cotton spinning mill; the Tianjin Military Academy; the Chinese Educational Mission to send students to study in the United States; and China's most modern army and navy, the Huai Army and the Beiyang Fleet, respectively. He also served as China's de facto foreign minister for the last quarter of the nineteenth century.

Frederick Townsend Ward, the American commander of the Ever-Victorious Army that had defended Shanghai against the Taipings, is often credited with helping China take the first step toward westernizing its military. Both the Xiang and Huai Armies soon purchased Western armaments, but remained administratively separate even though they belonged to the same country. This was a consequence of Manchu minority rule. A unified Han military force could easily threaten the dynasty. Therefore, the Manchus carefully kept their most effective Han forces divided. This system was adequate to suppress internal rebellions and prevent coups d'état, but it proved disastrous during war. Just as the Manchus preferred to pick off mutinous Han troops in detail, divided command allowed foreigners to dispose of Chinese forces sequentially.

In 1870 Li Hongzhang became governor-general of Zhili province, the location of Beijing, and retained this position for a quarter of a century. With the position came the responsibility for defending the capital and, as it turned out, conducting foreign affairs. Li became China's de facto foreign minister. In the 1870s, Li revived Chinese naval development, arguing that the Arrow War had proven Beijing to be more vulnerable from the coast than from its northwestern inland frontiers. In 1875, Li received central government funding to purchase ships from abroad, but far less than that allocated for inland border defense. Li's fleet became known as the Beiyang Fleet. It was based in Lüshun (Port Arthur) on the Liaodong Peninsula, the Manchurian promontory defining the northern shores of the Gulf of Bo Hai, while on the southern shores was the Shandong Peninsula, the location of the fleet's other base at Weihaiwei. These two naval bases allowed the Beiyang Fleet to guard the sea approaches to Beijing. The Qing eventually ordered the development of three other much less modernized fleets: the Guangzhou Fleet based at Guangzhou, the Nanyang Fleet based on the Yangzi River, and the Fuzhou Fleet based at the Fuzhou Shipyard in southeast China. In a policy parallel to that underlying the creation of provincial armies, each fleet remained administratively separate from the others so that a single military leader could not mutiny and turn the entire

navy against the Manchus. In the twentieth century, the Communists adopted a similar fleet structure.

Modernization included the creation of the internal capacity to build ships, manufacture armaments, produce iron and steel, and train officers. Shipyards were established in Shanghai, Fuzhou, and Tianjin; arsenals were built in these three cities as well as in Guangzhou, Nanjing, and other cities; and military academies were founded in Guangzhou, Shanghai, and elsewhere. Ships were the most complicated to build internally, so Li purchased a variety of ships of British, French, German, and domestic manufacture. By 1882, the Chinese navy was composed of fifty steamships. Half had been built by either the Shanghai or Fuzhou Shipyards and half had been purchased abroad, mainly from Britain and Germany. Not surprisingly, considering Li's political power, many of the best and most modern ships found their way into his Beiyang Fleet.

China's fleets competed rather than cooperated for scarce resources. As a result, by the early 1880s, the various Chinese fleets did not have standardized equipment or training, pursued no common strategy, lacked mechanisms to coordinate with each other, and so experienced great difficulty working jointly. In wartime, it was every fleet for itself. The Beiyang Fleet declined to assist the Nanyang Fleet in the Sino-French War (1883–5), and the Nanyang Fleet returned the favor in the First Sino-Japanese War (1894–5). Not surprisingly, China lost both conflicts. These military defeats marked the end of the Self-strengthening Movement. Nevertheless, the movement introduced to China the beginnings of modern industry and spread the study of Western technical subjects, which together were essential for China's subsequent economic development.

II. Financial Reform: The Imperial Maritime Customs

Beyond military modernization, reforms also addressed trade and the conduct of diplomacy. Although the Manchus desired mainly military modernization, their defeat in war forced other reforms as well. Because tax receipts were inadequate in times of crisis, the suppression of the mid-nineteenth-century Taiping Rebellion led to two new sets of taxes. On the local level, the government instituted the *lijin* (*likin*) tax, while on the national level, it levied a salt gabelle and a customs tax on imported goods. Local governments assessed a *lijin* tax on goods in transit. Eventually this tax, which, depending on the province, varied from 1 to 10 percent of the value of the goods, was also applied to production and even to sales. It raised the price of goods transported between provinces, often making domestic goods more expensive than foreign imports.

Although the *lijin* tax had a deleterious impact on Chinese economic development, it became such a lucrative source of local revenue that it remained in place until the Nationalist government finally abolished it in 1931. The central government collected about 20 percent of the *lijin* proceeds, while the bulk remained in the provinces and localities. As a result, the central government received only 40 percent of all tax revenues, or about 100 million taels out of total collections in the late nineteenth century of almost 250 million taels.

After the first Opium War, customs became standardized and were put under the administration of a new office, the Imperial Maritime Customs, founded in 1854. Although it was originally staffed by Chinese officials, by the early 1860s many of the customs officials were European. The Imperial Maritime Customs became the most well-run government of-

fice of the Qing government and also oversaw a variety of infrastructure projects, such as dredging waterways and maintaining wharves and harbor lights. Since foreigners paid most of the customs duties and dominated the leadership of the Imperial Maritime Customs, it soon funded many Chinese reforms.

The origin of the customs service predated the Arrow War by about five years. In 1853, Rutherford Alcock, the British consul in Shanghai, negotiated an agreement with Beijing allowing a foreign customs agent to collect and turn over customs duties to the Chinese government. This had several advantages for Beijing. First, it augmented the income of the central government. Second, in contrast to common Chinese practice, foreign members of the customs inspectorate did not take a cut of their collections but delivered them in toto to Beijing. This meant that the Manchus received

The Imperial Maritime Customs, founded in 1854, soon became one of the most important sources of income for the Chinese government. It also was in charge of dredging channels, maintaining lighthouses and harbor buoys, and building wharves, all of which led to a huge expansion of China's domestic and foreign trade. This is the Customs House at Hankou, located on the Yangzi River.

more tax income from foreign than from Han officials. The Imperial Maritime Customs regularized the collection of customs, guaranteed the payment of indemnities to the foreign powers, and secured future foreign loans to China. In 1863, a Briton, Sir Robert Hart, became the head of the Imperial Maritime Customs, a position he retained until 1908. This made him the longest-serving senior foreign employee of the Qing bureaucracy and a virtual one-man institution. Throughout his long term, Hart was intimately involved with numerous reform attempts.

On 6 November 1865, Hart wrote a letter urging the Manchus to adopt Western diplomatic practices, including sending representatives abroad. Not only could China better preserve its independence by having diplomats communicate directly with the European governments, but this interaction would propel further reforms. Hart also suggested that China take advantage of other recent advances, such as telegraphs, modern steamships, and railways. He warned that failure to adopt such reforms and technological advances would culminate in Western domination of China.

Hart's letter, in combination with other correspondence from the British diplomat and China expert Sir Thomas F. Wade, swayed the opinion of Prince Gong. Like Hart, Wade urged Prince Gong to promote the construction of railways, telegraphs, and mines; to encourage the westernization of military training; and to send diplomatic representatives abroad. Wade argued that embassies allowed China to make contact with foreign governments, which might assist China in times of need. Wade also suggested that China cease looking to past precedents to guide governmental policies.

In the end, Prince Gong decided to send China's first informal diplomatic mission to Europe, headed by Hart's Manchu Chinese-language secretary, Binchun (Pin-ch'un). In 1866, Hart accompanied this mission to various European countries, including France, Britain, Russia, Germany, and Sweden. While it was nonofficial, its official connections were widely known and Binchun held unofficial meetings with European government representatives. The Europeans treated the members of the mission well, and the Chinese recorded their impressions of Western technology, architecture, and social customs. However, the Qing government, with the notable exceptions of Zeng Guofan and Li Hongzhang, made no concerted effort to study Western institutions.

Meanwhile, the Imperial Maritime Customs focused on collecting fees on European goods imported into China. Initially, 40 percent of this revenue was devoted to paying off the indemnities imposed by the 1860 Treaties of Beijing; after 1866 the entire account went to the central government. The customs income from Shanghai soon became a major source of central governmental revenues, especially for emergency military funding such as Zuo Zongtang's extremely expensive reconquest of Xinjiang. Following the traditional Han strategy of pitting one barbarian against another, the Manchus leveraged the customs income from trade with the West to fund the military expedition to decimate the Muslim resistance. Because this revenue flow to Beijing was essential for the Qing government, it vigorously defended Shanghai from the Taipings.

Although the Manchus valued the customs revenue and followed Hart's technical suggestions for improving efficiency, they refused to adopt many of his other recommendations concerning infrastructure improvements like railways and telegraphs. Japan, in contrast, was already busy laying train and telegraph lines to create a comprehensive transportation and communication system. This difference would have military implications when China and Japan went to war in 1894 and the Qing dynasty found itself unable to deploy its troops rapidly for a lack of railways.

By 1875, there were some 400 foreigners working for the Maritime Customs Service. There were also many local employees, mostly Han Chinese, who studied English and learned about the West through contacts with foreign merchants. These Chinese formed a nucleus of pro-Western sympathizers in China. In 1896, it was the Maritime Customs Service that set up China's first modern postal service.

III. Foreign Policy Reform: The Zongli Yamen

In addition to sending their first mission abroad, the Manchus set up a special office to conduct diplomacy that would now take place in Beijing. Previously, the privilege of residing in the capital had been extended only to certain Jesuits in the Ming and early Qing periods, and to certain Russians attached to a Russian Ecclesiastical Mission and language school created under the 1727 Treaty of Kiakhta. (See Chapter 1, Section V.) All other un-Sinicized barbarians had been excluded from Beijing. Those Sinicized enough to conform to the tributary system were permitted in the capital for periodic but limited tribute missions, entailing the giving and receiving of presents and kowtowing before the emperor. All Western maritime powers had been required to work with the Reception Department of the Board of Rites (*Libu*), which administered relations with Sinified tributaries, such as the Koreans and the Siamese. However, because the Russians arrived by land, like the Mongols, they fell under the more important jurisdiction of the Court of Colonial Affairs (*Lifanyuan*), the special institution set up by the Manchus to deal with Inner Asian threats. (See Chapter 2, Sections I and III.)

The Europeans sought to change this institutional arrangement. The Western Europeans refused to perform the mandatory kowtow in Beijing, so they were not allowed in the city, while the Russians chafed at their exclusion from the growing maritime trade and the developing treaty port system. The Qing, in turn, resented the uncooperative attitude of the Europeans, who violated their norms of ethical behavior at every turn. After the first Opium War, the Chinese granted Westerners the right to communicate with the Court via the imperial commissioner in Guangzhou, who was fifteen days from Beijing by messenger. From the Chinese point of view, the intermediary function performed by the imperial commissioner provided a buffer between the throne and the barbarians. From the British point of view, the whim of the commis-

sioner determined whether or not and in what form their messages reached Beijing. Although the Treaty of Nanjing specified that the two sides were equals, in private Chinese officials still called the Europeans barbarians. The problem of communicating with Beijing became particularly serious during the Taiping Rebellion, which disrupted all mail courier service.

The Arrow War offered a long-awaited excuse to alter the situation. In 1857, the British focused on obtaining official diplomatic representation in the capital, the accepted Western practice for conducting foreign relations. This became an essential point in the peace negotiations for the Arrow War and a key term of the 1860 Treaties of Beijing. Immediately afterward, the British and French began to lobby for a new Chinese institution to conduct foreign affairs. They recommended that Prince Gong and his staff be institutionalized in the form of a Chinese foreign ministry. In

By the end of the nineteenth century, Chinese and foreigners were cooperating more frequently. This picture shows Customs students and their foreign teachers in Nanjing, circa 1900.

January 1861, Prince Gong recommended to the throne the creation of the "Office for the General Administration of the Affairs of the Different Nations" (*Zongli geguo shiwu yamen,* or Zongli Yamen for short), to be attached to the highest office, the Grand Council.

With the Nian bandits active to the north of the Yangzi River and the Taipings active to the south, Prince Gong argued that China needed to cooperate with the Europeans and Americans to suppress these critical antidynastic rebellions. Although the Xianfeng emperor agreed to Prince Gong's basic proposal on 20 January 1861, he changed the name to the "Office for the General Administration of the Trade Affairs of the Different Nations" (*zongli geguo tongshang shiwu yamen*). This change was intended to keep the foreigners at a proper distance, since, to the Chinese way of thinking, trade issues were not as important as political questions; in correspondence with foreigners, however, the word "trade" was dropped so that they would not be unnecessarily insulted. The Qing used these dual names to placate Han officials, on the one hand, and Westerners, on the other. The emperor also specified that this office be only temporary; its functions would revert to the Grand Council once the military crisis was over.

The Xianfeng emperor died in August 1861. When the Empress Dowager Cixi and Prince Gong jointly orchestrated a coup d'état in November 1861, Prince Gong became the head of both the Zongli Yamen and the Grand Council. The Zongli Yamen, instead of having only one grand councilor on its staff, became closely linked with the entire Grand Council. This reform unexpectedly increased its status, making it the main government institution for foreign affairs, with Prince Gong (1833–98) and Wenxiang (1818–76) as its most influential members. Both were generally respected by foreigners.

Following the defeat of the Taipings in 1864, the power of the Zongli Yamen gradually diminished. In the absence of a vital domestic threat, many Chinese officials thought that relations with foreigners were now expendable. Meanwhile, Self-strengtheners like Li Hongzhang began to acquire personal power over the conduct of foreign policy. Li, in particular, soon informally took over many functions of the Zongli Yamen. He dominated Chinese foreign affairs until China's defeat in the First Sino-Japanese War in 1895. Over the years, the Zongli Yamen lost its policy-making capacity with the declining political fortunes of Prince Gong and became little more than a bureaucratic office administering routine business with foreigners.

Staff of the Naval College, Customs staff, and Chinese officials, Nanjing, 1902.

IV. Educational Reform: China's First Embassy and Western Learning

To absorb military technology, the Manchus established various military educational institutions as well as language programs to enable officials to communicate with Europeans. A College of Foreign Languages was attached to the Zongli Yamen in 1862 for instruction in English (1862), French (1863), and Russian (1863), the languages of the primary economic and territorial beneficiaries of the Opium Wars. German would be added in 1872 and Japanese only in 1897. In the 1880s, courses in mathematics, astronomy, chemistry, physics, and mechanics became part of the curriculum. The Manchu Court and the Han bureaucracy focused on the technical subjects necessary to use and reproduce Western technology, particularly military technology. Virtually no one was interested in the Western institutional environment that produced the innovations and organized their citizenry to use them with such great effect.

In the past, the Han had adopted elements of other cultures, but according to their understanding, they never adopted core values or institutions from outsiders. In their view, Chinese civilization had always been technologically, militarily, economically, politically, and culturally superior to all others. In fact, China had absorbed a great deal from the outside—Buddhism, for example. More recently, China also had adopted much from the Manchus, including the banner system, dual Manchu–Han appointments, the Grand Council, the *Lifanyuan*, and separate banner examinations (all discussed in Part I). The Manchus even altered what future generations of Han defined as China, henceforth meaning not just the eighteen core provinces within the Great Wall, but also the lands of the expanded Qing empire.

Nor did the Han seem to recognize the Manchu innovations in empire building that made this possible.

The Manchus did not seek to point out their contributions, since part of their successful strategy for empire entailed blending in with their subject peoples, intermarrying with Inner Asians, mimicking Han culture, and Sinifying recalcitrant southern minorities. The Han ideology of empire rested on a Sinocentric view of undisputed and eternal Han superiority, as evidenced by millennia of brilliant Han achievements in all fields. These Han views gave no quarter to non-Han cultural achievements and so inhibited the Han from engaging in a deeper inquiry into the West. It took a century before the link between Western institutions and their military and economic power became clear to many Chinese.

Indicative of the lack of general Chinese curiosity about the West was the dearth of both translated Western works and Chinese travelogues. One notable exception was an early-nineteenth-century account written by the Chinese sailor Xie Qinggao (1765–1821), entitled *Hailu* or *Record of the Seas*. But this book was a narrative description of Xie's travels to Europe that did not inquire into the foundations of Western thinking. The scholar Wei Yuan published his seminal *Illustrated Gazetteer of the Maritime Countries* (*Haiguo tuzhi*) in 1842. (See the feature below.) In 1863, the missionary W. A. P. Martin completed his translation into Chinese of the standard Western work on international law, Henry Wheaton's *Elements of International Law*, published in Britain in 1836. But this was the West foisting books on China, not an indication of real interest.

Following Binchun's trip with Hart in 1866, several other Chinese delegations were sent abroad, including the

ILLUSTRATED GAZETTEER OF THE MARITIME COUNTRIES

Wei Yuan (1794–1856) was among the first Han officials of the Qing dynasty to make a serious attempt to study the West, explain it to his countrymen, and discuss the growing national security threat. His ideas became the basis for many future reforms. Wei was a minor official from Hunan who had passed the highest level of imperial examinations. Early in his career, he became engaged in a major editing project compiling numerous volumes of essays on social, political, and economic problems. In 1842, immediately after the end of the Opium War, he completed the first edition of *An Illustrated Gazetteer of the Maritime Countries* (*Haiguo tuzhi*) (also known as *Illustrated World Geography*). Expanded editions later appeared in 1847 and 1852, doubling its size from the original fifty to one hundred volumes. This is the most important work of the Qing dynasty analyzing the maritime dimension of national security overlooked by the continental preoccupations of the Manchus.

Wei Yuan saw a need both to study Western technology in order to use it to defend China and to study the West more broadly in order to learn how best to use barbarians to subdue other barbarians. He recommended military reorganization based on Ming dynasty, not Western, models and rejected the Western emphasis on trade as the basis for maritime relations. In this sense, the *Illustrated Gazetteer* constituted a revival of Han maritime traditions concerning Southeast Asia disrupted by the Manchus, who lacked a maritime tradition. Both the first and last of the book's sixteen sections emphasized the need for naval modernization. This reflected Wei Yuan's focus on coastal defense, which he considered to be central to China's failure in the Opium War. He warned that coastal defense depended on modern warships, which China must learn to construct by studying Western navies and ship-building facilities. For land warfare, he stressed the need to build Western artillery. His book helped encourage other Chinese to study and learn from the West.

Over and above military modernization, Wei believed China should craft better diplomatic strategies. His book introduced the history and customs of the West to Chinese intellectuals, making him one of the first Chinese officials to recognize that times were changing and that China had to study the West in order to defend its national security. Much of his source material for the first edition came from Lin Zexu, who had extensive dealings with the British in Lin's failed attempt to suppress the opium trade on the eve of the Opium War. On the basis of an improved understanding of the West, Wei recommended that China counterbalance dangerous foes with alliances. He was also one of the first Chinese officials to advocate allying with Russia in the event of a land war and with the United States in the event of a naval conflict. This alliance pattern would reappear repeatedly during the twentieth century, when both the Nationalists and Communists sought American help to defend against the Japanese invasion and when the Communists sought Soviet help during the Korean War.

Wei's many recommendations constituted an indictment of the Manchus for failing to defend China's long coastline. When Wei Yuan died in 1856, only a small number of Qing officials had put his ideas into practice. The next generation of Self-strengtheners, such as Zeng Guofan, Zuo Zongtang, and Li Hongzhang, and the following generation of late Qing reformers, such as Kang Youwei and Liang Qichao, would base many of their ideas on his recommendations. The former group focused on his recommendations for the westernization of China's military institutions, while the latter group examined the West more broadly to consider the reform of China's civil institutions as well. The role of Western ideas in Chinese development has remained an issue of heated debate ever since.

Meanwhile, the Japanese translated the *Illustrated Gazetteer* in 1854–6, producing both an abridged and a complete edition immediately after the publication of the final expanded Chinese edition. The work had an immediate and profound impact on Japanese thinking concerning the imperative to study the West and radically reform.

Burlingame Mission of 1868–71, the Chonghou Mission of 1870–2, and the Chinese commission to Peru and Cuba in 1873. (See Chapter 11.) Not until December 1876 did China send its first official embassy, recognized as such by Western countries, to establish a permanent overseas diplomatic presence. Its head, Guo Songtao, became China's first resident minister at the Court of St. James in England and later in France as well, returning to China in mid-1879. A brilliant student and an accomplished military adviser, Guo concluded that China could solve its foreign problems only through diplomacy. This was an unpopular position in China. From 1862 to 1874, he served in a variety of provincial postings, where he encouraged the development of railways, steamships, and the telegraph. From 1875 to 1877, he served in the Zongli Yamen. Although criticized for being too pro-Western, Li Hongzhang chose Guo to head China's first permanent embassy overseas. Given the anti-Western sentiments rampant in the Chinese bureaucracy at this time, the posting was potentially career terminating.

Xenophobes in Beijing supplied Guo with an assistant, Liu Xihong (Liu Hsi-hung), who was known for his antiforeign sentiments. Guo opened formal diplomatic relations with England and later with France, while Liu established relations with Germany. Guo was ordered to keep a diary, which was published as *The Record of an Envoy's Journey to the West* (*Shixi jicheng*), and was immediately attacked by conservatives for traitorously promoting the West. Beijing soon banned the book, although enough copies survived to influence later generations of Chinese intellectuals.

Guo had long admired Western technological achievements, but he went further to describe Western institutions, such as the British Parliament. Using traditional Chinese terminology, he emphasized the "ceremony" and "order" underlying Western institutions, suggesting that they had a worthy ethical basis. This, in turn, suggested the possibility of an alternative ethical basis to Confucianism. In China, such thinking was heresy. Some forty years later, other Chinese intellectuals during the 1919 May Fourth Movement argued that China should adopt not only Western technology but also some of its core values, such as democracy. Others gravitated to different strains of European thinking, particularly the Soviet interpretation of Marxism.

When discussing the strengths of European civilization, Guo emphasized international law. Unlike in China, where relations depended on the relative status of each person, institution, or ethnic group involved, in Europe the various states treated each other as equals. Guo noted that Western countries valued honor, discipline, and justice. The protection of these values permitted the orderly regulation of commerce. Instead of positing technology as the root of the West's wealth and power, Guo focused on the institutional basis. He concluded that China required not just modernization, but also westernization. This incensed his contemporaries, who had been credentialed by an examination system testing Confucian traditions of governance.

Finally, in perhaps his most profound departure from Chinese cultural traditions, Guo pointed to the prime role played by reason in European civilization and the wide availability of education even to commoners. He noted how, unlike his fellow Chinese, educated Europeans could rely on reason to make their own decisions. By contrast, he considered the average Chinese to be idle, ignorant, and corrupt. He believed it would be difficult for the Chinese to duplicate Western technological achievements until reason guided the thoughts and actions of the general population. As Guo remarked in despair in one of his letters from Europe: "Personally, I think there is something in the Chinese mind which is absolutely unintelligible."[2] As a first step on the long road to modernization via westernization, Guo believed China needed to adopt international law to regulate its foreign relations. Guo had come to the same conclusions as his Japanese contemporaries. His opinion, however, was very much in the minority and his ideas had little influence.

During the 1860s and 1870s, the Qing dynasty did begin to employ Protestant missionaries to work as translators in various Self-strengthening projects. In 1868 Zeng Guofan established a school to train translators at the Jiangnan Arsenal and make available Western works on technology and machinery. Meanwhile, missionaries worked to produce standardized Chinese-language textbooks, to be used in missionary schools, on astronomy, chemistry, geography, geology, history, language, mathematics, music, surveying, and zoology. These translators gradually created a vast new Chinese-language technical vocabulary to accommodate Western technical concepts and terminology. This is perhaps the most lasting contribution of the nineteenth-century Protestant missionaries in China, who altered the language spoken by the Chinese through the addition of thousands of new words. Like the Jesuits, who introduced Western mathematics and astronomy to the late Ming and early Qing Courts, these Protestant missionaries considered Western education as a means to spread Christianity. Instead, they wound up spreading a greater appreciation for Western science.

Western learning was brought to China mainly via foreign steamship companies. This 1920s photograph of Guangzhou shows a wide range of foreign steamships surrounded by local Chinese junks.

V. Governmental Restoration: Confucian Rectification

While some key Han provincial officials reacted to the civil and foreign wars with Self-strengthening in order to put Western military innovations at the service of the Qing state, other officials emphasized indigenous solutions to China's proliferating problems. These officials had faith in the universality of Han civilization. Some remained adamantly opposed to the introduction of modern technology, since to change any of the parts altered the entirety. This holistic view of the world hearkened back not only to Confucian beliefs but also to both the *yin* and *yang* framework and Daoism. According to the *yin* and *yang* model, the world was composed of opposites, each waxing and waning in inverse proportion to the other. This meant that any westernization of China would reverberate throughout the entire interlocking chain of human existence. Daoism stressed rule, not by decisive actions such as radical reforms, but by harmony with the environment, which the many rebellions had so clearly disrupted. This pervasive outlook saw China's problems less in terms of an asymmetry in military hardware and more in terms of an ethical degeneration within China, whose solution required a restoration of virtuous rule. This alone would halt the downturn in the dynastic cycle.

During the nineteenth century, the overwhelming majority of both Han and Manchus opposed westernization of Chinese institutions. Han officials had traditionally risen to power through academic success in the imperial examination system, while the Manchus had used this system to vet loyal administrators. Successful examination candidates devoted their early decades to the study of the Confucian Classics. An infiltration of Western subjects into the educational system eroded both the preeminence of their own educations and the power of Confucianism. They decried the adoption of Western technology as corrosive to both Chinese civilization and the dynasty; the restoration of Chinese primacy required a revival of such time-honored Confucian virtues as filial piety, righteousness, and harmony. These officials warned that those Chinese who adopted Western ways betrayed their own heritage.

In the nineteenth century, the most famous member of the group favoring a Confucian restoration was Woren (1804–71), a Mongol bannerman. He served as president of the Censorate, president of the Board of Works, tutor to the Tongzhi emperor, and chancellor of the Hanlin Academy. He rejected Western science in favor of geomancy, astrology, and a belief in ghosts and heavenly portents, and so opposed the introduction of mathematics and astronomy into the curriculum as foreign pollution. China, he believed, should focus on adherence to proper rituals and ethical codes, not on clever techniques or gadgets. He and his followers fought tooth and nail to limit the impact of the Self-strengtheners, whose changes, they feared, would permanently disrupt the cosmos. Although some of these restorationists did favor the use of some Western military technology, all of them vehemently opposed the introduction of Western institutions.

Government officials opposed westernization for other reasons as well. Some argued that the West would not necessarily sell the most up-to-date technology, so that China would always be behind. Others warned that the West hoped to dominate China through the spread of Western technology. Still others cited such social differences between China and Europe as the large disparity in population size to explain why westernization was unnecessary and potentially harmful, as it might lead to massive unemployment. Finally, concerns arose that the construction of modern buildings, railways, telegraph lines, and mines could seriously damage the cosmic order by violating the laws of *fengshui* and so should be avoided at all costs. Not until after the Sino-Japanese War did the general opposition to railways decline, when it became generally recognized that without interior lines of communication, China could not effectively deploy its forces on its own territory. Yet, there was still little recognition of the economic importance of railways.

Many officials feared that westernization would allow Christianity to make inroads. The Scottish Presbyterian Robert Morrison completed the first full Chinese translation of the Bible in 1823; it was heavily based on earlier partial Jesuit translations. Unlike China's native nonexclusive religions, such as Daoism and Buddhism, which tolerated multiple, layered belief systems, Christianity—like Islam—demanded an exclusive allegiance. Christianity required the faithful to sever ties with other religions, while its core beliefs cast doubt on the validity of the Confucian social hierarchy, which had imperial ancestors, not God, at its summit. Christianity demanded supreme loyalty not to the temporal figure of an emperor but to God, or, in the case of the Catholic Church, also to the pope in Rome; the Chinese literati of the Manchu Court correctly considered such ideas as a threat to the Confucian social order. Anti-Western officials argued that Christianity caused antigovernment rebellions, such as the quasi-Christian Taiping Rebellion; continuing westernization, they claimed, would inevitably lead to more and ever greater domestic unrest.

Some officials considered westernization to be an all-or-nothing proposition that, if introduced, would ultimately destroy Chinese civilization. Liu Xihong realized that the Western value system would erode Confucian values. He dismissed European civilization as being based on materialism, while Chinese civilization was based on philosophical ideals: "Foreigners consider material wealth as true wealth; China takes temperance as true wealth; Western nations think brute force is strength; China takes deference as strength. This is the real truth."[3] To Liu, material success reflected empty crassness, while Chinese traditions expressed ethical norms of behavior; generations later, the Chinese Communists repeated Liu's admonitions against Western acquisitiveness.

Many Chinese officials opposed westernization not out of contempt for Western ways, antiforeign prejudices, or personal interests vested in a Confucian status quo, but out of fear that the China they loved and the civilization they treasured would be irretrievably lost. Meanwhile, the inherent problems of minority rule at a time of a weakening mandate of heaven made westernization problematic for the Manchus. The overwhelming opposition to institutional reform by the Han literati populating the bureaucracy precluded westernization from the top, the path ultimately chosen by the Japanese. This left China with uncoordinated half-measures from the provinces.

Instead, many Manchus favored a Confucian restoration since it validated their rule by teaching loyalty to the emperor. During the Tongzhi emperor's reign, the government sponsored a revival of Confucianism. While this policy undoubtedly helped the Manchus to reassert short-term political control over their empire, it undermined the long-term goals of the Self-strengthening Movement. China willingly bought Western armaments and adopted Western technology, but it rejected the underlying modes of analysis, as well as the political and economic institutions, that made the Industrial Revolution possible in the first place and allowed the technology to be used so effectively. China's two-track policy of technology imports and Confucian revival would not solve the problem of protecting Chinese interests from the incursions of the great powers. However unsystematic the changes wrought by the Self-strengtheners, they irrevocably changed the China that Woren and his followers cherished and fought so hard to protect. The legacy of the Industrial Revolution has been highly corrosive to traditional societies everywhere. Throughout the rest of the nineteenth century and well into the twentieth century, many Chinese remained caught between a civilization that they revered and foreign technology that they craved.

Conclusions

The Self-strengthening Movement led to two important institutional reforms concerning the conduct of Chinese relations with the West: the creation of a quasi-foreign office, the Zongli Yamen, and the creation of a customs collection agency, the Maritime Customs Inspectorate. Defeat in the Opium and Arrow Wars forced these changes on China. Meanwhile, the Self-strengtheners focused on the military underpinnings of Western power and sought to replicate them in China, first by importing armaments and then by trying to produce them locally in Chinese arsenals and shipyards. They initiated these efforts during the great mid-century rebellions and used the imported technology to help restore order. As a result of this thinking, the measures promoted by the Self-strengtheners were limited in scope and did not attempt to understand the sources of Western innovation by examining its social, economic, and government institutions.

Those Chinese who went beyond these limited steps to acquire Western learning and those who developed extensive Western contacts often became suspect as traitors. The Communist term "spiritual pollution," leveled at those tainted with westernized ideas, has a long history going back at least to the Self-strengthening Movement. Much of the Han literati remained Confucian to the bones, so that curiosity about the West followed a very narrow channel to focus almost exclusively on armaments. When China's first ambassador to the West attempted to explain what he had seen to his countrymen, for many years they largely ignored him; meanwhile, Japan's most senior leaders of the Meiji period spent long periods abroad studying Western institutions and made this knowledge the basis for institutional reforms at home.

The Self-strengthening Movement attempted to employ Western technology, particularly military technology, without altering the fundamental institutional structure or Confucian bedrock of China. That is, they wanted some of the material fruits of Western civilization but not the institutional garden where they grew. Their motto was *"Zhong xue wei ti, Xi xue wei yong,"* or "Chinese learning for essential matters (*ti*), Western learning for practical matters (*yong*)." While this philosophy allowed for the adoption of some technological advances from the West, it refused to acknowledge that China might require fundamental social reforms to utilize the modern industrialized system created in the West. What the Self-strengtheners wanted was modernization, meaning the acquisition of the most up-to-date technology, but certainly not westernization, meaning the introduction of westernized institutions.

Chinese Self-strengtheners hoped to retain their civilization intact, not to disrupt its core values. Chinese resisted the encroachments of Western culture, adopting only those Western practices and technology necessary to keep foreigners at China's geographic and cultural periphery and thereby minimize any interaction. The Qing adopted westernizing reforms only for areas of direct and inescapable interaction,

namely, institutions concerning China's foreign relations, maritime customs, and the military. This was very much in keeping with their traditional method of empire that took advantage of barbarian traditions to maintain peace on the frontier: The Manchus attempted to use trade with the West just as they had used the *Lifanyuan*, Lama Buddhism, and intermarriage with Mongolians in order to retain power there.

BIBLIOGRAPHY

Ayers, William. *Chang Chih-tung and Educational Reform in China.* Cambridge, MA: Harvard University Press, 1971.

Banno, Masataka. *China and the West, 1858–1861: The Origins of the Tsungli Yamen.* Cambridge, MA: Harvard University Press, 1964.

Beasley, W. G. *The Meiji Restoration.* Stanford, CA: Stanford University Press, 1972.

Bennett, Adrian A. *John Fryer: The Introduction of Western Science and Technology into Nineteenth-Century China.* Cambridge, MA: Harvard University Press, 1967.

Chan, Wellington K. K. *Merchants, Mandarins and Modern Enterprise in late Ch'ing China.* Cambridge, MA: Harvard University Press, 1975.

Chu, Samuel C. *Reformer in Modern China, Chang Chien.* New York: Columbia University Press, 1965.

——— and Kwang-ching Liu, eds. *Li Hung-chang and China's Early Modernization.* Armonk, NY: M. E. Sharpe, 1994.

Cohen, Paul A. *Between Tradition and Modernity: Wang T'ao and Reform in Late Ch'ing China.* Cambridge, MA: Harvard University Press, 1974.

Crossley, Pamela Kyle. *Orphan Warriors: Three Manchu Generations and the End of the Qing World.* Princeton, NJ: Princeton University Press, 1990.

Elman, Benjamin A. *A Cultural History of Modern Science in China.* Cambridge, MA: Harvard University Press, 2006.

Feuerwerker, Albert. *China's Early Industrialization: Sheng Hsuan-huai (1844–1916) and Mandarin Enterprise.* Cambridge, MA: Harvard University Press, 1958.

Frodsham, J. D. *The First Chinese Embassy to the West.* London: Clarendon Press, 1974.

Hirakawa, Sukehiro. "Japan's Turn to the West." Translated by Bob Wakabayashi. In *The Cambridge History of Japan*, vol. 5, edited by Marius B. Jansen, 432–98. Cambridge: Cambridge University Press, 1989.

Hsü, Immanuel C. Y. *China's Entrance into the Family of Nations: The Diplomatic Phase 1858–1880.* Cambridge, MA: Harvard University Press, 1960.

Huenemann, Ralph William. *The Dragon and the Iron Horse: The Economics of Railroads in China, 1876–1937.* Cambridge, MA: Harvard University Press, 1984.

Jansen, Marius B. *The Making of Modern Japan.* Cambridge, MA: Harvard University Press, 2000.

Kennedy, Thomas. *The Arms of Kiangnan: Modernization in the Chinese Ordnance Industry, 1860–1895.* Boulder, CO: Westview Press, 1978.

Kuo, Ting-yee and Kwang-ching Liu. "Self-Strengthening: The Pursuit of Western Technology." In *The Cambridge History of China*, vol. 10, edited by Denis Twitchett and John K. Fairbank, 491–542. Cambridge: Cambridge University Press, 1978.

Leonard, Jane Kate. *Wei Yuan and China's Rediscovery of the Maritime World.* Cambridge, MA: Harvard University Press, 1984.

Morse, Hosea Ballou. *The International Relations of the Chinese Empire.* Vol. 2. Shanghai: Kelly and Walsh, 1918.

Ocko, Jonathan K. *Bureaucratic Reform in Provincial China: Ting Jih-ch'ang in Restoration Kiangsu, 1867–1870.* Cambridge, MA: Harvard University Press, 1983.

Porter, Jonathan. *Tseng Kuo-fan's Private Bureaucracy.* Berkeley: University of California Press, 1972.

Rankin, Mary. *Elite Activism and Political Transformation in China: Zhejiang Province, 1864–1911.* Stanford, CA: Stanford University Press, 1986.

Rawlinson, John L. "China's Failure to Coordinate Her Modern Fleets in the Late Nineteenth Century." In *Approaches to Modern Chinese History*, edited by Albert Feuerwerker, Rhoads Murphey, and Mary C. Wright, Berkeley: University of California Press, 1967, 105–32.

———— *China's Struggle for Naval Development, 1839–1895.* Cambridge, MA: Harvard University Press, 1967.

Rhoads, Edward J. M. *Manchus & Han: Ethnic Relations and Political Power in Late Qing and Early Republican China, 1861–1928.* Seattle: University of Washington Press, 2000.

Wright, Mary C. *The Last Stand of Chinese Conservatism: The T'ung-chih Restoration, 1862–1874.* Stanford, CA: Stanford University Press, 1957.

NOTES

1. Zeng Guofan's instructions to his sons upon leaving to settle the 1870 Tianjin Massacre. William James Hail, *Tsêng Kuo-fan and the Taiping Rebellion,* 2nd ed. (New York: Paragon, 1964), 353. Yale University, 1927. Bibliography: p. [372]–399. Hail, William James. 1964. Tsêng Kuo-fan and the Taiping Rebellion, with a short sketch of his later career. Yale historical publications, 18. New York: Paragon Book Reprint Corp.
2. Cited in J. D. Frodsham, *The First Chinese Embassy to the West* (London: Clarendon Press, 1974), xxxvii, xlii–xliv.
3. Ibid.

Chronology

1866	Binchun-Hart Mission
1867–70	Burlingame Mission
1868	Russia conquers Khanate of Bukhara
1869	Alcock Convention with Britain (not ratified)
1870	Tianjin Massacre
	Li Hongzhang made governor of Zhili
1871	Russian occupation of the Ili Valley
1873	Russia conquers Khanate of Khiva
1874	Japan sends punitive mission against Taiwan
1875	Tongzhi emperor dies; Guangxu emperor assumes the throne
	Margary Affair
1876	First official mission to Europe
	Yantai Convention with Britain (ratified 1885)
	Russia conquers Khanate of Kokand
1877	Yakub Beg dies
1878	End of Muslim Rebellion in Xinjiang
1879	Japanese annexation of Ryukyu Islands
	Treaty of Livadia (not ratified)
1881	Treaty of St. Petersburg
1883–5	Sino-French War over Vietnam
1884	Xinjiang becomes a Chinese province
1885	Taiwan becomes a Chinese province
1886	Burma becomes a British protectorate

11

Attacks on Chinese Sovereignty

On Reaching Hong Kong (1885)

The waters are those of Yao's time,
the sun is the same as Xia's,
also the cap and the gown I wear
are the uniform of Han.
Climbing the tower, I look all around—
this truly is my land,
yet on the great flags I do not see
our yellow dragon.[1]

Huang Zunxian (1848–1905),
poet, diplomat, reformer

Domestically, the Self-strengthening Movement allowed the Manchus to remain on the throne and in nominal control over a far-flung empire. Internationally, China sent its first official embassies overseas to Europe and entered into regular diplomatic contact with foreign countries. However, these reforms did little to address the sources of dynastic decline, namely, the terrible destruction from decades of civil war, population growth exceeding productivity, weakening central control over the civil bureaucracy and armed forces, increasingly visible corruption, declining Manchu military competence, and the shift in the international balance of power caused by the Industrial Revolution. Foreign policy high points of this period include two diplomatic initiatives, the Burlingame Mission sending China's first embassy abroad and the Alcock Convention attempting to establish juridically equal diplomatic relations with Britain; two causes célèbres involving the deaths of foreigners, the Tianjin Massacre and the Margary Affair; growing tensions with China's two closest neighbors, Japan and Russia, over Taiwan and Xinjiang, respectively; and finally, French colonization of the

Chinese tributary Annam (Vietnam) that culminated in the Sino-French War (1883–5).

I. The Burlingame Mission and the Alcock Convention

During the late 1860s and early 1870s, China began the lengthy and not altogether successful process of opening formal diplomatic relations with the West. The Guo Songtao embassy to Britain has already been discussed in the context of the institutional changes made during the Self-strengthening Movement (Chapter 10, Section IV). Other early attempts include the Burlingame Mission and the Alcock Convention.

Immediately after the Binchun-Hart Mission overseas in 1866, the Zongli Yamen appointed Anson Burlingame (1820–70), the former first American minister to China (1861–7), to lead China's second unofficial mission overseas in 1867. This may have been Burlingame's idea, since at his retirement party in Beijing, he evidently told Prince Gong that he would volunteer to assist China "as if he were China's envoy."[2] U.S. Secretary of State William Seward might have also put the idea in Burlingame's mind, since Seward suggested in a 1866 letter that China should send a diplomatic representative to Washington. In keeping with the Manchu pretense of joint Manchu–Han rule, the mission included Han and Manchu co-envoys; this was reportedly done at Robert Hart's suggestion so that the mission would be taken seriously.

The Burlingame Mission left on 25 February 1868 for California and then went on to Washington, D.C., where the members met President Andrew Johnson and Secretary of State Seward. On 28 July 1868, Burlingame apparently exceeded the authority granted by the Zongli

Yamen when he signed a treaty with Seward promising that the United States would not interfere in China. The treaty provided both countries most-favored-nation treatment with regard to residence and travel, as well as reciprocal rights of religious freedom and access to public schools. It allowed China to send consuls to Washington and laborers to work in the United States. While the treaty outlawed contract emigration because of its association with kidnapping Chinese for sale as coolie labor, it did not touch upon the issue of naturalization. China's first treaty negotiated on the basis of juridical equality went into effect with the exchange of ratifications in Beijing on 23 November 1869.

Burlingame's next stop was England, where he and his co-envoys met Queen Victoria. Here also, Burlingame lobbied for a formal British promise not to interfere in China. On 28 December 1868, the British government promised not to pressure China unduly in their ongoing negotiations on treaty revision. During 1869, Burlingame visited France, Denmark, and Sweden. In Prussia, he persuaded Chancellor Otto von Bismarck to make a similar statement of noninterference before moving on to Russia. Although the mission had an audience with Tsar Alexander II, soon afterward Burlingame contracted pneumonia and died on 23 February 1870. Perhaps due to his untimely death, Russia appears not to have made any promises to abstain from interfering in Chinese domestic affairs. Afterward, Burlingame's Manchu and Han Chinese co-envoys continued on alone to Brussels and Rome before returning to China later that year.

The Burlingame Mission gave China a much-needed breathing space, but contrary to Burlingame's expectations, the mission did not spur the study of the West in China; rather, it lent force to a traditionalist reaction. Once many of the key foreign powers assured Beijing that they would not demand immediate westernization, the conservatives within the government argued that rapid reforms were no longer necessary. The literati, in particular, opposed the wholesale adoption of Western learning, rightfully fearing that this would undermine the Confucian basis of their power. Instead of hastening China's modernization, therefore, the success of the Burlingame Mission may have impeded it.

The second unanticipated setback was the failure of the Alcock Convention. As the Burlingame Mission was winding down in 1869, the British minister to China, Rutherford Alcock, was conducting intensive negotiations with officials in Beijing concerning treaty revision. On 23 October 1869, the resulting Sino-British treaty granted China the right to set up a consulate on the British island of Hong Kong, increased the import duties on opium and silk paid to China, and amended the British most-favored-nation clauses to obligate Britain to abide by the most restrictive conditions negotiated

This typical Hong Kong street scene shows the commercial prosperity of the British colony.

by China with other countries. Finally, British citizens were given greater rights to live and work in China, while Beijing promised to adopt a commercial code. This treaty was far less one-sided than the treaties negotiated during the Opium Wars.

There was significant opposition to this convention in Britain. Hong Kong merchants, in particular, opposed higher tariffs and the presence of a Chinese consulate on British soil. Other foreign powers, but not the United States, objected to the precedent set by this convention. A combination of internal British interests hostile to the convention and antiforeign riots in China, the so-called Tianjin Massacre of 21 June 1870, culminated in a British refusal on 25 July 1870 to ratify the convention. The Chinese later attached special historical importance to this date as an example of Western mistreatment.

In the end, China's first attempts to build equal diplomatic relations succeeded with the United States but failed with the European powers. Confucian officials rejected the Zongli Yamen's attempt to negotiate equal treaties with foreigners. Westerners were equally convinced of their own cultural superiority and foreigners working in China were hesitant to give up their privileged position, especially before Beijing adopted a westernized legal system with compatible provisions for commercial, civil, and international law. As foreigners, they stood too low in the Confucian social hierarchy and the *guanxi* system to expect judgments in their favor within the Qing judicial system. Western demands for legal protections while in China became especially relevant at the time of the Tianjin Massacre, when many Chinese officials applauded the mob violence to rid the country of foreigners. In the end, opposition from both countries derailed China's first equal treaty with Britain.

II. The Tianjin Massacre (1870) and the Margary Affair (1875)

During the 1870s, two events seriously marred China's relations with France, Great Britain, and other major powers. First, a series of anti-Christian riots culminated in the Tianjin Massacre of 1870, in which about twenty foreigners, mostly French nationals, died. In response, the powers pressured Beijing to apologize and pay an indemnity. Second, the 1875

murder of a British official, Augustus Raymond Margary, increased Sino–British tensions and culminated in yet another Chinese apology and indemnity.

As a result of the French Treaty of Beijing that forced China to allow missionaries in the country, beginning in the 1860s Christians arrived in large numbers. Most came from France, Great Britain, and the United States. Missionaries were some of the first foreigners to venture outside the treaty ports, and they soon began buying land to build churches. They sought not only to spread religion but also to change social customs and to improve public health. They founded numerous churches, schools, universities, orphanages, and hospitals. Missionary schools made available Western education not only in religion but also in medicine and in a wide array of other subjects normally taught in the West but not in China. In particular, missionaries encouraged the education of girls and denounced the practice of footbinding. (See the feature below.)

FOOTBINDING

Han Chinese women bound their daughters' feet to make them more marriageable. The process involved bending the four small toes under the foot and breaking the bones. Approximately 10–15 percent of young girls died in the process. For men, women with small Lily Feet were thought to be more sexually desirable.

Of all the Chinese social practices, footbinding attracted particular attention of missionaries. Footbinding appalled Westerners, who could not understand how the Han could intentionally cripple their daughters, leaving them able to walk only with difficulty and pain. The many attempts of missionaries to ban the practice failed. Many Chinese considered their interference as another Western intrusion into China's domestic affairs.

The binding of the feet of Han Chinese girls began in the tenth century, first among entertainers and girls at the imperial Court and gradually spread among the literati. The practice spread from the rich to the poor and from urban to rural areas. By the late imperial period, footbinding was widespread throughout the Han population. Although the new republican government banned the practice after 1911, it continued in many rural areas until the Communists enforced harsher penalties in the 1950s. It did not end completely until the Cultural Revolution (1966–76), when Red Guards denounced women with bound feet and Mao Zedong labeled his political opponents as "old women with bound feet." In the 1990s, there were still old women in China hobbling on bound feet.

According to tradition, Li Yu (937–78), the last emperor of the Southern Tang dynasty, maintained a life of luxury and indolence at Court, where he had his favorite concubine bind her feet in silk and dance on a pearl-studded golden lotus platform. "Golden Lotus" became a synonym for bound feet and had powerful sexual connotations for Han men, who developed a fetish for small feet. Sexual manuals called "pillow books" described the use of bound feet during sexual intercourse.

Footbinding was a painful process beginning between the ages of five and eight, when mothers tightly bound the feet of their daughters, breaking all toes save the big toe in order to bend the arch over onto itself. This put the entire body weight on the outer heel. Tight binding cloth kept the feet in this position and prevented the bones from growing larger than 10 centimeters (3.9 inches) to create so-called Lotus Feet. The constant pain ended when the feet ceased growing, but walking remained painful so that the leg muscles tended to atrophy from lack of use. It took several years to complete the process, which often resulted in infection, gangrene, and death. As many as 10 to 15 percent of young girls who endured footbinding did not survive. Those who did were left to totter painfully on tiny feet, and forever tend infections and remove shedding skin from foul binding cloth. Bound feet required continued bandaging for support and special cleaning and care, since the practice often caused open sores and odors, which perfume was used to disguise.

Parents supported the practice in order to make their daughters more marriageable and also to provide a status symbol indicating an income sufficient not to require the physical labor of daughters. It was imperative that daughters marry since spinsters became a financial burden, while the failure to produce offspring violated the Confucian norms of filial piety and the requirements for ancestor worship. In the nineteenth and twentieth centuries, women with bound feet recounted their mothers' warnings that

In 1990, the authors visited Huhehaote (Hohhot), Inner Mongolia. While walking down a busy thoroughfare, they saw an elderly woman with bound feet walking down the street. The young man next to her was also clearly surprised by her appearance. While more and more rare, footbinding was practiced in China well into the 1920s and 1930s, and until it was outlawed in 1949, so there are still old women with bound feet in China.

Continued

they would die unmarried without bound feet and without children to tend their graves, so they would become "hungry ghosts" forced to wander for eternity. (See the feature on page 351.)

Many non-Han peoples in China rejected footbinding. These included the Manchus, the Tibetans, the Turkic peoples of Western China, the Mongols, and the Hakka. Since many of these people were nomadic, they could not afford to cripple their daughters. Many Hakka later moved to Taiwan, which explains why footbinding was less prevalent there. Initially, the Manchus tried to ban footbinding under the Shunzhi emperor (r. 1644–61), but the Han ignored the prohibition. The Kangxi emperor (r. 1662–1722) then revoked the ban rather than incur the wrath of the Han. Much later, the Empress Dowager Cixi (1835–1908) imposed a ban in 1902 that was also widely ignored.

The bound feet of Han women indicated their low status: They were crippled in order to satisfy the sexual fantasies of men. Female infanticide was another indicator. Likewise, during famines, little girls died in disproportionate numbers. To this day, the abortion of female fetuses continues to skew the gender distribution in the People's Republic of China.

Chinese from all walks of life intensely resented this interference. Officials believed that the Christian disrespect for social hierarchy and advocacy for the rights of man threatened social order. Educated Chinese immediately recognized the threat that Christianity posed for a Confucian government based on the mandate of heaven; for their family organization based on filial piety, ancestor worship, and collective responsibility; for the examination system based on the memorization of Han Classics; and for the cosmic equilibrium based on the emperor's ritual intercession between heaven and earth. They found tales of Christ's divinity to be ludicrous, given his relatively recent birth during the Han dynasty. Ordinary Chinese detested missionaries for destroying family unity and rejecting traditional Buddhist, Daoist, and ancestor-worship rites.

Christianity, like Confucianism, represented an entire way of life. Just as the Han historically assumed the role of educating their tributaries and frontier peoples in the ways of civilization, the Europeans and Americans sought to educate the Chinese in the norms of Western civilization. Unlike the Han, who generally waited for barbarians to come to them, Westerners aggressively explored the world and attempted to missionize those who never even desired contacts with the West. Christianity made a frontal assault on China's political and social order by rejecting the emperor as mediator between humanity and the cosmos. It put duty to God before duty to the state or to the family; made the individual soul, not the clan, the fundamental social unit composing society; and made the New and Old Testaments their central texts, not the Four Books or the Five Classics.

All Chinese, save a handful of converts, resented such views. After the settlement of the Opium Wars, antiforeign sentiments remained strong, particularly in Tianjin, where French troops continued to occupy the city until 1863 and were accused of abusing the populace. Throughout China, attacks on missionaries proliferated in the 1860s. Some were due

to Chinese superstition and xenophobia. Rumors abounded that the missionaries practiced magic on Chinese children and experimented on pilfered body parts: Missionaries were rumored to extract the eyes, bone marrow, and even souls of children in order to make medicine. Such rumors were more a projection of Chinese medicine, which used animal body parts in many remedies, than a reflection of European medicine that favored opiates. Others claimed that missionaries used drugs to force Chinese to convert. Faced with growing Chinese mob violence, the foreigners often responded in kind. In 1868, British naval forces seized the forts at Anping, Taiwan, demanding and receiving repayment for damage to Roman Catholic and Protestant churches. An estimated twenty-one Chinese were killed in this encounter.

By 1869, French missionaries in northern China had built a church and an orphanage in the city of Tianjin. The spreading rumors of French mistreatment were based on the small fee offered for each child delivered to the orphanage and the high mortality rate there. Because the nuns focused on baptizing sick children, undoubtedly many of the children delivered to them were seriously ill. When they died, however, the nuns were blamed for interfering in their fate. Responding to these rumors, Chonghou, the Manchu superintendent for trade in North China, inspected the French orphanage and found the rumors to be baseless. He established a committee to supervise the orphanage.

On 21 June 1870, the French consul in Tianjin, Henri Fontanier, insisted that Chonghou apologize to the French nuns for his inspection of the orphanage; but for a man to apologize to women went against Confucian ethics. Fontanier, ignoring Chonghou's timely warning to stay off the streets, panicked when he encountered the county magistrate of Tianjin, Liu Jie, who had been unable to disperse a mob that was gathering at the French church. Fontanier fired on Liu Jie, killing one of Liu's servants instead. The crowd erupted, killing

Fontanier, his assistant, two priests, ten nuns, three Russians, and approximately thirty Chinese Christian converts, and torching the French church and orphanage as well as four British and American churches. By the time the riot ended, eighteen French citizens had been killed. The foreign community was particularly outraged that the nuns had been stripped and sexually abused before being killed and burned, while the Frenchmen had been tortured and mutilated before being killed and dumped in a river. Although the French were the main target, the Chinese crowd hoped to eliminate other foreigners as well, chanting "Kill the French first, then the other foreigners."

When the foreign ministers of seven countries protested to Beijing, the Court initially assigned Zeng Guofan to resolve the matter, but his recommendation was considered to be too pro-Western. Zeng planned to sack all of the high Tianjin officials, including the circuit intendent, the prefect, and the district magistrate; execute the fifteen chief instigators; and exile twenty-one others. Conservative officials in Beijing condemned Zeng, who was quickly reassigned. Zeng's protégé, Li Hongzhang, replaced him as governor-general of Zhili and quickly agreed to pay France 400,000 taels in compensation, to send a mission of apology to France, to banish the prefect and magistrate, and to sentence eighteen rioters to capital punishment and twenty-five others to hard labor. In a one-for-one exchange, the number set to be executed exactly equaled the number of French dead. Beijing ordered Chonghou to Europe to deliver the official apology to the president of France. He was received at the palace of Versailles on 23 November 1871, where the incident was finally laid to rest.

The so-called Margary Affair was the second major international incident of the 1870s, this time between Britain and China. To counter the growing Russian penetration of Xinjiang, the British hoped to build a railway line from Burma into Western China as far north as the upper Yangzi River. Over the winter of 1874–5, a surveying team from India was scheduled to arrive in China, so the British sent Vice-Consul Augustus Raymond Margary into the interior to meet it, ignoring warnings from Chinese officials of the lawlessness of the area. After traveling up the Yangzi River, Margary journeyed through territory recently ravaged by the Panthay Rebellion toward the Sino-Burmese border. On 21 February 1875, when he was returning to China, an ambush killed Margary and five Chinese guards. There was substantial evidence that Margary's murder was premeditated in order to halt progress on the railway. The British demanded an investigation of the incident, an apology, and compensation for Margary's family. They also used the issue as a pretext to pressure China to discuss other outstanding questions, such as the right of foreign diplomats to obtain audiences with the emperor. To increase the pressure,

Britain withdrew its legation to Shanghai and threatened to sever diplomatic relations.

The Chinese agreed to establish their country's first diplomatic legation in Europe, headed by Guo Songtao, and his first assignment was to apologize for Margary's murder. While Chonghou had been China's first envoy to the West, Guo Songtao would be China's first minister. On 13 September 1876, Li Hongzhang and the British minister, Thomas Wade, signed the Yantai (Chefoo) Convention, which specified an indemnity of 200,000 taels for the families of the dead. This was an enormous sum, equaling fully one-half of the entire indemnity paid to France for the Tianjin Massacre. Other parts of the Yantai Convention were potentially more important: The Chinese government agreed to prepare regulations to govern relations between Chinese officials and foreign diplomats and to open four new ports to foreign trade. In return, the British agreed that only treaty ports would be exempt from local taxes (*lijin*); foreigners elsewhere would have to pay. Due to both international and domestic opposition to these terms, however, the British government did not ratify the Yantai Convention until 1885.

Li Hongzhang negotiated the settlements to both the Tianjin Massacre and the Margary Affair. Although his resolution for the Tianjin Massacre appeared harsher than Zeng's, Li actually kept the highest Chinese official, the circuit intendent, from being removed from office. Unlike Zeng, who tried to punish the actual culprits of the Tianjin Massacre, Li was more interested on devising a solution palatable to conservative officials in Beijing. Later, when solving the Margary Affair, Li quickly agreed to pay an indemnity and made vague promises to change the way Chinese officials treated foreigners. Again, this agreement did not resolve the underlying cause for conflict.

III. Japan and Taiwan (1871–4)

While Chinese leaders were focusing on resisting the West, their contemporaries in Japan were focusing on using Western methods in order to counter Western power. Unlike the Chinese, Japanese officials proved willing to adapt Western institutions to Japan. One of Japan's first actions was to reform its military. This, in turn, allowed for naval expansion both to the north, to Hokkaido and the Kurile Islands, and to the south, to the Ryukyu Islands, including Okinawa, and later to Taiwan (Formosa). (See Map 11.1.) Japan's southern maritime expansion came at China's expense.

Sino–Japanese diplomatic relations were opened on 24 July 1871 in accordance with Western norms for their treaties with each other, meaning on the basis of juridical

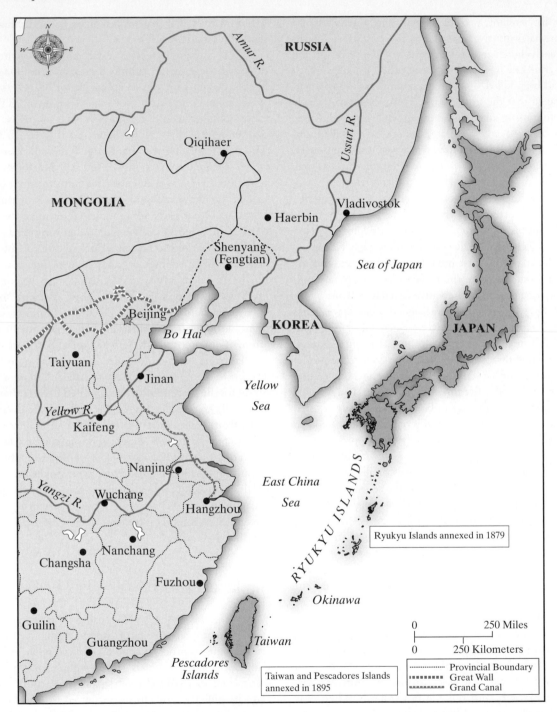

Map 11.1 Japanese Expansion

equality. Li Hongzhang and Zeng Guofan supported treaty relations with Japan, arguing that to do otherwise would transform a potential friend into an enemy. Many conservatives opposed the treaty because they regarded Japan as a tributary state. The treaty mandated trade at the various treaty ports, mutual consular jurisdiction, mediation to help the other against a hostile third party, and recognition of the territorial possessions of the other. Unfortunately, the two nations did not agree on which held sovereignty over the Ryukyu (Liuqiu in Chinese) Islands, which paid tribute to both.

China had already ceded the island of Hong Kong to Britain and Macao to Portugal. It had also lost control over vast but ill-defined Siberian and Central Asian territories to Russia. Japanese claims to the Ryukyu Islands for the first time put a Sinified tributary at risk. The Japanese referred to a group of over seventy islands stretching for more than 800 miles as the "Nansei Island Chain." Since the beginning of the Ming dynasty, these islands had paid tribute to China and had been registered as tributaries since 1372. Beginning in 1609, however, the Satsuma fief in Japan dominated these islands politically, but allowed the Ryukyu Islands to continue sending tribute missions to Beijing to avoid disrupting trade with China.

A massacre of fifty-four shipwrecked Ryukyu sailors by Taiwanese aborigines became the pretext for Japan to claim the island chain. Perhaps copying the European response to the Tianjin Massacre, Japan immediately protested to China on behalf of the sailors and their families. The Qing Court responded that the murders were an internal matter, since both the Ryukyu Islands and Taiwan were Chinese territory. When Beijing refused to take action against the Taiwanese aborigines, who it acknowledged were living in a part of China but stressed that this area had never before been under China's administrative control, the Japanese launched a punitive expedition to Taiwan.

In 1874, when the Japanese expedition occupied the northern coast of Taiwan, Beijing threatened to send its own ships but lacked adequate naval forces to respond. Chinese land forces were preoccupied putting down the Panthay, Donggan, and Xinjiang Muslim rebellions, so China settled for negotiations. The negotiators disagreed on whether or not Japan's naval expedition had broken the nonaggression provisions of the Sino-Japanese Treaty of 1871. The Japanese negotiator argued that China's lack of administrative control over the Taiwanese aborigines meant that there was no violation of the nonaggression clauses. The Chinese negotiators acquiesced to this Japanese interpretation and agreed not to condemn Japan's action. This set a precedent for foreign intervention in Chinese territories suffering from unrest and therefore not fully under Manchu control. When China agreed to pay a 500,000-tael indemnity both to cover the cost of Japan's expedition and to compensate the murdered Ryukyu sailors' families, this implied Japanese sovereignty. The last Ryukyu tribute mission traveled to China in 1875. In 1879, Japan ousted the royal family, annexed the islands, and incorporated them into Okinawa prefecture.

China's inability to protect its national security was no longer confined to its dealings with the West but now also included Japan, which seemed well on the road to contesting China's historic regional dominance. Beijing lacked a modern navy, since funds that might otherwise have been spent on the acquisition of capital ships had been expended suppressing the Muslim Rebellion in Xinjiang and resolving the Ili Crisis, discussed below. When the Manchu Court decided in 1874 to rebuild the Summer Palace, it siphoned off funds earmarked for naval development. This was the period when Li Hongzhang led a group of progressive Qing officials to push for building a proposed forty-eight-ship navy, arguing that Beijing was most vulnerable mainly from the coast, not from the Western borderlands. But because of the Russian threat in Xinjiang, the Qing continued to allocate most military funds to frontier and not coastal defense. Naval expenditures were wasted on incompatible equipment divided among uncoordinated commands.

IV. Russia and Xinjiang (1871–81)

In contrast to the Tianjin Massacre, the Margary Affair, and the massacre of the Ryukyu islanders, in which France, Britain, and Japan forced their will upon China, during the Ili Crisis (1871–81) China forced Russia to back down. In 1871 Russia occupied the Ili Valley in Western Xinjiang to prevent the Xinjiang Rebellion (1862–78) from spreading into Russian territory. (See Chapter 9, Section V.) To quell the rebellion, China deployed large forces under Zuo Zongtang and, much to Russia's surprise, restored order.

The Ili Valley was strategically and politically important, since the Tianshan Mountain Range ran east-west through Xinjiang, separating the Junggar Basin in the north from the Tarim Basin in the south, with the Muzart Pass to the south and the Talki Pass to the north linking the two basins. The Ili River valley ran east-west through the mountains linking Chinese with Russian territory. Thus, the Ili Valley controlled a prime invasion route to China as well as access to the Junggar Basin. Because the Tianshan Mountains were the last geographic barrier against Russia's ongoing expansion into Central Asia, the Manchus considered retention of Xinjiang vital to their empire's security. They expended enormous funds to retain Xinjiang but never won the allegiance of its inhabitants. By the early 1860s, more than a hundred years after the Qing conquest of Xinjiang in 1759, it was still a military colony with a military governor stationed at Ili.

Russia's goal in taking Ili was not only defensive, but also part of its rapid expansion into Central Asia. After the founding of the city of Vernyi in 1854, the Russians took Tashkent in 1865, subjugated the Uzbek Khanate of Bukhara in 1868, defeated the Uzbek Khanate of Khiva in 1873, and conquered the Uzbek Kokand Khanate in 1876. The Russian administrative system incorporated these areas as the governor-generalship of Turkestan established in 1867; the Central Asian border provinces of Semipalatinsk formed in 1854; Syr Darya and Semirech'e, both established in 1867; and three others in Uralsk, Turgai, and Akhmolinsk, all formed in 1868. The Ili Valley was the necessary invasion route for Russia to project power into Xinjiang. In June 1871, the governor-general of Russian Turkestan ordered troops to cross the Sino–Russian border to occupy Ili, and in 1873, Russia formally incorporated the area into the Russian provincial system as Kuldzha province. (See Map 5.2.)

The Russians were not eager to relinquish control over Xinjiang's mountain passes, since they gave Russia the strategic advantage in dealing with China and provided direct trade routes to Gansu, Shaanxi, and Mongolia. Therefore, the Russian price for withdrawal was high. Russia proposed that it retain control of the Muzart Pass, the most strategic part of the Ili Valley; acquire trading privileges throughout Xinjiang, Mongolia, and beyond the Great Wall into the heart of China; and receive a 5-million-ruble indemnity to defray the occupation costs. The Russians also proposed a separate agreement giving them the right to navigate the Songhua (Sungari) River, in Manchuria, as far inland as Potuna. China's diplomatic representative, Chonghou, agreed to these terms when he signed the Treaty of Livadia on 2 October 1879. As soon as China's government understood the treaty terms, however, it immediately repudiated the agreement. The resulting diplomatic row threatened to end in a war between Russia and China.

Meanwhile, the Tongzhi emperor had suddenly died in 1875, leaving no heir. Rumors circulated that his consort, who had died under mysterious circumstances shortly after her husband, had been pregnant. A power struggle erupted within the Manchu ruling house. In violation of Manchu rules, which required a candidate from the next generation, the new emperor was a three-year-old first cousin of the deceased emperor, and son of Cixi's favorite sister and Cixi's closest ally within the imperial family, Prince Chun, the younger brother of Prince Gong. Even after the child's selection, the controversy did not subside. When the deceased emperor's casket was interred in the Eastern Mausoleum in 1879, the official Wu Kedu committed suicide so that his final memorial would reach the throne. It did. In it, he accused Cixi of violating the laws of succession. Controversy spread throughout the empire. The Manchus had fought civil and foreign wars. Now the ruling clans fought among themselves. The last two Qing successions no longer followed the normal pattern of father to adult son but, for lack of any progeny, passed between cousins, casting doubt on their legitimacy. The last time an adult had succeeded to the throne was in 1851. (See Table 11.1.)

Although Chonghou appears to have kept officials in Beijing fully apprised of his ten-month-long negotiations, dynastic matters seem to have completely overshadowed his border negotiations. Once Chonghou signed the Treaty of Livadia and officials in Beijing finally focused on its contents, the Court refused to ratify it and condemned Chonghou to death. The foreign powers deplored such treatment of a diplomat, joined together in protest, and pressured the Court to rescind the sentence. However, Chinese outrage at the lopsided terms of the treaty made war with Russia appear imminent.

Russia had thousands of troops stationed near Ili and deployed twenty-three warships to China, but China had even more soldiers in the theater, since Zuo Zongtang had just put down the Muslim Rebellion in Xinjiang. The Qing put their most famous officers from the Taiping suppression in key positions and hired a former leader of the Ever-Victorious Army, Charles Gordon, to provide military advice. Russia, in contrast, had just fought a costly war with Turkey from 1877 to 1878 and had gotten a poor settlement at the multilateral Congress of Berlin. The costs of the war burdened the already faltering Russian economy. Then in 1879 Britain took control of Afghanistan, potentially threatening Russia's position in Central Asia. On top of this, Russia was in the midst of trying to revive the Three Emperors' League in Europe in order to break out of diplomatic isolation. A conflict with China might disrupt these delicate negotiations. In other words, this was a particularly bad time for Russia to go to war with China.

Diplomacy prevailed when Russia agreed to accept a new negotiator, Marquis Zeng Jize (the son of the famous general Zeng Guofan), who was serving as China's minister to Great Britain. His negotiations in St. Petersburg were acrimonious, but Russia preferred a large indemnity to an expensive war and restored most of the disputed territory for a 9-million-ruble indemnity. Russia curtailed its demands for greater trade privileges and dropped the provision concerning navigation rights on the Songhua River in Manchuria. As a result, the 24 February 1881 Treaty of St. Petersburg superseded the Treaty of Livadia. This halted, temporarily at least, Russia's expansion into China.

Despite the increased indemnity, the Chinese widely regarded the Treaty of St. Petersburg as a diplomatic victory because they had made one of the most powerful European nations back down. In reality, the treaty reinforced the precedent of diplomacy conducted not with a sound long-term strategy, but with the purse. China's repeated payments of large indemnities to mollify foreign powers ultimately retarded its own internal economic development. In 1884, soon after the Treaty of St. Petersburg, the Chinese govern-

Table 11.1   Late-Qing Successions

	1. Mianmu (1779–80)		
		1. Yiwei (1808–31) {	1. Zaizhi (adopted) {	1. Pulun b. 1874 / 2. Putong
			1. Zaichun (b. 1856; r. 1862–74) **Tongzhi emperor** {	1. Puyi (b. 1906; r. 1908–11; d. 1967) **Xuantong emperor** (adopted)*
		4. Yichu (b. 1831; r. 1851–61) **Xianfeng emperor** consort Cixi {	2. No name conferred (1858–61); died at time of Cixi's palace coup	
Jiaqing emperor (b. 1760 r. 1796–1820)	2. Mianning **Daoguang emperor** (b. 1872; r. 1821–50)		3. Zaitian (b. 1871; r. 1875–1908) **Guangxu emperor** (adopted) . {	1. Puyi (b. 1906; r. 1908–11; d. 1967) **Xuantong emperor** (adopted)*
		5. *Yizong*		
		6. Yixin, Prince Gong (1832–98) {	1. Zaicheng (1858–85) / 2. *Zaiying* {	1. Puwei, Prince Gong (adopted)†
		7. Yihuan, Prince Chun (1840–90) wife = Cixi's sister {	2. *Zaitian, Guangxu emperor*	
			5. Zaifeng, Prince Chun {	1. *Puyi, Xuantong emperor*
		8. Yihe (1844–68) {	1. Zaiying (adopted) {	1. *Puwei*†
	3. Miankai (1795–1840) {	1. Yizong (1831–89) (adopted) {	1. Zailian / 2. Zaiyi / 3. Zaiian	
	4. Mianxin (1805–28) {	1. Yizhi {	1. Zaiyi, Prince Duan's wife and Cixi's niece (adopted) {	1. Pujun b. 1886

Notes: This table shows the bewildering complexity of late-Qing successions due to the dramatic decline in imperial births. Names are written in *italics* for sons given up for adoption. Sons adopted into a family line are indicated by the phrase, (adopted).

All children of a particular generation share the same first character of their given names. Numbers indicate the birth order of sons. Most of those without descendants in the "Pu" generation have not been included.

*Puyi was adopted simultaneously as the son of the two previous childless emperors, Tongzhi and Guangxu.

†In January 1900 Puwei beame the adopted posthumous heir to the Tonzhi emperor but, as a result of his father's support for the Boxer Uprising, in November 1901 he was removed from the succession. He subsequently became the adopted Prince Gong.

Source: Hosea Ballou Morse, *The International Relations of the Chinese Empire*, vol. 2 (New York: Longmans, Green, 1918), 282; Arthur W. Hummel, *Emminent Chinese of the Ch'ing Period* (Washington, DC: U.S. Government Printing Office, 1943), passim; Jin Songqiao et al., comps., *Aixinjueluo zongpu* (Fengtian: Aixinjueluo Xiupuchu, 1938), 75–101.

ment made Xinjiang a regular province and incorporated it into the Chinese administrative system. Its diplomatic success with Russia seemed to indicate the validity of the Self-strengthening Movement. China's misplaced self-assurance, however, soon led to disaster with France in the Sino-French War. France, unlike Russia, was not beset by problems of diplomatic isolation, insufficient cash flows, or an inability to reach the battlefield in force.

V. France and Vietnam (1883–5)

China soon faced another European challenge on its periphery: French efforts to dominate the tributary state of Annam (north and central Vietnam). Flush from its success at Ili, the Chinese government hoped to use its recently modernized navy to force the French government to back down. But France had a state-of-the-art navy capable of efficiently deploying troops in the Vietnam theater and more than capable of countering the heterogeneous Chinese navies. The conflict proved to be one-sided. The Sino-French War in Vietnam (1883–5) would lead to China's loss of a second tributary state.

Vietnam had intermittently fallen under Chinese control as early as the reign of Han Wudi (140–87 BC) and again during the Tang dynasty (618–907). During the Qing period, Vietnam sent tributary missions to China. Beginning in the seventeenth century, however, Western influence in Vietnam increased with the arrival of the Jesuits. In 1859, antimissionary riots provided the French with an excuse to send troops, which transformed Vietnam's three southernmost provinces into a French colony in 1862. In 1874, France completed the task of turning Vietnam into a protectorate when it obtained the right to navigate the Red River in northern Vietnam. This agreement not only confirmed French control over Vietnam's foreign affairs, but also French domination over foreign trade with northern Vietnam. By 1880, the French had built forts along the Red River and stationed troops as far north as Hanoi and Haiphong. Faced with this growing threat, the government of Vietnam called on its suzerain, China, for assistance. Despite French opposition, Vietnam sent tributary missions to Beijing in 1877 and 1881.

Meanwhile, rebels from China began infiltrating Vietnam in 1882. (See Map 11.2.) Liu Yongfu (Liu Yung-fu), a Hakka born in Guangdong, dreamed of becoming a famous general of the Black Tiger militia. His troops rallied under a black flag and became known as the Black Flag Army, which was associated with the Heaven and Earth Society, an offshoot of the Taipings. For over a year, the Black Flag Army single-handedly opposed French forces in northern Vietnam. Although outnumbered, the Black Flag troops made effective use of guerrilla tactics.

The Qing dynasty could not ignore the request of a tributary to send troops, particularly after the loss of the Ryukyu Islands to Japan. Therefore, China intervened in 1883, stationing its forces close to the Sino-Vietnam border. The Chinese troops were more numerous than their French counterparts and the weapons they carried were modern, but their training remained inferior. In late 1883, the Qing infantry joined the fray in Vietnam almost a year after the Black Flag began to harass the French. Four months later, the French forced Liu Yongfu's guerrilla army to retreat back into China. In the spring of 1884 Li Hongzhang successfully negotiated a peace agreement, but the details did not reach troops on the ground and hostilities flared up again.

In August 1884 the French expanded the war to Taiwan, blockading the island and bombarding the forts at Jilong (Keelung), at its northern extremity. A much larger Chinese force under the former commander of the Anhui Army pressured the French to withdraw from the island. While Chinese land forces performed reasonably well, their naval forces did not. The China's Nanyang and Fuzhou fleets remained poorly trained and ill-equipped. The Beiyang Fleet, based far to the North in Manchuria, possessed state-of-the-art capital ships but refused to assist the South. On 23 August 1884, a French fleet of eight ships destroyed the Fuzhou Fleet in port at Fuzhou Harbor, just as the Japanese would destroy the Beiyang Fleet in its harbor during the Sino-Japanese War a decade later. The French proceeded to blockade the Nanyang Fleet on the Yangzi River, cutting the flow of tribute grain up the Grand Canal to the capital. Because the Beiyang Fleet ignored the requests by the Nanyang Fleet for assistance, the French navy never faced the most modern elements of the Chinese navy.

When the Qing officially declared war on France on 26 August 1884, the French made a second attempt to take Taiwan while maintaining the blockade of the Nanyang Fleet. French control over Taiwan was limited to the northern coast. Unlike the Ili Crisis, China became diplomatically isolated as Britain and Germany refused to assist Beijing while Russia and Japan continued to threaten China's northern frontier. Therefore, China called off the fighting on 4 April 1885 in order to allow Li Hongzhang to negotiate a settlement with the French minister in China.

The agreement, concluded on 9 June 1885, recognized all French treaties with Vietnam, transforming it into a French protectorate. The Sino-French War further eroded the tributary system. The peace settlement also entailed the opening of five more treaty ports along the southern border. In return, the French agreed to evacuate Taiwan and the Pescadore Islands, and China paid no indemnity. As in the

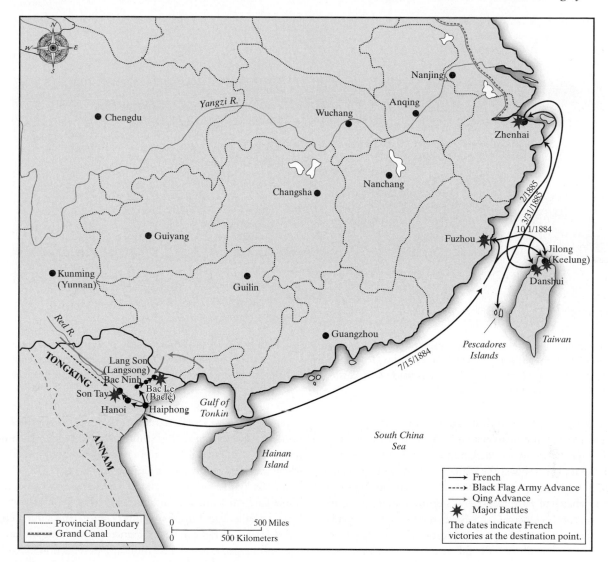

Map 11.2   Sino-French War (1883–5)

case of Russian intrusions into Xinjiang, the Qing responded to the crisis by formally integrating Taiwan into the Chinese administrative system, making it a province in 1885. A decade later, however, China lost the province to Japan.

Conclusions

The Self-strengthening Movement proved insufficient to defend vital Chinese interests. Western military and financial cooperation to put down the Taiping, Nian, Panthay, Donggan, and Muslim rebellions, and subsequent Western diplomatic support for the Burlingame Mission, all suggested a new era of reduced international tensions and an end to Chinese diplomatic isola-

tion. But the Tianjin Massacre, which scuttled the Alcock Convention and saddled China with a large indemnity, indicated underlying Sino-Western tensions and an inadequate Chinese strategy to deal with the West. The Qing Court relied on payments of indemnities. Such transfers of customs receipts to the foreign powers, while easy enough to do since they came from the foreign trade and were ultimately paid by Han Chinese, left China economically weakened and in no better position than before to protect its interests or to cope with future tensions.

After ceding the Ryukyu Islands to Japan without a fight, Chinese diplomats successfully forced Russian troops out of the Ili Valley. Although the terms of the Treaty of St. Petersburg gave Russia a small amount of territory in

This late-nineteenth-century photograph of Shanghai from across the Huangpu River in Pudong clearly shows the single main road running along the water, called the Bund (an Urdu word from India meaning "embankment"). By the end of the nineteenth century, the Bund had become the financial hub of East Asia, with almost all major corporate headquarters and financial institutions in China located there.

Western Xinjiang, the Manchus regained the most strategic areas. Their false sense of security quickly disappeared during the Sino-French War, when the Chinese land and naval forces failed to retain control over the Chinese tributary of Vietnam. Although Chinese forces increasingly relied on Western weaponry, they had yet to adopt a westernized military organization, strategy, or doctrine. Likewise, no attempt was made to restructure the economy or the educational system to make China capable of producing the full array of modern military and industrial technology, which depended on a modern industrial base. China's use of Western weapons and westernized diplomatic institutions brought limited results.

China's loss of the Ryukyu Islands and Vietnam threatened to undermine the tributary system and Chinese regional dominance. By the 1880s, a clear pattern of imperial decline was spreading along the frontiers. China would not be able to reverse this trend until after the founding of the People's Republic of China in 1949. In the meantime, its control continued to slip in Korea, Manchuria, Outer Mongolia, Inner Mongolia, Xinjiang, Tibet, and even in Shandong province, where the antidynastic Boxer Uprising originated. China's loss of the Ryukyu Islands to Japan and of Vietnam to France had immediate consequences in Southeast Asia: Soon afterward, Britain challenged Burma's tributary status and China conceded without a fight in 1886. France's success also undoubtedly encouraged Japan to take more aggressive action in Korea. Meanwhile, Russia drew lessons of its own, concluding that the lack of a railway to deploy troops along its long frontier with China had precluded a Russian victory in the Ili Crisis. The debate over building a Trans-Siberian railway assumed new urgency in Russia. The tsar mandated its construction a decade later in 1891, the next period when Russo-Chinese relations headed toward a crisis. In China, this succession of foreign policy crises fueled antiforeign sentiments.

BIBLIOGRAPHY

Cohen, Paul A. *China and Christianity: The Missionary Movement and the Growth of Chinese Antiforeignism, 1860–1870.* Cambridge, MA: Harvard University Press, 1963.

Eastman, Lloyd E. *Throne and Mandarins: China's Search for a Policy during the Sino-French Controversy 1880–1885.* Cambridge, MA: Harvard University Press, 1967.

Elleman, Bruce A. *Modern Chinese Warfare, 1795–1989.* London: Routledge, 2001.

Geyer, Dietrich. *Russian Imperialism: The Interaction of Domestic and Foreign Policy, 1860–1914.* Translated by Bruce Little. New Haven, CT: Yale University Press, 1987.

Hao, Yen-p'ing and Erh-ming Wang. "Changing Chinese Views of Western Relations, 1840-1895." In *The Cambridge History of China,* vol. 11, edited by John K. Fairbank and Kwang-ching Liu, 142–201. Cambridge: Cambridge University Press, 1980.

Hsü, Immanuel C. Y. *China's Entrance into the Family of Nations: The Diplomatic Phase 1858–1880.* Cambridge, MA: Harvard University Press, 1960.

———*The Ili Crisis: A Study of Sino-Russian Diplomacy 1871–1881.* Oxford: Clarendon Press, 1965.

——— "Late Ch'ing Foreign Relations, 1866–1905." In *The Cambridge History of China,* vol. 11, edited by John K. Fairbank and Kwang-ching Liu, 70–141. Cambridge: Cambridge University Press, 1980.

Iriye, Akira, "Japan's Drive to Great Power Status." In *The Cambridge History of Japan,* vol 5, edited by Marius B. Jansen, 721–82. Cambridge: Cambridge University Press, 1989.

Jelavich, Charles and Barbara Jelavich, eds. *Russia in the Far East 1876–1880: The Russo-Turkish War and the Kuldja Crisis as Seen through the Letters of A. G. Jomini to N. K. Giers.* Leiden: E. J. Brill, 1959.

LeDonne, John P. *The Russian Empire and the World, 1700–1917: The Geopolitics of Expansion and Containment.* London: Oxford University Press, 1996.

Liao Kwang-sheng. *Antiforeignism and Modernization in China, 1860–1980: The Linkage between Domestic Politics and Foreign Relations.* Hong Kong: Chinese University Press, 1984.

McAleavy, Henry. *Black Flags in Vietnam: The Story of a Chinese Intervention.* New York: Macmillan, 1968.

Morse, Hosea Ballou. *The International Relations of the Chinese Empire.* Vol. 2. Shanghai: Kelly and Walsh, 1918.

Paine, S. C. M. *Imperial Rivals: China, Russia, and Their Disputed Frontier.* Armonk, NY: M. E. Sharpe, 1996.

Williams, Frederick Wells. *Anson Burlingame and the First Chinese Mission for Foreign Powers.* New York: Russell & Russell, 1972.

Wright, Mary C. *The Last Stand of Chinese Conservatism: The T'ung-chih Restoration, 1862–1874.* Stanford, CA: Stanford University Press, 1957.

NOTES

1. Yao (r. 2357–2256 BC) was a legendary emperor considered a model Confucian monarch. The Xia dynasty (2205–1766 BC) exemplified the dynastic cycle with an exemplary early ruler and a tyrannical final ruler. The Han dynasty (206 BC–220 AD) laid many of the foundations of dynastic rule in China and is considered to be the classical period in Chinese history. Hong Kong was a British colony and therefore flew the British flag. Huang Zunxian, "On Reaching Hong Kong." In *An Anthology of Chinese Literature: Beginnings to 1911,* edited and translated by Stephen Owen, (New York: W. W. Norton, 1996), 1149. Copyright © 1996 by Stephen Owen and The Council for Cultural Planning and Development of the Executive Yuan of the Republic of China. Used by permission of W. W. Norton & Company, Inc.

2. Quoted in Immanuel C. Y. Hsü, *China's Entrance into the Family of Nations: The Diplomatic Phase 1858–1880* (Cambridge, MA: Harvard University Press, 1960), 168.

Chronology

1871	Russian occupation of Ili
1876	Treaty of Kanghwa; Japan opens Korea to foreign trade
1879	Japanese annexation of Ryukyu Islands
1881	Treaty of St. Petersburg
1882	Korean soldiers' mutiny
1883–5	Sino-French War
1884	Failed pro-Japanese coup d'état in Korea
1885	Treaty of Tianjin between China and Japan concerning Korea
1891	Construction of the Trans-Siberian Railway begins
1894	Tonghak Uprising in Korea
	Japanese treaty revision with Britain; end of the domestic phase of Meiji reforms
1894–5	Sino-Japanese War; beginning of the foreign policy phase of Meiji reforms
1895	Treaty of Shimonoseki
	Triple Intervention forcing retrocession of the Liaodong Peninsula
	France acquires a sphere of influence in South China
	End of Self-Strengthening Movement
1895–9	Scramble for Concessions
1896	Russo-Chinese alliance; Russia acquires railway concession in Manchuria
1897	Germany acquires a sphere of influence in Shandong province
1898	Russia establishes a railway concession on the Liaodong Peninsula
	Britain acquires a sphere of influence in the Yangzi River valley, central China, and a concession at Weihaiwei
	Japan acquires a sphere of influence in Fujian province
	Hundred Days' Reform
1899	United States proposes Open Door Policy

12

The First Sino-Japanese War

With a lifetime in battles' roar,
Who'd have thought death brings ease no more?
Three centuries a troubled place—
Here and afar lift grief's embrace!

Fall breeze, dress sword, a lone envoy cries.
Sunset, flags, a general sighs.
Ceaseless war reports come from afar.
Sirs, stay not idle as you are![1]

Deathbed poem by Li Hongzhang (1823–1901),
general, statesman, Self-strengthener

Until the First Sino-Japanese War (1894–5), the foreign policy record of the Self-strengthening period had been mixed. While the Burlingame Mission and the Ili Crisis seemed to have yielded positive outcomes, the Tianjin Crisis, Japan's annexation of the Ryukyu Islands, and the Sino-French War had all gone awry. In addition to the Manchus' fear of change, Han Confucianists remained ambivalent about the degree of modernization required. Prior to the war, the voices of the Self-strengtheners were very much in the minority. Li Hongzhang's recommendations, to revamp the imperial examination system and include technical subjects, were considered preposterous, and his attempts to promote railway construction were blocked. In the absence of central direction and in the face of widespread opposition, the reforms of the Self-strengtheners remained piecemeal, uncoordinated, and not necessarily complementary. In the military sphere, which the Self-strengtheners emphasized, the equipment was not standardized and most parts were not interchangeable. Provinces refused to share, let alone coordinate, their military assets with those of the other provinces. This division was particularly stark between North and South China. Just as the Beiyang Fleet

(literally, the North Sea Fleet) refused to aid the Nanyang Fleet (literally, the South Sea Fleet) in the Sino-French War, the Nanyang Fleet would now return the favor during the Sino-Japanese War.

I. The Korean Crisis

While China had been preoccupied with regaining the Ili Valley from Russia and fighting the French, a growing crisis had been brewing in its most important tributary, Korea. China had traditionally been Korea's protector, but the Manchus were experiencing increasing difficulties maintaining order at home, let alone abroad. The Yi dynasty (1392–1910) of Korea, like the Qing dynasty, had been beset by growing internal rebellions and foreign penetration. Japan and Russia were particularly active, since both considered the Korean Peninsula important to their own security: Prior to the completion of the Trans-Siberian Railway, Russia feared its Siberian possessions would be invaded from Korea, while Japan thought of the Korean Peninsula as the most likely disembarkation point for any forces invading its home islands. Neither wanted a foreign power to control Korea.

As with the Qing dynasty, the nineteenth century brought a succession of weak kings to the Korean throne. Corruption flourished. Impoverishment of the peasantry increased. The direct royal line died out in 1864 so that the child successor had dubious legitimacy, while his father, the regent, had even less. Factional strife extended to murder among the adult male members of the ruling clans, something that the Manchus managed to avoid. In 1875, Japan played the role that Britain played in China by opening Korea to foreign trade. Since 1867, China had been advising Korea to sign treaties with the Western powers to counter the growing influence of the Japanese. But the Koreans had their own conservative bureaucracy, which clung to tradition and wished to minimize outside contacts. When Japan forced the treaty port issue, however, China recommended signing the treaty. In 1876, Korea and Japan ratified the Treaty of Kanghwa opening three treaty ports to Japanese trade and granting Japanese citizens extraterritoriality and most-favored-nation treatment. But the treaty made no offer to collect customs from this trade, let alone to provide any customs duties to the Korean government. The treaty also proclaimed Korea to be a sovereign state in contravention to the Chinese claim to suzerainty. At the time, China did not dispute the issue because from 1871 to 1881 it was preoccupied by a looming war with Russia and from 1883 to 1885 it was at war with France.

In 1879, when Japan formally took control over the Ryukyu Islands, the Qing Court designated Li Hongzhang to oversee Chinese relations with Korea. In 1882 Korean soldiers mutinied over their government's failure to meet their payroll for more than a year. The rioters went on a rampage, killing all Japanese in their path. Both China and Japan responded by deploying troops in Korea. The conservative ex-regent, the virulently anti-Japanese Grand Prince Hŭngsŏn, took advantage of the turmoil to banish his son, King Kojong, and retake power. Grand Prince Hŭngsŏn sought Chinese sanction for his actions. Instead, the Chinese kidnapped him, keeping him under house arrest near Tianjin until 1885, and put his son back on the throne in the meantime. From the Chinese point of view, it had restored order in its tributary state. It then brokered a Korean-Japanese treaty, paralleling the settlement of the Tianjin Massacre. The 1882 Treaty of Chemulp'o mandated a Korean apology mission to Japan and an indemnity.

After the soldiers' mutiny, there was growing internal support for a Meiji-style reform program. When the Sino-French War broke out, China reduced its military presence in Korea and the reformers attempted a coup d'état in 1884. During an official banquet, they beheaded six ministers and their supporters, but the Chinese had enough troops to restore order in Seoul, which resulted in Japanese deaths. The incident ended with another Tianjin Massacre–type settlement, including a Korean apology and indemnity for Japan. This was the Seoul Protocol of 1885. The main negotiations, however, took place between China and Japan in Tianjin. Their 1885 Treaty of Tianjin called for a bilateral Chinese and Japanese troop withdrawal from Korea.

Behind the scenes, Chinese influence in Korea rapidly increased. For the first time since the Russian invasion of the Ili Valley in 1871, China had no immediate internal or external crisis diverting its attention from Korea. The Korean government had reservations about China's influence, so from 1884 on, it gravitated increasingly toward Russia to counterbalance both China and Japan. Meanwhile, Russia debated building a trans-Siberian railway to defend Siberia. In 1891, construction began. Diplomats around the world immediately realized that completion of this railway would alter the balance of power in East Asia, since Russia would be able to deploy troops efficiently all along China's northern borders. The Japanese, in particular, believed that they needed to solve the problem of Korea's instability before the Russians completed this railway.

Japan, like China, for many years had been preoccupied with its own internal problems. The Meiji reforms, creating westernized political, legal, military, economic, and educational institutions, were not completed until 1890 with the first session of the Diet. Thereafter, Japan focused on treaty revision with Great Britain. On 16 July 1894, Britain and Japan signed a precedent-setting agreement doing away with the unequal treaty system. Japan's strategy of westernization of its internal legal institutions removed any pretext for maintaining extraterritoriality or treating it differently from other Western nations. This was more successful than China's strategy of resistance. The unequal treaty system endured in China for another half century until 1943 with the West and through the late 1950s with Russia (the USSR). For Japan, treaty revision marked the end of the domestic phase of its strategy to counter the Western threat.

The year 1894 marked the outbreak of the greatest peasant rebellion in Korean history, the Tonghak or Eastern Learning Rebellion. In desperation, on 4 June 1894, the Korean government once again called on its suzerain for military aid. The Qing dynasty had to respond or lose its claim to Korea. The Japanese seized the opportunity to deploy even more troops and provoke a war with China. Although Japanese policy makers did not consider China to be in a position to threaten Japan directly, Russia was another matter. Persistent Russian eastward expansion suggested designs on Manchuria and the Korean Peninsula. Japan's fears turned out to be correct: Annexation of Korea and Manchuria remained a topic of discussion in the highest echelons of the Russian government. The Japanese decided to preempt Russia by taking Korea first.

Before the Japanese reinforcements arrived, Korean troops had already defeated the Tonghak rebels. But the Sino-Japanese troop deployments continued. On 25 June 1894, the representatives of the United States, Russia, France, and Great Britain in Seoul urged the simultaneous withdrawal of Chinese and Japanese troops. Li Hongzhang also tried to end the standoff by turning to Britain for help. Japan rejected all attempts to defuse the crisis, demanding that China cooperate with it to implement a Meiji reform package for Korea. But the Chinese refused. China had been unwilling to implement such reforms for itself, let alone for a tributary. On 22 June 1894, Japan announced that it would go it alone. By mid-July, the Japanese presented the Koreans with a governmental reorganization plan. On 23 July 1894, when the Korean government refused to cooperate, Japanese troops broke into the royal palace and took the royal family to the Japanese legation. They restored as regent Grand Prince Hǔngsǒn, the eighty-year-old father of King Kojong and the former hostage of Li Hongzhang. The grand prince would declare war on China on 27 July and requested military assistance from Japan.

II. The Hostilities

The Sino-Japanese War began on 25 July 1894, just nine days after the completion of the Japanese treaty revision with Great Britain. This war, like the Russo-Japanese War (1904–5) and the Pacific War (1941–5), began with a Japanese surprise naval attack—on 25 July 1894 in the vicinity of Feng Island—followed by separate declarations of war on 1 August 1894. (See Map 12.1.)

   Prior to the hostilities, no one outside Japan had questioned the truism that China was the great power of Asia. Then in a three-day period in mid-September 1894, Japan trounced China on both land and sea, earning the instant respect of the West, whose newspapers extolled Japan as the most recently arrived great power. In the Battle of P'yǒngyang, a former capital of Korea and the future capital of North Korea, the Japanese Army overran well-fortified Chinese positions in a two-day battle on 15–16 September. All the advantages were on the Chinese side: They had two months to prepare their positions, the Japanese had to cross a river in front of these positions, and the Chinese concentrated their most modern equipment and best forces there. Although the Chinese put up some of their stiffest resistance of the war, they failed to attack the Japanese as they crossed the river and were most vulnerable. Instead, they waited behind their fortified walls. Once across, the Imperial Japanese Army ripped the Chinese forces to shreds, shattering Chinese morale. The Chinese did not attempt to take another stand until they fled across the Yalu River, which they again allowed the Japanese to cross unopposed. The Chinese compounded their errors by consistently failing to destroy vital war materiel as they retreated. This helped compensate for the many shortcomings of the Japanese logistics.

   Chinese incompetence was derided in both Japan and the West. Chinese brutality reinforced these views. While the Japanese forces made great efforts to adhere to the 1864 Geneva Convention mandating protection for prisoners of war, the Chinese forces gave no quarter. They seemed to revel in mutilation. Disembowelment, excision of facial features, and extraction of livers were widespread. This was widely reported in the Western and Japanese press, creating a pervasive image of unrepentant and pointless Chinese barbarity. Equally counterproductive, Chinese officials kept reporting battlefield losses as victories. This added transparent deceit to military incompetence.

   The day after the Battle of P'yǒngyang, the second major battle of the war took place, this time between opposing naval forces. In the early 1890s, China's navy was over twice the size of Japan's, but it lacked a unified command and so could not count on cooperation from its many fleets. The Nanyang Fleet and the two smaller squadrons, based at Guangzhou and Fuzhou, quickly declared their neutrality in the Sino-Japanese War. In other words, South China refused to come to the aid of North China. This vividly demonstrated that even the core provinces of China were not unified by shared loyalties, and they left Li Hongzhang's Beiyang Fleet to fight the Japanese alone.

   In the late summer of 1894, the Japanese fleet had been trying to engage a very reluctant Beiyang Fleet, which the Japanese intercepted convoying troops to Korea. The fleets were roughly equivalent, with the Chinese possessing greater firepower and the Japanese greater speed. Yet, Japan sunk four out of the ten Chinese ships engaged, losing none of its own. The Chinese fleet fled, even while Beijing announced another victory. When the foreign advisers to the Beiyang Fleet reached port, they had a different story to tell. Corruption had left China's fleet supplied with ordnance of the wrong caliber, defective gunpowder, and inadequate coal supplies. A lack of translators had hindered the Chinese ships from executing basic naval formations. This permitted the Japanese fleet repeatedly to broadside the Chinese fleet. The Battle of the Yalu (also called the Battle of the Yellow Sea) demonstrated that the right equipment in the wrong hands can be useless.

   Japan successfully expelled Chinese forces from Korea, thereby achieving its initial war objective. Immediately after the battles of P'yǒngyang and the Yalu, the European press welcomed Japan's entry into the select ranks of the great powers. After P'yǒngyang, the rest of the war would be fought on Chinese territory and mostly in the Manchus' native Manchuria. With the Battle of the Yalu, Japan established command of the sea since the Chinese never again chose to contest it. This enabled Japan to deliver troops and supplies unopposed to the Asian mainland. This was critical, since without open sea lines of communication, Japan could not prosecute the war.

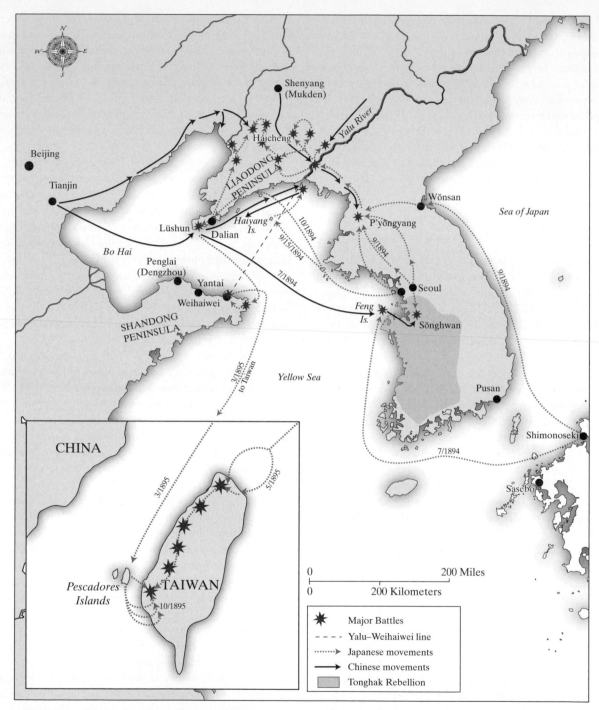

Map 12.1   Sino-Japanese War (1894–5)

One reason the Chinese navies did not perform well against Japan in the first Sino-Japanese War was that in 1893 the Empress Dowager Cixi diverted major portions of China's naval funds to rebuild the Marble Boat and surrounding gardens. Known as the "Boat of Purity and Ease," this pavilion was first erected in 1755 by the Qianlong emperor on the banks of the Kunming Lake in the Manchu Summer Palace to the northwest of Beijing (not to be confused with Yuanming Yuan, directly north of Beijing).

The second and final pair of major battles occurred over the winter of 1894–5. Japan took China's two key naval ports, located at the northern and southern gateposts to the Gulf of Bo Hai, controlling the sea approaches to Beijing. In the North, on 21 November 1894, the Imperial Japanese Army took the state-of-the-art fortress and naval refitting facilities at Lüshun (Port Arthur) on the Liaodong Peninsula, while on 12 February 1895, the Imperial Japanese Navy in combination with the Imperial Japanese Army took the port facilities at Weihaiwei on the Shandong Peninsula. Had the Chinese defended the fortresses at Lüshun, they could have inflicted huge losses on the Japanese, as the Russians would do a decade later in the Russo-Japanese War. Instead, the Beiyang Navy retired to Weihaiwei, where the Japanese fleet blockaded it in harbor.

China should have deployed its navy to attack Japan's vulnerable sea lines of communication rather than allow the fleet to be destroyed in port. Japan was a country of limited resources and limited manpower. Sinking even a small percentage of the Japanese troop transports might have changed the outcome of the war, particularly during the difficult winter campaign in Manchuria, where the Japanese supply situation was precarious. At a minimum, such a strategy would have greatly increased the cost of the war for Japan and prevented it from blockading the Beiyang Fleet in harbor and then sinking it. Flawed military strategy again lost the day for the Chinese. The destruction of the Beiyang Fleet undid China's main naval modernization effort of the preceding two decades. China would not attempt to re-create a first-class navy—until the 1990s.

Much of China's poor military performance can be attributed to the Han soldiers, who routinely fled from battle. Their Manchu overlords failed to equip, train, or even regularly pay them. Han soldiers had no particular loyalty to the Manchus and voted with their feet. Meanwhile, Chinese civilians routinely cooperated with Japanese forces, providing food and logistical assistance. Qing naval strategy focused on defense of the capital, not on destroying enemy forces or their logistical lines, while Japan demonstrated the critical importance of sea power; without command of the sea, Japan could not have deployed its troops at will. A key Japanese war objective became the long-term neutralization of Chinese sea power. The Japanese destruction of the Beiyang Fleet and the exaction of a large war indemnity prevented China from rebuilding its navy for a century.

After the debacle at Weihaiwei, Japan prepared for a pincer movement on Beijing, from Manchuria in the North and from Shandong province in the South. The loss of the naval refitting facilities at Lüshun left the Beiyang Navy unable to repair severely damaged ships. Japan also continued southward to take Taiwan and the Pescadore Islands. The anticipated pincer movement on Beijing was sufficient to bring the Qing dynasty to the bargaining table.

III. The Settlement

China would send three peace missions to Japan, two before the destruction of the Beiyang Fleet at Weihaiwei and the final one afterward. In the end, the Qing dynasty had to choose between settling the war on Japanese terms or risking a coup d'état by their own Han subjects. Li Hongzhang's military strategy had been to avoid war if possible and, after it broke out, to secure foreign mediation to broker a peace on Chinese terms. But once again, this strategy proved insufficient against foes of the Industrial Revolution era. Japan's victory reversed the long-standing balance of power in Asia, unseating China as the dominant regional power.

China, the Japanese thought, owed Japan respect. They demanded that China send representatives to Japan to make it clear that China was suing for peace. Under the tributary system, envoys had almost always gone to Beijing. Granting Japan's wish for respect was the last thing either the Manchus or the Han intended to do. Ever since the First Sino-Japanese War, the Chinese have made it a point of national policy not to accord the Japanese the respect to which the Japanese have felt entitled. This has been an enduring and major point of contention. For their part, a key Japanese war goal was to humiliate China. The Japanese relished a chance to turn the tables on China. Western nations have largely ignored the Sino-Japanese protocol wars because the Westerners have not understood their significance in face societies. Face remains a major component of the current acrimony over Japan's atrocities in World War II and its treatment of its own war dead.

For the initial peace delegation, China sent a German customs commissioner from Tianjin and a British journalist bearing a letter from Li Hongzhang to the Japanese prime minister, Itō Hirobumi. Itō refused even to receive an improperly accredited mission. If China would not negotiate seriously, Japan would continue the march on Beijing. The

foreign powers overwhelmingly sympathized with Japan. European norms for war termination called for high-ranking and properly accredited representatives to negotiate peace settlements. So, the fighting continued and the military situation did not improve.

For the second peace mission, China hired, at great expense as a special adviser, the former U.S. secretary of state, John Watson Foster (grandfather of the future U.S. secretary of state, John Foster Dulles). It also appointed two Han representatives, one a medium-ranking former minister to the United States, Spain, and Peru, and the other a man known primarily for the bounty he had offered per Japanese head delivered to him during his recent tenure as governor of Taiwan. Again, the purpose was to deny the Japanese the respect that the latter felt they had earned. Whereas the Manchus sent members of the imperial household, such as Prince Gong, to negotiate with the Western powers, they attempted to foist a motley assortment of flawed representatives on the Japanese. Again, the Manchus failed properly to accredit their representatives, who lacked the necessary plenipotentiary powers to negotiate a settlement, so the Japanese sent them packing.

This time, when the hostilities resumed, Japan took Weihaiwei and with it the Beiyang Navy. Had China appointed high-ranking and properly credentialed representatives for either of the earlier two peace missions, it might have preserved its navy. It also would have retained Taiwan and the Pescadore Islands, because the Japanese took these only in the final days of the war. In other words, Chinese desire to tweak the noses of the Japanese came at a very high price. Political separation of Taiwan from the mainland has effectively hemmed in Chinese naval ambitions to the present day. A major factor behind the current insistence by the People's Republic of China on its sovereignty over Taiwan relates to issues of naval containment. The geographic arc composed of the Kurile Islands, the Japanese archipelago, the Ryukyu Islands, and Taiwan continues to frustrate China's ambitions to project power from its coastline.

After the fall of Weihaiwei, the Qing Court finally became desperate enough to turn yet again to Li Hongzhang, the Self-strengthener who had done more than any of his countrymen to put China on the path to modernization. The Manchus and Han conservatives had blocked many of his efforts, including his attempt to encourage railway construction. During the war, the lack of railways greatly impeded China's ability to deploy troops. Li, unlike his jingoistic critics, who had been eager to put Japan in its place with a war, had done his best to avoid hostilities. He was well aware of Japan's modernization and westernization efforts. In the ensuing peace negotiations, Li told Prime Minister Itō Hirobumi, his Japanese counterpart and author of the Meiji Constitution, "What you have done

Li Hongzhang was the viceroy of Zhili during the First Sino-Japanese War and was sent to Japan to negotiate a peace treaty. During the April 1895 talks at Shimonoseki, Li was shot by an assassin and wounded below his left eye. The Japanese officials were so embarrassed by their failure to protect Li from attack that they softened the terms of the peace treaty. According to former U.S. Secretary of State John Foster, who was a special adviser to the Chinese during the negotiations, this made Li's injury "the most effective shedding of blood on the Chinese side during the entire war."[2]

for Japan I wanted to imitate for China. Had you been in my place you would know the unspeakable difficulties met with in China." Itō responded to Li: "When I was at Tientsin [Tianjin ten years earlier, settling the Korean problem] I gave you the friendly advice that many reforms were most important for your country but I regret very much that no change whatever has taken place."[3]

A failed assassination attempt against Li by a crazed Japanese assailant gave China unexpected leverage. On 17 April 1895, Li and Itō signed the Treaty of Shimonoseki. It marked the epochal reversal in the East Asian balance of power, since China was no longer dominant. Upstart Japan had attained primacy in East Asia, a position it retained even after World War II and to the present day. The main treaty points included (1) recognition of Korean independence; (2) a 200-million-tael indemnity; (3) the cession of Taiwan, the Pescadore Islands, and the Liaodong Peninsula; (4) the opening of four additional treaty ports; and (5) the right of foreigners to open factories, manufacturing plants, and other industrial enterprises, thereby opening up China to direct foreign investment, making possible rapid industrialization, especially in the treaty ports.

Provincial officials deluged the Qing Court with memorials urging rejection of the treaty. From Beijing's perspective, China's loss of Korea spelled the virtual end to the traditional tributary system, proving that China and the rest of Asia were being drawn inexorably into adopting Western notions of international law and westernized institutions to enforce it. China at the center, embodied in the name "Central Kingdom" or *Zhongguo*, was no more. Juxtaposed to Sinicization was another "ization," westernization. Japan had westernized in order to modernize. It had used westernization and modernization to defeat China on the battlefield. In doing so, it had proven that Sinification was not the one-way evolution assumed by the Han. The Sino-Japanese War overturned the Han assumption of the superiority of their civilization and undermined the Confucian bedrock of their culture. Henceforth, Chinese history would be a frustrating search for a suitable replacement for the Confucian ideology that had so long and so successfully guided Han thinking. The Han would later turn to nationalism and then communism, but with unsatisfactory results. Arguably, China has yet to recover the philosophical bearings that it lost in the First Sino-Japanese War.

Meanwhile, the large indemnity bankrolled Japanese military expansion. The money paid for the war plus a huge Japanese postwar rearmament program. Conversely, the indemnity prevented China from expending funds on its own armed forces. Japanese control of Taiwan and the Pescadore Islands marked the beginnings of the Japanese Empire that caused China such agony in the Second Sino-Japanese War (1937–45). Japanese colonization of Taiwan also marked the divergence of Taiwanese from Chinese history, since Japan implemented a Meiji-style reform program for Taiwan, which the Taiwanese did not resist. The Taiwanese economy developed rapidly under Japanese management, and Taiwanese-Japanese relations remained quite cordial. Japan's relations with Korea were another matter. The Koreans bitterly resisted the growing Japanese dominance over their country all the way to the end of World War II, and their animosity toward Japan has endured to the present day.

IV. The Triple Intervention

Li Hongzhang's strategy to secure foreign intervention to rein in Japan came to fruition shortly after the signing of the Treaty of Shimonoseki. Japan conveniently overreached when it demanded that the Liaodong Peninsula be included in the peace settlement, despite repeated warnings from the Japanese Foreign Ministry that the European powers would not permit Japan to occupy such a strategic position, controlling the northern sea approach to Beijing and potentially putting the Chinese capital under a direct Japanese military threat. The Russians repeatedly told the Foreign Ministry that they would not tolerate such an outcome, since a Japanese concession in southern Manchuria constrained Russia's own ambitions for Manchuria and a warm-water port on the Asian mainland. Prior to the development of icebreakers, Vladivostok remained frozen for an average of fifty-two days per year. This limitation put Russia in the market for a warm-water port either in Korea or in Manchuria. France was allied with Russia out of fear of Germany. This alliance meant that France would have to go along for the ride with any activist Russian foreign policy in East Asia. Germany, meanwhile, desired Russia to become bogged down in East Asia so that Germany could pursue its own expansionist agenda in Europe.

On 23 April 1895, just six days after the signing of the Treaty of Shimonoseki, the ministers of Russia, Germany, and France called on the Japanese Foreign Ministry to offer some "friendly advice." They recommended that Japan return the Liaodong Peninsula to China. This was the so-called Triple Intervention. Japan totaled the combined naval forces that Russia, Germany, and France could deploy in East Asia and backed down immediately. Japan was strong enough to take on China, but not a combination of some of the foremost powers of the day. As compensation for returning the Liaodong Peninsula, Japan pressured China into increasing its indemnity by 15 percent.

The Japanese public reacted with outrage. They believed that their diplomats had lost at the negotiating table what their brave soldiers had won on the battlefield. While Japan expelled China from Korea, the underlying problems of Korean instability and Russian East Asian ambitions remained. Japan and Russia would go to war over these issues a decade later in the Russo-Japanese War (1904–5), Japan's second war of Russian containment (see Chapter 13, Section V). The conservative Han literati were even more outraged by the outcome of the war. They used it to undermine Li Hongzhang, whose power would be eclipsed until these same conservatives landed China in another foreign policy fiasco, the Boxer Uprising of 1900, when Li would again be called upon to undo the mess (see Chapter 13, Sections II–IV).

Li remained wedded to the traditional Han strategy of barbarian management of setting one barbarian against another (*yi yi zhi yi*). When the Russians came to him to negotiate a Russo-Chinese alliance, Li was receptive. The terms turned out to be severe: Russia would protect China from Japan in return for a huge railway concession through the heart of Manchuria, allowing Russia to run the Trans-Siberian Railway from Lake Baikal straight to Vladivostok. Russia and China signed the treaty of alliance on 3 June 1896. Alas for China, Russia, not Japan, posed the most immediate territorial threat. On 27 March 1898, Russia demanded the same concession on the Liaodong Peninsula that it had helped force Japan to relinquish with the Triple Intervention. Russia then added a railway line to link Lüshun to the main Russian railway station at Harbin (Haerbin).

The 1896 Russo-Chinese agreement did not turn out to be much of an alliance. China regained sovereignty over these concessions from the USSR only in 1955, more than a decade after the Western powers renounced the treaty port system. In the end, the foreign intervention that Li sought yielded Russian instead of Japanese control over the Liaodong Peninsula, an increased indemnity to Japan, and vast Russian railway concessions through the dynastic homelands in Manchuria. The Harbin-Lüshun railway line ran very inauspiciously through the hallowed grounds of Shenyang (Mukden) in the vicinity of the original Qing imperial tombs, jeopardizing their carefully positioned *fengshui*. Again, the Chinese strategy had yielded the opposite of its intended outcome. China's failure in the Sino-Japanese War demonstrated that the age-old tributary system was dead. The postwar settlement then demonstrated that Han traditions of barbarian management were ineffective when applied to technologically superior foes. Setting one barbarian against another worked only when each was militarily inferior to China.

V. The Scramble for Concessions

The European powers carefully watched the Sino-Japanese War. Previously, many Westerners had remained hopeful that the Manchus would prove capable of implementing reforms to relieve China's increasingly visible poverty, its endemic official malfeasance, and its wholly inadequate infrastructure. China's conduct of the war, however, left no lingering illusions in the West: China had a military that sent soldiers off to war armed with bows and arrows, an army with no medical service, officers who mutilated prisoners, commanders who left supplies to the Japanese, first-class battleships that sat out the war in port, fleets that refused to respond to the call of their countrymen, and a government that focused on imperial celebrations for the sixtieth birthday of Cixi rather than on paying its soldiers. Western journalists filed reports initially expressing amazement, later disgust, and, before long, utter contempt.

Initial Western reports on Japan also expressed amazement—amazement that little Japan would be so stupid as to attack China. But soon they applauded Japan's professionalism in the field, its rapid military progress, and especially its highly successful modernization efforts at home. The Western press welcomed a new world power. Previously, many in the West had assumed industrialization to be the cultural monopoly of the Christian nations. After the war, such views fell by the wayside. Japan became a permanent member of the great powers' club.

By war's end, China was widely considered by the Western nations to be incapable of taking positive actions, so they stepped in to fill the power vacuum. While their main goal was to make money, the Western capitalists also considered their actions morally justified in the face of rotting Chinese political institutions. China's defeat led directly to a postwar Scramble for Concessions. The European powers and Japan vied to carve out spheres of influence, in which one power would implement the necessary modernization measures to develop the sphere's mineral resources and create the transportation grid to bring these resources to market. China gained from the creation of a modern infrastructure and from foreign investments in mining and industry, but the Chinese people intensely resented such foreign intrusions in their land and their own loss of control. Some Chinese favored a Meiji-style reform program, but they remained very much in the minority. Most of the Han literati and Manchus still had too strong a vested interest in the status quo.

Li's brainchild, the Triple Intervention, came at a price. France, the least enthusiastic participant, was the first to cash in. (See Map 12.2.) On 20 June 1895 it acquired a sphere of influence, including Yunnan, Guangxi, and Guangdong, that abutted its colony in Vietnam. In 1897, France added Hainan Island to its sphere of influence. Germany came next. In October 1895 it had acquired concessions in Hankou and Tianjin. Then in 1897 it acquired a large sphere of influence in Shandong province and, in particular, at Jiaozhou Bay and the city of Qingdao. (China's popular Tsingtao [Qingdao] Beer comes to us courtesy of the Germans.)

Russia was the last member of the Triple Intervention to secure compensation. It acquired the extensive Manchurian railway concessions and ports on the strategic Liaodong Peninsula. The original east-west link of the Trans-Siberian Railway cut through the rich heartland of northern Manchuria and controlled over 250,000 acres of Chinese territory, making this by far the largest foreign concession in China. In mileage it accounted for 45 percent of all foreign-owned railways in China in the 1920s. Contrary to the myth that Britain was the most voracious imperialist, it was merely the largest trading partner; in terms of territory, Russia was the greatest. As a result of the Scramble for Concessions, the pre–World War I breakdown of the railway mileage was as follows: the Chinese Eastern Railway (Russian), 1,073 miles; the South Manchurian Railway (originally Russian, but Japanese after the Russo-Japanese War), 709 miles; the Yunnan Railway (French), 289 miles; the Jiaozhou-Jinan (Kiaochow-Tsinan) Railway (German), 284 miles; and the Guangzhou-Kowloon Railway (British), 22 miles.[4] Finally, Belgium acquired the Beijing-Hankou Railway concession in 1897, and the United States secured the Guangzhou-Hankou Railway concession the following year.

Britain joined the Scramble for Concessions to counter the other powers. In February 1898, it secured a predominant interest over the Yangzi River valley. In June, a ninety-nine-year lease on the New Territories north of Kowloon expanded its permanent colony in Hong Kong and Kowloon. (The expiration of this lease triggered the return of Hong Kong and Kowloon to China in 1997.) It also expanded its sphere to include Shanxi, Henan, and Sichuan provinces. In addition, Britain responded to Russia's acquisition of Lüshun with its own lease of Weihaiwei. The concession treaty specified that Britain would withdraw from Weihaiwei as soon as Russia withdrew from Lüshun. This arrangement made Russia and Britain the sentinels to the sea approaches to Beijing. In 1899, Britain and Russia formalized their spheres of influence: Britain pledged not to seek railway concessions north of the Great Wall in return for a Russian promise not to do so in the Yangzi River valley. Meanwhile, Japan dominated Fujian province across the strait from its colony on Taiwan. In addition, it acquired a concession in Shashi, one of the cities removed from its demands in the negotiations for the Treaty of Shimonoseki. Thus, China's loss of the Sino-Japanese War caused a dramatic increase in the number of treaty ports and a corresponding increase in Chinese resentment and fears of partition. (See Table 12.1.)

The United States, preoccupied with the Spanish-American War of 1898, which brought it control over the Philippines, Puerto Rico, Guam, and Guantanamo Bay, was not a major participant in the Scramble for Concessions. Instead, in 1899 it rejected the division of China into exclusive spheres of influence by promoting the Open Door Policy. Most of the powers eventually gave nominal support to the policy, which called for the preservation of Chinese territorial integrity and equal international access to its treaty ports. In practice, they continued to curtail outside influence in their own

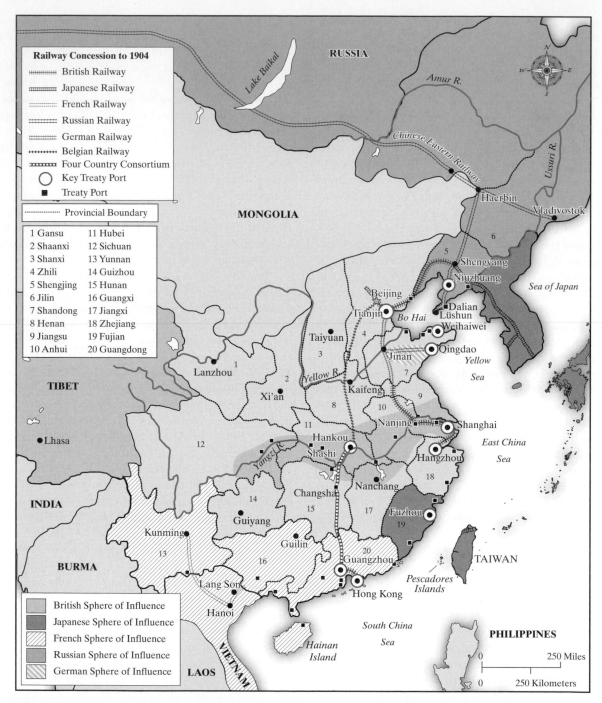

Map 12.2   Foreign Spheres of Influence in China

Table 12.1 Opening of Treaty Ports (1895–1911)

Date Opened	City (Pinyin)	City (Traditional Spelling)	Treaty	Signatories (In Addition to China)
1896	Suzhou	Soochow	1895 Treaty of Shimonoseki	Japan
1896	Hangzhou	Hangchow	1895 Treaty of Shimonoseki	Japan
1896	Shashi	Shasi	1895 Treaty of Shimonoseki	Japan
1897	Hekou	Hokow	1895 Commercial Agreement	France
1897	Simao	Szemao	1895 Commercial Agreement	France
1897	Wuzhou	Wuchow	1897 Burma Treaty	Britain
1897	Sanshui	Samshui	1897 Burma Treaty	Britain
1899	Nanjing	Nanking	1858 Treaty of Tianjin	France
1902	Tengyue	Tengyueh	1897 Burma Treaty	Britain
1904	Jiangmen	Kongmoon	1902 Commercial and Navigation Treaty	Britain
1904	Changsha	Changsha	1902 Commercial and Navigation Treaty	Britain
1906	Jiangzi	Gyangtse	1906 Tibet Supplemental Treaty	Britain
1906	Gedake	Gartok	1906 Tibet Supplemental Treaty	Britain
1906	Tieling	Tiehling	1905 Supplemental Treaty on Manchuria	Japan
	Xinmintun	Sinmin	1905 Supplemental Treaty on Manchuria	Japan
1906	Tongjiangzi	Tungkiang	1905 Supplemental Treaty on Manchuria	Japan
1906	Faku	Fakumen	1905 Supplemental Treaty on Manchuria	Japan
1907	Jilin	Kirin	1905 Supplemental Treaty on Manchuria	Japan
1907	Changchun	Changchun	1905 Supplemental Treaty on Manchuria	Japan
1907	Haerbin	Harbin	1905 Supplemental Treaty on Manchuria	Japan
1907	Manzhouli	Manchouli	1905 Supplemental Treaty on Manchuria	Japan
1907	Andong	Antung	1903 Commercial and Navigation Treaty	United States
1907	Dadonggou	Tatungkow	1903 Commercial and Navigation Treaty	Japan
1907	Qiqihaer	Tsitsihar	1905 Supplemental Treaty on Manchuria	Japan
1907	Aihun	Aigun	1905 Supplemental Treaty on Manchuria	Japan
1907	Fenghuangcheng	Fenghwang	1905 Supplemental Treaty on Manchuria	Japan
1907	Liaoyang	Liaoyang	1905 Supplemental Treaty on Manchuria	Japan
1908	Fengtian	Shengking	1903 Commercial and Navigation Treaty	Japan, United States
1909	Sanxing	Sansing	1905 Supplemental Treaty on Manchuria	Japan
1909	Longjingcun		1909 Tiumen River-Korean Border Treaty	Japan
1909	Juzijie		1909 Tiumen River-Korean Border Treaty	Japan
1909	Toudaogou		1909 Tiumen River-Korean Border Treaty	Japan
1909	Baicaogou		1909 Tiumen River-Korean Border Treaty	Japan
1910	Hunchun	Hunchun	1905 Supplemental Treaty on Manchuria	Japan
1910	Ningguta	Ninguta	1905 Supplemental Treaty on Manchuria	Japan
1910	Hailaer	Hailar	1905 Supplemental Treaty on Manchuria	Japan
(1916)	Zhangjiakou	Kalgan	1860 Treaty of Beijing	Russia

Note: During this period, Japan was the primary instigator. For 1843–94, see Table 7.3. We were unable to find traditional place names for all treaty ports.

Source: Haipeng Zhang, ed., *Zhongguo jindai shigao dituji* (Shanghai: Dituchubanshe, 1984), 83–4.

concession areas. The major issue between the United States and China concerned not concessions but Chinese immigration, which the United States had severely restricted in 1882 and banned altogether in 1888. These restrictions and the mistreatment of the Chinese who remained in the United States constituted an enduring source of tension until U.S. public attitudes changed and the immigration restrictions were lifted in 1943.

Meanwhile, it took decades for the foreign powers to develop their many concessions. Over the following century, the Chinese complained bitterly about them, yet foreign investments provided thousands of miles of railways and other infrastructure. When the foreigners left, the railways and treaty-port facilities remained to support China's economic development.

Conclusions

The Sino-Japanese War marked the end of the Confucian international order regulating East Asian relations. For better or for worse, a westernized framework for organizing international relations had been imposed on East Asia. The tributary system was dead. If the Opium Wars began this process, then the Sino-Japanese War finished it. For China the change was calamitous. Gone was its traditional position of regional primacy that provided the basis for the cherished beliefs concerning Sinocentrism, Han superiority, the preeminence of Chinese civilization, and the emperor as mediator between heaven and earth. This undermined both the Manchu mandate of heaven and the entire imperial system. Thus, the war had a far-reaching domestic impact.

Defeat by Japan rattled Han confidence in their understanding of the world far more profoundly than any barbarian-imposed defeat ever could. A former member of the Confucian order had abandoned that order for westernization and had used barbarism to defeat civilization. This is the reason why defeat in the Sino-Japanese War, in contrast to China's repeated defeats in the Opium, Arrow, and Sino-French wars, made such a profound impact on educated Chinese. The Manchus were living on borrowed time. The combination of the war and postwar proliferation of foreign concessions had an equally profound impact on ordinary Chinese who coalesced around the Boxer Uprising.

Because of its population, geographic extent, resources, shorter logistical lines, and long tradition of primacy, China should have won the war, but the Qing misconstrued the balance of power both in the world at large and in Asia. They believed that because they had always been dominant, they would remain so. They did not perceive the disconnect between their ambitious policy objective and their inability to achieve it using traditional methods. In a world in which China was no longer technologically supreme, time was not necessarily on its side. China's passive strategy during the Sino-Japanese War ceded the initiative to the Japanese, who chose the time and place of battle and so fought the war on their own terms. Japanese victory forced China to forfeit its claim to suzerainty over Korea, cede Taiwan and the Pescadore Islands, and fund future Japanese military expansion through the payment of an indemnity.

The combination of the destruction of the Beiyang Fleet and the imposition of a large indemnity precluded Chinese rearmament. Thus, the military imbalance resulting from the war became permanent. The Sino-Japanese War left the economies of several provinces devastated, the country deeply in debt, the Manchus discredited, and national defenses utterly compromised. The costs of the war increased Chinese indebtedness sevenfold and brought famine to North China. (See the feature on the next page.) The Manchus had no credibility at home or abroad, losing control not simply over tributary states but over the central provinces of China, where the great powers carved out ever larger spheres of influence during the postwar Scramble for Concessions. The Chinese government would not regain full sovereignty over its territory until the Communist victory in 1949.

Defeat vindicated the warnings of the Self-strengtheners. Ironically, the modernization projects that Li Hongzhang had so long promoted despite vehement opposition became widely accepted as a result of the war that destroyed his career. Broad sectors of the literati concluded that China must change and must change radically. Japan's total victory irrefutably demonstrated the superiority of Western technology and military institutions, and within two years, the emperor himself was in the thick of the reform movement of 1898. It is no coincidence that the Hundred Days' Reform of 1898, the 1900 Boxer Uprising, and a last-gasp Qing attempt at constitutional reform in the first decade of the twentieth century all followed in dizzying succession. Defeat by Japan broke the logjam that had long stalled reform efforts in China. Debate over the need for fundamental change has remained the focus of Chinese politics ever since. The Chinese have yet to find a completely satisfactory replacement for the Confucian ideology of empire that had guided their actions so successfully in the preindustrial era.

FAMINE

Famine has been the scourge of China. In 1926 the secretary of the International Famine Relief Commission wrote a book entitled *China: Land of Famine*, which counted 1,828 famines between 108 BC and 1911 AD, or nearly one per year. A common salutation in Chinese is "Have you eaten?" For all too many, it was not an idle question. The most common causes of famines were droughts, floods, and wars, with droughts generally more devastating than floods and warfare greatly exacerbating both. While droughts primarily afflicted North China, floods primarily affected South China. Increasing population magnified the devastation in both cases as people moved into ever more marginal and precarious lands. In addition, declining Qing finances precluded adequate investments in dikes and granaries, exacerbating the impact of bad weather cycles. Locust infestations also caused famines, most often in central and northern China.

The greatest cause of famine was not natural but man-made. It was warfare, which not only devastated agricultural lands and their population but also utterly disrupted famine relief efforts. The civil wars and foreign wars of the nineteenth and twentieth centuries disrupted vital agricultural routines, destroyed infrastructure, impoverished and incapacitated the central government, and brought environmental devastation. China has only recently been at peace with the end of the campaigns of the Maoist era that brought one of the greatest famines in Chinese history, the nationwide Great Famine (1959–61). One of the most important achievements of the People's Republic of China since the death of Mao has been the elimination of famine in China.

Until the creation of railways and telegraphs, it often took months before the news of a famine reached the capital. By the time famine relief from the outside reached the affected provinces, it was often too late for many. In 1876–9 and in 1920–1 the worst droughts since 1786 afflicted North China. In the first famine, an estimated 9.5 million died; in the second, 500,000 perished. The railway system that had been built between the two disasters made possible the rapid transmission of information and the distribution of food. In addition, Western countries paid 37 million Mexican dollars, or 40 percent of the famine relief costs, in 1920–1. This was an international relief effort of unprecedented scale at that time and a harbinger of later international famine relief efforts under the United Nations that have greatly reduced famine worldwide.

Whatever the cause of the crop failures—drought, flooding, locusts, or warfare—the ensuing tragedy followed a predictable pattern: Grain prices went through the roof while land prices went through the floor, wiping out the peasant economy in the process. Half-starved men roaming the barren land turned to banditry, while government forces responded with brutality. Others sold women and children to middlemen who prospered with a growing trade in slaves and prostitutes. In desperation, people stripped the vegetation of anything even semiedible, causing long-term environmental degradation. Bodies were left unburied, with the living too weak and the dead too numerous to inter properly. Disease and even cannibalism followed. Little girls died in disproportionate numbers, as they were the first to be sacrificed in a society that valued sons; this pattern persisted during the Maoist era. Refugees filled the roads. In 1877 a magistrate reported: "Men brutally butchered their own kin, mothers devoured their children, elder brothers their youngest, a grandson chopped his grandmother to pieces, a niece boiled and ate her own aunt. The mangled remains of those thus cruelly murdered were brought in evidence to my yamen again and again."[5]

The endemic warfare of the nineteenth and twentieth centuries brought famine to millions of Chinese.

Defeat in the Sino-Japanese War had dramatic repercussions for China, East Asia, and the world. This war marks the origin of the two-China problem. Henceforth, Taiwanese development diverged from that of the Chinese mainland. The war also marks the beginning of a long period of intrusive great power rivalries over the Korean Peninsula and endemic Korean instability, problems that have endured to the present. In addition, the war caused a fundamental reorientation of Russian foreign policy toward Asia, with massive investments in railway construction in Manchuria.

The war ushered in a long period of Russo–Japanese competition for empire in East Asia that continued through World War II; even today, Russia and Japan have yet to agree on sovereignty over the southernmost Kurile Islands. Finally, the war left a tragic legacy of Sino–Japanese animosity reinforced by an even more bitter Second Sino-Japanese War (1937–45). The world as China wanted it to be disappeared with the First Sino-Japanese War. Ever since, a central goal of Chinese foreign policy has been to reverse the outcome of the war, restore Chinese primacy, and contain Japan.

BIBLIOGRAPHY

Beasley, W. G. *Japanese Imperialism 1894–1945*. Oxford: Clarendon Press, 1987.

Bohr, Paul Richard. *Famine in China and The Missionary: Timothy Richard as Relief Administrator and Advocate of National Reform, 1876–1884*. Cambridge, MA: Harvard East Asia Center, 1972.

Conroy, Hilary. *The Japanese Seizure of Korea: 1868–1910: A Study of Realism and Idealism in International Relations*. Philadelphia: University of Pennsylvania Press, 1960.

Ding Richu. "Dowager Empress Cixi and Toshimichi: A Comparative Study of Modernization in China and Japan." In *China's Quest for Modernization: A Historical Perspective*, edited by Frederic Wakeman, Jr., and Wang Xi, 175–90. Berkeley: University of California Press, 1997.

Dorwart, Jeffrey, M. *The Pigtail War: American Involvement in the Sino-Japanese War of 1894–1895*. Amherst: University of Massachusetts Press, 1975.

Eastlake, Warrington and Yamada Yoshi-aki. *Heroic Japan: A History of the War between China & Japan*. 1897. Reprint, Washington: University Publications of America, 1979.

Eckert, Carter, et al. *Korea Old and New: A History*. Cambridge, MA: Cambridge University Press, 1990.

Elleman, Bruce A. *Modern Chinese Warfare, 1795–1989*. London: Routledge, 2001.

Hao, Yen-p'ing and Erh-min Wang. "Changing Chinese Views of Western Relations, 1840–1895." In *The Cambridge History of China*, vol 11, edited by John K. Fairbank and Kwang-ching Liu, 142–201. Cambridge: Cambridge University Press, 1980.

Hou, Chi-ming. *Foreign Investment and Economic Development in China, 1840–1937*. Cambridge, MA: Harvard University Press, 1965.

Iriye, Akira. "Japan's Drive to Great Power Status." In *The Cambridge History of Japan*, vol. 5, edited by Marius B. Jansen, 721–82. Cambridge: Cambridge University Press, 1989.

———*Japan & the Wider World*. London: Longman, 1997.

Kim, C. I. Eugene and Kan-kyo Kim. *Korea and the Politics of Imperialism 1876–1910*. Berkeley: University of California Press, 1967.

Langer, William L. *The Diplomacy of Imperialism 1890–1902*. 2nd ed. New York: Alfred A. Knopf, 1956.

Lensen, George Alexander. *Balance of Intrigue: International Rivalry in Korea & Manchuria, 1884–1899*. 2 vols. Tallahassee: University Presses of Florida, 1982.

Lone, Stewart. *Japan's First Modern War: Army and Society in the Conflict with China, 1894–95*. London: St. Martin's Press, 1994.

Mallory, Walter H. *China: Land of Famine*. New York: American Geographical Society, 1926.

Malozemoff, Andrew. *Russian Far Eastern Policy 1881–1904 with Special Emphasis on the Causes of the Russo-Japanese War*. Berkeley: University of California Press, 1958.

Nathan, Andrew James. "A History of the China International Famine Relief Commission." Cambridge, MA: Harvard East Asian Center, 1965.

Paine, S. C. M. *The Sino-Japanese War of 1894–1895: Perceptions, Power, and Primacy*. Cambridge: Cambridge University Press, 2003.

NOTES

1. Translated by the authors from the Chinese original found by Yu Minling at http://zh.wikipedia.org/wiki/%E6%9D%8E%E9%B8%BF%E7%AB%A0

2. Quoted in S. C. M. Paine, *The Sino-Japanese War of 1894–1895: Perceptions, Power, and Primacy* (Cambridge: Cambridge University Press, 2003), 260, 271.

3. Ibid.

4. Chi-ming Hou, *Foreign Investment and Economic Development in China, 1840–1937* (Cambridge, MA: Harvard University Press, 1965), 65.

5. Paul Richard Bohr, "Famine in China and the Missionary: Timothy Richard as Relief Administrator and Advocate of National Reform, 1876–1884," (Cambridge, MA: Harvard East Asian Center, 1972), 23.

Chronology

1894–5	Sino-Japanese War
1895–9	Scramble for Concessions
1895	Kang Youwei's Ten Thousand Word Memorial
1896	Chinese government sends first students to Japan
1898	Hundred Days' Reform
1899	Boxers active in Shandong
	U.S. Open Door Policy
1900	Destruction of sixty-four Manchu settlements on the Amur River
	Russian occupation of Manchuria
	Qing government declares war on foreign powers
	End of Boxer Uprising
1901	Boxer Protocol
	Death of Li Hongzhang
1904–5	Russo-Japanese War

13

The Attempt to Expel the Foreigners: The Boxer Uprising

Strong wine can't melt away
tears of care on our land;
to save these times we must depend
on talent beyond the common.

We will spend the blood that flows
from a hundred thousand skulls,
but we must exert our strength to turn
Heaven and Earth aright.[1]

Qiu Jin (1879–1907),
poetess, revolutionary martyr

The Manchus originally earned the mandate of heaven by establishing virtuous Confucian rule, fostering rural prosperity, restoring domestic tranquility, and expanding territorial conquests beyond any Han empire. In the late nineteenth century, none of these conditions held true. The Sino-Japanese War made clear to Chinese in the war zone the success of Japanese modernization programs. Han civilians and soldiers noted the stark contrast between the standard issue of equipment for each Japanese soldier and the failure of their government often even to pay, feed, or clothe, let alone equip, their own foot soldiers. In reaction, the central government orchestrated a major westernization program, the short-lived Hundred Days' Reform sponsored by the youthful Guangxu emperor (b. 1871, r. 1875–1908). But the Empress Dowager Cixi led the counterattack of the Han literati, whose livelihood depended on the status quo. Not surprisingly, another internal rebellion was soon in the making. The Society of Righteousness and Harmony (*Yihetuan*) emphasized willpower over technology and practiced traditional martial arts, so Westerners called them the Boxers. During May 1900, the Empress Dowager threw her support behind the Boxers, deflecting their rage away

from the Qing to focus instead on foreigners. While the dynasty survived the ensuing turmoil, Western defeat of the Boxers resulted in a new set of debilitating indemnities for China.

I. The Hundred Days' Reform

The Chinese became aware of Japanese modernization and westernization programs as a result of the Sino-Japanese War. Previously, educated Chinese who even knew about the Meiji reforms were generally contemptuous of them, but the rapid Japanese victory over China made some reconsider. In 1897, the College of Foreign Languages attached to the Zongli Yamen belatedly added Japanese to the curriculum.

In 1896, the Qing government sent an initial group of thirteen students to study in Japan. This would be the beginning of a wave of Chinese students studying there, including Sun Yat-sen, the founder of the Republic of China; Chiang Kai-shek, the future Nationalist Party leader; and Chen Duxiu, the founder of the Chinese Communist Party. Previously, generations of Japanese had gone to China to study, but now the Sino-Japanese War reversed the tide. From 1898 to the fall of the Qing dynasty in 1911, at least 25,000 Chinese studied in Japan. Japanese teachers flocked to China, where they taught Chinese the vocabulary of the new industrial world. Japan had been the first nation to translate Western terminology into characters, so many Western works in China were Japanese books retranslated into Chinese. The Chinese adopted Japan's character combinations to translate Western terminology. Thus, Japan became the filter though which many Chinese studied Western institutions.

A generation of Chinese reformers looked to Japan for models. The Hundred Days' Reform of 1898 was based on the Meiji reforms. Just as the Meiji emperor restored imperial rule in Japan, the Guangxu emperor sought this for China. But the Meiji emperor was the figurehead for a reform movement controlled by a ruling oligarchy, whereas the Guangxu emperor was hemmed in by a bureaucracy run by literati officials and manipulated by an aunt, whose combined interests were vested in the status quo.

Defeat in the Sino-Japanese War and the Scramble for Concessions spurred radical Chinese intellectuals. Kang Youwei, a political reformer from Guangdong, argued that Confucius was actually a reformer and appealed to the Manchu Court to implement westernizing reforms. Kang served primarily as a catalyst. Despite his lack of official position, he organized a Ten Thousand Word Memorial in 1895, signed by over 1,000 of those who had passed the highest level of the imperial examinations. It petitioned the imperial Court to implement wide-ranging institutional reforms. The reformers organized study groups and published newspapers to spread their ideas. Kang urged the Guangxu emperor to follow the examples of Peter the Great of Russia and the Meiji emperor of Japan, both leaders of autocratic countries that overcame their technological inferiority to surge forward and become major powers.

The Guangxu emperor was receptive. During the 103 days from 11 June to 21 September 1898, he issued a flurry of decrees westernizing educational, judicial, military, policing, and commercial institutions. For education, he abolished the eight-legged essay on the imperial examinations and mandated the establishment of military academies, westernized provincial schools, technical schools to support an industrial economy, and a preeminent center of westernized higher learning: the Imperial University in Beijing. For the government, he attempted to abolish redundant positions, streamline administration, broaden the flow of information, introduce modern budgetary procedures, and create government offices to promote agriculture, industry, and commerce. For the military, he ordered provincial reforms to create modern land and naval forces.

The reforms, however, did not include Kang's recommendations for a parliament or a constitution. Although the Manchus needed to restore their mandate to rule, there was no consensus on the abandonment of the Confucian basis for rule. The Manchus had originally cemented their moral authority to rule as guardians of Han civilization. Westernizing reforms entailed an abandonment of this role. Reforms that promised a more open political system representative of Han interests diluted Manchu control, which was already under siege. Opposition to the reforms was intense. Conservative Han bureaucrats and the Manchus joined forces in September 1898, when the Guangxu emperor announced that the

Manchu bannermen, like the Japanese samurai, would lose their stipends and, for the first time, have to earn their own living. While the Japanese reformers had the military power to suppress the ensuing Satsuma Rebellion of irate samurai in 1877, the Guangxu emperor had few loyal military forces at his disposal.

The Empress Dowager Cixi put an end to the reform movement on 21 September, when she orchestrated a palace coup, putting the Guangxu emperor under house arrest. She reclaimed control of the government, making herself regent for an allegedly seriously ill Guangxu emperor. In fact, she had him imprisoned on a small island in the imperial garden. According to some accounts, Yuan Shikai, a military protégé of Li Hongzhang, the former Chinese proconsul to Korea on the eve of the Sino-Japanese War and future president of China, had told Cixi that the reformers planned to have her arrested. The coup led to the execution of six of the most radical reformers. Kang fled abroad, where he continued to promote a constitutional monarchy patterned on Japan's Meiji reforms. The Empress Dowager Cixi rescinded most of the reform initiatives.

The swift reversal from reform to reaction was another unsettling indication of a dynasty losing control. There was nothing auspicious about the third regency by an emperor's minor concubine. Regardless of contemporary views of the capabilities of women, rule by women in imperial China was associated with dynastic disaster. According to the *Book of Odes*, "Wise man rears a wall / and a sly bitch downs it, / so nice to look at, elaborate in contriving? / No. Dirty, an owl, her tongue long as a dust-storm. / The stair-way, confusion not descended from heaven / but upsprung from women and eunuchs / from whom never good warning nor lesson." The next stanza admonishes, "Keep the hens out of public business, let'em stick to silk-worms and weaving."[2]

II. The Origins of the Boxer Movement

The combination of Chinese defeat in the Sino-Japanese War and the ensuing Scramble for Concessions simultaneously reaped a harvest of Chinese xenophobia and spurred the initial development of Chinese nationalism. The Chinese describe the Scramble for Concessions from 1895–9 as *guafen,* or "slicing up China like a ripe melon." The foreign presence became much more visible with the addition of new churches, the expansion of businesses, and the construction of foreign-financed railway lines. For many, the Western infrastructure disrupted the surrounding *fengshui,* which in

Western influence in China was particularly profound in matters relating to religion. Catholic and Protestant missionaries converted hundreds of thousands of Chinese to Christianity. This picture shows a Chinese pastor and his family living in Guangzhou. During the 1900 Boxer Uprising, over 30,000 Chinese converts were killed, a number over a hundred times greater than the foreign deaths.

turn disrupted the cosmos. They found evidence of this in the growing poverty and instability of China. Dissatisfied Han nationalists blamed both foreigners and Manchus for their country's ills.

The origin of the Boxers is obscure. They were a secret society, apparently an offshoot of the White Lotus Sect. The Boxer ideology was an amalgamation of elements of Daoism, allegiance to their own True Martial God, and reverence for certain famous historical figures. They were virulently anti-foreign, proposing the annihilation of all foreigners in China as well that of their local supporters. They rejected Western technology, spurning both westernization and modernization.

While unrest affected virtually all Chinese provinces in 1899, it was particularly severe in Shandong, which had suffered two years of drought and famine, followed by a devastating breach of the Yellow River dikes. The Boxers called themselves the Righteous and Harmonious Fists (*Yihequan*) in reference to their practice of martial arts. (See the feature below.) In the beginning, the Boxer groups were small, often hailing from the same village. Later, they became known as the Society of Righteousness and Harmony (*Yihetuan*).

The Boxers emphasized willpower over weapons and argued that invulnerability rituals neutralized Western weapons. Possession by various gods provided magical powers, immunity from bullets, and even the ability to fly. During the mid-1890s, a new Boxer school appeared in Shandong called the Armor of

MARTIAL ARTS: KUNGFU, TAI CHI, AND *QIGONG*

There are hundreds of different types of martial arts in China. Some of the most well known are kungfu (*gongfu*), Tai Chi (*taiji*), and the more dance-like and health-oriented *qigong*. Ever since the time of the Qin dynasty (221–6 BC), central governments have regularly sought to control the possession of weapons. Perhaps as a result, hand-to-hand combat became highly developed in China and profoundly influenced karate and judo in Japan and Tae Kwon Do in Korea.

In China the military arts include not only kungfu, but also less violent martial arts such as Tai Chi, which emphasizes "subduing the vigorous by the soft" and has 108 different movements that combine into sequences, generally of twenty to forty steps. *Qigong* is less violent still and rarely entails fighting; rather, it focuses on breathing, posture, and exercises to promote health and increase vitality. Today elderly Chinese can often be seen practicing *qigong* early in the morning in public parks.

Of China's many different schools of martial arts, the Shaolin order is probably most well known to Americans. It is said that this school dates to the sixth century AD, when a Buddhist priest from India named Bodhidharma, or Damo in Chinese, visited China. Because his disciples congregated at a temple in a newly planted forest, they became known as the "young-forest" (*shaolin*) school. To prepare the monks for deep Buddhist meditation, Damo taught a series of exercises intended to enhance the life force, or *qi*. The movements were based on the eighteen animals from Indo-Chinese iconography, including the tiger, deer, leopard, cobra, dragon, and others, and over time the exercises became codified into a system of self-defense known as "Shaolin kungfu."

In keeping with Buddhist traditions, the martial arts focused on self-defense. Over time, Daoist beliefs began to intermix with Buddhism, so that by the late nineteenth century, many practitioners of kungfu believed that chanting Daoist magical spells would make them impervious to gunfire. The Boxer Uprising in 1900 showed the limitations of kungfu as a defense against Western rifles when hundreds, if not thousands, of Boxers perished in futile bare-handed attacks against soldiers with Western rapid-fire rifles. The new government of the People's Republic of China outlawed the martial arts in 1949, but they continued to be widely practiced in Hong Kong, Singapore, and Taiwan. Hong Kong movies dating to the 1960s—in particular the 1973 Bruce Lee film *Enter the Dragon*, completed just before Lee's death—popularized kungfu in the United States. Since the early 1970s, numerous types of Chinese martial arts have become popular in the West.

the Golden Bell. It promised its followers that even uneducated peasants could learn Boxer techniques in as little as one day, and that after a three-night ritual Boxer warriors could face swords unarmed, and with further practice could withstand firearms. In addition to using traditional weapons, including swords and lances, Boxers often wore red or yellow charm-bearing turbans. In the late nineteenth century, many Asians remained highly superstitious, so Manchus and Han alike readily accepted the Boxers' claim to magical powers. When the Boxers applied their mind-over-matter tactics to Western firepower, however, the results were both predictable and tragic.

Although the Han opposed the Manchus, they both shared a love for Chinese civilization and a hatred for the Guangxu emperor's westernizing reforms. This created a common ground for the Boxers and reactionary elements within the Manchu Court and the Han bureaucracy. The Boxers associated China's accumulating ills with the growing foreign presence. They divided their foreign enemies into three categories: (1) Europeans, Americans, and Japanese; (2) Chinese who either were Christian converts or worked closely with foreigners; and (3) all Chinese who bought and/or used foreign-made goods.

The spread of Christianity in Shandong province became an increasing source of friction. In 1897, Boxers opposed Christian converts trying to build a church on the site of a former Buddhist temple. With the arrival of German troops in Shandong later that year and the creation of a German concession in Qingdao, foreigners began to support Christian converts. They favored Chinese converts in commerce and administration. This gave rise to a growing sense that the converts had taken advantage of this situation to promote their economic interests and their political influence. It exacerbated tensions between them and the rest of the population. In November 1899, roaming bands of Boxers attacked Christian converts throughout Western Shandong, and on 15 November, the Boxers burned a fortified Catholic village. Foreign pressure on Beijing to remove the governor of Shandong increased until his recall on 6 December. Although the new governor, the former general Yuan Shikai,

arrived in late December and immediately began suppressing the Boxers, the movement continued to grow. On 31 December 1899, a British missionary became the first foreign victim, dying at the hands of a mob.

Boxer influence gradually spread northward toward Beijing. Many local officials tolerated the Boxers as a legitimate form of the village militia. The deposed governor of Shandong, Yuxian, praised the Boxers to Court officials, who then recommended them to the Empress Dowager Cixi. For her, they were a potential threat, with their latent Han revanchism, but also a potential ally, with their extreme xenophobia. The Qing strategy was to redirect their antiforeign sentiments away from the dynasty and toward the expatriate community. It was a win-win strategy: If the Boxers were successful, they would banish the foreigners from China. If they were unsuccessful, the foreigners would rid China of a potential threat to the dynasty. Either way, the Manchus would attain their objective of strengthening their own position. Some government officials, however, such as Yuan Shikai, warned that encouraging the Boxers was a dangerous game.

III. The Boxer Uprising

Beginning in late 1899, the diplomatic community in Beijing, including Great Britain, France, Germany, and the United States, protested to the Zongli Yamen concerning China's failure to protect foreigners and Chinese converts from the Boxers. Although the Manchu Court reassured the representatives that it was suppressing Boxer activity, it covertly encouraged the attacks, which continued to spread in the direction of Beijing. By early 1900, the Manchus were supporting Boxer efforts to organize and drill citizen militias, while the Boxer groups gradually dropped their anti-Manchu rhetoric. During May 1900, the Boxers moved into the Beijing region, killing about seventy Roman Catholic converts only eighty miles from the capital. (See Map 13.1.)

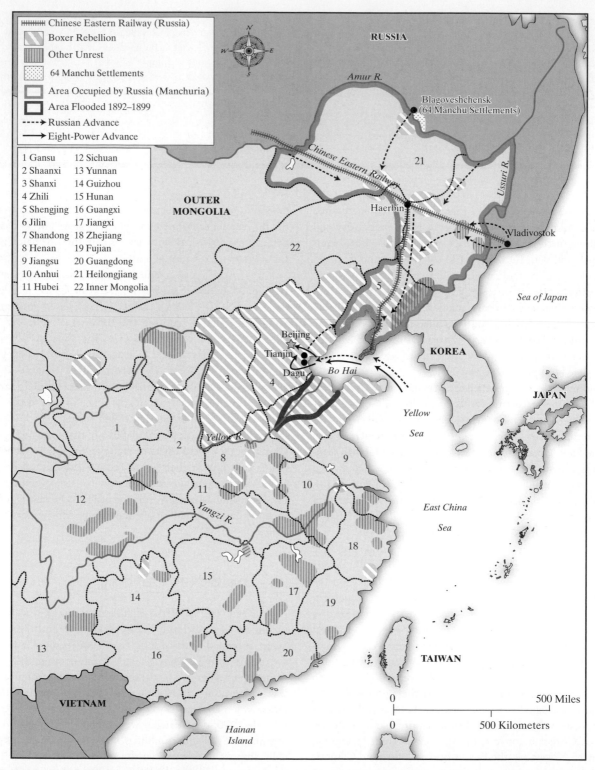

Map 13.1 Boxer Uprising (1900)

When the Qing government still failed to take action, the foreign ministers voted on 28 May to deploy additional troops. In early June, a combined force of nearly 2,000 troops from eight countries set out from the port of Tianjin to the capital, but Boxer militias and government troops forced it to return to Tianjin. Immediately afterward, the Court openly supported the Boxers. On 13 June, Boxer militias entered the capital, surrounded the foreign legations, cut the telegraph lines to Tianjin, and rendered the railways inoperable. They immediately burned many Western churches and foreign residences, exhumed Christian graveyards, and massacred or buried alive any Chinese converts they found. On 19 June, the Zongli Yamen warned all foreigners to leave Beijing by 20 June or face the consequences. When the deadline passed, Chinese troops began firing on the foreign legations. On 21 June 1900, an imperial edict declared war on all of the foreign powers. By doing so, the Manchus violated a basic principle of military strategy: Avoid attacking numerous strong enemies at one time.

The court reactionaries, led by a grandson of the Jiaqing emperor, Prince Duan (or Zaiyi), whose wife was the niece of the Empress Dowager, assumed command over tens of thousands of Boxers, while General Dong Fuxiang commanded the government troops. With the agreement of the Empress Dowager, rewards were offered to anyone who brought in a live foreigner for questioning before execution. Official propaganda explained that the removal of the foreigners would allow Chinese to live in peace. Opposing the Boxers in the legations were approximately 450 troops of an eight-nation military force, 475 civilians including 12 foreign ministers, and approximately 2,300 Chinese converts and 50 Chinese servants. By early July the foreigners' defenses were shrinking. The British legation became the last stronghold. Another very small force defended the Catholic Beitang Cathedral in north Beijing, where some 3,000 converts and 43 French and Italian marines held off a Boxer force of 10,000 for fifty-five days. The marines took advantage of the building's stone walls and the Boxers' faith in their immunity to gunfire to mow them down in droves. The Boxer leaders blamed the obvious failure of their mystical powers on the presence of women inside the cathedral, arguing that this "female pollution" had counteracted their powers.

For a time, those in Tianjin believed that the legations in Beijing had been overrun. Given China's vast superiority of forces and the inability of the defenders to resupply, this should have been the case. It turns out, however, that the commander in chief of the imperial troops in Beijing neither supported the Boxers nor openly defied the dynasty. Instead, he carried out a half-hearted siege. The Manchus had no intention of opening the adequately stocked imperial armories

Once the foreign nations intervened and the Chinese government turned against the Boxers, the capture and destruction of the Boxers was both rapid and brutal. Although no detailed records were kept, it is thought that over 100,000 Boxers perished.

and supplying the Boxers with modern weapons that could later be turned on the dynasty. Regional divisions also worsened during the uprising, with China's southern provinces declaring neutrality; Li Hongzhang in Guangdong province led the way, and Yuan Shikai in Shandong province and Governor-general Liu Kunyi of Jiangsu, Jiangxi, and Anhui provinces subsequently followed suit. South China avoided both the Boxer Uprising and the foreign reprisals.

As the Russians watched the unfolding events in China, they initially considered the unrest to be primarily a response to missionary and commercial activities, neither of which particularly concerned them. Therefore, Russia had not joined in the official protest against the spread of the movement in

January 1900. The unrest did not reach Manchuria until 23 June 1900, when the Court ordered the military governor of Fengtian province to organize the Boxers to cut the railway lines to prevent possible Russian troop deployments. In doing so, the Court needlessly created another foreign foe. The unrest soon spread to Heilongjiang province bordering Russia, which gained Russia's attention.

The foreign response was called the Eight-Nation Alliance and eventually totaled almost 54,000 troops; Japan sent over 20,000, Russia over 12,000, England around 12,000, and then France and the United States around 3,500 apiece. When the foreign community in Tianjin realized in late July that the legations were still holding out, a second force, the International Expeditionary Force of 18,000 troops, departed for Beijing on 4 August. It faced an estimated 50,000 Chinese opponents. Nevertheless, it made rapid progress. On 14 August, the allied troops breached Beijing's city wall and relieved the siege. As punishment for the Manchus, on 28 August 1900, allied forces threw open the sacred central gates of the Forbidden City and for the first time foreigners entered: Detachments from Russia, Japan, England, the United States, France, Germany, Italy, and Austria marched from the south gate straight through to the north gate. This fit the British tradition of overrunning Qing palaces. Unlike the Summer Palace in the Arrow War, the Forbidden City remained standing. But the damage to Qing prestige was enormous.

By late July, the Manchus realized their error. The Empress Dowager authorized the Zongli Yamen to open negotiations and arrange a cease-fire. On 27 July, she personally sent a present of ice, melons, and other fruit to the British minister, hoping that a solution might be found. When it became clear that negotiations were impossible, the Empress Dowager and her close officials fled Beijing for the inland city of Xi'an. During the Arrow War, she had fled to Manchuria, but in mid-July, Russia responded to the destruction of its railway concessions in Manchuria by deploying over 100,000 troops throughout the Manchu ancestral homeland. On the morning of 15 August 1900, the day after the International Expeditionary Force breached the walls of Beijing, and as the Empress Dowager fled the capital, she ordered the Guangxu emperor's favorite wife thrown down a well.

Meanwhile, within three months Russia occupied Manchuria, gaining possession of the Qing homelands and imperial tombs, an area of enormous symbolic importance to the dynasty. Per the terms of the 1858 Treaty of Aigun, there were sixty-four Manchu settlements on the Russian side of the Amur River but under Chinese jurisdiction. In the panic of the moment, local Russian authorities herded some 4,000 innocent Qing civilians into the Amur River, where most of them drowned. In 1909, when the Chinese demanded the return of this territory and an indemnity to cover the property losses, the Russian representative in Beijing refused on the grounds that the Manchus had left and therefore forfeited their property rights.

In the end, Russia's troop deployments far exceeded those of any other power because of the enormous Boxer damage to its very expensive Manchurian railway concessions, which constituted an investment roughly equivalent to 25 percent of the Russian government's budget over a three-year period. In all, two-thirds of its railway lines were damaged or destroyed, which made the Russians very reluctant to leave. The occupation began taking on the air of permanency, which was far more dangerous to China than the allied expeditionary forces. Russia alone intended to take territory. Discussions at the highest echelons of the Russian government concerned the maximum amount of territory that Russia should detach from China. Some thought Russia should limit itself to the relatively underpopulated northern Manchuria, while others had more ambitious plans. To the unanimous demands of the other foreign powers for a rapid troop withdrawal, the Russians responded with a policy of studied procrastination that lasted until the Japanese launched their second war of Russian containment, the Russo-Japanese War (1904–5), fought mainly on Chinese territory.

IV. The Boxer Protocol and the Economic Impact of the Indemnities

As the Manchus fled Beijing, they turned to a Han official to save them. The Empress Dowager once again called on Li Hongzhang, the great statesman, who had cleaned up her last mess with the Japanese. Li had negotiated the Treaty of Shimonoseki terminating the Sino-Japanese War; now he negotiated the Boxer Protocol ending the Boxer Uprising. He would die two months to the day after signing the 1901 Boxer Protocol, his last service to a dynasty that too often had rejected his timely advice, only to call on him to deal with the disastrous consequences.

Of the 231 foreigners killed during the Boxer Uprising, only about half were in Beijing or Tianjin. Many foreigners in the interior of China were completely helpless. In one well-known incident, the former governor of Shandong province whom the Empress Dowager reassigned as the governor of Shanxi province, Yuxian, rounded up all of the foreign missionaries and executed a total of forty-six, including fifteen men, twenty women, and eleven children. After the Boxer Uprising was over, foreign troops were sent to investigate many of the worst incidents. While the list of foreign dead is quite accurate, there is no corresponding account for all the Chinese dead. No one bothered to keep track. Thousands of Boxers and Chinese Christian converts perished.

On Christmas Eve 1900, Li Hongzhang began negotiations with the eleven foreign powers that had suffered losses but did not sign the final treaty until 7 September 1901, almost a year after his appointment. The first stumbling block was punishment of the high government officials implicated in the uprising. These were some of the Empress Dowager's closest allies. In a series of imperial edicts, the Empress Dowager agreed to exile her nephew-in-law Prince Duan, execute Yuxian, and execute, demote, and banish others. In addition to the punishment of highly placed officials in Beijing, 119 other minor officials were sentenced, many of them to death, for crimes against foreigners living in China's interior.

A second major issue concerned the size of the indemnity to compensate the foreign powers. The Boxer Protocol exacted the enormous sum of 450 million taels, approximately $333 million in 1900 dollars, to be paid over thirty-nine years. (See Table 13.1.) Russia received the lion's share of the indemnity, 29 percent, because of its huge railway losses. In descending order, shares of the indemnity were allocated to Germany, France, Great Britain, Japan, and the United States. The protocol relied on the standard Manchu remedy for altercations with the powers: mollify the barbarians with money. From the Manchu point of view, Han merchants, the group that sat at the bottom of the Confucian social order,

would ultimately finance the indemnity, which, as usual, was linked with foreign customs revenues.

The protocol also mandated the permanent deployment of foreign legation guards, the construction of twelve foreign garrisons between the coast and Beijing, and the destruction of the Dagu forts defending the approaches to the capital. Together these measures ensured access to the capital by foreign troops should the need arise. In other words, the treaty permanently undermined the defense of the capital. Additional articles set a two-year moratorium on the importation of foreign-made arms, suspended for five years imperial examinations in those cities where foreigners had perished, and mandated the barring from government of any Chinese officials who refused to repress crimes against foreigners. In keeping with the settlement of the Arrow War, the peace terms entailed the transformation of the Zongli Yamen into a more fully westernized Foreign Ministry.

Most notable about the Boxer Protocol was what it did not demand: The Manchus retained the throne, since the foreign powers were not willing to risk regime change. They understood that any new government would probably be more, not less, hostile to their presence in China. The Manchus had succeeded in their fallback position of using the foreigners to destroy the Boxers, but at the cost of further impairing their mandate to rule. The Qing remained on the throne, but only barely, since they had fled the capital; they were forced to apologize for the deaths of the German and Japanese ministers;

Table 13.1   Boxer Indemnity

Country	Percentage	Tael (Haiguan)	Foreign Currency	
Russia	28.97139	130,371,120	R	180,084,021
Germany	20.01567	90,070,515	Mrs	278,166,424
France	15.75072	70,878,240	Fr	265,793,400
Britain	11.24901	50,620,545	£	7,593,080
Japan	7.73180	34,793,100	¥	48,950,892
United States	7.31979	32,939,055	$	24,440,779
Italy	5.91489	26,617,005	Lire	99,803,769
Belgium	1.88541	8,484,345	Fr	31,816,294
Austria-Hungary	0.88976	4,003,920	Kr	10,394,092
Holland	0.17380	782,100	Fl	1,404,652
Spain	0.03007	135,315	Ps	507,431
Norway and Sweden	0.01396	62,820	£	9,423
Miscellaneous	0.03328	149,870	£	22,450
Total	100.00000	450,000,000		

Source: Zhaojin Ji, *A History of Modern Shanghai Banking: The Rise and Decline of China's Finance Capitalism* (Armonk, NY: M. E. Sharpe, 2003), 75.

foreign troops had violated the Forbidden City; and in a show of diplomatic equality, foreign envoys could now enter the Throne Hall of the Forbidden City. Like the many other attempts to resist foreign powers by force, this one also yielded the opposite of its intended outcome. Foreigners now had a stronger position in China than ever. In the long run, however, the Boxer movement constituted an important way station in the gradual development of Chinese nationalism. The movement spilled over local boundaries to move beyond community to nation and was spontaneous in development, reflecting a groundswell of domestic resentment against foreigners unifying persons of all walks of life and ethnicity.

V. The Aftermath: The Russo-Japanese War (1904–5)

The Boxer Uprising left Russia in occupation of Manchuria. Although the other foreign powers and China were unanimous in their demands for an immediate withdrawal, Russia set about negotiating an agreement with local Manchu officials in order to consolidate its administrative control over the three provinces constituting Manchuria. The Qing government refused to ratify it. Russia unilaterally took over the British customs administration at the treaty port of Yingkou but, unlike Britain, did not deliver the customs revenues to the Chinese government but kept them. While the other powers negotiated together in Beijing, Russia conducted bilateral negotiations with the Chinese representative in St. Petersburg in the hope of extending Russian control over Manchuria's administration and infrastructure. These talks went nowhere because the Chinese leaked treaty drafts to the other powers, which were outraged.

Meanwhile, the Japanese were particularly concerned about the Russian occupation of Manchuria, whose market Japan dominated. Most of the customs revenues being collected were on Japanese trade. Japan was well aware that Russia's colonial ambitions included Manchuria. Significantly, early in 1902, Japan and Britain signed a treaty of alliance, which exerted sufficient pressure on Russia so that it concluded a troop withdrawal agreement with China later that year. The withdrawal was scheduled to take place in three stages, but Russia never got beyond stage one.

Japan faced a rapidly closing window of opportunity. The Japanese believed that they had to secure a Russian troop withdrawal before the completion of the Trans-Siberian Railway irrevocably altered the East Asian balance of power and dashed Japanese dreams of empire. Japan repeatedly proposed a division of spheres of influence, with Japan dominant in Korea and Russia dominant in Manchuria, but the Russians did not want to limit their options. By 1904 the negotiations had gone nowhere and the Trans-Siberian Railway, although nearing completion, had yet to be double-tracked and was still missing the section around Lake Baikal, a lake the size of Switzerland.

On 8 February 1904 the Japanese launched a surprise attack on the Russian concession and naval base at Lüshun. (See Map 13.2.) The Chinese local population and the Manchu government both sympathized with the Japanese. Manchurians provided the Japanese with vital intelligence on Russian movements, harassed Russian lines of communication, and helped supply the Japanese army. Although the war was fought on Chinese territory, the Qing government proclaimed neutrality—a highly unusual situation in warfare. Essentially, the Manchus sat by while the belligerents laid waste to southern and eastern Manchuria. Neither Japan nor Russia wanted China in the war. The Japanese were loath to ally with the Chinese for fear of conjuring images of a "yellow peril" in impressionable Western minds. Chinese participation could have potentially threatened Western interests in China and drawn other Europeans into the conflict on Russia's side.

During the hostilities, the Japanese employed a highly effective network of Chinese spies, including the barber of the commanding Russian general. They also hired Chinese troops to harass the Russian rear and destroy the railway lines vital for Russian deployments and supplies. Included on the Japanese payroll were such key future Chinese political leaders as Yuan Shikai, who would later become president of the Republic of China, and the future Manchurian warlord Zhang Zuolin. Yuan and Zhang used the Russo-Japanese War to entrench their influence in North China.

The war went badly for the Russians. They also experienced a collapsing home front, with the 1905 outbreak of revolution in St. Petersburg spreading quickly to their empire in Poland. Russia sought a negotiated settlement. In the peace talks, it agreed to evacuate all troops from Manchuria, cede the southern half of its Manchurian railway concessions to Japan, but retain the major east-west railway line between Lake Baikal and Vladivostok. The Chinese public as well as the colonial peoples throughout Asia reveled in the defeat of a great European power by an Asian power, providing further impetus for Chinese students to flock to Japan. The impact of Japan's victory was equally profound in Southeast and South Asia and as far away as Africa, since it proved that selective westernizing reforms could succeed.

Although the war did secure a Russian troop withdrawal from Manchuria, it did so at the cost of expanding Japanese influence in Northeast Asia. The Japanese empire was firmly entrenched in Korea, which became a colony in 1910, and in southern Manchuria. Chinese neutrality excluded China from

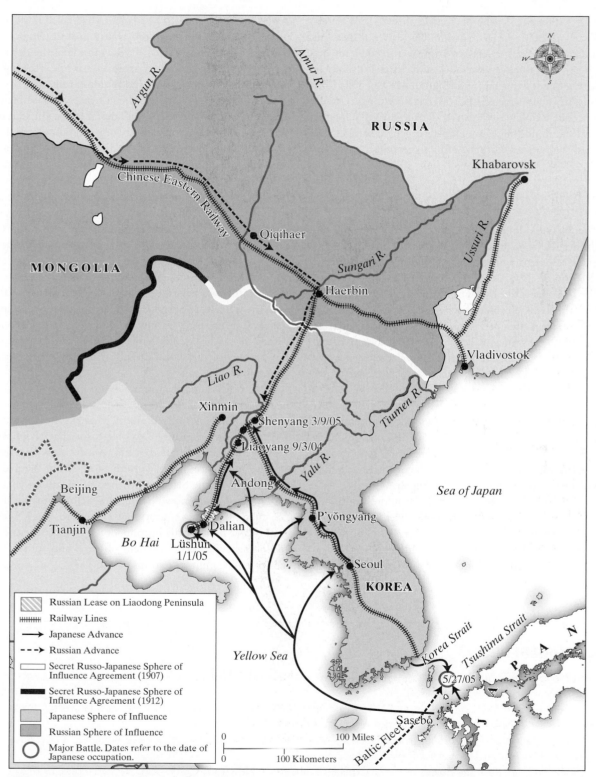

Map 13.2 Russo-Japanese War (1904–5)

the peace settlement. So the peace, like the war, was determined without Beijing's participation. Thereafter, Russia and Japan negotiated a series of agreements extending their respective spheres of influence westward, with Russia ultimately dominating Outer Mongolia and Japan, Inner Mongolia. The Manchus, by encouraging the Boxers, had unwittingly created an additional problem: The Russo-Japanese rivalry for the spoils of the imploding Qing empire began in earnest and continued throughout World War II and beyond.

Conclusions

With the Scramble for Concessions in full tilt, the Guangxu emperor decided to take matters into his own hands. He outlined a far-reaching reform program, the so-called Hundred Days' Reform of 1898. After one hundred days, the Empress Dowager Cixi placed the emperor under house arrest and had some of the key reformers executed. This was the first post–Opium War attempt at comprehensive reform directed from the top. Meanwhile, the Scramble for Concessions stirred a hornet's nest of antiforeign sentiments that coalesced in the Boxer Uprising. The Manchus successfully deflected Boxer xenophobia away from the dynasty and toward the foreign community. This was a strategy of hope that yielded another round of military defeat, indemnity, and foreign occupation. Worse still, the resulting Russian occupation of Manchuria precipitated the Russo-Japanese War, the devastation of the Manchurian war zone area, and the subsequent Russian and Japanese division of Manchuria and Mongolia.

The Manchus never recovered from the combined effects of the Sino-Japanese War and the Boxer Uprising. The Scramble for Concessions and the Boxer Protocol permanently impaired Qing sovereignty, with a proliferation of foreign spheres of influence and foreign troops permanently deployed in the capital. The Manchus had failed in their duty to preserve hallowed traditions and to protect China against barbarian incursions. Given the magnitude of the debacle, it is amazing that they survived at all. Meanwhile, growing Han nationalism threatened Manchu minority rule.

The Boxer Uprising was the last gasp of those Han and Manchus who totally rejected modernization. The efficacy of Western technology and military organization was no longer in dispute. The magnitude of the disaster helped form a consensus, even among the Han literati and Manchus, that China had to introduce its own Meiji reform program combining some degree of westernization with modernization. But if there was a consensus on the need to modernize, there remained much controversy surrounding westernization. The problem of which institutions to westernize and to what degree has continued to preoccupy the Chinese to the present day. At different times, the warlords, the Nationalists, and the Communists have all provided different answers. Today, as in the nineteenth and twentieth centuries, the question remains: Can the fruits of modernization be had without the garden in which they commonly grow? So far, the most modern nations of the world are also the most institutionally westernized.

No ready solution to China's problems appeared, short of radical reform. Like the defeat in the Sino-Japanese War, the Boxer debacle spurred another reform movement, very similar to the Hundred Days' Reform that the Empress Dowager Cixi had halted. China would now broaden its search for the origins of Western power from the gadgetry emphasized by the Self-strengtheners to the underlying educational and institutional basis. These reforms involved radical changes in the educational system to teach Western history and politics; the introduction of Western science and technology; the encouragement of travel and study abroad; and extensive military reforms.

BIBLIOGRAPHY

Cameron, Meribeth E. Thomas H. D. Mahoney and George E. McReynolds. *China, Japan and the Powers: A History of the Modern Far East.* New York: Ronald Press, 1960.

Chang, Hao. *Liang Ch'i-ch'ao and Intellectual Transition in China, 1890–1907.* Cambridge, MA: Harvard University Press, 1971.

Chen, Jerome. *Yuan Shih-k'ai.* 2nd ed. Stanford, CA: Stanford University Press, 1972.

Cohen, Paul A. *China and Christianity: The Missionary Movement and the Growth of Chinese Antiforeignism, 1860–1870.* Cambridge, MA: Harvard University Press, 1963.

———*History in Three Keys: The Boxers as Event, Experience, and Myth.* New York: Columbia University Press, 1998.

Connaughton, R. M. *The War of the Rising Sun and the Tumbling Bear: A Military History of the Russo-Japanese War 1904–5.* London: Routledge, 1988.

Duiker, William J. *Cultures in Collision: The Boxer Rebellion.* San Rafael, CA: Presidio Press, 1978.

Elleman, Bruce A. *Modern Chinese Warfare, 1795–1989.* London: Routledge, 2001.

Esherick, Joseph W. *The Origins of the Boxer Uprising.* Berkeley: University of California Press, 1987.

Geyer, Dietrich. *Russian Imperialism: The Interaction of Domestic and Foreign Policy, 1860–1914.* Translated by Bruce Little. New Haven, CT: Yale University Press, 1987.

Huang, Fu-ch'ing. *Chinese Students in Japan in the Late Ch'ing Period.* Tokyo: Centre for East Asian Cultural Studies, 1982.

Jansen, Marius B. *The Japanese and Sun Yat-sen.* Stanford, CA: Stanford University Press, 1954.

Kuo Ting-yee. *Sino-Japanese Relations, 1862–1927.* New York: Columbia University Press, 1965.

Kwong, Luke S. K. *A Mosaic of the Hundred Days: Personalities, Politics, and Ideas of 1898.* Cambridge, MA: Harvard University Press, 1984.

Lensen, George Alexander, ed. *Korea and Manchuria between Russia and Japan 1895–1904: The Observations of Sir Ernest Satow British Plenipotentiary to Japan (1895–1900) and China (1900–1906).* Tallahassee, FL: Diplomatic Press, 1966.

————*The Russo-Chinese War.* Tallahassee FL: Diplomatic Press, 1967.

Malozemoff, Andrew. *Russian Far Eastern Policy 1881–1904 with Special Emphasis on the Causes of the Russo-Japanese War.* Berkeley: University of California Press, 1958.

Nish, Ian. *The Origins of the Russo-Japanese War.* London: Longman, 1985.

Paine, S. C. M. *Imperial Rivals: China, Russia, and Their Disputed Frontier.* Armonk, NY: M. E. Sharpe, 1996.

Powell, Ralph L. *The Rise of Chinese Military Power, 1895–1912.* Princeton, NJ: Princeton University Press, 1955.

Purcell, Victor. *The Boxer Uprising: A Background Study.* Cambridge: Cambridge University Press, 1963.

Quested, Rosemary K. I. *"Matey" Imperialists? The Tsarist Russians in Manchuria 1895–1917.* Hong Kong: University of Hong Kong Press, 1982.

Reynolds, Douglas R. *China, 1898–1912: The Xinzheng Revolution and Japan.* Cambridge, MA: Harvard University Press, 1993.

Richardson, Philip. *Economic Change in China, c. 1800–1950.* Cambridge: Cambridge University Press, 1999.

Romanov, B. A. *Russia in Manchuria (1892–1906).* Translated by Susan Wilbur Jones. Ann Arbor, MI: American Council of Learned Societies, 1952.

Spector, Ivar. *The First Russian Revolution: Its Impact on Asia.* Englewood Cliffs, NJ: Prentice-Hall, 1962.

Tan, Chester C. *The Boxer Catastrophe.* New York: Columbia University Press, 1955.

Warner, Denis and Peggy Warner. *The Tide at Sunrise: A History of the Russo-Japanese War, 1904–1905.* London: Angus and Robertson, 1974.

Wehrle, Edmund S. *Britain, China, and the Antimissionary Riots, 1891–1900.* Minneapolis: University of Minnesota Press, 1966.

Westwood, J. N. *Russia against Japan, 1904–1905: A New Look at the Russo-Japanese War.* London: Macmillan, 1986.

White, John Albert. *The Diplomacy of the Russo-Japanese War.* Princeton, NJ: Princeton University Press, 1964.

Young, L. K. *British Policy in China: 1895–1902.* London: Clarendon Press, 1970.

NOTES

1. Qiu Jin, "On the Yellow Sea: A Man from Japan Sought Some Verses and Also Showed Me a Map of the Russo-Japanese War." In *An Anthology of Chinese Literature: Beginnings to 1911.* Edited by Stephen Owen, New York: W.W. Norton, 1996, 1151. Copyright © 1996 by Stephen Owen and The Council for Cultural Planning and Development of the Executive Yuan of the Republic of China. Used by permission of W. W. Norton & Company, Inc.

2. Ezra Pound, trans., *Shih-ching: The Classic Anthology Defined by Confucius.* Cambridge, MA: Harvard University Press, 194. Reprinted by permission of the publisher from THE CONFUCIAN ODES: THE CLASSIC ANTHOLOGY DEFINED BY CONFUCIUS by Ezra Pound, pp. 194–195. Cambridge, Mass.: Harvard University Press, Copyright © 1954, 1982 by the President and Fellows of Harvard College.

Chronology

1898	Hundred Days' Reform
1899–1900	Boxer Uprising
1901	Reform of examination system
	Boxer Protocol
	Zongli Yamen changed to Foreign Ministry
	Han–Manchu intermarriage permitted; footbinding discouraged
	Beginning of military reforms
1904–5	Russo-Japanese War
1905	Sun Yat-sen establishes the Tongmenghui in Tokyo
	Abolition of civil service examinations
	Mission sent to study foreign constitutions
1906	Eleven ministries replace the former Six Boards
1907	Twenty-eight Chinese naval officers sent to Great Britain
1908	Guangxu emperor dies; Xuantong emperor (Henry Puyi) assumes the throne
	Next day Cixi dies
1909	Provincial assemblies established
1910	Announcement of a plan to convene a National Assembly in three years
1911	Announcement of a plan to nationalize the railways
	Wuchang Uprising; beginning of the 1911 Revolution
	Outer Mongolia declares independence
1912	Establishment of the Republic of China
	Abdication of the Xuantong emperor; end of the Qing dynasty
	Yuan Shikai becomes provisional president in Beijing
	Death of the Meiji emperor

14

The 1911 Revolution

A dagger on my belt,
A cup of wine in my hand.
When the cup is drained, the dagger leaves its sheath,
And down falls my enemy's head.

****

As I pour a cupful to toast my dagger,
My singing splits the evening clouds.[1]

Liu Dabai (1880–1932),
teacher, revolutionary

The reforms undertaken by Beijing in the early twentieth century did nothing to reduce the spiraling anti-Manchu sentiments in China but, instead, weakened the institutional basis for Qing rule. The elimination of the imperial examination system undermined the authority of the Han literati, a key pillar of support for dynastic rule. Military reforms would prove even more dangerous to the dynasty, since the Manchus, for lack of alternatives, restored order by relying on provincial armies, which were raised, funded, and controlled by Han governors. But the Manchus were never able fully to assert their control over these armies, even though the Han provincial armies proved equally incapable of defending China from Japan or dealing effectively with the Boxer Uprising and its aftermath. During the ensuing Russo-Japanese War, Chinese military incapacity prevented China from participating in a war that devastated its territory. The Manchus, again for lack of alternatives, finally tried to create a modern unified army, which, in China, meant a Han army. This army soon applied its new skills against the Manchus.

I. The Reform Program of the Empress Dowager Cixi

The failure of the Boxer Uprising to expel the foreign presence from China demonstrated the inability of traditional Chinese institutions and practices to contain the foreign threat, while China's spiraling indemnities compromised its economic development. Broad segments of the imperial bureaucracy concluded that China had no alternative but radical change of its institutions and educational system. The initial reforms focused on education. (See Table 14.1.) In 1901, while the imperial Court was still in exile in Xi'an, it solicited its highest officials for reform proposals. In August, the Court formally abolished the examination requirement for the eight-legged essay, introduced questions concerning Western learning, and emphasized policy rather than the Classics. But those who administered the tests did not actually follow through with the changes. The Russo-Japanese War reinforced a pervasive sense of incapacity to deal with foreign threats, since the war was fought on Chinese territory but the Chinese had no say in its conduct or outcome. The end of hostilities gave renewed impetus to reform of the examination system, thought to be at the root of China's incapacity.

In 1905, the imperial examination system was abolished. Government employment and advancement would no longer be based on mastery of 2,000-year-old Classics but instead stressed job-related expertise. Classical education, once the best guarantee of financial security, became instantly worthless for government employment, overturning the social pyramid. Henceforth, an education in the humanities promised a life of genteel poverty rather than high position. In a stroke, the

Table 14.1   Late-Qing Reforms

Year	Political Reforms	Military Reforms	Educational Reforms	Legal Reforms	Economic Reforms
1901	Ministry of Foreign Affairs replaces Zongli Yamen Prohibition of sales of office	End of military examinations Creation of provincial training academies	Westernization of the examination system		Promotion of railway construction Order to draft laws on commerce
1902			Creation of a national syllabus Promotion of study abroad	Condemnation of footbinding Legalization of Han–Manchu intermarriage	
1903	Creation of Ministry of Commerce Creation of Ministry of Trade	Westernization of military training			Taxation of tobacco and liquor
1904		Edict to create a thirty-six-division unified national army	Higher military ranks opened to Han	Draft commercial code	
1905	Creation of Ministry of Police		Creation of a Ministry of Education		Opening of central mint and central bank with intent to standardize currency
1906	Edict to draft a constitution Eleven ministries replace the Six Boards			Prohibition of opium production, sale, and use	
1907	Manchuria integrated into the provincial system		National system for education of girls	Curtailment of Manchu financial privileges	
1908	Outline of a constitution issued			Draft criminal code completed	Committees for Reorganization of Financial Affairs established nationwide
1909	Provincial assemblies elected				Centralization of financial authority under the Ministry of Finance
1910	Convening of a National Assembly National Assembly passes its first budget	Reorganization of the navy			Only central bank to issue paper notes
1911		Creation of a General Staff		Draft civil code completed	Edict nationalizing railway system

Manchus had also eliminated a key pillar supporting their government: those Han officials whose classical education had given them a vested interested in the imperial status quo.

The reform, however, did not eliminate the legacy of the examination system, which endures to the present. Today the People's Republic of China holds an extraordinarily selective National College Entrance Examination that determines who and, more often, who will not attend college. As in the past, the exams are given over several days; they emphasize rote memorization and test mandatory subjects, although no

Prior to the educational reforms of 1905, which abolished the imperial examination system, the only modern schools in China were run by missionaries. The school in this photo (circa 1900) was funded by the American Board of Missions. Note, in particular, that the student body included both boys and girls.

longer exclusively the Classics.[2] Like the imperial examinations of the past, the current exams are closely linked to the future financial success of those tested. They alone determine college admission. As in the past, the pressure is intense. In postexamination Qing China, officials were encouraged to travel and study abroad. There was also a decentralized movement to establish new schools increasingly emphasizing the study of Western scientific and technological subjects. Thus, the Qing also lost control over education, which had previously been a government monopoly spreading the Confucian ideology of empire.

Russia's loss in the Russo-Japanese War (1904–5) demonstrated to the Chinese that the Meiji reforms had enabled a former member of the Confucian international system to defeat a major European power. This gave further impetus to reform in China. The reformers noted that Russia, the loser in the conflict, had an autocratic government, whereas Japan, like the major Western powers, had a constitutional monarchy. Liang Qichao (Liang Ch'i-ch'ao), one of the most articulate reformers, called for a constitutional monarchy. After the Hundred Days' Reform, when he and other followers of Kang Youwei fled to exile in Japan, he

had been deeply influenced by Japan's constitution and read many Western works in Japanese translation. The press and the urban gentry put increasing pressure on the government for constitutional reforms.

The Manchus soon introduced political reforms. Like the Meiji government, the Qing government established westernized ministries, including those concerning foreign affairs, commerce, police, and education. There was an attempt to reduce corruption by eliminating redundant offices, sinecures, and the sale of offices, as well as an attempt to cut the budget for palace expenses. Like the Meiji reforms, there were plans to westernize the country's commercial laws—heretofore a major source of Sino-Western friction. In 1905, the Qing government followed Japanese precedents to send a fact-finding mission abroad to study the constitutions of Japan, Britain, and Germany. The Japanese had done this in 1882–3 under Itō Hirobumi; whose trip culminated in a constitution in 1889.

The Chinese mission returned in 1906 to recommend a constitutional form of government, concluding that the Japanese political model would be most suitable for China. Plans were also underway to create a national legislature and corresponding provincial, prefectural, and district assemblies. The Qing variant of the Meiji model concentrated power in the person of the emperor, whereas in Japan, the emperor had a largely symbolic and legitimating role since a combination of civil and military elder statesmen actually set policy and ran the Japanese government. Within months of the mission's return, the Six Boards were expanded into eleven westernized, albeit Manchu-dominated, ministries. Social reforms included the end of the proscription of marriage between Manchus and Han, and new prohibitions on footbinding and opium.

Beginning in August 1901, the Qing also adopted military reforms, which they implemented much more rapidly than the civil reform program. Professional military education provided by newly established military academies replaced the imperial military examinations testing the Chinese Classics. The government established a central bureau to monitor military training throughout China. It reduced the size of the army in order to create a well-trained and more effective force. The Manchus also tried to reassert their control over these new institutions by making Manchu, not Han, appointments to senior positions. By 1904, the New Army reforms had been promulgated. By the fall of 1905, the New Army was composed of six divisions in North China. Within ten years, the government planned to create thirty-six divisions for a total peacetime army of approximately 500,000 men. Although these divisions were centralized under a General Staff in a newly created Ministry of War, local financing meant that each division was funded by its own province. By 1908, therefore, only about four military divisions were directly under Beijing's authority. For the Qing, this structure proved unworkable and dangerous.

The New Army differed greatly from traditional Chinese forces. Military service was no longer by conscription for life, but voluntary for three years on active duty and six years in the reserves. Soldiers were recruited from the same region where the division was located. They received relatively high pay and compensation for their families in case of death, injury, or lengthy service. Officers received more intensive training, which included a three-year course at a regional military primary school, followed by two more years at one of four national middle schools and, finally, a six-month tour of duty with an army division. Completion of this program made officers eligible to attend a special military high school. The two-year arms embargo mandated by the Boxer Protocol precluded the acquisition of armaments from abroad, so the Qing reformers emphasized domestic production. There were plans for three large arsenals to produce standardized weapons.

The Chinese government also planned a modern navy. In 1907, the Ministry of War added a naval department and planned to build four squadrons to defend the Gulf of Bo Hai, the Yellow Sea, the Zhoushan Archipelago off Shanghai, and the South China Sea. It sent twenty-eight sailors to Great Britain for training. The ministry also planned to reopen the Tianjin Naval College and establish other naval schools. In September 1909, the navy was transferred from the Ministry of War to a Navy Bureau. Later, on 4 December 1910, an imperial edict expanded it into a separate Ministry of the Navy.

The original date for completing the New Army reforms was 1916, but this was later optimistically pushed forward to 1912. In 1911, the year before the plan was scheduled to be completed, China's modern fighting strength approached 190,000 men, less than half of the targeted number. The Manchus were well aware that the New Army military reforms might become a threat to the dynasty, since the vast majority of recruits were Han. Therefore, in October 1905, they created schools for the sons of princes, imperial clansmen, and senior Manchu officials, and also established one division of Manchu Imperial Guards. During November 1910, service in this elite division was opened for the first time to Han Chinese. Although all of the divisions in the New Army were theoretically under the direct control of the Qing Court, by the outbreak of the 1911 Revolution the regional armies had become largely independent of Beijing.

The Qing military reforms were intended to strengthen and unify China against the foreign powers, but they also strengthened the Han opposition to Manchu rule. Before the reforms could be fully implemented, the Empress Dowager died. After a three-month illness she passed away in 1908, a day after the thirty-seven-year-old Guangxu emperor. The timing and suddenness of his death led to speculation that he might have been assassinated. The following year provincial assemblies were created, where pressure continued to mount on the Qing dynasty to promulgate a constitution and create a national legislature. In the short term, the reforms entailed significant tax increases that fell on a population that received no immediate tangible benefits. Rather, the taxes further eroded their incomes. Merchants and peasants responded by refusing to pay their taxes. Military salaries also fell, creating discontent among the rank and file. Strikes, unrest, and riots proliferated, and more of the population became politically radical.

II. Han Revolutionaries: Sun Yat-sen's Anti-Manchu Movement

Sun Zhongshan, who is better known in the West by the Cantonese rendering of his name, Sun Yat-sen, led a revolutionary movement based in South China. He greatly admired the leader of another South China–based rebel movement, Hong Xiuquan, emperor of the Taipings. While Hong was the last leader of a peasant rebellion that nearly toppled a dynasty, Sun was the first leader of a modern movement based on a political party that eventually transcended regional loyalties to acquire a national following.

Sun Yat-sen was born on 12 November 1866 to a peasant family near Guangzhou, in the southern province of Guangdong. Known to Chinese today as the father of the Chinese Republic, Sun was educated in China and the West and also lived in Japan. He understood the West from his years abroad, where he raised funds and organized a series of anti-Manchu movements, including the precursor to the Nationalist Party. Sun and his supporters played a notable role during the overthrow of the Manchus and the establishment of a republican government. Today, in an atypical instance of political agreement, Sun is a national hero in both the People's Republic of China and Taiwan.

Sun received a traditional early education, but at age thirteen he went to live with his brother in Honolulu, Hawaii, where he graduated from a missionary school in 1882 and briefly studied at Oahu College in 1883. Thereafter, he spent several years in Hong Kong before entering medical school in Guangzhou and later transferring to the Hong Kong College of Medicine for Chinese. Graduating in 1892 with a medical degree, Sun began his professional career in Macao. He then

U.S. immigration officials took this photograph of Sun Yat-sen in 1910. While he was not in China during the 10 October 1911 Revolution, when he returned he became China's first president, although he soon had to relinquish his post to Yuan Shikai.

In fall 1896, when Sun was visiting London to promote his program, agents of the Manchu dynasty detained him at the Chinese legation. After eleven days in captivity, the British Foreign Office pressured the Chinese legation to release him, whereupon Sun emerged as a hero. This event remains somewhat mysterious, since Sun apparently went to the Chinese legation of his own free will. Still, the story that he had been kidnapped made him instantly famous.

After the alleged kidnapping, Sun, like other famous reformers, including Karl Marx, spent many hours in the British Museum library writing revolutionary tracts. He developed his Three People's Principles while in London: People's Nationalism, People's Democracy, and People's Livelihood. Some consider them to have been based on Lincoln's Gettysburg Address, which emphasized government "of the people, by the people, and for the people." Sun's political views emphasized republican government based on the American model. In 1897 Sun moved to Japan, where he became deeply impressed by the Meiji reforms. The success of Japan's modernization efforts influenced many of Sun's generation. The number of Chinese students in Japan rose from 500 in 1902 to 13,000 in 1906. (See the feature on the next page.)

For the next ten years, Sun worked diligently to overthrow the Manchu dynasty. While in Tokyo, he took a major step on 20 August 1905, when he founded and became the first leader of the Tongmenghui, originally a coalition of heterogeneous groups dedicated to overthrowing the Manchus that gradually developed in the direction of a political party. Beginning with a membership of 70, most of them Chinese students studying in Japan, Sun's party grew to almost 1,000 by 1906. The Tongmenghui published the anti-Manchu newspapers *Twentieth Century China* and, later, the *People's Tribune*. These newspapers provided a forum for Chinese intellectuals to discuss China's return to Han rule. From 1906 through April 1911, the Tongmenghui actively fomented revolution; it was linked to ten unsuccessful uprisings in South China. Sun tried to broaden the scope of the organization by establishing a branch office in Shanghai on 13 July 1911. It soon forged links with New Army secret societies in Wuchang, located up the Yangzi River from Shanghai.

III. The Rights Recovery Movement

Initially, the treaty port press and the urban gentry particularly supported the Qing plans to promulgate a constitution. The gentry became actively involved in the creation of the recommended assemblies for local government, but the

moved in 1893 to Guangzhou, where he began his new career as an anti-Manchu revolutionary.

In Guangzhou, Sun first came in contact with anti-Manchu secret societies. Although supportive, Sun soon realized that his Western upbringing and education barred him from playing an important role in these societies, so in the fall of 1894, he returned to Honolulu, where he organized the Revive China Society. The society's charter was highly patriotic, stressing the dangers facing China, including both foreign ambitions and Manchu incompetence. After enlisting over one hundred overseas members, Sun returned to Hong Kong in early 1895 to set up a Chinese office. His basic program entailed expelling the Manchus, restoring Han rule, and creating a federal republic. Following an abortive anti-Manchu uprising in Guangzhou in 1895, Sun fled abroad.

electoral laws limited the vote mainly to degree holders and so excluded those most supportive of the reforms. Those excluded channeled their demands into a petition movement. When this proved ineffective, some increasingly supported the idea of revolution. Other members of the urban reformist elite supported the Rights Recovery Movement (*Shouhui liquan,* literally, the "recovery of profits and

rights"). They wanted to restore Chinese control over China's infrastructure, resource endowment, and manufacturing by buying or squeezing out foreign business interests. The movement soon focused on the railway system, largely financed and owned by foreign interests.

Foreign support for railway construction played an important though unintentional role in the denouement of

STUDY ABROAD

China's first group of students ever sent abroad to study went to the United States in 1872, but the undertaking so ruffled conservative feathers in Beijing that the students had to come home early and the Chinese Educational Mission to the United States was disbanded in 1881. Japan's stunning victory in the Sino-Japanese War (1894–5) then revived Chinese interests in study abroad, but this time in Japan, a familiar place within the Chinese cultural orbit. The wave of Chinese students that flooded Japan from 1898, right after the Hundred Days' Reform, until the outbreak of World War I in 1914 probably constituted the largest group of overseas students in world history up to that time. While the Japanese government had sent many officials on long sojourns to study the West, China sent its young. Those who returned would dominate key leadership positions in the Republican period.

In 1896, right after the Sino-Japanese War, thirteen Chinese went to Japan to study. By 1899 the number had surpassed 100 and included military officers, and by 1905 it had reached perhaps 10,000. Not only did the Chinese attend Japanese civilian and military educational institutions, but Japan also established special institutions for the Chinese. However, neither the institutions nor the students were suitably prepared, so students' experiences were very mixed. Nevertheless, most returned home with a deep appreciation of the force of Japanese nationalism and a growing sense of their own Chinese national identity. Through their labors, Japanese books proliferated on Chinese bookshelves and the Chinese increasingly learned about the West through a Japanese lens. Chinese revolutionaries in trouble at home often fled to Japan, including Kang Youwei and Sun Yat-sen, so that there was a strong revolutionary element among the students. Marxism spread to Asia via Japan, where key future Communist leaders studied, including Chen Duxiu, Li Da, Li Dazhao, and Zhou Enlai.

Although the Japanese welcomed the opportunity to show off their achievements to the Chinese and to host them at Japanese educational institutions, Sino-Japanese relations disintegrated during World War I over the disposition of German concessions in China. (See Chapter 16.) This dampened the allure of Japan as an educational destination of choice. Nevertheless, Japanese did not present the language barrier of Western languages, so many Chinese continued to study in Japan, most notably at its military institutions. Included in their number was Chiang Kai-shek and many other military leaders of the Republican period.

Few military leaders received their training in the United States. American influence was more important in technical subjects and the humanities. The United States was instrumental in redirecting the Boxer Indemnity to fund Chinese education both within China at Qinghua University and also abroad. In 1908, the U.S. Congress signed a bill creating Boxer indemnity scholarships, setting off a second wave of students to study in the United States between 1909 and the deepening of the Great Depression in 1930. Although the Chinese valued the scholarships, the U.S. Exclusion Act that remained in effect from 1882 to 1943, excluding Chinese from emigrating permanently to the United States, caused enduring ill will. Included in the second wave of students were such key Chinese intellectuals as Hu Shi of the May Fourth Movement and the top leadership of China's Foreign Ministry during most of the Republican period, such as Wellington Koo and C. T. Wang. After the Communist victory, many Western-educated Chinese heeded the call of patriotism to return home to help rebuild the motherland, only to be caught in the dragnet of Mao Zedong's many political campaigns.

After 1949, Taiwan continued the tradition of sending students to the United States. In fact, it sent many of its best students, who went on to serve in high government office; during Lee Teng-hui's presidency from 1988 to 2000, fourteen members of his cabinet held Ph.D.s from the United States. The People's Republic of China began sending its third wave of student to the United States in 1978 upon the signature of cross-cultural educational protocols. By 1988, China was sending more students than any other country to the United States. Many pursued Ph.D.s in the hard sciences. Included were the children of many of China's highest civil and military leaders. This third wave continues to the present and will surely have enormous implications for future Sino-American relations. While a number of students emigrated permanently to the United States after the Beijing Massacre in 1989, many others returned home to contribute to China's modernization. Since 1978, China has also sent many students to Europe and Japan.

the 1911 Revolution, also called the *Xinhai* Revolution after the lunar calendar's designation for the year 1911. During the Scramble for Concessions, the foreign powers staked out spheres of influence in which each developed the railways and mines to the exclusion of the others. While Japanese, Russian, and German interests were primarily in North China, British and French interests predominated in South and central China. Prior to 1911, provincial governments had a large stake in the development of railway lines through their territory. Over the years, local officials enjoyed financial benefits from the railways and developed important contacts with foreigners. As part of the late-Qing reforms, the Manchus attempted to consolidate China's many railways into one interconnecting national system. Local opposition to this plan overlapped with the beginning of the 1911 Revolution.

In contrast to the other powers, the United States abstained from carving out a sphere of influence and was also the first country to return its portion of the Boxer Indemnity by using the funds to establish Qinghua University in Beijing. Although the United States acquired a small concession area in Tianjin right after the Arrow War, it returned it to Chinese administration in 1880. Likewise, Washington never developed any railway concessions. Thus, at the time of the 1911 Revolution, the United States, alone among the great powers, did not have any railway or territorial concessions. Instead, Washington helped American commercial interests to expand in central China; U.S. companies were especially conspicuous in Shanghai and along the Yangzi River.

This gave the United States a pivotal geographic position, since its commercial interests were located directly between the Russian, Japanese, and German spheres of influence in the North and the British and French spheres of influence in the South. Through the application of the Open Door Policy, Washington tried to prevent China's dismemberment. The American-brokered 1905 Portsmouth Peace Treaty, terminating the Russo-Japanese War, gave lip service to the Open Door Policy, but it also reaffirmed the Russian possession of the Chinese Eastern Railway and the Japanese acquisition of the South Manchurian Railway (the southern part of the Chinese Eastern Railway), so Manchuria remained divided. Russia and Japan continued to carve up China, signing a series of secret agreements over the next decade in 1907, 1910, 1912, and 1916 that further defined their respective spheres deep into Inner and Outer Mongolia.

Washington backed the Manchu plan to nationalize Chinese railways in 1911 in the belief that central control over a unified railway network was essential for both reform and national integration. On 9 May 1911, a four-power banking consortium of British, French, German, and American investors signed a forty-year loan intended to buy out and unify the Guangzhou–Hankou and Hankou–Sichuan lines. This move threatened the expected profits of local investors, who accused Beijing of selling out China's interests to foreigners. It also outraged members of the Rights Recovery Movement, whose antiforeign program tapped into widely shared antiforeign sentiments. Qing proposals in June 1911 for railway nationalization in Henan, Hubei, Guangdong, and Sichuan all met with considerable opposition, with a general railway and industrial strike in Sichuan. During August, skirmishes between government troops and demonstrators resulted in thirty-two deaths. Since Hankou was the terminus of the two disputed Sichuan railway lines, people in this area—together with Hankou's sister cities of Wuchang and Hanyang (called collectively Wuhan)—had deep interests in the outcome of the dispute. Local gentry wanted to be reimbursed at 100 percent of their investment. The urban reform elite's inability to achieve its political program and the failure of the Rights Recovery Movement led to their further radicalization, fueled student activism, and spurred the development of political parties. The treaty port press closely followed these events. This added to the increasingly inflammatory mix of human passions and growing unrest among all segments of the population.

To offset unrest in Sichuan, the Qing government deployed large numbers of New Army troops to Wuchang. The arrival of these troops, who were young and predominantly Han, unexpectedly strengthened the anti-Manchu movement. An anti-Manchu rebellion was being secretly organized in the Russian concession when a premature bomb explosion alerted the police. Russian diplomatic reports from 1911 emphasized that a divided China would serve their territorial ambitions. Whether Russia actively supported the rebels is unclear, but certainly it had the most to lose if the railways were nationalized since it had the largest railway concessions. This accidental explosion precipitated the 1911 Revolution.

IV. The New Army and the Wuchang Rebellion

Although the westernizing reforms of the Qing government and the rising anti-Manchu Han nationalism constituted the underlying causes of the 1911 Revolution, the proximate cause was a military revolt of the Hubei New Army on 10 October 1911. It was concentrated in a major treaty port, and its recruits had a high literacy rate. Many revolutionary-minded youth wound up joining the army, since either they lacked the means to enter the new provincial schools or the schools could not accommodate all those interested in study. For these reasons, the New Army was particularly radical.

Those stationed in Wuhan were some of the best-educated soldiers in China. The force was well organized and cohesive; much of its officer corps had graduated from military schools, and some of these officers had joined anti-Manchu study groups and societies.

While the Wuchang uprising was poorly planned and executed, the response of local officials was even more inept. At a meeting held on 24 September 1911, plans for an uprising were discussed. The conspirators originally scheduled the rebellion for 6 October to coincide with the Chinese Mid-autumn Festival. Information leaks concerning this timing led to a postponement until late October at the earliest. But on 9 October, a bomb accidentally exploded at the revolutionaries' headquarters in the Russian concession in Hankou, and the police confiscated a membership list. The police, alarmed at the large number of New Army soldiers, immediately began rounding up suspects. This threatened the conspirators in the officer corps with almost certain arrest. In response, they sped up their timetable to strike before they were actually ready. The battalion representatives decided to go ahead with the uprising on the night of 10 October 1911. Xiong Bingkun, the chief representative of the Eighth Engineers Battalion, was one of the main leaders of the Wuchang uprising. During the early evening, Sergeant Xiong led a mutiny, killing all New Army officers who refused to go along with the rebellion.

The engineering battalion soon seized the main arsenal in Wuchang. This arsenal not only held weapons produced by the Hanyang factories, but also had foreign-made arms. Thereafter, the rebels attempted to neutralize forces loyal to the Qing by attacking the yamen of Governor-general Ruicheng. Fighting at the yamen was intense, but given sufficient time to bring up additional reinforcements, the loyalist troops could have defeated the revolutionaries, as had been the case in similar revolutionary outbreaks in Guangzhou and Sichuan. When shells began to fall within the yamen compound, however, Ruicheng boarded a warship anchored outside the city gates, leaving the local Qing commander in charge of defending the yamen. But the commander soon ordered his troops to retreat to the neighboring city of Hankou. Both decisions went against Qing military rules, which forbade officers to desert their posts. Due to the lack of organized resistance, the New Army took control of Wuchang by noon on 11 October 1911. The naval force sent to quell the rebellion mutinied, confirming that the revolutionaries were in charge. Although the core membership of the Wuhan New Army included fewer than 2,000 troops, within two days of taking control of Wuchang, the rebels had taken the sister cities of Hanyang and Hankou as well.

This inaction of the government troops gave the revolutionaries a much needed breathing space to consolidate their gains. They quickly formed a military government under Tang Hualong as civil governor. Tang had studied for a time in Japan, where he became a good friend of Liang Qichao. Later, as part of the late-Qing reforms, he helped establish the Hubei provincial assembly, where he became a major proponent of constitutional reform. Tang was instrumental in pressuring Li Yuanhong to accept the position of military governor of the revolutionary government.

Li Yuanhong had graduated from the Tianjin Naval Academy in 1889. He saw action in the Sino-Japanese War when his ship sank under enemy fire and he nearly drowned. After the war, he received army training in Japan. In 1906, as part of the late-Qing military reforms, he was stationed near Wuchang as the first commander of a brigade of the New Army in Hubei. Because all of the original coup leaders had either been injured by the bomb blast or were being held by the police outside of Wuchang, when the uprising started the mutineers forced Li at gun point to act as their leader. He procrastinated for three days before finally agreeing. When Li took charge, he became the military governor of the revolutionary government in Hubei. The revolutionaries declared the overthrow of Manchu rule and made all of Hubei province an independent republic. Telegrams bearing Li Yuanhong's name were sent to other provincial governments calling upon them to join the revolt against Beijing.

The nationalization of the railways remained a major concern. The telegrams referred to this proposed nationalization to warn that the Manchus were in the process of recentralizing their power and the Han might never get another chance to overthrow the dynasty. Meanwhile, Tang convinced the foreign consuls in Hankou to remain neutral. When Qing government troops requested foreign gunboats to support them by bombarding the revolutionaries, the foreign consuls refused. Once again, foreigners played a crucial role in determining the outcome of an internal uprising. During the Taiping Rebellion, foreign action had helped tip the balance in the favor of the Manchus. This time, it was foreign inaction that contributed to their fall.

V. The Collapse of the Qing Dynasty

The success of the Wuchang Uprising was as important symbolically as it was militarily. For the first time since the great rebellions of the mid-nineteenth century, a predominantly Han military force had defeated troops loyal to the Manchu Court. News of the successful revolt electrified the rest of the nation. After Li Yuanhong agreed to lead the Hubei rebellion, other anti-Manchu rebellions broke out throughout the country, especially in South China. (See Map 14.1 and Table 15.1.) Within six weeks, fifteen provinces, or approximately two-thirds of China's core area,

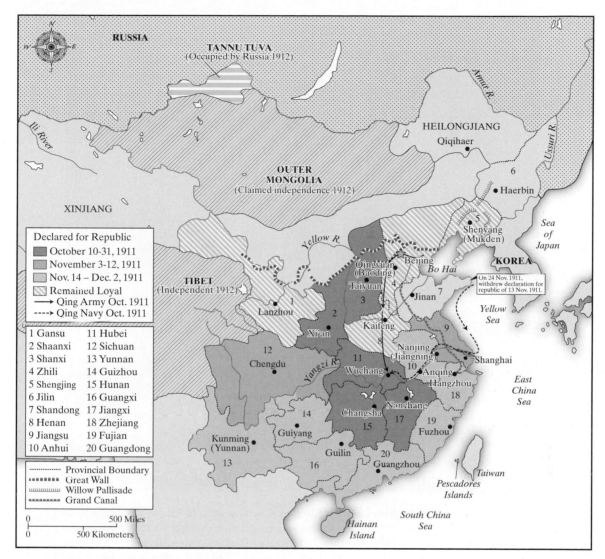

Map 14.1 1911 Revolution

had announced their defection from Qing rule. Anti-Manchu groups soon controlled much of the South, including the major river ports of Changsha and Shanghai. Although Beijing recovered Hankou on 2 November 1911 and Hanyang on 27 November, the loss of Shanghai in early November and of Nanjing in early December more than offset these imperial victories.

Following the success of the Wuchang Uprising, Sun Yat-sen cut short his fund-raising activities in Denver, Colorado, to rush to London and Paris to secure promises of diplomatic recognition should a republican government be established. He then returned to China, arriving just days before a provisional parliament was scheduled to meet in Shanghai to form a new government. On 29 December 1911, Sun was elected

as provisional president, and Li Yuanhong became provisional vice-president. Although revolutionaries and intellectuals such as Sun Yat-sen had long advocated revolution, the New Army made it a reality. Li's inclusion in the government reflected the importance of the Chinese military to the Republican government. As before, government rule seemed to rest on a combination of civil authority and military power. In reality, however, all power now resided in the army and the navy, because the new civil authorities lacked the means to enforce their will. On 1 January 1912, eighty-three days after the Wuchang Uprising, the Republic of China (ROC) was officially founded with Nanjing as its capital.

Soon after the ROC's founding, Yuan Shikai stepped in to fill the power vacuum. Yuan had originally been a protégé

On her deathbed in 1908, Empress Dowager Cixi placed the two-year-old Puyi on the throne; he is pictured here with his father, Prince Chun, and his younger brother. Without a strong ruler on the throne, within three years the Manchu dynasty had collapsed. During the domestic turmoil following President Yuan Shikai's death, there was an attempt to restore Puyi to the throne and revive the Qing dynasty. From 1 July to 12 July 1917, he ruled as the Xuantong emperor from the Forbidden City before being ousted; later, he became the puppet leader of Manchukuo under the Japanese. Henry Puyi survived World War II, spent ten years in a war criminals' camp, and then lived in Beijing from 1959 until his death from kidney cancer in 1967, working as a gardener at the Beijing Botanical Gardens.

of Li Hongzhang, serving as proconsul in Korea on the eve of the first Sino-Japanese War. After Li's death, Yuan rose to the rank of general in the Beiyang Army. He leveraged his command to help orchestrate the coup terminating the 1898 Hundred Day Reforms, to the satisfaction of his new benefactor, the Empress Dowager Cixi. As a reward, she made him governor of Shandong province, where he suppressed the Boxer Uprising. During the final period of Qing reforms, Yuan spearheaded the effort to transform Chinese adminis-

trative, educational, and economic institutions. Upon the Empress Dowager's death in 1908, however, he lost much of his power. Prince Chun, who served as the regent for his son, the two-year-old emperor Xuantong, was also the brother of the Guangxu emperor, whom Yuan had deposed. In 1909, Prince Chun ordered Yuan Shikai's retirement.

In 1911, however, when Prince Chun faced the Wuchang Uprising and the rapid spread of the anti-Manchu rebellion, he called on Yuan Shikai to use the latter's extensive military connections to save the dynasty. Yuan only accepted his new appointment as governor-general of Hunan and Hubei, the center of the rebellion, when the Qing promised to give him full power over the army and navy, plus unlimited financial backing. He also demanded and the Qing agreed to convene a national assembly responsible to a cabinet within a year and to grant an amnesty to republican revolutionaries. Thereafter, he packed the cabinet with his own loyalists and forced Prince Chun to resign his regency in favor of the powerless adoptive mother of the boy emperor. On 27 October 1911, Yuan assumed the title of imperial commissioner and on 1 November he became China's premier. With the help of two military aides—Feng Guozhang, in command of China's First Army, and Duan Qirui, in command of the Second Army—Yuan virtually became the military dictator of China. Feng Guozhang would later become the leader of the Zhili Clique, while Duan Qirui would become the leader of the Anhui Clique, two of the three main North China warlord cliques in the early 1920s. A third competing clique would be the Fengtian Clique under the Manchurian warlord Zhang Zuolin and, later, his son Zhang Xueliang.

To avoid a civil war, the Nanjing government petitioned Yuan to convince the Qing to abdicate. Yuan agreed, but on the condition that he be inaugurated as president of the new republic. Initially, the Manchus refused. Their change of heart came as a result of the assassination of the leader of the Imperial Clan party, Liangbi, in combination with a joint telegram organized by Duan Qirui and signed by forty Beiyang commanders urging the Manchus to abdicate for their own safety. Many Chinese diplomats abroad also advised the Manchus to step down. The Manchus found that they had no effective military support. As would later happen in the Russian Revolution in 1917, once the unpopular dynasty lost the allegiance of the military, it no longer had the coercive power necessary to retain the throne. The Manchu mandate to rule simply evaporated. On 12 February 1912 the Qing formally abdicated, on 13 February 1912 Sun Yat-sen resigned, and on 12 March 1912 Yuan was inaugurated as the new provisional president.

This arrangement successfully, although as it would turn out only temporarily, avoided a civil war. Yuan Shikai promised to honor the Republic and the new constitution, but the conditions were ripe for Yuan to recentralize dictatorial powers in his own hands. Furthermore, the transition from Manchu rule to Sun Yat-sen to Yuan Shikai was anything but democratic. The presidential title went to the man with the most effective army. This arrangement typified other warlord governments that followed. Ever since the 1911 Revolution, every successful government in China has had a strong military at its foundation. While modern governments in the West have generally emphasized civil control over the military, in the twentieth-century governments of China, military leaders held the highest executive office. This generalization applies to the warlords in the 1920s and 1930s, and to Chiang Kai-shek, Mao Zedong, and Deng Xiaoping.

Conclusions

The Boxer Uprising exhausted the Qing dynasty's traditional alternatives. For decades, the Qing avoided making comprehensive institutional reforms: First, they attempted modernization without westernization with the Self-strengthening reforms; then they attempted to strengthen the tributary system, only to lose both Vietnam and Korea to France and Japan, respectively; thereafter, they attempted to ally with Russia to contain Japan but simply lost the Liaodong Peninsula to Russia instead of to Japan; and finally, they attempted to encourage the Boxers to expel the foreigners, reaping instead an indemnity and foreign military deployments in the capital. These strategies of resistance to Western demands were ineffective, leading to huge indemnities.

The Manchus had long faced increasingly debilitating dilemmas. Military effectiveness required greater unity of command, but this would put dynastic overthrow within the reach of the Han. Trapped between the imperative to follow tradition in order to retain the mandate of heaven and the equally compelling imperative to reform in order to provide effective civil rule, the Manchu Court concluded that comprehensive westernizing civil and military reforms could no longer be avoided. But the Manchus remained extremely reluctant to implement political reforms, and so focused on educational, military, and economic reforms. In 1911, the general population burdened by the costs of reforms producing few benefits, political activists frustrated by a stalemated Rights Recovery Movement, and anti-Manchu elements of the New Army combined to call for an end to the dynasty. The Wuchang Uprising led to the abdication by the Manchus and the replacement of the imperial system of government with a westernized Republic.

In 1911, what began as a local mutiny quickly became a national rebellion because the Han refused to defend the dynasty. Manchu minority rule became utterly hollow, with nothing to support it. The warrior people who had ridden to victory in the mid-seventeenth century had lost their martial skills, any sense of purpose beyond the retention of privilege, and any vestige of legitimacy under either the traditional Confucian value system or the Western utilitarian value system. Under the former, they were unethical; under the latter, they were incompetent. The mathematics of the situation (a few million Manchus versus hundreds of millions of Han) scattered the house of cards to the winds. Outside of Manchuria, where for a brief period the Manchus served as puppets for the Japanese from 1931 to 1945, the Manchus became a nonpresence in Chinese politics. Because so many changed their surnames after 1911 and assimilated in order to avoid persecution, today it is difficult to distinguish people of Manchu ancestry from the Han.

The late-Qing military reforms greatly exacerbated the problem of local control in China. The Han commanded the modern military forces, while the Manchus no longer had their own effective armies of bannermen. The military reforms followed the general trend evident from the great mid-nineteenth century rebellions on: continued weakening of central control over the provinces and the rise of autonomous provincial armies. The 1911 Revolution was really a soldiers' mutiny supported by a naval mutiny. Although revolutionaries, such as the Nationalist Party leader Sun Yat-sen, attempted to take credit for the Qing's fall, he was not even in the country at the time. After the abdication of the Qing in 1912, many regional leaders claimed independence from any central authority and began to create autonomous fiefdoms. Given its origins, it should not be surprising that the 1911 Revolution did not create a truly democratic government. Instead, it helped usher in a period of even greater chaos and instability. This was the thirty-eight-year interregnum between the fall of the Qing dynasty and the founding of the Communist People's Republic of China that finally succeeded in restoring a strong central government to China and reuniting most of the territories of the Qing empire.

The 1911 Revolution vindicated the long-standing Manchu reluctance to promote westernizing reforms, since they became the first casualty of the reforms. Western powers demanded that the Manchus make westernizing reforms without apparently realizing that the prescription would prove fatal to the patient. Westerners have had great difficulty appreciating how corrosive their value system and institutional structures are to traditional cultures and elites. Nor do they adequately appreciate the turmoil entailed in abandoning hallowed traditions to chart a new path across an institutional void. Chinese, who perceive the world holistically, deeply appreciate the danger of tinkering with too many of the parts. Excessive reform, regardless of how noble the goal, can destroy the system that provides order and prevents chaos. In China, periods of dynastic decline, and especially of dynastic interregnum, have often been accompanied by warfare and famine.

In contrast, the Western analytical framework focuses on breaking down the parts, the very meaning of the word "analysis." Westerners often peddle the parts of their system on the international market without adequately appreciating their impact on the whole. In modern terminology, the Western program is called "nation building" and "state building," which are difficult to do. When reform calls for the creation of institutions that have never before existed in a society, there is rarely a consensus on what these institutions should look like or what kind of power-sharing arrangement—if any—should be established.

In the absence of strong institutions, such vital questions are often settled by force. The Chinese spent most of the next forty years embroiled in a variety of overlapping civil wars to answer such questions. These years of bloodshed and poverty conformed to the wrenching periods of dynastic change anticipated by the dynastic cycle. These were the dreaded years of *luan,* or chaos, when no government possessed the mandate of heaven, when no one interceded between man and the cosmos, and all suffered as a consequence. In other words, China's path to modernity has come at an enormous price.

BIBLIOGRAPHY

Bergère, Marie-Claire. *Sun Yat-sen.* Translated by Janet Lloyd. Stanford, CA: Stanford University Press, 1998.
Bieler, Stacey. *"Patriots" or "Traitors"? A History of American-Educated Chinese Students.* Armonk, NY: M. E. Sharpe, 2004.
Brunnert, H. S. and V. V. Hagelstrom. *Present Day Organisation of China.* Shanghai: Kelly and Walsh, 1912.
Cameron, Meribeth E. *The Reform Movement in China, 1898–1912.* New York: Octagon Books, 1963.
Chang Hao. *Liang Ch'i-ch'ao and Intellectual Transition in China.* Cambridge, MA: Harvard University Press, 1971.
———*Chinese Intellectuals in Crisis: The Search for Order and Meaning.* Berkeley: University of California Press, 1987.
Chen, Jerome. *Yuan Shih-k'ai.* 2nd ed. Stanford, CA: Stanford University Press, 1972.
Cohen, Paul and John Schrecker, eds. *Reform in Nineteenth Century China.* Cambridge, MA: Harvard University Press, 1975.
Dreyer, Edward L. *China at War, 1901–1949.* London: Longman, 1995.
Elman, Benjamin J. *A Cultural History of Civil Examinations in Late Imperial China.* Berkeley: University of California Press, 2000.
Esherick, Joseph W. *Reform and Revolution in China: The 1911 Revolution in Hunan and Hubei.* Berkeley: University of California Press, 1976.

Eto Shinkichi and Harold Z. Schiffrin, eds. *China's Republican Revolution.* Tokyo: Tokyo University Press, 1994.

Fung, Edmund S. K. *The Military Dimension of the Chinese Revolution: The New Army and Its Role in the Revolution of 1911.* Vancouver: University of British Columbia, 1980.

Furth, Charlotte, ed. *The Limits of Change: Essays on Conservative Alternatives in Republican China.* Cambridge, MA: Harvard University Press, 1976.

Jansen, Marius. "Japan and the Chinese Revolution of 1911." In *The Cambridge History of China: Late Ch'ing 1800–1911,* vol. 11, part 2, edited by John K. Fairbank and Kwang-ching Liu, 339–74. Cambridge: Cambridge University Press, 1980.

Kamachi, Noriko. *Reform in China: Huang Tsun-hsien and the Japanese Model.* Cambridge, MA: Harvard University Press, 1981.

Levenson, Joseph R. *Liang Ch'i-ch'ao and the Mind of Modern China.* Berkeley: University of California Press, 1970.

Liew, K. S. *Struggle for Democracy: Sung Chiao-jen and the 1911 Chinese Revolution.* Berkeley: University of California Press, 1971.

Lust, John. *The Revolutionary Army: A Chinese Nationalist Tract of 1903.* The Hague: Mouton, 1968.

MacKinnon, Stephen R. *Power and Politics in Late Imperial China: Yuan Shih-kai in Beijing and Tianjin, 1901–1908.* Berkeley: University of California Press, 1980.

McCord, Edward A. *The Power of the Gun: The Emergence of Modern Chinese Warlordism.* Berkeley: University of California Press, 1993.

Powell, Ralph L. *The Rise of Chinese Military Power, 1895–1912.* Princeton, NJ: Princeton University Press, 1955.

Price, Don C. *Russia and the Roots of the Chinese Revolution, 1896–1911.* Cambridge, MA: Harvard University Press, 1974.

Rankin, Mary Backus. *Early Chinese Revolutionaries: Radical Intellectuals in Shanghai and Chekiang.* Cambridge, MA: Harvard University Press, 1971.

Reynolds, Douglas R. *China, 1898–1912: The Xinzheng Revolution and Japan.* Cambridge, MA: Harvard University Press, 1993.

Rhoads, Edward J. M. *China's Republican Revolution: The Case of Kwangtung, 1895–1912.* Cambridge, MA: Harvard University Press, 1974.

Schiffrin, Harold. *Sun Yat-sen and the Origins of the Chinese Revolution.* Berkeley: University of California Press, 1968.

Schwartz, Benjamin. *In Search of Wealth and Power: Yen Fu and the West.* Cambridge, MA: Harvard University Press, 1964.

Wright, Mary Clabaugh, ed. *China in Revolution: The First Phase, 1900–1913.* New Haven, CT: Yale University Press, 1968.

NOTES

1. Liu wrote this poem prior to the Manchu overthrow as his promise to assassinate the emperor. Translated by Kai-yu Hsu, *Twentieth Century Chinese Poetry: An Anthology* (New York: Doubleday, 1963), 4.

2. Today all candidates must pass examinations in Chinese, mathematics, and a foreign language, usually English but also Russian or Japanese. For those specializing in the sciences, the three other mandatory subjects are physics, chemistry, and biology. For those specializing in the humanities and social sciences, they are history, geography, and political education.

Thematic Chronology (1912–49)

Decade	Politics	Economy	Diplomacy	Society	Culture
1900s	Abdication of Xuantong; establishment of Republic of China (1912) Anti–Yuan Shikai Second Revolution (1913) Anti–Yuan Shikai Third Revolution (1915–6) Sun Yat-sen's first Guangzhou government (1917–18) Founding of Nationalist Party (1919)	Nishihara loans (1917–18)	Tibet declares independence (1913) Japan seizes German concessions in Shandong (1914) Russia presents Twenty-one Demands concerning Mongolia (1914) Japan presents Twenty-one Demands (1915) Karakhan Manifesto (1919)	Zhang Zuolin takes control of Manchuria (1916)	May Fourth Movement (1919)
1920s	Sun Yat-sen's second Guangzhou government (1921–2) Founding of Chinese Communist Party (1921) First United Front (1923–7) Sun Yat-sen's third Guangzhou government (1923–5) Northern Expedition (1926–8) Central Plains War (1930) Xi'an Incident beginning Second United Front (1936–41) Nationalist government moves to Chongqing (1937)	Famine in northwest (1927–30), 3 mil. deaths Tariff autonomy agreements with United States (1928) Nanjing Decade (1928–37) Yangzi River flood (1931), 50 mil. displaced New famine (1936), 5 mil. deaths Yellow River flood from Nationalist breach of dikes (1938)	Establishment of Mongolian People's Government (1921) Nine-Power Treaty guaranteeing Open Door Policy (1922) Restoration of tsarist privileges to Soviet government (1924) Establishment of Mongolian People's Republic (1924) Sino-Soviet War over Chinese Eastern Railway (1929) Japanese invasion of Manchuria (1931–45) North China War (1933–5) Japanese invasion of intra-mural China (1937–45)	First Fengtian-Zhili War (1922) Second Fengtian-Zhili War (1924) Anti-imperialist May Thirtieth Movement (1925) Nationalist purge of Communists (1927) Nanchang Uprising (1927) Encirclement Campaigns (1931–4) Long March (1934) National Salvation League demonstrations (1935–6) Rape of Nanjing (1937)	Lu Xun's short stories become famous Ding Ling's novels become famous New Life Movement (1934) Mao writes most famous books on revolution
1940s	Rival government in Nanjing (1940) Establishment of People's Republic of China (1949)	Henan famine (1942–3), 5 mil. deaths Hyperinflation Chinese Communist Party (CCP) announces land reform (1946)	Britain and United States end extraterritoriality (1943) Japanese capitulation (1945) U.S. mediation of civil war (1945–7)	Rectification Campaign (1942–4) Renewal of Nationalist-CCP civil war (1945–9)	

Part III

The Republican Period, 1912–49

Part III begins with the collapse of the Qing dynasty in 1911, which produced an institutional vacuum. While the Han could agree on the restoration of Han rule, there was no consensus on the form this should take. Soon they turned on each other, ushering in over three decades of civil war in which millions of Chinese perished. In 1928, the Nationalist Party under Chiang Kai-shek succeeded in unifying the core provinces of China minus the empire—that is, minus Manchuria, Mongolia, Xinjiang, and Tibet. The civil wars, however, did not end but merely sparked foreign intervention, first by Japan and later by the Soviet Union and the United States. On 1 October 1949, this period ended when the Nationalists retreated to Taiwan and the Chinese Communist Party led by Mao Zedong founded the People's Republic of China.

Chapter 15 describes the creation of the Republic of China under Yuan Shikai and his controversial attempt to become the founding emperor of a new dynasty. These were also the years when Sun Yat-sen popularized his Three People's Principles that became the core ideology of the Nationalist Party. In the absence of strong institutions to resolve the growing disagreement over which model China should adopt for political and economic development, some resorted to coercion, rule by assassination, and, finally, civil war. In particular, Russia, for reasons of frontier security, and Japan, for reasons of trade, were deeply concerned with the outcome of this internal struggle. Although the interests of the Western powers were vested in the treaty port system, World War I (1914–18) and the Bolshevik Revolution (1917) soon completely overshadowed events in China.

Chapter 16 examines the postwar Paris Peace Conference. While Western and Russian attention remained riveted on Germany during World War I, the fledgling Chinese Republic tried its hand at diplomacy with disastrous results. Diplomats on the take signed treaties with Japan that could not be justified to an irate Chinese public. U.S. President Woodrow Wilson attempted to smooth over the sketchy diplomacy, only to be tarred in the Chinese press. The controversy focused on the return to Chinese sovereignty of the German concessions on the Shandong Peninsula. The diplomatic solution did not satisfy the Beijing government or the Chinese people. As a result, the U.S. mediation of the Shandong question at the Paris Peace Conference (1919) terminating World War I soured many Chinese intellectuals on American-style governance, and they increasingly turned to Soviet governmental models.

Chapter 17 focuses on the intellectual ferment in China. What should "new" China be? This was the period of the May Fourth Movement that radically transformed Chinese education. Classical Chinese, the written language of China's many dynasties, would be discarded for vernacular Chinese, meaning Mandarin, the North Chinese language spoken in the capital. The Bolshevik government that replaced the fallen Russian autocracy during 1917 was intent on expanding proletarian rule. Frustrated in Europe, the Russian Communists became active in Asia, where they were instrumental in founding Communist parties in China (1921), Outer Mongolia (1921), Japan (1922), and Korea (1925). Meanwhile, China's northern warlords fought a succession of wars entailing World War I–style combat to take control of the capital.

Chapter 18 describes how the Nationalist and Communist parties gained strength in the South while the northern warlords fought each other to exhaustion. In 1923 the two parties combined in the first united front to reunify China. The Soviet Union was intimately involved in aiding both while restoring its control over the former tsarist concessions in North China. Sun Yat-sen's sudden death in 1925 left a leadership vacuum at the head of the Nationalist Party that its military wing, under Chiang Kai-shek, soon filled. Chiang organized a Northern Expedition in 1926 to reunify the country. When he reached the Yangzi River port of Shanghai, he turned on his erstwhile Communist allies and systematically assassinated them. By 1928, he was largely successful in reunifying the core provinces of China. The reunification, however, did not represent centralized government, but rather a loose confederation of allied warlords.

MID-AUTUMN FESTIVAL

The Mid-Autumn Festival is the third most important holiday for the living after New Year's and the Dragon Boat Festival. Celebrated on the fifteenth day of the eighth moon of the lunar calendar, it usually occurs between mid-September and mid-October. The celebration originated in the worship of the moon during the Xia and Shang dynasties (2205–1122 BC). The Western and Eastern Zhou dynasty (1122–222 BC) emperors then established the custom of praying to the moon on the fifteenth night of the eighth lunar month. By the time of the Qing dynasty, Western Beijing had an altar to the moon, where the emperor offered annual sacrifices.

The festival eventually acquired an embedded political meaning: The Ming dynasty (1368–1644) used the festival to commemorate the Han Chinese rebels who had attempted to overthrow the preceding Mongol Yuan dynasty (1279–1368). According to legend, the rebels baked messages into the traditional moon cakes exchanged as gifts during the festival. The messages outlined their plans for attack so that on the night of the Moon Festival in 1353, the rebel leader Liu Bowen took over a key prefecture that would soon allow the Ming emperor, Zhu Yuanzhang, to overthrow the Mongols. In 1927, Mao Zedong tried to repeat this well-known event by instigating a peasant Autumn Harvest Uprising. (See Chapter 18, Section V.) Although he failed, when Mao finally did succeed in founding the People's Republic of China, he set National Day for 1 October 1949 to fall near the time of the Mid-Autumn Festival.

There are three main legends associated with the festival: The great archer Houyi shot down nine suns from the sky to prevent the earth from being incinerated and also built a jade palace for the Goddess of the Western Heaven. As a reward, he received the elixir of immortality on the condition that he fast for a year, but his beautiful wife, Chang'e, unable to control her curiosity, drank the elixir, whereupon she soared up to the moon, where she has remained ever since. On the fifteenth day of every lunar month, Houyi and Chang'e meet, the conjunction of *yin* and *yang*. Chang'e's picture adorns banners for the Mid-Autumn Festival. In addition, the PRC's current space program to explore the moon is named in her honor.

Another permanent resident of the moon, Wu Gang, was an unsatisfactory apprentice to an immortal. When he learned how to become one himself, his master punished him by sentencing him to chop down a cassia tree located on the moon. This proved an impossible task because the tree healed completely the same day, so Wu Gang is chopping still.

Finally, the most well-known legend concerns the rabbit Tu'er Ye. When three fairy sages transformed themselves into pitiful old men to beg food from a fox, a monkey, and a rabbit, the fox and monkey both fed the men, but the rabbit offered himself instead by jumping into a blazing fire. The rabbit's sacrifice so impressed the sages that they let him live forever in the Moon Palace, where he became the Jade Rabbit. When the U.S. astronauts landed on the moon, some Chinese wondered whether they might find Chang'e, Wu Gang, or Tu'er Ye.

The festival features many moon-shaped foods harvested in the fall such as apples, pears, peaches, grapes, pomegranates, melons, and oranges. Special foods include cooked taro, edible snails cooked in sweet basil, and water caltrope, a type of water chestnut. Round moon cakes are the most important. Although there are hundreds of types of moon cakes, they generally measure about three inches in diameter and about one and a half inches in thickness and are composed of a thin exterior pastry hiding a rich, dense filling. The fillings include lotus seed, melon seed, almond, bean paste, orange peel, and salted duck egg yolk. For ancestor worship, thirteen moon cakes are piled in a pyramid to symbolize the thirteen months of a complete lunar year, including the intercalary month.

The Nanjing Decade is the subject of Chapter 19. From the Northern Expedition in 1927 and the reunification of China in 1928 until the full-scale Japanese invasion of China proper in 1937, the Nationalist Party ruled from its capital in Nanjing. This relative security provided a short window to focus on internal reforms and state-building. Yet, this was also a decade fraught with domestic strife and foreign interference. Japanese concerns over the endemic instability in

China and territorial competition with the USSR culminated in the Japanese invasion of Manchuria in 1931 and the creation of the puppet state of Manchukuo (Manshūkoku in Japanese). Meanwhile, the Nationalist-Communist civil war continued unabated with a series of encirclement campaigns by the Nationalists. The Fifth Encirclement Campaign forced the Communists on the arduous retreat known as the Long March to desolate Yan'an, located on the northern periphery of China but close to Soviet sources of aid. In 1936, in order to expel Japan from Manchuria, the Nationalists and Communists formed a Second United Front. The Japanese regarded this as a direct threat to their national security and responded with a massive invasion of China proper in 1937.

During the course of this Second Sino-Japanese War, the focus of Chapter 20, the Japanese decimated Chiang's most well-trained and loyal forces. While they focused on fighting the conventional forces of the Nationalists, the Communists organized in the rural no-man's land, which Japan lacked the troops to garrison. The war destroyed the urban-based Nationalists' economy, leaving them severely weakened after the Japanese defeat in World War II. Once the United States declared war on Japan in 1941, both the Nationalists and Communists awaited the anticipated U.S. victory before resuming their civil war in force. The Nationalists' unwillingness to use their growing stockpiles of U.S. war materiel soured U.S.–Nationalist relations.

Chapter 21 discusses the final phase of China's long period of civil wars. From 1945 to 1949, the Nationalists and Communists fought a brutal civil war that brought the Communists to victory in Beijing and the Nationalists to exile on Taiwan. Initially, the United States attempted to mediate the conflict but succeeded only in tying itself to the increasingly corrupt Nationalist regime. When the United States withdrew from China in disgust, the Soviet Union continued to aid the Communists, while the Nationalists never recovered from their defeats in Manchuria. The coalitional structure of Nationalist rule meant that they were unable to combine their forces effectively. Instead, the Communists consistently defeated them in detail. Just as the revolutionaries brought down the Qing dynasty and just as the various warlords seized control, the Communists rose to power at the head of a conventional army.

Chronology

1911	Xinhai Revolution (10 October 1911–12 February 1912)
	Outer Mongolia declares independence
1912	Establishment of the Republic of China
	Yuan Shikai becomes provisional president in Beijing
1913	Anti–Yuan Shikai Second Revolution
	Yuan bans Tongmenghui; Sun Yat-sen goes into exile in Japan
	Tibet declares independence
1914–18	World War I
1914	Yuan prorogues the National Assembly
	Yuan declares Chinese neutrality in World War I
	Japan occupies German concessions on Shandong Peninsula
	Russia presents Twenty-one Demands concerning Mongolia
	Tongmenghui reorganized into forerunner of Nationalist Party
1915	Japan presents Twenty-one Demands, which becomes the Day of National Humiliation in China; beginning of anti-Japan movement
	Yuan made emperor
	Third Revolution in opposition to Yuan's attempt to become emperor
1916	Yuan abolishes the emperor system
	Zhang Zuolin establishes authority in Manchuria
	Yuan Shikai dies
	End of Third Revolution
	Li Yuanhong becomes president
	Restoration of the 1912 constitution and National Assembly
1917	Russian Revolution toppling the Romanov dynasty in March
	Failed restoration of the Qing dynasty under the former Xuantong emperor
	China declares war against Germany and Austria
	Establishment of the first Guangzhou government under Sun Yat-sen and Chen Jiongming
	Russian Revolution in November, bringing the Communists to power
1917–18	Nishihara loans to China
1918	Sun Yat-sen resigns from the Guangzhou government
	Election of the Anfu National Assembly
1919	Paris Peace Conference
	May Fourth Movement
	Founding of the Nationalist Party
1921	Establishment of the second Guangzhou government under Sun Yat-sen

The Founding of the Republic of China

Fellow human beings, wake up, wake up, wake up!
If you don't do what the American War of Independence did,
And stand up, refuse to pay taxes . . .
Never will you have the chance to change your destiny.[1]

Guo Moruo (1892–1978) poet, essayist,
playwright, historian, translator, ca. 1923

The 1911 Revolution marked the beginning of the Republican period (1912–49) in Chinese history. The Republican period was an interregnum between the Qing dynasty and the Communist People's Republic of China that finally succeeded in reunifying the Qing empire minus Outer Mongolia and Taiwan. In the interim, central power devolved to the provinces, where competing regional strongmen, known as "warlords," fought either to maintain their own autonomy or to expand their territory. This continued the devolution of central power begun during the great mid-nineteenth century rebellions, when the Qing dynasty allowed provincial authorities to create semiautonomous local armies that later became the nuclei of the warlord armies. Initially, General Yuan Shikai attempted to impose another dynasty in Beijing. His death in 1916 marked the beginning of the warlord period, and was characterized by worsening relations with Japan and an increasingly virulent nationalist movement among China's intellectuals and students. Sun Yat-sen tried to consolidate his political base in South China through a succession of governments in Guangzhou, while a North China power struggle erupted after Yuan's death.

I. The Republic under Yuan Shikai

The Republic, a nominally democratic form of government, had been born of a military uprising. At its head was a former Qing general, Yuan Shikai, who quickly assumed dictatorial powers more in the manner of traditional Chinese autocrats than in keeping with the westernized exterior of the new government. In light of the Manchu fall, Yuan Shikai quickly disbanded the New Army and transferred military power to generals personally loyal to him. Thereafter, he established his capital in Beijing and spent his first years as president trying to consolidate control both over China's now autonomous provinces and its far-flung dependencies and tributaries. Yuan's success was limited, especially with regard to the independence movement in South China and the imperial ambitions of his two closest neighbors, tsarist Russia and Japan, which vied for influence over the periphery of the former Qing empire

On 15 February 1912 the Nanjing Assembly unanimously elected Yuan Shikai as provisional president; Li Yuanhong became provisional vice-president five days later. Sun Yat-sen stepped down on the condition that Yuan rule from Nanjing. Yuan's power base, however, was in North China. Units of the Beiyang Army rioted in various northern cities, apparently to lend credence to Yuan's claim that the restoration of order required his presence in the North. The Nanjing government agreed that Yuan could rule from Beijing, where he was inaugurated as president of the Republic of China on 12 March 1912. As in previous periods of dynastic change, the imperial bureaucracy remained in place, and Yuan simply took over the reins of power from his Manchu predecessors. The enormous inertia of the imperial bureaucracy became a strong force of continuity and a key impediment to radical change.

Yuan sought more than simple personal aggrandizement; more importantly, he hoped to restore China to grandeur. He intended to emulate the Japanese model of economic development, which relied on centralized political control to impose controversial reforms, including the westernization of legal and financial institutions. As in Meiji Japan, Yuan hoped that the legal reforms would enable him to negotiate the end to extraterritoriality, while the financial reforms would create the basis for economic development. He also realized that economic development required an educated citizenry, hence his attempt to implement compulsory primary education for boys. In addition, he tried to promote economic development through improved agronomy, transportation, and credit availability. He took action on social issues, cracking down on opium smoking and production and promoting married women's rights. As in Japan, his program was controversial, but unlike the Meiji reformers, Yuan did not remain in power for a generation to complete the reforms. He soon became preoccupied, like the Empress Dowager before him, not with the creative exercise of power but with its retention.

As a former general, Yuan deftly asserted his control over the armed forces, recentralized power, and governed China through his *guanxi* network of hand-picked military officers. Once in office, armed force became the basis of his power. His decision to disband the New Army eliminated its role as a lightning rod for antigovernment opposition and also the possibility of its transformation into a national army. Yuan's decision to replace the New Army with a force loyal to him personally, not to China generally, was an important step toward warlord rule. In January 1913, Yuan went even further, placing all of the military governors directly under his authority in order to subsume them and their *guanxi* networks under his own. In the capital, he systematically undermined the power of the cabinet and then of the National Assembly, where the precursor of the Nationalist Party became a major obstacle to his plans.

During summer 1913, the so-called Second Revolution broke out. (See Map 15.1.) The elections in 1913 delivered a landslide victory in both houses of the parliament to this party. In response, it appears that supporters of Yuan Shikai had a key supporter of Sun Yat-sen, Song Jiaoren, assassinated. Song had been educated in Japan and had played a key role in forming the coalition of parties that united to become the precursor of the Nationalist Party in 25 August 1912. His plans for a Western parliamentary system of government threatened Yuan's hope to recentralize power under a dictatorial executive. A succession of mysterious deaths of those connected with the assassination ensued. When Yuan tried to finance his activities independently of the opposition-dominated parliament by seeking foreign loans, the legislature objected. Yuan then surrounded the parliament with troops, cashiered pro-opposition military governors, and on 6 May 1913 banned the party. Sun Yat-sen called for a Second Revolution. Seven provinces responded by declaring independence, but Yuan's troops defeated them in battle, while his generals established themselves as warlords along the Yangzi River. This ended the Second Revolution, but at the price of greatly exacerbated North–South tensions.

The opposition-dominated parliament remained determined to block Yuan's attempts to restore dynastic institutions. On 10 January 1914 Yuan dispensed with the National Assembly and the provincial assemblies altogether. He replaced the former with a loyal political council, with the northern warlord Duan Qirui serving as prime minister, and in May he extended his presidential term to ten years. In 1915 he attempted to dispense with the Republican government as well by proclaiming himself emperor. Yuan's restoration of imperial rule differed from Japan's Meiji restoration, in which

In 1912, General Yuan Shikai became the president of the Republic of China, after Sun Yat-sen, in return for convincing the Manchus to abdicate the throne. His presidency helped set the stage for the warlord period that followed, in particular as he doled out concessions to Russia and Japan in exchange for their support in his failed bid to become China's next emperor.

the emperor was a symbol of national authority legitimizing the work of powerful behind-the-scenes oligarch-bureaucrats. Yuan intended to exercise power personally.

Although Yuan's forces crushed the renegade provinces during the Second Revolution, beginning in late 1915 opposition to his plan to become emperor erupted. Yunnan declared independence on 25 December and Guizhou on 27 December. The rest of the provinces waited to see what would happen. When Yuan's supporters were unable to crush the rebels, Guangxi declared its independence on 15 March 1916, followed by Guangdong on 6 April, Zhejiang on 12 April, Shaanxi on 15 May, Sichuan on 22 May, and Hunan on 27 May. This became known as the Third Revolution. (See Map 15.2.) Yuan

refused to resign. Then on 6 June 1916, in the midst of the crisis, he suddenly died at the age of fifty-six of uremia, a severe impairment of the kidneys. (See Table 15.1.)

II. Relations with Russia, Japan, and Britain

In the aftermath of the Second Revolution, Yuan Shikai could ill afford foreign opposition to his plans, especially along China's northern borders. He tried to avoid foreign policy crises in order to focus on his domestic programs and to secure foreign loans to fund them. This strategy came at

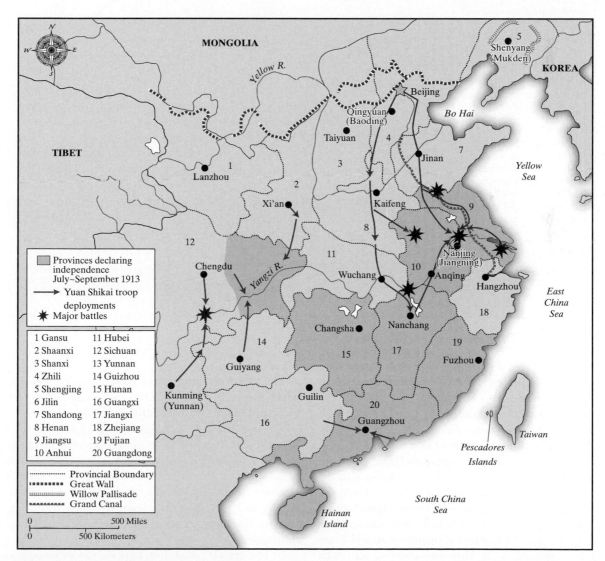

Map 15.1 Second Revolution (1913)

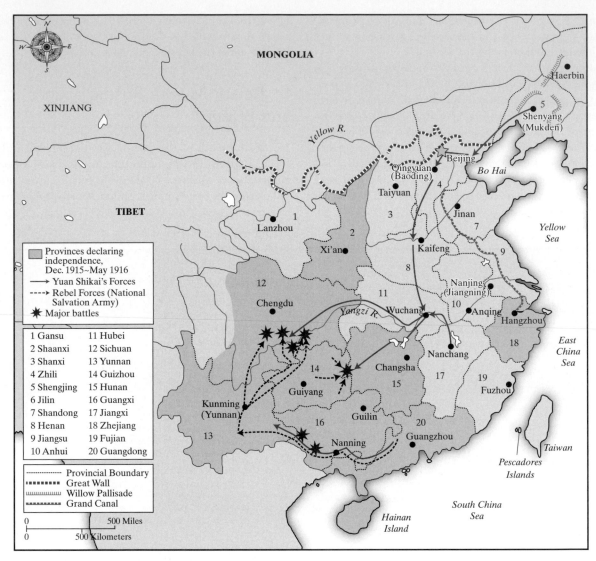

Map 15.2 Third Revolution (1915–16)

the price of deferring treaty revision, a feverently desired goal of Chinese nationalists. Yuan bought Russian, Japanese, and British support with a variety of agreements. Although his plans for dynastic restoration died with him, the secret treaties he signed retained the force of international law long after his death. Treaties with tsarist Russia and Japan greatly increased their spheres of influence. One set of treaties gave the Russians extensive rights and privileges in Outer Mongolia, transforming the region into a Russian protectorate. Another set increased Japan's hold over Manchuria and, following the outbreak of World War I, allowed Japan to usurp German control over concessions in Shandong province. To little effect, the United States protested these actions as violations of the Open Door Policy.

In the wake of the 1911 Revolution, Beijing renamed the Foreign Office the Ministry of Foreign Affairs and promoted Western-educated officials. Under this new leadership, the ministry established a commission to study China's treaties as the first step to renegotiate them on the basis of juridical equality. The Chinese government was determined to eliminate the so-called unequal treaties that established the concession system, guaranteed extraterritoriality and most-favored-nation treatment to foreigners, and set the country's tariffs. But Yuan Shikai ruled for just four years.

The dynastic chaos in China worked to Russia's advantage; Russia may even have assisted the New Army conspirators, who planned the Wuchang Uprising from the Russian

Table 15.1   The Three Revolutions (1911–16)
(dates show declarations of independence by province)

First Revolution	Second Revolution	Third Revolution
Fanned out from central China. Began with mutiny in Wuhan. Culminated in dynastic overthrow.	South China revolution. Yuan Shikai successfully deployed army to reverse opposition legislative victory. Increased power of army.	South China Revolution. Opposition to Yuan Shikai's attempt to become emperor. Army divided into factions. Warlord period began with death of Yuan on 6 June.
10 Oct. 1911 Hubei	15 July 1913 Jiangsu	25 Dec. 1915 Yunnan
22 Oct. 1911 Hunan	17 July 1913 Anhui	27 Dec. 1915 Guizhou
22 Oct. 1911 Shaanxi	18 July 1913 Guangdong	15 March 1916 Guangxi
29 Oct. 1911 Shanxi	18 July 1913 Jiangxi	6 April 1916 Guangdong
31 Oct. 1911 Jiangxi	19 July 1913 Fujian	12 April 1916 Zhejiang
31 Oct. 1911 Yunnan	25 July 1913 Hunan	15 May 1916 Shaanxi
4 Nov. 1911 Jiangsu	4 Aug. 1913 Sichuan	22 May 1916 Sichuan
4 Nov. 1911 Guizhou		27 May 1916 Hunan
5 Nov. 1911 Zhejiang		
7 Nov. 1911 Guangxi		
8 Nov. 1911 Anhui		
9 Nov. 1911 Guangdong		
11 Nov. 1911 Fujian		
12 Nov. 1911 Fengtian		
13 Nov. 1911 Shandong		
16 Nov. 1911 Jilin		
17 Nov. 1911 Heilongjiang		
27 Nov. 1911 Sichuan		
1 Dec. 1911 Mongolia		
6 Jan. 1912 Gansu		
7 Jan. 1912 Xinjiang		
Provinces not declaring independence from Manchus: Zhili, Henan. Tibet declares independence from China 1912.	Provinces not declaring independence from Yuan Shikai: Shandong, Hunan, Shanxi, Shaanxi, Hubei, Gansu, Xinjiang, Guizhou, Jilin, Fengtian, Heilongjiang Yunnan, Guangxi, Zhejiang Mongolia remained quasi-independent.	Provinces not declaring independence from Yuan Shikai: Zhili, Fengtian, Heilongjiang, Jilin, Gansu, Xinjiang, Shandong, Jiangsu, Anhui, Shanxi, Henan, Hubei, Jiangxi, Fujian.

Source: Limin Kuo, comp., *Zhongguo jindaishi cankao ditu* (Changsha: Hunan jiaoshu chubanshe, 1984), 41–2, 45; S. C. M. Paine, *Imperial Rivals: China, Russia, and Their Disputed Frontier* (Armonk, NY: M. E. Sharpe, 1996), 289.

concession. As soon as the 1911 Revolution broke out, tsarist Russia tried to take advantage of the ensuing Mongolian independence movement by negotiating two agreements in 1912 and 1913 to establish Outer Mongolian autonomy from China. In 1914, Russia presented Beijing with a list of Twenty-one Demands that would have made Outer Mongolia a de facto Russian protectorate. Yuan appeared willing to sign such a pact in order to gain Russia's backing for his own plan to become China's new monarch.

The Japanese were aghast at this dramatic expansion of Russian influence, including the transfer of hundreds of thousands of square miles of Chinese territory in Outer Mongolia to Russian control. They had already fought two wars to contain Russian expansion in East Asia—the First Sino-Japanese

War (1894–5) and the Russo-Japanese War (1904–5)—and believed that Japanese national security rested on containing further Russian expansion. On 18 January 1915, mirroring Russia's Twenty-one Demands, Tokyo presented Beijing with its much more famous Twenty-one Demands.

In addition to countering Russia, the Japanese government hoped to take advantage of the Western preoccupation with World War I to solidify its own position in China south of the Great Wall. The Japanese wanted (1) to assume control over the German concessions in Shandong province, which they had just taken from Germany by force; (2) to acquire mining and commercial privileges along the Yangzi River; (3) to expand their sphere of influence in Manchuria and Inner Mongolia as a counterweight to Russia; and (4) to prevent China from leasing additional coastal areas to other foreign powers. In a very controversial fifth set of demands, the Japanese sought a wide range of political rights, including the appointment of Japanese advisers throughout the Chinese government and police administration, Japanese domination of arms sales to China, and Japanese development of Fujian province across the strait from their colony of Taiwan.

On 13 March 1915, when the United States protested this attempt to dominate China politically, militarily, and economically, Japan modified its fifth set of demands. It no longer required China to accept Japanese police or an exclusive Japanese zone in Fujian province. On 28 April 1915, in the midst of the uproar, Japan publicly offered to restore the Shandong concession to China.

The Japanese were simultaneously negotiating with Sun Yat-sen's opposition government, but no known agreement was reached. Sun accused Yuan of secretly agreeing in advance to accept Russian and Japanese terms in return for their support for Yuan's ambitions to become China's new emperor. According to Sun: "In fact, the Twenty-one Demands were presented by Japan at his [Yuan's] own instigation; Japan did not, at the beginning, press him to accept these Demands."[2] According to this view, Japan delivered its conditions in the form of demands, instead of a formal treaty, in order to provide Yuan with a face-saving way to accept the terms, whereas in reality, Yuan agreed to all of them in advance to further his own political agenda.

The treaty encapsulating the Twenty-one Demands became an international issue when the Paris Peace Conference terminating World War I deliberated on the Shandong question. As Liang Qichao, the late-Qing revolutionary, later concluded, if China had openly resisted Japan in 1915, its claim at the Paris Peace Conference that Shandong should be returned directly to China would have been very strong. Instead, Yuan Shikai made the political calculation that he needed to focus on consolidating his own power domestically before he could take on Japan or Russia. From Japan's point of view, the new treaty would counterbalance tsarist Russian efforts to expand into Outer Mongolia. Taking Shandong from Germany also avenged Japan for German involvement in the Triple Intervention of 1895 that deprived Japan of the Liaodong Peninsula.

Yuan Shikai had no better luck dealing with Britain over Tibet. When news of the 1911 Revolution reached Tibet in 1912, the local population immediately expelled Chinese officials and troops from Lhasa for the first time since the eighteenth century. (See the feature below.) The Tibetans then sought British aid to protect their new-found independence. Although the British successfully pressured the Chinese into joining tripartite negotiations with Britain and Tibet, they were unable to secure Chinese ratification of the resulting Simla Convention of 1914. It became an Anglo-Tibetan agreement instead, dividing Tibet into Outer Tibet and Inner Tibet. The Dalai Lama would rule Outer Tibet with de facto autonomy but under nominal Chinese suzerainty. Inner Tibet, also known as Kham, encompassed the ethnic Tibetan regions of eastern Qinghai and Western Sichuan. It was given a more vague status, but with the Dalai Lama preeminent in religious affairs. While the British would not back the official independence that the Tibetans desired, they provided the Tibetans with sufficient military aid to keep the Chinese out and gain favorable terms of trade for themselves. Tibet did not return to Chinese rule until the People's Liberation Army occupied it beginning in 1950.

TIBETAN MINORITY

The Tibetans inhabit virtually inaccessible plateaus surrounded by mountains high above sea level. Only the main valley, the location of the capital, Lhasa, is suitable for cultivation; the other mountain valleys can support only grazing. The growing season is short and the rainfall scant, making for a harsh existence. Most Tibetans practice the Lama variant of Mahayana Buddhism that incorporates elements of ancient Tibetan shamanism and magic.

Buddhism probably came to Tibet in the seventh century. At that time, the Tibetan empire expanded into Nepal and Yunnan. Thereafter, it expanded northward to dominate the lucrative Silk Route trade as far north as Kashgar and as far east as Xi'an, the modern name for the Tang dynasty (618–907) capital, which the Tibetans sacked. Tibetan expansion ended with the assassination of their king in 842, while Tang dynasty emperors tried to buy peace on the frontier by marrying off Han princesses to the kings of Tibet. The Chinese have since claimed that these marriages document Tibet's tributary status. At the end of the twelfth century, many Indian Buddhists fled to Tibet to escape invading Muslim armies. When the Mongols established the Yuan dynasty (1279–1368) in China, they also extended their influence over Tibet, where Mongol domination continued until the Qing conquest of Tibet in the eighteenth century. The Mongols recognized the authority of Tibet's monks over both spiritual and temporal matters, giving enormous authority to the clergy.

During the early Qing dynasty, the Fifth Dalai Lama (1617–82) and the Seventh Dalai Lama (1708–57) reached an accommodation with the Qing. They ruled through a monastic bureaucracy that kept peace at home, power concentrated in key monastic institutions and a limited number of lay aristocratic clans, and Tibet demilitarized so that the Qing felt little need to interfere. The British invasion in 1903–4 that sent the Dalai Lama fleeing to Mongolia, however, awakened Chinese fears of border security. The Anglo-Russian rivalry for dominance of Central Asia had fueled British fears concerning the defense of India and resulted in a military expedition to Tibet. In response, the Chinese allowed the Dalai Lama to return home but rapidly reinvigorated their administration of Tibet and efforts at Sinification. When the Tibetans resisted, the Qing deployed their army, occupying Tibet in 1910 and sending the Dalai Lama back into exile, this time to India. Upon the fall of the Qing dynasty, the Dalai Lama raised an army and took control of Tibet in 1913. Tibet remained autonomous until 1950.

In the interim the Thirteenth Dalai Lama (1876–1933) tried to establish a centralized nation state, causing the Panchen Lama, the second most important incarnate lama after the Dalai Lama, to flee to China in 1924. Han nationalists accepted the Qing definition of China and wanted Tibet back. Prior to Nationalist reunification of China in 1927, governments in Beijing emphasized the "Harmonious Union of the Five Races," meaning the Han, the Manchu, the Mongols, the Tibetans, and the Muslims, and sometimes referred to the post-Qing government as the Republic of the Five Races. The Tibetans, like the Muslims and Mongols, understood this union to mean Han domination in practice. Thereafter, the Nationalists emphasized Sun Yat-sen's Three People's Principles, but given the numerous concerns of the new Nationalist government, there was little impact on Tibet. On the contrary, in the 1920s and 1930s, Tibetan Buddhism greatly influenced many Chinese, who found solace in the religion at a time when China devolved into chaos. The Nationalist government sought to cultivate ties with Tibet, sponsored a variety of joint educational institutions, and gave legal protection to Buddhist land holdings.

Tibet's approximately 2 million ethnic Tibetans occupy one of the most inaccessible regions in the world. Despite persistent attempts by China to dominate Tibet, the Tibetan people have so far resisted assimilation. In this photo, pro-Tibetan protesters are being arrested on 30 March 2008 outside the Chinese consulate in Kathmandu, Nepal.

Continued

In 1950, the People's Liberation Army invaded Tibet but initially tolerated Buddhist institutions. When China included Tibet in its land reform program that overturned the aristocratic-monastic social order, the Tibetans unsuccessfully revolted and the Fourteenth Dalai Lama (1935–   ) fled to India, where he has remained ever since. During the Cultural Revolution (1966–76), China tried to eradicate Tibetan culture as part of its campaign to eliminate the Four Olds—old ideas, old culture, old customs, and old habits. China shut down virtually all monasteries in this period and imprisoned many monks; numerous Tibetans perished. The Tibetans revolted again in the 1980s, which resulted in another wave of prison sentences and executions.

The flowering of Tibetan written culture occurred from the tenth through sixteenth centuries with the publication of numerous religious works. Judging from Tibet's architectural heritage, it reached the height of its prosperity during the early and middle period of Mongol domination from the thirteenth through sixteenth centuries. Numerous Buddhist temples and pagodas date to this period, but almost all were destroyed during the Cultural Revolution.

Traditionally, the Tibetans raised yaks, a beast resistant to the cold. They relied on yak milk and meat for food, the hair for textiles, and the live animal for transportation. Most of the population were serfs and lived in dire poverty. Up to one-third of the male population became monks, which meant that their maintenance depended in part on the alms of others. Foreigners who visited Lhasa in the nineteenth and early twentieth centuries were appalled by its filth. Human and animal excrement, garbage, and even dead animals littered the city streets. Few educational opportunities were available, so the vast majority of the population remained illiterate. Today one-fifth of Tibetans remain in poverty. In 1990, 45 percent of men over age fifteen remained illiterate, as did 80 percent of women of childbearing age. The Chinese have argued that their involvement in Tibet has been an attempt to drag the Tibetans into the modern world and to improve their standard of living. Administratively, the Chinese have divided the areas of Tibetan population into Tibet (formerly Outer Tibet), and Qinghai and Western Sichuan (formerly Inner Tibet). People's Liberation Army troops continue to garrison the region. A railway trunk line was completed in 2006 and will greatly facilitate Han migration to Tibet. The latest round of unrest began on 14 March 2008 to coincide with the forty-ninth anniversary of the 1959 uprising against Chinese rule.

III. The Founding of the Nationalist Party

All too quickly, the political compromise unraveled between the civil forces from South China affiliated with Sun Yat-sen and the military forces from North China under Yuan Shikai. Following the relocation of China's capital to Beijing, Sun and Yuan began to disagree on how the Republic of China should be governed. Sun then unsuccessfully attempted to create an alternate government in the South. He returned to Guangzhou, the capital of his native province of Guangdong, where the acting governor, Chen Jiongming, controlled the local troops. Yuan hoped to use Chen against Sun, but instead the two joined forces against Yuan in 1913. During the Second Revolution in 1913, when forces loyal to Yuan defeated the southern provinces, Sun Yat-sen fled to Japan, where he remained until the cascade of revolts in the last year of Yuan's rule.

While in Tokyo, Sun reorganized his party, the Tongmenghui, which had been active in the overthrow of the Manchus. On 8 July 1914, he renamed it the Chinese Revolutionary Party (*Zhongguo Gemingdang*). Its members vowed personal allegiance to Sun. They made him generalissimo of the Chinese Revolutionary Army, with powers much like those of the other Chinese warlords, except that his movement produced an ideology and a political party that ultimately transcended provincial boundaries to become a truly national movement.

Sun Yat-sen's political philosophy, known as the Three People's Principles, emphasized the three principles of nationalism, democracy, and the people's livelihood. These ideas became central to his political platform to reunify China. His earliest writings reveal the strong influence of his westernized education in Hong Kong and Hawaii, particularly concerning nationalism and democracy. In 1906 he defined nationalism as preventing foreign nations from violating Chinese sovereignty and interfering in its domestic affairs. This definition fit with the U.S. Open Door Policy. In December 1911 he urged the Chinese to foster nationalism in order to honor China and showcase the distinctive traits of the Chinese people.

In 1918, Sun presented a detailed definition of nationalism in his *Memoirs of a Chinese Revolutionary,* calling for a united Chinese Republic in order to combine China's various nationalities into a powerful nation. In 1919, he integrated President Woodrow Wilson's views on national self-determination into his Three People's Principles, calling on the Han "to merge in all sincerity with the Manchus, Mongols, Muslims, and Tibetans in one melting pot to create a new order of Chinese nationalism, just as America has produced the world's leading nationalism by melding scores of different people, black and white."[3] Sun continued to support Wilsonian nationalism in a later book, *China's Revolution,* published in early 1923, defining nationalism as "unity and equality of races within China, and China's rights among the nations of the world."[4] Both before and after World War I, his nationalistic goals included protecting Chinese sovereignty from foreign interference, guaranteeing the rights of China's ethnic minorities, and gradually melding these different groups into one nationality.

In late 1917, in opposition to the attempt by the northern warlord Duan Qirui to assert control over the government in Beijing, Chen Jiongming and Sun's party again combined forces. On 31 August 1917 Sun set up his first of three rival governments in Guangzhou. (See Table 15.2.) Sun called his government the Constitution Protection Movement and his military force the Constitution Protection Army, but he lacked direct control over his armed forces. These remained under the command of Chen Jiongming. Together they formed an alternate government to Beijing. Although Premier Duan Qirui in Beijing sent troops to destroy the Guangzhou government, infighting among the northern warlords prevented their success. This failure contributed to Duan's resignation on 22 November 1918.

As Chen Jiongming tried to create a consolidated military base in Guangdong and Fujian provinces, Sun Yat-sen soon ran into warlord troubles of his own. In May 1918, when the local power brokers in Guangzhou deprived Sun of authority within the new government, he left for Shanghai, where he reorganized his political party yet again. On 10 October 1919, on the eighth anniversary of the Wuchang Uprising, he renamed the party the Chinese Nationalist Party (*Zhongguo Guomindang,* Kuomintang or KMT). For simplic-

ity, from 1914 on, it will be referred to as the Nationalist Party and its members as Nationalists. This is the same party that long ruled Taiwan and remains a major political force there. By 1920, Chen defeated the rival warlord in Guangxi and Sun had plans to return to Guangzhou to set up a new government; from Guangzhou, he hoped to launch a military expedition northward to unite China. Sun returned to Guangzhou to his second opposition government, with himself as president, on 2 April 1921.

During most of these years, Sun's Guangzhou governments did not have a specific domestic or foreign policy program or even a clear plan on how to reunite China. Sun also lacked a well-organized army to defeat the northern warlords. This required funds, military advisers, and modern armaments. Although Sun tried to obtain foreign support, the major powers all recognized the Beijing government. Unifying China under the Nationalist Party became possible only after Sun allied with Moscow in January 1923 and received military aid from the Soviet-funded Communist International (Comintern).

IV. North China Warlord Intrigues

The factional infighting of the Republican period was extraordinarily complex. (See Table 15.3 and Map 15.3.) The rivalries were multilateral and both civil and military. In the World War I period, China north of the Yangzi River was split among three primary factions: the Anhui Clique, the Zhili Clique, and the Fengtian or Manchurian Clique. All were named after the provinces of origin of their leaders. In addition, there was the residual vice-president of Yuan Shikai's government, Li Yuanhong. The complexity of these factions reflected the underlying structure of power, which

Table 15.2 Guangzhou Governments of Sun Yat-sen

Government	Term of Rule	Reason for Creation	Reason for Dissolution
First government	August 1917–May 1918	Rump parliament, dissolved in Beijing, convenes in Guangzhou	Loss of military support
Second government	April 1921–June 1922	Military infighting allows rump parliament in Guangzhou to reinstate Sun	Chen Jiongming allied with Zhili Clique to force Sun's resignation
Third government	February 1923–March 1925	Yunnan and Guangxi warlords, and defectors from Chen's army oust Chen to restore Sun to power	Death of Sun Yat-sen

Table 15.3   Beijing Government (1916–20)

Period	President	Premier	Legislature	Key Issue
1916	Li Yuanhong (leader of 1911 Revolution in Wuhan)	Duan Qirui	Nationalist Party	Rivalry among president, premier, and legislature for control of Beijing government following death of Yuan Shikai.
July 1917	Failed Qing restoration			Beijing government disintegrated over whether to enter World War I and to accept Japanese loans. Attempt to restore dynasty during the power vacuum collapsed when Duan and Feng cooperated to restore the Beijing government.
August 1917	Feng Guozhang (Zhili Clique)	Duan Qirui (Anhui Clique)	Duan supporters	Sun Yat-sen formed the first Guangzhou government, creating a rival government in South China.
				Former members of the Yuan Shikai's *guanxi* network split into rival cliques over how to respond.
				Anhui Clique supported military reunification. Zhili Clique supported political unification.
1917–20	Figurehead	Figurehead		Duan in control from behind the scenes.

was personal, not institutional. It followed the traditional lines of *guanxi*. With the Qing's fall and the collapse of central institutions, the main ties holding China together were *guanxi*. With the exception of the Manchurian Clique, the primary Chinese factions were offshoots of Yuan Shikai's *guanxi* network, the so-called Beiyang Clique, which, in turn, was an offshoot of Li Hongzhang's Self-strengthening *guanxi* network. "Beiyang" referred to Yuan Shikai's Beiyang Army, which had formed the nucleus of his power but had been decapitated with his death.

Decapitation of a *guanxi* network meant a power struggle among its competing components and rival networks to reconstitute a personal power base under a successor. The lack of institutional mechanisms for succession in China has made the political process opaque to Chinese and foreigners alike. *Guanxi* networks are inherently secretive, since power revealed is power diminished. Conceptually, one can think of a *guanxi* network as a vast, prolific family tree, with all branches and generations alive simultaneously. The original ancestor sits at the head of the network of connections. He can call upon the next generation, or branches of the tree, who in turn call upon their subsidiary branches, and so on, even though he does not necessarily know the extent and strength of the *guanxi* networks of his subordinates; nor do the subordinates know the full extent or strength of the networks of their superiors.

Upon Yuan Shikai's death, Vice-president Li Yuanhong succeeded to the presidency on 7 June 1916, naming Duan

Qirui, Yuan's aide and powerful Beijing warlord, as his premier. There was an initial dispute over which constitution should prevail—the original 1912 constitution or Yuan's 1914 document providing much stronger presidential powers. President Li agreed to return to the 1912 constitution and restore the original National Assembly in exchange for promises by the southern provinces to rejoin the Republic. This compromise kept China nominally unified during late 1916 and early 1917, but the Republican government had authority, while warlords and their armies monopolized the real power.

Li Yuanhong and Duan Qirui both lacked the prestige of Yuan Shikai and proved unable to reglue the Republic. China fell into a ten-year period of civil war and chaos as Yuan's generals competed to reconstitute his *guanxi* network under their personal control. China quickly divided into regional governments under local warlords. The country also divided on North–South lines: In the North, a succession of warlord governments took control of Beijing; in the South, Sun Yat-sen founded his own republican government in Guangzhou, heavily dependent on the warlord Chen Jiongming.

Duan Qirui, who became the leader of the Anhui Clique, served as Yuan's minister of war, as his personal envoy to convince Li Yuanhong to serve as vice-president, and as the prime minister. By 1914, he became the most powerful supporter of Yuan Shikai, but his control over the promotions in the

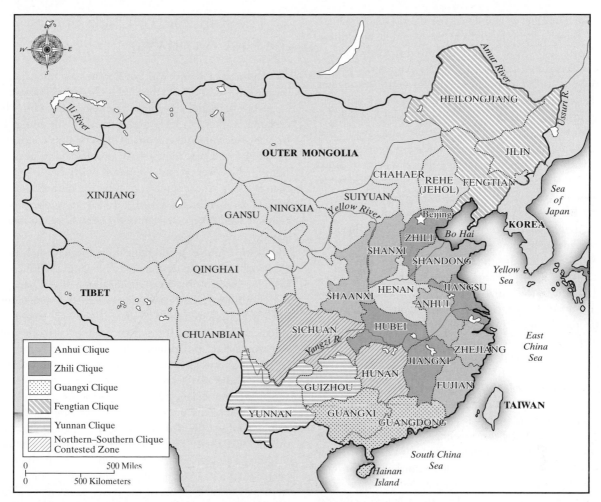

Map 15.3 Warlord Governments (1917–18)

Beiyang Army meant that many of the younger officers were more loyal to him than to Yuan. When Yuan tried to reassert his control over the military, Duan responded by opposing Yuan's plans to become monarch. The ensuing power struggle lasted until Yuan's sudden death. Although Vice-president Li Yuanhong assumed the presidency, Duan retained control over the Beiyang Army and sought to fund his army through his connections with Japan.

In the fall of 1916, another associate of Yuan Shikai, Cao Rulin, who had studied law at Waseda and Chūō universities in Tokyo and had diplomatic connections through his service in the Qing Foreign Ministry, presented Duan with a plan to reunify China by manipulating the foreign powers. Cao pledged his diplomatic connections to negotiate Japanese loans to underwrite Duan's army. To placate Britain, France, and the United States, Duan justified this

military modernization by acceding to the Entente's demands to enter World War I against Germany. Duan then turned to Japan for massive war loans. The newly modernized armies, however, would be used to reunify China, not to fight in Europe. The Japanese, in turn, wanted to maximize their sphere of influence in China while the European powers were preoccupied with the war in Europe. In return for the Nishihara loans negotiated from 1917 to 1918, Japan received valuable mining, banking, railway, armaments, and other contracts. No accurate records of the loans were ever made public because the Japan connection was extremely controversial.

Premier Duan Qirui's plan to dominate China backfired. When he declared war on Germany and Austro-Hungary without parliamentary approval, the legislature demanded his resignation. President Li Yuanhong agreed to resign, but a number of mainly northern pro-Duan provinces declared their independence from the Republic and threatened to attack Beijing. During the infighting, there was a brief attempt from 1 July to 12 July 1917 to revive the Qing dynasty by restoring to the throne the former Xuantong emperor (Henry Puyi). Duan put an end to this attempt by sending his army to Beijing. Li Yuanhong was compelled to resign, but was replaced by Duan's Beiyang Clique rival, Feng Guozhang. When Duan convened a new National Assembly packed with loyal supporters, the political parties of South China formed a separate government in Guangzhou under Sun Yat-sen. This was Sun's first Guangzhou government.

The Beiyang Army then split into the Anhui and Zhili Cliques. Duan wanted to launch a military expedition to suppress the Guangzhou government and his supporters became known as the Anhui Clique, named after his native province. His rivals became known as the Zhili Clique, named for the native province of its leader, another protégé of Yuan Shikai, Feng Guozhang, who favored a diplomatic solution to China's North–South division that did not require Japanese financing. Duan's inability to restore central control over Hunan and Sichuan provinces led to his forced resignation in the fall of 1917. But the Zhili Clique did not remain in power for long. Pressure from Duan forced the government to resume its military campaign to pacify Hubei and Hunan. On 19 March 1918, the majority of the Beiyang Army generals and eighteen military governors demanded that Duan be restored as premier, which occurred on 23 March 1918. Support from the Manchurian warlord and leader of the Fengtian Clique, Zhang Zuolin, also known for his Japanese connections, helped tip the balance of power in Duan's favor.

Thereafter, Duan ruled through a combination of military and civil authority. His Japanese-funded modernized military force, known as the Northwestern Frontier Army, was intended to reunify China, while his Anfu Club, named for Anfu Street, the location of its headquarters, marshaled supporters to dominate the parliament elected in 1918, the so-called Anfu Parliament that replaced the original 1912 parliament. Anfu Club discipline did not endure for long but succumbed to factionalism. Duan's insistence on a military rather than a negotiated reunification of China angered many, while his financial connections with Japan alienated Chinese nationalists. In the fall of 1918, Feng Guozhang resigned from the presidency and Duan Qirui from the premiership, but Duan continued to dominate the government from behind the scenes for the next two years. His popularity plummeted, however, as a result of his dealings with Japan, intrigues at home, and negotiations at the Paris Peace Conference terminating World War I.

V. The Republic of China Enters the First World War

The outbreak of World War I in Europe had immediate ramifications in East Asia. Japan carried out its obligations to Great Britain under the Anglo-Japanese alliance of 1902 by declaring war on Germany and Austria. By the end of 1914, Japanese forces had taken control of Germany's concession in Shandong province. Soon Tokyo consolidated its position by signing the Twenty-one Demands with Beijing. On 14 March 1917, almost three years after the outbreak of World War I, China finally severed diplomatic relations with Germany and Austria. Five months later, China formally declared war on 14 August 1917.

Many Chinese intellectuals and reformers, such as Liang Qichao, had long advocated that China join the Entente as a first step toward obtaining juridical equality. Chen Duxiu (Ch'en Tu-hsiu), the future leader of the Chinese Communist Party, supported the war effort in the hope that it would enhance China's world standing. Early participation in the war would have positioned China favorably at the anticipated peace negotiations to demand the restoration of the German and Austrian concessions.

China immediately received financial benefits for declaring war: Beijing discontinued paying Germany's and Austria's combined one-fifth share of the Boxer indemnity mandated by the 1901 Boxer Protocol. Thereafter, the United States, Belgium, France, Great Britain, Italy, Japan, Portugal, and, later, Russia all agreed to allow China to defer for five years all or part of their shares of the Boxer payments. These savings greatly increased the budget of the Beijing government, which was constantly in debt. Yet, the Chinese contribution to the war was minimal. China sent no troops to Europe. Approximately 100,000 Chinese laborers did travel to Europe to work for the Entente powers, but most of them had contracted to go before China declared war.

Japanese diplomats quickly foresaw the implications of China's declaration of war vis-à-vis Germany's concession in Shandong. To ensure that Japan did not lose its gains from the Twenty-one Demands, as had happened after the First Sino-Japanese War, Tokyo signed a series of secret agreements with most of the other Entente powers supporting the Twenty-one Demands and Japan's claims to Shandong. On 21 February 1917, Japan signed a secret agreement with Great Britain in which London promised to support Tokyo's claim to the Shandong concession in return for Japan's support for British claims to all of Germany's South Pacific islands. On 5 March 1917, Russia agreed to recognize the Twenty-one Demands in return for Japan's recognition of

Russia's preeminent position in Outer Mongolia. On 6 March 1917, Japan secretly agreed with France to work to persuade China to break off diplomatic relations with Germany and impound German ships. On 28 March 1917, Japan and Italy signed a similar secret agreement. Finally, on 2 November 1917, the United States and Japan exchanged what became known as the Lansing-Ishii Notes; Tokyo interpreted these notes to mean that the United States supported Japan's legitimate economic interests in China, while Washington emphasized Tokyo's promise to uphold the Open Door Policy. The United States was the only major power not to recognize Japan's Twenty-one Demands. Nevertheless, all of this diplomacy supported the Japanese claim over the Shandong concessions by treaties either tacitly recognizing Japan's economic interests in China or explicitly recognizing the Twenty-one Demands.

In September 1918, just three months prior to the formal beginning of the Paris Peace Conference, the Beijing government signed two additional secret agreements with Japan, recognizing the validity of those sections of the Twenty-one Demands pertaining to Shandong and to Japanese-funded railway construction. On 24 September 1918, Tokyo and Beijing exchanged confidential notes on the administration of Shandong and the construction of two new Japanese-financed railway lines. On 28 September 1918, they signed another secret agreement setting the railway loan and providing an immediate $9 million advance. Chinese acceptance of the money meant that under international law Beijing recognized the continued validity of the Twenty-one Demands as embodied in its 25 May 1915 treaty with Tokyo. This undermined the Chinese argument that Japan had forced the 1915 agreement on China as well as China's case for direct restitution of the Shandong concession from Germany, which was Beijing's original goal in declaring war on Germany and Austria.

Like Yuan Shikai, who signed agreements that endured long after his death, the northern warlord Duan Qirui, who was repeatedly in and out of power during the 1917–18 period, cut a deal with Japan that gave him immediate cash at the expense of his country's long-term interests. Once these deals were signed, they became international law. While preoccupied with these secret dealings with Japan, the Beijing government missed an historic opportunity to take advantage of the Russian Revolution in 1917 to restore Chinese sovereignty over Russia's vast concessions in Manchuria. This, however, would not have benefited Duan directly, but rather his rival, the Manchurian warlord Zhang Zuolin, so nothing came of it. In the warlord period, China was fractured by rival warlord *guanxi* networks whose primary interests were regional, not national.

The Sino-Japanese agreements were kept secret not only from the Chinese people, but also from China's own diplomatic representatives at the Paris Peace Conference. China's lead representative, V. K. Wellington Koo, apparently was not informed of their terms until January 1919. Although Washington had not recognized the Twenty-one Demands, it did recognize the rule of international law. China's own diplomacy left the American diplomats little room for maneuver. Not only had Japan signed agreements with all of the major Allied powers backing its claim to the Shandong concession, but it had concluded treaties with China during 1915 and 1918 that did likewise. Although the Chinese delegates tried to argue that Japan had compelled China to sign the Sino-Japanese agreements disposing of the Shandong concessions, Beijing's acceptance of a cash advance from Japan in 1918 undermined this argument. As the reformer Liang Qichao pointed out after the conclusion the Paris Peace Conference, the 1918 agreements rendered "China's trump card . . . at once ineffective."[5] When pieces of the convoluted diplomacy became public, the visceral popular outrage greatly amplified its importance.

Conclusions

The collapse of the Qing dynasty put institutional change at center stage on the political agenda. Determining the future course of Chinese politics was an inherently contentious but inescapable issue. In the absence of legitimate political institutions, these momentous decisions were ultimately resolved through political assassinations and on the battlefield, where military leaders marshaled rival armies and cobbled together rival governments on the basis of *guanxi*. For several decades, warlords buttressed by their own personal followings vied to control China. When warlords died, their followers dispersed, only to coalesce in some new combination around another. Therefore, few warlords left any institutional legacy. Their exclusive focus on the military elements of power meant little progress enhancing effective government administration. Only the Nationalists and, later, the Communists made significant progress on institution building.

Following the creation of a Republican government, President Yuan Shikai tried to install himself as China's new emperor. But the attempt found no public support. Yuan Shikai's sudden death in 1916 meant the decapitation of his vast *guanxi* network. His followers vied to take power for themselves. The Anhui Clique under Duan Qirui, the Zhili Clique under Feng Guozhang, the Manchurian Clique under Zhang Zuolin, and Li Yuanhong, Yuan's successor, played an intricate game of political chess to control North China. All but Zhang Zuolin were rival offshoots of Yuan Shikai's *guanxi* network. While these were the main North China warlords, in the period from 1912 to 1928 there were more than 1,300 Chinese in control of a personal army and a territorial base, meeting the minimum qualifications for a warlord.

Divisions between North and South China had become increasingly apparent ever since the Taiping Rebellion. The Taipings, the 1911 Revolution, and Sun Yat-sen's Guangzhou governments were all South China attempts to overthrow North China rule. In the final years of Qing rule, North–South divisions deepened when the South refused to rally behind the Manchus to expel the foreigners in the Boxer Uprising. During the early Republic, intermittent civil war undermined stability in the North. Competing factions shifted in and out of control over Beijing, which remained a symbol of central control and governmental legitimacy. In South China, Sun Yat-sen's Nationalist Party led a separatist movement that opposed Yuan Shikai's dicta-

torial powers, particularly after he tried to install himself as emperor. A succession of governments attempted to rule from Guangzhou. Most were under warlords allied with Sun's Nationalist Party.

The beginning of World War I in Europe seemed to offer China an unexpected opportunity to regain lost rights and privileges from the foreign powers. Chinese efforts first focused on Germany and Austria, the two central powers, which were quickly dispossessed of their concessions in China. The Bolshevik Revolution (1917) and the ensuing Russian Civil War (1918–22) seemed to offer the Chinese the chance to retake Russia's concessions. But with the European powers and the United States preoccupied with the war in Europe, Japan stepped in to fill the power vacuum in China. Japan offered Yuan Shikai and Duan Qirui the funds they needed to stay in power in exchange for expanded Japanese influence in China. However, once signed, these agreements obligated China under international law.

BIBLIOGRAPHY

Chen, Jerome. *Yuan Shih-k'ai.* 2nd ed. Stanford, CA: Stanford University Press, 1972.

Ch'i, Hsi-sheng. *Warlord Politics in China, 1916–1928.* Stanford, CA: Stanford University Press, 1976.

Deane, Hugh. *Good Deeds & Gunboats: Two Centuries of American-Chinese Encounters.* San Francisco: China Books & Periodicals, 1990.

Elleman, Bruce A. *Diplomacy and Deception: The Secret History of Sino-Soviet Diplomatic Relations, 1917–1927.* Armonk, NY: M. E. Sharpe, 1997.

———*Wilson and China: A Revised History of the Shandong Question.* Armonk, NY: M. E. Sharpe, 2002.

Ewing, Thomas. *Between the Hammer and the Anvil? Chinese and Russian Policies in Outer Mongolia 1911–1921.* Bloomington, IN: Research Institute for Inner Asian Studies, 1980.

Geyer, Dietrich. *Russian Imperialism: The Interaction of Domestic and Foreign Policy, 1860–1914.* Translated by Bruce Little. New Haven, CT: Yale University Press, 1987.

Goldstein, Melvyn C. *A History of Modern Tibet: The Demise of the Lamaist State.* Berkeley: University of California Press, 1989.

———*The Snow Lion and the Dragon: China, Tibet, and the Dalai Lama.* Berkeley: University of California Press, 1997.

Grunfeld, A. Tom. *The Making of Modern Tibet.* Rev. edition. Armonk, NY: M. E. Sharpe, 1996.

McCord, Edward A. *The Power of the Gun: The Emergence of Modern Chinese Warlordism.* Berkeley: University of California Press, 1993.

Nathan, Andrew J. *Peking Politics, 1918–1923: Factionalism and the Failure of Constitutionalism.* Berkeley: University of California Press, 1976.

Paine, S. C. M. *Imperial Rivals: China, Russia, and Their Disputed Frontier.* Armonk, NY: M. E. Sharpe, 1996.

Power, Brian. *The Puppet Emperor: The Life of Pu Yi, the Last Emperor of China.* New York: Universe, 1986.

Price, Ernest Batson. *The Russo-Japanese Treaties of 1907–1916 Concerning Manchuria and Mongolia.* 1933. Reprint, New York: AMS Press, 1971.

Robertson, James Oliver. *No Third Choice: Progressives in Republican Politics, 1916–1921.* New York: Garland, 1983.

Schiffrin, Harold. *Sun Yat-sen: Reluctant Revolutionary.* Boston: Little, Brown, 1980.

Sharman, Lyon. *Sun Yat-sen: His Life and Its Meaning.* Stanford, CA: Stanford University Press, 1968.

Sheridan, James E. *China in Disintegration: The Republican Era in Chinese History, 1912–1949.* New York: Free Press, 1975.

Tang, Peter S. H. *Russian and Soviet Policy in Manchuria and Outer Mongolia 1911–1930.* Durham, NC: Duke University Press, 1959.

Tuttle, Gray. *Tibetan Buddhists and the Making of Modern China.* New York: Columbia University Press, 2005.

Wei, Julie Lee, Ramon H. Myers, and Donald G. Gillin. *Prescriptions for Saving China: Selected Writings of Sun Yat-sen.* Stanford, CA: Hoover Institution Press, 1994.

Wilbur, C. Martin. *Sun Yat-sen: Frustrated Patriot.* New York: Columbia University Press, 1976.

Young, Ernest P. *The Presidency of Yuan Shih-k'ai: Liberalism and Dictatorship in Early Republican China.* Ann Arbor: University of Michigan Press, 1977.

Yu, George, T. *Party Politics in Republican China: The Kuomintang, 1912–1924.* Berkeley: University of California Press, 1966.

NOTES

1. Kuo Mojo, *The Works of Kuo,* vol. 1 trans. in Kai-yu Hsu, *Twentieth Century Chinese Poetry* (Garden City, NY: Doubleday, 1963), 29.
2. Sun Yat-sen, *The Vital Problem of China* (Taipei: China Cultural Service, 1953), 55.
3. Cited in Julie Lee Wei, Ramon H. Myers, and Donald G. Gillin, *Prescriptions for Saving China: Selected Writings of Sun Yat-sen* (Stanford, CA: Hoover Institution Press, 1994), 222–36.
4. Cited in Lyon Sharman, *Sun Yat-sen: His Life and Its Meaning* (Stanford, CA: Stanford University Press, 1968), 286–9.
5. Cited in Bruce A. Elleman, *Wilson and China: A Revised History of the Shandong Question* (Armonk, NY: M. E. Sharpe, 2002), 27.

Chronology

1897	Germany occupies Jiaozhou Harbor
1898	Germany establishes concession at Qingdao on Jiaozhou Bay
1914–18	World War I
1914	Yuan Shikai declares Chinese neutrality in World War I
	Japan declares war on Germany and Austria
	Japan occupies the German concession in the Shandong Peninsula
1915	Japan presents Twenty-one Demands, becomes Day of National Humiliation in China; beginning of the anti-Japanese movement
1917	Duan Qirui's government declares war on Germany and Austria
	Bolshevik Revolution in Russia
1918	Wilson issues Fourteen Points
	Duan Qirui's government signs secret agreements with Japan
1919	Versailles Peace Conference
	May Fourth Movement
1921	Establishment of the Chinese Communist Party
1921–2	Washington Conference
1922	Japan returns the Shandong concession to China

16

Versailles and Its Aftermath

When things come to this, what can they
do to us! What can they do to us!
Fortunately we have this star, a tiny point of light
Leading the traveler, hopeless to death,
across the desert night!
With the present destroyed,
The future shines before us.
Cast life aside and advance! Walk toward
the bright and brilliant end of our journey![1]

Anonymous anarchist, 1923

The Hundred Days' Reform, the fall of the Qing dynasty, and the three revolutions of the early Republican period fed a spreading intellectual ferment in China. At the settlement of World War I, U.S. President Woodrow Wilson's emphasis on national self-determination raised expectations in China for the return of foreign concessions, and particularly those of the defeated powers. Concession areas became an increasing focus not only for their infringement on Chinese sovereignty but because they accounted for a disproportionate percentage of China's modern sector dominated in this period by textiles. (See the feature below.) When the United States failed to support China's preferred method to return Germany's Shandong concessions to Chinese sovereignty, Chinese public opinion became vicerally anti-American. An outpouring of anti-Western and anti-Japanese Chinese nationalism marked the beginning of the May Fourth Movement. Chinese increasingly turned to the one great power not implicated in the Shandong imbroglio: Soviet Russia. Marxist study groups proliferated and, within two years, the Chinese Communist Party came into being with essential Soviet guidance and funding.

SILK PRODUCTION

In the first quarter of the twentieth century, silk remained China's primary export, to be overtaken by Manchuria's soybean products in the late 1920s. In 1920 silk goods accounted for 19 percent of Chinese exports, soybean products 13 percent, and tea less than 2 percent. Japanese competition, the invention of rayon, the Great Depression, and the refinement of cottons wreaked havoc on China's silk industry. Silk is perhaps China's oldest export, so old that the earliest East–West trade route became known as the Silk Route. According to legend, silk production became important as a result of the imperial patronage of the Yellow Emperor (r. 2697–2597 BC), himself perhaps an invention of Daoists of the third century BC. The Chinese have been weaving and exporting silk for thousands of years. During the Qing dynasty, Jiangsu and Jiangxi were the primary silk-producing provinces, where weavers increasingly lived in towns, particularly in Suzhou, Hangzhou, and Nanjing, and produced beautiful satins and velvets for luxurious clothing, and tapestry weaves for scrolls and woven portraits, as well as simpler items for regular clothing.

The production of silk cloth was the culmination of a long, labor-intensive, and highly specialized process. The mulberry-eating silkworm produced most silk. In the warmer parts of China, it reproduced nearly continuously

Continued

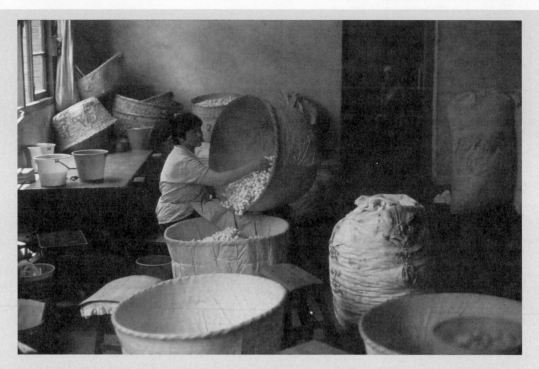

The production of silk in China dates back perhaps 5,000 years. After the *Bombyx mori* moth lays approximately 500 eggs, the larvae hatch and begin to eat mulberry leaves for about a month—becoming about 10,000 times heavier in the process—before the adult worm begins to spin a cocoon so as to go through metamorphosis into a moth. For its size, silk thread is incredibly strong, and in 1815 a New Orleans dentist first recommended that silk floss be used for cleaning teeth.

throughout the year, but it was susceptible to numerous devastating diseases. Careful monitoring and meticulous sanitation reduced the risk. One ounce of silkworm eggs produced 35,000 pounds of mature worms that ate one ton of mulberry leaves to produce 140 pounds of cocoons yielding 12 pounds of reeled silk. Silkworms matured in about forty days, when they made the desired cocoons, harvested a week later after the caterpillar transformed into a pupa. Cocoons were then exposed to the sun or subjected to a short steam treatment to kill the pupa and then air dried for up to two months before the silk could be reeled.

Reeling combined the threads from two or more cocoons to create raw silk. Different types of cloth required different thread thicknesses. Before reeling, cocoons were sorted by their quality and then softened through boiling so that the exposed end of the thread could be attached to the reel for winding. Thereafter, the silk was rewound to form skeins of uniform gauge and weight to be sent to a specialized shop for twisting. The degree and direction of the twist helped determine the appearance of the finished product. Although silk weaving techniques improved during the Qing dynasty, until the late nineteenth century the looms changed little. Setting up the loom, an extremely time-consuming and difficult process, entailed running from 90 to over 400 threads per inch to create the lengthwise threads for the finished cloth. Up to seven different crosswise threads created the pattern. Some woven silks were then dyed, while others were woven from dyed threads.

Over time there was increasing specialization of tasks: Silkworm farmers raised the caterpillars and then reeled their silk; others boiled and cleaned the reeled silk; still others dried and dyed the cleaned silk; the complicated threading of looms also became a highly skilled task; finally, other experts wove the cloth. Within the last two categories, there was further specialization by type of cloth being produced: figured patterns, plain weave, gauze, and brocade. Dye shops specialized by color: some devoted to blue dyes, others to red, some to bleaching and others to multicolored cloth. Dyeing required repeated phases of soaking, dyeing, pounding, and drying. The shrinkage during the dyeing process required careful pressing thereafter, another specialized occupation. By the 1920s, Shanghai dominated the silk reeling industry. From the late 1920s on, however, Japanese competition contributed to a decline in Chinese silk weaving.

I. Political Ferment and New Ideas

From the time of the Hundred Days' Reform on, people increasingly questioned old ideas and sought new ones. This meant a massive influx of foreign ideas and books and a noticeable exodus of Chinese seeking an education in Japan and the West. The Hundred Days' Reform and late-Qing reforms opened a discussion on parliamentary rule. With the fall of the dynasty, this discussion spread. Kang Youwei and Liang Qichao remained ardent supporters of public assemblies in order to remove the evils of private rule by autocrats or oligarchic rule by bureaucracies. China's initial experiences with public assemblies, however, did not go smoothly, as demonstrated by the three revolutions following in rapid succession upon the collapse of the Qing dynasty. Kang's and Liang's ideas did not provide a way to curtail the power of the independent militaries that dominated the scene in Republican China. They focused on the civil side of political power, not its interconnection with the military side.

At the turn of the century, the scholar Yan Fu translated key works of Western and especially British philosophy into Chinese. Most influential were those of Adam Smith, John Stuart Mill, Charles Darwin, and Herbert Spencer, who provided the analytical frameworks of laissez-faire economics, utilitarianism, biological evolution, and social Darwinism. Adam Smith, a Scotsman, explained economic prosperity in terms of individual competition to create economically efficient decisions. For Smith, prosperity welled up from below, with each individual making sound decisions, rather than flowing down from on high from an emperor in touch with the cosmos.

The British economist and philosopher John Stuart Mill made utility, not ethics, his core value. Whereas traditional Chinese philosophy focused on harmonizing human relations, Mill recommended decisions based on utility to the greatest number. According to Mill, freedom would yield correct principles as individuals strove for truth and false ideas fell by the wayside, but Mill's ideas concerning liberties, rights, and individualism contrasted with the traditional Chinese emphasis on interlocking social obligations and the primacy of group over individual rights.

Meanwhile, the British philosopher Herbert Spencer took the naturalist Charles Darwin's ideas concerning natural selection among organisms and applied this framework to human societies, so that the survival of the fittest applied not just to species but to nation-states and cultures. This philosophy became known as "social Darwinism." Many Chinese latched on to these ideas to explain both why China, especially in recent years, had not done well in the struggle among nations and how to extricate it from this predicament.

Whereas traditional Chinese philosophy explained political, social, and economic changes in terms of a balance between the forces of *yin* and *yang* in the cosmic order, these new Western ideas suggested that the pursuit of individual interests could be regulated by law to produce economic prosperity. Yan Fu concluded that freedom and democracy seemed to harmonize individual and group interests. Conversely, a failure to embrace these changes would condemn China to continuing decline. Yan's translations influenced a generation of Chinese intellectuals including the novelist Lu Xun, the professor and statesman Hu Shi (see Chapter 17), and the future leader of China, Mao Zedong.

At the turn of the century, as heavy industry took off in the West, more Chinese became interested in science. This was a natural extension of the technically minded preoccupations of the Self-strengtheners. Chinese of many different ideological persuasions latched on to science as essential for their country's future. Indeed, this conclusion has only strengthened over time. The analytical framework of science differed greatly from the traditional Chinese analytical framework embodied in the eight-legged essay. (See Table 16.1.) While the form of the eight-legged essay is almost poetic in nature, and is defined by a chronological sequence of earlier and then later parts, the Western mode of rhetoric is

Table 16.1   Chinese and Western Rhetoric

Eight-Legged Essay	Western Rhetoric
break open topic	background
receiving the topic	problem
beginning the discussion	hypothesis or proposed proposition
initial leg	means of testing
transition leg	evidence
middle leg	arguments as to what the evidence means
later leg	refutation of possible counterarguments
conclusion	conclusions and recommendations

Notes: The eight-legged essay is the traditional analytical format of the Confucian examination system. See Table 4.1, "Eight-Legged Essay Format," for an example of such an essay (Benjamin A. Elman, *A Cultural History of Civil Examinations in Late Imperial China* [Berkeley: University of California Press, 2000], 389–90). Copyright © 2000, The Regents of the University of California.

Source: Listed under "Western Rhetoric" is the standard organization of a scientific essay used in the West (Richard E. Nisbett, *The Geography of Thought: How Asians and Westerners Think Differently . . . and Why* [New York: Free Press, 2003], 196).

geared to making a proof based on evidence and deductive reasoning. The parts are defined not by chronology but by purpose and methodology. Each framework steered the mind into a specific way to analyze the world.

Anarchism, which came to China via Japan, became another powerful strain of thinking. Anarchists assassinated the occasional Manchu bureaucrat or imperial relative. But their importance was more social than political. Their stress on equality led to a complete reexamination of China's hierarchical social structure and to demands for the emancipation of the individual, which, in practice, meant the liberation of the individual from family obligations. In traditional China, these obligations constituted the social glue holding society together. For the anarchists, this was not social glue but enslavement. Transformation of the family entailed the liberation of women, who were the greatest beneficiaries of the whirlwind of ideas circulating through China. Within a generation, supporters of footbinding disappeared and the education of girls became accepted by virtually the entire political spectrum.

Amid this sea of change and cacophony of ideas, there were many concerned about retaining a Chinese identity. Self-criticism coexisted with veneration for a great people and a great culture. The Japanese had also faced this paradox when they embarked upon their westernization program, but they developed the concept of "national essence," which the Chinese then borrowed. National essence, however defined, provided an alternative to Confucianism and imperial orthodoxy. It would be based on a shared history and a common people, which together produced a shared national character. This idea eventually nourished a sense of nationalism, but the content of that nationalism would be a long time in forming, arguably continuing to the present day.

II. The Paris Peace Conference Examines the Shandong Question

Against this intellectual backdrop at home, world events continued apace. The Chinese public's expectations at the postwar peace talks were extraordinarily high. The Republic of China had joined the war anticipating that it would share in the fruits of victory and that diplomatic success in Europe would help rally a divided country around the central government. In January 1918, President Wilson made public his Fourteen Points for the postwar international order, emphasizing national self-determination and an end to secret diplomacy. This raised the hopes of the disenfranchised worldwide. Yet, under international law, China's treaty obli-

Mining engineer and, later, U.S. President Herbert Hoover was living in Tianjin, China, during the 1900 Boxer Uprising. Soon after the Boxers were defeated, this picture was taken showing a U.S. food distribution station for the poor in Beijing (circa 1902), an early example of international aid. Later, Hoover helped extend food aid to other countries, and in October 1914 he organized the Commission for Relief in Belgium to provide much-needed food aid to war-torn Europe.

gations could be altered only with the mutual consent of all the signatories.

At Paris, China, not Japan, was in a weak position. Unlike China, Japan had joined the Entente from the beginning, participated in the fighting, and expended large sums neutralizing German interests in Asia. Many members of the Entente considered the cancellation or deferment of the bulk of the Boxer Indemnity to have been more than sufficient recompense for China's minimal contribution to the war effort. Yet, at the opening of the talks, China's delegation asked the participating nations to discard almost a century of international treaties that China had signed under varying degrees of coercion to eliminate the unequal treaties, as Japan had done earlier.

The Chinese delegation had two sets of proposals, the first dealing with the return of Shandong from Germany and the second encompassing a much broader array of issues concerning "Re-adjustments with Friendly States." (See Map 16.1.) The Chinese delegation demanded that the foreign powers respect China's territorial integrity, not interfere in its domestic political affairs, and grant it full control over its economy. Many of these proposals were contentious, such as

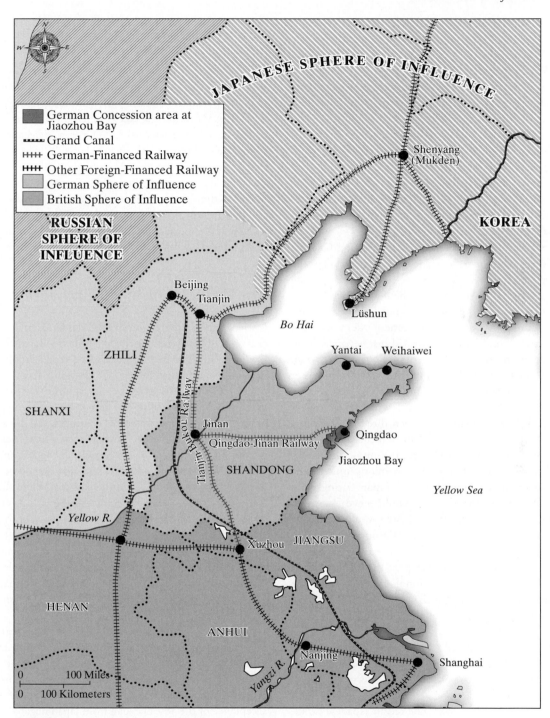

Map 16.1   German Concessions

the internationalization of the Manchurian railways and rivers and the gradual internationalization of the foreign settlements in preparation for their return to China. China's political proposals included the elimination of all legation guards, the removal of foreign troops, and the abolition of extraterritoriality. Finally, fiscal independence included the full restoration to China of the right to set and administer its own tariffs. If enacted, the Chinese delegation's proposals would have revolutionized China's international position. These proposals were modeled on Japan's achievement of juridical equality in 1894. But in contrast to Japan, China wanted juridical equality before it had a capable central government, let alone a functioning nationwide westernized judiciary or legal code.

In late January 1919, when the unsuspecting Chinese delegation first raised the issue of the direct restitution of the Shandong concession, the Japanese delegation revealed the heretofore secret 1918 agreements. These agreements jeopardized China's entire list of proposals, not just the few concerning Shandong, because the agreements demonstrated that the current Chinese government had just negotiated and signed treaties based on China's acceptance of the status quo.

At issue in the Shandong question was not whether Japan would retain the concession indefinitely, but whether Germany would return it to China directly or indirectly through Japan. The distinction between direct and indirect restitution was important to China, since if the Chinese delegation succeeded in gaining direct restitution of Shandong, this would have been tantamount to revoking unilaterally China's international agreements with Japan dating from 1915–18. Direct restitution also would have increased China's international standing, since China would have been dealing directly with Germany, a great European power, instead of Japan, which China persisted in treating as an inferior. Conversely, for Japan to take part in the restitution would grant Japan the international standing that the Chinese had consistently sought to deny it. For all of these reason, the Chinese regarded receiving Shandong from Japan as a great loss of face.

The Japanese were equally concerned with face. The Japanese delegation reminded their Chinese counterparts that Germany had been part of the Triple Intervention forcing Japan to restore the Liaodong Peninsula to China in 1895 after the First Sino-Japanese War. The recent Japanese expulsion of Germany from the Shandong concessions had partly settled the score. In Paris, Japan wanted to finish the job by forcing Germany to lose face by ceding Shandong to Japan, after which Japan would gain face by making the final return to China. For both China and Japan, Shandong was but the pretext in a long and bitter struggle fought diplomatically by means of face over the underlying issue of regional dominance. Most Westerners did not perceive this Sino-Japanese contest over face.

Because the transcripts of the Paris negotiations were kept secret, there was widespread public misunderstanding that the permanent cession of Shandong to Japan was at issue. This was never the case. Rather, the dispute focused on its direct or indirect return. The Chinese delegation at Paris deliberately obscured this by emphasizing instead the emotional importance of Shandong to the Chinese people and accusing Japan of wanting to retain the territory permanently. Although the Chinese delegation lost the diplomatic conflict, it won the propaganda war. It successfully secured for China the moral high ground, despite a far more complicated reality.

III. The Shandong Controversy

China's and Japan's incompatible demands at Paris meant that as soon as they broached the Shandong question, face would be in play. Beijing ordered its representatives not to bring up Shandong. Instead, Wellington Koo, who knew nothing of the 1918 secret treaties, ignored this order to demand the direct return of Shandong. The Japanese revelation of the 1918 agreements completely undermined his case.

Japan's demands for German possessions included the unconditional transfer of the Shandong concession, the railway running from Qingdao to Jinan, and the German islands in the Pacific Ocean north of the equator. When Wellington Koo tried to have Germany return the Shandong concession directly to China, the Japanese delegate revealed that Beijing and Tokyo had already concluded negotiations detailing the Japanese plans to restore the concessions to China. During the next three months, much additional information was released, including Japan's secret treaties with Great Britain, Russia, France, and Italy, as well as detailed information on its 1915 and 1918 agreements with China.

These documents undermined the American delegation's initial position on Shandong, forcing on it an entirely different negotiating strategy. Although the United States would have refused to recognize the secret Sino-Japanese agreements had they been coerced, the Beijing government's acceptance of the advance loan from Japan negated this interpretation of events. As British Prime Minister David Lloyd George was quick to point out, these obligations could not simply be ignored, since a world war had just been fought to uphold the sanctity of treaties. President Wilson took the lead in attempting to foster regional stability in East Asia, and to meet some of China's demands by encouraging China and Japan to negotiate a new treaty that would supersede the 1915 and 1918 agreements. He tried to craft a compromise that would, on the one hand, take into account Japan's commercial interests, which included the concession in Qingdao and the major thoroughfare through the province, the Qingdao-Jinan Railway, but would, on the other hand, guarantee China's sovereignty and political independence.

The Japanese delegation argued that full justice should be accorded to Japan, based "upon her sacrifices and achievements and upon the fact of actual occupation, involving [a] sense of national honor,"[2] that is, face. President Wilson tried to convince Japan to forego the Twenty-one Demands and to develop future relations based on respect for Chinese sovereignty. In particular, he wanted Japan to renounce all political privileges in China. He proposed circumventing the Twenty-one Demands with a Japanese statement that it would uphold Chinese sovereignty. The Japanese delegation agreed to Wilson's suggestion. In accordance with Wilson's compromise, Japan's relations with China would be regulated by the League of Nations, which Wilson assumed incorrectly that the United States would join.

Wilson convinced the Japanese to limit themselves to certain economic rights in Shandong, foregoing any military or political rights. This diplomatic solution avoided referring back to and thereby recognizing the 1915 and 1918 Sino-Japanese agreements infringing on Chinese sovereignty. But it did not resolve the underlying conflict concerning face: Giving face can produce a win-win solution, provided each side gives face to the other. The Japanese government opened a way to do this by agreeing to return the concessions, but the Chinese government was too weak to be equally magnanimous about the method of return. Weak Chinese governments are ill-equipped to give face to political foes, because face is a key currency of power in a *guanxi* system. Chinese political weakness eliminated the possibility of an amicable face-giving solution. This left a zero-sum-game solution whereby one side could win face only if the other side lost it. With that choice, the Japanese made sure that the Chinese were the losers.

IV. The Beijing Government's Reaction to the Compromise

In the end, the Paris Peace Conference did decide on China's behalf that Germany must give up to China "all the buildings, wharves and pontoons, barracks, forts, arms and munitions of war, vessels of all kinds, wireless telegraphy installations and other public property."[3] It also ordered Germany to return the ancient astronomical instruments

taken by German troops from Beijing in 1901. But the key exception was the Shandong concession itself, which Germany ceded to Japan for return to China.

The June 1919 Versailles Peace Treaty resulting from the Paris Peace Conference gave China many other benefits. It terminated all German and Austrian unequal treaties with China, returning all of Germany's property in Tianjin and Hankou and reaffirming the abolition of the German and Austrian shares of the Boxer Indemnity. As a result of Wilson's compromise, the Versailles Peace Treaty did not formally recognize Japan's 1915 and 1918 treaties, meaning that Japan was not guaranteed the special rights and economic privileges specified by these treaties. From the Chinese point of view, however, these benefits did not compensate for the indirect restitution of the Shandong concessions via Japan. Chinese criticism of the peace settlement was as immediate as it was vociferous.

On 30 April 1919, within four days of the news of the transfer of the Shandong concession to Japan, massive student demonstrations erupted. The Chinese public rebelled over China's perceived loss of face to Japan, a despised rival that many still regarded as an inferior. Their country's internal troubles heightened their resentment of Japan. Whereas warlords, corruption, and disunity characterized Chinese politics during the teens, World War I had brought great economic prosperity to Japan as it took over European markets in Asia. China's unending travails made Japan's economic, political, and diplomatic successes all the more galling to the Chinese. On May 4th, student groups marched through the foreign quarter in Beijing to protest at the American, British, French, and Italian legations. The police arrested thirty-two, and one student was killed. By 20 May 1919, what became known as the May Fourth Movement expanded: Students from middle schools and universities in Beijing went on strike and organized a boycott of Japanese goods. In early June another thousand students were arrested.

The May Fourth demonstrations had a tremendous impact in Beijing. Public outrage forced the resignation of senior officials in the Beijing government. The president was also under attack and threatened to resign. The Chinese public became increasingly critical of Wilson's role at Paris, where they believed their country had become a pawn in great power rivalries. Disenchantment with the United States opened China to other influences, such as Soviet propaganda, which was just reaching China for the first time. The Bolsheviks took power only in late 1917 with the expectations of a cascade of sympathetic Communist revolutions in war-torn Europe. When these revolutions failed to materialize, the Bolsheviks set their revolutionary sights on Asia.

Many of the leaders of the May Fourth Movement later became founders of the Chinese Communist Party. They included Chen Duxiu (Ch'en Tu-hsiu), who became the first leader of the party, and Li Dazhao (Li Ta-ch'ao), one of the first Chinese intellectuals to support Marxism. Although not at the head of the May Fourth Movement, Mao Zedong (Mao Tse-tung), the future leader of the People's Republic of China, was greatly influenced by the movement.

In June 1919, Beijing ignored the student-led demonstrations when it instructed its delegation in Paris to sign the Versailles Peace Treaty. Only at the last minute did Beijing rescind this order, much too late for the instructions to reach Paris in time. This made it appear that the Beijing government was trying to pin responsibility for the unpopular settlement on the delegates. The delegation had already decided, in an additional act of insubordination, not to sign regardless of orders. This refusal to sign gave these Western-trained diplomats enormous prestige at home, which translated into almost a free hand in setting the foreign policy of the Beijing government. This Anglo-American group controlled Chinese foreign policy during much of the Republican period, including both warlord rule in Beijing and Nationalist rule first in Nanjing and then later in Taipei, Taiwan. The Versailles Peace Treaty not only affected Chinese public attitudes, but also equally influenced the tenor of Chinese foreign policy. In particular, Chinese officials began to search for new foreign allies to use as leverage against the West. To many, Soviet Russia seemed a good fit.

V. The Long-term Impact of the Treaty of Versailles

The long-term impact of the Shandong decision was enormous. Not only did China refuse to sign the Versailles Peace Treaty, thereby delaying the return of the Shandong concession, but, quite unexpectedly, the controversy surrounding China's dissatisfaction helped convince the U.S. Senate not to join the League of Nations. This left in tatters the security system that Wilson had hoped would regulate not just Sino-Japanese relations but post–World War I international relations in general. It also circumscribed Washington's ability to help China in the future. As the United States became the focal point of public outrage, by extension this soured key segments of the Chinese population concerning the American development model of free-market capitalism and democracy. Representatives of Soviet Russia explained persuasively that imperialism and capitalism lay at the root of Chinese ills. The Soviet path to modernity seemed to offer an alternative to the increasingly tainted West, particularly as the Soviet

economy seemed to boom, while the West imploded. The Great Depression killed any Japanese interest in liberal Western models as well.

Public opinion in the United States, in China, and throughout much of the world condemned the Shandong resolutions even though few understood their contents, let alone their implications for China. The American press largely misunderstood and sensationalized Wilson's role, while the Chinese delegates turned on Wilson to blame him for their own mistakes and their government's corruption. Meanwhile, the reformers of the May Fourth Movement expressed outrage that China had not received equal treatment and justice at Paris. This created the perception that Woodrow Wilson and, by extension, the United States had betrayed China in its hour of need.

Ironically, Wilson, who had been China's strongest supporter of the Big Three (Britain, France, and the United States), received the lion's share of the public blame for the Shandong resolution. The Chinese delegates in Paris helped create this impression as a way to deflect blame from themselves and onto foreigners. On 28 July 1919, the *Peking Daily News* published a letter from the Chinese delegation to the U.S. Senate urging it not to ratify the Versailles Peace Treaty. The letter implied that the Shandong concession was being ceded to Japan in perpetuity, which was simply not true. However, American opponents of the League of Nations used this letter condemning the Shandong solution to argue successfully that the United States should not join the League of Nations, severely hampering that institution's future effectiveness.

The Chinese delegates publicly blamed Wilson for bringing China into the war with the false promise of overturning Japanese imperialism. They ignored his rebuttal that his compromise solution was in no way dependent upon the Twenty-one Demands of 1915 or on the later 1918 agreements. They also ignored the security system that Wilson hoped to create, whereby a group of nations under the framework of the League of Nations could help China and Japan regulate their relations. Without U.S. participation in the League, there would be no way to exert sufficient diplomatic pressure on Japan when it began to expand its sphere of influence in China in response to the onset of the Great Depression.

China's refusal to sign the Treaty of Versailles delayed the return of Shandong until 1922, when the final transfer was arranged during the Washington Conference (1921–2). The Shandong question, which had been the lightning rod of the May Fourth Movement and the spark contributing to the creation of the Chinese Communist Party in 1921, disappeared without any fanfare and with little publicity. In the end, just as had been agreed in Paris in 1919, Japan handed over the Shandong concession and the Qingdao–Jianan Railway was

Dependable institutions are essential to ensure stability in developing countries. Although Woodrow Wilson's goal of the United States joining the League of Nations failed, thus endangering China's long-term international security, efforts to create reliable internal security institutions were more successful. Here, new cadets are being trained to work for the Shanghai Municipal Police force.

organized as a joint venture. All of these arrangements were in line with Wilson's compromise settlement, which returned the concessions to China seventy-five years before the term stipulated in the original Sino-German agreement. He also convinced Japan to forego all political rights in Shandong gained by means of the Twenty-one Demands of 1915 and the secret agreements signed with China in 1918. Yet, the perception that Wilson had betrayed China endured.

Given the growing anti-Western sentiments in China, a major anti-Christian movement broke out in 1922 and lasted until 1927. Students formed an Anti-Christian Student Federation pressuring other students to leave mission schools, conducting repeated mass demonstrations, and, by 1926, killing missionaries and looting their missions. The controversy over the Shandong question left many Chinese predisposed to look favorably on Soviet economic, political, and military models. Then the Great Depression in the early

1930s dried up Western markets for Chinese and Japanese goods, revealed deep flaws in Western economic institutions, and reduced the appeal of Western democratic institutions unable to cope with skyrocketing unemployment rates. Soviet Russia seemed to offer all the answers. Both the Communist Party and the Nationalist Party turned to the Bolsheviks for advice, financing, and models to restore Chinese institutions.

Conclusions

Many in China had enormous expectations for the Paris Peace Conference terminating World War I. They hoped that foreign diplomatic success would help heal China's internal divisions and promote reunification. This strategy of hope ignored the fact that the Chinese delegation had a weak hand at the conference. Its stated policy was to reassert China's territorial integrity, preserve its sovereign rights, and regain full economic and fiscal independence. If the delegation had been successful, China would have eliminated all leased territories, including the Russian concession at Lüshun, the German/Japanese concession at Qingdao, and the British concession at Kowloon. The delegates also hoped to eliminate the deployment of foreign legation guards in Beijing, thus removing all remaining foreign troops from China, and to abolish all extraterritorial rights. Finally, fiscal independence would have allowed China to reestablish tariff autonomy.

These lofty ambitions failed to take into account China's own agreements. The Japanese government played a very deft game of diplomacy since it knew that the faltering Duan Qirui government would pounce on any loans, regardless of their diplomatic ramifications. For the other powers to have denied the validity of the Sino-Japanese agreements would have undermined international agreements in general and served as a precedent for eliminating almost a century's worth of treaties with China. World War I had just been fought, in part, over the sanctity of treaties. Therefore, the Western powers were in no position to treat treaty obligations lightly. In the end, the Japanese used the Western system of international law to defeat China diplomatically.

The cultural characteristic of face helps explain the otherwise inexplicably widespread outrage felt in China over the role played by Japan. Many Chinese still considered the Japanese as inferiors. Conversely, the Japanese were determined that China recognize the verdict of the First Sino-Japanese War: Japan was the dominant power of Asia, and China would have to treat it with respect. Each remained equally determined to enforce its norms of deference on the other, creating a zero-sum-game of diplomacy.

The Chinese public, instead of focusing on the domestic origins of their predicament, externalized the problem to blame first Japan and then the United States. Yet, neither foreign government was ultimately responsible for the musical-chairs sequence of governments in Beijing, in South China, and in the provinces in between. As noxious as the foreign concessions seemed, foreign capital had brought vital infrastructure, expertise, and expansion of China's small industrial base. Foreign concessions were not the root of China's problems; rather, the problem lay with China's lack of strong institutions in the aftermath of the destruction of the dynastic system of government. Prosperity required stability, which required laws and institutions. The latter were strictly domestic problems that could be solved only by the Chinese people.

While the turn-of-the-century intellectual ferment initially seemed to offer great promise, with numerous analytical frameworks to treat China's ills, as time wore on and the instability grew, it became clearer that the cure would not be so simple. The chaos of the early Republican period suggested that freedom and democracy could not easily be conjured. Economic prosperity seemed ever more elusive amid escalating warfare that tore apart rather than restored the social fabric. Justifiable and deeply felt frustration welled up as people sought culprits to blame for their predicament.

Chinese public outrage provided Soviet Russia with a unique opportunity to expand its influence at Western expense and, in doing so, to break out of its own diplomatic isolation. The widely accepted misconception that Wilson betrayed China at Versailles was instrumental to the success of the Soviet propaganda campaign. Unrealistic expectations in China led to a deep public sense of injury, expressed in waves of public demonstrations, adding to the turmoil of the warlord era. Public perceptions of betrayal at the Paris Peace Conference would lead many Chinese—not just future Communists, but also the leaders of the Nationalist Party—to turn to Soviet Russia for guidance. For many Chinese, the outcome at Paris set in motion a growing intellectual reorientation away from the capitalist and liberal-democratic West to the authoritarian and centrally planned economy of the Soviet Union.

BIBLIOGRAPHY

Chen, Jerome. *Yuan Shih-k'ai.* 2nd ed. Stanford, CA: Stanford University Press, 1972.

Ch'i, Hsi-sheng. *Warlord Politics in China, 1916–1928.* Stanford, CA: Stanford University Press, 1976.

Chu, Pao-chin. *V. K. Wellington Koo: A Case Study of China's Diplomat and Diplomacy of Nationalism.* Hong Kong: Chinese University Press, 1981.

Curry, Roy Watson. *Woodrow Wilson and Far Eastern Policy, 1913–1921.* New York: Bookman Associates, 1957.

Deane, Hugh. *Good Deeds & Gunboats: Two Centuries of American-Chinese Encounters.* San Francisco: China Books & Periodicals, 1990.

Dickinson, Frederick R. *War and National Reinvention: Japan in the Great War, 1914–1919.* Cambridge, MA: Harvard University Press, 1999.

Elleman, Bruce A. *Diplomacy and Deception: The Secret History of Sino-Soviet Diplomatic Relations, 1917–1927.* Armonk, NY: M. E. Sharpe, 1997.

———*Wilson and China: A Revised History of the Shandong Question.* Armonk, NY: M. E. Sharpe, 2002.

Fang Xing, Shi Qi, Jian Rui, and Want Shixin. "Cloth Processing in Suzhou and Songjiang." In *Chinese Capitalism, 1522–1840,* edited by Xu Dixin and Wu Chengming, translated by Li Zhengde, et al., 213–27. New York: St. Martin's Press, 2000.

———."Silk Weaving in Jiangsu and Zhejiang." In *Chinese Capitalism, 1522–1840,* edited by Xu Dixin and Wu Chengming, translated by Li Zhengde, et al., 203–12. New York: St. Martin's Press, 2000.

Fifield, Russell H. *Woodrow Wilson and the Far East.* New York: Thomas Y. Crowell, 1952.

Furth, Charlotte. "Intellectual Change: From the Reform Movement to the May Fourth Movement, 1895–1920." In *Cambridge History of China*, vol. 12, edited by John K. Fairbank and Albert Feuerwerker, 322–405. Cambridge: Cambridge University Press.

King, Wunsz. *Woodrow Wilson, Wellington Koo and the China Question at the Paris Peace Conference.* Leyden: W. Q. Sythoff, 1959.

———*China at the Paris Peace Conference in 1919.* New York: St. John's University Press, 1961.

Li Tien-yi. *Woodrow Wilson's China Policy.* New York: Twayne, 1952.

Nathan, Andrew J. *Peking Politics, 1918–1923: Factionalism and the Failure of Constitutionalism.* Berkeley: University of California Press, 1976.

Robertson, James Oliver. *No Third Choice: Progressives in Republican Politics, 1916–1921.* New York: Garland, 1983.

Schwartz, Benjamin. *In Search of Wealth & Power: Yen Fu and the West.* Cambridge, MA: Harvard University Press, 1964.

Sheridan, James E. *China in Disintegration: The Republican Era in Chinese History, 1912–1949.* New York: Free Press, 1975.

Xu Dixin and Wu Chengning, eds. *Chinese Capitalism, 1522–1840.* Translated by Li Zhengde, Liang Miaoru, and Li Siping. New York: St. Martin's Press, 2000.

Young, Ernest P. *The Presidency of Yuan Shih-k'ai: Liberalism and Dictatorship in Early Republican China.* Ann Arbor: University of Michigan Press, 1977.

Yu, George, T. *Party Politics in Republican China: The Kuomintang, 1912–1924.* Berkeley: University of California Press, 1966.

Zhang Yongjin. *China in the International System, 1918–20: The Middle Kingdom at the Periphery.* London: Macmillan, 1991.

NOTES

1. Cited in Edward S. Krebs, "The Chinese Anarchist Critique of Bolshevism during the 1920s," in *Roads Not Taken: The Struggle of Opposition Parties in Twentieth-Century China*, edited by Roger B. Jeans (Boulder, CO: Westview, 1992), 216.
2. Cited in Bruce A. Elleman, *Wilson and China: A Revised History of the Shandong Question.* (Armonk, NY: M. E. Sharpe, 2002), 81.
3. Ibid., 3–8.

Chronology

2–6 March 1919	Conference Founding the Comintern
4 May 1919	May Fourth Movement
28 June 1919	Treaty of Versailles
25 July 1919	Karakhan Manifesto
26 August 1919	Revised Karakhan Manifesto published in *Izvestiia*
14–20 July 1920	Anhui-Zhili War; Zhili Clique wins
13 March 1921	Establishment of the Mongolian People's Government
5 May 1921	Sun Yat-sen establishes his second Guangzhou government
23 July 1921	Establishment of the Chinese Communist Party
12 Nov. 1921–6 Feb. 1922	Washington Conference
4 February 1922	Sino-Japanese Treaty returning Shandong
6 February 1922	Nine-Power Treaty of the Washington Conference guaranteeing the Open Door Policy
29 Apr.–17 June 1922	First Fengtian-Zhili War; Zhili Clique wins
16 June 1922	Sun's Second Guangzhou government falls
26 January 1923	Establishment of the First United Front
1 March 1923	Sun establishes his third Guangzhou government
15 Sept.–3 Nov. 1924	Second Fengtian-Zhili War; Fengtian Clique wins
26 November 1924	Establishment of the Mongolian People's Republic

17

New Intellectual Currents

*"Without a good society, how can we have a good
government?"*
*"Without a good government, how can we have a good
society?"*
Such a set of chain, how can we untie?

*"If education is not good, how can we have good
politics?"*
"If politics is not good, how can we have education at all?"
Such a set of chain, how can we untie?

"If we do not destroy, how can we begin construction?"
"Without construction, how can we destroy?"
Such a set of chain, how can we untie?[1]

Hu Shi (1891–1962) May Fourth
Movement activist, scholar, statesman, 1927

Prior to 1919, a New Culture Movement emerged in
China. Initially, it focused on adapting Western learning
and science in order to address China's many problems
through a combined modernization and westernization program. In the two decades following the
Shandong decision and the ensuing May Fourth
Movement, however, China's focus increasingly
shifted toward Soviet models for political and economic development. The Bolsheviks rejected westernization, meaning Western European institutions,
promoting a Marxist critique of these institutions and
attempting instead to centralize political, economic,
and social institutions in the expectation of scientifi-
cally rationalizing them. Many Chinese intellectuals
saw in Soviet Russia an alternative path to modernity,
which would allow China to catch up to the West
without having to adopt any of the unwanted cultural
and institutional baggage. In particular, the outcome
of the Shandong question made Chinese youth receptive to Soviet promises of equal treatment. In the
spring of 1919 the Soviet Union founded the Communist International (Comintern) to promote world
revolution, and in 1921 Comintern representatives
helped found the Chinese Communist Party.

Education was at the heart of the New Culture Movement,
and Peking University, created in 1898 during the Hundred
Days' Reform, played an important role in this movement.
Professor Hu Shi, for example, argued that more Chinese
could learn to read and write if Classical Chinese was
replaced with vernacular (spoken) Chinese. Other Peking
University faculty included the writer Lu Xun and the first
head of the Chinese Communist Party, Chen Duxiu.
Pictured here is the interior of a schoolroom at Peking
University (circa 1902).

I. The New Culture Movement

Following the collapse of the Qing, many Chinese scholars advocated reforming Chinese culture through Western science and democracy in what became known as the New Culture Movement. Hu Shi, a professor at Peking University, became famous for suggesting that vernacular Chinese be used in writing instead of relying on Classical Chinese, which played a role akin to that of Latin in Europe. Hu Shi promoted writing in the spoken language so that books and newpapers would become accessible to anyone able to read Chinese characters. This reform vastly simplified the task of learning to read, raising the prospects for the first time in Chinese history of widespread literacy. Hu Shi rejected Confucianism and recommended a complete program of westernization, emphasizing liberalism, democracy, individualism, and scientific education. He popularized his ideas with two figures, Mr. Science and Mr. Democracy.

At this time, American academics, such as the philosopher and scholar John Dewey, were extremely popular in China. Dewey visited from 1919 to 1921, giving numerous public lectures. He advocated democratic principles as the basis for an industrial society and believed education should focus on solving current social problems. Some of China's most famous intellectuals, such as the founders of the Chinese Communist Party Chen Duxiu, Li Da, and Li Dazhao, and China's most famous radical author of the 1920s and 1930s, Lu Xun, were prominent in this westernizing movement. (See the feature below.)

AUTHOR LU XUN

Lu Xun (Lu Hsün) was the pen name of Zhou Shuren (1881–1936). Following the widespread criticism of Classical Chinese during the May Fourth Movement, Lu Xun became famous for writing "Diary of a Madman," the first popular story written in the spoken language.

Born in Zhejiang province, Lu Xun came from an impoverished gentry family. As a child, he developed an early love and a lifelong interest in folk tales, popular stories, art, and natural science. His father's death and ensuing financial problems, however, interrupted his early traditional education at the clan school of the Zhou family. Later, he passed the examination to attend the Jiangnan Naval Academy (1898–9), but soon transferred to and subsequently graduated from the Nanjing School of Railway and Mines (1899–1902). These two institutions set up to provide a westernized education greatly influenced Lu Xun, who became fascinated with Western science, philosophy, history, and literature. In 1902 Lu Xun won a scholarship to study language in Japan, and in 1904, in the hope of serving his country as a physician, he entered the Sendai Provincial Medical School; however, in 1906, right after the Russo-Japanese War, he dropped out. Chinese passivity during the war had appalled him. He concluded that he could best help change China not by treating one individual at a time but by writing to reach a mass audience.

In 1906 he returned home briefly for an arranged marriage before resuming residence in Japan, where from 1906 to 1909 he read numerous Western works in Japanese translation and became particularly influenced by Russian authors. He returned home in 1909, and from then to 1926 he took up a series of posts, initially as a teacher and later as a member of the Ministry of Education. From 1920 to 1926, he also worked as an instructor in Chinese literature at Peking University. Because the chaotic final years of the Qing dynasty and the early Republican period dashed his hopes for reform, he buried himself in research on ancient texts. The 1919 May Fourth Movement, however, revived his hopes and reform activities, and he wrote two collections of short stories between 1918 and 1926. These made him China's most famous living literary figure.

The deepening civil wars in China put an early end to his writing career, since his views satisfied neither the Nationalists nor the Communists, although he was revered posthumously by the Communists. Fame may have saved him from assassination by the Nationalists. Chiang Kai-shek's bloody purge of the Communists in 1927 appalled Lu Xun and caused him to flee to South China. As events in China went from bad to worse, Lu Xun's dreams of reform must have seemed increasingly remote. Rather than write his own essays, he translated numerous foreign works into Chinese until 1936, when he died of tuberculosis. He had a lifelong fascination with the world beyond China, writing: "Throughout the ages, the Chinese have had only two ways of looking at foreigners: up to them as superior beings or down on them as wild animals. They have never been able to treat them as friends, to consider them as people themselves."[2]

Lu Xun is best known for his many short stories and essays written in vernacular Chinese. In 1918, soon after the debate erupted over whether to publish in Classical or vernacular Chinese, Lu Xun published his most famous story in *New Youth* magazine (*Xin qingnian*), entitled "Diary of a Madman." He based it loosely on one with the same name by the Russian author Nikolai Gogol (1809–52), who described a simple office worker with delusions of being the king of Spain. Lu Xun wrote his story in the first person, which was unprecedented in Chinese literature. He condemned Confucianism as self-destructive, using the image of cannibalism to portray traditional Chinese culture as feeding on itself. The story's narrator recounts the diary of a deranged man obsessed with the fear that those around him are all cannibals. As his paranoia increases, he becomes convinced that sooner or later, he too will be eaten. The madman's diary ends with a plea to "save the children"—that is, a plea for China to change for the sake of future generations. "Diary of a Madman" has been called China's first Western-style story.

The story brought Lu Xun instant fame and tremendous influence in the May Fourth Movement. Many interpreted his stories as supporting the development of Communism. After 1949, his name became associated with a number of political campaigns, including the Cultural Revolution, when he was canonized by Marxist historians. After the death of Mao Zedong, however, ensuing generations increasingly read his works as criticisms of authoritarianism and as expressions of moral indignation at China's failure to reform.

The origin of the New Culture Movement dated to the anti-Japanese reaction following Japan's Twenty-one Demands in 1915. The day Beijing accepted the demands became known as National Humiliation Day. Although China signed equally onerous treaties with the other powers, these never became antiholidays commemorating the humiliations. The Chinese remained fixated on restoring their country's historical primacy in East Asia and putting Japan back in its place.

Chen Duxiu helped launch the beginning of the New Culture Movement with an opening essay for *New Youth* magazine, founded during the furor over the Twenty-one Demands. In a 1915 article, he called on youth and intellectuals to become politically and socially active to create a new society. Chen went on to become dean of Peking University's prestigious School of Arts and Letters in 1917 and one of China's most influential intellectuals. *New Youth* called on Chinese students to reject superstitions, adopt scientific reasoning instead, and follow Hu Shi's Mr. Science and Mr. Democracy. This emphasis on youth stood in stark contrast to the traditional Confucian focus on seniority and hierarchy. It also had implications for relations between the sexes and within families, including criticism of the subordination of women and an increasing unwillingness to subordinate the individual to the clan.

Chen Duxiu, like many other intellectuals at this time, hoped to restore China to its former status as a strong, independent nation. Initially, he looked to Western models. He advocated a combination of nationalistic pride in Chinese traditions and the utilitarian adoption of appropriate Japanese and Western institutions and practices. Although he supported China's participation in World War I in the hope of enhancing its international standing, he considered the final peace terms to be a national humiliation. Thereafter, he directed his disillusionment against the Western capitalist countries and Japan, as well as against Beijing, which he lambasted for failing to gain equal diplomatic treatment for China.

Initially, members of the New Culture Movement focused on a critique of traditional cultural models. Some soon recommended a Meiji-like reform program for China, but the Versailles settlement brought with it disgust for both the West and Japan as potential models for China. The students and intellectuals who became known as the "May Fourth generation" intensely felt their connection to the outside world and the prevailing currents of world revolution. Chinese newspapers carefully followed revolutionary movements in India, Vietnam, and especially Korea, where Korean revolutionaries proclaimed Independence Day on 1 May 1919 and rallies overflowed onto the streets to oppose Japanese rule. Many political activists felt that China again lagged behind the times, so they scheduled demonstrations on 4 May 1919 with the conscious intent to set in motion a popular movement to resist the great powers and foment political change.

II. The May Fourth Movement

On 4 May 1919, over 3,000 students gathered at Tiananmen, then the Gate of Heavenly Peace to the Forbidden City and now, with the Communist demolition of the surrounding neighborhoods, the site of Tiananmen Square. They came to protest both the Versailles settlement and the 1918 treaty by the Anfu Clique that recognized the Japanese right to the Shandong concessions. When the demonstrations led to an assault on a pro-Japanese official and the burning of the home of a cabinet minister, the government imprisoned hundreds of activists. Rather than dampening popular passions, in a spontaneous show of nationalism the unrest spread to over 200 other cities and 22 provinces, while in Shanghai merchants shut down for a week and workers in forty enterprises went on strike. (See Map 17.1.) The spreading unrest forced the Beijing government to release the imprisoned students, 1,150

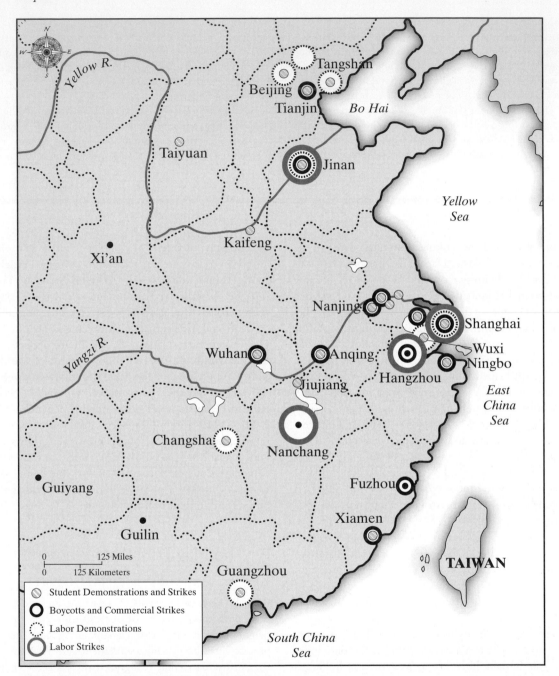

Map 17.1   May Fourth Movement (1919)

Map based on Jean Chesneaux, Françoise Le Barbier, and Marié-Claude Bergère *China from the 1911 Revolution to Liberation*, Paul Auster and Lydia Davis, trans. (NY: Pantheon Books, 1977), 66.

of whom left jail in a victory march that captured Chinese imaginations for years to come. These events dramatically widened the audience for the New Culture Movement, which soon became subsumed in the May Fourth Movement.

The year 1919 saw the creation of over 400 magazines, which spread news of the movement throughout China. Because these magazines were written in the vernacular, not Classical Chinese, they were accessible to a wide audience.

They provided articles on the latest trends in Western thinking and the development of the anticolonial movement outside China, as well as critiques of Chinese traditions and Confucianism in particular. The authors were bent on transforming Chinese culture. This approach departed from that of China's many dynasties, which had consistently defended Han civilization as unalterable. Ideas concerning individualism, liberty, democracy, equality, utilitarianism, socialism, and communism all ate away at the interlocking social obligations that had so long defined Chinese society. These new ideas released a generation of young people less bound by family obligations than in the past onto the political stage, where they clamored for change.

The May Fourth Movement had an enormous impact on subsequent Chinese intellectual, social, and political history. While the First Sino-Japanese War ushered in the creation of an indigenous press—as opposed to the foreign-owned press prior to the war—the May Fourth Movement brought a vernacular press and an even greater proliferation of newspapers and journals, so that for the first time one can speak of

China invented the printing press in the sixth century AD, and the first printed newspaper appeared in Beijing during the eighth century AD. During the New Culture Movement and especially with the May Fourth Movement, many newspapers and magazines began to discuss what development path was best for China. Following the widespread publication of the Karakhan Manifesto in China, much attention was turned to Soviet Russia and to the new Bolshevik form of government.

"public opinion" in China, meaning urban public opinion in this period. The May Fourth generation also compiled new and reprioritized anthologies of the Classical literature that restructured the prism through which the Chinese viewed their past and the Classics handed down from one generation to the next. These anthologies determined which literary works from China's rich literary tradition continued to be read and which gradually became forgotten.

Whereas the 1911 Revolution was a political revolution, the May Fourth Movement began the social revolution. It discredited Confucianism—already undermined as a political system with the loss of the First Sino-Japanese War—by undermining it as an ethical system as well. It rejected Confucian filial piety, which required the young to defer to the old, children to submit to their parents, and women to follow the dictates of men.

Its emphasis on radically changing the status of women in Chinese society put the so-called woman's question on the political agenda of all future political parties. The May Fourth generation rejected footbinding and arranged marriages and, for the first time in China's history, opened the political arena to women. Previously, with the exception of the perhaps apocryphal Mulan, the warrior-heroine and exemplar of Confucian values, the most famous women in Chinese history, such as the Tang dynasty Empress Wu (625–705) and the Empress Dowager Cixi (1835–1908), had been infamous—symbols of corruption, incapacity, and excess.

The May Fourth Movement also for the first time opened the political arena to the young. Student demonstrations would assume national importance during the May 30th Movement of 1925, the Nanjing Decade (1928–37), the Cultural Revolution (1966–76), and the Tiananmen Massacre (1989). Students in the democracy movement of 1989 consciously evoked the legacy of the May Fourth Movement by staging their most important demonstrations in Tiananmen Square in front of the Gate of Heavenly Peace, where the 1919 demonstrations had taken place.

The May Fourth Movement left an important political legacy. It couched solutions to China's numerous problems in terms of a nationalist agenda that set the tenor of future Chinese political debates. The united action by students, workers, and many other sections of society during 1919 to oppose the Versailles Peace Treaty forged a new nationalistic spirit. Previously, regional loyalties and Han–Manchu divisions had impeded the development of nationalism. For the first time in modern Chinese history and just a decade after the fall of the Qing dynasty, nationalism started to become a vital force in Chinese society. It appeared first among the urban educated elite. Over the course of the following decades, it gradually fanned out into the countryside. Those armies or political parties most capable of harnessing nationalism became the most successful in China's multilateral civil wars. These would be the Nationalist Party of Sun Yat-sen and the Communist Party of Chen Duxiu and Li Dazhao.

III. The Karakhan Manifesto and the Comintern

The Soviet Union attempted to capitalize on the political ferment in China by issuing the Karakhan Manifesto. On 25 July 1919, less than three months after the start of the May Fourth Movement, the Soviet government issued a manifesto signed by the deputy people's commissar, Lev Karakhan. In contrast to the other powers, this document pledged to meet all of China's many demands presented at the Paris Peace Conference. The date of its publication, 25 July, marked both the forty-ninth anniversary of the British refusal to ratify the Alcock Convention, one of China's first equal treaties (see Chapter 11), and the twenty-fifth anniversary of the start of the Sino-Japanese War, when China lost its traditional position of regional dominance to Japan (see Chapter 12). The dating contained the implicit message that, in contrast to imperial Britain and Japan, Soviet Russia would treat China justly.

Karakhan addressed his manifesto not only to the people of China but also to the governments of both South and North China, meaning Sun Yat-sen's government in Guangzhou and the warlord government in Beijing. Karakhan tailored his manifesto to capitalize on the Chinese disappointment over the recent events in Paris and specifically promised to renounce all annexations, indemnities, and subjugation of other nations, including all of tsarist Russia's unequal treaties, such as the 1896 Chinese Eastern Railway agreement, the 1901 Boxer Protocol, and Russia's 1907–16 agreements with Japan dividing Manchuria into a Russian and a Japanese sphere of influence. Most importantly, the Karakhan Manifesto promised the return gratis of the Chinese Eastern Railway, the largest foreign concession in China. It urged the Chinese people to escape the colonial destiny prescribed by the West by allying with the workers, the peasants, and the Red Army of Soviet Russia.

These Soviet offers made the Japanese demands at the Paris Peace Conference seem outrageous by comparison, fueling Chinese resentment. Wilson's apparent betrayal of China at Paris and the Soviet government's apparent offer of equality accelerated the growing interest in Soviet Russia. After the Karakhan Manifesto, Chinese publications featured numerous articles on the Russian Revolution and the Bolshevik ideology. The longer the delay in returning Shandong, the more appealing the Soviet offers became to Chinese intellectuals.

The Beijing government used the Karakhan Manifesto to pressure Japan and the United States into expediting the return of the Shandong concession and the Qingdao-Jinan Railway. At the Washington Conference (1921–2), convened to discuss arms limitations and regional security in East Asia, Beijing used Soviet Russia's apparent generosity to get better terms from Tokyo, which agreed to allow Beijing to redeem the railway, but it remained a joint venture in the interim.

Soviet Russia was not nearly as generous as its manifesto suggested. The new Soviet government, in the face of the same national security concerns as tsarist Russia, chose a remarkably similar strategy for empire by trying to expand further into the territories of the former Qing empire during periods of Chinese internal turmoil. (See Chapter 8, Section IV.) Questions concerning the content of the Karakhan Manifesto arose immediately upon the arrival in 1921 of the first official Soviet envoy to China, Aleksandr Paikes. He and his successors denied that there had ever been any promise to return the Chinese Eastern Railway but insisted that all tsarist treaties remained valid. The Soviet Union would not return the Chinese Eastern Railway to Chinese sovereignty until 1955, over a decade after the Western powers returned their final railway concessions. Paikes also urged that tripartite talks be convened in which Mongolia would be granted equal status with Russia and China per the terms of the 1915 tsarist tripartite treaty. The Beijing government argued that Outer Mongolia was not autonomous but an integral part of China.

During the Russian Civil War (1918–22) the Bolshevik Red Army was deployed to Outer Mongolia in pursuit of the tsarist-officered White armies. But after their defeat, the Red Army remained in Outer Mongolia to oversee its transition to Communism. Neither China nor Russia wanted a strong Mongolia on its long and vulnerable frontier, hence their rivalry for control. The date 13 March 1921 marked the creation of the Mongolian People's government, which became the first member of the Soviet bloc in 1924 with the creation of the Mongolian People's Republic. Although the Chinese did not realize it at the time, the loss of Outer Mongolia from the Chinese sphere of influence would be permanent.

The Soviet government apparently developed two versions of the Karakhan Manifesto, one for propaganda purposes and the other for secret diplomacy. It sent the original version to both the Beijing government and Sun Yat-sen's opposition government in Guangzhou and publicized it at that time to reach the Chinese people. A month later, on 26 August 1919, the Soviet newspaper, *Izvestiia,* published the same document containing no reference to the promised return of the Chinese Eastern Railway without compensation. China used the original version to extract concessions from Japan and the West, alleging better treatment from Soviet Russia, while Soviet Russia later used the edited version in its secret negotiations with the Beijing government to retain all tsarist privileges. Beijing never made the alterations public lest it appear inept yet again. Diplomatic blunders are difficult for any government to admit, but in face societies there is no recovery from public admissions of policy errors. Therefore, once duped, the Beijing government was stuck. The Chinese public never learned about the secret Sino-Soviet diplomacy, and so the myth of Sino-Soviet friendship was born.

IV. The Founding of the Chinese Communist Party

While Soviet representatives were negotiating with the Beijing government, Comintern agents sought out sympathetic intellectuals impressed by the first version of the Karakhan Manifesto. In early 1920, the twenty-seven-year-old Comintern representative, Grigorii Voitinskii, introduced himself to Li Dazhao at Peking University. Li Dazhao was a product of the westernized educational system established in Tianjin by the Self-strengthener Li Hongzhang. He became an early member of Sun Yat-sen's Tongmenghui and later studied at Waseda University in Japan. A vociferous critic of both the North China warlord governments in Beijing and Japanese policies in China, he became closely associated with Chen Duxiu and the New Culture Movement. He served as a professor and as a librarian at Peking University, where Mao Zedong later worked as his assistant. Initially, he favored Western constitutionalism as China's route to reform, but successive warlord governments discouraged this path. In late 1918, he turned to Marxism. Li took Voitinskii to Shanghai to meet Chen Duxiu.

Chen was in many ways the perfect choice to head a Chinese Communist movement. He was a well-known leader of the May Fourth Movement who gained notoriety for his arrest on 11 June 1919 and his eighty-three-day imprisonment. Upon his release, Chen lost his position at Peking University, whereupon he moved to Shanghai, the center of foreign capitalism. Chen not only had great prestige as one of China's most celebrated revolutionary leaders, but he was also unemployed. In his quest to save China, Chen explored utopianism, Wilsonian democracy, Christianity, and even John Dewey's guild socialism. Late in 1919, he published an article in *New Youth* calling on China to follow the American example and create a federal government from the ground up, with ordinary people establishing effective institutions of local government.

Chen did not know how to implement his plans. He complained in early 1920 that he wanted to create a new form of politics unconstrained by existing practices. Immediately after meeting Voitinskii that spring, Chen apparently found in Bolshevism what he was seeking: In May he published an article entitled "Workers' Consciousness," recommending that workers, as the most useful of all social classes, take control of politics, the military, and industry. By August, Chen was describing China's workers as an oppressed class, blaming capitalism for their enslavement, and prescribing revolution followed by a Leninist dictatorship of the proletariat.

Voitinskii also made contact with Sun Yat-sen. Most recently, Sun had been a political refugee living in the French concession in Shanghai. During October 1920, however, Sun returned to lead a new government in Guangzhou (his second of three—see Table 15.2). From this position, he hoped to challenge Beijing as the central government of China. Over the years, Sun had become increasingly disenchanted with Western constitutional democracies. The 1917 Bolshevik Revolution attracted his interest, particularly the civil-military and party organization that the Bolsheviks had used to such great effect to seize power. Sun offered Chen the chairmanship of his Education Committee. This gave Chen an unexpectedly early opportunity to promote his newly adopted Bolshevik ideas. After arriving in Guangzhou during the fall of 1920, Chen immediately founded a Marxist study group. He also helped edit the *Guangdong Masses Paper,* a small journal funded by the Guangzhou government. In the first edition, published in January 1921, Chen promoted socialism and the Russian Communist Party as the only embodiment of socialist ideals. This pro-Bolshevik Chinese-language article appeared only nine months after the widespread publication of the Karakhan Manifesto and Voitinskii's arrival in China, indicating how rapidly the Bolsheviks had cultivated ties with Sun Yat-sen.

When the revolutionary movement unexpectedly stalled in Europe, Soviet attention focused increasingly on Asia and the creation of Communist parties there. Its first success came with the creation of a Communist government in Outer Mongolia. But according to Leninism, Asian countries were too unindustrialized to support a true Communist revolution, so the Soviet Union advocated a united front strategy with all progressive parties in Asia to further the cause of revolution there. Soviet Russia relied on the Comintern to sponsor the creation of these Communist parties and forge united fronts. Communist parties were founded in Iran and Turkey in 1920; in Outer Mongolia and China in 1921; in Palestine and Japan in 1922; and in India and Korea in 1925. From Turkey all the way to Korea, Soviet Russia ringed itself with Communist parties.

The Dutch Comintern agent Henk Maring arrived in China in April 1921 and helped establish the Chinese

Communist Party (CCP) in July. Thereafter, his key goal became the creation of a United Front between the Chinese Communists and other nationalist groups, such as Sun Yat-sen's opposition government in South China. Together, they could promote revolution in China and also put pressure on the Beijing government to help Soviet Russia achieve its diplomatic goals.

After spending some time in Beijing, Maring traveled on 3 June 1921 to Shanghai, where he suggested that a party congress be held to found the CCP. Its First Party Congress took place in July. Because neither Chen Duxiu nor Li Dazhao could attend, Maring furnished the necessary funds and recommended a wide range of organizational principles based on a Leninist structure. Although Maring had little trouble getting his organizational changes accepted by the congress, he ran into stiff opposition when he suggested a ban on party members working for foreigners or capitalists,

or serving as government officials or members of parliament. In a Confucian society, intellectual achievements were the basis for government service. Maring's proposed ban would have cut off Chinese intellectuals from their traditional place in Chinese society. Even the party's newly elected leader, Chen Duxiu, was at that moment a government official in Sun's Guangzhou government, where he was serving as the secretary of education. In 1922, the Second Party Congress determined that party members could not become officials in capitalist governments without special permission. This meant that party members could not work in the Beijing government.

In a second document presented at the First Party Congress, the CCP outlined its plans for propaganda activities. Each area was to publish a union magazine, a daily and a weekly newspaper, and pamphlets and circulars for special occasions. Propaganda would be conducted in supplemen-

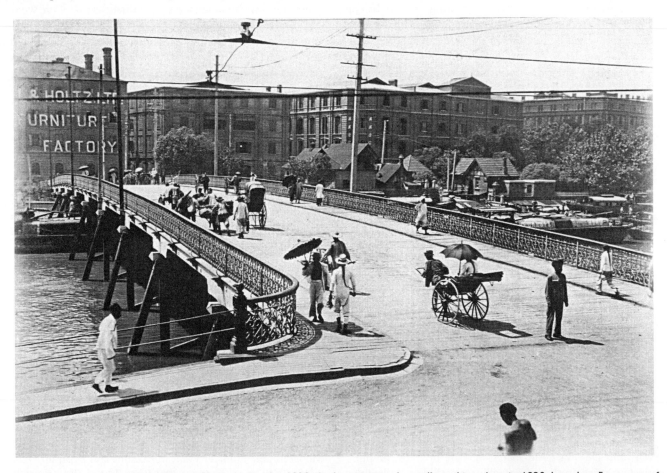

Unlike Europe and the United States, China during the 1920s had an extremely small working class; in 1920, less than 5 percent of China's population lived in cities, versus just over 50 percent in the United States. Many Chinese proletariat worked in foreign-owned factories, like these in Shanghai. Because of the lack of worker support, leaders of the CCP, like Mao Zedong, eventually turned to the peasants for support.

tary labor schools in order to teach workers how to form labor unions. Unions were to be formed at every factory that had over 200 workers and at least two CCP members.

Most importantly, Maring supported the United Front, which became the official policy of the Comintern. This prompted an acrimonious debate over the question of working with other parties. Some delegates argued that Sun Yat-sen's Three People's Principles resembled state socialism, but a majority considered Sun to be little better than a warlord and recommended his overthrow.

The First Party Congress elected Chen Duxiu in absentia as the party secretary, Zhang Guotao as the head of the Organizational Department, and Li Da as the head of the Propaganda Department. During the 1940s, Zhang became the highest-ranking defector from the Communists to the Nationalists; he rejected intrusive Soviet influence over the CCP. The party adopted a Leninist organization: a small, secretive, hierarchical and centralized party composed of professional revolutionaries. All new members had to be investigated by the local soviet, and discrimination by sex or nationality was banned. The following year, the CCP joined the Comintern. This required CCP leaders to make monthly reports to the Comintern headquarters in Moscow, as well as to other Asian countries in order to coordinate revolutionary activities in the region.

The CCP's resolution to join the Comintern meant the subordination of the Chinese revolution to Soviet revolutionary goals. Initially, the small size of the CCP and the ongoing Russian Civil War in Siberia protected the CCP from Soviet interference. The Chinese Communists were almost totally isolated from Moscow, as indicated by the profile of the student body at Moscow Communist University for Workers of the East. In the winter of 1921, there was not a single Chinese among the 601 international students. But this situation was temporary. In August 1921, when Chen returned to Shanghai to assume his duties as head of the CCP, he soon began to quarrel with Maring over the advisability of forming a United Front with Sun's Nationalist Party.

V. The Civil Wars in North China

During the warlord period from 1916 to 1926, the North China warlords exhausted each other with shifting alliances, constant infighting, and intermittent civil war that undermined North China's economy. (See Table 17.1 and Map 17.2.)

This fatal weakening of the North permitted forces from South China to launch a successful military expedition to reunify the country by 1928, at least on paper. North and South China warlords were equally preoccupied with the control of Beijing because of its symbolic importance as the traditional seat of legitimate government, its status as the capital of China's internationally recognized government, and its position for the collection of revenues. Control of the capital gave warlords a measure of legitimacy. The foreign powers, when faced with a bewildering succession of groups all claiming authority, made the highly practical decision to continue business as usual in Beijing where the Foreign Ministry's personnel had changed little despite the turmoil. The Beijing government alone among China's many warlord governments could raise foreign loans. The careers of Yuan Shikai and Duan Qirui demonstrated the importance of this power.

The Japanese helped bankroll the Anhui Clique warlord, Duan Qirui, in exchange for his cooperation on such diplomatic issues as the Shandong question. Duan's power base had also depended on another Japanese-funded warlord, Zhang Zuolin, the leader of the Fengtian Clique that controlled Manchuria. In 1918 Duan engineered the election of the Anfu Parliament, packed with his supporters. (See Chapter 15, Section IV.) In 1919, negotiations between North and South China continued concerning possible reunification, but no agreement was reached.

Table 17.1   North China Warlords in the 1920s

Name of Clique	Leader	Enemy	Foreign Supporter	
			Japan	Russia
Fengtian Clique (Manchuria)	Zhang Zuolin (assassinated 1928)	Shifting alliances	✓	✓
Anhui Clique	Duan Qirui*	Zhili Clique	✓	
(Anfu Club)	Xu Shuzheng		✓	
Zhili Clique	Feng Guozhang* (retired 1918)	Anhui Clique		
	Cao Kun*			
	Wu Peifu*		✓	
Feng Yuxiang	Feng Yuxiang	Shifting alliances	✓	✓

*Member of the *guanxi* network of Yuan Shikai.

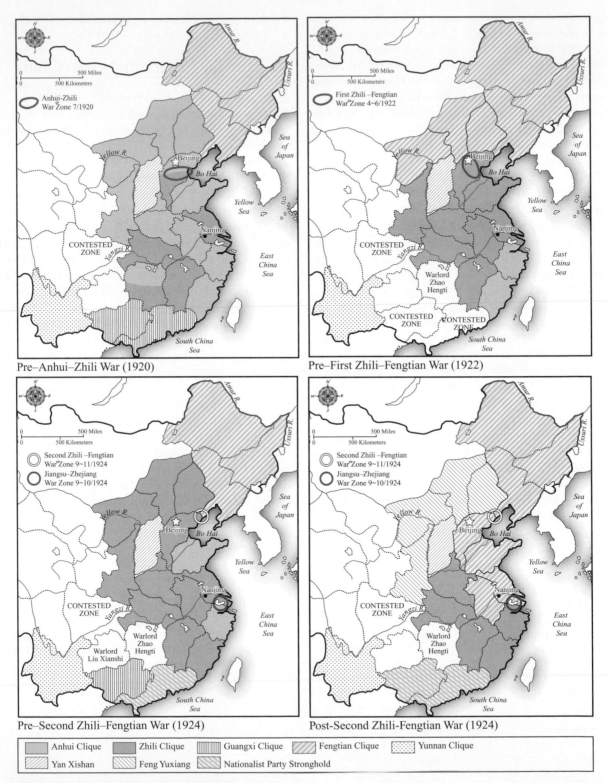

Pre–Anhui–Zhili War (1920)

Pre–First Zhili–Fengtian War (1922)

Pre–Second Zhili–Fengtian War (1924)

Post-Second Zhili-Fengtian War (1924)

Anhui Clique	Zhili Clique	Guangxi Clique	Fengtian Clique	Yunnan Clique
Yan Xishan	Feng Yuxiang	Nationalist Party Stronghold		

Map 17.2   Civil Wars in North China (1920–5)

Other northern warlords became increasingly critical of Duan, in particular Cao Kun and Wu Peifu, respectively the civil and military leaders of the Zhili Clique. Meanwhile, the warlord Xu Shuzheng rapidly expanded his power base in Outer Mongolia to threaten Zhang Zuolin. Xu had been a protégé of Duan Qirui, received formal military training in Japan, later served as Duan's liaison with the Fengtian Clique, and was a cofounder of the Anfu Club. In 1919 Xu tried to extend the Beijing government's rule over Outer Mongolia to counteract its growing autonomy, but he alienated the Mongols in the process. The Japanese were eager to fund his activities in order to undermine the growing Soviet influence in Mongolia. However, Zhang Zuolin considered the extension of the Beijing government's influence into neighboring Mongolia to threaten his own control over Manchuria.

Meanwhile, Cao Kun, yet another offshoot of Yuan Shikai's *guanxi* network, had risen quickly in the ranks of his benefactor's modernized army. Originally, he had been an ally of Duan Qirui, but gradually he slipped into the Zhili Clique. Cao felt increasingly threatened by Duan's growing military forces and also felt personal animosity to Xu Shuzheng. These tensions culminated in the brief Anhui-Zhili War from 14 to 20 July 1920 in which the Zhili and Fengtian cliques combined forces to defeat Duan Qirui's Anhui Clique. (See Table 17.2. Note the number of combatants and provinces affected by this and the following North China wars of the 1920s.) Their victory resulted in the dissolution of Duan's army and his Anfu Club, and made Cao Kun the undisputed civil leader of the Zhili Clique and Wu Peifu its undisputed military leader. Unfortunately, the two men did not see eye to eye on policy. Wu Peifu, another member of Yuan Shikai's *guanxi* network, had also risen through the military ranks to a position of great influence. He developed contacts with the Japanese during the Russo-Japanese War.

Table 17.2   Main North China Wars of the 1920s

War	Winning Alliance	Losing Alliance	Issue	Number of Combatants	Affected Provinces
Anhui-Zhili War (July 1920)	Zhili Fengtian	Anhui	Dominance of Beijing and Outer Mongolia	120,000[†]	7[*]
First Zhili-Fengtian War (April–May 1922)	Zhili Feng Yuxiang Chen Jiongming	Anhui Fengtian Sun Yat-sen	Dominance over Beijing and spreading influence in the South China	150,000+[†]	10[*]
Second Zhili-Fengtian War (Sept.–Nov. 1924)	Anhui Fengtian Sun Yat-sen Feng Yuxiang	Zhili	Dominance over North China and Manchuria, and spreading influence in South China Japanese get Feng to defect from Zhili to prevent this	450,000[†]	8[*]
Fengtian-Zhejiang War (Oct.–Nov. 1925)	Zhili, Anhui, Jiangsu, Jiangxi, Hubei	Fengtian	Dominance over Shanghai and Zhejiang province	?	5[†]
Fengtian-Feng Yuxiang War (Dec. 1925–Aug. 1926)	Zhili Fengtian	Feng Yuxiang	Dominance over Beijing, Tianjin, and northwest	600,000[‡]	8[‡]
Northern Expedition (July 1926–Dec. 1928)	Nationalists	North and South China warlords	Dominance over China	1,100,000[‡]	12[‡]

[*]The number of provinces encompassed by the war zone includes those involved not only in the war in question, but also in any other ongoing hostilities. The number of combatants applies only to the wars listed. Zhang Youyi, *Zhongguo jinday nongye shi ziliao*, vol. 2 (Beijing: Sanliandian, 1957), 609.

[†]Edward Dreyer, *China at War, 1901–1949* (London: Longman, 1995), 86, 101, 08, 110, 374–5.

[‡]Arthur Waldron, "War and the Rise of Nationalism in Twentieth-Century China," in *Warfare in China Since 1600*, edited by Kenneth Swope (Aldershot, UK: Ashgate, 2005), 308–9.

Because the Zhili and Fengtian cliques had in common only the desire to overthrow Duan Qirui, North China was no more stable after their victory than before. The Zhili Clique dominated the Beijing government during the next year and a half, when the Beijing government negotiated the Shandong treaty with Japan and began the long process of opening diplomatic relations with the Soviet government. The year 1921 marked the establishment of both Sun Yat-sen's second government in Guangzhou and the CCP.

In 1922, tensions again boiled over in North China. Wu Peifu of the Zhili Clique and Zhang Zuolin of the Fengtian Clique had a deep mutual animosity over who should dominate North China. Wu engaged in selective military campaigns against the warlords of Hunan and Sichuan in 1921 to secure his southern and Western flanks. Meanwhile, Zhang Zuolin had gradually been extending his influence from Manchuria into Zhili, the location of Beijing's and Wu Peifu's power base. Zhang Zuolin allied with his former enemies in the Anhui Clique, who hated the Zhili Clique more than they hated him. The Anhui Clique included powerful ties in Shanghai. Zhang also allied with Sun Yat-sen, who intended to launch a military expedition from the South. Zhang's goal was to reunite China under Manchurian hegemony. In response, the Zhili Clique combined forces with the northern warlord, Feng Yuxiang, and cultivated the Guangdong warlord and ally of Sun Yat-sen, Chen Jiongming, who soon expelled Sun Yat-sen, thus ending Sun's second government in Guangzhou. In the First Fengtian-Zhili War (29 April to 17 June 1922), Zhili emerged victorious and in control of most of North China, while Zhang was limited to his home base in Manchuria. Thereafter, Zhang tried to regroup with the help of Soviet and Japanese aid.

With the victory of the Zhili Clique, Cao Kun became president in October 1923, reportedly through bribes lavished on the members of the National Assembly. During his presidency, China opened diplomatic relations with the Soviet Union. The war had not resolved the issues of control over Manchuria or Shanghai because the remnants of the Anhui Clique had formed a triangular alliance with Zhang Zuolin in Manchuria and Sun Yat-sen in Guangzhou to establish the latter's third government in 1923. A move by the Zhili Clique to finish off the Anhui Clique would trigger this alliance, while a key member of this alliance, Zhang Zuolin, was eager to avenge his recent defeat by the Zhili Clique.

There was a failed attempt at a legislative unification of China. Cao Kun and Wu Peifu, the key leaders of the Zhili Clique, however, had increasingly divergent political plans. They vied for control in Beijing. While Cao had become separated from his military base of support, Wu focused on the military underpinnings of power. In 1923, Wu suddenly reversed his plans for a peaceful reunification of China in favor

of a military solution. He tried simultaneously to expand his influence into Fujian, Guangdong, and Sichuan and also prepared for a showdown with Zhang Zuolin. The civil side of Zhili rule under Cao Kun had become increasingly unpopular, given the clique's reputation for rampant corruption, while military officers had become increasingly disenchanted with Wu Peifu's military leadership. The Fengtian Clique once again allied with the Anhui Clique against the Zhili Clique. Fighting around Shanghai triggered the Anhui Clique's triangular alliance with both Zhang Zuolin and Sun Yat-sen. This was the Second Fengtian-Zhili War (15 September to 3 November 1924). Unlike the previous conflicts, this one rapidly became a large-scale war of attrition and trench warfare of the World War I variety. Wu Peifu's army numbered 170,000 and appeared undefeatable. But when Wu was already engaged in fighting, the commander of Zhili's Third Army, Feng Yuxiang, the so-called Christian warlord, mutinied and joined Zhang Zuolin. Warlords previously subordinate to the Zhili Clique then refused to rally.

The Japanese interfered with Wu's troop deployments and provided essential military aid to Zhang Zuolin. Japanese troops reportedly even intervened directly in the fighting. They were intent upon preventing a Zhili conquest of their sphere of influence in Manchuria, so they shifted the military balance accordingly. Feng occupied Beijing and unseated Cao Kun, but was soon forced to retreat to Kalgan, Inner Mongolia. The issue became who would head the Beijing government. Zhang Zuolin and Feng Yuxiang brought the Anhui Clique's Duan Qirui out of retirement for the task, but Duan soon tired of being a figurehead; he resigned in 1926 to devote his old age to the study of Buddhism.

Zhang Zuolin's forces continued south, precipitating the Fengtian-Zhejiang War in the summer and fall of 1925 for the control of Shanghai. Instead, Sun Chuanfang, the warlord of Zhejiang and member of the Zhili Clique, expelled the Fengtian forces from Shanghai and entrenched himself ever more firmly in control of the surrounding provinces. In late November 1925, Zhang Zuolin and Feng Yuxiang then had a falling out. The Zhili Clique's Wu Peifu allied with his recent enemy, Zhang Zuolin, to defeat Feng Yuxiang, who had earlier double-crossed both. This forced Feng temporarily into exile in the Soviet Union on 1 January 1926. Zhang Zuolin was not satisfied, however. In January 1926, he allied with Wu Peifu to destroy the remnants of Feng's army. During 1926, a much weakened Feng turned to the Nationalist Party. Zhang and Wu's cooperation increased in the face of the common threat posed by the Nationalist Northern Expedition of 1926. But by 1927, Feng and Zhang's armies had both turned on Wu Peifu, ending his military career.

This succession of events demonstrated that by 1926 the northern warlords managed only to play each other out. It also demonstrated the fatal weakness of power based primarily on *guanxi* networks and lacking sufficient institutional and ideological underpinnings. Alliances changed at the whim of volatile commanders focused mainly on personal gain. The constant turmoil in North China not only deflected attention from developments in South China but fatally weakened the armies of the North. This helped create the conditions for a reunification of China from an unexpected point on the compass: South China. The interregnum after the fall of the Qing dynasty followed the pattern of other periods of dynastic change in which military power, not civil authority, proved decisive. But military power without effective civil administration was at best temporary, hence the revolving door for the many warlord governments and alliances. By 1926, there were warlords in North China willing to ally with the Nationalists. This support was to play a crucial role in the Nationalists' decision to organize the Northern Expedition, which set out on 9 July 1926 to reunite China.

The constant warfare had a devastating impact on the economy and on living conditions. For the three decades prior to the 1920 Zhili-Anhui War that set off the real mayhem, land-tax and rent collections remained fairly constant. Thereafter, flooding, droughts, disrupted transportation, erratic marketing conditions, and public disorder became widespread, preventing normal economic activities. Warfare greatly exacerbated the periodic flooding and droughts typical of China's severe weather patterns by utterly disrupting the public works projects and relief efforts necessary to mitigate their effects. Unemployment skyrocketed, formerly productive farmland became wasteland, and warlords filled their armies with the desperate and the unemployed, paying them by printing money that sent inflation soaring. Formerly rare events became common, such as the sale of children, mass migrations, skyrocketing tenancy, endemic rural indebtedness, and the sale of women into prostitution. The wars produced the greatest flood of refugees since the Taiping Rebellion. Thus, there was a growing gap between the ideals of the May Fourth Movement and the realities facing urban and especially rural Chinese.

Conclusions

The end of the May Fourth Movement is marked either by the decline in student demonstrations in 1921 or by the more militant phase of student activism in 1924, when many joined the armed struggle to overthrow the Beijing government. Regardless, the movement left an indelible mark on Chinese history by setting in motion a social revo-lution. It transformed the political landscape with the reorganization of Sun Yat'sen's Nationalist Party and the creation of the CCP. Henceforth, nationalism became the rallying cry for all successful nationwide political movements in China. In social life, the New Culture Movement and vernacular Chinese were in and Confucianism as an ethical system was out. This set a course that would overturn the family system, whereby the young always deferred to the old and women always deferred to men. Instead, the emancipation of women and the empowerment of youth accelerated.

But destruction of the Confucian family system left a moral vacuum that the next generation strove to fill, Mao Zedong with his "new morality" based on the subordination to the party instead and Chiang Kai-shek with his attempt to hybridize Confucianism with modernity in his New Life Movement. (See Chapter 19, Section IV.) No new consensus emerged. Hu Shi presented the New Culture Movement as a Chinese Renaissance. But unlike the Renaissance in the West, which coalesced around shared core values, the New Culture Movement gave birth to multiple and competing visions for China's future.

The Karakhan Manifesto helped shift the course of China's internal debate toward the Soviet political model. In contrast to the demands by the Western powers to uphold treaties, the Soviet government promised a new and unexploitative way of conducting international relations. The Bolshevik promises to return the Chinese Eastern Railway gratis contrasted favorably with the Japanese attempts to retain control over the Shandong railway. The intermediary for this exchange of ideas was the Moscow-funded and controlled Comintern, which helped found the CCP in 1921.

In the end, many Chinese trusted the Bolsheviks' promises, thus creating a counterpoint to the myth that Wilson betrayed China. This second myth portrayed the Soviet Union as treating China equally. In reality, Soviet officials very quickly reasserted control over all of the tsarist concessions and expanded Russian influence over Outer Mongolia, but this diplomacy remained secret. For reasons of face, the Beijing government did not point out the Soviet alterations of the Karakhan Manifesto. By the 1930s, a global economic depression seemed to confirm the bankruptcy of conventional Western models for development, while the rise of two alternatives—communism and fascism—became increasingly appealing to many Chinese.

North China was riven by warfare: The Anhui-Zhili War in 1920 was followed by the First Fengtian-Zhili War of 1922 and then the Second Fengtian-Zhili War of 1924. None of the players seemed to disappear, but they succeeded only in weakening each other and despoiling the country they claimed to rule. They demonstrated the consequences of power that was

Table 17.3   Economic Impact of Warlord Armies (in Chinese dollars)

Year	Number of Soldiers	Total Expenditures
1916	500,000	$ 153,000,000
1918	1,000,000	203,000,000
1924	1,500,000	—
1925	1,500,000	600,000,000
1927	—	700,000,000
1928	2,200,000	800,000,000
1931	—	1,335,000,000
1937	2,233,000	—

Source: Edward R. Slack, Jr., *Opium, State, and Society: China's Narco-Economy and the Guomindang, 1924–1937* (Honolulu: University of Hawai'i Press, 2001), 171.

entirely personalized, without regular channels of law and institutions. *Guanxi* network competed with *guanxi* network, with some parts betraying others, only to have former enemies become temporary allies. Personalized rule brought no stability to China. During this tumultuous period, China became less effective at dealing with the foreign powers.

In dynastic terms, the warlord era was the disastrous interregnum that typified periods of dynastic change. As one of China's most revered poets, Li Bo, had written in the eighth century: "Kites and ravens peck men's guts, / fly with them dangling from their beaks / and hang them high / on boughs of barren trees. / The troops lie mud-smeared in grasses, / and the general acted all in vain. / Now I truly see that weapons/ are evil's tools: / the Sage will use them only / when he cannot do otherwise."[3] Constant fighting and huge warlord exactions to fund their armies left poverty and famine in their wake, with economic development an ever more elusive dream. (See Table 17.3.)

BIBLIOGRAPHY

Alitto, Guy S. *The Last Confucian: Liang Shu-ming and the Chinese Dilemma of Modernity.* Berkeley: University of California Press, 1979.

Ch'i, Hsi-sheng. *Warlord Politics in China, 1916–1928.* Stanford, CA: Stanford University Press, 1976.

Chow, Tse-tung. *The May Fourth Movement: Intellectual Revolution in Modern China.* Cambridge, MA: Harvard University Press, 1980.

Dallin, David J. *The Rise of Russia in Asia.* New Haven, CT: Archon Books, 1971.

Doleželová-Velingerová, Milena, Oldrich Kral, Graham Saunders, and Leo Ou-fan Lee, eds. *The Appropriation of Cultural Capital: China's May Fourth Project.* Cambridge, MA: Harvard University Press, 2001.

Dreyer, Edward L. *China at War, 1901–1949.* London: Longman, 1995.

Elleman, Bruce A. *Diplomacy and Deception: The Secret History of Sino-Soviet Diplomatic Relations, 1917-1927.* Armonk, NY: M. E. Sharpe, 1997.

Fairbank, John K., ed. *The Cambridge History of China*, vol. 12, *Republican China 1912–1949, Part I.* Cambridge: Cambridge University Press, 1983.

Feigon, Lee. *Chen Duxiu: Founder of the Chinese Communist Party.* Princeton, NJ: Princeton University Press, 1983.

Grieder, Jerome B. *Hu Shih and the Chinese Renaissance: Liberalism in the Chinese Revolution, 1917-1937.* Cambridge, MA: Harvard University Press, 1970.

Leong, Sow-theng. *Sino-Soviet Diplomatic Relations, 1917–1926.* Canberra: Australian National University Press, 1976.

Levenson, Joseph R. *Confucian China and Its Modern Fate.* 3 vols. Berkeley: University of California Press, 1958–65.

———*Liang Ch'i-ch'ao and the Mind of Modern China.* Berkeley: University of California Press, 1970.

McCormack, Gavan. *Chang Tso-lin in Northeast China, 1911–1928.* Stanford, CA: Stanford University Press, 1977.

Meisner, Maurice. *Li Ta-chao and the Origins of Chinese Marxism.* New York: Atheneum, 1977.

Myers, Ramon H. "The Agrarian System." In *The Cambridge History of China*, vol 13, edited by John K. Fairbank and Albert Feuerwerker, 230–69. Cambridge: Cambridge University Press, 1986.

Nathan, Andrew J. *Peking Politics, 1918–1923: Factionalism and the Failure of Constitutionalism*. Berkeley: University of California Press, 1976.

————"A Constitutional Republic: The Peking Government, 1916–28." In *The Cambridge History of China*, vol. 12, edited by John K. Fairbank, 259–83. Cambridge: Cambridge University Press, 1983.

Paine, S. C. M. *Imperial Rivals: China, Russia, and Their Disputed Frontier*. Armonk, NY: M. E. Sharpe, 1996.

Richardson, Philip. *Economic Change in China, c. 1800–1950*. Cambridge: Cambridge University Press, 1999.

Schwarcz, Vera. *The Chinese Enlightenment: Intellectuals and the Legacy of the May Fourth Movement of 1919*. Berkeley: University of California Press, 1986.

Schwartz, Benjamin. "Themes in Intellectual History: May Fourth and After." In *The Cambridge History of China*, vol. 12, edited by John K. Fairbank and Albert Feuerwerker, 406–51. Cambridge: Cambridge University Press, 1983.

Sheridan, James E. *Chinese Warlord: The Career of Feng Yu-hsiang*. Stanford, CA: Stanford University Press, 1966.

————*China in Disintegration: The Republican Era in Chinese History, 1912–1949*. New York: Free Press, 1975.

Uhalley, Stephen. *A History of the Chinese Communist Party*. Stanford, CA: Hoover Institution Press, 1988.

van de Ven, Hans. *From Friend to Comrade: The Founding of the Chinese Communist Party, 1920–1927*. Berkeley: University of California Press, 1991.

Waldron, Arthur. *From War to Nationalism: China's Turning Point, 1924–1925*. Cambridge: Cambridge University Press, 1995.

Wang, Y. C. *Chinese Intellectuals and the West: 1872–1942*. Chapel Hill: University of North Carolina Press, 1966.

Whiting, Allen S. *Soviet Policies in China, 1917–1924*. New York: Columbia University Press, 1954.

Yeh, Wen-hsin. *The Alienated Academy: Culture and Politics in Republican China, 1919–1937*. Cambridge, MA: Harvard University Press, 1990.

NOTES

1. Hu Shi, "A Second Song of Endeavor," cited in Stacey Bieler, *"Patriots" or "Traitors"? A History of American-Educated Chinese Students* (Armonk, NY: M. E. Sharpe, 2004), 251.

2. Cited in ibid., 17.

3. Li Bo, "South of the Walls We Fought," in *An Anthology of Chinese Literature: Beginnings to 1911*, Stephen Owen, ed. (New York: W. W. Norton, 1996), 244. From AN ANTHOLOGY OF CHINESE LITERATURE: BEGINNINGS TO 1911 edited and translated by Stephen Owen. Copyright © 1996 by Stephen Owen and The Council for Cultural Planning and Development of the Executive Yuan of the Republic of China. Used by permission of W. W. Norton & Company, Inc.

Chronology

26 January 1923	Sun-Joffe Pact; beginning of the First United Front (1923–7)
1 March 1923	Sun established his third government in Guangzhou
20–30 Jan. 1924	Nationalist Party's First National Congress
31 May 1924	Sino-Soviet treaty and secret protocol restoring tsarist privileges
16 June 1924	Establishment of the Whampoa Military Academy
15 Sept.–3 Nov. 1924	Second Fengtian-Zhili War
20 September 1924	Soviet-Zhang Zuolin Treaty giving Russia control over the Chinese Eastern Railway
7 October 1924	First Russian arms shipment arrives in Guangzhou
13 November 1924	Sun Yat-sen leaves for Beijing
26 November 1924	Founding of the Mongolian People's Republic
20 January 1925	Russo-Japanese treaty confirming spheres of influence in Manchuria
12 March 1925	Sun Yat-sen dies in Beijing
13 May 1925	Chiang Kai-shek made army commander in chief
30 May 1925	May Thirtieth Movement in opposition to imperialism
1 July 1925	Wang Jingwei assumes civil leadership of the Nationalist Party
20 March 1926	*Zhongshan* Incident; Chiang Kai-shek wrests control from Wang Jingwei
9 June 1926	Chiang appointed commander of the Northern Expedition
9 July 1926	Beginning of the Northern Expedition
December 1926	Chiang moves the Nationalist capital to Nanchang
26 December 1926	Britain announces a new China policy
3 January 1927	Britain returns its concession in Hankou
21 February 1927	Left Nationalists establish a rival government in Wuhan
22 March 1927	Nationalist forces take Shanghai
24 March 1927	Nationalist forces take Nanjing
	Nanjing Incident results in the death of foreigners
12 April 1927	Nationalist purge of Communists (White Terror)
18 April 1927	Nationalist government established in Nanjing
15 July 1927	Official end to the First United Front
1 August 1927	CCP Nanchang Uprising; founding of the People's Liberation Army
Aug.–Sept. 1927	CCP Autumn Harvest Uprising
October 1927	Mao Zedong sets up base area in Jinggangshan Mountains
11–13 Dec. 1927	Guangzhou Commune (also called "Canton" Commune)
7 April 1928	Resumption of the Northern Expedition
3 May 1928	Jinan Incident between Japanese and Nationalist forces
4 June 1928	Assassination of Zhang Zuolin
9 June 1928	Nationalist troops enter Beijing
29 December 1928	Zhang Xueliang comes to an agreement with the Nationalists
31 December 1928	Chiang proclaims national reunification complete

18

The Nationalist-Communist United Front

There is one sentence that can light a fire,
Or, when spoken, bring dire disasters.
Don't think that for five thousand years nobody has said it.
How can you be sure of a volcano's silence?
Perhaps one day, as if possessed by a spirit,
Suddenly out of the blue sky a thunder
Will explode:
"This is our China!"[1]

Wen Yiduo (1899–1946), assassinated,
professor, democrat, 1927

In North China the warlords had proven incapable of transforming operational success—the military defeat of the enemy—into strategic success with the creation of a unified and stable China. The civil and military elements of effective governance started to coalesce with the first Nationalist-Communist United Front. Sun Yat-sen agreed to the United Front strategy in January 1923 in order to create a military force capable of reuniting China. Success depended on Soviet aid, including funds, advisers, and arms via the Comintern, Soviet Russia's front organization for promoting communism abroad. After Sun Yat-sen died in 1925, Chiang Kai-shek became the commander in chief of the Nationalist Army on 5 June 1926. Whereas Sun had been a civil leader, Chiang was a military leader, and he attempted to reunify China by military means by launching the Northern Expedition in 1926, reaching Shanghai in 1927. On 12 April 1927, however, Chiang turned on his Soviet allies and purged the Nationalist Party of Communists and Communist sympathizers, summarily executing all he could find. He then launched the second phase of the Northern Expedition to take Beijing and force an alliance with the Fengtian Clique for a tenuous reunification of the core provinces of China plus Manchuria. The Nation-alists reunified China on paper and made significant progress institutionalizing their rule in the ensuing Nanjing Decade (1928–37), until the Japanese halted the process with their devastating invasion in 1937.

I. South China Diplomacy: The Origins of the First United Front

Both Sun Yat-sen and the heads of the various Beijing governments wished to reunite not just the core provinces of China, but the entire Qing empire. Soviet Russia deftly pursued multitrack negotiations designed to play off the Guangzhou, Beijing, and Manchurian governments against each other in order to consolidate a vast sphere of influence in Mongolia and Manchuria. The Soviet strategy entailed trading aid for desired concessions and then using each of these governments to put pressure on the others in order to consolidate incrementally its sphere of influence.

The roots of the United Front policy stretch back to 1917, when Sun Yat-sen publicly praised the Bolshevik Revolution. During 1918, the Russian foreign minister offered to form an alliance with Sun's first Guangzhou government as a way to exert pressure on the Beijing government in their ongoing negotiations. Support for the Nationalists fit the Soviet strategy of allying with nationalist movements as a way station on the path toward social revolution. During the Russian Civil War, Vladimir Lenin developed the original united-front strategy, whereby the Communists temporarily allied with a variety of so-called progressive social forces in order to achieve victory. After their victory in Russia, Lenin believed a succession of similar revolutions in neighboring countries must follow for Soviet Russia to

285

survive. By 1922, Soviet strategists considered China to be one of the most promising colonial countries for a successful revolution of national liberation, right behind Turkey, India, Persia, and Egypt. They hoped that China would soon become the second Communist state after Russia.

Sun did not care about world revolution, but focused single-mindedly on creating an ideology and a political organization under his leadership capable of uniting and administering China. This presupposed a China unified by military conquest, but Sun had not risen to power through the ranks of the old Qing military, as had Yuan Shikai, or through the ranks of its successor armies, as had the many warlords of North China. He was a civil, not a military, leader, yet his plans hinged on an effective Nationalist army. Although Sun would have preferred military support from the United States, England, or Canada, when these countries rejected his overtures, he turned to Soviet Russia as a last resort. Soviet promises of funding, military advisers, and arms then convinced Sun to establish a formal alliance with the CCP. The Western democracies failed to respond to this development because the restoration of war-torn Europe and the containment of Germany dominated their field of vision.

Sun remained fixated on a northern expedition to reunify China. He feared that an alliance with Soviet Russia might undermine this goal should the British counter the alliance by assisting one of the other warlords. So he tried to go it alone, but the first Northern Expedition did not go well. It left Guangzhou on 3 February 1922 but soon bogged down for lack of funds. Moscow's Communist Youth League sent its own representative, Sergei Dalin, to meet with Sun on 27 April 1922. While Sun wanted Soviet military aid, Dalin wanted Sun's cooperation in its diplomacy with the Beijing government, but Sun was reluctant to cede Mongolia and the Chinese Eastern Railway.

Meanwhile, the North China warlords were seeking allies throughout China as they drifted toward the First Fengtian-Zhili War (1922). When Sun allied with the Fengtian Clique out of a common desire to overthrow the government in Beijing, the Zhili Clique that controlled Beijing made a counteralliance with the Guangdong warlord, Chen Jiongming, who withdrew his military support from Sun. This caused Sun's second government in Guangzhou to fall on 16 June 1922. With the help of a young military cadet, Chiang Kai-shek, Sun sought refuge in Shanghai. This setback made Sun more receptive to Soviet offers.

After the Russian envoy, Aleksandr Paikes, left China, his replacement tried a different tactic. When Adolf Joffe's negotiations foundered with the Beijing government over the status of Outer Mongolia and of the Chinese Eastern Railway (see Chapter 17, Section III), he turned his attention to Sun

Yat-sen and the creation of a United Front. In mid-January 1923, Joffe traveled to Shanghai, where he met with Sun Yat-sen, who was between governments at the time and not in a position to be too choosy. On 26 January they formalized Sino-Soviet cooperation and officially inaugurated the First United Front[2] with the Sun-Joffe Pact. To relieve Nationalist suspicions of Soviet intentions, the agreement stated that China was not ripe for communism and Soviet Russia had no imperialistic designs on Outer Mongolia. Although it remained a part of China, Sun recognized the status quo, which in practice meant continued Soviet occupation. He also agreed to the joint management of the Chinese Eastern Railway.

Sun's agreement to these terms contributed to Moscow's ongoing negotiations with the Beijing government. The latter was demanding, per the terms of the Bolsheviks' original Karakhan Manifesto of 25 July 1919, a complete withdrawal of the Red Army from Outer Mongolia and a return of the Chinese Eastern Railway. In fact, with Sun's tacit support the Red Army stayed on in Outer Mongolia, which remained a Soviet puppet state until the USSR's collapse in 1991. In 1922, Sun was not in control of his base in Guangzhou, let alone Outer Mongolia or the Chinese Eastern Railway. So, he traded something he did not have for tangible Soviet aid. Like the Japanese loans to warlord governments in Beijing, this decision set international precedents that his successors would be unable to alter.

Sun also agreed to a United Front with the CCP, provided that the Communists joined the Nationalist Party as individuals, not as a bloc, rejecting an equal alliance. The Chinese Communists were not happy with such terms, but the Comintern ordered them to join the Nationalist Party anyway. The Chinese Communists took advantage of their improved relations with the Nationalists to promote labor unions and the urban labor movement; in this period, rural areas remained peripheral to the Communist strategy.

Thus, the Sun-Joffe Pact ceded the Soviets territorial concessions that they spent years fruitlessly trying to negotiate with a Beijing government more willing to cut deals with Japan than with the Soviet Union. It also extended Communist influence into South China via Communist infiltration of the Nationalist Party.

II. The Reorganization of the Nationalist Party

In return for these many concessions, Sun Yat-sen received financial and technical aid critical to the successful restructuring of the Nationalist Party. Upon the pact's signature,

Sun had the wherewithal to return to Guangzhou to form his third government. (See Table 15.2.) Sun envisioned state building as a three-stage process of military rule to reunify the country, followed by political tutelage under the Nationalist Party, and culminating in democratic, constitutional rule. During the tutelage stage that lasted arguably until the fully democratic 2000 Taiwanese presidential elections, the Nationalist Party took upon itself the task of ruling in the name of the people while educating and preparing them for self-government, starting at the local level and gradually working up to the national level.

Sun Yat-sen divided his government into five branches, subsequently outlined in the Nationalist Constitution. In addition to the executive, legislative, and judicial branches that structure most Western governments, he revived two imperial institutions that he called the "control branch" and the "examination branch." These harkened back to the Censorate and Board of Rites controlling internal surveillance and the imperial examinations respectively. The former performed as an ombudsman to ascertain the morals and performance of officials, while the latter vetted applicants for public jobs through civil service examinations.

The Nationalist Constitution, the platform of the Nationalist Party, and the opening line of the National Anthem all emphasized Sun Yat-sen's Three People's Principles of nationalism, democracy, and the people's livelihood. Nationalism embraced not only the many ethnic groups of China, but also freedom from imperialism. Democracy entailed elections and a five-branch government. The people's livelihood emphasized the government's obligation to provide its citizens with adequate food, shelter, clothing, and transportation. In practice, during the period of tutelage, the leadership of the Nationalist Party ruled supreme.

The Soviet Union provided the Nationalist Party with the institutional means to exercise party rule in practice. Moscow began to send military advisers, weapons, and funds to create a modern Nationalist Army, and the Comintern sent a team of advisers under Mikhail Borodin to reorganize the Nationalist Party. Sun patterned the Nationalist Army and political institutions on Soviet Russia's highly successful Leninist model. The Red Army had just finished reunifying the vast Russian empire, fighting off a variety of warlord armies within Russia and successfully parrying foreign intervention. Soviet civil leaders overcame these challenges to establish stable governmental institutions. For many Chinese, Russia seemed to offer the civil and military blueprint for their own country's reunification.

Soviet advisers transformed the Nationalist Party into a highly centralized and disciplined organization along the lines of the Bolshevik Party. They used the United Front to pair loyal Communists with Nationalist experts. This dual system fit with the use of political commissars that had been so effective in bringing the Bolsheviks to power and with Qing precedents that had paired Han and Manchu senior officials and was, in turn, based on Mongol practices. The Bolsheviks utilized the expertise of civil servants and military officers of the former tsarist government but paired such experts with politically reliable commissars. The USSR wanted the CCP to play this role in any Nationalist Party unification of China. It also wanted a fifth column in place to seize control later.

The Soviet advisers helped the Nationalists establish administrative institutions at the national, provincial, county, and local levels as well as a National Party Congress under the control of a Central Executive Committee authorized to act between the biannual congressional sessions. In Nationalist China, as in the Soviet Union, they established parallel institutions of party and government control. In January 1924, the First Congress of the Nationalist Party called for strict party discipline, a propaganda offensive, and a strong army to defeat both domestic opponents and foreign imperialism. The Three People's Principles were recrafted to take on a Communist spin. National liberation replaced nationalism, party control overshadowed democracy, and socialism colored the people's livelihood. As with the Bolsheviks, the Nationalist Party controlled the army.

Moscow funded and helped staff a Nationalist military academy on Whampoa Island, near Guangzhou. The Whampoa Military Academy opened on 16 June 1924. In the following year alone, an estimated 1,000 Soviet political advisers and military instructors arrived, while a Soviet general headed its military delegation. Between World War I and the Russian Civil War, these experts had gained ample military experience. The academy's first commandant, Chiang Kai-shek, had received his military training in Japan, while most of the Chinese instructors had been trained either in Japan or at one of China's elite military schools established during the Self-strengthening or late-Qing reform periods. Students at the Whampoa Military Academy received a rigorous six-month course that included technical training and political indoctrination. This Soviet assistance rapidly transformed Whampoa into the premier Chinese military school of the 1920s.

In keeping with Confucian educational traditions, masters continued to train their disciples; Chiang Kai-shek personally trained the first three classes of approximately 2,000 students. As his students, they owed him their allegiance. This dramatically expanded his *guanxi* network within the army. These men would become some of his

Trained in military schools in Japan, Chiang Kai-shek became the first commandant of the Soviet-funded Whampoa Military Academy in 1924. Chiang gained the loyalty of the first Whampoa graduates, who were later called the Whampoa Clique. Here Chiang is seen with Hu Hanmin (center), one of the strongest political leaders following Sun's death, and Wu Chaoshu (right), the British-trained head of the Nationalist Ministry of Foreign Affairs. This photograph may date to April 1927, just as Chiang was purging the Communists from the United Front.

most loyal supporters, known as the Whampoa Clique. Graduates soon saw action against Sun Yat-sen's nemesis, the Guangdong warlord Chen Jiongming, whose on-again-off-again support undermined Sun Yat-sen's first two governments. This time, when Chen tried to take advantage of Sun's absence in Beijing to attack the Guangzhou government, the new army handily defeated his larger but less well organized force.

In addition to forming a new army, Sun Yat-sen played an important diplomatic role in 1924. In the lead-up to the Second Fengtian-Zhili War, Sun allied again with the Fengtian Clique and remnants of the Anhui Clique to oppose the Zhili Clique's bid to reunify China. In November 1924, after Feng Yuxiang crippled the Zhili Clique with his defection, Feng, Zhang Zuolin, and the recently reinstated Duan Qirui invited Sun Yat-sen to come to Beijing to discuss the reunification of China under their auspices. Exploratory surgery in Beijing in late January 1925 revealed that Sun was suffering from inoperable cancer of the liver. This gave him less than two months to prepare his final political testament, exhorting his followers to reunite China under his principles and extolling the Sino-Soviet alliance. Sun's death on 12 March 1925 decapitated his vast *guanxi* network. As the many parts of this network succumbed to the gravitational pull of other leaders, it was unclear whether the Nationalist-Communist alliance would survive or whether the Communists would attempt to take control of the Nationalist Party.

III. North China Diplomacy: Beijing and Manchurian Warlords

Moscow successfully played off Beijing and the Manchurian warlord, Zhang Zuolin, against each other to consolidate its control over the Chinese Eastern Railway and Outer Mongolia. In 1924, Lev Karakhan, the USSR's new envoy to China, convinced Beijing to recognize the existence of the tsarist treaties with the expectation that they would be renegotiated at a conference to be convened almost a year later, but the two sides never reached an agreement on any amendments. This left the USSR with the tsarist treaty regime in place unchanged while reaping a harvest of favorable propaganda for publicly agreeing to renounce those same treaties.

Karakhan arrived in Beijing in September 1923. In early 1924, he implied that he would agree to Beijing's demands to abolish all of the tsarist unequal treaties, withdraw all Soviet troops from Outer Mongolia, and relinquish ownership of the Chinese Eastern Railway. In return, China recognized the USSR, breaking Moscow's almost total diplomatic isolation. Karakhan also agreed to a separate protocol stating that all former Sino-Russian treaties would not be enforced pending renegotiation. Implicit was Beijing's recognition of the legitimacy of these earlier agreements, although the terms were suspended. Through propaganda and pro-treaty demonstrations, both the Nationalists and the CCP pressured Beijing to sign the treaty and protocol.

At the suggestion of V. K. Wellington Koo, Beijing's foreign minister, Karakhan signed the Sino-Soviet treaty on 31 May 1924, the sixty-ninth anniversary of the failed Taiping 1855 Northern Expedition; hard-core Nationalists were undoubtedly upset by the implication that the North would defeat the South. While such dating tends to be considered coincidental in the West, in traditional Chinese thinking, where the cyclical conception of time and the traditional mode of analysis emphasized historical analogies to decipher the present, such overlapping dates contained carefully crafted messages.

Moscow took immediate advantage of the secret protocol. It retained all of tsarist Russia's special rights and privileges in China by delaying the convening of the official Sino-Soviet conference. Meanwhile it negotiated separate agreements with Japan and Zhang Zuolin, even while purging the Outer Mongolian leadership. As long as the conference did not convene, the Soviet Union's obligation under the 31 May 1924 treaty to remove its troops from Outer Mongolia and sell the Chinese Eastern Railway to China remained moot; even when the conference finally convened in August 1925, new treaties and conventions were never finalized, leaving the secret protocol in effect. As in the Shandong controversy, the diplomatic details were complex and kept secret from the Chinese public, which believed that the USSR had treated China better than had the United States.

Over the Beijing government's objections, Karakhan opened separate negotiations with Zhang Zuolin, signing a supplemental agreement with the Manchurian Autonomous Three Eastern Provinces on 20 September 1924. A secret protocol transferred control of the Chinese share of the railway from Beijing to Zhang and gave him the power to choose which Chinese officials would represent China in the joint commission running the railway. In return, Karakhan rewarded Zhang by changing the terms of the 1896 railway contract to reduce the original eighty-year lease to sixty years. At the end of sixty years, in 1956, the Autonomous Three Eastern Provinces of the Republic of China would receive back the railway and the surrounding railway property free of charge. Other changes included a provision that all profits from the railway would be divided equally between Moscow and Zhang's warlord government. Although this second secret protocol gave the appearance that Zhang would retain a half interest in the management of the railway, the USSR assumed majority control by reorganizing the railway administration so that it held most positions and by packing the upper administration with Soviet representatives.

Then, on 20 January 1925, the Soviet Union and Japan signed a treaty establishing political and economic relations and reaffirming the validity of the Portsmouth Peace Treaty of 5 September 1905, terminating the Russo-Japanese War. This meant that Tokyo acknowledged Soviet control over the Chinese Eastern Railway, while Moscow reaffirmed Japan's control of the South Manchurian Railway, thereby guaranteeing that neither would help the Chinese regain control over the Manchurian railway system.

Even more dangerous to China were the provisions dividing Manchuria into Japanese and Soviet spheres of influence by reconfirming Japanese-tsarist agreements dividing up Manchuria and Mongolia. This effectively undermined Washington's efforts to enforce the Open Door Policy and also contradicted the Russian propaganda excoriating foreign imperialism. When the Beijing government's new foreign minister, Wang Zhengting (Wang Cheng-t'ing), known as C. T. Wang, secretly protested the new Soviet-Japanese convention, Karakhan referred to China's 1915 treaty with Japan, the infamous Twenty-one Demands, to legitimate the Soviet-Japanese convention, something Wilson refused to do.

The Soviet Union also tightened its hold over Outer Mongolia during September 1924 with a purge that included the execution of the commander in chief of the Outer Mongolian Army as well the execution of five other prominent Mongol leaders. The spiritual leader of the Mongolian Lamaism also conveniently died in this period. By late September 1924, almost all non-Soviet foreigners had been expelled from Outer Mongolia. On 26 November 1924, the Mongolian People's Republic was founded and a new socialist constitution was promulgated.

The Soviet Union successfully followed a two-stage strategy. It established de facto control over Outer Mongolia and the Chinese Eastern Railway, and then it attempted to secure de jure control through parallel diplomacy with the Beijing, Guangzhou, and Manchurian governments. In the end, it divided and conquered. After Mao's victory in 1949, Stalin continued to refuse to renegotiate the unequal treaties with the People's Republic of China, a decision that contributed to the Sino-Soviet split in 1960.

IV. The Rise of Chiang Kai-shek and the Northern Expedition

Sun Yat-sen's *guanxi* network held the Nationalist Party together. As in other warlord governments, following his death in 1925, there was competition among his subordinates to take control of the party. In July, the Nationalists established a national government in Guangzhou and then reorganized the armed forces into the National Revolutionary Army. Wang Jingwei (Wang Ching-wei) became the leader of the left wing of the Nationalist Party, while Chiang Kai-shek became the leader of the right wing.

Wang, like many early party leaders, had been educated in Japan, where he met Sun Yat-sen and joined the Tongmenghui. He gained enormous national prestige for his failed assassination attempt in 1910 of the regent, Prince Chun, and had risen in the ranks of the Nationalist Party to become Sun's most trusted adviser. Wang advised Sun on his deathbed to sign a "will," which admonished Nationalist Party members to continue cooperation with the Soviet Union. Upon Sun's death, Wang took political control of the Nationalist Party. With the Comintern's backing, he began to purge the Nationalist Party of hundreds of anti-Soviet members.

Wang and other members of the left wing of the Nationalist Party attempted to take advantage of the seething labor unrest in China. During the spring of 1925, the May Thirtieth Movement erupted when a Japanese foreman killed a Shanghai worker during riots at a Japanese cotton mill. On 30 May, students from all over the city organized a protest outside a Shanghai police station. When the demonstrators refused to disperse, the police arrested three of them and four others were killed as the confrontation spiraled out of control. The demonstrations in Shanghai ignited anti-foreign protests throughout China. The movement quickly spread to Guangzhou, where a strike at the British concession on Shamian (Shameen) Island began on 20 June 1925. The CCP and the Nationalist Party organized a mass march of thousands of students, workers, and ordinary citizens, who converged on Shameen Island on 23 June. This demonstration ended in a massacre. The May Thirtieth Movement entailed a year-long boycott of Hong Kong, leaving 100,000 Chinese workers in Guangzhou unemployed. As Hong Kong trade imploded, losses mounted for British and Chinese interests alike.

While Wang Jingwei's faction tried to ride the tide of events to consolidate his control over the Nationalist Party, Chiang Kai-shek tried to make his own bid for power through the Nationalist military. Chiang had joined the Tongmenghui in 1908, and returned from Japan upon the outbreak of the 1911 Revolution to organize revolutionary forces. During these years in Shanghai he made formative connections in his *guanxi* network, including close ties with the Green Gang, the secret society dominating the Shanghai underworld. (See the feature on the next page.) After the Bolshevik Revolution, he became deeply impressed by the Soviets' combination of party and military organizations. In 1923, Sun sent Chiang to Moscow leading a delegation to study Soviet military institutions. Thereafter, Chiang replicated the Soviet political commissar system by embedding Nationalist Party loyalists in the army. As commandant of the Whampoa Military Academy, he worked closely with Soviet advisers to implement these reforms. On the eve of the May Thirtieth Movement, the Nationalist Party's Central Executive Committee made Chiang Kai-shek the commander in chief of the army with the mission of reuniting China by means of a second Northern Expedition.

Chiang used his position as commander of the First Army to consolidate his power base. In March 1926, he

SECRET SOCIETIES

The term "secret society" is of Western origin, originally meant to describe the many clandestine organizations in China. Secret societies provided *guanxi* networks for people on the move, such as peddlers, monks, and tradesmen. Secret society membership gave such people protection when they were away from home, substituting for the native place associations that fulfilled this function at home. Such associations were extremely important in China because they tended to resolve social conflicts more easily and quickly than the legal system did. Secret societies also protected local interests against those of outsiders. They created a *guanxi* network overarching the *guanxi* networks of clan and village. Elaborate initiation rituals and oaths of mutual assistance were typical.

Mutual defense societies often formed around preexisting local religious organizations, helping to account for the religious overtones of many secret societies. Sworn brotherhoods also developed into secret societies in the manner described in the popular stories from the *Romance of the Three Kingdoms* and *Water Margin*. There were relatively few secret societies until late in the reign of the Qianlong emperor, but as Chinese central institutions became increasingly enfeebled during the nineteenth century, the importance of secret societies grew.

Central governments have generally regarded secret societies with extreme suspicion and hostility because, more often than not, such organizations have opposed the traditional political order and government attempts at centralization. The Qing therefore condemned the religious views of secret societies as heterodox and warranting persecution. In the Qing period, the only exception to this rule was the Boxer Uprising, which ended badly for the Qing. The Communists also regarded secret societies as unwanted political competition, since the societies tended to focus on preserving the very local order and *guanxi* ties that communism sought to eradicate. The Nationalists, however, were riddled with secret societies. Sun Yat-sen had used the Triads to mobilize political support, while Chiang Kai-shek used the Green Gang, a Triad offshoot, to control Shanghai and assassinate the political opposition. Secret societies became heavily involved in the labor movement and in organized crime.

The Triads are among China's most long-lived and important secret societies. They emerged during the second half of the eighteenth century as a mutual aid society to cope with accelerating overpopulation and economic problems in Fujian province. Increasingly scarce resources set off local feuding, often between the many ethnic groups that make up South China. Over the years, the Triads spread throughout much of South China, particularly in Fujian, Guangdong, Guangxi, and Jiangxi provinces, where they expanded along the provincial frontiers and transportation routes. They had a significant Hakka membership. Feuding among the many ethnic groups populating South China is long-standing, and secret societies soon became involved. In addition, they became involved in various criminal activities. During the Republic period, the Triads became notorious for the latter. They moved from theft and extortion to prostitution, gambling, smuggling, and selling drugs. It is unclear how much of their growth came from opium smuggling in the nineteenth century, when foreigners imported opium but did not distribute it.

The Communists did their best to eliminate secret societies in the People's Republic of China, but they remained active in Hong Kong, Macao, and Taiwan. In Taiwan, secret societies have been deeply involved in the construction and entertainment industries. With the liberalization under Deng Xiaoping, secret societies returned to the People's Republic of China in the 1980s. Hong Kong Triads allegedly helped smuggle out dissidents after the Beijing Massacre in 1989. In the 1990s, the government of the People's Republic of China increasingly tried to limit secret society activities. In particular, it suppressed Falun Gong, a mystical Buddhism sect, after its demonstrations in 1999 demanding official status.

accused the Chinese Communists of sending a Nationalist naval vessel, *Zhongshan,* to kidnap him. He used this as a pretext to declare martial law, purge many top Communists from the military, put Soviet advisers under house arrest, and force Wang Jingwei into exile. This left Chiang in charge of government positions, to which he appointed key members of his own *guanxi* network.

On 15 May 1926, the Central Committee of the Nationalist Party issued new guidelines for the remaining Communists. These included registration of all Communist members of the Nationalist Party, restrictions on their serv-ing in high positions, and the demotion of many CCP members. As a result of this purge, the CCP lost much of its influence within the United Front. To no avail Chen Duxiu requested Comintern permission for the CCP to withdraw from the Nationalist Party.

On 9 July 1926, Chiang set the Northern Expedition in motion. (See Map 18.1 and Table 18.1.) The Nationalist Army rapidly moved north, taking Wuchang on the fifteenth anniversary of the 1911 Revolution, 10 October 1926, and expelling Wu Peifu from the central Yangzi Valley. Next, Chiang eliminated Sun Chuanfang, the warlord

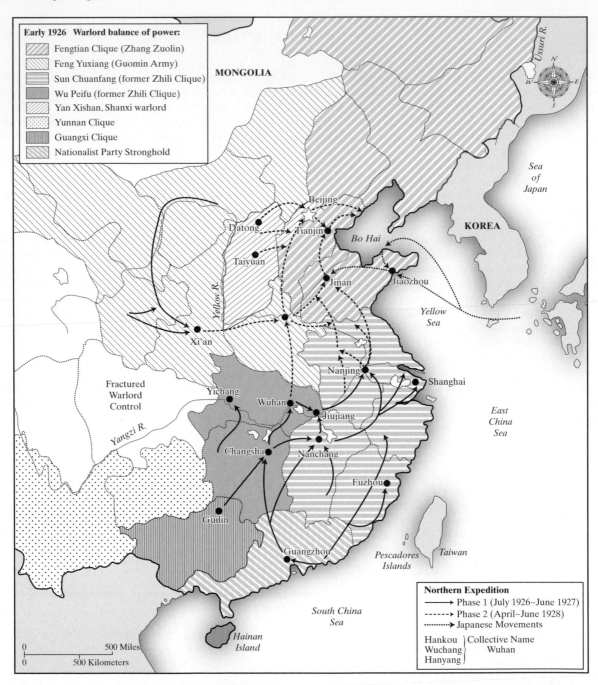

Map 18.1 Northern Expedition (1926–8)

governing the five southeastern provinces of Jiangsu, Zhejiang, Anhui, Jiangxi, and Fujian, which controlled the lower reaches of the Yangzi River; the trade emporium, Shanghai; and much of the central coastline of China. Sun Chuanfang had also received his military education in Japan, where for

a time he had been a member of the Tongmenghui, but after his return to China he gradually had become associated with the Zhili Clique. In the aftermath of the Second Fengtian-Zhili War, he commanded one of the two strongest armies of the Zhili Clique (Wu Peifu led the

Table 18.1 Warlord Coalitions during the Northern Expedition

Major Non-Nationalist Warlords Prior to the Northern Expedition

Leader	Territory	Events
Wu Peifu (Zhili Clique)	Henan, Hebei, part of Zhili, Hunan	Defeated in fall 1926
Sun Chuanfang (ex-Zhili Clique)	Nanjing, Jiangsu, Zhejiang, Fujian, Jiangxi, Anhui	Defeated in winter of 1926–7
Zhang Zuolin (Fengtian Clique)	Beijing, Manchuria, Zhili, Shandong	Allied with Sun Chuanfang
Yan Xishan	Shanxi	Allied with Sun Chuanfang
Feng Yuxiang	Northwest China	Supported purge of CCP

Main Rival Governments at the End of the First Stage of the Northern Expedition (1926–7)

Leader	Capital	Followers	Supporters of Purge of CCP Spring 1927	Consequences
Chiang Kai-shek	Nanchang (later Nanjing)	Right-wing Nationalists	✓	Alienated Soviet Union
Wang Jingwei	Wuhan	Left-wing Nationalists, CCP	✓	Reunification with Nanjing
Zhang Zuolin	Beijing	Manchurians	✓	Alienated Soviet Union

Nationalist Coalition During the Second Stage of the Northern Expedition (1928)

Leader	Territory	Consequences
Chiang Kai-shek	South China	Coalition expelled Zhang Zuolin from Beijing but
Feng Yuxiang	Northwest	Japanese murdered him on his return home. His son,
Yan Xishan	Shanxi	Zhang Xueliang, allied with Nationalists, creating
Li Zongren	Guangxi Clique	the nominal reunification of China

other). In December 1925, Sun Chuanfang declared his five provinces independent of the Beijing government and neutral in the anticipated Nationalist attempt to reunify China. But Chiang obliterated Sun's army. These successes put the Nationalists in control of Shanghai on 22 March and Nanjing on 24 March 1927, ending the first phase of the Northern Expedition.

Left-wing elements of the Nationalist Party capitalized on Chiang's absence from Guangzhou to consolidate their influence. In December 1926, Chiang responded by moving the capital to Nanchang, where he could oversee both military operations and civil rule. In January 1927, the Communists and other members of the Left Nationalists set up a rival government in Wuhan. For several months there were competing Nationalist governments. On 7 March 1927, Chiang sent a clear warning to Moscow not to attempt to direct the Chinese revolution. Soon afterward the Left Nationalists and the Communists took over the party's Central Committee, while Nationalist Party mem-

bers from Guangxi, the so-called Guangxi Clique, worked to overthrow Chiang.

V. The Beginning of the Nationalist-Communist Civil War

March 1927 was a very eventful month. The competition between the left and right wings of the Nationalist Party became increasingly intense. On 13 March, the Central Committee stripped Chiang Kai-shek of his chairmanships of the Political Committee, the Standing Committee, and the Military Council. His only remaining official post was his command over the expeditionary forces. On 21 March, the CCP orchestrated a general strike and armed insurrection in Shanghai in anticipation of the arrival of the Northern Expedition. As a result, 600,000 workers paralyzed the city so that Nationalist troops could enter the next day unopposed. Workers continued to organize. On 27 March

1,000 representatives of 300 union branches convened. The CCP urged the workers to disarm, to cooperate with the Nationalists, and to drop their more radical demands, such as the return of all foreign concessions to China. Simultaneously, a crisis with the foreign powers erupted. On 24 March, as the Nationalists took Nanjing, a contingent attacked the local foreign community, killing six, wounding many others, and destroying foreign property. British, American, French, Italian, and Japanese warships immediately retaliated by bombarding the city in what became known as the Nanjing Incident. Foreigners eventually attributed the killings to Communist sympathizers, which exonerated Chiang Kai-shek, but relations with the foreign powers remained tense.

Against this backdrop of social, labor, and diplomatic turmoil, the Comintern claimed its United Front to be on the verge of creating a national and social revolution in China. The Communists tried to undercut Chiang's position within the Nationalist Party, and workers seemed to be on the verge of seizing power. Meanwhile, as the Beijing government became increasingly concerned about the progress of the Northern Expedition and the possibility of a Communist seizure of power, it raided the Soviet embassy on 6 April 1927 and reported the discovery of proof that the USSR was plotting not only its overthrow but also Chiang's. Copies of these documents quickly found their way to Shanghai.

When Chiang demanded that the Comintern recall Borodin, the leader of the Soviet advisers, the Wuhan government stripped Chiang of his last official title as commander of the expeditionary forces. But Chiang was back in the heart of his own *guanxi* network, near his home province of Zhejiang and in the midst of his Shanghai connections. Instead of stepping down, on 5 April he issued orders to disarm all militia members in Shanghai who were not members of the Nationalist Army. This included many members of Shanghai CCP cells. On 12 April, Chiang joined forces with the underworld Green Gang and ordered a massacre of thousands of CCP members in Shanghai. This became known as the White Terror. The elimination of Communists from the Nationalist Party lasted for many months, entailed

Following Chiang Kai-shek's decision to purge the Communists from the United Front during April 1927, the Comintern representatives, including Mikhail Borodin (center), attempted to form a new government at Wuhan with Wang Jingwei (right), the head of the left wing of the Nationalist Party. Borodin's interpreter, Zhang Tailei, is sitting between them. When this new government failed, the Comintern advisers were forced to return to the USSR during late July 1927.

thousands of summary executions, and left the Nanjing government under the Right Nationalists. Included among the dead was Li Dazhao, a founder of the CCP. On 15 July, the Left Nationalists and the CCP split, marking the official end to the United Front. The Soviet military advisers soon returned home.

Over the summer of 1927, the Chinese Communists staged a last-ditch effort by ordering uprisings in Hunan, Hubei, Jiangxi, and Guangdong provinces. On 1 August, on the thirty-third anniversary of the formal beginning of the First Sino-Japanese War, they staged a mutiny among Nationalist troops at Nanchang, the capital of Jiangxi. The Nationalist Army put it down within four days. Nevertheless, the Nanchang Uprising is considered the origin of the People's Liberation Army of the CCP. The Communist survivors of the Nanchang Uprising, such as its leader, Zhu De, fled to rural areas in South China, where they joined with Mao Zedong to organize a peasant-based revolutionary movement.

Following the defeat at Nanchang, Communist leaders met in Hankou on 7 August 1927 to organize rebellions in Hubei and Hunan. This became known as the Autumn Harvest Uprising in the early fall of 1927. The future leader of the People's Republic of China, Mao Zedong, played a leading role in crafting a Communist strategy emphasizing land reform. But the CCP's Central Committee and the Comintern both rejected his emphasis on rural areas and demoted Mao after the uprising failed.

The last and most unsuccessful of the revolts occurred in Guangzhou, the capital of Guangdong. The Communists tried to take advantage of a local power vacuum caused by disagreements among the Guangdong and Guangxi warlords. The city had long been a center of activity for the Communists. They established the Guangzhou Commune (Canton Commune) that lasted from 11 to 13 December 1927. When the citizens of Guangzhou did not rise up to support it, the local warlords easily restored order. The common strategy of these failed uprisings had been to take control of urban areas in the expectation of spontaneous sympathetic revolts of the local population. These never occurred, so the weak Communist forces were easily annihilated.

Meanwhile, the Left Nationalist government in Wuhan dissolved in February 1928. Later that year, Chiang Kai-shek accepted many of its members, including Wang Jingwei, back into the Nationalist Party. In order to sponsor the reunification of the various Nationalist factions, in August 1927 Chiang temporarily stepped down as commander in chief of the National Revolutionary Army. In particular, the Guangxi warlords, Li Zongren and Bai Chongxi, also known as the Guangxi Clique, wanted Chiang out of power. They would

remain Chiang's key Nationalist rivals until the bitter end of the Chinese civil war in 1949.

During this hiatus in Chiang's career, he married Song Meiling, the U.S.-educated daughter of a wealthy Shanghai Protestant missionary family and younger sister of Sun Yat-sen's widow. Her brother, Song Ziwen, and her brother-in-law, Kong Xiangxi, would become central figures in Nationalist finance. The marriage extended Chiang's *guanxi* network into the U.S.-connected Christian convert community as well as into the wealthy Shanghai financial community, while his connection by marriage to Sun Yat-sen gave him greater prestige within the Nationalist Party.

At the request of the Nationalist leadership, on 6 January 1928, Chiang resumed command of the Northern Expedition. This second phase was in some ways more difficult than the first because the Nationalist Party was fundamentally a South China political movement and Chiang was now moving into North China. Chiang maintained his alliance with the northern warlord, Feng Yuxiang, who had betrayed his Soviet benefactors in late June 1927 in exchange for being made the Nationalist provincial leader of Henan. In February 1928, the Nationalists reorganized the army, dividing it among the party's four primary warlords: Chiang commanded the First Army, Feng Yuxiang led the Second Army, the Shanxi warlord Yan Xishan led the Third Army, and the Guangxi Clique warlord Li Zongren commanded the Fourth Army. Since the Zhili Clique armies of Wu Peifu and Sun Chuanfang had been defeated in the first phase of the Northern Expedition, the second phase focused on the elimination of the Manchuria warlord, Zhang Zuolin, who had taken Beijing after the defeat of Wu Peifu. In spring 1928, Chiang's troops entered Shandong and Zhang's forces were soon on the defensive.

Japan feared that a Nationalist occupation of Shandong province would undermine its special interests there. On 3 May 1928, Japanese and Nationalist forces clashed in Jinan in what became known as the Jinan Incident. The Japanese government then issued identical notes to the Beijing and Nationalist governments warning that it would not tolerate disorders in Manchuria, the focus of its economic interests in China. It specifically warned Zhang Zuolin that it would not allow his forces north of the Great Wall unless they retreated in good order. Zhang's attempted return home from Beijing ended in a fatal bomb explosion under his railway carriage on 4 June. It was set by senior officers of the Japanese army stationed in Manchuria, the Kantōgun or Kwantung Army. They hoped to seize control of Manchuria in order to force a reorientation of Japanese foreign policy. These plans would not reach fruition until 1931. In the meantime, Zhang's opium addict son Zhang Xueliang assumed

Following Sun Yat-sen's death in March 1925, he was buried in Beijing while a large mausoleum was being built in Nanjing, patterned on the Ming-era imperial tombs. On 1 June 1929, Sun's body was moved from Beijing to the completed mausoleum. Sun Yat-sen is revered in both the People's Republic of China and Taiwan, where he is considered the "Father of the Nation."

control over his father's fiefdom. Now fearing Japan, the son allied with the Nationalist Party in return for control over Rehe (Jehol) province. Thus, the Kantōgun's plans backfired.

To avoid further confrontations with Japan after the Jinan Incident, Chiang detoured around Shandong to capture Beijing on 9 June 1928. When Zhang Xueliang raised the Nationalist flag over Manchuria, the unification of China appeared complete. However, the unification existed in name only. In fact, Chiang succeeded only in negotiating a temporary alliance with the three strongest North China warlords: Feng Yuxiang, Yan Xishan, and Zhang Xueliang. This alliance was subject to change.

Meanwhile, on 18 April, the Nationalists—like the preceding Ming dynasty, the Taipings, and Sun Yat-sen—proclaimed Nanjing to be their capital. Like the last Han dynasty, the Ming, the Nationalists had also conquered China from the South. To reinforce the parallels, the Nationalists had Sun Yat-sen reburied next to the tomb of the founding Ming emperor in Nanjing. Then, in the manner of all new dynasties, the Nationalists reset the calendar so that 1912 became the first year of the Republic and 1928 became

year 17. Henceforth, the dating system would not be in terms of emperors, but in terms of political institutions. Taiwan still retains this dating system.

Conclusions

The Soviet Union played a crucial role in China's reunification. The success of the Northern Expedition hinged on a reorganized and adequately equipped military. To secure vital Soviet aid, Sun negotiated away the northernmost portions of the former Qing empire and agreed to allow Communists into the Nationalist Party. This meant an extension of Soviet influence in Outer Mongolia, Manchuria, and within the Nationalist Party. The agreements signed with the USSR remained in effect long after Sun's death.

The Soviet Union provided numerous military advisers to set up the Whampoa Military Academy, which trained many of the Nationalists' and Communists' most important future civil and political leaders. Without Soviet assistance, it seems highly unlikely that the Nationalists could have trained the large number of officers needed to staff the new

Nationalist Army. As commandant of the academy, Chiang Kai-shek developed a substantial *guanxi* network with the students and faculty at Whampoa, which subsequently became known as the Whampoa Clique. Soviet advisers were instrumental in reorganizing the Nationalist Party along Soviet institutional lines, meaning that Soviet influence extended to Nationalist civil institutions. The political commissar system embedded party representatives in the structure of the army, while the centralization of the party organization made it more effective at executing strategy. Finally, the Soviet Union provided weapons and ammunition vital to the success of the Northern Expedition.

In return for this essential Soviet aid, Chiang tolerated a United Front. As Chiang organized the military forces to reunify China, the Communists organized a rapidly expanding urban labor movement that took over Shanghai on the eve of the arrival of Chiang's troops. With the impending success of the Northern Expedition, the left and right wings of the Nationalist Party split into rival governments in Wuhan and Nanchang, respectively, each anticipating victory. Chiang seized the moment to eradicate Communist influence in the Nationalist Party and over the urban labor movement. He turned on his Soviet benefactors, expelled them from the country, and engaged elements of the Shanghai underworld to slaughter all suspected Communists and labor leaders. Chiang successfully employed Han traditions of barbarian management to play off one foreign power against the others. Soviet military assistance allowed him to reunite South China, which provided the prospect of a unified and effective central government.

Reunification in combination with an increasingly antiforeign labor movement put pressure on the Western powers to begin negotiations on the return of their concessions to Chinese sovereignty. During the Northern Expedition, the Nationalists forced foreigners to evacuate their concessions in Hankou and Jiujiang in early 1927. Soon afterward, Great Britain opened negotiations for their permanent return to Chinese sovereignty and agreed to discuss the status of its other concessions. Chiang then broke with Moscow and purged his former Communist allies. Resuming the Northern Expedition, this time without Soviet assistance, Chiang unified China in 1928. Although the Japanese prevented his occupation of Manchuria, their ill-timed assassination of Zhang Zuolin backfired by propelling Zhang Xueliang to ally with Chiang.

The Nationalists' reunification of China was nominal for several reasons. They had neither a united government nor a united military. Chiang's purge of the Communists in April 1927 eliminated Communist influence within the party but did not end its factional divisions. The Nationalist Army lacked a unified command and was really a loose coalition of autonomous warlords: Since the fall of the Qing dynasty, Yan Xishan had been in control of Shanxi province, whose geography created a strategic enclave, easy to defend and difficult to take. He cooperated with the Nationalists on his own terms. Feng Yuxiang's power base remained in northwest China, where frictions with the Soviet Union and rival warlords determined his ardor for the Nationalists. Similarly, Zhang Xueliang's loyalties to the Nationalists reflected the magnitude of the Japanese threat to Manchuria. Nationalist influence in North China remained tenuous, and Chiang was not secure even in South China. The Guangxi Clique remained in firm control of Guangxi province and had an alternate political program. Chiang's *guanxi* network, in contrast to that of Sun Yat-sen, which had been based in Guangdong province, centered on the lower reaches of the Yangzi River and particularly on Shanghai. For this reason, throughout the rest of the Chinese civil war, Chiang made heroic efforts to defend Shanghai.

Chiang's success to a large degree paralleled the strategies of other warlord leaders: By forming strategic alliances first with Feng Yuxiang and Yan Xishan, and later with Zhang Xueliang, he was able to proclaim China unified on 31 December 1928, when in fact his control actually rested on a precarious coalition. In other words, Chiang had simply initiated a new consolidated phase of warlordism. As before, the Nationalist government had little choice but to placate the various regional powers in order to secure their cooperation. The political instability took a terrible toll on the Chinese population. In the famine of 1927, 3 to 6 million died and 60 million were affected in northwest China. Warfare meant no famine relief.

Sun Yat-sen's military and political legacy was profound. His creation of an opposition government in Guangzhou divided China, while his 1923 alliance with Soviet Russia enabled his successor to reunify it on paper. But this alliance with Moscow came at a price: Russia consolidated its control over Outer Mongolia and the Chinese Eastern Railway. This led to Japanese countermeasures to protect their sphere of influence in Manchuria from the spread of communism. The USSR did not take kindly to Chiang's purges in 1927, but set about cultivating warlord alternatives along its frontiers and aiding the CCP in South China. In 1929, the Nationalists even went to war against the USSR in an unsuccessful attempt to undo Sun's legacy of Soviet control over the Chinese Eastern Railway. This inspired further Japanese countermeasures. Japan had already fought two wars to contain Russia (see Chapters 12 and 13, Section V), and a third war now loomed on the horizon.

BIBLIOGRAPHY

Chan, Anthony B. *Arming the Chinese: Western Armaments Trade in Warlord China*. Vancouver: University of British Columbia Press, 1982.

Chesneaux, Jean. *The Chinese Labor Movement, 1919–1927*. Translated by H. M. Wright. Stanford, CA: Stanford University Press, 1968.

Ch'i, Hsi-sheng. *Warlord Politics in China, 1916–1928*. Stanford, CA: Stanford University Press, 1976.

Elleman, Bruce A. *Diplomacy and Deception: The Secret History of Sino-Soviet Diplomatic Relations, 1917–1927*. Armonk, NY: M. E. Sharpe, 1997.

Forbes, Andrew D. W. *Warlords and Muslims in Chinese Central Asia: A Political History of Republican Sinkiang 1911–1949*. Cambridge: Cambridge University Press, 1986.

Gillin, Donald G. *Warlord Yen Hsi-shan in Shansi Province 1911–1949*. Princeton, NJ: Princeton University Press, 1967.

Guillermaz, Jacques. *A History of the Chinese Communist Party 1921–1949*. Translated by Anne Destiny. New York: Random House, 1972.

Hall, J. C. S. *The Yunnan Provincial Faction 1927–1937*. Canberra: Australian National University, 1976.

Jordan, Donald A. *The Northern Expedition: China's National Revolution of 1926–1928*. Honolulu: University of Hawai'i Press, 1976.

Kapp, Robert A. *Szechwan and the Chinese Republic: Provincial Militarism and Central Power, 1911–1938*. New Haven, CT: Yale University Press, 1973.

Lary, Diana. *Region and Nation: The Kwangsi Clique in Chinese Politics 1925–1937*. Cambridge: Cambridge University Press, 1974.

———*Warlord Soldiers, Chinese Common Soldiers, 1911–1935*. New York: Cambridge University Press, 1985.

Leong, Sow-theng. *Sino-Soviet Diplomatic Relations, 1917–1926*. Canberra: Australian National University Press, 1976.

Liu, F. F. *A Military History of Modern China 1924–1949*. Port Washington, NY: Kennikat Press, 1956.

Luk, Michael Y. L. *The Origins of Chinese Bolshevism: An Ideology in the Making, 1920–1928*. Oxford: Oxford University Press, 1990.

Lutz, Jessie Gregory. *Chinese Politics and Christian Missions: The Anti-Christian Movements of 1920–1928*. Notre Dame, IN: Cross Roads Books, 1988.

Martin, Brian G. *The Shanghai Green Gang: Politics and Organized Crime, 1919–1937*. Berkeley: University of California Press, 1996.

McCord, Edward A. *The Power of the Gun: The Emergence of Modern Chinese Warlordism*. Berkeley: University of California Press, 1993.

McCormack, Gavan. *Chang Tso-lin in Northeast China, 1911–1928*. Stanford, CA: Stanford University Press, 1977.

Murray, Dian H. and Qin Baoqi. *The Origins of the Tiandihui: The Chinese Triads in Legend and History*. Stanford, CA: Stanford University Press, 1994.

Myers, Ramon. "The Chinese State during the Republican Era." In *The Modern Chinese State*, edited by David Shambaugh, 42–71. Cambridge: Cambridge University Press, 2000.

Nathan, Andrew J. *Peking Politics, 1918–1923: Factionalism and the Failure of Constitutionalism*. Berkeley: University of California Press, 1976.

Olivier, Bernard Vincent. *The Implementation of China's National Policy in the Northeastern Provinces*. Lewiston, NY: Edwin Mellen Press, 1993.

Price, Jane L. *Cadres, Commanders, and Commissars: The Training of the Chinese Communist Leadership, 1920–1945*. Boulder, CO: Westview Press, 1976.

Pye, Lucian. *Warlord Politics: Conflict and Coalition in the Modernization of Republican China*. New York: Praeger, 1971.

Rigby, Richard. *The May Thirtieth Movement: Events and Themes*. Canberra: Australian National University Press, 1980.

Saich, Tony. *The Origins of the First United Front in China: The Role of Sneevliet (Alias Maring)*. Leiden: Brill, 1991.

———and Hans van de Ven, eds. *The Rise to Power of the Chinese Communist Party: Documents and Analysis*. Armonk, NY: M. E. Sharpe, 1996.

Sheridan, James E. *Chinese Warlord: The Career of Feng Yu-hsiang*. Stanford, CA: Stanford University Press, 1966.

————*China in Disintegration: The Republican Era in Chinese History, 1912–1949.* New York: Free Press, 1975.

So, Wai-chor. *The Kuomintang Left in the National Revolution, 1924–1931.* Oxford: Oxford University Press, 1991.

Sutton, Donald. *Provincial Militarism and the Chinese Republic: The Yunnan Army, 1905–1925.* Ann Arbor: University of Michigan Press, 1980.

Tien, Hung-mao. *Government and Politics in Kuomintang China 1927–1937.* Stanford, CA: Stanford University Press, 1972.

————"Factional Politics in Kuomintang China, 1928–1937: An Interpretation." In *China at the Crossroads: Nationalists and Communists, 1927–1949,* edited by F. Gilbert Chan, 19–36. Boulder, CO: Westview Press, 1980.

Tung, William L. *The Political Institutions of Modern China.* The Hague: Martinus Nijhoff, 1968.

Wilbur, C. Martin. *The Nationalist Revolution in China, 1923–1928.* Cambridge: Cambridge University Press, 1984.

————and Julie Lien-ying How. *Missionaries of Revolution: Soviet Advisers and Nationalist China, 1920–1927.* Cambridge, MA: Harvard University Press, 1989.

Wou, Odoric. *Militarism in Modern China: The Career of Wu P'ei-fu, 1916–1939.* Folkstone, England: Dawson and Sons, 1978.

Yu, George, T. *Party Politics in Republican China: The Kuomintang, 1912–1924.* Berkeley: University of California Press, 1966.

NOTES

1. Wen Yiduo, "One Sentence," in *The Columbia Anthology of Modern Chinese Literature*, edited by Joseph S. M. Lau and Howard Goldblatt (New York: Columbia University Press, 1995), 507. From *The Columbia Anthology of Modern Chinese Literature,* by Victor Mair, Copyright © 1995, Columbia University Press. Reprinted with permission of the publisher.
2. After it fell apart in 1927, there would be a Second United Front formed in 1936.

Chronology

4 June 1928	Japanese assassination of Zhang Zuolin
25 July 1928	Tariff autonomy agreements with the United States
29 December 1928	National reunification complete with Zhang Xueliang agreement
11 July–22 Dec. 1929	Sino-Soviet War over Chinese Eastern Railway
Sept.–Dec. 1929	Guangxi Clique and Feng Yuxiang fight Chiang Kai-shek
24 October 1929	Wall Street stock market crash: Great Depression begins
April–November 1930	Central Plains War
Spring–summer 1930	Operational failure of the Li Lisan line
5 Nov.–27 Dec. 1930	First Encirclement Campaign
March–May 1931	Second Encirclement Campaign
July–October 1931	Third Encirclement Campaign
18 September 1931	Manchurian Incident; beginning of Second Sino-Japanese War
7 January 1932	United States adopts Non-recognition doctrine
28 January 1932	First Shanghai Incident; Japanese assault on Shanghai
1 March 1932	Manchukuo declaration of independence
May 1932–spring 1933	Fourth Encirclement Campaign
2 December 1932	China and the Soviet Union restore relations severed in 1927
1933–5	North China War
January 1933	Japan invades Rehe and Hebei
20 January 1933	Adolf Hitler comes to power
5 March–30 May 1933	War of the Great Wall
27 March 1933	Japanese withdrawal from the League of Nations
31 May 1933	Sino-Japanese Tanggu Peace
Oct. 1933–April 1934	Fifth Encirclement Campaign
19 February 1934	Beginning of New Life Movement
16 October 1934	Beginning of the Long March
6–8 January 1935	Zunyi Conference
May 1935	Japan sets up an autonomous government in Inner Mongolia
24 November 1935	Japan set up an autonomous government in East Hebei
11 December 1935	Japan sets up the Hebei-Chahar government
24 November 1936	German-Japanese Anti-Comintern Pact
7 December 1936	Mao becomes chairman of the Central Military Council
12 December 1936	Xi'an Incident: Second United Front
7 July 1937	Marco Polo Bridge Incident: escalation of Sino-Japanese War
13 August 1937	Second Shanghai Incident

19

The Nanjing Decade

High officials amuse themselves with showy New
Life events.
How can such greedy officials revive the dead soul
of the nation?
They have no concern for home or country.
The whole city just rushes out to watch the kites.[1]

Chen Duxiu (1879–1942), founder of the CCP,
written from a Nationalist jail
cell in Nanjing, 1934

The Nanjing Decade represented the high point of Nationalist rule, when the Nanjing government had nominal control over the entire country. Compared to the preceding turbulent decade of military reunification and the ensuing decade of Japanese invasion and occupation, the Nanjing Decade was one of comparative stability. The task of creating a modern China was daunting, however, and the U.S. stock market crash in 1929 soon ushered in the Great Depression. This led to proliferating trade barriers and staggering unemployment rates in the West, leading the Nationalists to adopt a hybrid system based on Leninist party organization supplemented by the fascist model of state-sponsored private enterprise and supported by Nazi military aid. But the relative stability of the Nanjing decade was turbulent by any normal standards. In 1929 the Nationalists lost the Sino-Soviet railway war in Manchuria, leaving the USSR in charge. This prompted third-party intervention. In 1931 Japan invaded and rapidly occupied all of Manchuria, forcing the USSR back within its own borders. Meanwhile, Chiang's numerous anti-Communist campaigns finally forced the CCP to retreat from South China on the Long March to Yan'an, located on the barren North China frontier with Outer Mongolia. The weakening of the CCP, coupled with Japanese expansion, convinced

Chiang to reassess his position of hostility to the Soviet Union. In 1936 he opened a Second United Front with the Communists to oppose Japan.

I. Elimination of the Unequal Treaties with the Western Powers

The Nanjing government made treaty revision a top priority by continuing the Beijing government's strategy of using the USSR's supposed renunciation of its unequal treaties to influence the other powers. Beijing had already made notable progress. In 1925, the signatories of the 1922 Nine-Power Treaty at the Washington Conference agreed to allow China to set its own tariffs starting in 1929 and to renegotiate the relevant treaties. Beginning in 1926, Beijing applied pressure selectively on specific countries to abolish their other unequal treaties, acting unilaterally against small countries, like Belgium, but more cautiously against larger countries, like France, Britain, and the United States. Belgium and Spain soon complied.

By the end of January 1927, Great Britain agreed to put the concessions under Chinese jurisdiction, in this case the Beijing government, thus making all British missionaries subject to Chinese law and prohibiting them from owning land, and making British subjects liable for Chinese taxation. This would have greatly reduced the scope of extraterritoriality and autonomy of the concession areas. Like the Alcock Convention fifty-seven years earlier (Chapter 11, Section I), this equal treaty was not ratified, this time because the Northern Expedition overthrew the Beijing government. Meanwhile, the Nationalists and Great Britain engaged in similar negotiations over the British concessions at Hankou and Jiujiang, areas in Central China under Nationalist, not Beijing's, control.

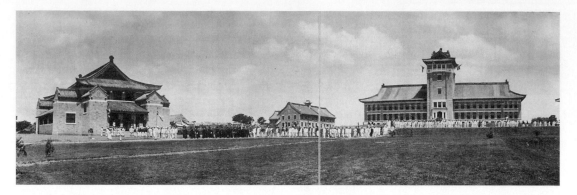

The Nanjing Decade witnessed many educational successes. The University of Nanking, established in 1888 by a consortium of American churches, quickly became one of China's premier institutions of higher learning. Its faculty included the American author Pearl S. Buck, winner of the Nobel Prize in Literature (1938), whose books presented a sympathetic view of China's development.

The Nationalists, like the many warlord cliques in and out of power in Beijing, adopted the Foreign Ministry of the Beijing government. This followed the Han tradition of retaining the officials of the previous dynasty to serve the new one. From an administrative viewpoint, Beijing actually absorbed Nanjing, not the reverse; hence, foreign policies changed little. The Nanjing government even adopted Beijing's formula: It announced in early 1928 that it would recognize all of China's treaties but that it reserved the right to abrogate unilaterally those detrimental to Chinese interests. It soon notified Portugal, Italy, and Denmark that their treaties were a dead letter.

During the summer of 1928, C. T. Wang became the new Nationalist foreign minister, while Wellington Koo remained China's most influential diplomat. Wang effectively merged the diplomatic corps of the Beijing and Nanjing governments. He threatened to put foreigners under Chinese jurisdiction if their respective governments did not renegotiate the unequal treaties, in effect an ultimatum either to negotiate or to lose their rights. Belgium, Italy, Denmark, Spain, Portugal, and Mexico quickly agreed to eliminate their right to extraterritoriality by 1 January 1930. Together, the Beijing and Nanjing governments reduced the number of foreign countries enjoying extraterritoriality from nineteen to nine. Sweden, Peru, Brazil, and Japan declined to renegotiate their treaties. This meant that China did not recognize extraterritoriality for these countries, but the practice continued until a dispute arose. The remaining three Western countries—the United States, Great Britain, and France—continued to negotiate, while the USSR claimed unimpaired extraterritoriality for its officials. This effectively included all Soviet citizens in China, because only government representatives could travel there.

The United States recognized Chinese tariff autonomy on 25 July 1928, but offered to abolish extraterritoriality only gradually over a ten-year period while China adopted a westernized legal system. War with Japan, however, overtook these negotiations. In World War II, the issue of Chinese cooperation to defeat Japan completely overshadowed extraterritoriality for the West. On the thirty-first anniversary of the 1911 Revolution on 10 October 1942, Britain agreed with Chiang Kai-shek's Chongqing government to eliminate its unequal treaties. Not to be outdone, Japan followed suit on 9 January 1943 with the Wang Jingwei puppet government in an attempt to shift Chinese support from Chiang's to Wang's government. Great Britain and the United States formally ended their extraterritoriality on 11 January 1943. Thereafter, between 1943 and 1947, the Chinese government completed its goal of negotiating new treaties with a number of smaller countries. This left only the USSR with its original tsarist-era privileges intact.

II. The Russo-Japanese Rivalry Over Manchuria

In the 1920s, the Nanjing government also tried to renegotiate its treaties with Russia to eliminate all tsarist-era privileges. Beginning in March 1929, the Nanjing government tried to open negotiations with the USSR on the Chinese Eastern Railway. After Moscow refused, the Nationalists unilaterally took control of the railway and authorized a raid on the Soviet consulate in Haerbin (Harbin) in May. This paralleled the 1927 raid on the Soviet embassy that led to the collapse of the First United Front and the rupture in Sino-Soviet diplomatic relations. Again the Nationalists used confiscated documents to accuse Moscow of sponsoring subversive Communist activities. In July, the Nanjing government closed down a variety of organizations representing Soviet economic interests in Manchuria. The Soviet government protested on 13 July 1929, giving Zhang Xueliang's Mukden government and the Nanjing government three days to respond. When they failed to do so, the USSR severed diplomatic relations with China and organized a Special Far Eastern Army. The Sino-Soviet War of 1929 was short, but intense (11 July–22 December). On the Soviet side, the Special Far Eastern Red Army consisted of 100,000 troops supported by tanks and aircraft. On the Chinese side, Zhang Xueliang deployed 60,000 men and the Nationalist Army stood ready to support him, but the fighting was one-sided, with the Chinese sustaining enormous casualties.

From the end of August through November 1929, the Soviet government tried to restore the status quo ante bellum, but negotiations with Nanjing soon deadlocked. Moscow turned to Zhang Xueliang's government in Mukden. On 26 November, Mukden broke with Nanjing to negotiate with the Soviet government. This forced Nanjing to capitulate. On 22 December 1929 the Soviet and Nanjing governments signed a protocol at Khabarovsk ceding the USSR majority control over the Chinese Eastern Railway and guaranteeing Soviet consulates extraterritoriality. Thus, the Nationalist government officially recognized Soviet retention of the unequal treaties concerning the tsarist sphere of interest in China. The Nationalist strategy of armed resistance had strengthened, not weakened, Soviet influence throughout Manchuria. In its following five-year plan, the Soviet government stressed the development of Siberia, mandating major infrastructure investments and the settlement of the frontier area. Stalin used his collectivization of agriculture in European Russia to relocate at least 5 million peasants to camps in Siberia and the Arctic. Many soon populated the long and disputed borders with China, in part, as a means of border defense.

Meanwhile, Sino-Soviet negotiations progressed slowly. In June 1931 there were reports that China had agreed to repurchase the Chinese Eastern Railway gradually by allowing Soviet goods into Manchuria duty-free. This solution was attractive to the cash-strapped Nationalists but alarming to the Japanese because duty-free Soviet goods would undersell their own products and because the agreement threatened to erode the Japanese sphere of influence in Manchuria recognized by previous Soviet-Japanese treaties.

In June 1928, the Japanese army in Manchuria, the Kantōgun, had acted unilaterally in a misguided attempt to protect Japanese interests by assassinating Zhang Xueliang's father, Zhang Zuolin. On 18 September 1931, in the so-called Manchurian Incident, officers of the Kantōgun used an explosion on the Southern Manchuria Railway south of Mukden as a pretext to invade and occupy all three provinces of Manchuria. (See Map 19.1.) In fact, Japanese troops, not Chinese insurgents, set the charges. Interestingly on 15 September 1931, three days before the Manchurian Incident, Chiang Kai-shek ordered the bulk of Zhang Xueliang's Northeastern forces to leave Mukden and move south. In Zhang Xueliang's moment of dire need, Chiang remained uncommitted, perhaps hoping that, in retribution for the 1929 Sino-Soviet War, the Japanese would eliminate the Russians from Manchuria and then withdraw or, if they did not, events would at least clip the wings of the Fengtian Clique. In the end, Chiang got more than he bargained for.

In Japan, the military had become increasingly dissatisfied with their Foreign Ministry's long-standing policy of cooperation with the West. The Great Depression followed by the Western response of protectionism had devastated the Japanese economy. Japan's many warnings of Soviet expansion and Communist insurgency in China had fallen on deaf ears; the West was preoccupied with post–World War I reconstruction, the containment of Germany, and the economic collapse resulting from the Great Depression. Japan's military concluded that cooperation with the West had reached a dead end and increasingly believed that the restoration of Japanese prosperity depended on economic self-sufficiency. This could be provided by an empire of sufficient size. Stabilizing China's economy was necessary for Japan's own prosperity, but this required political stability, which in turn required a stable buffer state to cut off Soviet influence.

The Manchurian Incident constituted a de facto coup d'état in Japan. It ended the Meiji Restoration policy of cooperation with the West and ushered in a succession of governments increasingly reflecting the position of the Japanese military. This decision had enormous consequences not only for China and Japan, but also for Asia and ultimately for the United States and the other Western powers as well. During the next five months, the Kantōgun quickly overran and occupied Manchuria, meeting only sporadic resistance. In late December 1931, Zhang Xueliang followed Chiang Kai-shek's order to give up his rule over Manchuria without a fight by deploying his forces south of the Great Wall. Apparently Chiang thought he could organize a diplomatic offensive in which the foreign powers would pressure Japan to withdraw. In 1932, Japan took Harbin, the Soviet administrative center in Manchuria, thereby threatening the Soviet sphere of

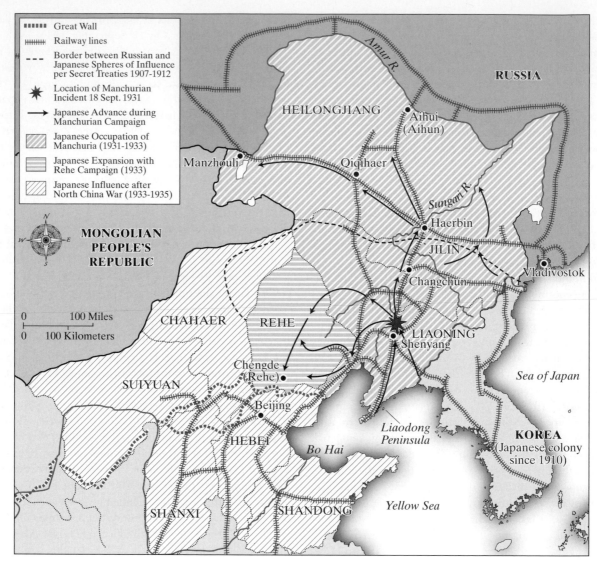

Map 19.1   Japanese Occupation of Manchuria (1931–3) and the North China War (1933–5)

influence. Meanwhile, on 28 January 1932, Japanese forces fought Nationalist troops in Shanghai in the so-called First Shanghai Incident. The Nationalist forces fought hard but were unable to match the Japanese and retreated within the month. The Western powers then helped broker an armistice signed on 5 May 1932, establishing a neutral zone around the city.

In the interim, Japan conquered Manchuria and on 1 March 1932 established the puppet state of Manchukuo, ostensibly under the rule of the Manchus. Japanese forces conducted a special operation to kidnap the last Qing ruler, the emperor Xuantong, also known as Henry Puyi, from his retirement in Tianjin to play a cameo role as emperor of

Manchukuo. During August 1932, Japan formally recognized Manchukuo as an independent country, but Great Britain, most European countries, and the United States refused to go along; on 7 January 1932, Washington announced the Non-recognition Doctrine, stating that it would not recognize any new situation in China resulting from warfare, that is, the occupation of Manchuria and subsequent establishment of Manchukuo. Instead of recognizing Manchukuo, the League of Nations sent the Lytton Commission to investigate. The Japanese delegation defended Japan's action as an attempt to contain the spread of Soviet communism and to restore stability, but in February 1933, the League of Nation adopted the Lytton report condemning

Japan's actions. Without U.S. membership, however, the League had limited leverage over Japan. In March, Japan withdrew from the League in protest.

The Japanese did not stop; in January 1933 they absorbed Rehe, the traditional summer retreat of the Manchu emperors. By April, they consolidated control over northeast China. That month they moved south of the Great Wall into the core provinces of China. This was the War of the Great Wall that took place between 5 March and 30 May 1933, when the Japanese cleared out all Chinese forces immediately south of the Great Wall. During May 1933, the Chinese sued for peace at Tanggu, right outside of Tianjin. The Tanggu Peace of 31 May 1933 was signed nine years to the day after the 1924 Sino-Soviet Treaty returning the Chinese Eastern Railway to Soviet control—an implicit message that all territorial losses were permanent. It made eastern Hebei a demilitarized zone, thus leaving Tianjin and Beijing undefended.

The boundaries of Manchukuo incorporated most of China's northeastern provinces of Heilongjiang, Jilin, Liaoning (Fengtian), and Rehe. Yet, the creation of this large buffer state—greater than the combined territory of France, Germany, Great Britain, and Italy—did not sate the Japanese appetite for expansionism. The fighting continued. Together these campaigns from 1933 to 1935 comprised the North China War. During 1935 Japan created three puppet states in North China: the East Hebei Autonomous Government, the Hebei-Chahar Political Council, and an Inner Mongolian government under Prince De (Demchukdonggrub). Nanjing disputed the loss of Inner Mongolia and, on 24 November 1936, successfully ousted Prince De. This victory inflamed Chinese nationalism and fueled public hopes that China could now challenge Japan successfully.

Meanwhile, Moscow made a long overdue reassessment of its position in Manchuria. Given the rise of fascism in Germany, it decided that, rather than attempt to defend the Chinese Eastern Railway against a Japanese army in occupation, it would sell the concession to the Manchukuo government for a profit. It did so in 1935. Thus, the Japanese succeeded where the Chinese failed: They removed Soviet influence from Manchuria. Japan's strategy, however, boomeranged. Its invasion of Manchuria and North China pressured the Nanjing government into seeking better relations with both the USSR and the CCP. This Nationalist strategy precipitated Japan's invasion of China proper in 1937. That invasion would so weaken the Nationalists that it greatly facilitated the postwar Communist rise to power, which created the Japanese nightmare scenario of a unified Communist China under Soviet tutelage.

III. The Military Side of Nation Building: Uprisings and Encirclement Campaigns

Interfering with the Nationalists' ability to deal with the Soviet Union and Japan was an ongoing power struggle between Chiang Kai-shek and the many competing elements of his coalition. Chiang wanted to create a unified military and government under the Nationalist Party. Some members of his coalition, such as the Guangxi Clique, shared this ambition, but with themselves, not Chiang, in control. Others wanted to retain their regional autonomy. This applied to Yan Xishan, the warlord of Shanxi, and to Feng Yuxiang, who controlled the strategic corridor separating Manchuria from China.

During the Nanjing Decade, Chiang Kai-shek tried to consolidate control over his heterogeneous army by demanding a unified command. The coalition members balked. The Guangxi Clique rebelled. (See Table 19.1.) Then Feng Yuxiang declared his independence on 20 May 1929, so that Chiang fought Feng simultaneously with the Soviet railway war. Chiang also tried to undermine the Guangxi Clique by separating its political leaders from their troops. In January 1930, the Guangxi Clique unsuccessfully resisted by attacking the Guangdong warlord, Zhang Fakui. Wang Jingwei, the leader of the Left Nationalists, then tried to establish a rival government in Beijing. He forged a coalition unified by a shared dislike of Chiang but without a common positive program. The coalition included the Guangxi Clique, its recent enemy the Guangdong warlord Zhang Fakui, Yan Xishan, and Feng Yuxiang. The resulting Central Plains War (April through November 1930) may have been the bloodiest phase of the Chinese civil war thus far. Chiang drove the Guangxi and Guangdong cliques back to their home provinces, where they attempted to create a rival government in Guangzhou in May 1931. The Japanese invasion of Manchuria later that year restored their allegiance to Nanjing in the face of a common enemy. Nevertheless, until the Communist victory in 1949, the Guangxi Clique remained the most important alternative to Chiang's rule.

Chiang cemented his victory in the Central Plains War by convincing the formerly neutral Manchurian warlord, Zhang Xueliang, to join his side. Together, they eliminated Feng Yuxiang and Yan Xishan. Feng's army was incorporated into the Nationalist Army, while Yan's troops returned to Shanxi. This effectively finished Feng's career. The Japanese invasion, however, restored Yan to power in Shanxi as another Nationalist coalition formed around a common hatred of Japan but again lacked a positive program.

Table 19.1   Political Instability during the Nanjing Decade

Attempts to Overthrow Chiang Kai-shek:

Year	Leader(s)	Event
1929	Li Zongren	Guangxi Uprising
1929	Feng Yuxiang	First Henan Uprising
1929	Feng Yuxiang	Second Henan Uprising
1929	Tang Shengzhi	Zhengzhou Mutiny
1930	Yan Xishan, Feng Yuxiang, Li Zongren, Wang Jingwei, Zhang Fakui	Central Plain War
1931	Li Zongren, Wang Jingwei	Rival government in Guangzhou
1933	Feng Yuxiang	Chahar Uprising
1933	Communists	Fujian People's Government
1936	Li Zongren	Guangdong-Guangxi Crisis

Nationalist-Communist Civil War:		*Japanese Invasion:*	
Year	Event	Year	Event
1930	First Encirclement Campaign		
1931	Second Encirclement Campaign	1931	Invasion of Manchuria
1931	Third Encirclement Campaign	1932	Assault on Shanghai
1932–3	Fourth Encirclement Campaign	1933	Invasion of Rehe, Hebei
1933–4	Fifth Encirclement Campaign	1933	War of the Great Wall
1936	Xi'an Incident	1937	Full-Scale Invasion of China

The Soviet victory over the Nationalists in the 1929 railway war had heartened the CCP. It adopted the Li Lisan line, announced on 7 December 1929. In a strategy reminiscent of the failed Nanchang Uprising, the Autumn Harvest Uprising, and the Guangzhou Commune, it called for attacks on Changsha, Nanchang, and Wuhan, the major cities in the middle reaches of the Yangzi River valley, in order to set off a cascade of urban rebellions that would bring the Communists to power. Li Lisan had been one of the founding members of the CCP and was a well-known labor organizer. He helped lead the ill-fated Nanchang Uprising, was closely connected with the Soviet Union, and from mid-1928 through 1930 dominated CCP policymaking.

Chen Duxiu, the former head of the CCP, had attacked Li Lisan's proposal, as well as most CCP policies, since his demotion in 1927; he accused Moscow of using the Chinese Communists to serve its own ends. The party expelled Chen as a Trotskyite on 15 December 1929. Leon Trotsky was the internationalist rival of Stalin expelled from the Communist Party of the Soviet Union in 1927, in part, over differences on the China policy. Yet, as Chen predicted, the assumption of sympathetic urban rebellions remained as false as in the

1927 uprisings. The capture of Changsha on 27 July 1930 by Peng Dehuai, who would later lead Chinese forces in the Korean War (1950–3), ended within a week, while the Communists were unable to stage rebellions in Nanchang or Wuhan. With these failures, Li was sent for intensive reeducation to Moscow, where he remained until the Red Army overran Manchuria in the final days of World War II.

The Communists' inability to attract a sustained urban following led to a reassessment of their strategy. Instead of focusing on securing urban base areas, which tended to be Nationalist strongholds, they gradually turned their attention to China's vast hinterland to build rural base areas wherever they could cultivate local support. This new emphasis on remote rural areas was a strategy not of choice but of necessity. The CCP had proven unable to take or hold cities. This change in strategy would be gradual and adopted only after heated and divisive debates.

Mao Zedong and Zhu De established the most successful early South China base areas, moving from the Jinggang Mountains on the Jiangxi-Hunan border across the Gan River to establish the famous Jiangxi Soviet, straddling the Jiangxi-Fujian border. The Communists took advantage of Chiang

Kai-shek's preoccupation with the Central Plains War, followed by the Japanese invasion of Manchuria, to organize the Jiangxi Soviet, and others in the Dabie mountains of the Hubei-Anhui-Hunan border area, in the Hunan-Hubei-Jiangxi border area, in the Hunan-West Hubei area, and elsewhere. Most of these base areas were located in geographically remote areas straddling the borders of two or three provinces, where provincial authority had always been weak and the people were often extremely poor. Such areas created the opportunity for the Communists to establish defensible sanctuaries that were costly for the Nationalists to attack. To fund defenses, the Communists confiscated the land of the rich, redistributed it to the poor, and collected taxes from these new and presumably grateful small landholders. Many in the party doubted that the peasantry would remain loyal for long. However, compared to the Nationalists, who promised the peasants little but increasing taxation and conscription, the Communist program proved more popular. The peasants provided not only food and manpower to the Communists, but also information about enemy activities.

In the Jiangxi Soviet, Zhu De commanded the military, while Mao served as the ranking political commissar. Bitter disputes raged within the Communist leadership over the proper relationship between the party and the army, the role of base areas, and land reform. It was finally agreed in 1929 that the army had both a military and a political role. It had to defeat the enemy and also to secure the allegiance of the vast uncommitted civilian population. Zhu and Mao attempted to cultivate peasant support by conducting land reform, which entailed the widespread executions of landowners, but continued executions and expropriations of smaller landholders threatened to alienate too much of the rural population. In the end, the Communists permitted private land ownership but distributed among more numerous small landholders. The promise of land reform and the redress of injustice helped the Communist forces to grow rapidly, from thousands to tens of thousands, but continued rural control required a balance of terror and consent that proved highly unstable in practice. By 1930, the Jiangxi Soviet was composed of about a dozen liberated areas, and the Chinese Red Army (renamed the People's Liberation Army [PLA] after World War II) had grown to approximately 60,000 to 65,000 men.

In response, Chiang launched a succession of encirclement campaigns to eliminate these base areas and to annihilate the Communist forces. (See Map 19.2.) The First Encirclement Campaign, begun on 5 December 1930, was an unsuccessful attempt to dislodge the soviets in Jiangxi province. The Second Encirclement Campaign, from May to June 1931, and the Third Encirclement Campaign, from July to October 1931, attempted to eliminate the

soviets from Jiangxi and Fujian, but the Japanese invasion of Manchuria brought the latter campaign to a premature halt. The Fourth Encirclement Campaign, beginning in May 1932, successfully dislodged the border region soviets in Hubei-Henan-Anhui and Fujian, but the Japanese invasion of Rehe and the War of the Great Wall, both in 1933, forced the Nationalists to limit this campaign until after the Sino-Japanese Tanggu Peace of 31 May 1933.

In October 1933, Chiang launched his highly successful Fifth Encirclement Campaign, which culminated in the Communist exodus from Jiangxi on the Long March (1934–5) to the barren imperial periphery in Yan'an, Shaanxi. The Nationalists adopted a blockhouse strategy with the assistance of German military advisers, who had replaced the Soviet advisers expelled in 1927. With a combined force of 700,000 men, the Nationalists gradually encircled the Communist-controlled areas, where continuing Communist purges and heavy-handed requisitioning had alienated the populace. Mao increasingly advocated using guerrilla tactics in opposition to the party's Central Executive Committee, which was under pressure from the Comintern to employ conventional positional warfare. Mao lost this ideological battle and was removed from the Red Army's command structure in 1932. The Maoist vision of military strategy did not prevail until after the Fifth Encirclement Campaign virtually obliterated the Communist forces in a battle of positional warfare.

In the resulting year-long 6,000-mile Communist retreat from South China, only 10,000 of the 100,000 troops that belonged to the Jiangxi Soviet made it to Yan'an in October 1935. In reality, there were three Long Marches because the Nationalists flushed three separate CCP armies out of South China that made their way separately to Yan'an. Two other armies began their Long March in 1932 as a result of the Fourth Encirclement Campaign. The survivors of these three armies converged in eastern Gansu in the fall of 1936 and in 1937 established the main CCP base area in Yan'an.

Although the CCP later treated this as a heroic era, in reality the Long March was a strategic disaster. Exile in Yan'an gave Mao time to reflect and to write some of his most famous political tracts. Nationalists also herded other fleeing Communists into Guizhou and Sichuan, provinces resistant to Nanjing's control. Pursuit of the Communists gave Chiang the pretext to occupy and take control of these provinces without fighting the local warlords. When the Communists fled to Shaanxi, Chiang may have calculated that this province lay too far beyond the Nationalist sphere of influence and too close to the Soviet Union, and that the Japanese would probably eliminate the Communists for him anyway. While continuing to disrupt the Communists' supply lines, the Nationalists desperately needed to turn their attention to the civil side of

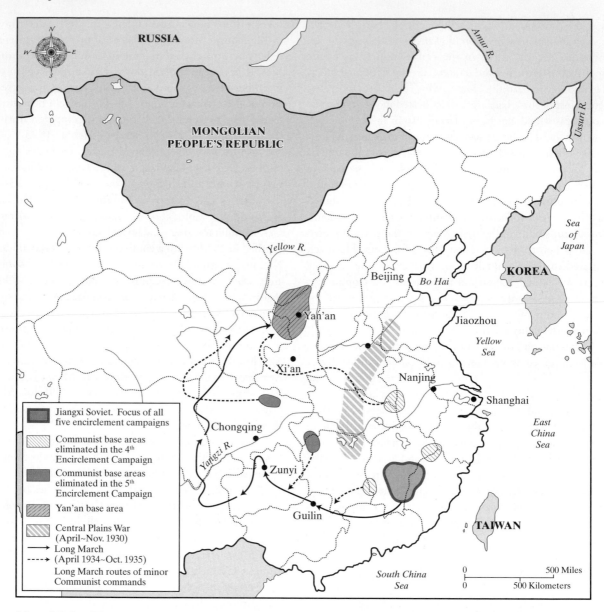

Map 19.2   The Five Encirclement Campaigns (1930–4) and the Long March (1934–5)

nation building. Chiang's underestimation of the Communist threat in Yan'an proved to be a critical error.

IV. The Civil Side of Nation Building: Nationalist and Communist Ideology

The relationship between civil and military power had been ambiguous under the Nationalists. Sun Yat-sen had been a civil leader in search of an effective military. Chiang provided the military, only to become a military leader in search of civil allegiance. The Military Affairs Commission that led the Northern Expedition to victory had been disbanded in 1928 in anticipation of a change to civil rule. Constant warfare intervened, so a far more centralized Military Affairs Commission was reestablished in 1932 firmly under Chiang's control. It oversaw all matters related to defense and eventually controlled the civilian economy in a relentless pursuit of resources to maintain an army against gathering foes. (See the feature on pages 310 and 311.)

During the Nanjing Decade, the Nationalists attempted to create a broad array of civil institutions. In 1931 they introduced a westernized civil service system and civil service examinations. They also introduced comprehensive westernized codes of civil litigation and administrative, civil, and criminal law. They drafted a massive land reform law in keeping with Sun Yat-sen's land-to-the-tiller ideology, whose implementation began with comprehensive land surveys. They encouraged the development of credit and agricultural cooperatives, programs in agronomy, and investment in China's long-neglected irrigation and levee infrastructure. Together these reforms helped produce an improved harvest in 1936.

In keeping with Western practices, the Nationalists established three levels of financial administration, at the national, provincial, and county levels, and earmarked specific taxes to fund each level of government. They made great efforts to unify and stabilize the currency. Considerable economic development also took place. The government sponsored the development of coal mining, the chemical industry, and heavy industry. From 1928 to 1934, civil expenses as a proportion of the Nationalist budget more than tripled, from 8 percent to 25 percent. The

Nationalists also promoted the education of both girls and boys. The trajectory of these reforms followed the highly successful westernizing reforms of Meiji Japan. Japan, however, had had nearly three decades of peace to complete its reforms.

The Nationalist Party attempted to centralize provincial and local administration. It reinstituted the Qing dynasty's *baojia* system to establish control over the countryside. (See Chapter 2, Section IV.) Unlike the Qing, which had used the system initially for tax collection and law enforcement, the Nationalists needed accurate household registers primarily for military conscription and secondarily to mobilize labor for public works projects. The Nationalists also attempted to form a constabulary force, known as the Peace Preservation Corps, to maintain public order.

Chiang needed popular support to provide the legitimacy that new institutions often lack. Although nationalism was increasingly strong among China's literate elite and urban population, the countryside retained its regional loyalties, which helps explain the persistence of warlord rule. In the midst of the Fifth Encirclement Campaign in 1934, Chiang attempted to broaden his popularity by launching the New Life Movement. It emphasized the traditional

Peasants weathered the high inflation of the war years better than did urban workers because they produced and owned tangible goods. Pictured here, a woman gathers the straw after the grain harvest in central China. Straw was used for thatching, sandal making, basketry, and animal feed. Yet peasants were also the primary victims of famines and floods. The 1931 Yangzi River flood displaced over 50 million people—or about one in four Chinese peasants—and killed almost 4 million.

NATIONALIST GOVERNMENT

(ca. 1941)

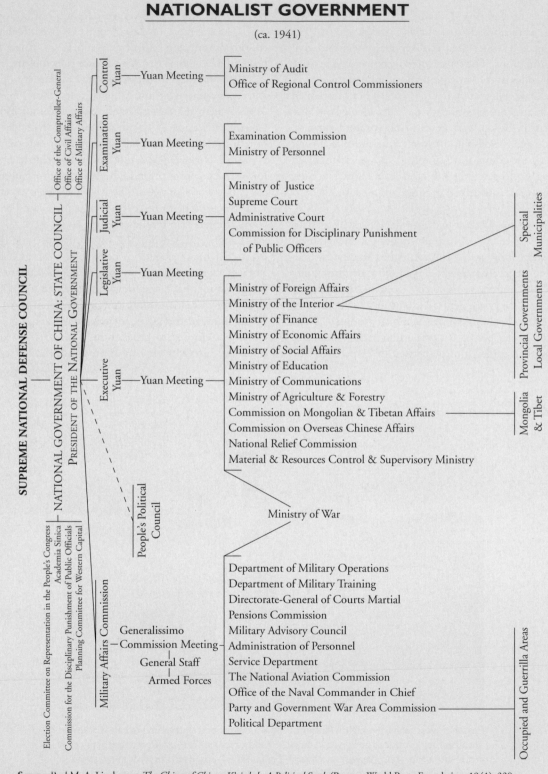

Source: Paul M. A. Linebarger, *The China of Chiang K'ai-shek: A Political Study* (Boston: World Peace Foundation, 1941), 330.

NATIONALIST PARTY CONGRESS

(ca. 1941)

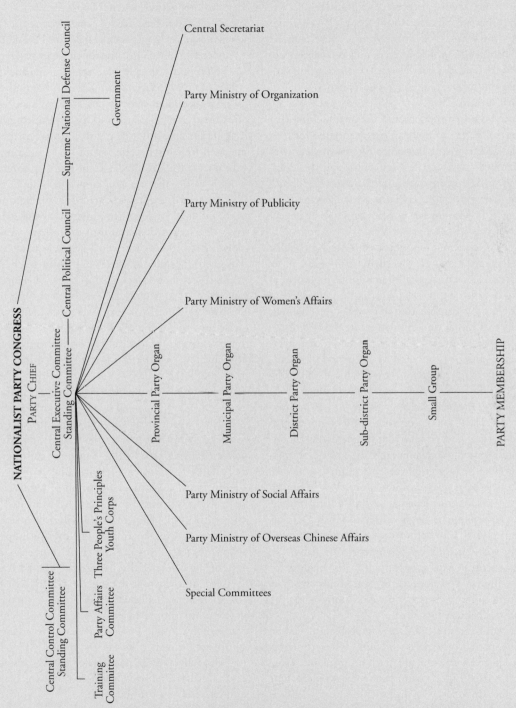

Source: Paul M. A. Linebarger, *The China of Chiang K'ai-shek: A Political Study* (Boston: World Peace Foundation, 1941), 331.

Confucian values of moral righteousness, respect for authority, and proper decorum but sought to harmonize them with such twentieth-century concerns as modernity, science, and nationalism. To the Three People's Principles Chiang added the Three Transformations. These entailed progress in cultural life, militarization, and economic productivity. In other words, the Three Transformations included ideological, military, and civil components.

Like communism, the New Life Movement was an attempt to create the first modern and national identity that would allow the Chinese to unite to defeat internal foes, regionalists, the Japanese, and any other foreign powers with imperialistic ambitions. Both the Nationalists and the Communists hoped to find strength in unity and to end China's long period of dynastic decline, civil unrest, and foreign invasion. The New Life Movement, unlike communism, never became widely accepted.

The reality of endemic feuding within the Nationalist Party, a ceaseless civil war, and the Japanese invasion made the party's lofty goals seem cynical to many (see the poem at the beginning of this chapter). The economy remained in desperate straits from a combination of the ongoing civil war, the Great Depression that undermined trade, the loss of the Manchurian market after the Japanese invasion, and gyrations in currency values, exacerbated in this period by fluctuations in international silver prices. This produced collapsing prices for agricultural commodities and manufactured goods just at the time that the Nationalist government was improving its ability to collect taxes. Together these events spelled disaster for both rural and urban living standards. As the internationally recognized government of China, the Nationalist government became responsible for the country's many ills and the convenient scapegoat for those groups not in power. As Chinese resentment over Japanese expansionism intensified, ordinary citizens increasingly criticized Chiang's focus on finishing the civil war before opposing the Japanese. While Chiang wished to defeat one enemy at a time, the public rallied around slogans excoriating the Nationalists for killing fellow Chinese. The sloganeering was highly effective, but the resulting military strategy proved disastrous for the sloganeers and the Nationalists alike.

The Communists also faced daunting problems. Warfare brought famine, particularly in North China, where droughts and famines occurred with regularity even in peacetime. During the Communists' flight north, they held an important Politburo Conference in Zunyi, Guizhou, in January 1935. It marked both the final burial of the Li Lisan Line and the continuing rise to power of Mao Zedong. Mao became a member of the Politburo's Standing Committee, where he denounced former party leaders for adopting erroneous tactics that re-

sulted in the loss of the Jiangxi Soviet and the near-destruction of the Red Army. Mao's close relationship with Zhou Enlai dates to this period, when Zhou provided critical support at the Zunyi Conference. Zhou soon became the CCP's de facto foreign minister, a position he held until his death in 1976. By October 1935, Mao became the de facto leader of the CCP.

During the decade Mao spent in Shaanxi from 1935 to 1945, often called the Yan'an Period, Mao solidified his control. His comrades credited him with military and political genius because of his early and forceful insistence on guerrilla warfare as opposed to the disastrous positional warfare recommended by Moscow. In Yan'an he focused on the political education of his comrades in his particular brand of revolutionary theory that became known as Mao Zedong Thought. Mao's guerrilla strategy of people's war became commonly accepted. It was a defensive strategy that enabled the Communists to leverage their position of military weakness to wear down their opponents' much stronger conventional forces. His guerrilla bands attacked weak Japanese or Nationalist elements along their long logistical lines. This forced a dilemma upon the Japanese and the Nationalists both to concentrate their forces, since small units were vulnerable, and also to disperse these larger forces throughout the country in a frustrating attempt to protect railway lines and roadways. In effect, the Japanese became the prisoners of urban China because they lacked the manpower to garrison rural China, while the Nationalists proved unable to rally support in the countryside, so that they too remained holed up in urban centers.

Mao was a great student of traditional Han military strategy as outlined by Sunzi and in *The Romance of the Three Kingdoms*, the Ming classic on shifting alliances and multilateral warfare. Despite his avowed rejection of Confucianism and his persecution of Confucianists, he followed its traditions, developed by Mencius, emphasizing the cultivation of loyalties by winning hearts and minds. Mencius had analyzed the fall of the emperors Jie and Zhou, the last monarchs of their respective dynasties: "It was through losing the people that Jie and Zhou lost the Empire, and through losing the people's hearts that they lost the people."[2] Elsewhere Mencius wrote that "good education wins their hearts."[3] Mao followed this Confucian tradition by emphasizing propaganda to educate the masses in order to win their hearts and minds. Mao's literary interests also reflected the passions of China's traditional scholar elite; his literary forms followed Classical Chinese models, and he became a prolific poet.

Once Mao became accepted as the primary leader, he ruled much like a traditional Confucian monarch and followed Legalist traditions. Many even referred to him as China's new emperor, suggesting that the Communists constituted yet another dynasty. Mao persecuted Confucianism in order to destroy family loyalties and the *guanxi* networks of warlords, Nationalists, and regionalists, and replace them with one overarching loyalty to the Communist state. His rejection of Confucian deference to age and family loyalties was an attempt to secure the support of those on the bottom rungs of Confucian society—the young, the poor, and the female—to win the civil war and then to institutionalize Communist power and loyalty to the state thereafter. Mao did not eliminate *guanxi;* rather, he eliminated opposing *guanxi* networks. Mao ultimately took a much more comprehensive approach than the Nationalists to nation building. While both parties focused on projecting power from the top down through society, the Communists also sought to organize popular support from the bottom up. The Communists focused on propaganda work to a much greater extent than did the Nationalists, and they aimed this propaganda at China's vast peasantry.

V. The Xi'an Incident and the Second United Front

From 1927 to 1936, Chiang Kai-shek considered the Communists rather than the Japanese to pose the most dangerous threat. He called Japan an "external disease of the skin" but the CCP a potentially terminal internal disease. He feared that striking Japan before eliminating his internal foes might be suicidal. Ensuing events would prove him right.

In the early 1930s, Europe had become increasingly tense with the rise of fascism in Italy and Germany. Moscow looked with particular apprehension upon Nazi Germany on its European borders and imperial Japan on its Asia borders. On 24 November 1936, the Germans and Japanese signed an Anti-Comintern Pact that threatened a two-front war on the Soviet Union. Stalin suddenly desperately needed the Chinese to cease fighting each other in order to unite against Japan and thereby deter Japan from invading Russia. This was not an idle conjecture since Japan had intervened aggressively in the Russian Civil War (1918–22) and was the last foreign country to evacuate, when its troops finally left Sakhalin Island in 1925. Ever since the Russo-Japanese War, Japanese army war plans had made Russia the main enemy and focused on a land grab in Siberia. Within two weeks of the Anti-Comintern Pact, the Soviet Union was brokering the settlement of the so-called Xi'an Incident.

In the two years since the last encirclement campaign against the Communists, Chiang Kai-shek consolidated his rule in South China sufficiently to begin a sixth and final campaign to wipe out the Communists in remote Shaanxi.

This required the cooperation of the generals of North China, where Chiang's authority remained weak. When Chiang arrived in Xi'an on 4 December 1936 to discuss the campaign plan with Zhang Xueliang, the exiled Manchurian warlord; Yan Xishan, the Shanxi warlord; and Yang Hucheng, the Shaanxi warlord, the generals mutinied, took Chiang hostage on 12 December, and weighed the pros and cons of executing him. This became known as the Xi'an Incident.

The Soviet Union was deeply involved with the mutiny. It encouraged collaboration between the CCP and the mutineers, and contained CCP demands to execute Chiang for fear that the Nationalist armed forces would disintegrate, leaving little to prevent the Japanese from invading Siberia. Stalin wanted the Nationalists and Communists to cooperate to fight Japan so that Russia would never have to do so. Stalin insisted that Mao drop his desired plan to execute Chiang and instead send an emissary to negotiate a second Nationalist-Communist united front.

Since 1935, the CCP had repeatedly proposed uniting (temporarily) with the Nationalists in order to oppose Japan. In early 1932, it had declared war against Japan and organized an insurgency in Manchuria, but within several years, the Japanese had chased any surviving guerrillas across the Soviet border. Regardless, this resistance gave the Communists a huge propaganda advantage over the extremely unpopular Nationalist strategy of appeasement. In late 1935, massive student demonstrations in Beijing denounced the Nationalist foreign policy toward Japan. By June 1936, National Salvation Leagues were being set up throughout China to pressure the Nationalists to take a more aggressive stance against Japan, but Chiang resisted the growing popular pressure and student demonstrations throughout urban China.

The Soviets held a trump card: They had Chiang Kai-shek's only legitimate son, who had been educated in Russia since 1925; they returned him only after Chiang publicly implemented the United Front policy. The son was irreplaceable since Chiang could no longer father children, as was evident from his childless marriage in 1927 to Song Meiling. Therefore, his dynasty depended on the return of his son, Chiang Ching-kuo. Chiang Kai-shek was released on Christmas Day 1936. He quickly returned to Nanjing, where he had his captors, Zhang Xueliang and Yang Hucheng, arrested. Zhang remained under house arrest for many decades in China and Taiwan. Yang Hucheng was not so lucky. He and his immediate family were all imprisoned and eventually shot in 1949 as the Nationalists fled to Taiwan.

The United Front forced a reorientation of Chiang Kai-shek's military strategy from fighting the Communists, a shared objective with Japan, to fighting Japan. This transformed him into a dire enemy of Japan, which had warned him repeatedly to stay clear of the Communists. Japanese foreign policy in China had long focused on the containment and, if possible, rollback of Russian influence in East Asia. In the 1930s, they perceived the Chinese Communists to be Russian proxies. With the Second United Front, the Nationalists acquired guilt by association. In May 1937, Chiang hired the recently retired U.S. army captain Claire Lee Chennault, a vocal proponent of air power, to create a Nationalist air force, while the Germans agreed to provide $100 million in weapons.

The Xi'an Incident may have offered Chiang a convenient pretext to make a policy reversal. His long-standing focus on destroying his domestic opposition rather than opposing Japanese aggression had become so unpopular that it seemed unlikely that he could retain power if he did not establish his anti-Japanese and nationalist credentials. In the months following the Xi'an Incident, the Chinese Communists promised to cease destabilizing the Nanjing government, to replace all soviets with democratic governments, to integrate the Red Army into a National Revolutionary Army, and, most importantly, to put their troops under the command of the Nanjing government's Military Commission.

The Nationalist-Communist alliance quickly exacerbated Soviet-Japanese and Sino-Japanese tensions. Japan accused Moscow of orchestrating the Xi'an Incident. In early July 1937, the Japanese garrison near Beijing (then called Peiping) began to conduct field exercises, a privilege based on the 1901 Boxer Protocol that allowed foreign troops to be stationed between Tianjin and Beijing. On 7 July 1937, after receiving fire from Chinese troops, a Japanese unit reported one of its soldiers missing in the vicinity of Marco Polo Bridge, south of Beijing. The Japanese officers, thinking that the missing man might have been captured by the Chinese, demanded a search of the nearby town of Wanping. Previously, the Nationalists had backed down during such incidents. With the creation of the Second United Front, tensions rapidly escalated into a general war. When the local Chinese officers refused to allow the Japanese to search Wanping, the Japanese bombarded it, but their garrison numbered only 10,000 in contrast to the opposing Chinese force of 100,000. When the Chinese successfully repulsed the Japanese and counterattacked, the Japanese responded massively. The Japanese War Ministry mobilized five divisions so that its strength in North China soon reached 100,000.

This so-called Marco Polo Bridge Incident started out as a minor skirmish between Nationalist and Japanese troops but soon escalated into all-out war. On 17 July 1937, Chiang Kai-shek declared that China had no choice but to struggle for national survival. He called for resistance on the part of the Chinese people, but the Nationalist Army was unprepared to face the Japanese. Strategists in Tokyo optimistically predicted that the entire campaign would last only three months, but they were not prepared either. By 1945 they still had not pacified the China theater.

Conclusions

The nominal reunification of China did not end the dozen years of civil war following the death of Yuan Shikai. The so-called Nanjing Decade, dating from the end of the Northern Expedition in 1928 until the Japanese invasion in 1937, marked the high point of Nationalist rule, but it included at least nine coups and countercoups within the Nationalist leadership, five encirclement campaigns against the Communists, and the Japanese invasion of Manchuria and North China. The decade was anything but peaceful.

Much of the country, especially in the North, remained outside of Nanjing's control. Although the Nanjing government succeeded in forcing many of the foreign powers to give up their unequal treaties, the USSR and Japan were the two crucial exceptions. When China lost the 1929 war, the Japanese feared a rapid expansion of Soviet influence in Manchuria. They used the Manchurian Incident in 1931 as a pretext for a massive invasion and occupation of the region, with plans for long-term colonization. They formalized these plans with the creation of the puppet state of Manchukuo under Puyi, the last Manchu emperor. In 1935 the USSR sold the Chinese Eastern Railway to Japan, giving Tokyo full control over Manchuria to use as a base to expand southward. These foreign affairs debacles had an enormous impact on China's domestic situation, with the general population increasingly determined to resist the Japanese.

The Nationalists were far more successful at creating the military institutions to conquer an empire than at creating the necessary civil institutions to retain the empire thereafter. The last conquerors of China, the Manchus, had been more successful in engineering this transition. They had adopted Han civilization and the dynastic system in order to cement the loyalties of their subjects. Chiang had great difficulty forging loyalties. He put together various coalitions against a succession of common threats, but the coalitions did not endure after the defeat of the shared enemy. He tried to craft a positive program out of Sun Yat-sen's Three People's Principles and his own New Life Movement, but they proved insufficient to overcome China's endemic regionalism. He was able to unite South China, but his North China allies feared his dominance and so prevented him from reuniting North and South China.

The Chinese Communists, not out of choice but out of dire necessity, tried to organize both from the top down, to centralize party control in accordance with Soviet models, and from the bottom up in a hearts-and-minds propaganda campaign to win the allegiance of the rural population. By contrast, the Nationalist Party was fundamentally an urban movement that never was able to extend its control over the countryside beyond the rural elite. In the Fifth Encirclement Campaign, Chiang Kai-shek nearly annihilated the CCP, forcing its flight in 1934 on the Long March to northwest China. From Yan'an, the Chinese Communists could make contact with the Soviet Union and later receive crucial military and financial aid.

In 1936, when Chiang was on the verge of engaging in a sixth encirclement campaign, the murky Xi'an Incident occurred. Chiang made an about-face on strategy to pursue closer ties with the USSR and a Second United Front with the CCP to fight the Japanese. The Second United Front backfired for all parties except the USSR, which correctly anticipated that Japan would become so bogged down in China that it would not attack Siberia. Japan followed the Soviet script, responding to the threat of increasing Communist influence with a full-scale invasion that proved more lethal to the Nationalists than to Japan's real enemies, the Communists, while Chiang was overextended fighting two deadly enemies. The Communists would eventually win the civil war in 1949, and in the 1960s, Mao even thanked a visiting Japanese dignitary for making the Communist victory possible. Victory came at the price of a brutal Japanese occupation that left the CCP in possession of an economically devastated homeland.

BIBLIOGRAPHY

Chang, Jung and Jon Halliday. *Mao: the Unknown Story.* New York: Alfred A. Knopf, 2005.

Coble, Parks M. *The Shanghai Capitalists and the Nationalist Government, 1927–1937.* 2nd ed. Cambridge, MA: Harvard University Press, 1986.

———*Facing Japan: Chinese Politics and Japanese Imperialism, 1931–1937.* Cambridge, MA: Harvard University Press, 1992.

Crowley, James B. *Japan's Quest for Autonomy: National Security and Foreign Policy, 1930–1938.* Princeton, NJ: Princeton University Press, 1966.

Dreyer, Edward L. *China at War, 1901–1949.* London: Longman, 1995.

Duara, Prasenjit. *Culture, Power, and the State: Rural North China, 1900–1942.* Stanford, CA: Stanford University Press, 1988.

Eastman, Lloyd. *The Abortive Revolution: China under Nationalist Rule, 1927–1937.* Cambridge, MA: Harvard University Press, 1974.

———"Nationalist China during the Nanking Decade 1927–1937." In *The Cambridge History of China,* vol. 13, edited by John K. Fairbank and Albert Feuerwerker, 116–67. Cambridge: Cambridge University Press, 1986.

———Jerome Ch'en, Suzanne Pepper, and Lyman P. Van Slyke, eds. *The Nationalist Era in China.* Cambridge: Cambridge University Press, 1991.

Fenby, Jonathan. *Chiang Kai-shek: China's Generalissimo and the Nation He Lost.* New York: Carol & Graf, 2003.

Feuerwerker, Albert. *Economic Trends in the Republic of China, 1912–1949.* Ann Arbor: University of Michigan Press, 1977.

Furuya, Keiji. *Chiang Kai-shek: His Life and Times.* Translated and abridged by Chun-ming Chang. New York: St. John's University Press, 1981.

Guillermaz, Jacques. *A History of the Chinese Communist Party 1921–1949.* Translated by Anne Destiny. New York: Random House, 1972.

Harrison, James. *The Long March to Power: A History of the Chinese Communist Party, 1921–72.* New York: Praeger, 1972.

Hsiao, Tso-liang. *Power Relations within the Chinese Communes Movement, 1930–1934.* Seattle: University of Washington Press, 1961.

Israel, John. *Student Nationalism in China, 1927–1937.* Stanford, CA: Stanford University Press, 1966.

Kataoka, Tetsuya. *Resistance and Revolution in China: The Communists and the Second United Front.* Berkeley: University of California Press, 1974.

Kim, Ilpyong J. *The Politics of Chinese Communism: Kiangsi under Soviet Rule.* Berkeley: University of California Press, 1974.

Kirby, William Corbon. *Germany and Republican China.* Stanford, CA: Stanford University Press, 1984.

Myers, Ramon H. "The Agrarian System." In *The Cambridge History of China,* vol. 13, edited by John K. Fairbank and Albert Feuerwerker, 230–69. Cambridge: Cambridge University Press, 1986.

Price, Jane L. *Cadres, Commanders, and Commissars: The Training of the Chinese Communist Leadership, 1920–1945.* Boulder, CO: Westview Press, 1976.

Rawski, Thomas. *Economic Growth in Prewar China.* Berkeley: University of California Press, 1989.

Schram, Stuart. *The Thought of Mao Tse-tung.* Cambridge: Cambridge University Press, 1989.

Selden, Mark. *The Yenan Way in Revolutionary China.* Cambridge, MA: Harvard University Press, 1971.

Sih, Paul K. T., ed. *The Strenuous Decade. China's Nation-building Efforts 1927–1939.* New York: St. Johns University Press, 1970.

Thomas, S. Bernard. *Labor and the Chinese Revolution: Class Strategies and Contradictions of Chinese Communism, 1928–1948.* Ann Arbor: University of Michigan Press, 1983.

Tien, Hung-mao. *Government and Politics in Kuomintang China, 1927–1937.* Stanford, CA: Stanford University Press, 1972.

van de Ven, Hans. "New States of War: Communist and Nationalist Warfare and State Building (1928–1934)." In *Warfare in Chinese History,* edited by van de Ven, 321–97. Leiden: Brill, 2000.

Van Slyke, Lyman P. *Enemies and Friends: The United Front in Chinese Communist History.* Stanford, CA: Stanford University Press, 1967.

Wei, William. *Counterrevolution in China: The Nationalists in Jiangxi during the Soviet Period.* Ann Arbor: University of Michigan Press, 1985.

Wu, Tien-wei. *The Sian Incident: A Pivotal Point in Modern Chinese History.* Ann Arbor: University of Michigan Press, 1976.

Wylie, Ramond F. *The Emergence of Maoism: Mao Tse-tung, Ch'en Po-ta, and the Search for Chinese Theory, 1935–1945.* Stanford, CA: Stanford University Press, 1980.

Yang, Benjamin. *From Revolution to Politics: Chinese Communists on the Long March.* Boulder, CO: Westview Press, 1990.

Young, Arthur N. *China's Nation-building Effort, 1927–1937: The Financial and Economic Record.* Stanford, CA: Hoover Institution Press, 1971.

NOTES

1. "New Life" refers to the Nationalists' New Life Movement and "kites" refers to a kite-flying festival in the city. Translated by Hans van de Ven, "New States of War: Communist and Nationalist Warfare and State Building (1928–1934)," in *Warfare in Chinese History,* edited by van de Ven (Leiden: Brill, 2000), 370.

2. *Mencius,* D. C. Lau, trans. (London: Penguin Books, 1970), 121. Transliterations have been converted to *pinyin.*

3. Ibid., 184.

Chronology

7 July 1937	Marco Polo Bridge Incident; escalation of the Second Sino-Japanese War
13 Aug.–12 Nov. 1937	Second Shanghai Incident, also called Battle for Shanghai
21 August 1937	Nationalist-Soviet Nonaggression Treaty
30 October 1937	Nationalist government moves to Chongqing
13 December 1937	Japanese occupation of Nanjing; beginning of Rape of Nanjing
March–20 May 1938	Xuzhou Campaign
7 June 1938	Nationalists breach Yellow River dikes
31 July–10 Aug 1938	Zhanggufeng Incident; Soviet-Japanese border clash
21 October 1938	Guangzhou falls
25 October 1938	Wuhan falls
November 1938	Completion of the Burma Route
11 May–15 Sept. 1939	Nomonhan Incident; Soviet-Japanese border clash
23 August 1939	German-Soviet Nonaggression Pact
1 September 1939	Japan sets up the Mongol Autonomous Government
	Germany invades Poland; beginning of World War II
30 March 1940	Wang Jingwei heads the puppet government in Nanjing
20 Aug.–5 Dec. 1940	Hundred Regiments' Campaign
6–13 January 1941	New Fourth Army Incident, effective end of Second United Front
13 April 1941	Japanese-Soviet Neutrality Pact
17 April 1941	United States begins providing military aid to the Nationalists
22 June 1941	German invasion of Russia
25 July 1941	United States freezes Japanese assets in the United States
28 July 1941	Japan invades southern French Indochina
1 August 1941	U.S. oil embargo on Japan
7 December 1941	Japanese attack on Pearl Harbor; beginning of the Pacific War
11 January 1943	United States and Britain sign agreements with Nationalists to end extraterritoriality in China
Spring–winter 1944	Ichigo Offensive to clear the land route from Korea to Hanoi
13 October 1944	Soviet annexation of Tannu Tuva
4–11 February 1945	Yalta Conference
7 May 1945	Unconditional surrender of Germany
6 August 1945	U.S. atomic bombing of Hiroshima
8 August 1945	Soviet invasion of Manchuria
9 August 1945	U.S. atomic bombing of Nagasaki
14 August 1945	Nationalist-Soviet Friendship Treaty
15 August 1945	Japanese capitulation; end of Sino-Japanese War and World War II

20

The Second Sino-Japanese War

The Chinese have generally portrayed what they call the War of Resistance against Japan as an anti-imperialist struggle against Japanese aggression; the more neutral name used here—the Second Sino-Japanese War—emphasizes that there were two belligerents. Western histories tend to ignore the Sino-Japanese War altogether, focusing on the post–Pearl Harbor phase of World War II without understanding the Sino-Japanese War antecedents. The reality was far more complicated than any of these accounts. The Soviet Union considered Asia to be one theater in its global struggle to spread communism, and it hoped that China would become a cooperative communist state. But

the USSR was also engaged in a long-standing regional conflict with Japan for spheres of influence in Manchuria and Mongolia. Japan intervened in China to stabilize Manchuria, which, from Tokyo's point of view, was the most vital part of the former Qing empire. Meanwhile, the formation of the Second United Front did not end the civil war in China, because the Communists and Nationalists retained antithetical goals and the collapse of the dynastic system left an institutional void that both sides strove to fill. Thus, there were three ongoing "nested" wars: a global world war; a regional Sino-Japanese War; and a domestic Nationalist-Communist civil war. For Chinese civilians these were truly hideous years as famine, refugees, and disease all followed in the wake of war. Millions of Chinese died and millions more became homeless. The Nationalists proved incapable of defeating the Japanese unassisted, but their refusal to capitulate meant that Japan could not win the war either. So hostilities dragged on for fifteen long years, becoming increasingly bitter and brutal.

I. Great Power Rivalries Over China

The Second Sino-Japanese War did not begin in 1937 but rather with the Manchurian Incident in 1931 because once Japan initiated military operations, it never stopped. After the occupation and pacification of Manchuria came the North China War (1933–5), which the Nationalists chose not to fight but regional forces did. During the campaign, Japanese forces moved south of the Great Wall into the core provinces of China. (See Chapter 19 Section II.)

China became the battleground for great power rivalries. The Great Depression made communist ideology particularly threatening to Tokyo, which feared its spread among Japan's hard-pressed population. In contrast, the USSR considered the Depression an opportunity to spread revolution. Japan looked upon the escalating Chinese civil war with growing apprehension. It needed a stable China to integrate the two countries' economies to sustain growth. Initially, Moscow desired a disintegrating China so that it could seize frontier territories and promote a Communist revolution in an environment of economic turmoil and endemic warfare. But with the rise of Nazi Germany, the USSR wanted China to counterbalance Japan to prevent a two-front war.

The Japanese doubted Chiang Kai-shek's ability to win the civil war. Over the years, they had become increasingly skeptical that any Chinese could restore effective internal administration. The perceived incompetence of their fellow Asians harkened back to a famous essay written by the renowned Meiji-era writer and philosopher Fukuzawa Yukichi in 1885 entitled "On Saying Good-bye to Asia." The remedy would be for Japan to bring modernity and prosperity to Asia.

The Japanese considered the creation of Manchukuo to be a great success, and with success came arrogance. Under Zhang Xueliang's warlord administration, the region had been in economic chaos, with all seizable resources funneled into the military and printed money making up any shortfalls. Japan changed this situation. It restored order, stabilized the currency, made massive infrastructure investments, and over the course of the war transformed Manchuria into the most industrialized region in Asia outside Japan. In the process, it catapulted its own economy out of the Great Depression. The rest of China, however, continued to churn. Instead of stopping with Manchuria, Japanese forces kept on going and showed no signs of stopping. Chiang had assumed that Japan would stop and that he could reach a negotiated settlement, given his and Japan's shared antipathy for communism. Insatiable Japanese expansion precluded this outcome, leaving Chiang little choice but to form a Second United Front.

Japan considered the creation of Manchukuo to be a direct response to the Soviet occupation of Outer Mongolia and to the ongoing Communist infiltration of Xinjiang. To protect its vast investments, in 1936 Tokyo announced plans to resettle 5 million Japanese mainly along the Manchukuo-Soviet border. Meanwhile, in the USSR, the Great Purge caused the forced migration of millions of Soviet citizens to prison camps in Siberia, likewise located mainly along the Soviet border with Manchukuo. Each country strove to prevent the other from striking first in an anticipated Soviet-Japanese war.

Moscow responded to Japan's occupation of Manchuria by consolidating its own sphere of influence. After selling the Chinese Eastern Railway to Manchukuo in 1935, it tightened its hold over Outer Mongolia by signing a ten-year Protocol of Mutual Assistance on 12 March 1936. Tokyo considered this protocol to be an anti-Japanese military alliance. Simultaneously, the USSR increased its influence over Xinjiang, signing secret treaties with the local Xinjiang warlord, Sheng Shicai, in 1934 and 1936. Then came the Second United Front, aimed at expelling Japan from the lands of the former Qing empire. It also raised the prospect of a Communist-dominated China. During the Xi'an Incident, Tokyo warned Nanjing that an alliance with the Communists would compel Japan to respond in kind. Tokyo's response was the Marco Polo Bridge Incident, in which a skirmish between Japanese and Nationalist troops rapidly escalated into a full-scale China-wide war. It escalated because, unlike in the past, Chiang Kai-shek did not back down.

On 30 July 1937 Beijing and Tianjin fell to Japan. On 13 August hostilities erupted in Shanghai, where Chiang's German-trained troops were concentrated, outnumbering Japanese forces ten to one. Chiang initiated this confrontation, the so-called Second Shanghai Incident, ordering his air force to bomb Japanese warships in the harbor, but the bombs hit residential neighborhoods instead. Tokyo responded by sending massive reinforcements to expand operations in central China. Chiang's troops fought for three months. In the end he lost a quarter of a million men, half of his forces deployed at Shanghai. Their elimination meant the loss of his best-trained troops and left the road to Nanjing open. The Japanese price for peace was recognition of Manchukuo, a price that neither Chiang nor Mao could pay, given the depth of public sentiments against Japan. The longer the war went on, the deeper these sentiments became. In desperation, Chiang turned to the USSR for help. On 21 August 1937, Nanjing and Moscow signed a non-aggression pact, allegedly with a secret section detailing closer political and military links. In March 1938, the Soviet government loaned the Nationalists $50 million. The Japanese military strategy of relentless expansion precluded the negotiated settlement they sought and reinforced rather than weakened the United Front. Conversely, Chiang's growing ties with the Communists only fueled Japan's fury. So, the war continued to escalate.

When the Japanese invaded China proper in 1937, they expected the Chinese to react as they had during the First Sino-Japanese War and during the occupation of Manchuria, but Japan was no longer fighting an alien Manchu regime or on the imperial periphery in Manchuria. It was fighting a Han government in Han China. The Japanese invasion triggered a revulsion so deep that politically it greatly strengthened the Nationalist warlord coalition even while it obliterated

Following a Japanese attack on Shanghai's South Station on 28 August 1937, a terrified baby appears to be one of the only survivors. Later, claims were made that the Chinese photographer staged this picture, and a segment from the propaganda film *Battle of China* shows a man carrying this same baby toward the platform, not away from it. An estimated 136 million Americans saw this picture in *Life* magazine or in one of the 800 American newspapers that reprinted it. For many this image symbolized China's fight against Japan.

Chiang's armies. While Japan could dominate the cities and the intervening railway lines, the countryside swarmed with marauding Nationalist and Communist guerrillas. During the Nanjing Decade, both the Communists and the Nationalists had increasingly tried to stir feelings of nationalism as a vehicle to power. Japanese actions played right into this strategy.

Border tensions spiraled between the Soviet and Japanese spheres of influence. While a military clash in August 1938 at Zhanggufeng on the Manchukuo-Korean-Soviet border ended in stalemate, a pitched battle on the Outer Mongolian-Manchukuo frontier at Nomonhan became an important turning point in Japanese strategy. From May to September 1939, massive armored divisions engaged in battle at Nomonhan. Soviet forces prevailed only after sustaining heavy casualties, but the Japanese suffered a staggering 73 percent casualty rate, losing over 18,000 men. This was a military disaster for Japan. Previ-

ously, army war plans had called for a northern advance against Russia. After Nomonhan, there was increasing support for the navy war plan for a southern advance in the South Pacific, the strategy that led to the Japanese attack on Pearl Harbor. Germany seized the opportunity to deflect Soviet attention. In August 1939, Germany and the USSR signed a nonaggression pact. The combination of defeat on the field and German-Soviet diplomacy ended Japanese hopes of eliminating the Soviet threat to the north. On 15 September 1939, the Soviet Union and Japan signed an armistice agreement, ending the Nomonhan Incident.

Subsequently, Soviet officials expressed their willingness to forego active support for either side in the Chinese civil war in exchange for Japan's agreement not to annihilate the Chinese Communists. They proposed an exchange of Soviet noninterference in a Japanese advance south into Indochina in return for Tokyo's acquiescence to future Soviet incursions into Afghanistan. Japan later agreed to a Soviet free hand in Xinjiang. The negotiations culminated in the Neutrality Pact of 13 April 1941. It stipulated that Moscow would recognize Manchukuo and Tokyo would recognize Soviet hegemony over Outer Mongolia. The treaty secured Japan's strategic rear to the north. Two months later, in June, Germany attacked the USSR. This meant that Japan could pursue its war against China with little fear of Soviet intervention.

II. The Regional War and the Civil War

Against this backdrop of Soviet-Japanese rivalries, Japan and China fought a regional war for control over China. Within this war was a long-standing civil war between the Nationalists and the Communists and, before long, the civil and regional wars became a theater in an overarching global war.

After Shanghai fell, in rapid succession the Japanese took Datong in September, Taiyuan in November, and Jinan in December 1937. The Chinese retreat became a rout. Following the occupation of Nanjing in mid-December 1937, the Japanese forces controlled all access to and traffic along the Yangzi River. When the Chinese did not capitulate with the fall of their capital, the Japanese attempted to cow the Chinese population into submission. In a repeat of the Manchu massacre of Ming loyalists in Yangzhou before taking Nanjing in 1645, Japanese officers oversaw the massacre of what the Chinese claim was over 300,000 prisoners of war and civilians in the so-called Rape of Nanjing. The Japanese believed that terrorizing innocents would cause the Chinese to capitulate. This strategy backfired. Instead of capitulation, it led to a contagion of virulently anti-Japanese nationalism that has persisted to the present day and gave Japan an international reputation for barbarity. Japan's unwillingness to make a formal apology for the Nanjing Massacre remains an enduring source of Sino-Japanese hostility.

The Xuzhou Campaign (March–May 1938) followed the fall of Nanjing. It was larger than most battles of World War II, involving some 600,000 combatants. Victory put Japan in possession of North China and the Yangzi River valley, but at the cost of further developing Chinese nationalism. Li Zongren, the leader of the Guangxi Clique, recreated a Nationalist army out of a motley array of poorly trained regional forces, mostly from areas far to the south of the fighting. In an attempt to break Chinese morale, the Japanese promised to give no quarter to those fleeing the field. Instead of creating paralysis, the threats steeled the

will to resist. Although Li Zongren's troops had vastly inferior equipment and training compared to the Japanese, they fought with heroism. Tens of thousands of Chinese died, including nine generals; only one was from Shandong, the location of the battle. In other words, Chinese forces were fighting for China, not, as in the past, strictly for their native place. (See Map 20.1.)

Chiang lost his main armies once with the fall of Nanjing and now a second time during the Xuzhou Campaign. In June 1938, in an act of desperation, he ordered the breach of Yellow River dikes at Huayuankou (near Zhengzhou). Approximately 800,000 drowned, and millions became refugees. The Japanese simply detoured around the flooded areas, butchering any civilians in their path. For the next decade the Yellow River ran outside of its dikes, leaving misery in its wake. A sign of imperial legitimacy was the ability to control the waters and maintain the dikes. Chiang's strategically ineffective breach of the Yellow River dikes weakened the Nationalist mandate of heaven. In addition, the Nationalist decision in November 1938 to torch the refugee-filled city of Changsha rather than to let it fall to Japan intact became a symbol of Nationalist brutality toward the general population. (See the feature on page 323.)

The Sino-Japanese War was a disaster for China. After sixteen months of battle following the Marco Polo Bridge Incident, the Japanese controlled North China, most of the Yangzi River Basin, and as far south as Guangzhou. They established three puppet governments to rule these areas: On 27 October 1937, they founded the Mongolian Autonomous Government to administer Chahar and Suiyuan provinces; on 14 December 1937, they set up a provisional Chinese government in Beijing to rule Hubei, Henan, and Shandong, but also linked with Chahar and Suiyuan; on 28 March 1938, they established a government in Nanjing with jurisdiction over Jiangsu, Zhejiang, and Anhui. Then in 1940, Japan consolidated the Beijing and Nanjing governments under Wang Jingwei, a pro-Soviet supporter of Sun Yat-sen and a key Nationalist leader. The new government recognized Manchukuo and gave Japan the right to send troops to oppose communism in China. In return, Japan, Manchukuo, and Japan's major European allies, including Germany and Italy, recognized Wang's government in Nanjing.

During the Nationalists' forced retreat, they temporarily increased their support for the United Front by providing financial and military aid to the Communists, which opened new opportunities for the latter. In May 1938, Mao Zedong began advocating the establishment of guerrilla bases in rural, so-called peripheral, areas where there were few Japanese troops. Mao's military strategy envisioned a rapidly expand-

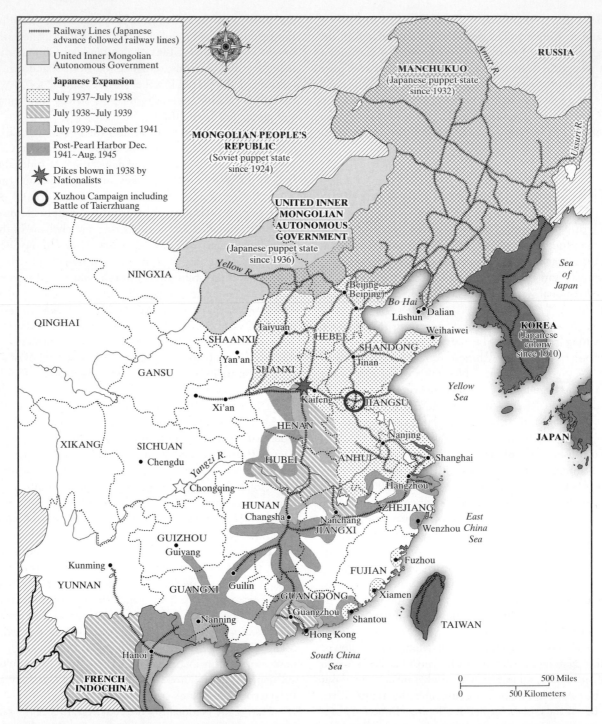

Map 20.1   Sino-Japanese War (1937–45)

ing guerrilla army that would eventually be able to repel enemy attacks. While securing these base areas, the CCP mobilized the local population into mass organizations. By 1938, they had established over ten base areas in the Japanese rear, mostly in North China. The dispersion in rural areas put the Communists out of contact with the Japanese forces, which were concentrated in the cities and along the transportation routes connecting them.

YELLOW RIVER FLOODING

The Yellow River valley is the cradle of Han civilization. The river acquired its name about 2,000 years ago when the expansion of farming during the Qin and Han dynasties into the grasslands along the river and the felling of trees on its banks resulted in soil erosion and sedimentation that turned the river water a yellow color. Over the years, sedimentation made the river bottom rise above its former banks, creating an eternal battle between the gravitational pull of the water toward the lowest lands and people building and maintaining levees to contain the rising waters. The sediments have created rich farmland, so the lower course of the river, the part most prone to flooding, is heavily populated and agriculturally highly productive. The river forms the second longest river system after the Yangzi River. It runs nearly 3,000 miles from the Qinghai-Tibet plateau through North China to the sea. Its intersection with the Grand Canal requires a complicated and high-maintenance series of levees. The Grand Canal, completed during the Sui dynasty (581–618), was the major North-South transportation artery; it was vital to supply the capital with food and tax revenues from South China.

For thousands of years, the Chinese have tried to master the Yellow River through an extensive dike system and periodic dredging. Success has depended on persistence, mass labor, and extensive government funds. Each year 1,600 million tons of silt flow down its course to expand the Shandong Peninsula. Between 1194 and 1983, this created over 11,000 square kilometers of new land. Even in the best circumstances, the river has been difficult to contain because sediment continually builds up on the river floor and heavy rains push the waters ever higher up the levees. In the two millennia preceding the Communist Revolution, there were over 1,500 recorded breaches of the dikes. In periods of declining dynastic fortunes and civil wars, the dikes have not been maintained and disaster has followed. There have been at least seven major changes in course and many more minor changes in the last two millennia. Each of these changes has left a swath of human misery between the old and new channels. The last major shift, between 1853 and 1855, resulted in part from a failure to maintain the levees during the Taiping Rebellion; the flooding then helped precipitate the Nian Rebellion. A less radical change in course occurred in 1938, when Chiang Kai-shek had the dikes destroyed at Huanyankou, Henan, to halt the advancing Japanese Army. In the ensuing flooding, about 1 million Chinese drowned and 11 million were without food or shelter. Only in 1947, with U.S. aid, were the dikes repaired.

Except for the 564 years between 1289 and 1853, and the eight years between 1939–47 when the Nationalists deliberately breached the dikes, the Yellow River has always emptied into the sea on the northern side of the Shandong Peninsula. Containing the river has required the organization and mobilization of a huge labor force. Some have argued that the vast system for dikes, flood control, and irrigation to propagate rice is the origin of "Oriental despotism," meaning that an autocratic state was necessary to maintain such a complex and expensive system in ancient times. Others have argued that the Chinese created this vast hydraulic system in ancient times in order to increase agricultural productivity to feed their vast armies. These interpretations are controversial, but the problem of flood control remains very real. The Chinese continue to suffer major floods.

By 1943, the CCP controlled about 155,000 square miles of the 345,000 that comprised occupied China. In contrast, the Japanese actually controlled about 82,000 square miles, while the Nationalists had been reduced to only 41,000. Most of the remaining 67,000 square miles was either barren or guerrilla areas. Japan simply lacked the manpower to garrison rural China. Nevertheless, the Communist forces were no more able than the Nationalist armies to defeat the Japanese in conventional battles. Their 1940 Hundred Regiments' Campaign against Japanese strongholds in northern China boomeranged as badly as any Nationalist strategy. Japanese counterattacks devastated the Communist Eighth Route Army, which reportedly sustained 100,000 casualties. Japan then responded with a devastatingly effective pacification program called the Three Alls Strategy: burn all, kill all, plunder all, causing untold civilian misery. Thereafter, the CCP abandoned conventional warfare for dispersed guerrilla warfare to harass isolated Japanese units. While this strategy could not win the war, it greatly increased the costs to Japan. The strategy left Japanese and Nationalist main forces to fight and weaken each other while the CCP made revolution in the remote countryside.

The Nationalist Party, with its urban power base, bore the brunt of the Japanese offensive throughout China, while the Communists found sanctuary in remote base areas. Like the Communists, the Nationalists lacked the capacity to undertake a counteroffensive against the Japanese. With the growing influence of the Communists in the countryside, the Nationalists restricted Communist political activities, outlawed their sponsorship of mass organizations, and criticized them for reneging on promises to put their forces under Nationalist command.

Increasing tensions culminated in the New Fourth Army Incident in January 1941 when the Communist-led Fourth Army defied orders from Chiang to deploy north of the Yangzi River. Nationalist forces ambushed it but proved unable to disband the New Fourth Army, while the spectacle of Chinese fighting Chinese alienated many supporters. The Nationalists bore the brunt of the blame. As the incumbent government, the Nationalists also bore the blame for the failure to defeat the Japanese and for the misery of the tens of millions of refugees fleeing the hostilities.

Negotiations between the two ceased; the Nationalists tried to cut off supplies to the Communist armies; hand-picked government troops blockaded the Communist base in northern Shaanxi. The United Front limped along in name only. This uneasy stalemate continued through May 1944, when U.S.-brokered talks in Xi'an renewed negotiations between Nationalist and Communist representatives. In July 1944, the United States sent an Army Observation Group, known as the Dixie Mission, to evaluate the CCP's political and military capabilities in the hope of establishing air bases to bomb Japan. While certain members of the mission, like the State Department representative John S. Service, were very positive about the Communists' chances of taking power, leaders in Washington were much more wary about allying with the CCP.

III. The Global War

The invasion of China proved far more costly than Japan had ever imagined. Despite its virtually uninterrupted victories, the Nationalists and Communists continued to resist. Their inland locations, however, interfered with the delivery of military supplies. As soon as Chiang moved his capital to Chongqing, he attempted to reorganize the Nationalist Army. But his only link with the outside was the Burma Road, a 715-mile path cut through the steep mountain gorges of southwest China. Opened in December 1938, it allowed supplies to be shipped from Rangoon. In 1941, Chiang, along with the USSR, became a major recipient of U.S. Lend-Lease aid. Japan was determined to stop the flow of supplies, so it began to penetrate farther into Southeast Asia. After the fall of France, the Vichy government agreed to halt all aid to the Nationalists via French Indochina and permit Japan to use its air bases. In September 1940, Japanese troops moved into northern Indochina. Soon afterward, Tokyo called on the British to close the Burma Road. Hard pressed by the Germans in Europe, the British agreed.

Washington responded to the Japanese invasion of China proper with a growing list of embargoed products. It hoped not only to deter Japan from further aggression, but also to force it to roll back its zone of occupation. Like Chiang's agreement to the Second United Front and the Japanese invasion of China, this strategy of deterrence also backfired. The Japanese government, far from being deterred, concluded that it had to expand its empire as rapidly as possible. After the United States imposed an oil embargo in retaliation for the Japanese occupation of southern Indochina, the Japanese government concluded that it would have to take the oil fields of the Dutch East Indies (Indonesia). It assumed that the United States would interfere militarily from its bases in the Philippines, which sat astride the vital sea lanes between Japan and the Dutch East Indies, and perhaps Britain would also intervene—hence the strategy for the simultaneous preemptive attacks against Pearl Harbor, the Philippines, and British Malaya.

Japan had been unable to extricate itself from the China quagmire militarily or diplomatically. It then tried to overcome its strategic overextension by cutting off Chiang from foreign aid, while also expanding its own resource base throughout the South Pacific, and preempting U.S. intervention by attacking Pearl Harbor. As in China, Japan incorrectly gauged the reaction of those attacked. Contrary to expectations, the United States did not withdraw from Asia but launched a war of annihilation. After Pearl Harbor, U.S. aid to China rose from $26 million to a total of $1.3 billion by the end of the war, while U.S. credit to China reached $500 million. Once Washington declared war on 8 December 1941, Chiang correctly calculated that the United States would defeat Japan so that he could focus on his primary goal of annihilating the Communists. For similar reasons, the Communists also husbanded their resources.

Both the Nationalists and the Communists continued to employ the traditional Han strategy for barbarian management that had been so successful for Chiang in the civil wars prior to 1937. Ironically, the strategy developed for use against frontier people proved far more effective against Han warlord regimes than against industrialized foreign foes. Instead of successfully playing off Russian and Japanese aggressors against each other, China became the victim of both. Chiang's unwillingness to fight the Japanese after Pearl Harbor despite massive U.S. aid alienated his richest foreign benefactor, while Mao became entangled in Soviet foreign policy during the Korean War (1950–3). Barbarian management, so effective in the preindustrial era, did not play well in international relations after the Industrial Revolution.

Washington appointed General Joseph Warren Stilwell to coordinate the U.S.-Nationalist war effort against Japan. He soon developed an intense loathing for Chiang, whom he referred to as "peanut" in reference to Chiang's bald head.

When General "Vinegar Joe" Stilwell insisted that Chiang Kai-shek order his reserves to fight the Japanese in Burma, Chiang demanded that Washington withdraw Stilwell, which it did, sending the more compliant Major General Albert C. Wedemeyer instead. In this picture, camouflaged Chinese soldiers repel a charge of 50,000 Japanese along the Salween River on the Thai-Burmese border.

Likewise, Stilwell's loss of Chiang's remaining German-trained troops (equal to one-third of his reserves) in the Burma campaign in 1942 did not endear him to Chiang. Conflict over military strategy between Chiang and Stilwell became acute, and centered on Stilwell's belief that Chiang should redeploy the 400,000 troops blockading the Communists to fight Japan. In June 1942, when promised U.S. aid failed to arrive on schedule, Chiang threatened to sign a separate peace treaty with Japan, an attempt to play Japan off against the United States in another round of barbarian management. After he engineered Stilwell's recall, Chiang ended reforms to create a constitution. With Stilwell gone, there was no longer a need to keep up any pretense of democratic government.

After the U.S. Navy's victory at the Battle of Midway in early June 1942, Japan remained on the defensive for the duration of the war. The U.S. island-hopping campaign forced Japan to divert troops from China to the Pacific. The Battle for Guadalcanal in December 1942 forced Japan to halt its plans for a major offensive on the Nationalist capital at Chongqing. In 1944 Japan launched one final offensive in China, Operation Ichigo, in order to open a land link to Indochina. Japan had to suspend this successful operation in

order to redeploy forces to protect its home islands against the anticipated U.S. invasion. From the U.S. perspective, the Battle for the Marianas during the summer of 1944 made the China theater irrelevant for its war against Japan. Airfields in the Marianas meant that the United States no longer needed Chinese airfields to bomb Japan.

IV. Soviet Efforts to Expand Their Sphere of Influence

After the German invasion of the USSR, Stalin closed the border with Xinjiang. This wreaked havoc with the Xinjiang economy, so the local warlord, Sheng Shicai, started casting about for another benefactor. Until the German invasion, Xinjiang had been a de facto Soviet protectorate, with Soviet natural resource extraction and air and other military bases. In 1943 Sheng, in desperation, allowed the Nationalists to set up a provincial headquarters, the first time any central government of China had done so since the fall of the Qing dynasty. By 1944, Chiang was able to remove Sheng from power. That year, the war in Europe was going well enough for Stalin to respond to the removal of Sheng Shicai by supporting a rebellion in northwestern Xinjiang. This led to the division of the province, with the creation of the East Turkestan Republic along the Soviet border. Its territory contained some of the largest and richest mineral deposits in the province, and its very name indicated its Soviet orientation. It was located "east" of Russian, not Chinese, Turkestan. (See Map 21.1.)

Meanwhile, Stalin's refusal to allow Lend-Lease shipments for China across the Soviet-Xinjiang border indicated his continued adherence to his secret agreement with Japan not to aid the Nationalists in return for Japan's promise not to overrun the CCP's base in Yan'an. Under the 1941 Soviet-Japanese Neutrality Pact, Soviet-Japanese trade continued throughout the war. In particular, Russia provided Japan with vital oil supplies from Sakhalin Island, circumventing the U.S. embargo that had precipitated the attack on Pearl Harbor. Whereas desperation to defeat Germany propelled Russia to ally with the United States in Europe, in Asia there was no equivalent threat to Soviet survival. Instead, Stalin hoped to delay the end of the Pacific War until after the defeat of Germany, when he could turn his attention from Europe to expand Russia's sphere of influence in China. In the meantime, continued U.S.-Japanese fighting served to weaken both enemies. To protract the Pacific War, at different times Stalin aided the Nationalists, the Communists, Japan, and the United States.

During the war, Stalin was able to absorb Tannu Tuva, formerly northwestern Mongolia. Like Outer Mongolia, it had long been officially recognized as Chinese territory. Russian influence had been growing since the final decade of tsarist rule. The Soviets had made Tannu Tuva a protectorate in 1926, followed by official annexation on 13 October 1944. The area was twice the size of Portugal, constituted a strategic plateau for the defense of Siberia, and contained rich gold and other mineral deposits.

The global war also settled the fate of Outer Mongolia. Given Outer Mongolia's landlocked location, and in the absence of neighbors willing to leave it to its own devices, true independence was impossible. It would remain part of either the Soviet or Chinese sphere of influence. As the defeat of Japan drew near, Chiang Kai-shek anticipated a resumption of all-out civil war. Therefore, he attempted to negotiate an alliance with Stalin to preclude Soviet aid to the CCP. At the 1945 Yalta Conference, Russia, the United States, and Britain agreed to preserve the status quo in Outer Mongolia, which the United States interpreted to mean that Outer Mongolia remained an integral part of China per the terms of the 31 May 1924 Sino-Soviet Treaty. Stalin, however, interpreted the status quo to refer to the many Sino-Russian unequal treaties and the 1924 secret protocol making Outer Mongolia a Soviet protectorate.

In the Nationalist-Soviet negotiations of 1945, Chiang traded Outer Mongolian independence for a Soviet promise not to aid the CCP and in anticipation of Soviet participation in the war against Japan. But Nationalist diplomats secretly acknowledged that independence actually meant that Outer Mongolia had become part of the Soviet sphere of influence. In addition, the Nationalists accepted Outer Mongolia's expanded borders gained from Manchukuo as a result of the 1941 Soviet-Japanese Neutrality Pact as well as Soviet retention of the vast tsarist sphere of influence in Manchuria; the Russians resumed majority control over the Chinese Eastern Railway and the port of Lüshun, as well as an exclusive concession at the port of Dalian. They signed the Nationalist-Soviet Friendship Treaty on 14 August 1945, the day before the Japanese capitulation.

These major Nationalist concessions presupposed that the Soviet military effort against Japan would be substantial. According to Chiang's way of thinking, granting Stalin extensive rights over Manchuria would make him fight that much harder; Japanese and Soviet mutual destruction was almost assured. However, President Harry Truman's decision to drop two atomic bombs in combination with the 1.7-million-man Soviet invasion of Manchuria brought about an unexpectedly rapid Japanese capitulation. As a result, the Red Army's war against Japan lasted less than a week. This proved as disastrous for the Nationalists as it was beneficial for the Communists. Chiang's many concessions to Stalin expanded the Soviet sphere of influence over the old Qing frontier areas, while Stalin did not honor his commitments. Once Chiang granted Outer Mongolia its independence from China during January 1946, as per the Nationalist-Soviet Friendship Treaty, it became permanent, both in fact and under international law. After Stalin got what he wanted, Soviet troops allowed the CCP's People's Liberation Army to form a base of operations in Manchuria behind its lines and thus safe from the Nationalists. By May 1946, the Chinese Communists began to consolidate control over this vital region.

Manchuria had largely escaped the destruction of the Sino-Japanese War. The Japanese had made enormous infrastructure investments, so Manchuria had surpassed Shanghai to become the most industrialized part of China. In 1944–5 Manchuria alone produced 8.5 times more pig iron than had ever been produced in China proper in a single year. In the same period it produced 2.5 times more electricity and 8.5 times more cement. In 1944, 3.5 million tons of soybeans were harvested, meaning an agricultural surplus to feed a large army.[2] In addition, Manchuria had China's best railway system, greatly facilitating troop deployments. After the Japanese capitulation, the Communists fanned out from Manchuria to conquer the rest of China.

V. Impact on the Chinese Population

As the war went on, the Chinese civilian economy collapsed. Economic statistics for the Japanese empire showed rapid growth prior to 1937. Its economy stayed at this plateau until 1941 but rapidly imploded when the United States joined the war. After Pearl Harbor, the situation for average Chinese dramatically worsened, since as the Japanese became desperate, they sucked additional military resources out of China to fight the United States; left short-handed, Japanese troops treated civilians in all theaters of the war with increasing brutality. The years from 1941 on were truly desperate years in China.

From 1937 to 1941, refugees flooded into the once-hated foreign concession areas in China's coastal cities that had suddenly become sanctuaries before the invading Japanese armies. After the outbreak of the global war in 1941, Japan took over the concession areas and put the foreign occupants in internment camps; many American civilians were subsequently traded for Japanese civilians being held in U.S. relocation centers. Meanwhile, in rural China, civilians fled before each Japanese offensive, causing a massive population relocation from coastal to northern China and gutting the agrarian economy. Over 95 million Chinese became refugees during the war, while 2 to 3 million residents of Henan died in the famine of 1942–3 because the war precluded relief efforts to mitigate the effects of the drought. (See Table 20.1.)

With the Japanese occupation of Shanghai and the other coastal and Yangzi River cities in 1937, the Nationalists lost their economy and their tax base. Although some companies relocated to Chongqing, most did not. Yet, the funds required to field huge armies only increased, so the Nationalists resorted to printing money. This was an economic strategy not of choice but of necessity, yet its effect would be to erode

Table 20.1 Refugees and Homeless during the Second Sino-Japanese War (1937–45)

Province or City	Number of Refugees	% of Population
Anhui	2,688,242	12.23
Beijing (Hebei)	400,000	15.45
Chahar	225,673	11.08
Fujian	1,065,469	9.25
Guangdong	4,280,266	13.76
Guangxi	2,562,400	20.37
Hubei	7,690,000	30.13
Hebei	6,774,000	23.99
Henan	14,533,200	43.49
Hunan	13,073,209	42.73
Jiangsu	12,502,633	34.83
Jiangxi	1,360,045	9.55
Manchuria	4,297,100	12.12
Nanjing (Jiangsu)	335,634	32.90
Shandong	11,760,644	30.71
Shanghai (Jiangsu)	531,431	13.80
Shanxi	4,753,842	41.06
Suiyuan	695,715	38.20
Tianjin (Hebei)	200,000	10.00
Wuhan (Hubei)	534,040	43.56
Zhejiang	5,185,210	23.90
Total	95,448,753	26.17

Source: Stephen MacKinnon, "Refugee Flight at the Outset of the Anti-Japanese War," in *Scars of War: The Impact of Warfare on Modern China*, Diana Lary and Stephen MacKinnon, eds. (Vancouver: University of British Columbia Press, 2001), 122. Reprinted with permission of the Publisher from *Scars of War: The Impact of Warfare on Modern China* by Diana Lary and Stephen MacKinnon. University of British Columbia Press © 2001. All rights reserved by the publisher.

Table 20.2   Price Indices in Nationalist- and Communist-Controlled China

Year	Nationalist Areas	Yan'an
1937	100	100
1938	145	143
1939	323	237
1940	724	500
1941	1,980	2,200
1942	6,620	9,900
1943	22,800	119,900
1944	75,500	564,700
1945	179,000	N/A

Source: Lyman van Slyke, "The Chinese Communist Movement during the Sino-Japanese War 1937–1945," in *The Cambridge History of China,* vol. 13, Denis Twitchett and John K. Fairbank, eds. (Cambridge: Cambridge University Press, 1986), 685.

the Nationalist base of support. It produced staggering rates of inflation, wiping out savings and impeding commerce. Conspicuously wealthy Nationalist functionaries, flaunting their privileges before a desperately poor general population, alienated public support. The Communists also resorted to inflationary policies in Yan'an, but they retained a greater degree of popular respect. (See Table 20.2) There were no Communists flaunting their wealth—they had no wealth. Rather, they lived with the rural population, shared its miseries, and increasingly convinced the peasantry that, compared to the Nationalists, the Communists represented the better bet.

In order to extract more resources from the faltering economy, the Nationalists reorganized their military and government in January 1939, concentrating ever more military, political, and economic power in the hands of Chiang Kai-shek. In the new Nationalist capital of Chongqing, Chiang became director-general of the Nationalist Party, making him the Nationalists' supreme civil and military leader. Assuming the full trappings of a dictator further undermined Chiang's popularity. As the military situation became ever more dire, Chiang's secret police became more blatant in their brutality.

The Nationalists, as the incumbent and dictatorial government that was a law unto itself, reaped the blame for failing to defeat the Japanese and mitigate the human misery, as well as for imposing corrupt and inept rule. The Communists remained immune to such criticisms. Increasingly, the Chinese public looked upon the Nationalists as a criminal organization. For instance, although the Nationalists had outlawed opium in 1927, their underworld supporters took over the trade, so that, in practice, the ban became a very lucrative Nationalist-controlled mo-

During June 1941, the Japanese bombed Chongqing, the Nationalist wartime capital, creating mass panic. Hundreds, perhaps thousands, of Chinese died while attempting to flee to safety, many times more than would have been killed by the Japanese bombs.

Table 20.3   Deaths from Civil Wars and Foreign Invasion (1917–45)

Years	Civil and Foreign Wars	Noncombatant Deaths	Combatant Deaths	Famine Deaths
1917–28	Warlord killings	450,000	178,000*	6,000,000*
1921–8	Nationalist killings	139,000		
1923–8	Communist killings	43,000		
1929–37†	Warlord killings	350,000	406,000	6,500,000†
1929–37	Nationalist killings	1,524,000		
1939–37	Communist killings	850,000		
1937–45	Warlord killings	110,000	7,140,000	2,250,000
1937–45	Japanese killings	3,949,000		
1937–45	Nationalist killings	5,907,000		
1937–45	Communist killings	250,000		
	Subtotals:	13,572,000	7,724,000	14,750,000
Total deaths in all three categories:				36,046,000

*Combatant and famine deaths pertain to the entire 1917–28 period.

†Includes flood and famine victims.

Source: R. J. Rummel, *China's Bloody Century: Genocide and Mass Murder Since 1900* (New Brunswick, NJ: Transaction Publishers, 1991), 24–5. Rummel provides low, intermediate, and high estimates. We have used his intermediate estimates.

nopoly. As the Japanese moved south, they tried to take over the drug trade. After the Communists lost their Nationalist subsidies with the 1941 New Fourth Army Incident, they too increasingly relied on drug revenues, with a key difference: They effectively cracked down on opium consumption within their base areas. In contrast, the ubiquitous opium dens of Nationalist-controlled territories seemed to be a powerful indicator of Nationalist hypocrisy and corruption. When the Nationalists resorted to the highly inflationary printing of money and engaged in ever more confiscatory requisitioning, this only fed these perceptions.

The Second Sino-Japanese War left China a wasteland. Over 7 million Chinese soldiers perished. In addition, the regional war with Japan took the lives of nearly 4 million noncombatants, while the civil war took the lives of 6 million more. The Nationalists' responsibility for the overwhelming majority of the noncombatant deaths further eroded their support (See Table 20.3).

Conclusions

Following the Xi'an Incident, Chiang Kai-shek agreed to the second Nationalist-Communist United Front, this time against Japan. In response to Nanjing's apparent alliance with Moscow and following the Marco Polo Bridge Incident, Tokyo authorized the occupation of North China. Chiang felt compelled to ride the tide of Chinese nationalism to take action against Japan. Beginning in August 1937, fighting also erupted in central China. Japanese forces occupied Nanjing in mid-December 1937. The Japanese Rape of Nanjing, far from undermining China's resolve, served only to fuel Chinese resistance. Chiang moved the capital up the Yangzi River to Chongqing. In October 1938 the Japanese took Wuhan, thus consolidating control throughout central China.

In the 1930s, the USSR and Japan once again defined their respective spheres of influence in China. In this division, Moscow retained control over Outer Mongolia, while Tokyo gained control over all of Manchuria. By means of the 1941 Soviet-Japanese Neutrality Pact, Moscow agreed to cease supplying the Nationalists and also to stop anti-Japanese activities by the Chinese Communists. In return, Tokyo agreed to accept unchallenged Communist control over three provinces in northwestern China. This left the Chinese Communist forces intact at the end of the war. The agreement also freed Japan to move south, sparking war with the United States.

The U.S. entry into the Pacific War in late 1941 allowed the Nationalists to retain control of Chongqing. Chiang based his military and diplomatic policies on the traditional Han methods of barbarian management. He hoped to set his foes on each other so that he could wait on the sidelines and take control of China after the anticipated U.S. victory over Japan. At the end of World War II, Chiang believed that he had finessed both the United States and the USSR. He successfully put off repeated American demands for an offensive until after Japan surrendered. In the final days of the war, he also cut a deal with Stalin in return for vague promises of Soviet cooperation to help undermine the Chinese Communists. The 14 August 1945 Friendship Treaty with the USSR, in combination with the Yalta Agreement, meant that Chiang ceded full control over Outer Mongolia and recognized extensive Soviet concessions in Manchuria in return for Stalin's promise to support only the Nationalists.

The U.S. use of the atomic bomb and the USSR's rapid entry into the war, both during early August 1945, were major reasons leading to Japan's surrender. The war ended over a year earlier than expected, long before Chiang had a chance to extend his control over North China. On 8 August the USSR declared war on Japan, pouring over a million men into Manchuria and rapidly occupying the region. Then it delayed the entry of the Nationalist forces while it allowed the Chinese Communists to consolidate control over the region. Soviet-controlled Manchuria soon became the base from which the CCP would fight its way to power.

The final death toll for the Sino-Japanese War was staggering. Estimates of Chinese war deaths from 1937 to 1945 exceeded 10 million. Ninety-five million Chinese became refugees, creating the largest forced migration in Chinese history. Chiang's United Front strategy, Japan's strategy of invasion in 1937, the U.S. strategy of deterrence, and Chiang's dealings with Stalin had all yielded the opposite of their intended outcomes. When Chiang's actions unwittingly triggered the Japanese invasion, the Japanese atrocities then inflamed Chinese nationalism. Meanwhile, the U.S. trade embargo and Stalin's secret diplomacy triggered Japan's southward advance, which Stalin then used to secure his hold over Outer Mongolia. Arguably, Stalin was the only world leader who received a large return in Asia based on a relatively small military investment. Japan's brutality toward civilians in the war against China and in World War II has left an enduring legacy of fear of and hostility to Japan throughout Asia.

BIBLIOGRAPHY

Bagby, Wesley M. *The Eagle-Dragon Alliance: America's Relations with China in World War II.* Newark: University of Delaware Press, 1992.

Barnett, A. Doak. *China on the Eve of Communist Takeover.* New York: Praeger, 1963.

Benson, Linda. *The Ili Rebellion: The Moslem Challenge to Chinese Authority in Xinjiang, 1944–1949.* Armonk, NY: M. E. Sharpe.

Benton, Gregor. "Comparative Perspectives: North and Central China in the Anti-Japanese Resistance." In *North China at War: The Social Ecology of Revolution 1937–1945,* edited by Feng Chongyi and David S. G. Goodman, 185–224. Lanham, MD: Rowan & Littlefield, 2000.

Boyle, John Hunter. *China and Japan at War: The Politics of Collaboration.* Stanford, CA: Stanford University Press, 1972.

Brush, Lucien M., M. Gordon Wolman, and L. M. Brush, eds. *Taming the Yellow River: Silt and Floods: Proceedings of a Bilateral Seminar on Problems in the Lower Reaches of the Yellow River, China.* Dordrecht: Kluwer Academic, 1987.

Ch'en, Jerome. *Mao and the Chinese Revolution.* London: Oxford University Press, 1965.

Ch'i, Shi-sheng. *Nationalist China at War: Military Defeats and Political Collapse, 1937–1945.* Ann Arbor: University of Michigan Press, 1982.

Eastman, Lloyd. *Seeds of Destruction: Nationalist China in War and Revolution 1937–1949.* Stanford, CA: Stanford University Press, 1984.

———. "Nationalist China during the Sino-Japanese War 1937–1945." In *The Cambridge History of China,* vol. 13, John K. Fairbank and Albert Feuerwerker, eds., 547–608. Cambridge: Cambridge University Press, 1986.

———, Jerome Ch'en, Suzanne Pepper, and Lyman P. Van Slyke, eds. *The Nationalist Era in China.* Cambridge: Cambridge University Press, 1991.

Elleman, Bruce A. "The Final Consolidation of the USSR's Sphere of Interest in Outer Mongolia." In *Mongolia in the Twentieth Century: Landlocked Cosmopolitan,* edited by Stephen Kotkin and Bruce A. Elleman, 123–36. Armonk, NY: M. E. Sharpe, 1999.

———*Modern Chinese Warfare, 1795–1989.* London: Routledge, 2001.

———*Japanese-American Civilian Prisoner Exchanges and Detention Camps, 1941–45.* London: Routledge, 2006.

Elvin, Mark. *The Retreat of the Elephants: An Environmental History of China.* New Haven, CT: Yale University Press, 2004.

Forbes, Andrew D. W. *Warlords and Muslims in Chinese Central Asia: A Political History of Republican Sinkiang 1911–1949.* Cambridge: Cambridge University Press, 1986.

Garver, John. *Chinese-Soviet Relations, 1937–1945: The Diplomacy of Chinese Nationalism.* Oxford: Oxford University Press, 1988.

Harrison, James. *The Long March to Power: A History of the Chinese Communist Party, 1921–72.* New York: Praeger, 1972.

Hasegawa, Tsuyoshi. *Racing the Enemy: Stalin, Truman, and the Surrender of Japan.* Cambridge, MA: Harvard University Press, 2005.

Hsiung, James C. and Steven I. Levine, eds. *China's Bitter Victory: The War with Japan 1937–1945.* Armonk, NY: M. E. Sharpe, 1992.

Jansen, Marius. *Japan and China. From War to Peace, 1894–1972.* New York: Rand McNally, 1975.

Johnson, Chalmers. *Peasant Nationalism and Communist Power: The Emergence of Revolutionary China, 1937–1945.* Stanford, CA: Stanford University Press, 1982.

Lary, Diana. "Defending China: The Battles of the Xuzhou Campaign." In *Warfare in Chinese History*, edited by Hans van de Ven, 398–427. Leiden: Brill, 2000.

——— *China's Republic.* Cambridge: Cambridge University Press, 2007.

Li, Lincoln. *The Japanese Army in North China, 1937–1941: Problems of Political and Economic Control.* Oxford: Oxford University Press, 1975.

Paine, S. C. M. *Imperial Rivals: China, Russia, and Their Disputed Frontier.* Armonk, NY: M. E. Sharpe, 1996.

Saich, Tony and Hans van de Ven, eds. *New Perspectives on the Chinese Communist Revolution.* Armonk, NY: M. E. Sharpe, 1995.

Selden, Mark. *The Yenan Way in Revolutionary China.* Cambridge, MA: Harvard University Press, 1971.

Shum, Kui-kwong. *The Chinese Communists' Road to Power: The Anti-Japanese National United Front, 1935–1945.* Oxford: Oxford University Press, 1988.

Slack, Edward R., Jr. *Opium, State, and Society: China's Narco-Economy and the Guomindang, 1924–1937.* Honolulu: University of Hawai'i Press, 2001.

Tuchman, Barbara. *Stilwell and the American Experience in China, 1911–1945.* New York: Macmillan, 1970.

Van Slyke, Lyman. "The Chinese Communist Movement during the Sino-Japanese War 1937–1945." In *The Cambridge History of China*, vol. 13, edited by John K. Fairbank and Albert Feuerwerker, 609–722. Cambridge: Cambridge University Press, 1986.

Wakeman, Frederic, Jr. *Policing Shanghai 1927–1937.* Berkeley: University of California Press, 1995.

Wang, David D. *Under the Soviet Shadow: The Yining Incident: Ethnic Conflicts and International Rivalry in Xinjiang 1944–1949.* Hong Kong: Chinese University Press, 1999.

Young, Arthur N. *China's Wartime Finance and Inflation, 1937–1945.* Cambridge, MA: Harvard University Press, 1965.

NOTES

1. Dai Wangshu, "Written on a Prison Wall," in *The Columbia Anthology of Modern Chinese Literature*, Joseph S. M. Lau and Howard Goldblatt, eds. (New York: Columbia University Press, 1995), 514. From The Columbia Anthology of Modern Chinese Literature, by Victor Mair. Copyright © 1995, Columbia University Press. Reprinted with permission of the publisher.

2. Lloyd E. Eastman, *Seeds of Destruction: Nationalist China in War and Revolution 1937–1949* (Stanford, CA: Stanford University Press, 1984), 224; Oleg B. Borisov, *The Soviet Union and the Manchurian Revolutionary Base, 1945–1949* (in Russian) (Moscow: Mysl', 1975), 49, 53–4, 57.

Chronology

8 August 1945	Soviet declaration of war on Japan and invasion of Manchuria
14 August 1945	Soviet-Nationalist Friendship Treaty
15 August 1945	Japanese capitulation; end of Sino-Japanese War
26 Aug.–11 Oct. 1945	CCP-Nationalist talks in Chongqing about joint rule
9 September 1945	Surrender of Japanese troops in China
19 September 1945	Communist strategy: expand in the North, defend in the South
October–December 1945	Renewal of the civil war in eleven provinces
23 Dec. 1945–7 Jan. 1947	Marshall Mission
6 January 1946	Nationalists recognize Outer Mongolian independence
10 January 1946	Marshall brokers cease-fire agreement, excludes Manchuria and South China
11–31 January 1946	Political Consultative Conference to resolve CCP-Nationalist differences
3 May 1946	Completion of Soviet evacuation from Manchuria
4 May 1946	CCP land reform announcement
7 June 1946	U.S.-brokered truce in Manchuria
July 1946	Resumption of full-scale civil war
17 July–13 Sept. 1947	CCP National Land Conference
1 September 1947	CCP shifts to nationwide counteroffensive
10 October 1947	CCP "Outline Land Law of China"
25–8 Dec. 1947	Mao warns against overly militant land reform
25 May 1948	Mao orders moderation of land reform
8–13 September 1948	CCP shifts focus from rural to urban areas
12 Sept.–2 Nov. 1948	Liaoyang-Shenyang Campaign expelling Nationalists from Manchuria
6 Nov. 1948–10 Jan. 1949	Huai-Hai Campaign opening the way to the Yangzi River
21 Nov. 1948–31 Jan. 1949	Beiping-Tianjin Campaign
6–8 January 1949	Further moderation of land reform to win support in South China
31 January 1949	PLA enters Beijing
25 February 1949	Mutiny of the Nationalist flagship
20 April 1949	PLA crosses the Yangzi River
23 April 1949	PLA enters Nanjing
27 May 1949	PLA enters Shanghai
1 October 1949	Establishment of the People's Republic of China
10 December 1949	Chiang Kai-shek flies to exile in Taiwan

21

The Civil War: Nationalists versus Communists

You, suffering Chinese peasants,
carrying on your back a rotten ancient tradition
Under the quickening steps of history,
you succumb in silence, you struggle;
Power of many kinds rises and disappears;
nobody can tell how Dao changes;
The different types of guns uniformly rob you of life;
like a tornado at night.[1]

Du Yunxie (1918–2002), poet, veteran

Outside intervention in China's former empire—first by the Soviet Union in Outer Mongolia, then by Japan with its invasion of Manchuria in 1931, and again by the Soviet Union with its brokered Second United Front, and finally by the full-scale Japanese invasion of China proper—impeded the reunification of China under the Nationalists. Chiang's unwillingness to cede Manchuria to the Japanese cost him the Sino-Japanese War, while his unwillingness to cede it to the Communists cost him the civil war. The outbreak of the Cold War following World War II formed the backdrop to this final stage of China's long civil war that had begun with the collapse of the Qing dynasty. The United States and the Soviet Union competed to fill the political vacuum left by the demise of the Japanese empire with its allied states. No amount of U.S. aid or help of advisers seemed adequate to save the Nationalists from either the Communists or themselves. The civil war ended in 1949 with the creation of the People's Republic of China (PRC) and the retreat of the Nationalist Party to Taiwan, where it remains to this day as the largest political party of the Republic of China (ROC).

I. Renewal of the Civil War

After the failed Hundred Regiments' Campaign in 1940 and the entry of the United States into the war against Japan, the Communists ceased fighting the Japanese main forces and instead concentrated on gathering support in the countryside. The many Japanese engagements in China after 1940 were aimed mainly at Nationalist forces. Thus, the Sino-Japanese War started to shift the internal balance of power within China away from the Nationalists. At the beginning of World War II, Communist forces totaled approximately 300,000 soldiers compared to the Nationalist postwar force of 2.5 million. By early 1945, however, the CCP claimed to have 1.2 million members, while its two main armies, the Eighth Route and New Fourth armies, claimed to have 900,000 troops. Although these numbers were probably greatly inflated, they still indicated dramatic growth. (See Table 21.1.)

On 9 August 1945, the day the United States dropped its second atomic bomb on Japan and the day after the Soviet invasion of Manchuria, Mao Zedong declared the beginning of the People's Liberation Army's (PLA) anti-Japanese offensive. On 10 August, the commander of the PLA, Zhu De, ordered the seizure of urban areas. Striking deep into Manchuria, PLA commander Lin Biao quickly expanded the CCP's control into the heart of Japan's colonial empire so that within two weeks, CCP-controlled territory almost doubled. By late August the Communist held an area with a population of 100 million. Not only did the Communists obtain Japanese weapons as they disarmed Japanese units, but the CCP now controlled some of the most productive territory in China with a rail system ideally suited for rapid troop deployments.

Table 21.1   Growth in Communist Party Membership

No.* Date		Location	CCP Membership	General Secretary (or Equivalent)	Party Line
1st	late July–early Aug 1921	Shanghai, Jiaxing	53	Chen Duxiu	Chen elected general secretary; thirteen members attended
2nd	16–23 July 1922	Shanghai	195	Chen Duxiu	Join Comintern; United Front with Nationalists
3rd	12–20 June 1923	Guangzhou	420		"Bloc within" strategy: CCP members to join GMD
4th	11–22 January 1925	Shanghai	9,000	Chen Duxiu	Secretariat established
5th	27 Apr.–9 May 1927	Wuhan	57,900	Chen Duxiu	Political Bureau set up; ended United Front after purge
6th	18 June–11 July 1928	Moscow	40,000	Xiang Zhongfa	Li Lisan line; tensions with Mao's peasant strategy
7th	23 Apr.–11 June 1945	Yan'an	1,210,000	Mao Zedong	Mao Zedong Thought; increasing centralization
8th	15–27 Sept. 1956	Beijing	10,730,000	Mao Zedong	Mass political campaigns, Great Leap Forward, etc.
9th	1–24 Apr. 1969	Beijing	22,000,000	Mao Zedong	Ascendant military; Lin Biao named Mao's successor
10th	24–8 Aug. 1973	Beijing	28,000,000	Mao Zedong	Gang of Four at height of power
11th	12–18 Aug. 1977	Beijing	35,000,000	Hua Guofeng	Succession struggle; Deng Xiaoping reinstated
12th	1–11 Sept. 1982	Beijing	39,650,000	Hu Yaobang	Deng consolidates power through appointments
13th	25 Oct.–1 Nov. 1987	Beijing	46,000,000	Zhao Ziyang	Third Generation takes control[†]
14th	12–18 Oct. 1992	Beijing	51,000,000	Jiang Zemin	Rapid economic market reforms
15th	12–18 Sept. 1997	Beijing	60,417,000	Jiang Zemin	Plans to close state-owned enterprises
16th	8–15 Nov. 2002	Beijing	66,355,000	Hu Jintao	Rise of Fourth Generation.[†]

Note: Since 1992, Party congresses have been on a regular schedule.

GMD = Nationalist Party (*Guomindang*)

*No. = National Party Congress number.

[†]First Generation = Mao; Second Generation = Deng (first two generations both of the Long March vintage); Third Generation = Jiang (children at the time of the Long March); Fourth Generation = Hu (born after the Long March).

Source: Himeta Mitsuyoshi et al, *Chyūkoku nijyū seikishi* (Tokyo: Tokyo University Press, 2000), 164; R. Keith Schoppa, *The Columbia Guide to Modern Chinese History* (New York: Columbia University Press, 2000), 308–11; "National Congress of the Communist Party of China," *Wikipedia,* http://en.wikipedia.org/wiki/Template:Politics_of_the_People%27s_Republic_of_China; http://www.chinatoday.com/org/cpc/; http://www.terra.es/personal2/monolith/china2.htm/.

Stalin pressured Mao Zedong to fly to Chongqing to negotiate with the Nationalists. Mao insisted on retaining control over those areas liberated by the PLA, which included most of North China, Inner Mongolia, and a number of eastern cities, areas where Nationalist influence was extremely weak. Chiang Kai-shek refused, incorrectly assuming that Stalin would honor his recent agreement not to support the Communists. Mao and Chiang did agree on 10 October 1945, the thirty-fourth anniversary of the collapse of the Qing dynasty, to support the formation of a Political Consultative Conference to resolve their differences. Although this conference convened in Nanjing on 11 January 1946, it quickly deadlocked.

While Mao was still in Chongqing, the arrival of a Soviet delegation in Yan'an prompted a CCP reassessment of its military strategy. The Soviets wanted the CCP to focus on taking control not of South China but of Manchuria as the Soviet Red Army withdrew. On 21 October 1945, Mao ordered all Communist forces south of the Yangzi River to redeploy to North China, where he intended to win the civil war. Thereafter, the CCP began to destroy railways and other transportation lines in order to slow down any future Nationalist advance. The Communists employed a "horizontal plan," while the Nationalists relied on a "vertical" one. The horizontal plan called for conquering a strip of land along the Yellow River from Shaanxi province all the way to the sea in order to create a barrier against the Nationalist Army, while the vertical plan entailed the interruption of any horizontal plan by confining the Communists to northwest China. The U.S. Marine Corps, however, prevented the PLA from fully executing its plan by landing at Tianjin in September to accept the Japanese surrender and moving into North China to occupy Beijing and Qingdao in October. These U.S. forces held these strategic positions until the very last months of the civil war in the spring of 1949. The U.S. deployed these forces primarily to repatriate the Imperial Japanese Army but secondarily in the vain hope of slowing the outbreak of the civil war.

The Nationalists were unprepared for the rapid Japanese surrender that followed within a week of the dropping of two atomic bombs and the Soviet invasion of Manchuria. Their troops were mainly deployed in inland locations in South and Central China, far from the liberated areas where they needed to preempt a Communist takeover of North China. U.S. planes began to airlift 110,000 Nationalist troops to Beijing and Nanjing, blocking Chinese Communist attempts to retake China's traditional capitals from the Japanese. Chiang Kai-shek insisted on retaking Manchuria despite its location far from his own power base along the Yangzi River but much nearer to Yan'an and the Soviet border. The Sino-Japanese War, after all, had been fought over Chinese sovereignty of Manchuria. (See Map 21.1.)

Yet, Manchuria was a singularly inhospitable environment for him to fight the Communists. In the warlord period, the

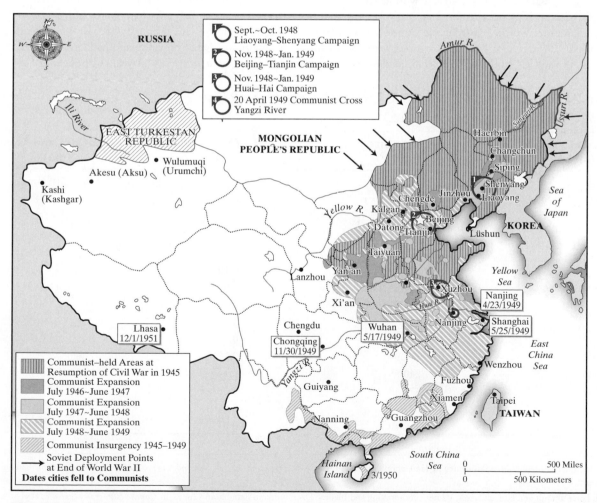

Map 21.1 Chinese Civil War (1945–9)

Zhang family had carefully kept the Nationalists out; in the succeeding Manchukuo period, the Japanese had likewise excluded the Nationalists and also had wiped out the potentially sympathetic local elite. The elite who remained were considered collaborators. Land ownership was more concentrated than elsewhere in China, so the Communist program of land reform was particularly attractive to the local population. (See Tables 21.2 and 21.3.) The Nationals were particularly ill-equipped to garner public support because of the long-standing divisions between North and South China. Many of Chiang's troops and Chiang himself did not even speak Mandarin, the language of North China. Mao's home province was Hunan, so even he spoke Mandarin with a heavy accent. Choosing Manchuria as the initial theater for the resumption of the civil war played to Mao's strengths and to Chiang's weaknesses.

Once again, Washington provided crucial aid: The U.S. Navy transported two complete Chinese armies from South China. Moscow, however, in accordance with its secret protocol with Chiang Kai-shek, retained control over the main Manchurian ports, which it closed to the United States and the Nationalists. Other major Manchurian cities were already in the hands of the CCP. In November 1945, Nationalist troops gradually advanced northward along the Tianjin-Shenyang Railway, while Communist forces slowed their progress. When confronted with the prospect of Manchuria entirely under CCP control, Chiang petitioned the Red Army to remain longer. Stalin agreed.

Stalin, whose primary focus remained Germany and Eastern Europe, did not wish events in Manchuria to sour relations with the United States at this time. Therefore, he did not allow the Communists to concentrate their troops in highly visible cities. Instead, the PLA consolidated its control over large swaths of rural areas. Conversely, the Nationalists, who had no rural bases in Manchuria, were concentrated in urban areas. In November 1945, Nationalist forces moved into Rehe province, pushing the Communists northward. To placate the United States while the issue of Mongolian independence remained unsettled, the USSR gave permission for an airlift of Nationalist troops into Shenyang in December. By the end of the month, the Nationalists had gained control over the crucial Shenyang railroad and occupied such important North China cities as Beijing, Tianjin, Shenyang, and Datong, while the PLA retained power in Kalgan, in Chahar province, and had large forces in Shanxi, Hubei, and Rehe provinces, as well as throughout Manchuria.

Table 21.2   Concentration of Land Ownership in China, 1930s
(1 *mu* = 733.5 square yards = 6.6 acres)

Size of Holding (*mu*)	Average Size (*mu*)	Percent of Households (*mu*)	Percent of Land Owned (*mu*)
landless	0.00	25.80	0.00
0 >−5	2.65	26.42	6.21
6–10	7.23	17.80	11.42
11–15	12.25	9.77	10.63
16–20	17.42	5.93	9.17
21–30	24.33	6.10	13.17
31–50	38.01	4.60	15.54
51–70	58.59	1.61	8.38
71–100	82.61	0.98	7.16
101–150	120.21	0.54	5.71
151–200	171.97	0.18	2.76
201–300	240.95	0.14	3.17
301–500	378.40	0.08	2.63
501–1,000	671.87	0.01	2.30
1,001+	1,752.60	0.01	1.75
Total	11.04	100.00	100.00

Note: One-quarter of all households owned no land, another quarter owned about 6 percent of the land, and 5 percent of the households owned about 25 percent.

Source: Loren Brandt and Barbara Sands, "Land Concentration and Income Distribution in Republican China," in *Chinese History in Economic Perspective*, Thomas G. Rawski and Lillian M. Li, eds. (Berkeley: University of California Press, 1992), 182. Copyright © 1992, The Regents of the University of California.

Table 21.3 Concentration of Land Ownership by Region, 1930s
Percentage distribution by size of farms operated, 1934–5
(1 *mou* or *mu* = 733.5 square yards = 6.6 acres)

Province	<10 *mu*	10–29.9 *mu*	30–49.9 *mu*	50–99.9 *mu*	>100 *mu*
Northwest					
Chahar	1.4	7.9	2.2	8.9	79.6
Suiyuan	9.3	33.3	16.2	18.4	22.8
Shaanxi	38.7	35.9	12.8	10.1	2.5
Manchuria*					
Liaoning	19.9	21.4	23.8	20.1	14.9
Jilin	7.4	16.6	27.6	22.6	25.8
Heilongjiang	5.9	9.7	16.5	22.9	45.0
North					
Shanxi	16.9	41.0	20.3	16.1	5.7
Hebei	40.0	41.4	10.8	6.1	1.7
Shandong	49.7	38.5	7.9	3.3	0.6
Henan	47.9	34.6	9.5	6.2	1.8
East					
Jiangsu	52.3	38.1	5.8	2.5	1.3
Anhui	47.0	38.2	9.6	4.5	0.7
Zhejiang	67.0	27.8	3.5	1.4	0.3
Central					
Hubei	60.4	32.0	5.5	1.8	0.2
Hunan	56.5	33.4	6.3	3.1	0.8
Jiangxi	54.2	41.6	3.7	0.5	†
Southeast					
Fujian	71.8	24.8	2.5	0.8	0.1
Guangdong	87.4	12.3	0.3	†	—
Guangxi	51.1	37.7	7.2	3.0	0.9

The statistics show disproportionately concentrated landholdings in Manchuria. In contrast, land was far more evenly distributed in South China. No statistics were available for the northwestern provinces of Ningxia, Qinghai, and Gansu or for the southwestern provinces of Guizhou, Yunnan, and Sichuan.

*Feuerwerker provides all of the statistics except those from Manchuria. Levine provides the latter. Feuerwerker's statistics are measured in *mou*, an alternate pronunciation for *mu*. Levine, however, uses data measured in *shang*, a term used in Manchuria to designate the amount of land that one person could cultivate in a day. Therefore, the figure varied by terrain. In southern Liaoning, 1 *shang* equaled 6 *mu* and in northern Liaoning 10 *mu*, while in the more northerly provinces of Jilin and Heilongjiang, it equaled 12 *mu* (Jiaoyubu chongbian guoyu cidian bianji weiyuanhui, comp., *Guoyu cidian*, vol. 5 [Taipei: Taibei shangwu yinshuguan, 1980], 4167). Like Feuerwerker, Levine provides five classes of holdings, divided as follows: smallholders with 1 *shang* or 1–3 *shang*, middleholders with 3–5 or 5–10 *shang*, and large landowners with over 10 *shang*. We have inserted Levine's statistics under Feuerwerker's headings, although the categories do not correspond exactly.

†Less than 0.05 percent.

Source: Albert Feuerwerker, "Economic Trends, 1912–49," in *The Cambridge History of China*, vol. 12, edited by John K. Fairbank (Cambridge: Cambridge University Press, 1983), 82; Steven I. Levine, *Anvil of Victory: The Communist Revolution in Manchuria, 1945–1948* (New York: Columbia University Press, 1987), 201.

U.S. logistical support and Soviet acquiescence to the air-lift of Nationalist troops made possible Nationalist gains in North China. Without the help of the U.S. Navy and the U.S. Air Force, Nationalist forces could not have moved into North China so quickly. Washington also continued to provide extensive military assistance. Moscow, on the other hand, while not actively helping the Nationalists, granted them permission to enter Manchuria but excluded the Nationalists' rapidly growing navy. With U.S. help and Soviet acquiescence, Chiang was able to reassert nominal control over most of China. To many, the Nationalist victory seemed complete.

II. U.S. Diplomatic Intervention

On several occasions during the Pacific War, the United States had tried to encourage the Nationalists and Communists to settle their differences politically by forming a coalition government. During spring 1944, President Franklin D. Roosevelt had sent Vice President Henry A. Wallace for discussions with Chiang Kai-shek about reconciling their differences, and in 1944 Major General Patrick J. Hurley tried to strengthen Chinese military effectiveness against Japan by combining Nationalist and Communist forces. Both attempts failed. Instead, Chiang turned to Stalin to try secretly to gain an edge over Mao.

In December 1945, President Harry S. Truman appointed General George C. Marshall as his special envoy to China in order to negotiate a cease-fire between the Nationalists and the Communists, as well as a reduction in their armed forces. Truman also urged the peaceful reunification of China under the auspices of the Political Consultative Conference to create a coalition government, as agreed to earlier by Chiang and Mao. No Chinese dynasty had ever risen to power in this manner. In practice, the two sides had mutually exclusive objectives: the full control of all of the lands of the former Qing empire. Neither wanted a coalition government, but rather the annihilation of the other. The United States failed either to play the role of a neutral broker or to provide massive support for the Nationalists. This helped to create the worst possible outcome, with both sides becoming increasingly anti-American. In early 1947, the Marshall Mission ended in failure.

Although the U.S. government recognized the Nationalists as the only official government of China, its direct military support gradually declined. U.S. troop numbers in China dropped from a high of 113,000 in 1945 to 12,000 by the end of 1946. The United States used its massive amount of World War II surplus military equipment in Asia to outfit thirty-nine Nationalist Army divisions by late 1945. Washington also contributed $500 million to the United Nations Relief and Rehabilitation Administration's program for China, which distributed most of this money to Nationalist-controlled areas. Finally, in August 1946, the U.S. government sold the Nationalists war surplus worth $900 million for a mere $175 million. This war surplus included ships, trucks, airplanes, and communications equipment, so the Nationalists had both an air force and a navy, while the Communists had neither. Nonetheless, U.S. aid was limited, since U.S. forces were not engaged in efforts to halt the gradual spread of Communist influence. This spread accelerated with the Soviet withdrawal from Manchuria beginning in mid-March 1946, when the Communists were quick to fill the power vacuum. Elsewhere in North China, Communist forces successfully occupied sections of Shandong and Jiangsu provinces.

The CCP's decision to try to secure Manchuria was, in the view of General Marshall, a violation of the U.S.-brokered cease-fire. He negotiated one last cease-fire beginning 7 June 1946. The truce halted the highly successful Nationalist offensive at the Songhua (Sungari) River. The Communists took advantage of the cease-fire to resume organizing the Manchurian countryside, while the Nationalists remained confined to the cities, where, in the face of constant warfare, the economy had not improved but worsened. Urban economic life withered when the cities were cut off from the surrounding countryside and from other cities. The local population blamed those in charge, meaning the Nationalists. After the 7 June truce, Nationalist forces would never again regain their momentum when full-scale hostilities resumed in July 1946. In January 1947, Marshall gave up on his mediation efforts and requested to be recalled. Upon his return, President Truman made him secretary of state. Then, on 29 January 1947, the United States notified Nanjing that it would end all of its efforts to mediate the Chinese civil war. It concluded that a coalition government, however desirable, was simply not feasible.

In July 1947, General Albert C. Wedemeyer was sent on a fact-finding mission to China. He arrived soon after the Nationalist-controlled State Council formally outlawed the CCP. Wedemeyer believed that the Nationalists could not win the war unless they minimized the corruption that had arisen from the absence of national institutions and from a shattered economy. Yet, neither problem could be solved in wartime, which greatly magnified both. The Nationalist *guanxi* network was too fragile to survive the U.S. cure so that, once again, all of the U.S. reform proposals were nonstarters.

Secretary of State Marshall insisted that the United States not send combat troops to join the fighting. He cautioned that the renunciation of the unequal treaties in 1943 meant that Washington had given up all rights to send U.S.

By 1945, Mao Zedong was generally accepted as the senior leader of the CCP. U.S. efforts to support a coalition government by the Nationalists and Communists failed, and with Soviet help, the Chinese Communists were soon entrenched in Manchuria. From there, they launched a repeat of Japan's invasion strategy and eventually took control over all of continental China.

ships into Chinese waters and would appear imperialistic if it sought Nationalist permission to do so. Meanwhile, the Soviet Union continued to block U.S. entry into Manchurian ports. Truman also opposed sending combat troops. There was no public support to do so and no hope of military success given the unpopularity of the Nationalists, the size of the theater, and the magnitude of U.S. commitments in Europe. Therefore, the United States limited its support for the Nationalists to economic aid. Even this rapidly declined.

Stark images of Nationalist brutality and incompetence helped undermine U.S. public support, while Western photographers were not privy to images of the Communists' vicious treatment of their political opponents. As the Cold War heated up globally, the Nationalists' fragile loyalty to the United States, their diplomatic dabbling with the USSR, their police-state governance, and their economic incompetence triggered a reassessment in Washington. Chiang was no longer considered to be a useful ally but rather a political liability. The United States left him to his fate, providing just enough aid, U.S. policymakers hoped, so that when he fell,

he, not they, would be blamed for the creation of a Communist China. How the United States could have spent so much—approximately $3.9 billion supporting Chiang—and achieved so little haunted U.S. policymakers for some time. Chiang incorrectly assumed that the gravy train would continue. He could not imagine that Washington could write off these sunk costs and accept the consequences of a unified Communist China hostile to the economic and political system that the United States hoped to make the hallmarks of the postwar global order.

III. Soviet Intervention

The Soviet Union also intervened in the Chinese civil war in order to shape the postwar order on its Central Asian and Siberian borders. At different times it aided both the Communists and the Nationalists. In the final days of World War II, Stalin negotiated a friendship treaty with Chiang and continued to recognize the Nationalist government. Although

Stalin provided crucial Japanese war material to the Communists, he delayed the CCP seizure of Manchurian cities until after he had consolidated Soviet gains in Eastern Europe and Outer Mongolia. As the USSR repeatedly delayed the arrival of Nationalist troops in Manchuria, it used this time to strip the region of much of its infrastructure, which hurt the Nationalists, with their urban-focused strategy, in the short run and the Communists in the long run. In Xinjiang the Soviets supported a breakaway regime, the East Turkestan Republic (Chapter 20, Section IV), while consolidating their control over Outer Mongolia. On the one hand, the Soviets desired a Communist China; on the other hand, they retained the tsarist impulse toward empire and the imperial aversion to strong neighbors.

Stalin faced competing concerns. Most important, he did not want events in Asia to have a negative impact on the consolidation of his control over Eastern Europe. Europe was central to post–World War II Soviet national security. Asia was not. Second, he shared the security concerns of his tsarist predecessors that came with the geographic location of Russia. There were long borders to defend in very unstable regions of the world. The Soviets, like the tsars before them, engaged in the traditional foreign policy strategy of a great continental power. This entailed preventing the rise of any major power on their borders. Neighbors should be kept weak and dependent. Funding both sides in the Chinese civil war served this purpose. If each side exhausted the other, Stalin could trade with the higher bidder. Ideally, neither would triumph to create a strong, unified China, so Stalin's policy was to delay this eventuality as long as possible.

Stalin continued to deal with the Nationalists until the Outer Mongolians held their mock plebiscite. The logistics of trying to poll a nomadic people were impossible. The voting result was ludicrously high—unanimous, it was said—in favor of independence from China. Once the Nationalists had officially recognized Outer Mongolian independence in January 1946, Stalin had less reason to mollify Chiang Kai-shek. Under international law, the Nationalists could not retract their recognition of Outer Mongolia even if Stalin did not subsequently keep his end of the bargain. This is when Stalin belatedly started to supply the Communists with Japanese war surplus. In the interim, the Nationalists staged a very successful offensive. Thus, to secure Outer Mongolia, Stalin had nearly sacrificed the CCP, which angered Mao.

The U.S.-brokered cease-fire and Chiang's request for a six-month delay in the Soviet troop withdrawal provided the USSR the opportunity to collect war reparations from Japan in the form of heavy machinery removed from Manchurian factories and mines. Estimates of the economic losses to China range in the billions of dollars. Shipment of the equipment to the USSR required a working railway system. Therefore, it sent numerous railway experts, who repaired the railway system and trained thousands of Chinese to operate it. This put the Manchurian transportation system firmly under the control of the CCP. When Soviet forces withdrew in May 1946, the Communists controlled the northern two-thirds of Manchuria, which coincided with the old tsarist sphere of influence. Manchuria's deindustrialization served to replace Soviet wartime losses and to provide one more obstacle to the restoration of China as a great power.

Once the Communists received the Japanese military surplus, they were able at long last to make the transition from a guerrilla force to a strong conventional army. Without the equipment, they could not have fought the conventional battles that defeated the Nationalist armies and drove them into retreat to Taiwan. Conversely, although the United States had provided the Nationalists with all of the necessary equipment to field a large conventional army, this military aid did not address the underlying coalitional structure of Nationalist rule, the tremendous loss of prestige suffered during their constant defeats during the Sino-Japanese War, or the endemic malfeasance of Nationalist leaders whether in military or civil office. The implosion of the urban Chinese economy left the Nationalists without an economic base and soon without a political base. The Communist strategy targeted cities to erode public support from within. Desperation fueled corruption, and the Nationalists reaped the blame. The postwar economic collapse, particularly in the cities, helps explain the Nationalist loss of the civil war.

After the Long March, the many years in exile on the rural periphery of China had forced the Communists to focus on cultivating rural support or die on the vine. Their preferred strategy, based on Communist ideology, had been to secure control over the urban areas to stage a proletarian revolution, but this strategy had nearly cost the Communists utter destruction in the 1920s and 1930s. Ironically, the Sino-Japanese War had given the Communists a much-needed breathing space. While the Imperial Japanese Army focused on fighting the conventional forces of the Nationalists, the Communists conducted a reassessment and turned to a Maoist guerrilla strategy emphasizing the countryside and China's vast rural population. The Soviet military equipment was essential to enable this grassroots revolution to seize power. The Nationalists, even in their weakened state, still possessed vast, well-equipped armies that had to be defeated conventionally. A successful offensive required vehicles, tanks, and artillery. These items could not be conjured from rural peasant China.

IV. The Nationalist Economic Implosion

The Nationalist Party never recovered from the economic effects of its expulsion from its coastal urban power base. The party was fundamentally an urban movement. It derived much of its wealth from China's coastal cities, where it represented the commercial interests of the modern sectors of the urban economy. The Japanese destroyed the economic underpinnings of its power. When they forced the Nationalists to flee ever further inland, the economy imploded. With no revenues to support taxation, the Nationalists resorted to a common policy of beleaguered governments: they printed money. With an enormous army to pay and a war to fight, the Nationalist Party had staggering expenses but a negligible revenue base. As the war with Japan dragged on, Nationalist printing presses churned out worthless currency. Rampant inflation destroyed carefully accumulated savings. In doing so, hyperinflation undermined the urban and rural social order. (See Table 21.4.) This was when the Nationalist Party became synonymous with gross corruption. Since rural areas still operated in large measure on barter transactions, inflation was more detrimental to the urban than the rural economy. This meant that inflation hurt the Nationalists more than the Communists.

Another part of the Nationalist power base was rural landed interests. Its coalitional nature magnified the influence of regional power brokers. This, in turn, greatly complicated Nationalist rule. Chiang Kai-shek united the country in name, but Nationalist unity rested on a fragile coalition of regional warlords unified by a common fear of the Japanese and the Communists, not by a shared positive reform agenda. Each warlord retained an army personally loyal to him, giving each varying leverage in his dealings with Chiang Kai-shek. None wanted his own base of power eliminated. Therefore, within the Nationalist Party, there was strong resistance to the centralization of power.

During the Sino-Japanese War, Chiang consistently rejected U.S. military advice to unify the command of his armies. In 1947, as the tide of the civil war turned against him, Chiang belatedly ordered the elimination of warlord remnants and personal armies. In response, thousands of decommissioned officers defected with their troops to the Communists. The structure of power in China remained personalistic, not institutional, so troops remained loyal not to their government but to their commander. Once Mao had defeated Chiang, he turned on the warlord remnants to obliterate these last *guanxi* networks of the old order. During the Korean War (1950–3), Mao deployed Nationalist turncoat units to the front, where they either fought or were eliminated.

Chiang Kai-shek's rural elite power base was also highly resistant to land reform. Any land redistribution would have been their loss. While the Nationalists had initiated land reform during the Nanjing Decade, the escalation of the war with Japan in 1937 made the land reform law a dead letter. Had Chiang continued to pursue land reform, some warlords would have defected and others might have combined to overthrow him. It is no coincidence that the Nationalist Party did not resume land reform until it fled to Taiwan,

Table 21.4 Hyperinflation

Date	Issuing of Gold Yuan (100 Million)	Issuing Index (31 Aug. 1948 = 1)	Shanghai Wholesale Price Index (1937 = 1)
31 August 1948	5.44	1.00	1.64
September 1948	12.02	2.21	1.97
October 1948	18.50	3.40	2.20
November 1948	33.94	6.24	25.43
December 1948	83.20	15.29	35.84
January 1949	208.70	38.28	128.76
February 1949	597.30	109.80	897.78
March 1949	1,961.30	360.53	4,053.20
April 1949	51,612.40	9,487.57	83,820.00
May 1949	679,458.00	124,900.37*	2,102,000.00

* First week.

Source: Zhaojin Ji, *A History of Modern Shanghai Banking: The Rise and Decline of China's Finance Capitalism* (Armonk, NY: M. E. Sharpe, 2003), 235.

The average urban Chinese was attracted to the Communists by economic factors as much as or more than belief in the Soviet philosophy. Rampant inflation forced prices up by a factor of ten during 1948 alone, and there was widespread unemployment. The Nationalist government seemed unable to solve these problems, while the Communists claimed they could once they had taken power.

where it redistributed the land not of party loyalists, but of the local Taiwanese. The Communists, in contrast, used land reform to rally support in the countryside. The Chinese peasantry did not understand that collectivization was the ultimate goal. As in the Bolshevik Revolution of 1917, the peasantry took the bait of land reform only to lose all their land after the revolution.

Following the end of the Marshall Mission, ever-growing economic problems in the Nationalist-controlled areas continued to erode Chiang's political legitimacy at the same time as his military campaign in Manchuria began to falter. China's economic turmoil directly benefited the CCP, since average Chinese began to see in the Communists a possible solution to China's staggering problems. Mao identified a clear culprit: the capitalist rich allied with Chiang. He had a simple solution: punish the rich and confiscate their wealth. He also provided instant gratification: the redistribution of wealth and particularly of land. This ideology fused righteous indignation and jealousy to overturn the old social order in China. Chinese students played a key role in this grand strategy, since the Communists targeted high school and college

students, China's idealistic youth. These young people accepted the Communists' simple black-and-white but highly reductionist propaganda message that ascribed China's many ills to Chiang. These young people provided vital intelligence to the Communists, while their many demonstrations got the Communist message out to a broad urban audience including workers and the middle class.

Chiang also lost the support of many business leaders. The failure of the Nationalist economic program became integral to its collapse. Following World War II, inflation in China was out of control. Between September 1945 and February 1947, wholesale prices in Shanghai increased thirtyfold. A 171-pound bag of rice costing only 12 yuan in 1937 sold for 6.7 million yuan by early June 1948 and for an incredible 63 million yuan in August 1948. Wheelbarrows supplanted purses on shopping expeditions. The resulting financial chaos precluded ordinary business transactions, let alone economic growth. This destroyed small businesses and entrepreneurs.

Although the Nationalist government tried to check inflation by imposing price and wage ceilings, and later by imposing food rationing, this was unsuccessful because these laws did not address the underlying problem of shattered production. Uncontrolled inflation increased unemployment. During 1946, unemployment reaching an unprecedented 30 percent even in the national capital of Nanjing. This, in turn, led to a rapid increase in the number of industrial strikes, which further reduced production. These factors worked to the advantage of the Communists, who tirelessly infiltrated labor unions to turn them against the Nationalists. The Nationalist government was rotting from within and was no longer able to rally popular support from without.

V. The Communist Victory

As Nationalist rule imploded, the Communists orchestrated an increasingly effective campaign to rally popular support. Soviet history offered a very powerful model for Mao. The Bolsheviks had won the Russian Civil War in large measure with an extremely popular land reform program that their bourgeois enemies could not match without undermining their middle- and upper-class support. The Chinese Communists likewise tried to manipulate the land issue.

On 4 May 1946, the Communists announced a land reform program that went beyond rent reduction to redistributing property. They held a National Land Conference in Hebei over the summer of 1947 to draft a land reform law. The draft law, published on 10 October, mandated the confiscation of landlords' lands and movable property. Mao warned against alienating farmers by overly radical land reform and on 25 May 1948 ordered the moderation of the campaign. Unlike in Russia, land ownership was not very concentrated in China. Most landowners held small plots. The Communists needed to retain the sympathies of this large independent farmer population in order to win the civil war. There was further moderation of the land reform law in January 1949, mandating rent and interest reductions, not land redistribution. These changes were aimed at winning sympathies in South China, where land ownership was more widespread than in North China. The campaign was managed well enough that, in comparison to the endemic maladministration of the Nationalists, the Communists seemed a better choice.

As a result of growing defections, Nationalist forces began to decline in number. In contrast, the PLA experienced enormous growth, from an estimated half million in mid-1945 to 1.3 million in mid-1946, 2 million in mid-1947, 2.8 million in mid-1948, and 4 million in early 1949. Success in the field led to an evolution of Communist military strategy. In September 1945, the Communists decided to concentrate the PLA in Manchuria, while the Nationalists remained divided among three competing objectives: to eliminate warlord remnants in South China, to consolidate their control over the vast areas recently evacuated by the Japanese, and to conduct a major offensive in Manchuria. This allowed the PLA to concentrate against just a part of the Nationalist forces. By September 1947, Mao could announce a change in military strategy from a strategic defensive to a nationwide counteroffensive. A year later, the Communists shifted their military focus from rural to urban China.

Manchuria proved to be the decisive theater in the Chinese civil war, meaning that the Nationalists lost the war there. (See Table 21.5.) With U.S. assistance, Chiang Kai-shek deployed the cream of his army in the hopes of reconstituting the entire Qing empire. He positioned his troops to defend cities that soon became isolated from each other and cut off from the long Nationalist supply lines to the south. The Communist strategy entailed taking control of the surrounding countryside, cutting the transportation links between the cities, and allowing the urban economies to collapse and public disaffection with Nationalist rule to set in before picking off the Nationalist armies one at a time. Although the Communist military strategy caused the economic collapse of the cities, urban populations blamed the Nationalists for the ensuing hardships.

The coalitional nature of Nationalist rule meant that Nationalist armies often did not come to each other's rescue. Chiang's military strategy reinforced this tendency by rarely ordering the relief of besieged cities. Rather, Chiang Kai-shek followed Sunzi's strategy of leaving his own troops with no escape route in order to force them to fight. Instead, individual Nationalist troops, and sometimes entire armies, defected to the Communists, who welcomed them since Mao followed Sunzi's complementary strategy of never putting enemy troops on death ground, but instead giving them an out so that they would not need to fight to the death. This helped encourage massive Nationalist defections, and defectors were treated well by the CCP. Once the Communists took power and could deal with their potential enemies from a position of strength, they systematically eliminated former Nationalists troops, if not in the Korean War, then during the many ensuing political campaigns of the Communist period.

After the U.S.-brokered cease-fire in June 1946, the Communists had, in equal measure, cultivated and coerced the support of the Manchurian populace. During late 1947 and early 1948, the PLA under Lin Biao killed, wounded, or captured an estimated 150,000 Nationalist troops. It pushed the rest into a small triangle bounded by the cities of Jinzhou, Changchun, and Shenyang. The PLA took Harbin (Haerbin) and by May 1948 had cleared most Nationalists from

Table 21.5   Campaigns of the Chinese Civil War (1945–9)

Dates	Campaign	Significance
Oct.–Dec. 1945	Outbreak of hostilities in eleven provinces	Renewal of full-scale civil war
January–6 June 1946	Nationalist offensive in Manchuria	Rapid offensive to the Sungari River
6 June–July 1946	Cease-fire	Nationalists permanently lose their momentum
January 1947	Start of CCP Manchurian counteroffensive	Harbinger of a turning tide
19 March 1947	Yan'an falls to the Nationalists	Symbolism of the loss of CCP headquarters
May–June 1947	Siping Campaign (Manchuria)	Final important Nationalist victory
March–September 1948	CCP offensive in Shandong	Another harbinger of a turning tide
12 Sept.–2 Nov. 1948	Liaoyang-Shenyang Campaign	Manchuria falls to the Communists; the tide turns
21 Nov. 1948–31 Jan. 1949	Beiping-Tianjin Campaign	CCP takes the traditional capital and North China
Nov. 1948–Jan. 1949	Huai-Hai Campaign (Anhui)	Simultaneous losses shatter the Nationalist morale
20 April 1949	Communists cross the Yangzi River	CCP moves into Nationalist South China heartland
23 April 1949	Nanjing falls to the Communists	Fall of the Nationalist capital
May 16–17 1949	Wuhan falls to the Communists	CCP takes a key industrial center
25 May 1949	Shanghai falls to the Communists	CCP takes the most important commercial center
1 October 1949	Mao Zedong proclaims the PRC	Reasonable hopes for a Nationalist victory gone
30 November 1949	Chongqing falls to the Communists	Fall of the Nationalist capital
10 December 1949	Chiang Kai-shek flees to Taiwan	Official Nationalist presence on the mainland gone
March 1950	Hainan Island falls to the CCP	Taiwan seems next
25 June 1950	Outbreak of the Korean War	United States prevents PRC invasion of Taiwan
1 December 1951	Llasa falls to the CCP	China reoccupies Tibet after a forty-year hiatus

Note: The shaded area indicates the Manchurian phase of the civil war. It also corresponds to the first four years of the conflict. In the next and final year, the Communists took all of China south of Manchuria. After they took Manchuria, Nationalist power imploded.

Manchuria. By fall 1948 the PLA surpassed the Nationalist army in size, with 3 million versus 2.9 million men. The Nationalists lost Jinzhou on 14 October, Changchun on 18 October, and Shenyang on 2 November 1948.

Chiang had suffered catastrophic losses in the field three times during the Sino-Japanese War: in late 1937 in the fight for Shanghai and Nanjing, a second time during the Xuzhou Campaign in 1938, and again during the Ichigo Campaign of 1944. From 1948 to 1949, the Communists decimated his fourth set of armies in Manchuria. Spurred on by their success, Mao announced that the PLA was no longer a guerrilla army but was now ready to fight a conventional war. Following the PLA victory in Manchuria, Communist forces spread south into China proper. Fighting was concentrated in the Beijing-Tianjin area; the so-called Beiping-Tianjin Campaign brought an estimated 900,000 Communist troops out of Manchuria to oppose 600,000 Nationalist troops. By January 1949, Tianjin and Beijing both fell without a fight. Nationalist morale was collapsing. The Nationalist general Fu Zuoyi surrendered with 200,000 troops. This brought Nationalist losses to 1.5 million men between September 1948 and January 1949.

An even more important Communist victory occurred in the Huai-Hai Campaign, the largest battle of the civil war, involving over 1 million combatants and fought simultaneously with the Beiping-Tianjin Campaign. Communist forces moved into Jiangsu and Anhui provinces, while Chiang, in recognition of the importance of the road to Nanjing, stationed 400,000 of his best troops near Xuzhou. Even though they enjoyed air superiority and had better equipment, the Nationalists' morale was low and two divisions went over to the Communists. In November 1948, the Communists wiped out another 100,000 Nationalist troops. Finally, on 15 December 1948, after sixty-five days of fighting, the Commu-

While the PLA had begun as a guerrilla force, by 1948 they were able to adopt conventional warfare to invade China proper from their Manchurian base. To some, it looked as if China might follow Germany's example and divide at the Yangzi River into a North and a South, similar in size but with the North Communist and the South Nationalist. However, when the Nationalist Navy mutinied, it allowed the Communists to cross the Yangzi River and take Shanghai, thereby forcing the Nationalists to retreat to Taiwan.

nists took Xuzhou, opening the road south to the Yangzi River and on to Nanjing.

This still left the Nationalists in possession of their traditional power base, South China. They alone had a navy and an air force to interdict troops crossing the Yangzi River. If the Communists could not cross, they could not take South China. Li Zongren, the leader of the Guangxi Clique, urged Chiang to cooperate in its defense. (See the feature on the next page.) Chiang, however, feared this rival power base and focused on the defense of Shanghai instead. In effect, Chiang preferred to cede South China to the Communists rather than to his Nationalist rivals. Consistent with his strategy throughout the civil war, Chiang made another static defense of a city, this time of his power base, Shanghai. The Communist counterstrategy of surrounding and strangling the cities remained highly effective.

On 25 February 1949, the Nationalist flagship, *Chongqing,* mutinied, becoming another symbol of the waning Nationalist mandate to rule. By the end of April 1949, much of the rest of the Nationalist fleet guarding the Yangzi River also defected. On 20 April, Communist forces crossed the Yangzi to overrun Nanjing three days later. Thereafter,

the PLA began the task of consolidating control over all of mainland China, taking Shanghai and Wuhan in May, Xi'an and Changsha in August, Guangzhou in October, and finally Chongqing in November 1949.

The PLA's rapid advance forced the remaining Nationalist units to retreat to Taiwan, where the Nationalist Party continued its anti-Communist struggle. Chiang Kai-shek claimed that his Republican government remained the legitimate government of all of China. Meanwhile, in late September 1949, Mao Zedong assembled a new Political Consultative Conference that elected him as chairman of the central government and once again made Beijing the capital. On 1 October 1949, Mao officially proclaimed the creation of the People's Republic of China from the Gate of Heavenly Peace to the Forbidden City, the imperial seat of the Qing dynasty. He told the huge crowd: "The Chinese people have stood up . . . nobody will insult us again,"[2] meaning the end of the long period beginning with the Opium Wars that the Chinese call the "era of humiliations." The Republican period had ended for mainland China. The era of two Chinas had begun.

ZHUANG MINORITY

Li Zongren is the most famous member of China's largest ethnic minority group, the Zhuang. Today most Zhuang live in the Zhuang Autonomous Region in Guangxi province, but there are also communities in Guangdong, Yunnan, and Guizhou. While most Zhuang follow their traditional religion based on the worship of spirits and ancestors, some practice Buddhism, Daoism, Christianity, or Islam, so that language, not religion, distinguishes the Zhuang. They belong to the Northern Dai ethnic group and linguistically are divided into two very distinct dialect groups. In the past, their use of written language was limited to transcribing prayers and songs, but in 1955 the PRC government developed a transcription system for their language based on the Latin alphabet. The Zhuang used to wear distinct clothing that now appears only on special occasions. Their most famous handicrafts are brocades; their most important festivals include the Spring Festival, the Devil Festival, and the Ox Soul Festival.

The Zhuang became an officially recognized ethnic group only under the Communists. In 1949 the PRC changed the character used to write "Zhuang," which contained the highly pejorative dog radical and also indicated a type of wild dog. The simplified character used in the PRC means "strong." Under China's previous governments, many Zhuang disguised their identity in order to escape the discrimination accorded to China's so-called southern barbarians. This has led to some dispute over their origins.

The Zhuang believe that they came from outside Guangxi. According to this view, the Zhuang, like the Miao, originally inhabited areas far to the north but left Central China perhaps 5,000 years ago. During the many Chinese dynasties from the Han dynasty on, the Zhuang continued to resist Han Chinese rule but suffered repeated defeats, fleeing ever farther south. More recently, PRC scholars have argued that archeological remains demonstrate that the Zhuang originated in Guangxi or at least intermarried with the local population.

In any case, warfare with the Han forced continued southward migrations around 1100 AD, when different groups fled to Indochina and became known as the Lao, Thai, and Shan peoples and the Zhuang of South China. Others fled to Burma and as far afield as India. The Qing dynasty never fully pacified the Zhuang areas. Indeed, the Taiping rebels found them to be a receptive audience. In the Republican period, the Zhuang were key supporters of the Guangxi Clique, which was among the most powerful warlord cliques within the Nationalist coalition and presented an alternative to Chiang Kai-shek's rule. Li Zongren was one of Chiang's most powerful rivals. During the Second Sino-Japanese War, the 1944 Ichigo Offensive of the Japanese went through Zhuang territories to face stiff guerrilla resistance.

In the 1920s and 1930s, the Zhuang had been the most consistent Communist supporters of any ethnic group in Guangxi. Nationalist hostility to the Guangxi Clique inadvertently encouraged this trend. Perhaps to reward their loyalty, in 1952 the government designated the Western half of Guangxi as the Zhuang Autonomous Prefecture. In 1958, the government expanded the area to encompass all of Guangxi, renaming it the Guangxi Zhuang Autonomous Zone, which became one of the five provincial-level autonomous regions. This set a precedent far short of independence that was useful against China's more separatist nationalities, such as the Tibetans, the Uighurs, and the Mongols.

The campaign against the Four Olds during the Cultural Revolution targeted minority people for preserving their traditions. The Zhuang retaliated by trying to depose the Guangxi party secretary. In the ensuing battles, 90,000 perished and cannibalism was apparently practiced on victims. Guangxi was among the most violent provinces during the Cultural Revolution. During the Sino-Vietnamese War, China invaded Vietnam over the Western Guangxi border and the cross-border shelling did not end until the 1980s. This slowed the adoption of the economic reforms of the Deng Restoration. The province remains poor and cut off, with an inadequate road and rail system.

Conclusions

An army mutiny supported by a naval mutiny precipitated the collapse of the Qing dynasty in 1911, while a naval mutiny allowed the Communists to cross the Yangzi River to unify North and South China in 1949. The thirty-eight-year interregnum between imperial and Communist rule was one of almost continuous civil war. The North China warlords so weakened each other in the civil wars of the early 1920s that the Nationalists were able to launch the Northern Expedition from South China that achieved nominal unification in 1928. In reality, the Nationalists were a heterogeneous coalition of South China warlords with marginal influence over North China. During the Nanjing Decade from 1928 until the Japanese invasion of China proper in 1937, Chiang engaged in constant internal warfare to consolidate control over this coalition and to eliminate the Communists in a series of five Encirclement Campaigns culminating in the Long March (1934–5).

The post–World War II phase of the civil war resumed a Nationalist-Communist conflict dating back to Chiang's 1927 purge during the Northern Expedition. With the escalation of the Second Sino-Japanese War in 1937, the Japanese main forces focused on destroying the Nationalists, while the Communists organized rural China behind Japanese lines. In the final months of the Sino-Japanese War, the Communist base of operations in North China shifted to Manchuria, the most highly industrialized part of Asia outside of Japan. During late August 1945, Mao and Chiang tried to negotiate a settlement but failed. All U.S. efforts to establish a coalition government also failed. In January 1947, Washington withdrew the Marshall Mission and called off all further American attempts to bring about a peaceful resolution to the Chinese civil war; U.S. financial support to the Nationalists continued, but at substantially lower levels. The subsequent Communist victory changed the equation in the Cold War with the Western perception that the so-called Sino-Soviet bloc constituted an effective anti-Western alliance.

To win the civil war, the Communists used Manchuria's food, industrial goods, and military supplies to build up the PLA. The Manchurian theater pitted Communist strengths against Nationalist weaknesses. This was the only theater where Communist and Nationalist forces were roughly equal. Everywhere else the Nationalists had the advantage, so the Communists concentrated their main forces in Manchuria, while the Nationalist forces remained dispersed throughout China. The long Japanese occupation destroyed the indigenous Manchurian elite, which was most likely to support Nationalist rule, while, as Southerners, the Nationalists had difficulty recruiting Northerners' support. In contrast to the distant Nationalist base of support, Yan'an was adjacent to both Manchuria and the Communists' foreign patron, the USSR. At the end of the war, the USSR retained Outer Mongolia and occupied Manchuria, thus giving the CCP easy access to the Northeast.

Until the final year of the civil war, the most likely outcome seemed to be the division of China at the Yangzi River into two roughly equal states: a Communist North China and a Nationalist South China. Stalin supported this outcome, because splitting China into two hostile parts, like the division of Germany and Korea, would have kept it weak, preoccupied, and unable to threaten the Soviet Union. Mao and Chiang, however, both rejected this outcome, pressing for full reunification.

Once the Nationalists started losing, their mandate of heaven evaporated like that of the Qing dynasty before them. Their inability to defeat the Japanese or restore domestic prosperity had already severely weakened their legitimacy. Their devastating and highly symbolic breaching of the Yellow River dikes in 1938 in an unsuccessful attempt to halt the Japanese demonstrated a callousness—in Confucian

terms, a lack of humaneness—toward the very people in whose interest they were supposed to rule. The major features of Nationalist rule were those of failing dynasties: civil war, foreign invasion, natural disasters, famine, corruption, and hyperinflation.

The Chinese became increasingly united in their disgust with the Nationalists, not in their loyalty to the Communists. Popular perceptions of the main foreign patrons of each side reinforced such views. Ever since the Shandong controversy at the end of World War I (Chapter 16), there had been a growing perception that the West continued to treat the Chinese as a subject people. The Nationalists came to be viewed as puppets of the United States. In contrast, ever since the publication of the Karakhan Manifesto (Chapter 17), many Chinese believed that the USSR had done more than any other nation to help China in its time of greatest need. When the Nationalists started to lose the civil war in Manchuria, there was a growing sense that their mandate to rule had disappeared. Nationalist units defected in droves to serve the ascendant new Communist dynasty.

In Western military history, mass defections are highly unusual. In both world wars, the Germans fought on long after any reasonable hope of victory was gone. In World War II they fought all the way to Berlin. Yet in China, mass defections were common, in part, because of the personalistic, not institutional, origins of military loyalties, so that defecting commanders took their troops with them. Nationalist defections escalated after the loss of Manchuria, one of the most distant theaters from their power base in South China. Of the five years of civil war following 1945, four were devoted to the struggle for Manchuria, while the Communists wrapped up the rest of the country—virtually an entire continent—in one year.

The Communist victory was a combination of conventional warfare and enemy defections. Like ascendant dynasties of the past, they rose to power on the basis of peasant armies convinced of the righteousness of their cause and the corruption of their adversaries. The Chinese Communists very astutely turned a strategy of the weak into a formula for victory. Instead of trying to create a power base strictly from the top down, as the Nationalist had, the Communists also focused on creating support or at least acquiescence from the bottom up. Through trial and error, they fine-tuned their land reform policy to attract sufficient rural support to win the civil war. But after the civil war, Mao, like Stalin, then took this land away again in a massive collectivization campaign. Thus, the Chinese peasantry lost the very material possession that they valued the most.

The Communists also harnessed nationalism. Chinese nationalism had been long in coming. During the Qing dynasty, there had been little sense of nation in China. Rather, loyalties remained rooted in home villages—what the Chinese referred to as their "native place." This meant that when the Qing dynasty collapsed, central rule did not naturally reconstitute itself. Instead, in the absence of a strong center, China atomized into a plethora of competing provinces ruled by warlords. Many of these warlords simply hoped to retain their autonomy. Unlike the regionalists, both the Nationalists and the Communists attempted to craft an ideology to create a binding sense of nation. Both shared the ambition of reunifying all lands of the old Qing empire by means of Han nationalism.

The Nationalists in 1928 succeeded in unifying China militarily, just as the Communists did in 1949. The key intervening event between these two unifications was the Second Sino-Japanese War. The Japanese invasion and occupation were long and brutal. Unlike the Manchus, who emphasized their patronage of Han traditions, the Japanese made clear their utter contempt for the Han. The Japanese unwittingly spurred the development of a strong sense of unity among the Han. During the Northern Expedition, during the Long March, and particularly during the post–World War II phase of the Chinese civil war, the Nationalists and Communists tried to instill a common ideology to inspire and rally a nation.

When Mao Zedong came to power after the long and turbulent interregnum of the Republican period, he ruled over a people who had increasingly acquired a modern sense of nation. This transformation, however, was still not complete. Strong North-South divisions remained, and there was as yet no consensus on what precise form modern China should take. As in the fall of the Qing dynasty, the victors raised the specter of imperialism to play on Han xenophobia. Anti-Western Han nationalism limited the effectiveness of U.S. aid to the Nationalists. Yet, it was not the West that had engaged in territorial expansion in Outer Mongolia and Manchuria, but fellow Communists in the Soviet Union.

With the creation of the People's Republic of China, the PLA began consolidating Communist control throughout the lands of the former Qing empire. The non-Han populations of Inner Mongolia, Xinjiang, and Tibet by and large rejected the new Han sense of nationalism. They desired independence but lacked the military means to gain it. For the first time since the collapse of the Qing dynasty, the core provinces of Han China as well as most of Qing Inner Asia had been reunited under the control of a government in Beijing. The long interregnum ended with the creation of the new Communist dynasty. Mao ruled the country with the power of an emperor until his death, writing poetry comparing himself to the greatest emperors of China. (See his poem at the beginning of Chapter 22.) The CCP elite played the role of the imperial clan. Communism replaced Confucianism as the binding ideology of the nation. In accordance with notions of *yin* and *yang*, while many of the key details changed—some forces strengthened, while others weakened—an overarching continuity remained.

BIBLIOGRAPHY

Barnett, A. Doak. *China on the Eve of Communist Takeover.* New York: Praeger, 1963.

Benson, Linda. *The Ili Rebellion: The Moslem Challenge to Chinese Authority in Xinjiang 1944–1949.* Armonk, NY: M. E. Sharpe, 1990.

Bianco, Lucien. "Peasant Responses to CCP Mobilization Policies, 1937–1945." In *New Perspectives on the Chinese Communist Revolution,* edited by Tony Saich and Hans van de Ven, 175–88. Armonk, NY: M. E. Sharpe, 1995.

Chang, Gordon. *Friends, Enemies: The United States, China, and the Soviet Union, 1948–1972.* Stanford, CA: Stanford University Press, 1990.

Chassin, Lionel Max. *The Communist Conquest of China: A History of the Civil War 1945–1949.* Translated by Timothy Osato and Louis Gelas. Cambridge, MA: Harvard University Press, 1965.

Chen, Yung-fa. *Making Revolution: The Communist Movement in Eastern and Central China, 1937–1945.* Berkeley: University of California Press, 1986.

Eastman, Lloyd E. *Seeds of Destruction: Nationalist China in War and Revolution 1937–1949.* Stanford, CA: Stanford University Press, 1984.

———. "Nationalist China during the Sino-Japanese War 1937–1945." In *The Cambridge History of China,* vol. 13, edited by John K. Fairbank and Albert Feuerwerker, 547–608. Cambridge: Cambridge University Press, 1986.

Forbes, Andrew D. W. *Warlords and Muslims in Chinese Central Asia: A Political History of Republican Sinkiang 1911–1949*. Cambridge: Cambridge University Press, 1986.

Garthoff, Raymond L. "Sino-Soviet Military Relations, 1945–66." In *Sino-Soviet Military Relations*, edited by Raymond L. Garthoff, 82–99. New York: Praeger, 1966.

Garver, John W. *Chinese-Soviet Relations 1937–1945: The Diplomacy of Chinese Nationalism*. New York: Oxford University Press, 1988.

Jeans, Roger B., ed. *Roads Not Taken: The Struggle of Opposition Parties in Twentieth-Century China*. Boulder, CO: Westview Press, 1992.

Kaup, Katherine Palmer. *Creating the Zhuang: Ethnic Politics in China*. Boulder, CO: Lynne Rienner, 2000.

Lary, Diana. "Defending China: The Battles of the Xuzhou Campaign." In *Warfare in Chinese History*, edited by Hans van de Ven, 398–427. Leiden: Brill, 2000.

Ledovsky, A. M. *The USSR, the USA, and the People's Revolution in China*. Translated by Nadezhda Burova. Moscow: Progress Publishers, 1982.

Levine, Steven I. *Anvil of Victory: The Communist Revolution in Manchuria, 1945–1948*. New York: Columbia University Press, 1987.

———."Mobilizing for War: Rural Revolution in Manchuria as an Instrument for War." In *Single Sparks: China's Rural Revolutions*, edited by Kathleen Hartford and Steven M. Goldstein, 151–75. Armonk, NY: M. E. Sharpe, 1989.

Murray, Brian. "Stalin, the Cold War, and the Division of China: A Multiarchival Mystery." *Cold War International History Project*. Working Paper no. 12, The Wilson Center, Washington, DC. June 1995.

Myers, Ramon. "The Chinese State during the Republican Era." In *The Modern Chinese State*, edited by David Shambaugh, 42–71. Cambridge: Cambridge University Press, 2000.

Olivier, Bernard Vincent. *The Implementation of China's National Policy in the Northeastern Provinces*. Lewiston, NY: Edwin Mellen Press, 1993.

Pepper, Suzanne. "The KMT-CCP Conflict 1945–1949." In *The Cambridge History of China*, vol. 13, edited by John K, Fairbank and Albert Feuerwerker, 723–88. Cambridge: Cambridge University Press, 1986.

Ryan, Mark A., David Michael Finkelstein, and Michael A. McDevitt. eds. *Chinese Warfighting: The PLA Experience Since 1949*. Armonk, NY: M. E. Sharpe, 2003.

Saich, Tony and Hans van de Ven, eds. *The Rise to Power of the Chinese Communist Party: Documents and Analysis*. Armonk, NY: M. E. Sharpe, 1996.

Short, Philip. *Mao: A Life*. New York: Henry Holt, 1999.

Terrill, Ross. *Mao: A Biography*. Rev. ed. Stanford, CA: Stanford University Press, 1999.

Tsou, T'ang. *America's Failure in China, 1941–50*. Chicago: University of Chicago Press, 1963.

Tung, William L. *The Political Institutions of Modern China*. The Hague: Martinus Nijhoff, 1968.

Westad, Odd Arne. *Decisive Encounters: The Chinese Civil War, 1946–1950*. Stanford, CA: Stanford University Press, 2003.

Yick, Joseph K. S. *Making Urban Revolution in China: The CCP-GMD Struggle for Beiping-Tianjin, 1945–1949*. Armonk, NY: M. E. Sharpe, 1995.

NOTES

1. Du Yunxie, "The Sandaled Soldier," in *Twentieth Century Chinese Poetry*, Kai-yu Hsu, trans. (Garden City, NY: Doubleday, 1963), 228.
2. Cited in Ross Terrill, *Mao: A Biography*, rev. ed. (Stanford, CA: Stanford University Press, 1999), 226.

Thematic Chronology (1949–2008)

Decade	Politics	Economy	Diplomacy	Society	Taiwan
1940s	Establishment of the PRC (1949)		Soviet Union recognizes PRC (1949)		Brutal suppression of anti-Nationalist demonstrations (1947)
1950s	Three-Antis Campaign (1951) Five-Antis Campaign (1952) Hundred Flowers Campaign (1956) Anti-Rightist Campaign (1957) Great Leap Forward (1958)	Land reform law (1950) Establishment of agricultural collectives (1953) First five-year plan (1953–7) Great Famine (1959–61)	Britain recognizes PRC (1950) Sino-Soviet Friendship Treaty (1950) Korean War (1950–3) Soviet Union returns concessions (1952–5)	PRC occupies Tibet (1951) Tibetan Uprising (1959)	Land reform (1953) First Taiwan Strait Crisis (1954–5) Second Taiwan Strait Crisis (1958)
1960s	Mao Zedong's leadership challenged Successful test of the atomic bomb (1964) Successful test of the nuclear bomb (1967)		Sino-Soviet split (1960) Sino-Indian Border War (1962) Sino-Soviet Border War (1969)	Cultural Revolution (1966–76)	
1970s	Death of Lin Biao (1971) Death of Mao Zedong; arrest of Gang of Four (1976) Democracy Wall posters (1978–9)	Tangshan earthquake (1976) Four Modernizations (1977)	Shanghai and Sino-Japanese Communiqués (1972) Agreements to restore diplomatic relations with the United States and Japan (1978) Sino-Vietnamese War (1979)		PRC replaces Taiwan at UN (1971) Taiwanese economic miracle U.S. changes recognition from Taiwan to PRC (1979)
1980s	Tiananmen Massacre (1989)	Opening of Special Economic Zones (1980) Land reform (1984)	PRC renounces Sino-Soviet Friendship Treaty (1980) Anglo-Chinese declaration on return of Hong Kong (1984)	Revitalization of Chinese cinema Pro-democracy student movement (1986–9)	End of Nationalist one-party monopoly (1986) Taiwanese permitted to visit PRC (1987)
1990s	Death of Deng Xiaoping (1997)		PRC test fires missiles off Taiwan on the eve of presidential elections (1996)	Introduction of bar exams (1986)	Reform of legislature (1989)
2000s	Transfer of power from Jiang Zemin to Hu Jintao (2004)	Sichuan earthquake (2008), over 70,000 deaths	PRC and Taiwan admitted to the World Trade Organization (2001)	Lawyers Law (1996)	Democratic Progressive Party wins the presidency (2000)

Part IV

China and Taiwan in the Postwar Era

Part IV examines events following the Communist victory in the Chinese civil war. Mao Zedong's first goal became establishing his own legitimacy. He confirmed his mandate of heaven by reunifying China, adopting a comprehensive domestic reform program to restore rural and urban prosperity, and reestablishing an independent foreign policy ending China's era of humiliation.

Chapter 22 describes the Communists' early attempts to institutionalize their military victory in order to make it permanent. This entailed the reunification of the lands of the former Qing empire, the rectification of the party, the collectivization of agriculture, the nationalization of industry, and the cultivation of the Sino-Soviet alliance. Meanwhile, the Nationalists tried to preserve their opposition government on Taiwan through comprehensive economic reforms.

Chapter 23 examines the Korean War, which broke out within a year of the Communist victory. Kim Il Sung, the ruler of North Korea, secured Soviet and Chinese support to invade South Korea. When the war went badly for Kim, Mao decided to project Chinese influence into the former tributary zone of the Qing empire. Mao had no intention of allowing the United States, the former benefactor of Chiang Kai-shek, to entrench itself on the Korean Peninsula. Mao took advantage of the war both to eliminate potential domestic critics and to dispose of remnant warlord and Nationalist armies by deploying them to the front lines. At war's end, China had for the first time fought the Western powers to a stalemate. The combination of victory in the civil war and success in the Korean War greatly strengthened Mao's mandate of heaven. He had demonstrated through action his worthiness to rule.

GRAVE SWEEPING DAY AND DOUBLE NINTH FESTIVAL

Just as the New Year's celebrations, the Dragon Boat Festival, and the Mid-Autumn Festival are the three most important holidays for the living, for the dead the most important ones are the Grave—or Tomb—Sweeping Day (*Qingming jie*) and the Double Ninth Festival (*Chongyang jie*). Both festivals fall according to the lunar calendar, so that Grave Sweeping Day is usually observed on 4 or 5 April, while the Double Ninth Festival occurs sometime in October. In 1935 the Nationalist government designated Grave Sweeping Day as an official holiday, and in 1966 it designated Double Ninth Day as Senior Citizen's Day. By chance, 5 April coincided with Chiang Kai-shek's death in 1975. While neither holiday is officially celebrated in the PRC, the Communist government no longer interferes with their observance, in contrast to the Cultural Revolution, when the Red Guards vandalized many grave sites.

Ancestor worship reflects the belief that the dead still have physical needs, that ancestors can assist the living if these needs are met, and that ancestors can influence a person's fortune. Ancestor worship is perhaps the original religion of China. (Buddhism, Islam, Christianity, and Judaism were all imported from outside China, while its main indigenous schools of thought, Confucianism and Daoism, have more in common with philosophies than religions.)

Continued

Grave Sweeping Day is held during early April. After the body has fully decomposed, the tomb is opened and the bones are collected and put in an urn. If a Chinese man died overseas, his bones were sent back to his ancestral home for reburial. This holiday was officially celebrated for the first time in the PRC on 4 April 2008.

Confucianism reflects this early emphasis on ancestor worship by its own focus on filial piety and ritual observances to ancestors. Confucius thought that societies not based on ancestor worship would soon disintegrate.

Ancestor worship begins with a proper grave. Experts in *fengshui* or geomancy determine the best location, often siting the grave in relation to nearby streams, rivers, trees, and mountains. Facing south toward pine groves is considered particularly auspicious. Instead of a headstone, a small stone tablet is usually placed at the foot of the grave, recording the person's name, date of birth, and date of death.

Cleaning the grave includes weeding, dusting the tablet, and adding new flowers. In a simple ritual, the head of the household or eldest son kowtows three times with a wine cup in hand and then pours the wine on the ground. Other members of the family then follow, usually in descending order by age and position within the family. Incense and food can be placed in front of the tablet. Food offerings can include a whole chicken, hard-boiled eggs, and dim sum pastries. Three sets of chopsticks and three Chinese wine cups are arranged near the food.

In addition to burning incense in front of the tablet, paper facsimiles of everyday objects are burned, including paper money and, in recent years, eyeglasses, cameras, cars, cell phones, and even paper mistresses. If the ancestor smoked, a lit cigarette is a suitable offering. Then firecrackers are set off to scare away evil spirits and to alert the deceased that their needs have been met. Ignored ancestors can turn into demons, the inspiration for many Chinese horror films.

The Double Ninth Festival also honors ancestors. It is sometimes called Double *Yang* because the number 9 is related to the *yang* principle of the sun. Also known as Autumn Remembrance, this festival is similar to Grave Sweeping Day because families also visit the graves of ancestors to clear them and offer sacrifices. The festival is linked with a legend dating to the Han dynasty about a famous musician and his disciple. One day, the magician warned his disciple that on the ninth day of the ninth month he and his entire family would perish unless they brought the berries from the pepper-acacia tree to a high mountain. The disciple obeyed. In his absence, his house and all his livestock were destroyed, so the flight had saved him. Therefore, it is common to go hiking on this holiday, which is why it is sometimes called the "Climbing Up on High" festival.

Chapter 24 discusses the Chinese quest for foreign policy independence from the USSR. Stalin's successor, Nikita Khrushchev, and Mao competed for leadership of the Communist bloc. As the senior, Mao believed he should lead. These tensions produced in the 1960 Sino-Soviet split that shattered the unity of the international Communist movement. Meanwhile, tensions with India culminated in war in 1962. Domestically, Mao attempted to accelerate the pace of economic development to close the gap between China and the developed countries. The poorly conceived economic policies of the Great Leap Forward (1958–60) brought famine, not prosperity, and nearly cost Mao his rule.

Mao launched the Cultural Revolution (1966–76) in an attempt to restore himself to power, the subject of Chapter 25. He tried to transfer primary Han loyalties from the family to the CCP. Although his policies scattered families throughout the countryside and the prison system, amazingly the Han family survived. After Sino-Soviet tensions erupted in war in 1969 and the Soviet Union considered employing nuclear weapons, there was a Sino-American rapprochement under President Richard Nixon. This, in combination with the militarization of the Sino-Soviet border, put enormous and permanent economic pressure on the Soviet Union.

Chapter 26 turns to the succession crisis and the economic reforms following Mao's death. Stalinists, technocrats, and ideologues all competed for influence. Mao's declining health precipitated a succession crisis that began with Lin Biao's mysterious death, apparently while trying to flee to the USSR. Mao's death marked the end of the Cultural Revolution. The succession struggle entailed the demise of the Gang of Four, the ideologues, and the rise to power of the technocrats under Deng Xiaoping. Thereafter, China fought Vietnam to undermine its ties with the Soviet Union. Meanwhile, Taiwan initiated a comprehensive economic reform package that created a standard of living far surpassing that of China. In response, Deng adopted an economic reform program of his own that laid the basis for rapid growth and increasing prosperity after decades of stagnation. The Deng Xiaoping Restoration greatly strengthened the Communist mandate of heaven.

Chapter 27 examines the impact of the breakup of the Soviet Union. Mikhail Gorbachev's promotion of public discussion in Russia gave rise to similar expectations in China. Students began demonstrating in Tiananmen Square, demanding that their government democratize, while China's minorities grew restive. When the government deployed the army to put down the demonstrations with lethal force, the domestic and international reaction was so overwhelmingly hostile that Tiananmen weakened the Communist mandate of heaven. Afterward, the government relied increasingly on Han nationalism to shore up its rule. This was displayed most visibly in the suppression of unrest in Xinjiang and Tibet and in relations with the West. Most gratifying to Chinese nationalism was the return of Hong Kong and Macao to Chinese sovereignty, marking the end of the treaty port system era.

Chapter 28 turns to problems of governance in the absence of a preeminent leader. Following the death of Deng Xiaoping, it was unclear whether the rapid economic growth rate could be maintained. The easy phase of economic reform had ended, leaving such intractable problems as overpopulation, money-losing state-run enterprises, environmental degradation, and water and energy shortages. While the September 2004 handover of power from Jiang Zemin to Hu Jintao was peaceful, Taiwan's comprehensive political reforms had resulted in full democratization in the 2000 presidential elections that brought the opposition party to power. Once again, comparisons between Taiwan and the PRC were unfavorable for China. PRC-ROC relations improved with greater governmental, commercial, and private contacts, but PRC arms acquisitions were increasingly tailored to a possible invasion of Taiwan.

Chronology

1942–4	First CCP Rectification Campaign
28 February 1947	Brutal suppression of an anti-Nationalist demonstration in Taiwan
1947–8	Second CCP Rectification Campaign
12 April 1949	Rent reduction for tenant farmers on Taiwan
21–30 September 1949	Chinese People's Political Consultative Conference opens in Beijing to establish the government
1 October 1949	Creation of the PRC with Mao as chairman and Zhou Enlai as premier
2 October 1949	Soviet Union recognizes the PRC
3 October 1949	United States continues to recognize the Nationalist government
10 December 1949	Chiang Kai-shek departs for Taiwan
16 December 1949	Mao arrives in Moscow
13 January 1950	Great Britain recognizes the PRC
14 February 1950	Sino-Soviet Friendship Treaty
25 June 1950	North Korea invades South Korea
27 June 1950	United States sends the Seventh Fleet to the Taiwan Strait
30 June 1950	Publication of the Land Reform Law
8 October 1950	China decides to intervene in the Korean War
21 February 1951	Publication of the law punishing counterrevolutionaries
1 December 1951	PLA enters Lhasa, the Tibetan capital
7 Dec. 1951–4 July 1952	Three-Antis Campaign
15 December 1951	Law on agricultural cooperatives
1 Feb. 1952–15 July 1952	Five-Antis Campaign
21 February 1952	Campaign against counterrevolutionaries
10 January 1953	Land redistribution on Taiwan, compensated for with stocks and bonds
16 December 1953	Law establishing agricultural production collectives

22

The Communist Victory

But Alas! Qin Shihuang and Han Wudi
Were lacking in literary grace,
And Tang Taizhong and Song Taizu
Had little poetry in their souls;
And Genghis Khan,
Proud Son of Heaven for a day,
Knew only shooting eagles, bow outstretched.
All are past and gone!
For truly great men
Look to this age alone.[1]

Mao Zedong, (1893–1976), comparing himself to the
five greatest emperors of the Qin, Han, Tang, Song,
and Mongol dynasties, respectively, 1936

The 1 October 1949 founding of the People's Republic of China did not resolve China's problems. As the Nationalist Party's survival on Taiwan inaugurated the era of two Chinas, Mao Zedong succeeded in reuniting North and South China and much of the Qing empire, with the two major exceptions of Outer Mongolia and Taiwan. This, and Nationalist control of the offshore islands of Jinmen and Mazu, which had always been considered an integral part of China and had never been ceded to Japan, denied Mao the total victory he sought and the unencumbered mandate from heaven this would have conferred. For Mao, the situation was dangerous, since he believed Chiang Kai-shek's many pronouncements that the Nationalist Party was awaiting an opportune moment to invade the mainland. The Communists had won the civil war but had yet to consolidate their political control throughout the country. They started with the economy through land reform and the nationalization of industry and commerce. This vulnerable period in CCP rule coincided with the honeymoon period of the Sino-Soviet alliance.

I. The Formation of the People's Republic of China

During the thirty-eight years since the fall of the Qing dynasty, China lacked a unified central government. The reunification of China was unexpected and, to a large degree, unwelcome to Stalin, whose diplomacy during the late 1940s had focused on playing the Nationalists and Communists off against each other. Instead of a weak China, which would remain dependent on Stalin, the creation of the People's Republic of China in 1949 implied a vigorous new Communist dynasty that might challenge Soviet leadership of the international Communist movement. For the first time since the death of the Qianlong emperor in the eighteenth century, China might consistently pursue an active and independent foreign policy. Such a state might follow China's traditional policy of regional hegemony, setting it on a collision course with Soviet ambitions.

The goals of eliminating any Nationalist remnants and reconstituting the Qing empire consumed China's leaders after the liberation. The Communist victory had been unprecedented in its rapidity: Between April 1949, when the PLA first crossed the Yangzi River, and October 1949, PLA forces moved along the eastern seaboard from Shanghai all the way to Guangzhou far more quickly than the Northern Expedition's reverse campaign in the 1920s. In December 1949, the PLA reached Chengdu, in Sichuan province, bordering on Tibet. This completed the reunification of the core provinces of Han China, albeit just two-fifths of the maximum extent of the old Qing empire.

After sending troops to Tibet in 1950, the PRC forced the Fourteenth Dalai Lama to sign a 1951 agreement acknowledging Chinese sovereignty. Many outsiders portrayed China's occupation of Tibet as an act of conquest and empire building, since the Tibetans were ethnically and culturally distinct from the Han Chinese, had been autonomous since 1911, and did not want to be reabsorbed into the Chinese empire. PRC leaders, however, considered Tibet to have been an integral part of China since the Yuan dynasty in the thirteenth century. But the invasion of Tibet eliminated a buffer zone between China and India and would later lead to tensions and war. The PRC acquired control over Xinjiang, an area constituting about one-sixth of the entire land mass of China, under murky circumstances. As Nationalist power imploded, Soviet influence over the breakaway East Turkestan Republic in Xinjiang grew. Over the summer of 1949, a Soviet plane carrying virtually all the leaders of the republic crashed, killing all on board, and in October 1949 the PLA marched into Urumchi, the capital of Xinjiang. By 1955, the PRC proclaimed Xinjiang as one of its autonomous regions. Reassertion of Han control greatly extended China's borders with the USSR. As in Tibet, these borders would become the site of a future border war.

Although the PRC managed to absorb all of Tibet, Xinjiang, and South China minus some offshore islands, it failed to achieve its objective of total reunification. The PLA was not able to take Outer Mongolia or Taiwan. Stalin was unwilling to discuss the former, so the Mongolian People's Republic remained part of the Soviet sphere of influence and the continuing object of Chinese irredentism. As for Taiwan, the Nationalist Party's survival potentially threatened the Communists' mandate of heaven. As long as Taiwan remained separate, it constituted an alternative to Communist rule. The Nationalists also retained a foothold close to the mainland by fortifying the offshore islands of Jinmen (Quemoy) and Mazu (Matsu).

During this period, there was minimal open factionalism or internal dissent within the CCP. Its main leaders—Mao Zedong, Zhou Enlai, Zhu De, Liu Shaoqi, Deng Xiaoping, Lin Biao, and Peng Dehuai—had known each other during the difficult years of the Long March and the Second Sino-Japanese War and had cooperated effectively to win the civil war. But the party had grown dramatically during this period, so that there were literally millions of new members. There was no guarantee that the new members all shared the political ideals of the CCP leadership. In the past, rectification campaigns had followed periods of rapid party growth. The term "rectification" referred to the correction of incorrect work styles. The Communists believed that those who called themselves Communists had to share the same political program. Those who did not should be expelled from the party lest

Mao Zedong's portrait hangs above the main gateway to the Forbidden City, right off Tiananmen Square, the same spot where the PRC was founded on 1 October 1949. According to Peking guidebooks from the late 1940s, Chiang Kai-shek's portrait hung at this very place until the Communist forces took it down and replaced it with Mao's portrait.

they corrupt it. This paralleled the Qing suppression of so-called heterodox sects.

This process began during the 1942–4 Rectification Campaign at Yan'an, when the CCP emphasized an ideological program known as Mao Zedong Thought in order to unify the party under Mao's leadership. The Rectification Campaign focused on educating new members, expelling those with differing ideas, and promoting reliable cadres. This campaign emphasized undermining those favoring a united front and opposing Mao's focus on the peasantry. Rectification was achieved through a combination of "thought reform," coercion, and executions. It was assumed that the unity of organization required the unity of thought. The campaign attempted to instill mass conformity in order to create a highly effective party organization capable of extending its rule throughout China.

In theory, rectification implied education, not coercion, and redemption, not punishment. The CCP wanted to avoid the brutality of the Stalinist purges. The emphasis on reeducation, not execution, as had been the case in the Soviet purges, was linked to Confucian traditions honoring education as the best way to produce model human behavior. Nevertheless, in practice, coercion, punishment, and execution played highly visible roles in China as well. In 1944, the party called off the campaign when it devolved into a witch hunt that created a climate of terror, described at the time as "excesses." Thereafter, each of Mao's mass movements included rectification campaigns that terrorized many innocent people. This tactic, however brutal, proved highly effective at making the party responsive to Mao and preventing the rise of potential rivals. The 1942–4 campaign increased Mao's personal power by eliminating Soviet-educated rivals.

From 1947 to 1948, a second Rectification Campaign changed the rural party organization and land reform. This took place at the turning point in the Chinese civil war. To win, the Communists needed a carefully crafted land program that would be sufficient to induce mass support but not so sweeping that it would alienate China's numerous small landowners. This campaign focused on the grassroots implementation of land reform. There was considerable tension in the party concerning the relative emphasis on ideological conformity versus economic efficiency. Mao emphasized the former, while his successor, Deng Xiaoping, would focus on the latter. The Korean War, which broke out in 1950, made both economic efficiency and ideological conformity essential for the survival of the CCP. (See the feature below.)

PEKING OPERA

While the CCP used the rectification campaigns to enforce ideological conformity among elites, it encouraged conformity from the grass roots through education and cultural events. Throughout the Chinese civil war, the Communists performed didactic plays before peasants and troops. They also relied on traditional cultural forms such as Peking opera, particularly during the Cultural Revolution.

In the West, Peking opera is the most famous form of Chinese opera. In China, Kunqu opera, which highlights the poetry of the Ming and Qing dynasties and greatly influenced Peking opera, is actually the most famous, while Guangzhou opera is widespread in South China and many expatriate Chinese communities. In addition, there are hundreds of other types, each differentiated by its instrumentation, music, and acting styles and the incorporation of the local dialect, local folk tales, and traditions.

Theater rapidly developed during the Yuan and particularly the Ming dynasty and increasingly emphasized multiple operatic roles. During the Qing dynasty, Hangzhou became the cultural center of opera until the Taiping Rebellion devastated the city. Peking opera originated with the eightieth birthday festivities for the Qianlong emperor in 1790, when performers presented the Anhui and Hubei operatic tradition that would evolve and dominate the repertoire performed in the capital to acquire the name "Peking opera." Among the most famous Qing-period operas is *The Peach Blossom Fan*.

While opera is a form of high culture in the Anglophone West, Chinese from all walks of life have enjoyed opera, which includes not only singing, acting, and Chinese instrumentation, but also dancing, mime, stylized movements, and acrobatics. The lack of props makes possible outdoor performances, so that performances typically took place in the village markets as well as in city theaters. The scripts were usually based on beloved folk tales, legends, or adaptations of literary classics such as the *Romance of the Three Kingdoms*.

The Communists tried to take over this art form to popularize their social programs, producing operas with highly didactic messages during the Chinese civil war and the Maoist era thereafter. This proved very effective in a country with a high illiteracy rate. Although Mao Zedong was a great opera fan, opera reforms starting in 1964 banned many traditional scripts, for instance ghost dramas, a genre based on the spirits of the unjustly killed avenging their deaths. His wife, Jiang Qing, became deeply involved in replacing the traditional repertoire with a heavy dose of communist iconography during the Cultural Revolution. Of the eight model plays that Jiang Qing selected, five were Peking operas.

In traditional Peking opera, there are four categories of characters: men, women, painted faces, and clowns. In keeping with China's civil-military traditions, the male characters fall into two types: scholar-officials and warriors, with the latter performing highly skilled acrobatics. A further division, reflecting China's Confucian traditions, is the segregation of those playing old men

Continued

Elaborate costumes and traditional music are just part of the Peking opera's repertoire, which can also include singing, dancing, and acrobatics. While Peking opera has 1,400 different distinct works, during the Cultural Revolution most were banned. Only during the 1980s was it once again acceptable to stage some of the other operas. Meanwhile, the Taiwanese government subsidized traditional Peking opera, although over time it became influenced by local Taiwanese opera styles.

versus young men. Traditionally, men also played female roles, which included elderly women, aristocrats, ladies' maids, warriors, and comedians. In keeping with Chinese traditions of *yin* and *yang*, painted faces and clown roles represented opposites, with the former including heroes and demons. Each role incorporated a familiar style of makeup, mime, costuming, and singing that allowed audiences immediately to recognize the type of character. The stories of Chinese opera were part of the social fabric of the local community.

II. Land Reform and Agrarian Policies

Mao regarded collectivization as essential to prevent a reversion to capitalism. According to Communist ideology, peasants were a backward-thinking class with an inherent desire for private property, which created the basis for the social inequalities that underlay capitalism. Stalinist ideology emphasized the rapid development of heavy industry funded by resources extracted from the countryside. During the civil war, Mao had been flexible on reform in order not to create too many enemies at once. After he defeated the Nationalists, he could focus on restructuring the countryside. (See Table 22.1.) In a manner that closely paralleled the Soviet Union's mixed economy under the New Economic Policy during the 1920s and its forced-draft industrialization of the 1930s, Mao intended to harness all of China's resources to transform it into a great power capable of protecting its vital interests and projecting its power abroad. This required major infrastructure investments, a strong military, and loyalty throughout the population.

Mao in his Common Program of October 1949 called for a mixed capitalist-socialist economy to restore production and rebuild China after so many decades of warfare. During this early period, he sought to use the expertise of businesspeople to make the economy function. Chinese who had been educated abroad were urged to come home to help rebuild. In the countryside, Mao initially took a comparatively benign approach to former landlords, demanding the parceling out of their land but generally not their execution. The Communists seized the historic moment following their victory in the civil war to ride the wave of popular expectations for a better

Table 22.1   Primary Land Reform Laws

Date	Law	Significance
4 May 1946	CCP announces plans for land reform	Garners growing rural support
17 July–13 September 1947	CCP National Land Conference	Helps undermine Nationalist support
10 October 1947	Outline Land Law for China	Mandates land redistribution
1947–9	Various moderations of land reform allowing for greater private ownership	Garners support of owners of small properties, especially in South China
30 June 1950	Land reform law	Establishes peasant associations
15 December 1951	Draft law on agricultural cooperatives	Establishes peasant cooperatives
16 December 1953	Law on agricultural production collectives	Establishes production collectives
17–30 August 1958	Creation of people's communes	Causes all land ownership to revert to the state
18–22 December 1978	Deng Xiaoping's agricultural reforms	Dismantles Mao's collectivization

Note: The CCP took a flexible approach to land reform to win the civil war (see the boxed area above). Upon victory, however, it eliminated all private land ownership. After three decades of rural stagnation and the death of Mao Zedong, Deng Xiaoping reversed the collectivization of the countryside (see the shaded area above). Thereafter, agricultural production boomed.

future to implement far-reaching reforms before people reverted to old patterns of behavior. The first order of business was the restoration of law and order in the countryside after decades of warfare. The rural population supported the Communists' campaign of bandit suppression, which was largely successful by 1951. This entailed the growth of local organizations such as people's militia units. The Communists simultaneously set up village-level peasant associations to implement popular party programs, such as highly progressive tax rates, the land-to-the-tiller program carefully matching land parcels with the individuals who worked them, the promotion of mutual aid teams to share equipment and know-how, and credit cooperatives to provide wide access to credit.

The Communists established village-level offices for the CCP, the Woman's Association, and the Youth League. By empowering the formerly powerless—the rural poor, women, and the young—the CCP created a majority favoring its land redistribution programs and capable, by sheer numbers, of enforcing the party's will on the former rural elite, who stood to lose everything. Upward mobility for the many trumped downward mobility for the few.

It took time for all these pieces to fall in place, so land redistribution occurred gradually. The Land Reform Law of June 1950 encouraged poor peasants to organize peasant associations, which then classified each rural resident as a (1) landlord, (2) rich peasant, (3) middle peasant, (4) poor peasant, or (5) landless laborer. Not surprisingly, poor peasants willingly took the lead. During so-called struggle sessions, they pressured landlords, rich peasants, and even middle peasants to give up their land. In this initial phase of the land redistribution process, completed by October 1952, five to fifteen households joined together into a collective.

Although the Communists claimed that they were bringing economic justice to rural China, the actual situation was more complex. Class relations were not fixed; rather, family prosperity changed with each generation. A Chinese proverb says: "No family remains rich for three generations; no family remains poor for three generations." Under the best circumstances, there was not enough land to employ the entire rural population as farmers. Years of warfare had created enormous rural grievances. Warfare and inequities in the distribution of land greatly heightened these preexisting tensions. The Nationalists had done little to address the rural crisis, but had increasingly dragooned rural youth into the army, had relied on confiscatory rural taxation to fund that army, and had done little to curtail abuses inflicted by their followers on the struggling rural population.

Land ownership, however, was not particularly concentrated compared to that in Russia or Europe, where Marx had drawn his original models. In South and Central China, the Nationalist heartland, land holdings were generally small but intensively farmed. (See Table 21.2 and Table 21.3.) North China, which was outside the Nationalist sphere of influence, had the most unequal land distribution, but such land distributions were not fixed. Nevertheless, the Communists adhered to the Marxist paradigm of rigid class membership that justified brutality against the prosperous. With the onset of the Korean War, Mao wanted to remove any remaining internal enemies. By the completion of land reform, 2–5 million landowners had been executed and land ownership became a capital crime.

According to the Resolution on Mutual Aid and Cooperatives for Agricultural Production adopted in December 1951, after the completion of land reform, peasant families could join together to form collectives. Referred to as Agricultural

Producers' Cooperatives, they jointly made labor assignments and shared equipment. By 1953, about one-sixth of the peasant population worked on collectives. Over time, the size of the government-sponsored cooperatives rose from a dozen families, to 50 or more in 1953, to as many as 300 in 1955. That year the government monopolized the purchase of agricultural products and ensured the distribution of food to urban areas by a system of urban rationing. Mao intended to take advantage of economies of scale in order to maximize production while minimizing costs. This had certain parallels with the USSR's forced collectivization of the 1930s, which facilitated tax collection and also streamlined the Communist government's rural bureaucracy.

The final phase of collectivization took place faster than Mao expected. In July 1955, 16.9 million peasant households worked on collective farms. Five months later, the number had risen to 70 million households, or approximately 60 percent of the country's 110 million rural households. By 1956, collectivization had been completed, although peasants retained title to their land. With the creation of People's Communes during the Great Leap Forward, land ownership reverted to the communes controlled by local governments. Despite these agricultural reforms, average grain yields in the 1949–58 period were lower than those in the 1931–7 period. Yet, the 1930s encompassed years of civil war.

Mao's decision to collectivize agriculture reversed his promise of land ownership to the dispossessed made during the civil war. The age-old peasant dream of land ownership became more elusive than ever. Collectivization allowed the Communists to do what no other Chinese government had ever done: Central administration penetrated deep into the countryside to control the peasantry from the bottom up. Mao placed the entire rural population in CCP-run organizations, taking over their very places of work. Control over the countryside enabled Beijing to collect more taxes, which it used to rebuild the country's neglected infrastructure, finance the military, and develop heavy industry. The result was a massive transfer of wealth from rural to urban China.

Membership and status within the new Communist-sponsored organizations depended on class background, with the promotion of poor peasants to positions of local authority. China, far from becoming a classless society, became a finely graded hierarchy where access to employment, social services, education, consumer products, and party membership depended on heredity and social class. Anyone opposing Communist rule became a class enemy and risked imprisonment, if not execution. Although Mao attacked Confucianism, he reestablished an equally hierarchical social order.

Collectivization undermined the traditional landlord *guanxi* system that had formerly controlled rural life. A new class of Communist cadres replaced the traditional rural elite, on whose *guanxi* networks warlordism had depended. In doing so, the Communists simultaneously destroyed the old China that they so detested and rooted out the last remnants of Nationalist influence. But the Communists did not get rid of *guanxi*; rather, they made it the monopoly of the CCP. Rule remained personalistic but now focused on those constituting the vanguard of the revolution.

III. The Nationalization of Industry and Commerce

The nationalization of private property occurred much earlier and more rapidly in urban than rural areas. When the Communists took power in 1949, only one-fifth of the Chinese economy was under direct or indirect state control. The Communists quickly instituted a system of joint state management of private enterprises. Almost overnight the government nationalized heavy industry. (See Table 22.2.) Foreign trade,

Table 22.2   Speed of Economic Reorganization
Changing Proportion of Five Economic Components of GNI, 1952–66
(total value of GNI = 100)

Year	State	Cooperative	State-Private	Capitalist	Individual
1952	19.1	1.5	0.7	6.9	71.8
1953	23.9	2.5	0.9	7.9	64.8
1954	26.8	4.8	2.1	5.3	61.0
1955	28.0	14.1	2.8	3.5	51.6
1956	32.2	53.7	7.3	—	7.1
1966	33.2	56.4	7.6	—	2.8

Note: The shaded area shows the period when individuals and capitalist enterprises accounted for more than half of the gross national income (GNI). Note the rapidity of the nationalization and collectivization process.

Source: Ting Gong, *The Politics of Corruption in Contemporary China: An Analysis of Policy Outcomes* (Westport, CT: Praeger, 1994), 80.

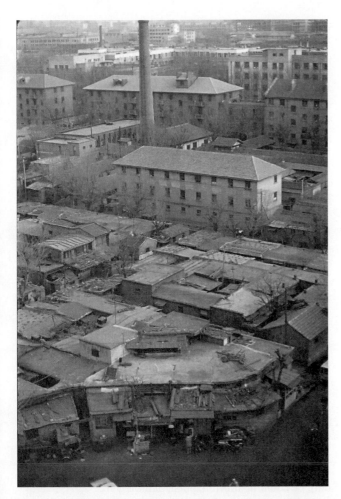

After the nationalization of most large industries during the early 1950s, factories and urban housing existed side by side. Adopting a variation of the *baojia* system, work units (called *danwei*) provided a worker's housing, food, and salary and so could be used to ensure loyalty to the state.

banking, the transportation system, and most large-scale commerce all became state monopolies. After forty years of waiting, the central government finally nationalized the railway system. By 1953, the state jointly managed one-third of all businesses, and only one-sixth of the businesses remained completely independent of state control. Industrial development became a national priority. These policies helped restore China's urban economy, but the demands of the Korean War would soon stretch the economy to its limits.

The government instituted a policy of "peaceful transformation," entailing the selection of industries for a joint state-private management scheme. This plan had many parallels with earlier foreign-operated joint management companies, in that Beijing retained majority control while the former owners remained in a managerial capacity. For the time being, the former owners, in return for their cooperation, received a nominal fixed return on their investment. These policies resulted in the de facto nationalization of Chinese industry, but their gradual implementation minimized any visible social friction. Many businesspeople were eager to see China prosper and thought that the CCP might solve the problem of China's terrible instability, so there was no large-scale organized opposition to this policy, which allowed Mao slowly to erode the power of the country's business elite.

The Korean War provided a pretext, accepted by the population, for extreme measures. The CCP took advantage of this opportunity to prevent the reemergence of competing economic centers that might challenge Communist rule. In December 1950, during the "Resist America and Aid Korea" campaign, the Communist government froze foreign business assets, charging many businesspeople with tax evasion. Payment of inflated tax bills forced some to sell out at artificially low prices. The new government required most other foreigners, including teachers, missionaries, and aid workers, to leave China at this time, cutting off virtually all contacts with the non-Communist outside.

Soon afterward, the "Suppression of Counterrevolutionaries" campaign began in 1951. Millions of Chinese were accused of collaborating with the Nationalists. Accused spies were arrested, and eventually hundreds of thousands, or perhaps even millions, of people were imprisoned or executed. Businesspeople were considered particularly untrustworthy, and Beijing nationalized their businesses. The transformation from private to state-owned industry created new problems: Like the former imperial officials, some Communist cadres were tempted to use their new powers for personal gain. The campaign also targeted labor unions in an effort to maximize essential military production. The CCP promised workers that the state would better protect their rights than self-interested labor leaders. Similar to the *baojia* system, people were organized by *danwei*, or work units, under the control of loyal Communists.

PRC entry into the Korean War also created an imperative for the CCP to consolidate control over the home front via the equivalent of a third Rectification Campaign. In 1950, the CCP focused on streamlining local administration in order to restore production and cultivate popular support. This second stage entailed a three-pronged attack aimed at cadres, the bourgeoisie, and intellectuals. The Three-Antis Campaign from late 1951 until mid-1952 sought to root out corruption, waste, and bureaucracy by removing corrupt Communist officials who profited from business connections. In particular, it targeted former Nationalist officials, who were generally removed from office once they trained their replacements. Since it was unclear whether the Nationalists would enter the Korean War as part of the UN force, the campaign sought to root out potential spies in wartime. It also attempted to eliminate violations of the law and of party discipline.

The Five-Antis Campaign against bribery, tax evasion, fraud, theft of public property, and the use of state secrets for personal enrichment targeted businesspeople charged with tax evasion and cheating the government. The campaign, ostensibly meant to eliminate corruption in the private sector, in reality eliminated what was left of the business community. Business leaders were forced in struggle sessions to confess real or imaginary crimes and to denounce each other. They were also subject to arbitrary and heavy fines. In the new registry of class backgrounds composed of sixty different categories, businesspeople found themselves at the top of a list of those considered objectionable. Children of businesspeople were also singled out. Far from establishing a classless society, the Communists created a caste system where birth, not merit, determined status.

For intellectuals, there was a separate campaign of thought reform. Intellectuals had been active in past revolutionary movements, so that the Communists believed it essential to secure their loyalty. In combination with collectivization, this attack on flawed cadres, businesspeople, intellectuals, and Nationalist remnants effectively consolidated Communist control over China. The government replaced private industry and entrepreneurs in most cities and towns with state-owned enterprises and businesses managed by employee-worker committees. These reforms produced a dramatic surge in state revenue, which the state used to fund the military and the CCP. With loans from the Soviet Union and the diversion of money from rural to urban areas, heavy industry became the focus of China's first five-year plan. Industrial production soared.

IV. Diplomatic Isolation and the Sino-Soviet Alliance

After 1949 only a few Western countries, such as Great Britain, and a somewhat larger number of Asian countries, such as neighboring India, recognized the PRC. Britain did so out of concern for its vulnerable colony of Hong Kong. The United States, however, refused and imposed a trade embargo. This left Mao with only the Soviet Union for assistance. During this honeymoon period of the Sino-Soviet alliance, Mao preferred isolation from the West in order to cleanse China of imperial influence and to eliminate any remaining domestic enemies. As long as both China and the Soviet Union focused on recovering from wartime devastation, their interests remained more or less compatible. Stalin immediately recognized China's new

government, but given his country's enormous commitments in Eastern Europe, he provided less help than desired.

For years Stalin had turned down Mao's repeated requests to travel to Moscow, but once Mao assumed power, Stalin relented. This was Mao's first trip abroad. He arrived in Moscow in December 1949 for eight weeks of talks. The two leaders agreed on the need for mutual defense. Stalin appeared willing to help Mao create a modern air force and navy. They also discussed whether to renegotiate the terms of the 1945 Yalta Agreement and the Sino-Soviet Friendship Treaty signed by the Nationalists. For Mao, this question was important not only to determine the status of Manchuria and Xinjiang, where the USSR had acquired important privileges, but also to determine the future of Outer Mongolia, which the Nationalists had granted formal independence. Stalin rejected modification of the Yalta Agreement, while Mao agreed to respect the terms of the 1945 friendship treaty but hoped that particular issues would be renegotiated.

This setup gave Stalin enormous diplomatic leverage. Simply by refusing to discuss certain issues, he could retain the status quo that favored Soviet interests; this technique had much in common with the Soviet diplomacy of the 1920s, when a similar refusal to negotiate new treaties enabled the retention of the old tsarist terms. In 1950 Stalin avoided discussing Outer Mongolia altogether, which by default remained in the Soviet sphere of influence, while the Soviet troops stationed in Outer Mongolia posed a potential security risk to Beijing, located just one day's drive from the Sino-Mongolian border. But given Mao's diplomatic isolation, he could ill afford to alienate the USSR.

Mao needed a security pact with Stalin to deter Japan and the United States. As Mao and Stalin shared an interest in keeping the United States off the Asian mainland, they coordinated to support North Korean ambitions to reunify the Korean Peninsula. On 7 January 1950, the PRC and North Korea signed a series of agreements and during late January met to discuss military matters. Beijing quickly agreed to repatriate the battle-hardened Korean troops who had participated in the Manchurian phase of the Chinese civil war. The USSR and the PRC signed their own thirty-year friendship treaty on 14 February 1950, almost five years to the day after the Yalta Treaty, thus tacitly recognizing its terms. The USSR agreed to provide China with a military alliance, credits of $300 million, and military and industrial advisers. During the 1950s, it sent thousands of advisers. It also agreed in principle to return Lüshun (Port Arthur) and Dalian (Dairen). Both pledged to fight along side the other in the event of a third-party attack.

Despite official Nationalist and Communist public pronouncements to the contrary, the USSR retained the tsarist unequal-treaty regime, including such privileges as extraterritoriality and retention of the former tsarist concessions, most notably the Chinese Eastern Railway. Extraterritoriality and concessions were two of the most resented features of Western imperialism. Conversely, the CCP's primary foreign enemies, the Western powers, had given up their privileged positions in China by 1943; the Western exceptions to this generalization were British Hong Kong and Portuguese Macao, which remained colonies until 1997 and 1999, respectively. While PRC propaganda sheets designated the United States as the key international foe, Washington had never maintained concessions and so had nothing to return. Rather, the U.S. government had promoted the Open Door Policy to halt China's division into spheres of influence.

V. Land Reform on Taiwan

Japan renounced its sovereignty over Taiwan at the end of World War II, while the United States facilitated the evacuation of Nationalists troops to the island. Unlike mainland China's, Taiwan's economy had not been shattered. The Japanese had maintained stability during their rule, and the U.S. bombing campaign to defeat Japan had largely bypassed the island. When the first Nationalist troops arrived in October 1945, they encountered immediate problems with the local population, many of whom did not feel a common identity with the Nationalist refugees from the Asian mainland. Most educated Taiwanese used Japanese. Although they also spoke a Chinese dialect, it was the South China language of Fujian province, which was unintelligible to speakers of the North China language of Mandarin or to Chiang's allies from Shanghai or Guangzhou.

A major anti-Nationalist uprising broke out on 28 February 1947, the so-called February 28 Incident, during a police crackdown on cigarette smuggling. Investigators tried to confiscate one woman's entire supply; she resisted; one of the policemen hit her with the butt of his pistol. One thing led to another, with riots erupting in Taipei, its port city of Keelung (Jilong), and then spread to other cities throughout Taiwan. These riots resulted in the death or injury of approximately 1,000 recent immigrants from the mainland. The ensuing government repression caused the death or injury of over 8,000 Taiwanese. In sharp contrast to Nationalist practices on the mainland, which tended to ignore such incidents, this time the embattled leadership concluded that the army general in charge of suppressing the unrest had used excessive force and subsequently had him executed.

The Nationalist Party had learned certain lessons from its defeat on the mainland. It was well aware of the precariousness of its situation. While it monopolized politics on the national level until the 1980s, it held local elections starting in 1946 and elections for the provincial assembly starting in 1951. Thus, the Nationalist Party early on in Taiwan created a hybrid government that mixed elements of a democracy with its autocratic one-party rule. Government studies concluded that the civil war had been lost because of widespread corruption and hyperinflation that destroyed public support. The solution on Taiwan would be economic growth through price stability and land reform.

The Nationalist Party embarked on land reform in Taiwan in 1948, with the sale of public land that had formerly belonged to Japanese landlords, and carried out additional land sales in 1952–8. In April 1949, another land reform law mandated rent reduction for tenant farmers, previously set at 37.5 percent of the yearly crop. These reforms caused land prices to plunge, which enabled the Nationalist Party to adopt a land-to-the-tiller program in 1953. This program required landlords to sell land to their tenants at artificially low rates. Between 1953 and 1955, the number of individual landholders increased from just over 400,000 families to almost 600,000 families. As a result, the percentage of farmers on Taiwan owning land rose from 25 to 35 percent.

Land reform was not accomplished without bloodshed: Taiwanese landowners were no more eager to give up their holdings than were those on the mainland. But politically, land reform was more feasible on Taiwan than on the mainland because the Nationalists were redistributing land not of their own elite, but of the Taiwanese, and possessed an army to implement the program. Expropriated landlords received bonds that most owners assumed would soon become worthless, but economic growth in Taiwan eventually made the bonds very valuable. As a result, land reform permanently reduced the economic and political influence of landlords, made land available to recent arrivals from the mainland, and allowed the Nationalists to rule successfully. It also removed one of the major sources of economic inequality in Taiwan. Memories of this bloody era still linger.

Meanwhile, the Nationalist Party imposed tight controls on speculation, especially in the sale of rice, the main food staple. In this reform as well, it relied on earlier precedents. In particular, a January 1946 reform created a provincial food bureau to ensure an adequate supply of rice. These controls enabled the Nationalist Party to guarantee food supplies during its precarious early years on Taiwan. Nationalist officials even received a rice credit as part of their yearly salary.

For industrial development, the Nationalists focused on an import-substitution and value-added strategy. They erected a tariff wall to protect infant industries in order to substitute locally made consumer goods for imported ones. In addition, they sought to develop export industries to profit from value added to raw materials being processed. In the early years, Taiwan focused on the development of light industry and the production of consumer goods that would most rapidly improve the local standard of living. It would not focus on heavy industry until the 1960s. These economic policies stood in stark contrast to the Soviet model for industrial development followed by mainland China, emphasizing heavy industry and the production of war materiel over consumer goods.

All of these early political and economic reforms among Taiwan's 6 million people helped ease the dislocations from the sudden influx of 600,000 Nationalist soldiers and another 600,000 refugees in 1949. With such a large military, Chiang Kai-shek could control domestic politics. After the outbreak of the Korean War, U.S. purse strings reopened. In 1951, U.S. aid to Taiwan amounted to 10 percent of the island's entire GNP. Many Taiwanese political and scientific leaders went to the United States for advanced degrees, often in the sciences and engineering.

The Communists intended to retake Taiwan soon after the liberation of Central and South China. Prior to the outbreak of the Korean War, Washington anticipated this eventuality and had not intended to intervene. The eruption of the Korean War changed the situation. In 1950, the Truman administration and the Democratic Party were reeling from Republican charges spearheaded by Senator Joseph McCarthy of having "lost" China to communism. With the North Korean invasion of South Korea, Truman appeared to be on the verge of losing a second Asian country to communism in less than a year, so he immediately intervened in the Korean War and sent the Seventh Fleet to the Taiwan Strait. Henceforth, the United States strove to prevent a mainland invasion of Taiwan, which gave the Nationalists a much-needed breathing space.

In contrast to the PRC's rejection of Han traditions and Western liberalism, Taiwan became a unique hybrid of Confucian China, Meiji Japan, and U.S. scientific education. It attempted to infuse Confucian ethical values into its primary educational system, to follow the example of Meiji Japan to work within the international economic and legal systems, and to send students to the United States to study in its graduate programs. Taiwan's economic growth took off while the Communists became consumed by political campaigns, so that by the 1980s the GNP of the tiny island was approximately half that of the huge mainland, creating an astronomical difference in per capita standards of living. Meanwhile, Taiwanese political leaders continued to move the government slowly toward democracy. The so-called Taiwan Miracle had begun.

Conclusions

With the Nationalist Party on Taiwan, an uncertain alliance with the USSR to the north and northwest, and diplomatic isolation from most Western countries, the CCP had to solve China's problems largely on its own. As a first step, Mao began the process of creating cooperatives, collectives, and peasant communes in order to transfer wealth from rural to urban China to fund heavy industry. Land reform entailed the executions of millions of former landowners. The CCP nationalized much of the urban private sector with the establishment of state monopolies on banking, transportation, and commerce.

Simultaneously, Mao launched the Three- and Five-Antis Campaigns aimed at consolidating Communist control over its own cadres, Nationalist remnants, businesspeople, and intellectuals. The political campaigns resulted in the expulsion of 10 percent of the party membership and the execution of hundreds of thousands, and possibly of millions. (See Table 27.1.) Mao's coercive approach to dissent and his elimination of entire social groups was in keeping with China's ancient Legalist traditions, in which state interests were paramount. His persecution of those labeled as counterrevolutionaries paralleled the Qing suppression of heterodox sects.

Meanwhile, on Taiwan, the Nationalist government-in-exile implemented policies that, if adopted in China immediately after World War II, might have saved the regime. In particular, the Nationalists implemented a comprehensive land reform package in order to equalize holdings. With the reorganization of rural Taiwan and the development of the existing Japanese colonial industrial base, the Nationalists thrived. For mainland China, Chiang Kai-shek continued to portray Taiwan as a viable alternative to Communist rule. The accidental amalgam in Taiwan of Han culture with Japanese organization and U.S. technology proved to be highly successful.

BIBLIOGRAPHY

Bennett, Gordon. *Yundong: Mass Campaigns in Chinese Communist Leadership.* Berkeley: University of California Press, 1976.
Chao, Kang. *Agricultural Production in Communist China, 1949–1965.* Madison: University of Wisconsin Press, 1971.
———*Capital Formation in Mainland China, 1952–1965.* Berkeley: University of California Press, 1974.
Ch'en, Theodore Hsi-en. *Thought Reform of the Chinese Intellectual.* Hong Kong: Hong Kong University Press, 1960.

Copper, John F. *Taiwan: Nation-State or Province?* 4th ed. Boulder, CO: Westview Press, 2003.

Dai Qing. *Wang Shiwei and "Wild Lilies": Rectification and Purges in the Chinese Communist Party 1942–1944*. Edited by David E. Apter et al., translated by Nancy Liu et al., and compiled by Song Jinshou. Armonk, NY: M. E. Sharpe, 1994.

Dreyer, June Teufel. *China's Forty Millions: Minority Nationalities and National Integration in the People's Republic of China*. Cambridge, MA: Harvard University Press, 1976.

Dittmer, Lowell. *China's Continuous Revolution: The Post-Liberation Epoch, 1949–1981*. Berkeley: University of California Press, 1987.

Domes, Jürgen. *The Internal Politics of China 1949–1972*. Translated by Rüdiger Machetzki. New York: Praeger, 1973.

———*Socialism in the Countryside: Rural Societal Politics of the People's Republic of China, 1945–1979*. Translated by Margitta Wendling. London: C. Hurst, 1980.

Friedman, Edward, Paul G. Pickowicz, Mark Selden, and Kay Ann Johnson. eds. *Chinese Village, Socialist State*. New Haven, CT: Yale University Press, 1991.

Griffin, P. *Chinese Communist Treatment of Counterrevolutionaries*. Princeton, NJ: Princeton University Press, 1976.

Gurley, John G. *China's Economy and the Maoist Strategy*. New York: Monthly Review Press, 1966.

Harding, Henry. *Organizing China: The Problem of Bureaucracy, 1949–1976*. Stanford, CA: Stanford University Press, 1981.

Ho, Ping-t'i. *Studies on the Population of China, 1368–1953*. Cambridge, MA: Harvard University Press, 1959.

Kirby, Richard J. R. *Urbanization in China: Town and Country in a Developing Economy, 1949–2000 A.D.* New York: Columbia University Press, 1974.

Lardy, Nicholas R. *Agriculture in China's Modern Economic Development*. Cambridge: Cambridge University Press, 1983.

———and Kenneth Lieberthal, eds. *Chen Yun's Strategy for China's Development*. Armonk, NY: M. E. Sharpe, 1983.

Liu, Ta-chung. *The Economy of the Chinese Mainland: National Income and Economic Development, 1933–1959*. Princeton, NJ: Princeton University Press, 1965.

Oi, Jean C. *State and Peasant in Contemporary China: The Political Economy of Village Government*. Berkeley: University of California Press, 1989.

Richardson, Philip. *Economic Change in China, c. 1800–1950*. Cambridge: Cambridge University Press, 1999.

Rubinstein, Murray A., ed. *Taiwan: A New History*. Armonk, NY: M. E. Sharpe, 1999.

Shue, Vivienne. *Peasant China in Transition: The Dynamics of Development toward Socialism, 1949–1956*. Berkeley: University of California Press, 1980.

Teiwes, Frederick C. "Establishment and Consolidation of the New Regime." In *The Cambridge History of China*, vol. 14, edited by Roderick MacFarquhar and John K. Fairbank, 51–143. Cambridge: Cambridge University Press, 1987.

———*Politics and Purges in China: Rectification and the Decline of Party Norms, 1950–1965*. 2nd ed. Armonk, NY: M. E. Sharpe, 1993.

———and Warren Sun, eds. *The Politics of Agricultural Cooperativiztion in China: Mao, Deng Zihui, and the "High Tide" of 1955*. Armonk, NY: M. E. Sharpe, 1993.

Tsou, Tang. *Embroilment over Quemoy: Mao, Chiang, and Dulles*. Salt Lake City: University of Utah, 1959.

Wakeman, Frederic, Jr. *History and Will: Philosophical Perspectives of Mao Tse-tung's Thought*. Berkeley: University of California Press, 1973.

White, Lynn T., III. *Careers in Shanghai: The Social Guidance of Personal Energies in a Developing Chinese City, 1949–1966*. Berkeley: University of California Press, 1978.

Wong, John, *Land Reform in the People's Republic of China: Institutional Transformation in Agriculture*. New York: Praeger, 1973.

Yang, Martin M. C. *Socioeconomic Results of Land Reform in Taiwan*. Honolulu: University of Hawaii Press, 1970.

NOTES

1. Mao Zedong, "Snow," in Ross Terrill, *Mao: A Biography*, rev. ed. (Stanford, CA: Stanford University Press, 1999), 170; Geremie R. Barmé, *Shades of Mao: The Posthumous Cult of the Great Leader* (Armonk, NY: M. E. Sharpe, 1996), 3–4.

Chronology

1946–54	French Indochina War
15 August 1948	Establishment of the Republic of Korea
2 September 1948	Establishment of the Democratic People's Republic of Korea
14 February 1950	Sino-Soviet Friendship Treaty
3 March–23 April 1950	Campaign to take Hainan Island
25 June 1950	North Korean invasion of South Korea
27 June 1950	U.S. sends Seventh Fleet to the Taiwan Strait
15 September 1950	Inch'ŏn landing
18 October 1950	Mao Zedong orders army across the Korean border
21 February 1951	Publication of the law punishing counterrevolutionaries
10 July 1951	Korean War armistice talks begin
8 December 1951	Beginning of Three Antis Campaign
1 February 1952	Beginning of Five Antis Campaign
31 December 1952	Soviet Union returns railway concessions to China
15 February 1953	Decision for rapid collectivization
5 March 1953	Joseph Stalin dies
15 March 1953	Soviet agreement to help build 141 projects in China
27 July 1953	End of the Korean War
20 July 1954	Geneva agreement ending the French Indochina War
1953–7	First Five-Year Plan in China
25 May 1955	Soviet return of naval base at Lüshun, Manchuria

23

The Korean War

What miracle is there that we cannot create?
Which enemy is there whom we cannot defeat?
Ah, flood, don't dream of riding
Higher and faster than the dike we build.

Now that the flood bows before us,
Like some of these stubborn people who,
Having received a heavy blow from us,
Just begin to rub their eyes with their hands.

Look, what a great change
Has already occurred on our Chinese soil;
Look, how we six hundred million people
So closely share our hardships and our fortune![1]

He Qifang (1912–1977), poet, journalist,
literary critic, veteran (1954)

In the nineteenth century, Korea was surrounded by three empires—those of China, Japan, and Russia—whose power required the Korean government to ally with at least one of them in order to survive the intrusions of the others. Until the forcible Japanese annexation of Korea in 1910, China had been the patron of choice. In the second half of the twentieth century, however, the Cold War transformed the international alliance system into a Western bloc and a Communist bloc. The end of World War II marked the beginning of an era of unprecedented U.S. involvement in East Asia, including the two major hot wars of the Cold War: the Korean War (1950–3) and the Vietnam War (1961–75). In the case of Korea, Japan's defeat in World War II left a power vacuum and competing governments emerging in the North and South: North Korea was under Kim Il Sung and allied with the Soviet Union, while South Korea was under Syngman Rhee and looked to the United States for support. On 25 June 1950, North Korea launched a

full-scale armored invasion of South Korea. U.S. influence at the United Nations was at its height, and a massive UN intervention made Korea a major theater of the Cold War and the test case for the postwar U.S. strategy of the containment of communism. The United States provided enormous military aid to South Korea, including combat forces, which prompted Chinese intervention and resulted in a stalemate. For Stalin, the Korean War seemed a low-risk venture to exclude the United States from the northeastern Asian mainland while tying down both the United States and China and allowing the USSR a breathing space to consolidate its control over Eastern Europe.

I. The Outbreak of the Korean War

The end of World War II left Korea divided along the 38th parallel into Soviet and U.S. occupation zones. The Korean people shared great bitterness over the Japanese colonial experience but lacked a common positive vision. Communist influence was quite strong in North Korea, with the return of the many Koreans who had served with the Communists in the Chinese civil war and resisted the Japanese occupation in Manchuria and Korea; Kim Il Sung had also received military training in the USSR. Yet, Korea's large Christian population created potential ties with the West.

Because the two zones could not agree on the form of government for a unified Korea, each zone established its own, creating a Communist North and an authoritarian anti-Communist South. As in China, Washington hoped to form a coalition government. But Syngman Rhee and Kim Il Sung refused to negotiate in good faith.

The Soviets assumed a military solution and had armed North Korea accordingly, while the United States kept South Korea militarily weak to prevent it from invading the North. During a UN-sponsored vote in May 1948, which the North Korean government boycotted, the South Koreans elected the First National Assembly. Formal establishment of the Republic of Korea (ROK) with its capital in Seoul occurred on 15 August. On 2 September, the North Koreans proclaimed the Democratic People's Republic of Korea (DPRK) with its capital in P'yŏngyang. Although the United States helped create and train the South Korean Army, it did not provide modern weapons or an air force, and the leader of South Korea, Syngman Rhee, lacked military experience. Later that year, the United States withdrew its last two divisions from Korea.

During January 1950, Washington made two important foreign policy announcements concerning East Asia. First, Secretary of State Dean Acheson appeared to exclude Korea from the U.S. first line of defense in Asia, which he extended from the Aleutians through Japan and Okinawa and down to the Philippines. Second, the U.S. government indicated that it would not send any additional aid to the Nationalist government exiled on Taiwan. In March 1950, the PRC launched a successful amphibious invasion of Hainan Island, and the United States expected Taiwan to be next. Such actions suggested a U.S. retreat from the East Asian mainland.

Stalin had taken a special interest in North Korea after World War II. Although the Soviet-Korean border was only twelve miles long, the Korean Peninsula was a potential invasion route into the USSR from China as well as Japan. As protection, Stalin provided Kim Il Sung with the airplanes, tanks, and artillery that Syngman Rhee lacked. During Mao's trip to Moscow in January 1950, Kim Il Sung repeatedly sought Soviet approval for an invasion of South Korea. Stalin finally discussed it with Mao, who agreed to aid Kim.

A civil war had already broken out in Korea. During the last nine months of 1949 and the first half of 1950, there was constant fighting along the 38th parallel. Then in the early hours of 25 June 1950, the North launched a full-scale invasion. The South Korean Army had nothing to counter the Soviet-made tanks and rapidly retreated down the peninsula. The Western allies considered Stalin responsible for the attack, feared he would do likewise in Europe if unopposed in Korea, and so immediately banded together to support South Korea. Kim, Stalin, and Mao had all failed to understand both domestic politics in the United States and the Western alliance system. The Truman administration, faced with a communist victory in Korea so soon after Mao's triumph in China, concluded that it could not afford to lose a second Asian country to communism in less than a year. It organized a powerful UN-sponsored coalition to intervene quickly and massively to destroy Kim's predictions of a rapid victory. Kim had triggered a massive third-party intervention.

Washington also immediately deployed the Seventh Fleet to the Taiwan Strait to ensure that the Korean conflict was not a feint to cover a Chinese attack on Taiwan. Within a matter of days, the Cold War's territorial and political divisions of East Asia had been established. The PRC denounced the U.S. naval deployment as armed aggression, while Taiwan unexpectedly regained America's full support. Soon, U.S. money began to pour into the island and helped jump-start its economy, while China had to delay its own economic recovery to fight yet another war. Initially, the outbreak of hostilities played into the hands of Stalin, not Mao. Not only did the war reaffirm Stalin's position as the leader of the Communist bloc, but Chinese, not Soviet, soldiers tied down Western forces.

The war also temporarily pushed aside the myriad problems that would later undermine the Sino-Soviet alliance. Stalin hesitated to help Mao retake Taiwan. The island was too far afield from Stalin's continental interests, and a divided China meant a preoccupied China less likely to reestablish itself as a great power and challenge the Soviet Union. The Korean War also delayed discussions on the renunciation of Soviet concessions and privileges in China. These included the Soviet Navy's exclusive use of Lüshun as a warm-water port; the continued Soviet management of the Chinese Eastern Railway; and a long list of unresolved border issues including disputed islands in the Amur River, Soviet troop deployments in Xinjiang, and the contested status of Outer Mongolia.

Stalin left Mao to fight the UN, initially providing only minimal assistance. Eventually, troops from fifteen other nations—including Great Britain, France, Australia, New Zealand, Thailand, Canada, Greece, Turkey, and the Philippines—joined the UN effort. The bulk of the UN forces, however, were American and South Korean. Before the allied troops could reach the theater, North Korea capitalized on surprise to take 90 percent of the Korean Peninsula, surrounding UN forces in the vicinity of Pusan, on the extreme south. South Korea fought hard, but it lacked the artillery and tanks to halt the invasion.

II. The Chinese Decision to Intervene

On 15 September 1950, the UN counteroffensive began with General Douglas MacArthur's successful amphibious landing behind the North Korean lines at Inch'ŏn, the port

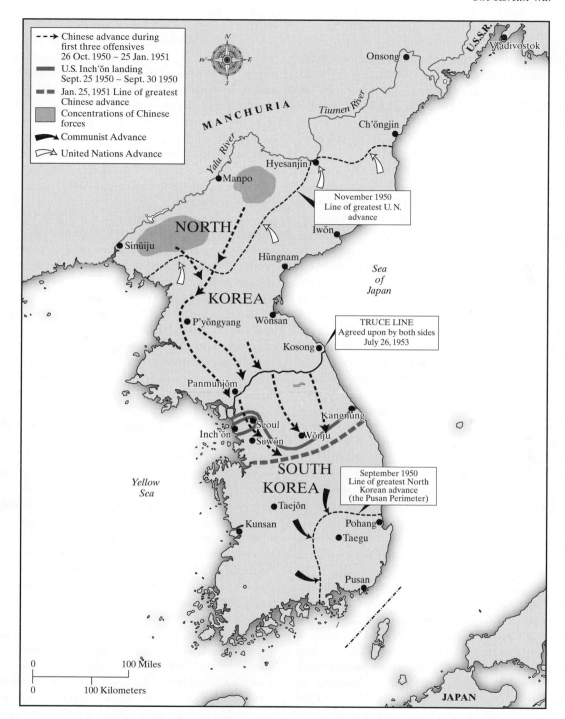

Map 23.1 Korean War (1950–3)

city of Seoul, and a coordinated counterattack from Pusan. (See Map 23.1.) UN forces sent the North Korean Army into a full retreat up the peninsula. On 30 September the South Korean Army crossed the 38th parallel, and on 19 October, UN forces occupied the North Korean capital of P'yŏngyang. With the success at Inch'ŏn, Washington expanded its policy objective from restoration of the prewar status quo to reunification of the peninsula under Syngman

Rhee. As soon as the South Korean Army crossed the 38th parallel and General MacArthur issued his ultimatum to Kim Il Sung demanding unconditional surrender, Mao decided to intervene. Under no circumstances would Mao acquiesce to a hostile great power forming a base on China's border. This would be true for Korea and later for Vietnam. The lessons of the recent war with Japan, whose continental base of operations had been in Korea, were simply too vivid.

Shortly after the Inch'ŏn landing, Mao had a senior military officer, commander Nie Rongzhen, and a senior civil official, Premier Zhou Enlai, relay a message: China would intervene if the UN forces crossed the 38th parallel. Washington dismissed this warning on the grounds that China was too weak to contemplate taking on the UN coalition. U.S. analysts grossly underestimated the value China put on maintaining a buffer zone in Korea. Mao equated victory in Korea with his own long-term political survival.

Upon the outbreak of the war, Mao immediately deployed a massive force in Manchuria, fearful that the war might spill across the border into China. Thereafter, he continued to send reinforcements. Once the Chinese invasion was underway, Stalin reneged on an earlier promise to provide the invading Chinese Army with air cover, resulting in high Chinese casualties. Stalin had been shocked by the massive U.S. intervention and feared further escalation. He did not want to risk Soviet pilots coming into contact with U.S. forces and possibly triggering a wider and far more dangerous global conflict. Mao believed he had little choice but to go ahead without the benefit of Soviet air cover, because he could not afford either to lose Korea or alienate the USSR, whose continued military assistance would be essential to prosecute the war. But this Soviet reversal of a firm promise angered Mao.

On 25 October, South Korean forces arrived at the Yalu River bordering China. Soon afterward, UN forces began to encounter occasional Chinese troops, but they ignored this warning sign of Chinese intervention. Between 14 October and 1 November 1950, tens of thousands of PLA soldiers secretly crossed the Yalu River. The ensuing counterattack took the UN forces by surprise. Intelligence estimates of the number of Chinese troops in North Korea in October 1950 varied between 15,000 and 20,000. Only much later were these numbers revised upward to 250,000, with as many as 700,000 Chinese troops operating in North Korea at the peak of the war.

The UN forces were soon in a retreat that lasted until January 1951 and ended only after they recrossed the 38th parallel and once again lost the city of Seoul to the Communist forces. While the PLA could claim victory, it came at a high cost, with hundreds of thousands of Chinese troops killed or wounded, including the death of Mao's son, Mao Anying. Chinese successes encouraged Mao to duplicate the earlier U.S. mistake by expanding his war objective from restoration of the prewar status quo to reunification of the peninsula under Kim Il Sung. The supreme commander of the Chinese forces, Peng Dehuai, disagreed, foreseeing that China lacked the logistical capabilities to sustain long supply lines deep into South Korea. Mao overruled him.

Mao also underestimated the lethality of U.S. air power and seemed to ignore the U.S. nuclear arsenal. Over the course of his career, Mao made a number of famous remarks minimizing the dangers of atomic and nuclear weapons. In the late 1950s, when Prime Minister Jawaharlal Nehru of India expressed his fear that an atomic war would annihilate mankind, Mao related, "I said that if the worst came to worst and half of mankind died, the other half would remain while imperialism would be razed to the ground and the whole world could become socialist."[2] Nehru's jaw dropped. Similar remarks later made to Stalin's successor, Nikita Khrushchev, had an identical effect.

Reunification exceeded the PLA's military capacity. UN forces orchestrated a counterattack on 25 January 1951 that routed the Communist forces. As Peng predicted, China's logistical lines proved inadequate. This time Chinese and North Korean troops fled north together. The UN attack shattered North Korean morale, and an intensive bombing campaign destroyed both the North Korean infrastructure and its ability to prosecute the war. Responsibility for continuing the war now fell directly on Mao's shoulders. He rejected advice to accept a UN-sanctioned cease-fire; rather, he demanded another major military victory. The Chinese forces were unable to retain their positions, however, and Seoul changed hands for the last time when it fell again to UN forces on 14 March.

Following China's intervention, General MacArthur openly defied Washington by arguing that Chinese territory should be attacked. On 11 April 1951, President Truman publicly relieved him of his position as Allied Commander of the UN forces in Korea. Initially, the deadlock continued unchanged under General Matthew B. Ridgway, as additional Chinese offensives in April and May 1951 also failed. In danger of being outflanked and surrounded, the Chinese troops retreated; the retreat quickly turned into a rout; and UN estimates of Chinese casualties were over 100,000. Following the defeat of China's fifth and sixth offensives, the

PLA assumed defensive positions just north of the 38th parallel.

By late January 1951, there were calls within both the Chinese and North Korean leadership to end the war. The UN subjected North Korea to a brutal bombing campaign; the Korean population was starving, and China had endured enormous casualties. According to Premier Zhou Enlai, the Korean War cost China more than the entire Second Sino-Japanese War. China had committed 73 percent of its military forces, devoted 60 percent of its railway boxcar capacity to the war, and delayed national reconstruction. Stalin, however, had no reason to quit. He suffered neither bombings nor casualties and was profiting from lucrative arms sales even while Mao was tying down the Western alliance far away from Stalin's concerns in Eastern Europe. The war also prevented China from rivaling Soviet power either along their long mutual border or within the international Communist movement.

The UN decision to halt its offensive in July 1951 to negotiate peace gave the Chinese the breathing space they needed to dig into the mountainous North Korean terrain. The Chinese and the North Koreans created a complex network of trenches, tunnels, and bunkers in the hills overlooking the UN positions. Henceforth, China might still be unable to deliver victory in the sense of defeating Syngman Rhee, but it could prevent defeat by stopping the UN forces from advancing up the peninsula.

III. The Soviet War Protraction Strategy

Prior to China's intervention, Stalin feared that the Korean War might escalate into a direct confrontation between the USSR and the United States. As long as this was a possibility, he remained cautious. Once the Chinese intervened and, more importantly, once they dug in after the UN halted its offensive, Stalin no longer faced the possibility of UN forces advancing up to his vulnerable Siberian border. This opened an array of enticing possibilities. With China entrenched, Stalin saw enormous benefits in protracting the conflict.

China required Soviet heavy artillery, tanks, and aircraft in order to prosecute the war. This did not come cheaply but required payments in goods and raw materials. To obtain these required extensive agricultural and commercial reforms (discussed in Chapter 22) in order to extract maximum resources from the Chinese economy. The economic and human costs of the Korean War caused much hardship in China. Because most Soviet military assistance did not arrive until after the main offensives had ended, the Chinese relied on their numerical superiority to compensate for the lack of modern weapons. This meant high casualty rates. For the final two years of the war, the line of demarcation hardly changed, but the U.S. Air Force showered bombs on North Korea and the Chinese stationed there.

During the long stalemate, Stalin envisioned a high-reward but low-risk war protraction strategy. The hostilities provided a way to weaken both a despised enemy, the United States, and a potential rival, China. A conflict in Asia, a theater remote from Moscow's primary national security interests in Europe, provided Stalin with a much-needed breathing space to consolidate control over Eastern Europe and rebuild after the devastation of World War II. Washington was pouring its forces and economic resources into the sinkhole of Asia, while an increasingly unpopular war weakened the Truman administration at home, where most Americans wanted their troops returned. Finally, the military stalemate that developed during the final two years of the war made the U.S. military appear weak and ineffective, while Chinese diplomatic isolation and dependence on Soviet military supplies glued China to its alliance and kept it at odds with the United States. The war left such bitterness between China and the United States that it would take two decades before there was a diplomatic rapprochement under President Richard Nixon.

Peace negotiations opened on 10 July 1951, almost exactly one year after the start of the war. The talks bogged down almost immediately over the repatriation of prisoners of war (POWs) and remained stuck on this issue for fifteen months. Washington took the position that there should be no forced repatriations of POWs, while the Communists considered this to be a violation of the 1949 Geneva Convention. Treaties had a special historical significance for China, since the Western powers had used treaties as their primary mechanism to dominate China in the nineteenth and early twentieth centuries. The CCP derived much of its domestic legitimacy from its expulsion of the imperialist powers. Premier Zhou Enlai wanted to postpone the issue until after the armistice but Stalin disagreed, accusing the Chinese of kowtowing to yet another Western violation of international law.

The UN announcement that only 70,000 of its 132,000 Communist POWs wished to return home, while the rest wished to remain in South Korea or go to Taiwan, shocked the Chinese and North Koreans. It suggested widespread discontent within their militaries. For some this was a second defection. Mao sent to the front lines of Korea many former

Nationalist troops, who had defected to his side during the Chinese civil war. Lacking any other important ally, Mao could not easily ignore Soviet wishes. China depended on their military assistance, which provided almost 90 percent of its munitions. The Chinese could not jeopardize their relations with the Soviet Union at this time. So, the Korean War dragged on for two more years.

IV. War Termination

War termination had to await the death of Stalin in 1953, when his successors recognized that the war had resulted in the encirclement of the USSR, including the strengthening of the Western alliance in the form of a far stronger North Atlantic Treaty Organization (NATO), the rearmament of the United States and permanent mobilization of the U.S. military, and the creation of a vast network of overseas U.S. military bases. There were also troubles within the Soviet empire requiring immediate attention. In March 1953 alone, over 100,000 East Germans fled to the West. For the USSR, Germany was the linchpin of its national security and the East German regime was crumbling. Uprisings had also broken out in Czechoslovakia and Bulgaria, along with an unprecedented prison riot in the Soviet Union. The new leadership concluded that it needed to settle the war in Korea so that it could focus its attention on internal problems, most immediately on political succession in Moscow.

Within two weeks of Stalin's death on 5 March 1953, his successors signaled that they wanted to terminate the war. There was an immediate exchange of sick POWs without a corresponding demand for forced repatriations. Premier Zhou Enlai traveled to Moscow for Stalin's funeral, and the two countries worked out the details of their war termination strategy. Within four months, an armistice had been negotiated and signed despite Syngman Rhee's doing everything in his power to scuttle the settlement in a vain attempt to reunite the peninsula under his leadership. The Communists ultimately ignored his many provocations, including his mass release of Communist POWs on 17 June 1953, thus preventing their forced repatriation. Although the Communists issued the expected protests, they still signed the final armistice agreement on 27 July 1953. Washington silenced Syngman Rhee's objections with a strengthened defense treaty and a generous long-term economic aid package that would fund South Korea's government for decades.

The war restored China's traditional influence, often described as tributary relations, over the northern half of the Korean Peninsula. Kim Il Sung, who had not originally desired direct Chinese intervention, had become utterly dependent on their military assistance. The war's devastation left him far worse off than before the hostilities, when he had controlled the most industrialized part of Korea and the strongest military forces. U.S. bombing leveled his country's agricultural and industrial infrastructure. By war's end, the United States had expanded its target list to include his dike and irrigation system; after the war, U.S. dollars poured into the South.

China's position within the socialist camp became much stronger. At the 1950 Stalin-Mao talks, Mao deferred to Stalin. During the Korean War, the Soviet Union demanded that the PRC pay full rates for Soviet military aid. Following Stalin's death and the Korean armistice, however, Mao expected greater respect. Leadership of the international Communist movement was up for grabs, and Mao now saw himself, not Stalin's successor, Nikita Khrushchev, as the most senior Communist leader.

The PLA's success in the Korean War furthered China's ambition to reassert its historic claim to primacy in Asia. During the hostilities, China had rapidly increased its military assistance to the Viet Minh, providing them with crucial aid in their war to expel the French from Indochina (Vietnam), much as the Soviet Union had aided the CCP during the Chinese civil war. China played the role of a great power at the 1954 Geneva Conference settling the First Indochina War, when it helped broker a French withdrawal. The combination of the Chinese victory in Korea and its growing participation in Vietnam gave Mao great regional influence. Thereafter, China continued to support North Vietnam in its struggle against the United States and South Vietnam in the Vietnam War. Between 1965 and 1969, China deployed over 300,000 troops to North Vietnam to man the antiaircraft units responsible for a large percentage of downed U.S. aircraft, to run engineering units to restore bombed rail lines, and to train North Vietnamese pilots. Not only did China assist the North Vietnamese, it also hoped to drive a wedge between Vietnam and the USSR, thereby dominating Southeast Asia. Thus, with the Korean War, China was on the path to restoring its traditional primacy in East Asia, usurped by Japan in the First Sino-Japanese War of 1894–5.

But the cost of the Korean War was heavy. While Chinese forces succeeded in pushing the UN forces back below the 38th parallel, estimates of those killed and wounded ranged in the millions for the Chinese and North Korean side. These contrast to the much smaller, although still extraordinarily high, estimate of 996,937 casualties for the UN side. Mao had also lost his chance to retake Taiwan; he remained diplomatically isolated; and he had become extremely dependent on the Soviet Union. The one-China policy followed by both the PRC and Taiwan meant that there was only one seat in the UN for the internationally recognized government of China. Taiwan would occupy that seat until 1971, when the 1969 Sino-Soviet border war in combination with the U.S. desire to withdraw from the Vietnam War changed the balance of power in East Asia and undermined international support for Taiwan's continued representation in the UN.

V. The Domestic Consequences of the War

The PRC government used the Korean War not only to reestablish China as a major regional power but also to advance its own domestic agenda. With the end of the war, PLA commander Peng Dehuai returned home, receiving a hero's welcome and a mass celebration in Beijing on 11 August 1953. He was later named as one of the PRC's ten marshals, second in command only to Zhu De. The CCP hailed China's success in holding the united Western armies at bay as the first great Chinese victory against a foreign foe since the Mongol invasions. The war reinforced the verdict of the Chinese civil war that the era of humiliation that had begun with the Opium Wars had indeed ended. The PLA's ability to fight a coalition of the strongest powers of the West to a stalemate—presented in China as an undisputed Chinese victory—greatly strengthened Mao's mandate of heaven. He had already achieved the remarkable feat of reuniting much of the greater Qing empire, a task that had eluded his countrymen for the two generations since the fall of the Manchus. Immediately after the reunification of China, Mao had reestablished China's place in the world by fighting the world's most economically developed countries. His countrymen rallied to his support with a renewed feeling of national pride.

The combination of these successes added greatly to the already growing cult of Mao as a leader of enormous wisdom and personal competence. He appeared to be China's new and virtuous emperor during the early and most promising phase of the dynastic cycle. In the 1930s, Mao had favored a peasant strategy rejected by the Soviet Union, with its Leninist emphasis on urban areas. The CCP had paid dearly for adhering so long to the Soviet line. Mao proved these people wrong. Then at Yan'an, during the darkest years of Communist rule, Mao had written voluminously on Communist military strategy, making confident predictions of victory. The Communist victory in the civil war seemed to vindicate him once again.

Military victory gave rise to the cult of Stalin and the cult of Mao, the former in World War II and the latter in the Chinese civil war and Korean war. Both leaders used victory in war to cement rule at home and abroad. Victory gave Mao the mandate to transform the Chinese state and society. Internationally, Maoist propaganda aimed at Chinese citizens and a foreign audience became so effective that his military and soon his economic strategies would gain adherents throughout the developing world. For many, Maoism seemed to offer an alternative to Western capitalistic and democratic models. Initially, China would support revolution just in Vietnam. By the early 1960s, however, China would actively promote its model for revolution and economic development in Southeast Asia and Africa.

Domestically, when the Korean War began, the Communists had only just taken power over their own vast, war-torn country. They had yet to eliminate the many Nationalist remnants, particularly in South China, nor had they fully established a central government, let alone the many institutions of provincial and local government. Decades of warfare had devastated both the countryside and the cities, so that an enormous task of reconstruction lay ahead. The twin problems of rural poverty and nation building loomed large on the horizon during the long interregnum between the Qing dynasty and the establishment of the PRC. The nearly four decades of intervening warfare had greatly magnified these problems, so that the CCP faced a daunting domestic agenda. Despite the Korean War, the Communists established central governmental institutions. (See the feature on the next page.)

When the Communists seized power, they allowed other small political parties to continue to exist. During the Korean War, Mao used the state of war as a pretext for eliminating his remaining political opponents. The conflict was the backdrop to the collectivization of agriculture and the antirightist campaigns of the early 1950s (discussed in Chapter 22, Sections II and III). War provided the justification for harsh measures, including the execution of several million accused landlords and rightists. Mao also sent former Nationalist supporters to the killing fields of Korea. The combination of these antirightist campaigns and collectivization wiped out any significant residual support for the Nationalists. The CCP effectively used the state of war to justify the silencing of dissent at home, and all the remaining nominally independent parties grew weaker over time until they disappeared.

The war, however, delayed the task of internal reconstruction. Much of the Soviet aid came in the form of loans. Therefore, the general Chinese population actually paid for the Chinese side of the war effort. This turned out to be expensive, consuming 30 to 40 percent of the government budget and further depressing the already marginal Chinese standard of living. The Korean War had become the sinkhole for Chinese government spending, delaying the introduction of the first Five-Year Plan (1953–7).

CHINESE GOVERNMENT

CCP Structure

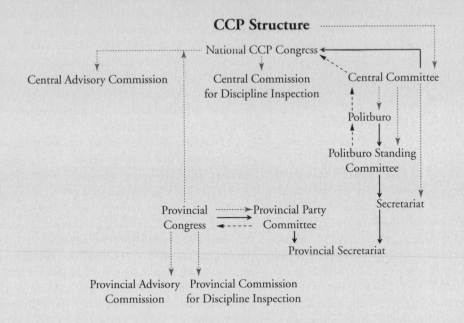

PRC State Structure

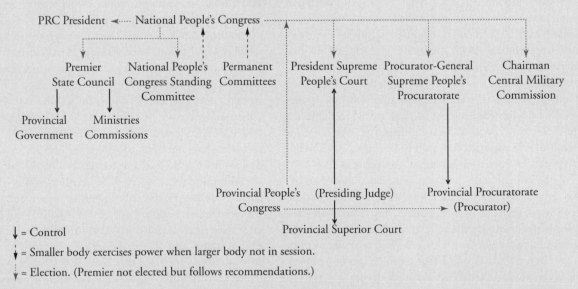

↓ = Control

↓ = Smaller body exercises power when larger body not in session.

↓ = Election. (Premier not elected but follows recommendations.)

Source: Colin Mackerras, *The New Cambridge Handbook of Contemporary China* (Cambridge: Cambridge University Press, 2001), 88, 95. Reprinted with permission of Cambridge University Press.

Even though the PRC probably sustained over a million casualties in the Korean War, Mao Zedong's success in fighting the UN armies to a standstill was portrayed as China's first military victory against the West since the Opium Wars. The Cult of Mao led to the erection of hundreds of Mao statues all over China, and different localities competed to see who could build the largest one; to this day, the twenty-four-meter-tall statue in Kashgar, Xinjiang, built in 1968 at the height of the Cultural Revolution, is one of the country's largest. During the late 1980s, many of them were quietly taken down. However, in 2008 it was reported that the largest statue of Mao ever, at 183 meters, would be built in Changsha, Hunan, the capital of the province where Mao was born.

Conclusions

The Chinese claimed victory in the Korean War. Not only had they assisted their socialist ally, Kim Il Sung, but they had countered a great power alliance. They achieved their minimum war objective of retaining North Korea as a buffer zone, and they also extended their influence over Kim Il Sung, who initially had been very wary of China. Following the signing of the final truce in July 1953, mass celebrations honored the return of Chinese forces. Although the Chinese claims of victory were inflated, the Korean War significantly altered the balance of power in East Asia. China had demonstrated that it was capable of pursuing an active and effective foreign policy for the first time since the eighteenth century.

The unanticipated UN intervention dashed both Stalin's hope for a no-risk, low-cost adventure and Mao's plan to focus on domestic reconstruction. As UN troops rapidly approached the Sino-Korean border, Mao intervened. At any one time, an estimated 700,000 Chinese troops were stationed in Korea. China began the war as a satellite of the USSR and a suppliant for Soviet aid. Stalin served as the main arms supplier, but the Chinese bore the brunt of the fighting and paid for the Soviet war surplus with real goods that they desperately needed for their own economy. China, an extremely poor country, ended up paying an estimated $1.3 billion for Soviet equipment and supplies. On the Communist side, most of the fighting and the financial burden fell on China, while its local ally, North Korea, was utterly devastated. Mao also incurred an unexpected cost: While he gained North Korea as a sphere of influence, he lost Taiwan.

The real victors of the war were Chiang Kai-shek and South Korea, while the real losers were Kim Il Sung and the USSR. Chiang, without even participating, had been pulled under the U.S. nuclear umbrella and reconnected with the U.S. economic lifeline. Taiwan was far more secure after the war than before, when a mainland occupation seemed imminent. Kim ultimately lost because his postwar situation—U.S.

troops entrenched in South Korea and U.S. money bankrolling the South Korean government—was far inferior to the prewar situation of a destitute and militarily weak South Korea. The USSR also lost because it transformed the rapidly demobilizing United States of the late 1940s into a permanently mobilized military superpower with basing privileges throughout the world, including Europe.

The death of Stalin marked the end of the honeymoon period in Sino-Soviet relations. Mao did not respect Stalin's successors, who were not sufficiently aggressive for Mao's tastes. Immediately after the war, China demanded that the Soviet Union leave Manchuria. From 1953 to 1955, the USSR lost control of the Chinese Eastern Railway and its base at Lüshun. With a massive Chinese army still mobilized for the Korean War, Stalin's successors, who had yet to decide which one of them would rule, were in no position to resist. China's foreign policy also changed. When Mao finally had the chance to pursue the domestic reconstruction deferred by the Korea War, China's economy began to grow and Soviet aid was no longer so important: Within a matter of years, Mao broke with Moscow in the 1960 Sino-Soviet split. This event unexpectedly ended what many in the West had assumed would be a permanent monolithic era in international communism.

BIBLIOGRAPHY

Chang, Gordon H. *Friends and Enemies: The United States, China, and the Soviet Union, 1948–1972.* Stanford, CA: Stanford University Press, 1990.

Chen, Jian. *China's Road to the Korean War: The Making of the Sino-American Confrontation.* New York: Columbia University Press, 1994.

Clayton, David. *Imperialism Revisited: Political and Economic Relations between Britain and China, 1950–54.* New York: St. Martin's Press, 1997.

Cohen, Warren. *East Asia at the Center: Four Thousand Years of Engagement with the World.* New York: Columbia University Press, 2000.

Cumings, Bruce. *Korea's Place in the Sun: A Modern History.* New York: W. W. Norton, 1997.

Foot, Rosemary. *A Substitute for Victory: The Politics of Peacemaking at the Korean Armistice Talks.* Ithaca, NY: Cornell University Press, 1990.

George, Alexander L. *The Chinese Army in Action: The Korean War and Its Aftermath.* New York: Columbia University Press, 1967.

Goncharov, Sergei N. John W. Lewis, and Xue Litai. *Uncertain Partners: Stalin, Mao, and the Korean War.* Stanford, CA: Stanford University Press, 1994.

Li Xiaobing, Allan R. Millett, and Bin Yu, trans. and eds. *Mao's Generals Remember Korea.* Lawrence: University of Kansas Press, 2001.

Mastny, Vojtech. *The Cold War and Soviet Insecurity: The Stalin Years.* New York: Oxford University Press, 1996.

Ryan, Mark A. David Michael Finkelstein, and Michael A. McDevitt, eds. *Chinese Warfighting: The PLA Experience Since 1949.* Armonk, NY: M. E. Sharpe, 2003.

Short, Philip. *Mao: A Life.* New York: Henry Holt, 1999.

Stueck, William W. *Rethinking the Korean War: A New Diplomatic and Strategic History.* Princeton, NJ: Princeton University Press, 2002

Terrill, Ross. *Mao: A Biography.* Stanford, CA: Stanford University Press, 1999.

Weathersby, Kathryn. "Stalin, Mao, and the End of the Korean War." In *Brothers in Arms: The Rise and Fall of the Sino-Soviet Alliance 1945–1963,* edited by Odd Arne Westad, 90–116. Stanford, CA: Stanford University Press, 1998.

Whiting, Allen Seuss. *China Crosses the Yalu: The Decision to Enter the Korean War.* New York: Macmillan, 1960.

Xiang, Lanxin. *Recasting the Imperial Far East: Britain and America in China, 1945–1950.* Armonk, NY: M. E. Sharpe, 1995.

Zhai, Qiang. "Transplanting the Chinese Model: Chinese Military Advisers and the First Vietnam War, 1950–1954." In *Chinese Warfare since 1600,* edited by Kenneth Swope, 445–73. Aldershot, England: Ashgate, 2005.

Zhang, Shu Guang. *Mao's Military Romanticism: China and the Korean War, 1950–1953*. Lawrence: University of Kansas Press, 1995.

Zhang, Xiaoming. "The Vietnam War, 1964–1969." In *Chinese Warfare since 1600*, edited by Kenneth Swope, 473–504. Aldershot, England: Ashgate, 2005.

NOTES

1. He Qifang, "I Seem to Hear the Roar of the Waves: To the Flood Fighter of Hankou," in *Twentieth Century Chinese Poetry*, Kai-yu Hsu, trans. (Garden City, NY: Doubleday, 1963), 212.
2. Quoted in Ross Terrill, *Mao: A Biography*, rev. ed. (Stanford, CA: Stanford University Press, 1999), 268.

Chronology

30 December 1949	India recognizes the PRC
1 December 1951	PLA enters Lhasa, the Tibetan capital
1 January 1953	Implementation of the First Five-Year Plan (1953–7)
15 March 1953	Soviet agreement to help build 141 projects in China
8 August 1953	Soviet Union successfully tests a nuclear weapon
28 September 1953	Sino-Soviet Economic Cooperation Agreement
29 April 1954	India recognizes Chinese sovereignty over Tibet
3 Sept. 1954–1 May 1955	First Taiwan Straight Crisis
2 December 1954	U.S.-Taiwan Mutual Defense Treaty
18–24 April 1955	Bandung Conference
24 February 1956	Khrushchev's Secret Speech at the Twentieth Party Congress
2 May 1956	Mao's speech launching the Hundred Flowers Campaign
Fall 1956	Unrest in Poland and Hungary
8 June 1957	Beginning of the Anti-Rightist Campaign; end of the Hundred Flowers Campaign
26 August 1957	Successful Soviet test of an intercontinental ballistic missile
15–27 Sept. 1956	Eighth Party Congress approves the Second Five-Year Plan (1958–62)
4 October 1957	Successful Soviet launch of *Sputnik*
15 October 1957	Sino-Soviet Defense Technology Treaty to provide nuclear weapons technology to China
5–23 May 1958	CCP Congress announces the beginning of the Great Leap Forward
23 Aug.–6 Oct. 1958	Second Taiwan Straight Crisis
1959–61	Great Famine
9 January 1959	Promulgation of the Regulation on Household Registration concerning the *hukou* system
27 Jan.–5 Feb. 1959	Khrushchev announces a policy of peaceful coexistence at the Twenty-First Party Congress
12–30 March 1959	Tibet revolts against Chinese rule; Dalai Lama flees to India
18–28 April 1959	Chinese People's Congress replaces Mao with Liu Shaoqi as the state chairman
20 June 1959	Soviet Union renounces the Sino-Soviet Defense Technology Treaty
14 July 1959	Peng Dehuai circulates a letter criticizing Mao and the Great Leap Forward
2–16 August 1959	Lushan Conference; dispute over the Great Leap Forward
8 September 1959	China rejects the McMahon Line as the Sino-Indian boundary
15–27 Sept. 1959	U.S.-Soviet détente with Nikita Khrushchev's visit to the United States
1960–1	Rectification Campaigns
16 April 1960	China criticizes the Soviet policy of peaceful coexistence
16 July 1960	Soviet Union recalls advisers from China; beginning of the Sino-Soviet Split
20 Oct.–22 Nov. 1962	Sino-Indian Border War
16 October 1964	China successfully tests an atomic bomb
17 June 1967	China successfully tests a hydrogen bomb
18 May 1974	India successfully tests an atomic device
11 May 1998	India successfully tests an atomic bomb
28 May 1998	Pakistan successfully tests atomic bomb

24

Mao's Quest for World Leadership

Grain scattered on the ground,
Potato leaves withered,
Strong young people have left to make steel,
Only my children and old women reap the crops.
How can they pass the coming year?
Allow me to raise my voice for the people![1]

Marshal Peng Dehuai (1898–1974) on the famine
following the Great Leap Forward

At the end of the Korean War, the Chinese Communists stood at the pinnacle of their achievements, proclaiming victory in the civil war and in a major foreign war. They freed China of the discredited old order and were poised to begin the arduous task of constructing a new order. Mao initially followed the Soviet model despite deteriorating relations with the USSR. The First Five-Year Plan (1953–7) focused on the collectivization of agriculture to promote heavy industry through the transfer of wealth from rural to urban China. In 1956 Mao launched the Hundred Flowers Campaign (1956–7) in part to test the level of discontent within China. The scope of the ensuing criticism of the CCP surprised the Communist leadership. Mao promoted the Great Leap Forward (1958–60) in a utopian attempt to maintain both political and economic control, to address the lagging agricultural growth rates left by the First Five-Year Plan, and to close as rapidly as possible the economic gap with the Soviet Union. Fear of the USSR convinced Mao to hasten domestic construction, just as fear of capitalist-fascist encirclement had impelled Stalin to accelerate Soviet economic development in the 1930s. In both cases, their respective populations paid the price for forced-draft industrialization.

I. The Hundred Flowers Campaign

Concerns about agriculture formed the backdrop to the Hundred Flowers Campaign. The First Five-Year Plan, adopted at the end of the Korean War, followed the Soviet model for economic development emphasizing the rapid growth of heavy industry and centralized planning to achieve it. With the assistance of numerous Soviet technical advisers and the industrial and infrastructure endowment left by the Japanese, the plan achieved high industrial growth rates, but agriculture lagged. The Korean War required enormous sacrifices from the Chinese population. Although the First Five-Year Plan increased production, huge population growth meant that per capita output remained low. Collectivization had improved government control over the countryside but had not dramatically improved yields. Rural growth remained inadequate to sustain rapid industrial development, while growing Sino-Soviet tensions spurred Beijing to catch up economically and militarily. To stir the necessary revolutionary fervor, Mao cultivated the support of educated Chinese.

In February 1956, Premier Nikita Khrushchev delivered his so-called Secret Speech attacking Stalin before the Twentieth Party Congress of the Soviet Union. The speech infuriated Mao because the criticism leveled against Stalin's personality cult applied equally to the cult of Mao. Much to his dismay, the Secret Speech led to de-Stalinization in the USSR and an attempt in Hungary to overthrow the socialist government. Although Mao supported Soviet military intervention to crush the Hungarian uprising, the use of force by one socialist state against another set a precedent. It suggested that Moscow might be willing to do the same in other cases, perhaps even against China. The Soviets would later make this explicit in the 1968 Brezhnev Doctrine, justifying such interventions. There also remained a strong pro-Soviet element in the CCP, creating the possibility of party members conspiring with the Soviet Union against Mao.

The Hundred Flowers Movement began in May 1956, ostensibly to liberate China's intellectuals, especially its scientific community, so as to motivate them to work harder for the state. Economic development required the commitment of educated Chinese. The Hundred Flowers Campaign gave experts and professionals a degree of freedom to express themselves and to organize their activities. It encouraged them to believe that the CCP valued their opinions. Intellectuals initially responded cautiously, remembering the consequences of previous political campaigns.

At the Eighth Party Congress of the CCP in September 1956, revisions of the constitution removed references to Mao Zedong Thought; during the Cultural Revolution, ten years later, the denunciation of Liu Shaoqi would center on these deletions. The Congress also rejected Mao's desire for greatly accelerated economic development policies. In February 1957, almost a year to the day after Khrushchev's Secret Speech denouncing Stalin, Mao proclaimed criticism to be good and, if well intentioned, to be a source of national strength. At the time, mounting shortages and inflation cast a shadow on Mao's policy choices and dampened enthusiasm for the Soviet development model.

Gradually, exchanges of opinion became increasingly frank and soon extended beyond professionals to include students and workers. In May 1957 the press reported widespread criticism of the CCP, while labor and student unrest escalated. Students fanned out into the factories and the countryside to spread their message. Criticism focused on the insulation of the party from the general population, its failure to impose the rule of law on its own members, its close ties with the USSR, its continuing internal factionalism, and its monopolization of political power; meanwhile, the leaders of the Peasant's and Worker's Party and the Democratic League expressed their desire for a multiparty political system. The charges resembled those leveled against Chiang Kai-shek during the civil war. Mao had incorrectly assumed an underlying sympathy of intellectuals and experts with the CCP without taking into account the effects of his repeated political campaigns of the early 1950s that had disproportionately targeted these groups.

When criticism far exceeded his expectations, Mao replaced the Hundred Flowers Campaign in June 1957 with a combination of a rectification campaign for party members, suppression of the labor unrest, and an Anti-Rightist Campaign against intellectuals, the latter organized by the CCP general secretary, Deng Xiaoping. (See the feature on the next page.) This constituted a major policy reversal that validated the criticisms of such party leaders as Liu Shaoqi, who had warned against political liberalization. Although Mao recognized the importance of strengthening party relations with the general population, he did not foresee the underlying hostility of students, intellectuals, and workers to party policies, which undermined Mao's own position and fueled tensions within the party. Continuing bad economic news and a reduction in Soviet aid as the USSR strove to restore order in Eastern Europe encouraged CCP leaders to close their ranks to weather the growing economic crisis at home.

Without warning, many of the most outspoken critics during the Hundred Flowers Campaign lost their positions and party membership; some were imprisoned, and others were exiled. This quelled any opposition from the scientific community to the acceleration of collectivization and the new practices in agronomy that would soon follow. Some Chinese concluded that they had been duped by Mao in a movement designed not to learn the truth, but to ferret out any emerging antigovernment opposition.

II. The Great Leap Forward

The Hundred Flowers Campaign and the Anti-Rightist Campaign led to a third and even larger movement, the Great Leap Forward, named after the Soviet Great Leap Forward of 1929 that commemorated Stalin's fiftieth birthday with a campaign to consolidate his rule and initiate the cult of Stalin.[2] The Chinese Great Leap Forward signaled that Mao, not Khrushchev, was the rightful leader of the Communist bloc.

Mao began his Great Leap against the backdrop of the USSR's successful launch of *Sputnik* on 4 October 1957, only days after the 1 October anniversary of the PRC's founding. The satellite was a key step in the development of intercontinental ballistic missiles, which would allow Moscow to deliver nuclear weapons anywhere on earth, while Beijing lacked any means to retaliate. Almost immediately after the launch, Mao began to call for an accelerated drive to modernize China. He openly criticized the USSR for relying too much on heavy industry (e.g., *Sputnik*) and too little on collective agriculture. In particular, he called for the rapid construction of people's communes. The first such commune was named "Sputnik" as a challenge to Moscow.

During a three-month period at the end of 1958, Mao consolidated China's 750,000 collective farms into 24,000 communes, reorganizing nearly one-sixth of humanity in the process. To keep people on the communes, the government simultaneously greatly strengthened the *hukou* system, an internal passport and residence scheme, which was an amalgamation of China's traditional *baojia* controls and the

AUTHOR DING LING

One of the main targets of the Anti-Rightist Campaign was Ding Ling (1904–86), China's most famous female author of the twentieth century. She was born into a landowning family, but her father soon died. Her mother became a militant feminist who joined the CCP in 1927. Ding Ling received a good education and attended a high school run by Chen Duxiu, the founder of the CCP. In 1924 she studied in the Communist-dominated literature department at Shanghai University but soon moved to Beijing, where she took classes at Peking University; met her future husband, the poet Hu Yepin; joined various left-leaning and anarchist organizations; came under the spell of such Russian and French authors as Gorky, Tolstoy, Flaubert, and Maupassant; and began writing short stories and novels. In 1928, she published her first and widely acclaimed anthology of short stories, reflecting her experiences as a student and a rebellious young woman intent upon making her own way through life. These themes resonated among the members of her transitional generation, who were in the process of abandoning the traditional Confucian hierarchy of their elders and straining to envision a less confining world for their children.

While her husband became increasingly involved in revolutionary activities, Ding Ling focused on writing, producing another widely acclaimed anthology of short stories in 1929 as well as other literary works. After her return to Shanghai, her husband joined the CCP in 1930 and that year she gave birth to a son. As her husband's literary career foundered, he became increasingly involved in his revolutionary activities until the Nationalists arrested him, along with four other left-leaning writers, and executed them in 1931. Afterward Ding Ling no longer focused on her literary career, but on fomenting revolution. She joined the CCP around 1933, and her literary works increasingly reflected the Communist themes of class and political consciousness.

The Nationalists imprisoned her from 1933 to 1935, unwittingly causing an even greater interest in her works, many of which were published during this period, when she was presumed dead. In 1937 she fled to the Communist base in Yan'an, where Mao personally welcomed her. There she formed the Women's National Salvation Association and became deeply involved in organizational and propaganda work, as well as romantically involved with the key military leader Peng Dehuai. During the Rectification Campaign of 1942–4, she initially attempted to correct party officials for failing to follow through on their ideals and for perpetuating women's subordination. But soon she became the subject of rectification and was demoted; nevertheless, her literary career flourished. She based her novel *The Sun Shines over Sangkan River,* published in 1948, on her experiences in 1946 and 1947, witnessing the implementation of land reform in Chahar, Inner Mongolia, and Hebei. The novel described the complex social relations during land reform. In 1951 the book became the first Chinese work to win the Stalin Prize, but she wrote little fiction thereafter, focusing on works spreading the Communist message instead.

In the late 1940s and early 1950s, she held senior positions in China's key women's and literary organizations, including the editorship of the main journal elaborating the CCP's cultural policies. In the 1950s, she became increasingly at odds with other members of the literary establishment over the issue of artistic freedom. Books, she believed, should reflect a writer's feelings, not official orthodoxy. She was among those to voice criticisms during the Hundred Flowers Campaign and suffer for her frankness. She became a principal literary target of the ensuing Anti-Rightist Campaign in 1957. When she refused to make a self-criticism, she lost her official posts and in 1959 was assigned to a two-year stint in Manchuria of "reform through labor." By 1960 she had recanted, only to be imprisoned during the Cultural Revolution from 1970 to 1975. Upon her release, she remained in the public eye for her still extremely popular fiction.

Soviet internal passport system. Only urban residents received grain rations because the communes were expected to be self-sufficient, while only those with an urban *hukou* could get the ration coupons necessary to acquire food. For out-of-town visitors, official permission was necessary to acquire such ration coupons. This kept the peasants not only in rural areas but on their assigned commune. These government-imposed administrative structures supplanted the rural *guanxi* networks centered on the village that had traditionally governed rural life. Peasants no longer even had the autonomy to raise their own food. The collectivization of the countryside reduced the incentives to produce while providing few limits to consumption. Official propaganda in fall 1958 proclaimed a food surplus and urged Chinese to eat their fill. Long before the year was out, the peasants had consumed their food supply for the entire year.

The communes introduced new agricultural practices, following the theories of the Soviet geneticist Trofim Denisovich Lysenko, who had applied the Marxist class framework to the study of genetics. He rejected "fascist" theories of crop and animal heredity, arguing instead that plants acquired characteristics directly from their surrounding environment. Therefore, the Chinese attributed the 1950 potato virus to environmental factors, ignoring China's own research on the potato blight until many years later, in 1979. Another prophet of the new agricultural science was Vasilii Williams, a professor at the

Moscow Agricultural Academy, who rejected the use of chemical fertilizers, recommending crop rotation with fields lying fallow two out of every three years. Other Soviet agronomists emphasized deep plowing, or furrows four to five feet deep.

Mao had become enamored of Williams' ideas while still at Yan'an and had subsequently adopted those of Lysenko as well. While the capitalist world was using chemical fertilizers and hybrids to obtain record yields, Mao chose the Soviet model for agriculture, which was based on social theory, not hard science. Mao added a twist of his own, pest control, calling for the extermination of the Four Pests: sparrows, rats, mosquitoes, and flies. Whole communities turned out to beat drums to prevent the frightened sparrows from alighting until they fell to earth from exhaustion. By April 1960, enough sparrows had been eliminated so that bed bugs were substituted for birds. Mao did not recognize the connection between birds and insect control, and in the absence of effective predators, insects ravaged the crops.

Mao also called for more irrigation. This required more dams. He wanted small reservoirs throughout the country, which entailed the resettlement of those living on the lands soon to be flooded. The construction of the Xin'anjiang reservoir in north Zhejiang alone forced the relocation of 300,000 people, who were often evicted and then left to fend for themselves. Hastily built dams, however, often broke, with cata-strophic results. Most of the county-level dams were breached within two to three years, and the major dam built on the Yellow River quickly silted up. Then, during the heavy rains of August 1975, the Banqiao and Shimantan dams in Zhumadian, Henan, broke, killing 240,000 people. Reportedly, this was the most catastrophic dam failure in history.

Mao's goal was to increase the agricultural surplus to fund heavy industry. Instead of relying on large-scale factories, however, he promoted backyard foundries, where peasants could manufacture goods for themselves. Mao set ludicrously high production quotas, originally with the promise of surpassing British production in fifteen years and then in just seven years. Quotas became all-important. In order to meet the steel quotas, many villages and towns forced people to give up their iron tools and utensils to melt them down in the backyard forges. Although quotas were met and in many cases exceeded, the metal produced was of poor quality and often useless. Necessary implements had been turned into unusable ingots. The industrialization program put huge demands on labor, which Mao provided by encouraging women to engage in remunerative work.

The campaign to build dams and produce steel continued through the autumn harvest of 1958. This meant that grain rotted in the fields for lack of labor. Over the winter of

During the Great Leap Forward, the PRC focused on heavy industry at the expense of light industry. Only during the 1980s did a thriving market in consumer goods, like this clothing store in Harbin (Haerbin), Manchuria, begin to provide a wider variety and greater choice to the average Chinese consumer.

1958–9, local granaries emptied throughout China. Mao did not believe that there was a grain shortage; rather, he believed that the peasants were hiding grain. Instead of making food available from the central granaries, he sent inspection teams to punish hoarders and confiscate their harvests. He acted on the basis of optimistic production reports from local officials seeking to curry favor with their superiors. Mao might have considered reports of a drought affecting Manchuria from late 1958 to the spring of 1959 that delayed the planting and reports of flooding in South China during the spring of 1959. Instead, he tried to secure more funds for industrialization from trade revenues by doubling grain exports from 1958 to 1960 and reducing food imports. He also tried to gain international influence by donating grain to North Korea, North Vietnam, and Albania. By increasing food exports, Mao intended to vindicate his policies and, in doing so, demonstrate his leadership of the international Communist movement.

Minister of Defense and hero of the Korean War Peng Dehuai was one of the few high-ranking leaders to call attention to the impending famine. Unlike either Mao Zedong or Liu Shaoqi, a key promoter of the Great Leap Forward, Peng was the son of poor peasants whose own brother had died of starvation. Mao and Liu were the children of middle-class farmers who had been prosperous enough to provide them with a private education. At the Lushan Conference in August 1959, Peng spoke out, detailing the failures of the Great Leap Forward and accusing Mao of petty-bourgeois fanaticism. Peng had gained enormous prestige for his service during the Korean War. Later, he told his niece, "I have experienced famine. I know the taste of it and it frightens me! We have fought decades of war and the people, poorly clothed and poorly fed, have spilt their blood and sweat to help us so that the Communist Party could win over the country and seize power. How can we let them suffer again, this time from hunger?"[3]

When Peng criticized Mao in a letter circulated at the Lushan Conference, two days later Khrushchev did likewise, indicating possible coordination between Moscow and the pro-Soviet faction within the CCP. Peng favored cultivating better relations with Moscow, while Mao contemplated a complete break. Because Peng's criticisms were valid and many of the other Politburo members were ready to support him, Mao staged a preemptive attack, accusing Peng of placing the PLA before the party. While Mao excelled at political intrigue, Peng did not.

Provincial governors throughout China backed Mao's policies. The upper leadership of the CCP was implicated in the policy choices as well. At Lushan, Mao received the backing of his most essential supporters: the majority of his generals. Peng was in the minority. This gave Mao the required coercive power to forge ahead. A renewed Anti-Rightist Campaign began immediately after the Lushan summit. Within the month, Peng Dehuai had written a self-criticism and was under house arrest. Lin Biao, who replaced him as defense minister, made the restoration of the cult of Mao a priority. He required soldiers to memorize an anthology of excerpts from Mao's collected works that became known as the *Little Red Book*. (See the feature on page 396.) Rectification was the order of the day. The Great Leap Forward continued, while Mao retained control over the CCP with PLA backing.

III. The Great Famine (1959–61)

The harvest was worse in 1959 than in 1958. The state responded by increasing the requisitioning quotas so that, in many areas, it took the entire harvest. This meant widespread famine by the end of 1959 and widespread death by early 1960. China had long been a land afflicted by famine, particularly in the North, where droughts occurred regularly. In the past, such famines has been regional because warfare and climatic conditions had been regional. The Great Leap Forward marked the first time in Chinese history that a national campaign had undermined agriculture everywhere to create a nationwide famine of truly stupendous proportions. Harrowing memories never left those who survived.

By spring 1960, many surviving peasants were too weak to plant new crops. Under such dire circumstances, the peasantry had not given up their crops willingly. As in the Soviet collectivization campaign, terror was necessary to take enough food to feed the cities. After the countryside was stripped of food, cannibalism ensued. Usually this involved corpses, particularly of dead children. But murder also occurred. The famine imposed dire choices on families. Many ceased feeding their daughters before their sons. This meant that a disproportionate number of girls starved to death. To prevent parents from abandoning their children, the state provided little assistance for orphans.

Xinyang prefecture of Henan province had become famous in April 1958 with the establishment of China's first commune. Xinyang party leaders were ardent believers in China's new agricultural programs. They ignored the signs of famine in the fall of 1959, permanently silencing those who dared disagree. By the winter of 1959–60, peasants were eating bark, grass seeds, and weeds. In response, the local CCP redoubled its search for grain hoarders. Estimates vary on the number of those who died, ranging from 1 to 4 million out of a population of 8 million. In the worst-hit counties of Xinyang, two-thirds of the population allegedly perished.

A major power struggle was brewing. Economic disaster brought the Rectification Campaign of 1960–1. In April

1959, Liu Shaoqi had replaced Mao as chairman of the PRC, while Mao remained chairman of the party. In early 1961, Liu Shaoqi and other senior leaders sent fact-finding missions to the countryside. Zhou Enlai and Deng Xiaoping reported widespread starvation. Some argued that the communes should be abandoned. Others, including Mao's eventual successor, Hua Guofeng, dismissed such reports as lies. Liu Shaoqi successfully introduced the reforms that ended the famine. They became known as the "Three Freedoms, One Guarantee": Peasants could raise their own animals, cultivate small private plots, and trade food, with the exception of grain, in return for their guarantee to supply grain to the state. This was very much in keeping with the Soviet Union's response to the postcollectivization famine of the 1930s, which also had permitted the private plots that subsequently became the mainstay of its food supply. In China, 7 percent of cultivated land would be dedicated to private plots. In addition, the Chinese abandoned the Soviet pseudoscience of Lysenko and Williams. With the partial restoration of private farming, production started to recover.

In 1962, China made large purchases of grain from Canada and Australia so that the famine ended by the fall, although consumption remained at subsistence levels.

In 1961, articles critical of Mao began to appear in the press. By the middle of the year, Mao made a self-criticism. Then in 1962, during the annual August retreat of the CCP at the coastal resort Beidaihe, Mao launched a counterattack against Liu Shaoqi and General Secretary Deng Xiaoping. The Communist leadership split: Deng launched his Four Clean Ups Campaign aimed at party members who had hoarded grain during the famine, while Mao launched his Socialist Education Campaign (1962–5) against capitalist roaders. Such divisions slowed the recovery.

It is very difficult to measure the number of deaths resulting from the Great Famine. The most reliable estimate, leaked by the Chinese government years later, set the death toll at the big round number of 30 million. Nearly one-quarter of the fatalities involved peasant girls, who died at a much higher rate than boys. This is consistent with the disproportionate number of female fetuses aborted in China and the dispropor-

Table 24.1 Worst Famines in Chinese History (1842–2009)

Year	Deaths (millions)	Affected Population (millions)	Affected Provinces
1849	15		Zhili, Hubei, Zhejiang, Gansu[*]
1851–2			Widespread[*]
1853–5			Shandong, change in course of Yellow R.[*]
1857	8		Shandong[*]
1867			General crop failure[*]
1876–9	9.5		Shandong, Zhili, Henan, Shaanxi, Shanxi[†]
1920–1	0.5	20	North China[‡]
1927	3	60	Northwest China[§§]
1934			Two-thirds of country hurt by drought/floods[*]
1936	5		Sichuan[§§]
1941	2.5		Sichuan[§§]
1943	5		Henan[§]
1946	4 (Hunan)	30	Nationwide[*]
1960–1		30	Nationwide[§]
1978			Major drought[‖]

Note: Statistics are provided when available. Since Mao's death, the major causes of past famines have continued—droughts in the North and flooding of the Yellow and Yangzi rivers—but the government has avoided famine since 1978 (over 30 years and counting) through more effective disaster relief.

[*]Colin Mackerras, *Modern China: A Chronology from 1842 to the Present* (San Francisco: W. H. Freeman, 1982), 41, 49, 51, 57, 65, 107, 131, 133, 135, 137, 352, 353, 421.

[†]Andrew James Nathan, "A History of the China International Famine Relief Commission" Cambridge, MA: Harvard University, East Asian Center, 1965.

[‡]Penny Kane, *Famine in China, 1959–1961: Demographic and Social Implications* (New York: St. Martin's Press, 1988), 36.

[§§]Donald Hyndman and David Hyndman, *Natural Hazards and Disasters,* 2nd ed. (Belmont: CA: Brooks/Cole, 2009), 263.

[§]Jasper Becker, *Hungry Ghosts: Mao's Secret Famine* (New York: Free Press, 1996), 13–22, 274.

[‖]Colin Mackerras, *The New Cambridge Handbook of Contemporary China* (Cambridge: Cambridge University Press, 2001), 17.

tionately high numbers of girls populating orphanages. People valued sons more than daughters. In the 1980s, the System Reform Institute was charged with making a more accurate count. According to leaked reports, it concluded that between 43 and 46 million people had died, but the findings were never published. Allegedly, the death tolls were 7.8 million in Henan, 8 million in Anhui, 7.5 million in Shandong, 9 million in Sichuan, and 0.9 million for Qinghai, making a total of 33.2 million for just these five provinces. Put another way, 5 percent of China's rural population perished. Deaths in the Great Famine dwarfed even those of the second largest famine in Chinese history, the prolonged drought in North China during 1876–9 that had claimed 9.5 million lives. (See Table 24.1.)

Both the Great Famine in China and the famine of 1932–3 in the Ukraine, the traditional breadbasket of the Russian empire, were direct results of the combination of collectivization and forced-draft industrialization. Both broke the back of any lingering peasant resistance to Communist rule, but at a steep cost in terms of human lives and in permanently stagnant agricultural production. This, in turn, retarded the industrial development of both countries. Nevertheless, collectivization firmly entrenched the power of the Communist Party in the countryside.

As in the USSR, the CCP instituted an internal passport system and set up food rationing and special distribution networks to serve the Communist elite that overwhelmingly lived in the cities. Party members suffered the least during both famines because they lived in separate housing complexes with their own cafeterias. These communal kitchens continued to receive food even while the peasants who produced it starved. Thus, the famine in China was largely a rural phenomenon. Nor could peasants flee the countryside because entry into urban areas required permission and food rations in cities required a local registered domicile listed in their internal passport. Rationing coupons were valid only locally and only for a short period of time. The Communist Party in both countries had a stranglehold over the movements of the citizenry.

Although Mao employed a rural strategy to bring the CCP to power during the Chinese civil war, thereafter the Communists entrenched themselves in the cities at the expense of the peasantry. As in the Russian Revolution, the Communist alliance with the peasantry had been temporary. Immediately after the revolution, the Communists reclaimed the land and requisitioned its products. Mao's economic strategy for industrial development did not deliver prosperity. Even the Soviet Union sharply criticized the economics of the

Private cars were rare in China from the 1950s on. The bicycle became the most widespread and cheapest transportation option for the average Chinese. With its sturdy frame and wide tires, a typical bicycle could easily carry the rider plus several hundred pounds of additional goods, ranging from entire pigs to bricks to baskets. In 2001 China still had over 500 million bicycles, but by 2008 there were almost 25 million privately owned cars, a number that is doubling every four years.

Great Leap Forward. The Great Leap Forward was one of the most ill-conceived government policies in human history. It delivered not industrial development, its goal, but nationwide famine, followed by agricultural stagnation.

IV. The Sino-Soviet Split

Stalin's death in 1953 offered Mao the opportunity to claim the leadership of the international Communist movement. At the time, Mao was the most senior Communist leader. He had a large army deployed near the Sino-Soviet border. His troops had fought the UN to a stalemate. His was the most populous Communist country. His revolutionary model based on the peasantry, not Lenin's based on the urban labor movement, seemed most appropriate for the world's developing countries.

Stalin's successors, however, resisted Mao's attempt to take control of a movement their country had created. From the Soviet point of view, the Chinese were singularly ungrateful considering the enormous and vital Soviet technical assistance provided ever since the founding of the CCP in 1921. In the 1940s the USSR had extended its influence deep into Xinjiang, Outer Mongolia, and Manchuria, raising the prospect of Soviet encirclement of the capital. It took the Korean War and Stalin's death for the withdrawal of Soviet troops from Manchuria. Yet, Outer Mongolia and the many disputed sections of the Sino-Soviet border remained under Soviet control.

Mao pressed Khrushchev to eliminate extraterritoriality and all unequal treaties. Because there were no private citizens in Communist countries—all were state employees—most Soviet citizens in China enjoyed diplomatic immunity, something Western businessmen never claimed. The Soviet government used its own definition of "socialist internationalism" to justify the expansion of this privilege. Under socialist internationalism, all distinctions between national and international interests were irrelevant because the interests of socialist countries were assumed to be identical. By definition, one socialist country could not exploit another. Between 1950 and 1960, the USSR sent 10,000 advisers to China. All enjoyed extraterritoriality and diplomatic immunity. This, in combination with Chinese diplomatic isolation, meant that the privileged Soviet position was far more comprehensive than had been the case for any other nation. The USSR retained these privileges until the Sino-Soviet split of 1960, when it withdrew its last 1,390 advisers.

Tensions brewed. Khrushchev's Secret Speech soon threatened Mao's leadership position in China. In 1957, the USSR offered to help China develop nuclear weapons, but at the price of establishing Soviet submarine and naval bases in Chinese coastal cities. Meanwhile, Khrushchev embarked on a new foreign policy aimed at easing tensions with the West; Mao feared that such ties might strengthen at Chinese expense.

Soon Mao deliberately fueled tensions with the United States to convey to his citizens the urgency of the economic reforms of the Great Leap Forward. On 23 August 1958, Mao touched off the Taiwan Strait Crisis by shelling the Nationalist-held island of Jinmen (Quemoy), located just off the coast of Fujian province. Even though the United States was preoccupied by the aftermath of the 1957 Suez Crisis between Egypt and a coalition of Israel, Britain, and France over control of the Suez Canal, it still deployed six aircraft carriers armed with nuclear weapons, raising the possibility of a U.S.-Soviet confrontation on behalf of their respective allies.

This was actually the Second Taiwan Strait Crisis. The first had occurred from 1954 to 1955, when Mao shelled Jinmen in order to fuel the revolution at home and to force Chiang Kai-shek to halt the Nationalist blockade off the Chinese coast. Ever since 1949, the Nationalists had been harassing PRC shipping. The United States signed a defense treaty with Taiwan on 2 December 1954 in the midst of the crisis. The PRC then took all formerly Nationalist-occupied islands off the Zhejiang coast, although the Nationalist blockade remained in effect, though with shrinking geographic coverage.

Mao used the Second Taiwan Strait crisis both to rally support at home for his domestic programs and to warn the USSR of the dangers of cooperating with the United States by making the analogy with its last and disastrous attempt to cooperate with an adversary on the eve of World War II. To drive home this point, he deliberately began shelling Taiwan on the nineteenth anniversary of the German-Soviet Non-aggression Pact. Mao was making a bid to take control over the international Communist movement. Instead, the USSR renounced the Sino-Soviet Defense Technology Treaty that would have provided nuclear weapons. This occurred two months before the 1959 Lushan Conference, where there was some question of whether the USSR had advance warning of Peng Dehuai's denunciation of Mao.

In 1959, Khrushchev visited the United States. On the way home, he stopped off in China to celebrate its tenth anniversary. There he tactlessly referred to the United States and the USSR as the world's two great powers and pointedly did not include China. Equally tactlessly, he came to the Beijing summit bearing gifts for the deposed marshal, Peng Dehuai, and continued to criticize Mao for the Great Leap Forward. Mao needed a pretext to neutralize the pro-Soviet faction within the CCP that wished to abandon the Great Leap Forward and return to the Soviet models of the Second Five-Year Plan. In opposition to the new Soviet policy of "peaceful coexistence" with the West, Mao called for the expansion of the socialist camp by whatever means, including military.

Despite the rhetoric of communism denying the possibility of imperialism by Communist states, China and the USSR were engaged in a traditional competition for continental empire as well as an increasingly global competition for influence within the international Communist movement. Tensions continued to escalate until the USSR unilaterally withdrew many of its advisers. This left numerous factories and projects unfinished. Then, in August 1960, the PRC appears to have unilaterally abolished Soviet extraterritoriality, whereupon the Soviet Union recalled all of its remaining advisers at the height of the Great Famine.

The timing of the 1960 Sino-Soviet split was not related to any policy change on the Soviet side, but rather on the Chinese side. From the time of the disputed 1919 Karakhan Manifesto on, China had accumulated an inventory of grievances against the Soviet Union. After the Great Leap Forward, Mao came under growing criticism within the CCP and particularly from high-ranking members who advocated cordial relations with the Soviet Union and the adoption of orthodox Soviet economic policies. One of these was Marshal Peng Dehuai, who tried to pin the responsibility for the Great Leap Forward on Mao. This act opened the possibility that Peng might try to use his *guanxi* network within the PLA to stage a coup. Instead, Mao used the generals to oust Peng.

The Sino-Soviet split became public in 1960 when the Soviet and Chinese presses exchanged diatribes in a competition for the sympathies of the many recently independent countries in the wave of decolonization following World War II. The anti-Soviet propaganda campaign accompanying the split presented the Chinese people with a jarring image of Soviet imperialism. The formerly greatest benefactor of China had suddenly become its greatest predator. Mao portrayed the Soviet Union as an insatiable imperial power that had entrenched itself in Outer Mongolia, Manchuria, Xinjiang, Vietnam, and India in order to encircle China.

Although the Sino-Soviet split had ideological elements—such as the role of communes, the use of force against Communist countries, and Khrushchev's plans for peaceful coexistence with the West—the underlying issues were Mao's attempt to take control of the worldwide Communist movement following Stalin's death and limit Soviet influence in China. The public vitriol did not increase Mao's international standing; instead, the dispute undermined the international prestige of communism, and split the international movement into pro-Soviet and pro-Chinese factions.

V. The Sino-Indian War of 1962

Just as territorial issues bedeviled Sino-Soviet relations, they also caused tensions in Sino-Indian relations. India considered South and Southeast Asia as its traditional sphere of influence: All of these nations had acquired Buddhism from India. Yet, China claimed much of the same area: Burma, Thailand, Nepal, Vietnam, and Tibet had all once been Qing tributaries.

In the case of Tibet, although no Dalai Lama had ever kowtowed to a Qing emperor, the Qing had, at different times, been deeply involved in the selection of the Dalai Lama and the administration of Tibet. As in the Sino-Soviet rivalry, China and India each wanted to limit the access of any other great power to its sphere. During the long interregnum between the Qing dynasty and the PRC, Tibet had been independent of Chinese control. With the Communist victory in 1949, the CCP focused on reasserting Han control over the frontiers of the former Qing empire. In 1950 Tibet was next on the list.

Traditionally, India faced no threats from the northeast. Tibet had long been friendly; geography kept it isolated; and Chinese influence was indirect. The Chinese occupation of Tibet in 1951 created a permanent change in Indian national security. At the time, the Indian government pursued a strategy of cultivating Chinese friendship under the assumption that China would reciprocate: India had been among the first countries to extend official diplomatic recognition to the new Communist government and it acceded to China's conquest of Tibet, creating a mutual border between China and India. Later, during the Korean War, the Indian government acted as intermediary for China with the UN. Mao, however, regarded India as a lackey of the West for succumbing to colonialism for so many centuries, and he ridiculed Indians for revering Mahatma Gandhi and his call for a nonviolent revolution.

In 1953, Zhou Enlai proposed the Five Principles of Peaceful Coexistence, emphasizing mutual noninterference in the domestic affairs of the other, as well as equal and mutually beneficial relations. In 1954, he and Indian Prime Minister Jawaharlal Nehru signed an agreement concerning Tibet in which India formally recognized Chinese sovereignty over Tibet in exchange for Chinese friendship. Alas for India, under international law, recognition of sovereignty was permanent, while Chinese friendship was fickle. Finally, in 1955, India invited Zhou Enlai to represent China at the Bandung Conference, where China courted the nonaligned nations by stating, among other things, that overseas Chinese owed their allegiance to their home nation, not to China. This conference also gave Zhou a public venue to promote Chinese leadership abroad with a platform advocating peace, the abolition of nuclear weapons, universal representation in the UN, and arms reduction. The ten-point Bandung Declaration, representing twenty-nine countries and over half of the world's population, incorporated China's Five Principles of Peaceful Coexistence.

Meanwhile, Chinese collectivization of agriculture sparked a revolt of the Tibetan population of Western Sichuan province in 1954. The PRC responded with continued collectivization, the confiscation of herd animals, and the destruction of Lamaist monasteries. As in China proper, collectivization did not bring increased yields but resulted in stagnation. Although the Chinese also made infrastructure

Even as China invested heavily in high technology to make its own atomic bomb, a range of lower-tech developments were also adopted. Here, a public bus is powered by methane stored in a large rubber bag on the roof, which gradually deflates as the gas is used up. Sichuan province, where this picture was taken, has large supplies of natural gas. Methane can also be collected as an unwelcome by-product from coal mines.

investments and introduced economic reforms to improve the Tibetan standard of living, many Tibetans resented Chinese interference. The Tibetan population of Sichuan rebelled again in 1956 and rural unrest continued to spread toward Lhasa in 1958, until Lhasa also rose up in March 1959.

The Chinese government responded to the revolt by deploying the PLA and imposing the policies of the Great Leap Forward. This spelled the end to nomadism, with the population forced onto communes and their herds taken away in 1959. Many Tibetans considered Mao's agricultural policies to be an attempt to destroy their culture. The ecology of Tibet was not suited to the settled agricultural practices demanded by the CCP. As a result, as many as one in five Tibetans died of starvation. In 1962 the Panchen Lama, one of the most revered figures of Tibetan Buddhism, issued a report accusing the Chinese of attempting to destroy the Tibetan nationality, that is, of practicing genocide. The report landed the Panchen Lama in jail, where he remained until 1977.

Despite Chinese protests, India granted sanctuary in 1959 to the Dalai Lama, the spiritual leader of Tibet. In India, the Dalai Lama remained politically active. At the time, the United States was funneling aid to the Tibetan rebels as a minor operation in the global Cold War against the Soviet Union and its allies. The Chinese believed that the Indians supported this covert aid. China responded to the spreading unrest with a brutal pacification campaign entailing summary executions, torture, forced resettlement, reprisals, and the systematic destruction of monasteries. During the Cultural Revolution, the Chinese would ban and severely punish even the private practice of Lamaism. Neighboring Indians were appalled. From their point of view, the Chinese provided nothing in return for Indian friendship.

Sino-Indian border tensions began to increase. On 17 July 1954, the Chinese government demanded the Barahoti section of the border, also claimed by the Indians, as part of Uttar Pradesh province. (See Map 24.1.) On 28 June 1955, soon after the successful conclusion of the Bandung Conference, the Indian government protested a Chinese incursion into this area. China denied the charge. However, during 1956, China took possession of the Tunjun La and Shipki La passes. In 1958, the Indian government first learned of the completion of a Chinese road across the Ladakh region of the volatile province of Jammu and Kashmir, claimed by both India and Pakistan. The Chinese were building a road in order to facilitate their escalating pacification of Tibet so that they could encircle Tibet via Xinjiang. India protested to no

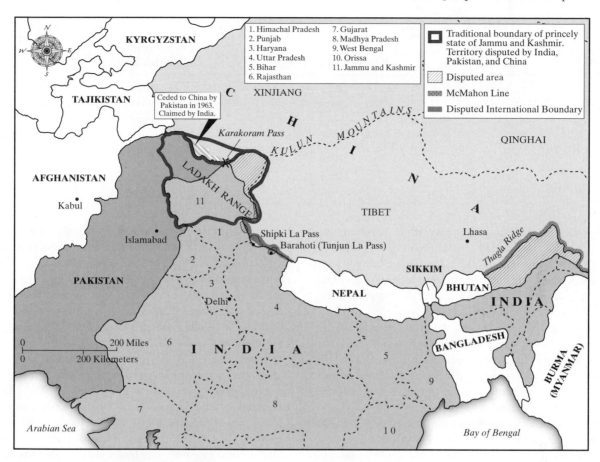

Map 24.1 Sino-Indian War (1962)

effect. Likewise, on 24 August 1958, the Indian government protested the publication of Chinese maps showing large areas along the Sino-Indian border as Chinese territory.

In November 1958, China denied that it had ever signed agreements defining the border with India. This suggested a unilateral rejection of such treaties as the Kashmir-Tibetan Treaty of 1842 detailing the Ladakh boundary, the Anglo-Chinese Convention of 1890 detailing the Sikkim boundary, and, most importantly for India, the 1914 McMahon Line, agreed to by China, Tibet, and India, setting the eastern border from Bhutan to Burma. On 8 September 1959, Zhou Enlai stated that the McMahon Line constituted a British policy of aggression against Tibet, that it was illegal, and that it had never been recognized by any Chinese government. China's elimination of Tibet as a buffer state suggested to many Indians that it had aggressive designs on Indian territory. Clashes erupted in 1959 along the westernmost section of the border south of the Kunlun Mountains in what India considered to be Himachal Pradesh

province. Soon, fighting also erupted far to the southeast near Bhutan. The disputed land to the west comprised approximately 15,000 square miles, while that to the east approximated 25,000 square miles.

During 1962, following India's decision to deploy troops close to the border, China put troops on Thagla Ridge, just north of the McMahon Line near the eastern border. On 22 September 1962, when Indian troops attempted to repel the PLA, they triggered a PLA blitzkrieg on 20 October, followed by a unilateral Chinese cease-fire on 22 November. India tried to negotiate a return to the prewar lines of demarcation, but China would not do so unconditionally. All attempts to solve the underlying Sino-Indian border problems failed, and talks did not reopen until 1979. From 1962 to 1979, Beijing supported anti-Indian movements throughout South Asia.

China's hard line in dealing with India reflected its general inflexibility on all border issues. In the nineteenth century Russia had taken vast Chinese lands in the North, while the Western powers had established treaty ports and spheres

Table 24.2   Acquisition of Nuclear Weapons

Country	Atomic Bomb Test	Thermonuclear Bomb Test
United States	1945	1952
Soviet Union	1949	1953
Great Britain	1952	1957
France	1960	1968
China	1964	1967
India	1974	
Pakistan	1998	

of influence throughout China proper. In the twentieth century, Japan had attempted to dominate Manchuria and coastal China, while Russia had taken Outer Mongolia and occupied Xinjiang for a time. China lost enormous territories during these years and so had acute sensitivity regarding national boundaries. The Chinese government considered the Tibetans to be utterly backward and in desperate need of a Communist revolution, while control over Tibet precluded invasion from that quarter. Moreover, Tibetan resources were essential for Chinese economic development. Tibet accounts for 40 percent of China's known mineral resources and approximately 13 percent of its territory.

There was also a Sino-Soviet dimension to Sino-Indian tensions. During the late 1950s, Khrushchev granted generous credits to India and the two countries signed a five-year trade agreement on 16 November 1958. Yet, Khrushchev refused to gratify China on any territorial issues or to provide the technology to produce an atomic bomb. Then he backed India in the Sino-Indian border dispute. Since China also had border claims against the USSR, Khrushchev did not want to set a precedent by backing Chinese claims against India. Mao, for his part, feared that the Soviet Union would combine with India to surround and restrict Chinese actions. Atomic weapons magnified these fears. China's only hope would be to shore up its own border defenses. While China focused on preventing bordering nations from forming anti-Chinese alliances with the Soviet Union, India and the USSR had cordial relations, in large measure, to counterbalance their mutual fears of China. China's victory over India demonstrated its ability to retain, and even expand, its territory. It also served as a warning to Moscow that China's other territorial disagreements would not be ignored forever. China attacked India just as Soviet-Indian relations were warming, yet the Soviet Union did not actively come to India's aid. Thus, China demonstrated to India the limits of Soviet-Indian cooperation.

China's quick military victory over India reverberated throughout Asia. One of the first countries to respond was Pakistan. The two countries quickly signed a Sino-Pakistan border agreement in which Pakistan ceded territory in Kashmir to China. In 1965 the PRC supported Pakistan during the Pakistani-Indian war over Kashmir. China's victory also sent a clear message to the countries of Southeast Asia—many of them former Chinese tributary states—that the PLA was now both willing and able to reassert Chinese influence abroad. China's detonation of an atomic bomb in October 1964 reemphasized its independent foreign policy. The 1962 border war overturned Indian foreign policy, spurring India to develop atomic weapons in 1974. (See Table 24.2.) Fear of India then spurred China to help Pakistan become an atomic power, making it the only Muslim state with atomic weapons. In 1998, India and Pakistan both successfully tested atomic weapons. The bitter Indian-Pakistani dispute over Kashmir provided an eternal pretext for war, now with the potential to go nuclear. In short, Sino-Indian tensions had global consequences.

Conclusions

With the Hundred Flowers Campaign, the Great Leap Forward, the Sino-Soviet split, and the war with India, the Chinese government demonstrated the independence of its domestic and foreign policy from Western, Soviet, or Indian influence. For the first time since the Opium Wars, the Chinese government was charting a completely independent, if not a particularly wise, course of action. No foreign power forced these choices upon China; in fact, they were taken against foreign advice. Mao reunified China. Next, he sought leadership of international communism.

In the Hundred Flowers Campaign, Mao sought mild dissent within the intellectual community to restore public enthusiasm for Communist rule. To his dismay, he discovered widespread public dissatisfaction. He responded with jail sentences in the ensuing Anti-Rightist Campaign. This muzzled the opinion of experts, which made possible the unwise agronomy, economics, and industrialization practices of the Great Leap Forward. China's Western-trained experts knew better but could say nothing. In the Great Leap Forward, Mao attempted to chart a new path to economic development. He followed the Soviet model, putting the peasantry under strict government control by forcing them onto communes so that he could redistribute income away from agriculture to industry. But unlike Stalin, Mao attempted to decentralize industry throughout the countryside as well. In both countries, the result—widespread famine—was similar, only more severe in China. Mao hoped to catch up economically with the USSR so that he could challenge its leadership of the international Communist movement on the basis of both economic production and ideological correctness. Mao, in the tradition of the Legalists, ignored the human costs of his attempt to reorganize the social structure of China. The needs of the state apparently justified all.

Initially, the Chinese population enthusiastically participated in the Great Leap Forward with the expectation of prosperity around the corner. The combination of collectivization, a plague of insects, politically correct agronomy, and excessive agricultural requisitioning to feed the cities, however, led to a nationwide famine throughout rural China. The policy choices of the CCP brought famine, not wealth. As a result of Mao's failed attempt at social engineering, 30 million Chinese perished, a large percentage of them peasant girls, whose parents sacrificed them before their brothers. The reward for peasant support for the Communist Revolution was collectivization, starvation, and economic deprivation.

The Great Leap Forward was an enormous debacle on numerous levels: It undermined agricultural and industrial production; greatly exacerbated tensions with the USSR; weakened popular support for the Communists; drove a wedge between urban and rural China; and threatened the cult of Mao. In April 1959 Mao relinquished his position as head of state to Liu Shaoqi, although he retained his chairmanship of the tarnished CCP. Khrushchev took advantage of Mao's failed policies to undercut his claims to leadership both of China and of the international Communist movement. Pro-Soviet sympathizers within the CCP, such as Peng Dehuai, favored rapprochement with the USSR. Mao's divisive policies split the party into two hostile factions. All of this put Mao under extreme pressure to retain his hold on power.

The policies of the Great Leap Forward split not only the CCP but also the international Communist movement. Mao demanded nuclear technology from the USSR. In return, the USSR demanded basing rights for Soviet warships and submarines in Chinese ports. Mao demanded an end to Soviet rapprochement with the West. Khrushchev warned Mao that the Great Leap Forward would not work. While Mao proclaimed it to have been a huge success, Khrushchev admonished him for bringing China to the brink of ruin. When Mao precipitated the Taiwan Strait Crisis to stir domestic nationalistic passions in support of the Great Leap Forward, he created an international crisis with the potential to escalate into a U.S.-Soviet nuclear confrontation. The economic policies of the Great Leap Forward in combination with the nuclear brinkmanship of the Taiwan Strait Crisis appalled the Soviet leaders, who concluded that further economic aid to China would endanger Soviet national security. By 1960 they had withdrawn all of their advisers, leaving many large development projects unfinished. The Sino-Soviet split became public in a propaganda war fought in the international press.

Finally, even though in the early 1950s India was one of China's most ardent supporters, and the two countries pledged to coexist peacefully, the long-term impact of the Sino-Indian border war produced profound international ramifications. Within a few years, India would acquire atomic weapons to counterbalance the nuclear threat from China, while China would then agree to help Pakistan to acquire atomic weapons to neutralize India. The end result was nuclear arms proliferation and an arms race on one of China's most vulnerable borders.

BIBLIOGRAPHY

Bachman, David. *Bureaucracy, Economy, and Leadership in China: The Institutional Origins of the Great Leap Forward.* Cambridge: Cambridge University Press, 1991.

Becker, Jasper. *Hungry Ghosts: Mao's Secret Famine.* New York: Free Press, 1996.

Chang, Jung and Jon Halliday, *Mao: The Unknown Story.* New York: Alfred A. Knopf, 2005.

Chao, Kang. *Agricultural Production in Communist China, 1949–1965.* Madison: University of Wisconsin Press, 1971.

Christensen, Thomas J. *Useful Adversaries: Grand Strategy, Domestic Mobilization, and Sino-American Conflict, 1947–1958.* Princeton, NJ: Princeton University Press, 1996.

Clark, M. Gardner. *The Development of China's Steel Industry and Soviet Technical Aid.* Ithaca, NY: Cornell University Press, 1973.

Conquest, Robert. *Harvest of Sorrow.* Oxford: Oxford University Press, 1986.

Dittmer, Lowell. *Sino-Soviet Normalization and Its International Implications, 1945–2000.* Seattle: University of Washington Press, 1992.

Doolin, Dennis J. *Territorial Claims in the Sino-Soviet Conflict: Documents and Analysis.* Stanford, CA: Stanford University Press, 1965.

Eckstein, Alexander. *China's Economic Revolution.* Cambridge: Cambridge University Press, 1977.

Garthoff, Raymond. *Sino-Soviet Military Relations.* New York: Praeger, 1966.

Garver, John W. *Protracted Contest: Sino-Indian Rivalry in the Twentieth Century.* Seattle: University of Washington Press, 2001.

Ginsburgs, George. *Sino-Soviet Territorial Dispute.* Oxford: Oxford University Press, 1968.

Gittings, John. *Survey of the Sino-Soviet Dispute.* Oxford: Oxford University Press, 1968.

Goldstein, Melvyn C. *A History of Modern Tibet, 1913–1952.* Berkeley: University of California Press, 1989.

Grunfeld, A. Tom, *The Making of Modern Tibet*, rev. ed. Armonk, NY: M. E. Sharpe, 1996.

Heimsath, Charles H. and Surjit Mansingh. *A Diplomatic History of Modern India.* Bombay: Allied Publishers, 1971.

Hoffmann, Steven A. *India and the China Crisis.* Berkeley: University of California Press, 1990.

Jian, Chen. *Mao's China & the Cold War.* Chapel Hill: University of North Carolina Press, 2001.

Kane, Penny. *Famine in China, 1959–61. Demographic and Social Implications.* Basingstoke, England: Macmillan, 1988.

Knight, John and Lina Song. *The Rural–Urban Divide: Economic Disparities in China.* Oxford: Oxford University Press, 1999.

Li, Zhisui, *The Private Life of Chairman Mao.* Translated by Tai Hung-chao. New York: Random House, 1994.

MacFarquhar, Roderick, ed. *The Hundred Flowers Campaign and the Chinese Intellectuals.* New York: Praeger, 1960.

———*The Origins of the Cultural Revolution.* Vols. 1, 2. New York: Columbia University Press, 1974–83.

Maxwell, Neville. *India's China War.* London: Cape, 1970.

Middleton, Drew. *The Duel of Giants: China and Russia in Asia.* New York: Charles Scribner's Sons, 1978.

Perkins, Dwight H., ed. *Rural Small-scale Industry in the People's Republic of China.* Berkeley: University of California Press, 1977.

Printz, Peggy and Paul Steinle. *Commune: Life in Rural China.* New York: Dodd, Mead, 1977.

Sandhu, Bhim. *Unresolved Conflict: China and India.* New Delhi: Radiant Publishers, 1988.

Schapiro, Judith. *Mao's War against Nature: Politics and the Environment in Revolutionary China.* Cambridge: Cambridge University Press, 2001.

Sheehan, Jackie, *Chinese Workers: A New History.* London: Routledge, 1998.

Short, Philip. *Mao: A Life.* New York: Henry Holt, 1999.

Teiwes, Frederick C. *Politics and Purges in China: Rectification and the Decline of Party Norms, 1950–1965.* 2nd ed. Armonk, NY: M. E. Sharpe, 1993.

———*China's Road to Disaster: Mao, Central Politicians, and Provincial Leaders in the Unfolding of the Great Leap Forward 1955–1959.* Armonk, NY: M. E. Sharpe, 1999.

Terrill, Ross. *Mao: A Biography.* Rev. edition. Stanford, CA: Stanford University Press, 1999.

Trivedi, Ram Naresh. *Sino-Indian Border Dispute and Its Impact on Indo-Pakistani Relations.* New Delhi: Associated Publishing House, 1977.

Tsou, Tang. *Embroilment over Quemoy: Mao, Chiang, and Dulles.* Salt Lake City: University of Utah Press, 1959.

Unger, Jonathan. *The Transformation of Rural China.* Armonk, NY: M. E. Sharpe, 2002.

Wang, Fei-ling. *Organizing through Division and Exclusion: China's Hukou System.* Stanford, CA: Stanford University Press, 2005.

Whitson, William W. *The Chinese Military and the Political Leaders and the Distribution of Power in China, 1956–1971.* Santa Monica, CA: Rand, 1972.

Zagoria, Donald. *The Sino-Soviet Conflict, 1956–1961.* Princeton, NJ: Princeton University Press, 1962.

NOTES

1. Cited in Jasper Becker, *Hungry Ghosts: Mao's Secret Famine* (New York: Free Press, 1996), 88, 320.
2. Moshe Lewin, *Russian Peasants and Soviet Power: A Study of Collectivization* (New York: W. W. Norton, 1969), 450.
3. Quoted by Jasper Becker, *Hungry Ghosts: Mao's Secret Famine* (New York: Free Press, 1996), 88.

Chronology

27 April 1959	Liu Shaoqi replaces Mao as head of state
January 1961	Publication of Wu Han's play, *Hai Rui Dismissed from Office*
16 October 1964	China successfully tests its first atomic bomb
10 November 1965	First attack on Wu Han's play; beginning of the Cultural Revolution
1 May 1966	Official beginning of the Cultural Revolution
20 June 1966	Red Guards begin attacks on the Four Old Things
23 October 1966	Liu Shaoqi and Deng Xiaoping submit self-criticisms
17 June 1967	China successfully tests its first hydrogen bomb
5 September 1968	Revolutionary committees set up throughout China
31 October 1968	Dismissal of Liu Shaoqi and expulsion from the CCP
12 November 1968	Announcement of the Brezhnev Doctrine
2 March 1969	Sino-Soviet fighting on Zhenbao Island
1–24 April 1969	Ninth Party Congress
June–August 1969	Sino-Soviet fighting in the Xinjiang Uighur autonomous region
8 July 1969	Sino-Soviet fighting near Khabarovsk
12 November 1969	Liu Shaoqi dies in prison
14 April 1971	United States announces loosening of trade restrictions for PRC
9–11 July 1971	Secret visit of Henry Kissinger to Beijing
25 October 1971	PRC to replace Taiwan at the United Nations
21–7 February 1972	Richard Nixon visits China
27 February 1972	Shanghai Communiqué and Lin Biao's death announced
25–30 September 1972	Prime Minister Tanaka Kakue visits China
29 September 1972	Sino-Japanese Communiqué restoring relations
27 January 1973	Paris Peace Agreement settling the Vietnam War
16 December 1978	Communiqué on the Establishment of Diplomatic Relations between China and the United States
17 August 1982	Joint Communiqué on the Question of Arms Sales to Taiwan

25

The Cultural Revolution

Song of Wisdom

Another joy, the spell of high ideals,
Drew me through many a twisting mile of thorn.
To suffer for ideals is no pain;
But oh, to see them mocked and scorned!

Now nothing remains but remorse —
Daily punishment for past pride.
When the glory of the sky stands condemned,
In this wasteland, what color can survive?[1]

Mu Dan (1918–1977), poet
translator, veteran, 1976

With the breathtaking failure of the Great Leap Forward and growing realization within the CCP leadership that it had caused the Great Famine, Mao feared for his political survival due to a slackening in revolutionary momentum and an entrenched Communist bureaucracy. Mao used the Cultural Revolution to eliminate the pro-Soviet faction in the Chinese leadership and those who had reversed his economic policies to end the Great Famine. He also took advantage of the Cultural Revolution to reorient China's foreign policy away from the Soviet Union and seek rapprochement with the United States, an extremely controversial about-face that could have easily undermined Mao's mandate to rule. Unlike the Great Famine, however, which hit China's rural areas most severely, the Cultural Revolution took its greatest toll on cities and towns, and in particular on the emerging modern sectors of the urban economy. It would undermine economic development for well over a decade, as the most knowledgeable teachers and professionals were ostracized, exiled to the countryside for years of manual labor, or even killed, requiring years to reconstitute the educational institutions that existed on the

eve of the Cultural Revolution. The movement also nearly set off a nuclear war with the Soviet Union.

I. Mao's Weakened Position

In the early 1960s, Mao was still in the process of consolidating his control over the CCP and also over the military. As in the early years of Manchu rule, leadership remained to some extent collective. Important decisions were made after some discussion among the top leaders. The Hundred Flowers Campaign indicated a strong undercurrent of dissent among Chinese intellectuals and CCP members. Then the Great Famine greatly magnified this dissatisfaction. Such Soviet leaders as Nikita Khrushchev had made clear their poor opinion of Mao's policies. The problem of agricultural stagnation also confounded Khrushchev, whose failure at agricultural reform coupled with the 1962 Cuban Missile Crisis, when he caved in to U.S. pressure and removed Soviet nuclear missiles from Cuba, culminated in his ouster in 1964. The potential relevance of this precedent to Mao's continued rule could not have been lost on the Chinese leadership.

The Great Famine proved extremely divisive, so that the leadership had begun to coalesce around very different policies. There was a strong pro-Soviet group that hoped to emulate the Soviet model for economic development. There was an even stronger and virulently nationalistic group that emphasized the imperialistic nature of Soviet foreign policy and rejected all Soviet models for foreign or domestic policy. This group of ideologues believed that China should follow its own indigenous route to modernization without westernization or Sovietization. There was also another emerging group of bureaucrats who saw a technocratic route to prosperity by emphasizing scientific expertise over ideology. This disagreement concerned the USSR's and China's optimal route to modernization. There was no disagreement that China needed to acquire and then be able to produce its own state-of-the-art technology in all fields and especially for the military. All groups intended to transform China into a great power second to none, but they disagreed over the appropriate strategy to realize this objective. Mao stayed in power by playing off these groups against each other.

There was enormous disagreement on the policies necessary to promote economic recovery. By 1960, China's agricultural output had dropped to 75 percent of its pre–Great Leap Forward level. Between 1959 and 1961, the Chinese population had fallen by 13.5 million. Industrial production had also imploded, with heavy industry even more severely affected than light industry: Between 1961 and 1962, heavy industrial production dropped by 47 percent. The technocrats blamed these problems on the policies of the Great Leap Forward, while the anti-Soviet group blamed them on the sudden withdrawal of Soviet advisers. The ideologues blamed faltering revolutionary spirit and bureaucratic sclerosis, and demanded further rectification of the CCP and mass political education.

For a time, the technocrats, or economic rationalists, came to the fore. Deng Xiaoping was one of the leaders of this group, which focused on economic performance over ideological rectitude and recommended material incentives to spur production and the reward of professional expertise. To Mao, such policies seemed to promote at best a pale image of the Soviet paradigm and at worst a restoration of bourgeois rule. Yet, he was under siege in the party for causing the Great Famine and was forced to make self-criticisms during the spring of 1959. This undercut his mandate to rule. Policy reversals are difficult in all societies, but particularly so in a face society where power is exercised not primarily through institutions, but through personalistic ties of *guanxi*. Those whose shortcomings become known by definition lose face, which erodes *guanxi*, thus shrinking the person's power base—hence the enormous implications of self-criticism during the CCP's many rectification campaigns. Those forced into self-criticism were potentially permanently compromised. Mao also lost tremendous face when Liu Shaoqi replaced him as head of state in April 1959.

When the Sino-Soviet split became public, this further eroded Mao's mandate to rule. Until then, despite the many frictions, Beijing had portrayed the Soviet Union as a close and reliable ally. New realities suggested that Communist orthodoxy was wrong on numerous counts. Although Mao could still manipulate the party apparatus as chairman of the CCP, his power over the government had greatly diminished. Between 1961 and 1966, he convened only one meeting of the Central Committee of the CCP. The other members of the Politburo started to ignore his views. He no longer was

often seen in public with foreign visitors or even with his own people. Liu Shaoqi and Deng Xiaoping stressed the restoration of bureaucratic normalcy.

This infighting at the top over key domestic and foreign policy issues formed the backdrop to the Cultural Revolution. The *guanxi* networks of key leaders were combining into hostile coalitions. Through 1966, Mao was on the losing side until he started to organize a revitalized set of *guanxi* networks in his support. These included the military, radical intellectuals, and students. He began the movement by working through the Shanghai media and stirring up Shanghai students in order to bypass the central government that had diminished his power. With the revolution over and the Great Famine the most recent achievement of the CCP, enormous social tensions arose from the increasingly visible disconnect between the utopian promises of communism and the stark reality of enduring poverty, inequality, and corruption. Mao would attempt to blame his enemies for the CCP's failure to match their ideals with reality. For most Chinese, who were not part of any of these high-level *guanxi* networks, the major division in China seemed to be between the emerging highly privileged Communist elite and their children, on the one hand, and the vast majority of the population on the other. The elite had access to educational opportunities, hospital care, jobs, food, and housing far beyond the means of the majority of the population. As in the civil war, Mao used jealousy against his enemies with lethal results. Before, it had been the evil wealthy Nationalists; now it would be the privileged Communist elite. He would play off the deep popular frustrations to eliminate his rivals.

II. The Phases of the Cultural Revolution

The demotion of Marshal Peng Dehuai in 1959 had been highly unpopular among the general public. The pretext for the Cultural Revolution was a not so subtle attack on Mao for dismissing Peng, disguised, as is so often the case in China, in art or poetry. The vice-mayor of Beijing, Wu Han, wrote a play about Hai Rui (Hai Jui), a loyal Ming dynasty official dismissed for daring justly to criticize the emperor. The play, *Hai Rui Dismissed from Office* (*Hai Rui baguan*), implied that Mao was a modern-day emperor, who had cashiered Peng unfairly for daring to speak the truth about the Great Leap Forward. Intellectuals started a movement at Peking University, where big-character posters appeared criticizing the government. Mao instigated a withering counterattack on Wu Han that rapidly broadened to attacks on revisionist intellectuals in general and, from there, to attacks on revisionists within the CCP. Soon big-character posters appeared denouncing revisionists. Wu Han would die during the Cultural Revolution.

Mao's chief allies were Lin Biao, who commanded the PLA; Chen Boda, who served as chief ideologue and interpreter of Mao Zedong Thought; and his third wife (some accounts say fourth, counting an unconsummated arranged marriage at age fourteen), an actress turned revolutionary called Jiang Qing (real name Li Shumeng; stage name Lan Ping) who had aspirations to reshape Chinese culture. Chen Boda and Jiang Qing formed the cultural wing of Mao's emerging *guanxi* network, important for setting ideological orthodoxy and for mass mobilization. Institutionally, their position resembled that of court favorites in past imperial dynasties. Jiang Qing has been compared to the Empress Dowager Cixi because of her enormous influence over Mao's decisions. This triumvirate—Chen Boda, Lin Biao, and Jiang Qing—deflected the wave of public resentment concerning the deprivations from the Great Leap Forward, jealousy over the privileges of Communist cadres, and disenchantment of China's youth over inadequate job opportunities, against the technocratic and the pro-Soviet factions.

From 1965 to 1966, Mao focused on removing his rivals in Beijing. He circumvented the CCP's administrative structure by mobilizing China's vast population of urban youth and harnessing their idealism, fervor, and political naiveté to remove his political opponents: Mao's *Little Red Book,* first published in 1966, of revolutionary quotations became their source of wisdom. (See the feature below.) First among his enemies were those who had ended the Great Famine and, in doing so, showed up the economic incompetence underlying the Great Leap Forward. This meant Liu Shaoqi, who prior to the Cultural Revolution had authority on a par with that of Mao and, in the absence of the Cultural Revolution, might have eventually unseated him.

Zhou Enlai announced the beginning of the Great Proletarian Cultural Revolution at a huge demonstration at Tiananmen Square celebrating International Workers' Day on 1 May 1966. He called on China's students to rally behind Mao. By this time, the cult of Mao, which had its origins in the Yan'an era, was so strong that many Chinese youth, who in the absence of life experiences that would have allowed them to think more independently, assumed that Mao was always right. Mao had China's urban youth organized into quasi-military units of Red Guards, which he set upon the local CCP administrative structure that increasingly had hindered his efforts to transform China. They were to root out those belonging to any of the so-called Four Bad Elements (*si lei fenzi*): the descendants of landlords, wealthy peasants, counterrevolutionaries, or other rotten elements. Over the summer and fall of 1966, the Red Guards held eight mass rallies in Tiananmen Square, where millions of Chinese youth from cities throughout China converged to hear Lin Biao, Chen Boda, Jiang Qing, and Zhou Enlai. Through mid-1968, Mao relied on these young people to spearhead his revolution, first in Beijing and by late 1966 throughout the country. Ironically, the members of the Red Guard came not from the proletariat, as Communist ideology would imply, but were the children of professionals.

Apparently Mao envisioned enthusiastic youthful critics inspiring sincere recantations by chastised party officials to pro-

MAO'S LITTLE RED BOOK

The *Quotations from Chairman Mao Zedong,* first published in 1966 as a pocket-sized book with a bright red plastic cover, became known, over the course of its numerous reprintings, as *The Little Red Book.* Marshal Lin Biao compiled the quotations of Mao to create a convenient anthology for indoctrinating new PLA recruits. The Red Guards of the Cultural Revolution, however, latched on to it and were rarely without their copies. A generation of Chinese schoolchildren grew up memorizing this anthology, just as their great-grandparents had memorized the Confucian Classics. Unlike the Confucian Classics, which were complex and intended for the literary education of the elite, Mao's quotations were written in simple language aimed at the political education of a mass audience. The purpose of *The Little Red Book* was the same as that of the Classics: to create loyalty to the existing political order.

   The Little Red Book contained thirty-three chapters of quotations from Mao organized topically. Chapter titles included "The Communist Party," "Classes and Class Struggle," "Imperialism and All Reactionaries Are Paper Tigers," "People's War," "The People's Army," "The Mass Line," "Self-Reliance and Arduous Struggle," "Methods of Thinking and Methods of Work," "Correcting Mistaken Ideas," and "Criticism and Self-Criticism." Six chapters specifically concerned the military and five the CCP. According to the opening chapter, "The Chinese Communist Party is the core of leadership of the whole Chinese people. Without this core, the cause of socialism cannot be victorious."[2]

The following chapter on class struggle offered cold comfort to those with the misfortune to be born into the wrong class: "Classes struggle, some classes triumph, others are eliminated."[3] For those with the illusion that they could think independently, Mao responded: "In class society everyone lives as a member of a particular class, and every kind of thinking, without exception, is stamped with the brand of a class."[4] In keeping with the *yin* and *yang* traditions of coexisting opposites, Mao extolled the "people's democratic dictatorship"[5] that was at once a democracy and a dictatorship. He rejected the notion that historical development could be peaceful: "The seizure of power by armed force, the settlement of the issue by war, is the central task and the highest form of revolution."[6] But he was optimistic that the destructive power of modern weaponry had been exaggerated: "The atom bomb is a paper tiger which the U.S. reactionaries use to scare people. It looks terrible, but in fact it isn't. Of course, the atom bomb is a weapon of mass slaughter, but the outcome of a war is decided by the people, not by one or two new types of weapon."[7]

In keeping with the Han tradition of the subordination of the individual to the family, Mao replaced the family with the CCP: "We must affirm anew the discipline of the Party, namely: (1) the individual is subordinate to the organization; (2) the minority is subordinate to the majority; (3) the lower level is subordinate to the higher level; and (4) the entire membership is subordinate to the Central Committee."[8] For the minority peoples of China, this did not depart from the traditional pattern of Han domination. As in the past, China remained hierarchical and the control of the very top of the social and political pyramid was now defined by CCP position.

duce a reformed and effective party. Instead, the Red Guard attacks undermined party authority and organizations of all kinds to produce anarchy. The Red Guards could not agree among themselves and were soon reduced to infighting and uncoordinated but brutal attacks on others. Instead of the rectification that Mao intended, lawlessness extended from the capital to the provinces. Restoration of order was extremely difficult and did not occur fully until after Mao's death. Arguably the authority of the CCP never recovered fully from the combined effects of the Great Famine and the Cultural Revolution.

The Cultural Revolution moved through phases. In the first phase, Mao relied on those who knew least about the Great Famine: the idealistic teenage children of the Communist elite. These young people had spent their lives in the urban areas least affected by the famine and had been raised by parents who had not dared discuss the disastrous policies pursued by the Communist government. In urban areas, Chinese students began joining the Red Guards and criticizing what they claimed were the old ideas of many government officials. They denounced the Four Olds: old ideas, old culture, old customs, and old habits. Initially they attacked their teachers, the authority figures of children's lives and of China's Confucian past. In doing so, they gutted the educational system. As proof of their zeal, the Red Guards ravaged China's artistic heritage, finding destruction easier to accomplish than construction. Red Guards destroyed ancient buildings, libraries, art treasures, historical and religious sites, museums, historic homes, and books from the previous dynasties, proclaiming that these artifacts represented impediments to China's future progress. Many of China's greatest artistic treasures were lost. Red Guards did not limit themselves to vandalism but engaged in widespread murder of those with Western educations or previous Western contacts, as well as any considered in some way bourgeois.

Students became some of Mao's most reliable supporters during the Cultural Revolution. Wearing military-style clothing and sporting large Mao buttons, the Red Guards attacked Communist bureaucrats for not following the true path to communism, as set forth by Mao Zedong in his *Little Red Book*.

In the next phase, Mao increasingly emphasized class struggle and the need to eradicate class enemies. He turned from intellectuals to the Communist elite. University-age Red Guards, often too old to be the children of the Communist elite that had come to power over the previous decade, then attacked the heads of the CCP subunits and so-called capitalist-roaders. Without well-placed parents, they had no qualms about widening their attacks to include the Communist elite. Mao used the Cultural Revolution to undermine his political opponents, especially Peng Dehuai of the pro-Soviet faction and Liu Shaoqi of the technocratic faction. Mao's wife, Jiang Qing, had Peng arrested and tried by the Red Guards. Thereafter, she helped orchestrate the destruction of Mao's other potential rivals, including Liu Shaoqi, who lost his position as head of state and in October 1968 was expelled from the party. Neither Peng nor Liu survived the turmoil but died under arrest, the former beaten to death and the latter from psychological abuse and withheld medical attention.

As disorder spread throughout the country, there were pitched battles among the Red Guard factions and the terror became so random that no one was immune. As this infighting devolved into a new civil war in the provincial cities and towns, Mao called on the army under Lin Biao to restore order and demobilize the Red Guards, which were disbanded in 1968. (See Table 25.1.) As a price for PLA support, Lin Biao's officers acquired a plurality of leadership appointments made at the Ninth Party Congress in April 1969. At this time, Lin Biao also secured the coveted position of Mao's successor, originally promised in 1966 but now formally written into the constitution. Thus, Lin combined the civil and military positions of his fallen enemies, Liu Shaoqi and Peng Dehuai. The rapid expansion of the PLA indicated the primacy of its internal garrisoning duties over national defense. All of this gave the PLA enormous authority, which potentially threatened Mao's authority over the long term. Its dominance also threatened the long-term interests of the cultural *guanxi* network under Jiang Qing and Chen Boda and the surviving Communist cadres under Zhou Enlai. Thus, these *guanxi* networks competed with each other even while cooperating with Mao.

As part of the Cultural Revolution, from 1967 to 1978 the government forced 17 million urban youth, mainly middle school and high school graduates, to work in the countryside, the "up to the mountains and down to the countryside youth," also known as the Sent Down Generation. Many were separated from their families for over a decade. Few remained in rural areas when they were allowed to return home in 1979. The program was intended to relieve urban unemployment while promoting rural development. In practice, it caused enormous bitterness among those separated from their families. This program differed from the government's reduction of the urban population by 26 million between 1961 and 1963. On that occasion, recent rural arrivals were forced to return to the countryside, while during the Cultural Revolution, the children of long-term urban residents were sent to the countryside.

In addition to urban youth, by 1969 the Communist elite of the 1950s and early 1960s had been scattered throughout the countryside to perform manual labor or serve out prison terms; the educational system had been devastated, with those lacking instruction attempting to educate others; economic production had again imploded; the status and power of the army had grown immeasurably; and Mao had become China's new emperor, in reality if not in name. Like the Bolshevik elite that brought revolution to Russia, the first-generation Communist elite had been sacrificed on the altar of the supreme leader's quest for personal rule. Stalin and Mao eliminated those most familiar with their past and in doing so attempted to control public memory. Whereas Stalin had most of his early compatriots shot, Mao, following Confucian preferences, subjected his to coercive reeducation. In each country, the purged were often sent to sparsely populated frontiers as a first line of defense. At the Ninth Party Congress in 1969, there was a 60 percent turnover of the previous Politburo, a 70 percent turnover of the previous Central Committee, a 70–80 percent turnover of the regional and provincial leaders, and a much larger military and Red Guard presence throughout the party. Mao's Great Purge was now complete.

The impact of the Cultural Revolution in urban versus rural areas differed. In rural areas, the Cultural Revolution brought important benefits. Barefoot doctors made their impact during this period when, for the first time in Chinese history, they provided medical care in many villages and immunized children nationwide against common ailments. Mortality rates from these diseases, which declined dramatically during the Cultural Revolution, have been gradually increasing again ever since the elimination of barefoot doctors in 1981.

The Cultural Revolution also encouraged communes to establish high schools and junior high schools throughout rural China, while the radicalization of the commune system removed any financial incentives for parents to keep their children at home to work. These wider educational opportunities for rural China came from shifting educational resources away from elite urban schools for the privileged. In 1965 China had 14.4 million secondary school students. This grew to 68.9 million in the 1977–8 academic year. The market reforms under Deng Xiaoping resulted in numerous secondary school closures, 23,700 schools in 1980 alone, as well as the reappearance of strong financial incentives for parents to keep their children at work in the fields both to bring in income and to save on growing school fees.

Table 25.1 Army Officers Serving in the Government (Percentages)

Year	CCP First Secretaries in Provinces	Leadership Groups in Provinces	Central Committee	Politburo
1956	21		35	30
1965		11		
1966	25			
1969			45	40
1971	72	62		
1973		49	24	24
1975	38			
1977			30	31
1978	31	12		
1982		3	22	21
1983	5			
1985	0	0	15	18
1987		0	17	11
1992			24	9
1997			22	13

Note: The shaded area indicates the period of maximum military influence, which corresponds to the height of the Cultural Revolution and the deployment of the PLA to restore order.

Source: Lynn T. White III, *Unstately Power: Local Causes of China's Intellectual, Legal, and Governmental Reforms*, vol. 2 (Armonk, NY: M. F. Sharpe, 1998), 326.

Rural areas also benefited from the cultural focus of the Cultural Revolution through increasing cultural and sports activities. These medical, educational, and cultural programs all benefited the poorest the most. From the rural point of view, the Cultural Revolution targeted the urban privileged.

III. The PLA and the Restoration of Order

The release of Red Guards uprooted the CCP bureaucracy, particularly in urban China, but at the cost of economic paralysis in urban areas and stagnant production in rural areas. Local officials responded to calls for an offensive against the Four Bad Elements with a scramble to come up with suitable quotas of victims, many of whom were summarily executed along with their children. Local officials responded to the campaign against the Four Olds by targeting China's minority populations for preserving their traditions in the face of another attempt at sinification. Some of the worst violence took place in areas with large minority populations, such as Guangxi and Guangdong.

Having broken the power structure arrayed against him, Mao sought to reestablish his supremacy. He did so by using

the most traditional military service, the army, which still relied on minimally equipped foot soldiers, unlike the air force or navy, which required more highly educated personnel to fly the planes and deploy the ships. Mao sought not professional competence but ideological loyalty from the army, which dwarfed the other two military services in size. Mao had long-standing ties with the army not only from his days as a guerrilla but, more importantly, as a key military theorist of international standing and the architect of the Communist victory in the civil war. Mao used his connections within the army to ensure the appointment of officers loyal to him. As disorder spread throughout China, spontaneous conflicts broke out between Red Guard and army units. In 1967 Mao deployed more than half of the army to restore order.

Mao had already set up the institutional requirements for success. The CCP had come to power through the victory of arms. It had increased its legitimacy through foreign military intervention in Korea. The top leadership of the CCP coincided with the military leadership of the civil war years. In other words, like the Manchus before them, the PRC did not initially have a civil government, but rather a military government. China had a huge land force of 2.5 million men that was far too large to be engaged strictly in national defense. Like the Manchus, the Communists relied on the army to occupy the country and retain the throne. They devoted enormous funds for this purpose. The PLA's budget averaged between 20 and 40 percent of government revenues. Control over these funds made the PLA one of the strongest groups within the government and made the leaders of the PLA, such as Peng Dehuai and Lin Biao, some of the most influential politicians. The faction controlling the military held the reins of power.

Politically, the PLA leadership was subordinate to the precursor to the Central Military Commission, where Mao served as chairman and which was under the direct control of the Party Central Committee. Peng Dehuai headed the Ministry of National Defense from 1954 until his purge in 1959, whereupon Lin Biao succeeded him. Both played prominent roles in fighting the Chinese civil war, while Peng led China to victory in Korea. The PLA, in turn, exercised control over the country by establishing military regions. Each such region overlapped two or three of China's twenty-six provinces and autonomous regions. Like the USSR, the Chinese government designated the central parts of its empire as provinces and the incompletely integrated periphery as autonomous regions. The military regions were devised to overlap populous Han provinces and non-Han autonomous areas to prevent rebellions.

Mao watched with misgivings the spread of Soviet military education and the increasing emphasis on professional qualifications over ideological correctness. The creation of a new network of military schools and academies emphasized professional military education, which had an enormous impact on all branches of the military, and many PLA officers had received further advanced training in the USSR. This meant that many officers remained loyal to Soviet military doctrine as well as to Soviet political and economic models even after Mao rejected them. China's military academies, in addition to teaching military subjects, supervised the political indoctrination of PLA officers. In keeping with the Leninist political commissar system, membership in the CCP continued to be widespread throughout the PLA officer corps.

The Korean War, *Sputnik*, and increasing tensions with the USSR all demonstrated the need to modernize the PLA. Chinese soldiers had suffered grievously from UN firepower and from China's inability to provide adequate air cover; *Sputnik* indicated that Moscow could send nuclear weapons–tipped ballistic missiles around the globe; and deteriorating relations made the defense of China's northern frontiers a top priority. China's First Five-Year Plan (1953–7) provided the PLA with a wide range of modern military equipment, while the country strove to become independent of munitions purchases from the Soviet Union. The 1960

Sino-Soviet split had a particularly severe impact on the PLA, and especially on the air force and navy, which relied on the USSR for virtually all of their equipment and fuel. By the early 1960s, however, China was able to produce a broader range of planes, tanks, and patrol boats.

After the Korean War, Peng Dehuai attempted to professionalize the army. Beginning in 1955, the PLA adopted a new table of ranks for the officer corps based on the Soviet system. For the first time, salaries were paid in money instead of in goods and services, with relatively high salaries for officers, transforming the military into a desirable profession. High rank and salary were key elements of *guanxi*. Later, Mao would argue that these reforms undermined the revolutionary unity of the PLA. In fact, they increased the military's leverage vis-à-vis the government.

In 1965 Lin Biao, with Mao's blessing, again eliminated ranks and made officers cadres in order to undercut the emerging personal power bases of potential rivals. He restored the Leninist commissar system by revitalizing political departments throughout the PLA. Under Lin's stewardship, China defeated India in the 1962 war and successfully tested its first atomic weapon on 16 October 1964, giving the military enormous prestige. In contrast to the increasingly sclerotic CCP, the military seemed full of vigor. The revitalized army, with its big budget, new array of equipment, officer corps loyal to Mao, and renewed emphasis on ideological correctness, had the Red Guards under control within the year, but at the cost of untold numbers of casualties.

IV. The 1969 Sino-Soviet Border Conflict

Much of the radicalism of Mao's desired policies stemmed from a fear of capitalist restoration in China that originated from lessons he drew from recent Soviet experiences. He viewed the restoration of private plots of land, de-Stalinization, the rehabilitation of political prisoners, political liberalization, and rapprochement with the West under Khrushchev as proof that the revisionists had taken over the Communist Party of the USSR. He saw a similar pattern emerging after the Great Leap Forward, with a growing emphasis on expertise over ideology and material incentives over equality, and was determined to nip such trends in the bud. By 1969, he seemed to have undermined the power of the Soviet faction and planned to announce his victory over the revisionists with great fanfare at the Ninth Party Congress in April 1969. A foreign policy success against the USSR would demonstrate his leadership.

The Soviet invasion of Czechoslovakia in 1968, squelching an attempt to democratize, and the Soviet declaration of the Brezhnev Doctrine justifying such Soviet intervention in wavering socialist states, set a precedent for Soviet intervention elsewhere. Border security reemerged as a major issue. After the Sino-Soviet split, relations continued to deteriorate, especially in Central Asia. In 1963, the USSR accused China of setting up labor camps (called *laogai*) in Xinjiang, suppressing minorities, and persecuting minority spokesmen and Soviet nationals. The *laogai* labor camp system mirrored Qing dynasty institutions of military exile, which had entailed deportation of criminals to remote outposts of the empire. During the 1960s, Beijing carried out a number of large-scale programs in its Central Asian territories, including colonizing disputed areas with army veterans, resettling nomadic tribes, and using the Cultural Revolution as a pretext to send large numbers of Han to labor camps along the frontiers. In the past, such Han migrations into non-Han lands had often sparked rebellions and secession movements. To escape China's grip, Xinjiang residents fled across the border to the USSR; as many as 60,000 crossed in 1962 alone. Most were non-Han who made up the bulk of Xinjiang's population and had the same ethnicities as the Soviet population across the border. Beijing accused Moscow of trying to subvert Xinjiang.

Mao's numerous public statements dismissing the human costs of using nuclear weapons raised doubts in the Soviet Union about Mao's mental stability. As a result, Moscow built up its military power in East Asia. In September 1964, Soviet leaders stated pointedly that they would use nuclear weapons to defend their borders. During the Cultural Revolution, China responded by building enormous bomb shelters in Beijing, which later became the nucleus of the city's subway system. The USSR rapidly increased its troop deployments on its Asian frontiers from seventeen divisions in 1965, to twenty-seven divisions in 1969, and peaking at forty-eight divisions by the mid-1970s. Two to three divisions were also stationed in Mongolia.

At the time of the announcement of the Brezhnev Doctrine, China began publicly to accuse the USSR of being an imperialistic country. On the heels of the purge of the technocrats in China came the elimination of the Soviet-educated elite. With Mao's main opponents either arrested or dead, and with the bulk of the Moscow-trained cadres either sent down to the countryside or imprisoned in camps, there was little opposition to Mao's call to oppose the USSR. He sponsored noisy demonstrations in front of the Soviet Embassy. Anti-Soviet hysteria became a pretext for the purges and part of Mao's strategy to blame China's mounting domestic problems on Moscow. Like the Beijing governments of the early Republican period, which considered the United States responsible for many of their country's ills, Mao heaped the blame on his heretofore primary foreign benefactor, the USSR.

Tensions escalated, with thousands of border clashes reported between 1964 and March 1969, when, on the eve of the Ninth Party Congress, Mao precipitated a major border clash. Soviet troops controlled over 600 of the 700 small riverine islands, many of them taken from China when Japan controlled Manchuria in the 1930s and then occupied by Soviet troops in World War II. These conflicts were small in scope, but they continued to escalate. This, coupled with China's domestic turmoil and the USSR's invasion of a fellow socialist country, helped set the stage for a series of battles during 1969 in which the PLA fought the vaunted Red Army. The PLA's self-proclaimed success, in turn, gave Mao sufficient face to make an even more radical shift in Chinese foreign policy. He did so at tremendous risk when the Soviet Union reportedly approached the United States about a possible nuclear strike on China.

In March 1969, a succession of border incidents occurred along the Ussuri and Amur rivers, which form the easternmost sections of the Sino-Soviet border. The Chinese had long disputed Soviet sovereignty over many islands on their side of the main channel of these rivers. Under customary international law and in accordance with Soviet treaties setting its river borders in Europe, the Chinese demands were reasonable, but Moscow refused to compromise. It did not want to set a precedent of withdrawing from disputed territory that might have a ripple effect elsewhere in its vast empire. At that time, Soviet and Japanese diplomats were embroiled in the so-called Northern Territories Dispute over the status of the Kurile Islands, which the Red Army occupied after Japan's surrender.

The Chinese appear to have precipitated the first major clash. It took place on 2 March 1969, on the mile-long Ussuri River island of Zhenbao (Chen Pao or, in Russian, Damansky Island), claimed by both the Soviet Union and China. During the night of 1–2 March, approximately 300 specially trained PLA troops secretly fortified the island. When fighting erupted the next morning, the Chinese killed approximately thirty Russians and took another nineteen prisoner. Soviet reinforcements arrived later to expel the Chinese from the island. During a second clash two weeks later, on 14–15 March, the Red Army attacked China, with an estimated 60 Russian casualties and as many as 800 Chinese casualties in the nine-hour firefight. Both the USSR and the PRC claimed victory. In Beijing, Lin Biao's crack troops were credited with saving the Chinese people, while in Moscow there were mass anti-Chinese demonstrations before the Chinese embassy. Subsequently, other Sino-Soviet clashes occurred on the Amur River island of Bacha (Pa ch'a or Goldinsky in Russian) and in Xinjiang.

The possibility of a full-scale war appeared increasingly likely. Negotiations to end the conflict opened during June 1969 but were interrupted by a 13 August clash along the Xinjiang-Kazakhstan border. On 11 September, with a major

Sino-Soviet war looming on the horizon, Soviet Premier Aleksei Kosygin flew to Beijing to meet with Premier Zhou Enlai. Like the tributaries of the past, the Russians went to Beijing, not the reverse. During a four-hour meeting, they agreed that the status quo of the borders would be maintained and there would be no further armed confrontations. More substantial talks began in late October 1969 but made little headway. By the mid-1970s, Moscow had increased its troop strength along the border to more than a million men, equipping them with both conventional and nuclear weapons; it made additional naval deployments in the Pacific; and in European Russia it deployed a first-strike missile system that could reach China.

Although the 1969 Sino-Soviet border conflicts were inconclusive, Mao made it clear that he would not bow before Soviet military power or accept the Brezhnev Doctrine. He repeatedly dismissed the lethality of nuclear weapons, implying that China had population to spare. The PLA, by holding the Red Army at bay, had proved sufficient to defend China's borders from the reputedly first-rate Soviet troops. Once again Mao had made a major foe back down, gaining the necessary face to set China's foreign policy on a new and radical course: rapprochement with the United States and Japan.

V. Sino-American Rapprochement

Washington policymakers realized that the bitterness of Sino-Soviet border conflict had opened new diplomatic possibilities. The United States had become bogged down in the Vietnam War (1961–75), which had become extremely unpopular at home, and wanted to withdraw. Yet, it also wanted to maintain pressure on the Soviet Union to win the Cold War. While U.S. policymakers hoped to play what they called the "China card" against the Soviet Union, Mao also intended to play the capitalist card against Moscow.

After the North Vietnamese Tet Offensive in 1968, the American public put intense pressure on the U.S. government to extricate itself from the Vietnam War. Prior to the 1969 Sino-Soviet border conflict, fear of Chinese intervention in Vietnam on the scale of the Korean War had made the United States very reluctant to invade North Vietnam, mine its key harbors, or bomb close to the Chinese border. This had given the North Vietnamese a sanctuary where they could operate at will. After 1969, however, the U.S. government realized that there was no longer any possibility of a Chinese invasion of North Vietnam; with the Red Army poised on China's northern border, China could not afford to risk a two-front war for the sake of the North Vietnamese. This permitted a much more aggressive U.S. military strategy in Vietnam, including expanding the areas subject to bombing and mining.

Sino-Soviet tensions also presented President Richard Nixon with a rare opportunity to combine forces with China to exert greater pressure on the USSR and, over the long term, induce its economic collapse. On 4 August 1969, President Nixon called Moscow the main aggressor in the Sino-Soviet border conflict and argued that a Chinese defeat would be contrary to U.S. interests. This comment indicated a shift from the U.S. policy of isolating China. In 1971, U.S. Secretary of State Henry Kissinger made a secret trip to Beijing in preparation for President Nixon's trip the next year. Nixon had two objectives: extrication from the Vietnam War and victory in the Cold War against the USSR.

In what must have seemed to many Chinese as an American tributary mission, President Nixon flew to China in 1972 to meet with Mao. They signed the Shanghai Communiqué, the first of three communiqués issued in 1972, 1978, and 1982. The Shanghai Communiqué provided two interpretations of the status of Taiwan. While China again declared Taiwan to be its province, the United States agreed not to challenge the view shared by "all Chinese" on both sides of the Taiwan Strait that "there is but one China and that Taiwan is part of China."[9] Over the ensuing decades, particularly after the Taiwanese government allowed its citizens to visit China in 1987, many Taiwanese changed their minds, concluding that the one China did not include Taiwan. The Shanghai Communiqué also provided for exchanges between the United States and China. While formal diplomatic relations would not be reestablished until 1979, the subject of the second communiqué, the long period of Sino-American estrangement had ended. On 25 October 1971, Taiwan lost its seat at the United Nations. Henceforth, the PRC sat on the Security Council as one of the five privileged nations to possess veto power, along with the Soviet Union, the United States, France, and Great Britain, the victorious powers at the end of World War II when the United Nations was established. Most countries soon changed from recognizing Taiwan to recognizing the PRC. A third communiqué would limit U.S. arms sales to Taiwan.

Immediately after opening relations with China, Nixon visited Moscow, where he warned General Secretary Leonid Brezhnev that Washington would consider a Soviet attack on China an attack against U.S. interests. Implicit in the Sino-American rapprochement was a degree of military cooperation against the Soviet Union. China had come around to the U.S. view that the USSR constituted the main enemy. Growing U.S. cooperation with the PRC also signaled a U.S. shift from unconditional support of Taiwan that caused extreme apprehension among Taiwan's Nationalist elite.

The Cultural Revolution paved the way for a major transition in China's foreign policy, just as the 1969 border clashes with the USSR ended all hope for a return to the former Sino-Soviet monolith. By the early 1970s, Mao signaled a complete break with the USSR and the opening of diplomatic relations with the United States. Here, teams of people are clearing the snow and ice in preparation for President Nixon's 1972 visit to China.

Chairman Mao welcomes President Nixon to China. The signing of the Shanghai Communiqué, in which the United States agreed that Taiwan was part of China, opened the door for further cooperation by the two countries against their mutual enemy the USSR.

President Richard Nixon and his wife were taken to the theater by Mao's wife, Jiang Qing, where they saw a performance of the 1964 ballet "The Red Detachment of Women." This ballet was turned into a Peking opera during the later years of the Cultural Revolution. Its focus on a peasant girl on Hainan Island attempting to join the CCP, and its theme of good versus evil were emblematic of the Cultural Revolution.

Nixon's China diplomacy stunned the Japanese leadership and caused the fall of its government. The failure of Nixon's administration to consult or even provide advance warning to Japan, its primary regional ally, concerning the reversal of its East Asian foreign policy left Prime Minister Satō Eisaku in the lurch. Public pressure required Satō to respond forcefully, but he did not want to abandon Taiwan; instead, he resigned, causing the cabinet to fall. His successor, Prime Minister Tanaka Kakuei, in consultation with Washington and in response to intense domestic pressure, visited Beijing in September 1972, where he signed agreements normalizing Sino-Japanese relations. Mao actively courted the Japanese, muting the anti-Japanese propaganda in China and renouncing all demands for a war indemnity. Taiwan responded in outrage by severing its relations with Japan, but cooler heads prevailed and Japan and Taiwan immediately established semiofficial organizations that functioned as embassies. In 1978, Japan and China would sign another agreement officially terminating the Sino-Japanese War.

This geopolitical shift put even more pressure on Moscow, since the USSR and Japan had outstanding border disputes of their own, specifically the southernmost Kurile Islands just north of the Japanese island of Hokkaido. U.S.-Chinese-Japanese cooperation encircled the USSR on both its eastern and Western frontiers, hemmed in the Soviet fleet in the Pacific, and thereby reduced it to a defensive posture. While China toned down the propaganda war on Japan, its verbal attacks on Moscow became increasingly shrill throughout the 1970s. In February 1974, Mao publicly called for a Third World coalition against the Soviet Union. China prepared for a possible war with the USSR by building an extensive network of tunnels for bomb shelters in its major cities. In addition to defending its borders with over a million troops, Mao authorized the removal of its nuclear research facilities from Lop Nor, which was uncomfortably close to Xinjiang's border with the USSR, to a more remote location in Tibet. Meanwhile, Chinese missile technology made rapid advances. By 1973, Beijing was producing medium-range missiles capable of striking Moscow and Leningrad.

Border incidents continued throughout the 1970s, resulting in occasional fatalities. Moscow tried to use these confrontations to pressure Beijing to renegotiate the 1950 Sino-Soviet Treaty. When Beijing showed no interest in renewing this accord, the Soviet Union increased its troop concentrations along the Sino-Soviet and Sino-Mongolian borders. Brezhnev announced that the Soviet Union was prepared to use the Red Army against China on behalf of its socialist allies. This was a warning to China not to interfere in Mongolia or Vietnam at a time when Sino-Vietnamese relations were deteriorating. Sino-Soviet tensions spawned a variety of proxy wars in Southeast Asia, most notably in Cambodia and Laos, where each side supported its own faction in ongoing civil wars.

Mao implemented an about-face in foreign policy while simultaneously retaining the mandate of heaven. During the one and a half decades between 1960 and 1976, Mao went from a foreign policy of close alliance with the Soviet Union to the brink of nuclear war; from propaganda portraying the United States and Japan as the sources of global evil, past and present, to détente with both; and from a domestic policy of creating socialism in isolation to opening the door, however slightly, to the West. Little was left of Mao's original foreign policy program.

Mao's retention of power was a major feat of political calculation. He realigned Chinese foreign policy in order to use one set of barbarians, the United States and Japan, to play off another, the USSR. His policy shift proved to be prescient. It enabled China and the United States to encircle the USSR. Soviet militarization of its eastern and Western borders proved to be a greater economic burden than the inefficient Soviet economy could bear. Chinese troop dispositions, their growing military capabilities, and their enormous numerical superiority along the frontier forced Moscow into extremely expensive troop deployments in a part of its empire from which it drew few revenues. In contrast, Manchuria is one of the most productive regions of China, so that it naturally had a far greater population than the Soviet Far East. The USSR completed its strategic overextension with its 1979 invasion of Afghanistan. Both American and Chinese leaders were eager to exploit Moscow's weakness and push it over the edge. These cumulative expenses helped cause the implosion and collapse of the USSR in 1991, an event that would have implications for the survival of the CCP as well. While Mao rejected the Soviet foreign policy paradigm, he retained the Soviet model for economic development. The about-face on economic policies would await his successor, Deng Xiaoping.

Conclusions

The Cultural Revolution began as Mao's fight for political survival in the disastrous aftermath of the Great Leap Forward and ended with China's search for a new modus vivendi with the United States and Japan. In the wake of the Great Famine, three factions competed for power in China: The

Stalinists represented key elements of the military, the technocrats focused on economic development, and the ideologues were under Mao. Mao enlisted the support of idealistic young people to circumvent the emerging CCP bureaucracy. He ousted the technocrats, destroyed the Stalinists, and put the ideologues in power for the next decade. While the collectivization campaign of the Great Leap Forward had wreaked havoc on rural China, the Red Guards of the Cultural Revolution threw away urban China's human capital—the educated and professionally competent citizens necessary to run a modern economy.

During the course of the Cultural Revolution, Mao used a series of public campaigns to isolate and destroy his political enemies. He undermined key rivals such as Peng Dehuai and Liu Shaoqi to replace them with hand-picked men like Lin Biao, who then died mysteriously in a plane crash on 13 September 1971 while apparently attempting to flee to the USSR. Mao's purges eliminated from power the last of the pro-Soviet generation, sending many into exile along the contested frontiers with the Soviet Union. Mao short-circuited the institutions that by law should have governed China. From 7 July 1966 until 13 January 1975, neither the National People's Congress nor its Standing Committee ever met. Mao succeeded in his primary objective, which was to remain in power, whatever the costs. Like the Empress Dowager Cixi and like Chiang Kai-shek before him, Mao pitted competing factions against each other so as to divide and rule. Like Cixi and Chiang, he did so at great cost to his country and countrymen.

While the intent of the Cultural Revolution had been not only to keep Mao in power but also to counter bureaucratization in order to restore revolutionary vigor, it resulted in a resurgence of *guanxi* networks. When institutions and lines of authority collapsed under the onslaught of the Red Guards, people fell back on *guanxi* to survive. There was a proliferation of idioms to describe the functions of *guanxi* in the Maoist era: Things were accomplished through "the back door": *zou houmen* or "going through the back door" and *kai houmen* or "opening the back door" meant reliance on personal connections. This required connections in key places: *zhao shuren* meant "to find an acquaintance," while *gao guanxi* and *la guanxi* both meant "to make connections." Nepotism was referred to as "petticoat connections" (*qundai guanxi*), literally meaning connected through one's female relatives. Thus, while anti-corruption campaigns proliferated in the Communist era, the problem of corruption has continued to grow. (See Table 25.2.) The Cultural Revolution brought another unanticipated consequence: economic contraction. In 1976 alone, China's GNP shrank by 2.7 percent, while urban

Table 25.2   Anticorruption Campaigns under Mao Zedong and Deng Xiaoping

Year	Name of Campaign
1951	Three-Antis Campaign
1952	Five-Antis Campaign
1963–5	Socialist Education Movement
1966–76	Cultural Revolution
1980–1	Campaign to Curb Official Privileges and Unhealthy Tendencies in the Party
1982	Campaign Resolutely to Crack Down on Economic Crimes
1983	Campaign to Eradicate Housing Irregularities by Officials
1984–5	Campaign to Stop Officials from Engaging in Commercial Activities
1986–7	Campaign to Punish Violations of Laws and to Discipline the Party and the State
1988–9	Campaign to Build a Clean Government and Curb Corruption
1991	Anticorruption Campaign
1994	Anticorruption Campaign
1996	Anticorruption Campaign

Source: Ting Gong, *The Politics of Corruption in Contemporary China: An Analysis of Policy Outcomes* (Westport, CT: Praeger, 1994), xv–xvi; Xiaobo Lü, *Cadres and Corruption: The Organizational Involution of the Chinese Communist Party* (Stanford, CA: Stanford University Press, 2000), 223.

wages declined from an average of 628 to 605 *yuan* from 1968 to 1976.

In the mid-1960s, tensions with the USSR were particularly sharp along China's Central Asian borders. During the late 1960s the scene of the Sino-Soviet fighting shifted farther north and east, to the Ussuri and Amur rivers. Mao sponsored a nationwide anti-Soviet campaign to prepare the country for a possible war. During 1969, a series of border incidents along the Ussuri and Amur rivers proved that China could hold its own against the Red Army. This opened new diplomatic possibilities for Mao. He sought out the United States and Japan while giving the appearance that they had approached him. Having them travel to China followed the choreography of tributary missions in the past, when foreign dignitaries visited Beijing to pay their respects to the emperor of China.

While rapprochement with the United States and Japan initially focused on geopolitical issues concerning the USSR, Mao's successors would refocus his policy on the development of trade. After Mao's death in 1976, which marked the end of the Cultural Revolution, the technocrats, who had long waited in the wings for an opportunity to make a comeback, seized the reins of power. Not long after Mao's death, a 1 November 1977 issue of *The*

People's Daily (*Renmin Ribao*) identified the USSR as China's most dangerous enemy while presenting the United States and Japan as allies. A generation of Chinese had been traumatized by the self-inflicted wounds of the Great Leap Forward and the Cultural Revolution. There are no reliable figures on the deaths that resulted from the Cultural Revolution. Estimates all range in the millions. It was widely known that Chinese living standards and the quality of life had imploded. As a result, there was an emerging consensus within the CCP that the political campaigns of the preceding two decades had not brought China prosperity, but rather to the brink of ruin. They only awaited the death of their emperor to act.

The trauma of the Cultural Revolution scarred all those who survived it, from small children whose parents were ripped away from them; to the school-age children who never received a normal education; to young adults who were banned from higher education and professional accomplishment; to adults whose homes, families, and livelihoods were stripped from them. Although famine did not reappear, hunger remained endemic in rural China. Grain production would not reach pre–Great Leap Forward levels until 1978, two years after Mao's death and the end of the Cultural Revolution. For the last twenty years of Mao's rule, living standards in China stagnated.

BIBLIOGRAPHY

An, Tai Sung. *The Sino-Soviet Territorial Dispute.* Philadelphia: Westminster Press, 1973.

Armstrong, J. D. *Revolutionary Diplomacy: Chinese Foreign Policy and the United Front Doctrine.* Berkeley: University of California Press, 1977.

Becker, Jasper. *Hungry Ghosts: Mao's Secret Famine.* New York: Free Press, 1996.

Bernstein, Thomas P. *Up to the Mountains and Down to the Villages: The Transfer of Youth from Urban to Rural China.* New Haven, CT: Yale University Press, 1977.

Chan, Anita. *Children of Mao: Personality Development and Political Activism in the Red Guard Generation.* Seattle: University of Washington Press, 1985.

Chang, Jung. *Wild Swans: Three Daughters of China.* New York: Doubleday, 1991.

————and Jon Halliday. *Mao: The Unknown Story.* New York: Alfred A. Knopf, 2005.

Cheng, Nien. *Life and Death in Shanghai.* New York: Grove Press, 1986.

Cohen, Warren I. *East Asia at the Center.* New York: Columbia University Press, 2000.

Dittner, Lowell. *Sino-Soviet Normalization and Its International Implications, 1945–2000.* Seattle: University of Washington Press, 1992.

————*Liu Shao-ch'i and the Chinese Cultural Revolution.* Rev. ed. Armonk, NY: M. E. Sharpe, 1998.

Domes, Jürgen. *The Government and Politics of the People's Republic of China: A Time of Transition.* Boulder, CO: Westview Press, 1985.

————*Peng Te-huai: The Man and the Image.* Stanford, CA: Stanford University Press, 1985.

Esherick, Joseph W., Paul G. Piskowicz, and Andrew G. Walder, eds. *The Chinese Cultural Revolution as History.* Stanford, CA: Stanford University Press, 2006.

Gao, Mobo C. F. *Gao Village: A Portrait of Rural Life in Modern China.* Honolulu: University of Hawai'i Press, 1999.

Garver, John. *China's Decision for Rapprochement with the United States, 1968–1971.* Boulder, CO: Westview Press, 1982.

Gong, Ting. *The Politics of Corruption in Contemporary China: An Analysis of Policy Outcomes.* Westport, CT: Praeger, 1994.

Harding, Harry. "The Chinese State in Crisis." In *The Cambridge History of China,* vol. 15, edited by Roderick MacFarquhar and John K. Fairbank, 107–217. Cambridge: Cambridge University Press, 1991.

Joseph, William A., Christin Wong, and David Zweig, eds. *New Perspectives on the Cultural Revolution.* Cambridge, MA: Harvard University Press, 1991.

Lee, Hong Yung. *The Politics of the Chinese Cultural Revolution: A Case Study.* Berkeley: University of California Press, 1978.

Low, Alfred D. *The Sino-Soviet Confrontation since Mao Zedong: Dispute, Detente, or Conflict?* New York: Columbia University Press, 1987.

Lü, Xiaobo. *Cadres and Corruption: The Organizational Involution of the Chinese Communist Party.* Stanford, CA: Stanford University Press, 2000.

MacFarquhar, Roderick. *The Origins of the Cultural Revolution.* 3 vols. New York: Columbia University Press, 1974–97.

Nelson, Harvey W. *The Chinese Military System: An Organizational Study of the Chinese People's Liberation Army.* Boulder, CO: Westview Press, 1977.

Perry, Elizabeth J. and Li Xun. *Proletarian Power: Shanghai in the Cultural Revolution.* Boulder, CO: Westview Press, 1997.

Robinson, Thomas. "China Confronts the Soviet Union: Warfare and Diplomacy on China's Inner Asian Frontiers." In *The Cambridge History of China,* vol. 15, edited by Roderick MacFarquhar and John K. Fairbank, 218–304. Cambridge: Cambridge University Press, 1991.

Ryan, Mark A., David Michael Finkelstein, and Michael A. McDevitt, eds. *Chinese Warfighting: The PLA Experience Since 1949.* Armonk, NY: M. E. Sharpe, 2003.

Seybolt, Peter J., ed. *The Rustication of Urban Youth in China: A Social Experiment.* White Plains, NY: M. E. Sharpe, 1977.

————*Politics and Purges in China: Rectification and the Decline of Party Norms, 1950–1965.* 2nd ed. Armonk, NY: M. E. Sharpe, 1993.

Seymour, James D. and Richard Anderson. *New Ghosts, Old Ghosts: Prisons and Labor Reform Camps in China.* Armonk, NY: M. E. Sharpe, 1998.

Thurston, Ann F. *Enemies of the People: The Ordeal of the Intellectuals in China's Great Cultural Revolution.* Cambridge, MA: Harvard University Press, 1988.

Unger, Jonathan. *The Transformation of Rural China*. Armonk, NY: M. E. Sharpe, 2002.

White, Lynn T., III. *Policies of Chaos: The Organizational Causes of Violence in China's Cultural Revolution*. Princeton, NJ: Princeton University Press, 1989.

Whitson, William W. with Huang Chen-hsia. *The Chinese High Command: A History of Communist Military Politics, 1927–1971*. New York: Praeger, 1973.

Wich, Richard. *Sino-Soviet Crisis Politics: A Study of Political Change and Communications*. Cambridge, MA: Harvard University Press, 1980.

Yang Xiguang and Susan McFadden. *Captive Spirits: Prisoners of the Cultural Revolution*. Oxford: Oxford University Press, 1997.

Zagoria, Donald. *The Sino-Soviet Conflict, 1956–1961*. Princeton, NJ: Princeton University Press, 1962.

Zweig. *Agrarian Radicalism in China, 1968–1981*. Cambridge, MA: Harvard University Press, 1989.

NOTES

1. Mu Dan, "Song of Wisdom." In *The Columbia Anthology of Modern Chinese Literature*, Joseph S. M. Lau and Howard Goldblatt, eds. (New York: Columbia University Press, 1995), 534.
2. Mao Zedong, *Quotations from Chairman Mao Tse-tung* (Beijing: Foreign Language Press, 1972), 2.
3. Ibid., 8.
4. Ibid., 8.
5. Ibid., 39.
6. Ibid., 61.
7. Ibid., 140.
8. Ibid., 255.
9. "Joint Communiqué, 28 February 1972, http://edition.cnn.com/SPECIALS/cold.war/episodes/15/documents/us.china/.

Chronology

20 July 1967	Wuhan mutiny
13 September 1971	Death of Lin Biao
25 October 1971	UN to replace Taiwan with the PRC
21–7 February 1972	Richard Nixon visits China
18 January 1974	Beginning of Jiang Qing's Criticize Lin Biao and Confucius Campaign
8 January 1975	Deng Xiaoping becomes party vice-chairman
13 January 1975	Zhou Enlai proclaims the Four Modernizations
5 April 1975	Chiang Kai-shek dies; Chiang Ching-kuo succeeds to presidency
1975–9	Cambodian–Vietnamese War
8 January 1976	Zhou Enlai dies
5 April 1976	First Tiananmen Incident: crowd paying last respects to Zhou forcibly dispersed
7 April 1976	Deng Xiaoping fired; Hua Guofeng becomes premier
28 July 1976	Tangshan, Hebei earthquake, 240,000 deaths
9 September 1976	Mao Zedong dies
6 October 1976	Arrest of the Gang of Four
7 October 1976	Hua Guofeng becomes party chairman
21 July 1977	Deng reinstated
12–8 August 1977	End of Cultural Revolution and adoption of Four Modernizations proclaimed at Eleventh Party Congress
November 1977	Production Responsibility System introduced in part of Anhui province
May 1978	Beginning of mass exodus of Vietnam's Chinese population
12 August 1978	Sino-Japanese peace and friendship treaty signed
2 November 1978	Soviet-Vietnamese security treaty
19 November 1978	First Democracy Wall posters appear
18–22 December 1978	Third Plenum; Deng Xiaoping and technocrats take control
1 January 1979	Normalization of Sino-U.S. relations
10 January 1979	Cambodian government set up under Vietnamese Army
17 Feb.–5 Mar. 1979	Sino-Vietnamese War
3 April 1979	PRC renounces Sino-Soviet Friendship Treaty effective 11 April 1980
6 December 1979	Democracy Wall outlawed
27 December 1979	Soviet invasion of Afghanistan; war continues until 1989
23–9 February 1980	Hu Yaobang becomes general secretary of the CCP; Liu Shaoqi exonerated
2–7 August 1980	Independent job searches legalized
26 August 1980	Opening of Special Economic Zones
30 Aug.–10 Sept. 1980	Zhao Ziyang replaces Hua Guofeng as premier
25 January 1981	End of trial of Gang of Four
27–9 June 1981	Hu Yaobang replaces Hua Guofeng as chairman of the Central Committee; Deng made chairman of the Central Military Commission
11 January 1982	Deng announces One Country, Two Systems doctrine
1 January 1984	Land reform providing fifteen-year land titles, transferability, and credit
10 May 1984	Liberalization of government-operated businesses
June 1985	Completion of transformation of communes into village governments

26

The Deng Xiaoping Restoration

You must be mad
To want to be an empress!
Here's a mirror to look at yourself
And see what you really are.
You've got together a little gang
To stir up trouble all the time,
Hoodwinking the people, capering about.
But your days are numbered. . . .
Whoever dares oppose our Premier
Is like a mad dog barking at the sun—
Wake up to reality![1]

Eulogy to Premier Zhou Enlai
attacking Jiang Qing and the Gang of Four

Mao used the Cultural Revolution to entrench himself in power, yet he could not escape his own mortality. As his declining health became obvious to all, the issue of succession became increasingly urgent. The Cultural Revolution had put in power the ideologues, such as Mao's wife, Jiang Qing, but at the pleasure of the military under Lin Biao, who provided the essential coercive force. Mao designated Lin Biao as his successor, but after the PLA suppressed the worst of the unrest, Mao sought to curtail Lin's power; to this day, Lin Biao's death while fleeing to the USSR remains one of the most mysterious events of this period. The Cultural Revolution ended with Mao's death, and the technocrats under Deng Xiaoping quickly wrested control from the ideologues. In 1978, Deng promoted his Four Modernizations program, adopting domestic and foreign policies that became known as the Open Door, in a belated attempt to catch up with Taiwan's economic growth. To implement his reforms, he accelerated generational change within the leadership. China's economy boomed, creating an appearance of domestic stability and the prospects for

widespread prosperity for the first time since the early Qing dynasty. Deng Xiaoping continued Mao's foreign policy, however, including a gradual opening to Japan and the West against a backdrop of continuing tensions with the USSR. In 1979, Washington recognized Beijing as China's legitimate government and affirmed that there was only one China. Deng took a hard line vis-à-vis the USSR, denouncing its invasion of Afghanistan and pitting the PLA against Vietnam to undermine a new Soviet-Vietnamese alliance. A weakened Soviet Union was central to Deng's plans because he believed that China could not reform successfully with a strong, interventionist USSR on its borders.

I. The Impending Succession, the Fall of Lin Biao, and the Death of Mao

The PLA gained great political power as a result of the Cultural Revolution, and its commanding officer was positioned to succeed Mao. Lin Biao was one of the most famous Chinese Communist leaders after Mao. In 1925 he joined the Socialist Youth League and enrolled in the Whampoa Military Academy, where he met Zhou Enlai, who later became one of Lin's patrons. At age twenty, Lin participated in the Northern Expedition, joined the CCP, and helped lead the failed Nanchang Uprising marking the PLA's creation. During the 1930s, he headed the CCP's military academy in Yan'an. Just as the position of commandant of the Whampoa Military Academy provided Chiang Kai-shek with a vast *guanxi* network within the Nationalist Army, Lin's position at the Yan'an military academy gave him extensive contacts among the rapidly growing PLA officer corps. When Lin spent three years (1939–42) in a Soviet hospital, he apparently developed strong personal and ideological ties with the USSR. During the civil war, Lin led the PLA to victory in Manchuria, the decisive theater of the war, and then to victory throughout North China. Although he declined to command Chinese forces during the Korean War, his Fourth Field Army played a major role. He was the main beneficiary of Peng Dehuai's fall from grace in 1959, assuming the position of minister of defense.

During the 1960s, Lin demonstrated sycophantic loyalty to Mao by pushing the cult of Mao and Mao's *Little Red Book*. Lin and Mao emphasized ideological rectitude over both economic performance and professional expertise, as well as the promotion of national and anticolonial revolutions throughout the Third World. Lin survived the PLA purge of 1967, when power was decentralized and regional commanders were given control over their armies. During the Cultural Revolution, the PLA was charged with organizing provincial and municipal revolutionary committees to promote the movement.

In Wuhan, the PLA interpreted this assignment to include the suppression of the most radical organizations that threatened public order. When fighting erupted in 1967, the PLA restored order but at the cost of many lives. Although Beijing intervened to restore the radicals to power, elements of the army forces in Wuhan mutinied, kidnapping key leaders of the radicals on 20 July in what became known as the July 20th Incident. Beijing immediately mobilized air, ground, and naval forces to attack the city. Unlike the 1911 Revolution, however, this Wuhan rebellion failed because units loyal to Beijing were willing to intervene, but the threat from shifting military loyalties could not have been lost on Mao and others. Lin Biao's origins as a Hubei native born near Wuhan may have helped him at this juncture, since he may have been seen as a military leader acceptable to both Wuhan and Beijing.

In recognition of the army's key role in restoring order during the Cultural Revolution, in April 1969 the Ninth Party Congress named nine serving military officers and three former marshals to the twenty-five-man Politburo to create a nearly equal division of power between the PLA and the CCP. Lin was at the height of his influence, with his name written into the revised constitution as Mao's successor. Tensions with the USSR were extreme. As long as China remained diplomatically isolated, the PLA was central to parrying the Soviet threat. Mao charted a course of rapprochement with the United States, a strategy designed both to counter the USSR and to undercut the growing domestic threat of PLA domination of the government.

As Mao aged and his own death approached, he became increasingly worried about being overthrown. Those in the number two position, such as Liu Shaoqi and Lin Biao, did not last long. Although Mao and Lin had been comrades in arms since the 1920s, in the late 1960s Mao's growing paranoia and their differences over foreign policy ultimately cost Lin his life. A committed Communist, Lin originally opposed both Soviet "socialist imperialism" and U.S. "capitalist imperialism." In the early 1970s, he decried Mao's attempts to open relations with the United States, demanding political purity. With the restoration of order within China and the prospects of cooperation from the United States to counter the USSR, Mao had the leverage to reduce the PLA's political influence. Mao, with the help of Zhou Enlai, removed generals loyal to Lin by making use of the division in the armed forces between the new, more modernized and professionalized services—the air force and the navy—and the most traditional service, the army. Mao's loyalists dominated the army, while many regional commanders were suspicious of Lin's ultra-leftism.

It is unclear whether Lin attempted to organize a military coup or whether his son (an ambitious young man in his mid-twenties) sought to assassinate Mao. Perhaps Lin foresaw the consequences of his fall from grace and simply sought to flee. Whatever the case, just two months after Kissinger's secret visit to Beijing, Lin died in a plane crash over Mongolia. The USSR found the plane wreckage but never clarified what it discovered at the crash site. Nor is it certain that Lin was ever on the plane or even alive at the time. His last public appearance had been in June, while his alleged death was in September 1971. According to one interpretation, Lin's disappearance in 1971 suggests that he had become an impediment to Mao's strategy to use the United States to undermine the USSR. Another interpretation, the one supported by the PRC, accuses Lin of trying to wrest power from Mao. Others portray Lin as yet another pawn sacrificed in Mao's never-ending quest to retain power.

Lin's fall was a major turning point in the Cultural Revolution. It came during a wave of purges of the top CCP leadership, removing fully one-third from office and eliminating all of Mao's major potential rivals. In 1974 the key ideologues, who later became known as the Gang of Four, cooperated with Mao to launch the "Criticize Lin, Criticize Confucius" campaign. Mao's wife, who clearly hoped to succeed him, needed to weaken the Chinese prejudice against female leadership so evident in the poem at the beginning of this chapter but emanating from Confucianism, whose Five Relationships emphasized the subordination of women.

The propaganda campaign was soon overtaken not by the succession of Mao, but of Zhou Enlai. With Zhou's diagnosis of terminal cancer in 1972, it became imperative to find a replacement with the necessary technical expertise to manage the economy. While Mao dominated ideological matters, Zhou, rightly or wrongly, had been credited as being the party pragmatist and sympathizer with the technocrats. In addition to the CCP, the PLA was also purged in 1971–2. This required cooperation of key elements of the military, who apparently demanded as their price a return to more pragmatic economic policies and the restoration of such technocrats as Deng Xiaoping, who had been purged by Lin Biao as an early critic of the Cultural Revolution. This confluence of events allowed Deng to return to power. The technocrats seized the opportunity to purge leftist PLA officers. The ideologues remained implacably hostile, but they could take solace in the impending death of Zhou and the weakening of the military due to further factional infighting.

During 1975, the one year that Deng was in charge, he launched the Four Modernizations campaign for agriculture, industry, defense, and science and technology in order to restore economic stability. The death of Zhou, however, precipitated Deng's second fall from power and the end game to the succession struggle. Simply put, if Deng had remained in power to oversee the succession at Mao's death, he would have radically reformed the ideological-revolutionary government that Mao intended to make his political legacy. Therefore, Mao removed Deng immediately after Zhou's death, replacing him with a key beneficiary of the Cultural Revolution to ensure political continuity and maintain the factionalized leadership that allowed Mao to divide and rule. Mao chose not a member of the Gang of Four, but a rival to their political aspirations, Hua Guofeng. This change ushered in the final stage of the Cultural Revolution.

From 1972 until Mao's death in 1976, the intensity of the Cultural Revolution gradually diminished. Although no other leader directly challenged Mao, his declining health prevented him from launching any major political initiatives. During some weeks he could keep a normal schedule; during others, he languished in bed. By 1974 he was nearly blind and often only his nurses could understand his words—and sometimes not even they. The ill health of China's leaders did not inspire confidence in the regime's claim that it retained the mandate of heaven.

China remained on autopilot in anticipation of the implosion of Mao's *guanxi* network upon his demise. Those with their sights set on the succession hoped to harvest enough parts of this network to replace the Great Helmsman. An emerging majority in the upper echelons of the government yearned for stability and desired economic growth, not the ideological obsessions that had turned China upside down. Mao's generation was rapidly passing from the scene. Liu Shaoqi died in 1969, Lin Biao in 1971, and Peng Dehuai in 1974. In 1976 Zhou died on 8 January, Zhu De on 6 July, and Mao Zedong

himself on 9 September. Three weeks after Zhu De's death, the massive Tangshan earthquake killed hundreds of thousands of people in North China, while over the summer the Yellow River flooded seven times. Constant unrest was caused by ideologues and technocrats alike. In traditional China these were the unmistakable signs of dynastic succession.

II. The Rise to Power of Deng Xiaoping

Within a month of Mao's death, the moderates under Hua Guofeng wrested power from the radical ideologues. The Eleventh National Party Congress in August 1977 officially declared the Cultural Revolution to be over. The majority rejected the policies of the ideologues. Mao's purges and tensions with the Soviet Union undermined the Stalinists. By default, this left the technocrats in the strongest position. As loyal members of the CCP, who intended to use the party as their vehicle to power, they had a problem. The Chinese people had reaped negligible rewards for their two decades of excruciating suffering from the Great Leap Forward through the Cultural Revolution—both central policies of the CCP. Mao's successors needed to distance the CCP and its icon, Mao, from these policy disasters.

As a solution, the technocrats singled out Mao's widow, Jiang Qing, and three of her political allies to become scapegoats for the ills of an era. Jiang Qing had been an actress when she met and married Mao in 1939. Mao was twenty years her senior and had abandoned his first two sets of children as his career took him from place to place. Most died as small children. Although Jiang promised never to become involved with politics, she helped to precipitate the Cultural Revolution when she and Yao Wenyuan, a CCP official, denounced the play *Hai Rui Dismissed from Office* for being critical of Mao. Thereafter, she formed a faction that pushed for increasingly radical policies, especially in culture, where she was responsible for imposing revolutionary genres on all art forms in China. But Jiang remained peripheral to key political decisions in economic and foreign policy. She had negligible ties with the military, so she lacked the power to enforce, but relied instead on the approval of Mao and implementation by others.

Although Jiang Qing was certainly guilty of extremism, she was not responsible for the wide array of policies that had collectively rocked China. Moreover, she was incapable of acting without Mao's personal approval. Yet, she fit the role of scapegoat. According to Han traditions, the reigns of empresses are notorious for misgovernment. After Mao's death, Jiang failed in her bid to take power. On 6 October

1976, she and her closest associates were arrested. In addition to Jiang and Yao, this included two Politburo members, Wang Hongwen and Zhang Chunqiao. In 1980, the so-called Gang of Four were publicly tried and imprisoned.

Although the CCP tried to keep Mao's image intact, the number and seriousness of the errors made during his tenure could not help but impinge on his legacy. Conversely, Deng, who had been purged twice during the Cultural Revolution, used his image of resiliency through great adversity to promote his economic alternative to Maoism. Deng would complement Mao's foreign policy innovations with the domestic policy innovations for which he became famous. In doing so, he attempted to restore the virtue of Communist rule. This fit the scenario of previous restoration periods, when a particularly vibrant emperor reversed the symptoms of dynastic decline and restored the dynasty to a path of righteousness.

In the aftermath of Jiang Qing's fall from power, Hua Guofeng became the CCP chairman and Deng Xiaoping became the deputy chairman. More importantly, Deng soon became the chief of the PLA General Staff, undoubtedly through his strong military ties dating to the 1920s. Deng helped to orchestrate the attacks on the Gang of Four. Since he had been out of power during most of the years of the Cultural Revolution and his family had so clearly suffered, he could not be blamed for the lunacy of the era: His eldest son remained permanently confined to a wheelchair from a fall from a fourth-story window and a denial of proper medical care afterward, both courtesy of the Red Guards. Other leaders of the CCP, however, had benefited from the turmoil—Hua Guofeng, in particular. Hua had been a strong ally of Mao from the time of Lin Biao's disappearance in 1971 to Mao's death in 1976 and owed his rapid rise to the purge of others.

Criticism of the Gang of Four had a secondary goal: It weakened Hua's position and indirectly tarnished Mao's reputation without destroying it. Between 1977 and 1978, Deng solidified his power base so that in September 1980, a Deng loyalist, Zhao Ziyang, replaced Hua as premier. A year later, in June 1981, a second Deng ally, Hu Yaobang, became chairman of the Central Committee. It is unclear how Deng engineered these changes since Hua Guofeng had all the official titles that Deng conspicuously lacked. One can only speculate that Deng's extensive *guanxi* network in the PLA proved decisive. As an indication of this, Deng Xiaoping became chairman of the Central Military Commission, which arguably was and remains the most powerful body in the Chinese government because it controls the PLA, the ultimate arbiter in Chinese politics.

Foreign policy proved critical in lining up the PLA behind Deng Xiaoping. China's poor showing on the battlefield convinced military leaders of the need to modernize their weaponry and transformed them into essential supporters of Deng Xiaoping's economic reforms. The Sino-Vietnamese War was China's fourth major conflict of the post-1949 period concerning regional dominance. The previous three had been the Korean War (1950–3), the Sino-Indian War (1962), and the Sino-Soviet border conflict (1969). All took place on China's frontiers, where Beijing attempted to assert itself vis-à-vis its neighbors.

During the Vietnam War (1961–75), China provided North Vietnam with crucial economic and military aid, estimated at $20 billion for the 1950–78 period, plus 320,000 army personnel. But Vietnam's reunification in 1975 changed Sino-Vietnamese relations. Just as Stalin had misgivings about a unified China, Mao had misgivings about a unified Vietnam. In 1975, when China refused to increase its support, Le Duan, the secretary-general of the Communist Party of Vietnam, accused it of hostility to Vietnam. In comparison to China's $200 million aid package, the Soviet Union promised $3 billion. Vietnam therefore aligned its foreign policy with Moscow, not Beijing. In 1976, Chinese internal turmoil caused frictions on the Sino-Vietnamese border, while anti-Han discrimination in Vietnam caused a wave of Han Vietnamese refugees to flee over the Chinese border in 1978. Additional tensions arose from mutual claims to sovereignty over the Paracel and Spratly Islands in the South China Sea as well as from Vietnam's December 1978 invasion of Cambodia (Kampuchea), China's client state.

There were grave concerns in China of a possible encirclement from the Soviet-Vietnam alliance in combination with Sino-Indian tensions. Before China could pursue potentially destabilizing domestic reforms, its borders had to be secure. An alliance with Vietnam would enable Moscow to put pressure on China's southern border, forcing China to relieve pressure on the Sino-Soviet border in the north. Moscow also made a concerted effort to improve relations with the other Southeast Asian countries bordering on China. In 1978, Vietnam requested membership in the Council for Mutual Economic Assistance (Comecon), the Soviet organization to coordinate economic policies among its allies. By August 1978 as many as 4,000 Soviet advisers were in Vietnam; in September the Soviet Union began to provide increased arms shipments; and on 2 November the two countries signed a Treaty of Friendship and Cooperation. Hanoi was particularly eager to cement relations with Moscow to counter the Sino-American rapprochement. Its December 1978 invasion of Cambodia was meant to preclude a two-front war. The Soviet-Vietnamese treaty was therefore aimed at China. It called for immediate consultations in the event of an attack against either. Reportedly, it also included a secret protocol granting Soviet forces access to Vietnam's airfields and port facilities.

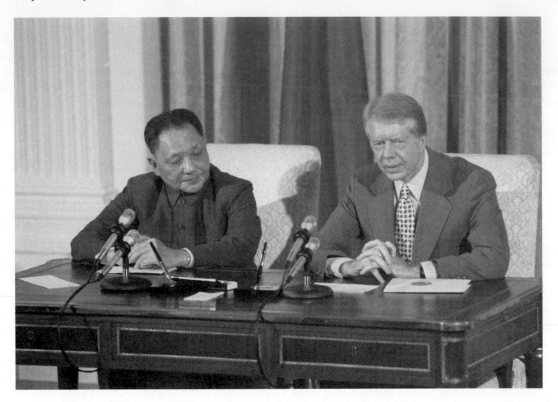

On 1 January 1979, Deng Xiaoping and President Jimmy Carter signed a treaty in Washington restoring full diplomatic relations between China and the United States. Carter supported Deng's goal of breaking a recent Soviet-Vietnamese security pact, and Chinese forces invaded Vietnam in mid-February. Moscow's decision not to intervene convinced Hanoi that the security pact with the USSR was dead.

China immediately responded by solidifying its relations with the United States. Deng Xiaoping flew to Washington to sign a treaty on 1 January 1979 restoring full diplomatic relations. U.S. President Jimmy Carter shared Deng's desire to weaken the Soviet-Vietnamese alliance. On 15 February 1979, just one day after the twenty-ninth anniversary of the Mao-Stalin agreement on Mongolia, and on the first day that China could officially renounce the thirty-year Sino-Soviet Treaty of Friendship, Alliance, and Mutual Assistance, Deng declared that China planned to conduct a limited attack on Vietnam. But Deng also put 1.5 million troops along the Soviet border on an emergency war alert in order to prevent Soviet intervention on Vietnam's behalf.

Vietnam's November 1978 security treaty with the Soviet Union and its December 1978 invasion of Cambodia prompted the Chinese invasion to prevent the Vietnamese attempt to change the balance of power in Southeast Asia. By 7 January 1979 the Vietnamese forces had secured the Cambodian capital of Phnom Penh. Five weeks later, on 17 February 1979, Chinese forces invaded Vietnam. (See Map 26.1.) By early

March, 120,000 Chinese were facing an equal number of Vietnamese. After three weeks of intense fighting, China occupied the provincial capitals of three of Vietnam's six provinces on its borders and deployed over 250,000 men.

When Beijing announced a troop withdrawal on 5 March 1979, the twenty-sixth anniversary of Stalin's death, the primary goal of the offensive appeared to remain unmet. Vietnam's military potential remained intact. Casualties on both sides were high. To most outsiders, Chinese forces seemed to have been worsted in the conflict. In the war, China's intended audience was not Hanoi but Moscow. China used the hostilities to confirm that Moscow would not honor its treaty obligations to intervene on Vietnam's behalf. This greatly diminished any fear that the USSR and Vietnam might combine to put effective military pressure on China's southern frontier. Once China assured itself of the hollowness of the Soviet-Vietnamese alliance, it set about reshaping Sino-Soviet relations.

On 3 April 1979, Beijing renounced the 1950 Sino-Soviet friendship treaty effective upon the expiration of its

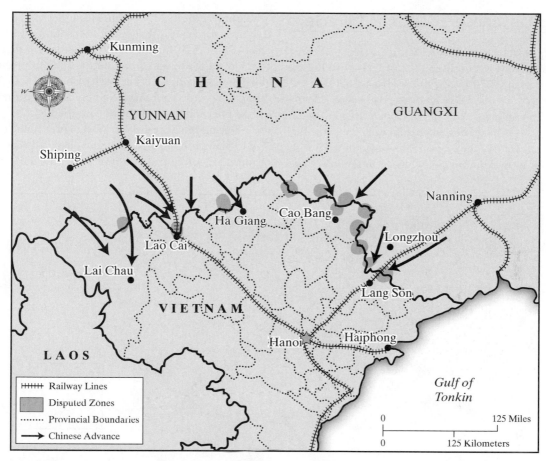

Map 26.1 Sino-Vietnamese War (1979)

thirty-year term in 1980. This marked the formal end to the Sino-Soviet alliance. Despite the highly visible Sino-Soviet split during the 1960s, the 1950 friendship treaty had remained in force throughout. As the end of its term approached, the Soviet Union redoubled its efforts to renew the treaty. It allied with Vietnam in 1978 in part to pressure China. In the aftermath of the Sino-Vietnamese War, however, Beijing referred to Moscow as a "paper polar bear." Although Sino-Soviet negotiations began in October 1979, Beijing broke them off on 20 January 1980 in response to the Soviet invasion of Afghanistan. Through the early 1980s, China insisted that normalization of relations with the USSR required the prior resolution of their disputes concerning Mongolia, Afghanistan, and Southeast Asia.

China's poor military showing in Vietnam led to comprehensive reforms jettisoning the Maoist military doctrine of people's war in preference for a more professionalized and streamlined military. During the three-week war, over 50,000 Chinese had died, perhaps even exceeding the 58,000 U.S. deaths during the entire Vietnam War. These losses clinched Deng Xiaoping's case that China had to modernize to be either strong or prosperous. Most importantly, Deng restored civilian control over the military. During the Cultural Revolution, the PLA had assumed enormous political responsibilities. Deng curtailed its role in internal security, civil construction, and railway engineering and restored central control over the regional military commanders.

China's invasion of Vietnam had terrible consequences for the large Han population living there, whose loyalties the Vietnamese government now suspected; 80 percent of the 1.4 million refugees fleeing Vietnam in the immediate aftermath of the war were ethnically Han Chinese. Several hundred thousand fled into China; others became known as the "boat people" as they fled by sea. Territorial issues between China and Vietnam have endured, with competing claims to the Paracel and Spratly Islands and armed incidents and unilateral seizures of territory in 1988 and 1992.

III. The Taiwanese Economic Miracle

Chinese rapprochement with the United States had enormous repercussions for the Republic of China (ROC) on Taiwan. (See Map 26.2.) Events in the global Cold War had caused Washington to reverse its plans to abandon Chiang after 1949. Taiwan benefited from its close relations with the United States, as U.S. aid flowed into Taiwan's economy. But the reprieve granted by the Korean War ended in 1979 with the U.S. shift in recognition from Taiwan to the PRC. The

end game of the Cold War caused another U.S. reassessment with equally far-reaching implications for Taiwan. With the Sino-Soviet Split in 1960 and the border conflict in 1969, the United States wanted to use the PRC to precipitate the long-awaited collapse of the Soviet Union. It wanted to play the China card. This entailed distancing itself from Taiwan as the price for rapprochement with the PRC.

During the Korean War, Washington funneled massive aid to Taiwan in order to restore its shattered economy. This happened rapidly and at a time when the Taiwanese most

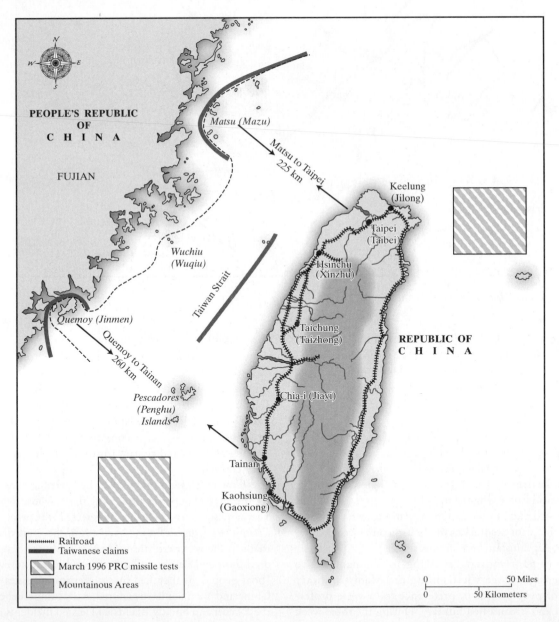

Map 26.2   Taiwan

needed it. Although fifty years of Japanese colonization had left a basic modern infrastructure that survived the war largely intact, the economy had been tied to the Japanese empire and the export of such primary products as sugar, rice, and pineapples. These were inadequate to provide prosperity. The Japanese had made great strides in developing railway, telephone, irrigation, legal, banking, commercial, public health, and educational systems. They formed village cooperatives to improve farming methods and promoted an efficient commercial market network. When the Pacific War started to go badly for Japan, Taiwanese professionals took over more senior positions within the colonial economy and government.

Even so, when the Nationalists took power, Taiwan had an annual per capita income of less than $100, putting it on a par with India. It had no industrial base beyond some small textile factories, a few modern sugar refineries, and other food processing plants, and 60 percent of the workforce was employed in agriculture. War left the island suffering from acute inflation, shortages, and a massive population influx from the mainland. The defeat of Japan eliminated Taiwan's main market, and the loss of the civil war soon eliminated China as well. The Nationalists were

extremely vulnerable when the Korean War suddenly changed their economic and security prospects. The Nationalists, acutely aware of their many failings during the Chinese civil war, focused on land reform (discussed in Chapter 22, Section V) and inflation control to solidify their rule. This had been accomplished by 1953.

A large percentage of those in charge of Taiwan's economic planning had advanced degrees from the United States. They relied on advice from Chinese-born academics holding important positions in the United States. Taiwanese planners concluded that they should emulate the Japanese model for economic development. Initially, they focused on an import-substitution strategy. This entailed import restrictions to enable Taiwanese infant industries to become established. In contrast to the PRC, which focused on heavy industry, Taiwanese planners emphasized light industry, particularly textiles. Soon they also developed the capacity to produce bicycles, flour, cement, and other goods for the domestic consumer market. All of these items were intended to increase the general standard of living in Taiwan as the basis for further economic growth. Production was not aimed specifically at military production, the focus of

The "Taiwan miracle" was partly Japanese, since Japan had left Taiwan in 1945 with a comprehensive infrastructure; partly American, since the United States had educated many of Taiwan's top leaders and invested heavily in the Taiwanese economy; and partly Chinese, since the Nationalists from the mainland and the local Taiwanese people worked together for a long time to create a viable economy. This scene of downtown Taipei in the 1980s shows the end results of this mixture.

the Soviet model for economic development that the PRC continued to follow.

By 1960, Taiwanese planners had shifted from import substitution to export promotion. They introduced economic reforms to remove tariff walls, foreign exchange controls, and restrictions on direct foreign investment. They also provided tax incentives for targeted export industries, made massive infrastructure investments, and turned to the development of heavy industry. By 1965, U.S. aid was down to 2 percent of Taiwan's GNP and a generation of political and technological leaders, particularly engineers and scientists, had received advanced degrees in the United States and returned home with their expertise. Taiwan's economy also benefited from all the U.S. procurements necessary to prosecute the Korean and Vietnam wars. In the 1970s and 1980s, Taipei targeted Ten Major Projects to improve the island's infrastructure, including a superhighway system, an international airport, two state-of-the-art port facilities, modernization of the railway system, construction of two nuclear power plants, an integrated steel mill, and shipbuilding facilities. These investments provided economic efficiencies that helped counteract the dramatic rise in oil prices resulting from the 1973 international oil embargo by the Organization of Petroleum Exporting Countries. From 1974 to 1984, Taiwan had the second highest economic growth rate in the world after Singapore.

The rapidly growing economies of Taiwan, Singapore, Hong Kong, and South Korea collectively became known as Asia's Little Tigers or the Four Little Dragons. During the 1950s, real GNP growth in Taiwan exceeded 7 percent per year, while in the 1960s and 1970s it reached almost 10 percent. The percentage of the economy devoted to agricultural production dropped quickly, from about a third in the 1950s to only 3 percent in the 1970s. Meanwhile, the share of industry in the economy increased from about 25 percent to 35 percent. Taiwanese businesses were among the first in Asia to emphasize the development of hi-tech industries and soon became third, behind the United States and Japan, in computer hardware manufacturing. In particular, Taiwan took advantage of the East Asian sea lanes passing by its shores to create a globalized domestic economy; its Evergreen Shipping Company soon became one of the largest container companies in the world.

In order to work efficiently in the global economy, Taiwan has adopted international law wholesale. Conformity to international law had been the key issue bedeviling Sino-Western relations since the time of the Qing dynasty. In Taiwan, business relations do not rely primarily on *guanxi,* as they so often do in the PRC. While business contacts remain important, the ultimate arbiter of business relations is not *guanxi* but contract law before a duly appointed judiciary. In

contrast, the PRC did not reform its legal system until after its application in 1984 to join the General Agreement on Tariff and Trade (GATT), the predecessor of the World Trade Organization (WTO). It would take China fifteen years to implement the required legal reforms allowing it to become a full member of the WTO on 10 November 2001. Taiwan secured its membership one day later, not because of long-standing deficiencies in its own legal system, but because the PRC used its international influence to make sure that it was admitted first. This was a matter of face and international prestige for the PRC to mask the inferiority, compared to Taiwan, of its economic performance and legal and political reforms. From the Opium Wars until the Deng Xiaoping period, most governments of mainland China had rejected international law, considering it to be simply a tool of Western domination.

While bicycles were prevalent in the PRC, in Taiwan motor scooters and private cars made the economy run. Here, one of the island's thousands of privately owned and operated automotive stores specializes in selling moped parts.

The most spectacular change in Taiwanese society has been the rapidly growing prosperity of the general population, to the point where the International Monetary Fund reclassified Taiwan in 1997 as an advanced economy. Although there are many rich people on Taiwan, fully half of the population considers itself to be part of the middle class. In 2000, Taiwan's 22 million people created a GNP over one-quarter that of the PRC, with its 1.2 billion people. This translated into a GNP per capita in China of $1,000 versus $16,000 for Taiwan, putting Taiwan on a par with Spain. Even accounting for the greater purchasing power of $1,000 in the PRC than in Taiwan, the difference in standards of living remains dramatic. Taiwan's foreign exchange reserves became so large in the late 1980s (hitting $70 billion) that they approximated half of the GNP of the PRC at that time. Some joked that Taiwan could soon buy back the PRC piece by piece.

These successes became known as the "Taiwanese economic miracle." A small island nation with few natural resources and a tenuous international standing catapulted itself in two generations from poverty into the ranks of the most developed nations. The miracle was a hybrid of Han culture, originating primarily from South China and Fujian province; Meiji Japanese agricultural and business models; technical expertise from higher education in the United States; and Nationalist Party leadership. Although the Nationalists lost the civil war, they seemed to have won the peace. However, there was a dark side to this miracle. The Nationalists ruled under martial law until 1987. Official figures from 1949–87 show 29,407 arrests, and perhaps 10–15 percent of those arrested were executed. Until the 1960s, mainlanders, comprising only 15 percent of the population, occupied all key political, military, police, and state-run economic positions, effectively excluding the native Taiwanese majority. Into the 1980s, elements of the Nationalist Party continued to rely on underworld gangs for contract killings of political opponents and critics.

IV. Deng Xiaoping's Agricultural Reforms

The economic miracle in Taiwan put great pressure on the PRC to change. How could it be that an island with 1/50th of its population, less than 1/250th of its land mass, and no special resource endowment could have a GNP half that of the entire PRC? The economic statistics were damning. To compete with Taiwan, Deng Xiaoping coupled Mao's foreign policy of Sino-American rapprochement with a radical redirection of economic policy. In August 1977, the Eleventh Party Congress adopted Deng's reform program, known as the Four Modernizations. It had first been proposed by Zhou Enlai in 1975 and put into effect by Deng, but it ended within the year because of Zhou's death and Deng's demotion.

In 1978, during the Third Plenum, Deng Xiaoping and the technocrats seized power. They rode the wave of deep popular discontent beginning in late 1978, when Chinese citizens anonymously pasted big-character posters on city walls, called the Democracy Wall Movement, with messages critical of Mao's policies during the Cultural Revolution. This public outpouring confirmed Deng's recommendation to act swiftly. The government announced that three decades of communism had

Table 26.1 Comparison of Urban and Rural Income and Consumption

	Net Income Per Capita			Consumption Per Capita		
Year	Urban	Rural	Urban (Rural = 100)	Urban	Rural	Urban (Rural = 100)
1967				251	110	2.28
1970				260	114	2.28
1975				324	124	2.61
1980	439	191	2.30	468	173	2.71
1985	749	398	1.88	802	347	2.31
1990	1,523	686	2.22	1,686	571	2.95
1995	4,288	1,578	2.72	5,044	1,479	3.41

Note: Knight and Song provide complete figures for the 1967–95 period. Between 1982 and 1985 rural and urban incomes reached their greatest equality, with urban workers earning just under twice as much as their rural counterparts. In the 1990s, the inequalities between urban and rural standards of living grew rapidly.

Source: John Knight and Lina Song, *The Rural–Urban Divide and Economic Disparities and Interactions in China* (Oxford: Oxford University Press, 1999), 29.

Table 26.2 Growth in Per Capita Gross Domestic Product (Yuan)

Year	Per Capita GDP
1979	417
1980	460
1981	489
1982	525
1983	580
1984	692
1985	853
1986	956
1987	1,104
1988	1,355
1989	1,512
1990	1,634
1991	1,879
1992	2,287
1993	2,939
1994	3,923
1995	4,854
1996	5,576
1997	6,054
1998	6,308
1999	6,551
2000	7,086
2001	7,651
2002	8,214
2003	9,073

Source: National Bureau of Statistics of China, 2006.

remolded most of the Four Bad Elements—descendants of landlords, rich peasants, capitalist-roaders, and rotten elements. At the end of 1978, over 4 million in the countryside still suffered legally sanctioned discrimination because of their class origin. This number was reduced to 50,000, although class origin remained part of their permanent records.

To create incentives to produce, farm prices were increased and bonuses and piece rates were mandated. In 1979, the government began to keep more accurate statistics to monitor its economic progress; enterprises were allowed to retain a portion of their profits to fund wage incentives; and from 1979 to 1981 state procurement prices for agriculture increased. Deng oversaw the dismantling over a five-year period of the commune system imposed during the Great Leap Forward. Individual families became responsible for

agricultural production. In 1985, the government relaxed its procurement rules to introduce contract purchasing, creating a mix of state and market prices for agriculture. Households contracted with the state to rent land on a semipermanent basis with the obligation to sell a proportion of their crop to the state. Once they met these obligations, they were free to dispose of any surplus as they saw fit. This led to the appearance of a wide variety of private markets. Land was assigned to families and became inheritable. Mandatory procurement, however, remained for three key crops: grain, cotton, and cooking oil. Grain prices were not deregulated until 1992.

The decollectivized agriculture from 1978 to 1984 created an unusual one-time improvement in agricultural productivity that benefited all. As a result, it narrowed the gap between urban and rural standards of living. (See Table 26.1.) Whereas from 1957 to 1978 grain production rose at a rate of 2.6 percent per annum, from 1979 to 1984 it doubled, to 4.9 percent per annum, transforming China from a net food importer into a net exporter. Cash incomes quadrupled. (See Table 26.2.) Standards of living improved. People ate better. They actually had money to invest. From 1978 to 1984, crop and livestock production increased by 49 percent. This rapid increase in agricultural efficiency and production lifted at least 100 million Chinese out of poverty; the poverty rate fell from 33 percent to 11 percent of the rural population during 1978–84. From 1985 to 1991, however, Beijing minimized increases in agricultural procurement prices to focus on improving urban standards of living, and the gap between rural and urban living standards again widened.

V. Deng Xiaoping's Industrial Reforms

In 1978, priority shifted from heavy to light industry. Deng introduced the Industrial Responsibility System, allowing companies to retain a percentage of their profits to reinvest at their own discretion. Plant managers could hire, fire, and set wages and prices within certain ranges. Wages and salaries became linked to performance. By 1984, only 30–40 percent of industrial production remained under central planning, while 20 percent was entirely market driven. The rest was under some degree of central control. China experienced double-digit industrial growth rates, and urban wages increased. (See Table 26.3.) In 1984, the government streamlined the tax regulations for enterprises, decentralized production targets increasingly to the enterprise level, and in 1985 reformed wages in public enterprises. In 1992 the government put increasing pressure on state-owned enterprises to reform their managerial practices.

In 1980 China opened four Special Economic Zones to experiment with market-oriented reforms and to attract

Table 26.3   Indices of Workers' Wages

Year	Index (1978 = 100)			Index (Preceding Year = 100)		
	Total	State-Owned Organizations	Urban Collective-Owned Organizations	State-Owned Organizations	Urban Collective-Owned Organizations	Non-State-Owned Non-Collective-Owned Organizations
1980	135.8	134.0	144.2	118.6	123.3	
1985	243.1	227.2	311.7	121.6	123.0	163.9
1990	518.7	495.9	579.8	113.4	108.7	135.7
1995	1,423.8	1,297.2	1,179.6	117.4	115.5	140.0
2000	1,873.1	1,624.3	917.2	106.3	95.5	121.3
2003	2,591.6	2,068.2	827.7	108.3	100.2	124.7

Note: These statistics show the general and dramatic rise in wages since the Deng Xiaoping reforms. The wage rise was most pronounced in the private sector.
Source: National Bureau of Statistics of China, 2006.

foreign investment. These zones were placed next to overseas Chinese communities: in Shenzhen, on the border with Hong Kong; in Zhuhai, outside of Macao; in Xiamen, located in Fujian, the native province for many Taiwanese; and in Shantou, the native place of many other overseas Chinese. Their location was intended to maximize connections with the vast Chinese diaspora, while the regulations administering the zones were intended to attract Western, Japanese, and Taiwanese investment. The government also reduced protectionism and repeatedly devalued its currency to encourage trade and investment. The Special Economic Zones provided a filter for the introduction of more market-oriented economic policies. Successful practices were then spread nationwide. By the end of 1993, when the government prohibited the creation of any new zones, there were already 9,000. By then, land and labor prices in the zones were not always competitive with those outside, so that there was increasing foreign investments in the PRC's regular economy.

The Chinese government followed the Japanese economic model for prosperity emphasizing the export of consumer goods. From 1987 on, China began registering trade surpluses. Like postwar Japan, China increasingly tried to promote high-technology industries. In 1983 it targeted the electrical and electronics sectors for export growth. In 1986 the government started investing in high-technology research; in 1991 it expanded the high-technology districts; in 1992 it promoted service sector development; in 1993 it began reforming the banking system; and in 1994 it reformed the educational system.

Meanwhile, in 1983 and 1988, new regulations concerning investment incentives specifically targeted Taiwan in an economic strategy to tie Taiwan's prosperity to that of the

mainland and, in so doing, promote the long-term prospects for reunification through economic integration. In 1982, in an effort to promote Hong Kong investment and also reunification, Deng Xiaoping publicized his One Country, Two Systems doctrine that would allow Hong Kong and Taiwan to retain their economic system under Chinese sovereignty. That year, Britain agreed to negotiate with China on the future of its colony, Hong Kong.

To train the professionals necessary to run a modern economy, for the first time since the 1930s China sent thousands of students to study abroad. These included the children of China's civil and military leadership. They would become China's Meiji generation of students, who would selectively apply what they had learned from their studies and seen in their travels. Increasing Western influence produced a short-lived campaign in 1983 against foreign Spiritual Pollution, but it lacked the bite of the earlier Maoist campaigns. Meanwhile, the West often saw China in terms of its cuisine. (See the feature on the next page.)

Many Communist loyalists were uneasy about the reforms. Tax exemptions, low wages, the freedom to hire and fire, and the prospect of joint Sino–foreign company ownership distinguished the Special Economic Zones from the rest of China. In addition, fourteen coastal cities were opened to foreign commerce. To the ideologues and the Stalinists, this all smacked of the treaty port era. In 1984 a debate emerged over the question of whether Marxism was dead given that the government had abandoned so much of its economic paradigm. Deng Xiaoping's 1987 pronouncement that central planning would no longer drive economic development constituted a de facto abandonment of the Soviet model for economic development. Arguably, it also constituted the abandonment of communism, given the economic definition

CHINESE CUISINE

In recent years, China's inexpensive manufactures have come to represent a significant percentage of the household goods, clothing, and electronics consumed in the West, while its cultural exports include movies made by an extraordinary generation of film makers as well as fiction. China has not only reopened to Western civilization but also has had an enduring presence in the West. Even during the long years of Chinese isolation, Westerners enjoyed China's cuisine, one of the world's greatest cuisines, provided by the many overseas Chinese living around the globe. For many foreigners, this cuisine is the most identifiable and most enjoyed Chinese

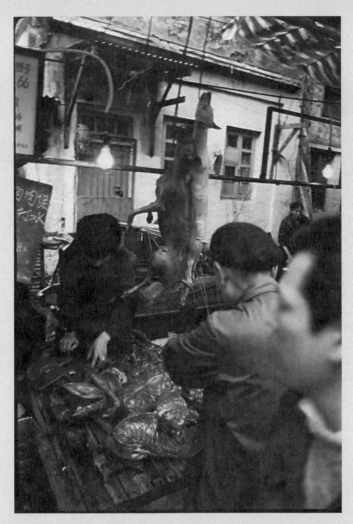

Deng Xiaoping's economic reforms during the 1980s began to spur massive growth rates in the PRC. Much of this growth was simply catching up to where China should have been if the Cultural Revolution had not occurred. Standards of living gradually increased, and consumer goods became more widely available. Here, a butcher in southern China is selling dog meat, which has been a popular Chinese dish for thousands of years, especially during the winter, when it is thought to produce greater body heat.

Continued

cultural export. Few Westerners realize that China has not one but eight major cuisines. Cantonese is the most well known in the West because most Chinese emigrants came from Guangdong and dominate Chinese restaurants abroad. Most dishes are mild, with numerous and often unusual ingredients, fresh seafood, and dried or salted, preserved foods. The Cantonese are known among their fellow Chinese for their delight in eating almost anything. Exotic ingredients include snakes, chicken feet, worms, insects, and dogs. The Cantonese are famous for dim sum, usually served on Sundays at brunch. "Dim sum" refers to a whole range of small dishes served with tea, often delivered on trolleys to allow diners to pick and choose.

With the reopening of China, other regional cuisines have become more well known abroad. Sichuanese cuisine, in contrast to Cantonese food, is famous for its spicy peppers, although not all of its dishes are hot. Pickled, salted, dried, and smoked, preserved ingredients are also common. Famous dishes include *Mapo dofu* (Ma-po's Tofu), a spicy tofu dish, and *Gongbao jiding* (Kung Pao chicken), a spicy chicken, peanut, and dried hot pepper dish. The other six major cuisines are Anhui, Hunan, Fujian, Jiangsu, Shandong, and Zhejiang cuisines. Most Chinese culinary traditions derive from the Shandong cuisine of the Yellow River delta, the cradle of Chinese civilization.

A Chinese meal consists of the main food—meaning a staple carbohydrate (rice, noodles, or steamed buns)—plus various and often numerous dishes, with no special importance accorded to meat versus vegetables. While rice is the staple of South China, noodles and steamed buns are the staples of North China. Most dishes are composed of bite-sized pieces, the exception being fish, which are usually served whole. Diners all have their own rice bowls but share all other dishes and traditionally use their own chopsticks to eat from them, although serving utensils are increasingly used. There is also more talk of using reusable chopsticks to decrease deforestation.

Desserts receive far less emphasis than in Western cuisine, and meals do not end with sweets but with soup or possibly fruit. Hot tea and hot water are common drinks, not cold beverages, which are thought to impede digestion. Boiled water also ensures that the drink is safe for consumption, since tap water remains unsafe to drink without boiling. Uncooked food is rarely served since night soil has been the traditional fertilizer; serving uncooked food risks spreading hepatitis, a disease endemic in mainland China.

Most dishes are steamed, stir-fried, or deep-fried in the belief that short cooking time enhances the flavor. Basic flavorings for most Chinese dishes include soy sauce, light and dark rice vinegar, sesame oil, rice wine, ginger root, spring onion, garlic, sugar, salt, cornstarch, and monosodium glutamate. Pork is the staple meat, and cooking oil is the staple fat. Westerners are less familiar with Chinese breakfasts than with dinner and lunch fare. Common breakfast dishes include eggs hard boiled in tea, rice porridge, pickled vegetables, rice balls, and dough pastry.

---

of the concept. In 1992 Deng tried to demonstrate that the market was not a capitalist institution—markets, however, are the basis for capitalism—and in 1994 he emphasized that his country was "building socialism with Chinese characteristics." Yet, his reforms produced economic development in China based on markets, not socialism, and were more akin to the state capitalism of Meiji Japan than to the socialism of Karl Marx or Vladimir Lenin. To many in the West, it seemed that China was taking up where it left off in the 1930s.

Deng Xiaoping's reforms were breathtakingly successful. On the eve of the reforms, foreign trade accounted for 13 percent of Chinese GDP, and in terms of international trade, China ranked thirty-second in the world. Two decades later, in the late 1990s, trade had grown to 30 percent of GDP, and China ranked tenth in international trade and possessed one of the world's largest merchant marines to deliver its bounty throughout the globe. Its trade had grown over ten times. China was no longer exporting primary products, but rather manufactured goods. It also had attracted enormous foreign investments. Whereas prior to Deng Xiaoping's reforms China had needed to adjust its annual growth targets downward, in 1993 it adjusted anticipated growth statistics upward from 6 percent to 8–9 percent in the Eighth Five-Year Plan. By the late 1990s, China had absorbed 40 percent of the foreign investments made in all developing countries. Sino-foreign ventures accounted for half of China's imports and one-third of its exports. About two-thirds of this investment came from overseas Chinese, mainly from Hong Kong and Taiwan. Thus, Deng's strategy of ensnaring Taiwan economically was successful.

On the negative side, there was a decline in major infrastructure investments in rural areas, such as irrigation and flood control. There was a growing disparity between urban and rural incomes and between coastal and inland incomes. Those employed outside of agriculture earned four times more than those who remained on the land. In industry, retained profits greatly decreased state revenues, leading to a growing deficit. This was coupled with problems revaluating the yuan and an initital growing trade deficit that later turned into a large surplus. The construction boom entailed shortages and inflation, and state-run industries performed poorly. Lifting price controls also caused inflation, which reached 10 percent, while corruption and bad bank loans grew.

Deng Xiaoping, like Chiang Kai-shek, rejected political liberalization. While he initially used the public malaise to promote his economic reform program, he ignored the popular demands for democracy. In March 1979, after a successful trip to the United States normalizing relations and after the end of the Sino-Vietnamese War, Deng rapidly suppressed the Democracy Wall movement, removing the posters and silencing their authors. In September 1980, he had the constitution amended to revoke the right to display big-character posters. As a loyal Communist, he may have been correct: Only a decade later in the Soviet Union, President Mikhail Gorbachev's call for *glasnost* (openness) ended in the collapse of the Communist government.

Deng hoped to reduce tensions with the West to focus on domestic reforms. On 11 January 1982, he made it clear that the One Country, Two Systems doctrine applied equally to Hong Kong and Taiwan, keeping tensions with Taiwan low during his tenure. His main legacies were foreign policy continuity with Mao's realignment, the abandonment of Mao's ideological bent in domestic policy, an emphasis on technical expertise, and the market-oriented economic reforms that lifted millions of Chinese out of poverty. In many ways, his reforms followed the economic model of the state-sponsored, export-based strategy to prosperity of Asia's Little Tigers—South Korea, Taiwan, Singapore, and Hong Kong—whose post–World War II growth rates had been so extraordinary. The Little Tigers, in turn, had largely followed the path of Meiji Japan.

Conclusions

The 1970s were a watershed both for the PRC and the ROC. By means of the Cultural Revolution, Mao Zedong remained in power but at a tremendous human and material cost. He reoriented Chinese foreign policy away from the USSR to the formerly demonized West. Powerful elements within the CCP opposed this shift, including major segments of the military. When Mao curtailed the power of the military, his proclaimed successor, Lin Biao, died mysteriously in a plane crash over Mongolia. Five years later, Mao could not escape his own mortality. This presented his successors with the dilemma of maintaining the CCP as their vehicle to power while distancing themselves from disastrous policies pursued in its name. As a solution, Mao's widow,

Jiang Qing, and three of her closest supporters, the so-called Gang of Four, were blamed for the excesses of the Cultural Revolution. Blaming four individuals obviated the need to search more broadly for the groups, institutions, and beliefs responsible for policies that had not benefited the general population, but instead had caused the deaths of tens of millions of Chinese.

The technocrats under Deng Xiaoping took charge. They maintained foreign policy continuity by further improving relations with the United States, both to exert pressure on the Soviet Union and to pursue economic reforms at home. This culminated in 1979 with the normalization of relations with the United States and the renunciation of the Sino-Soviet friendship treaty. The Sino-Vietnamese War of 1979 precipitated this reorientation in the following sense: The Soviet Union had shown itself incapable of or unwilling to honor its treaty obligation to come to the defense of Vietnam, indicating that it posed less of a military threat to China than in the past. This gave China the foreign policy latitude to restore relations with the United States at the Soviet Union's expense. The war transformed the Chinese military into a key advocate of economic reform in order to modernize the armed forces that had performed so poorly against Vietnam.

Meanwhile, the leaders of the ROC had been carrying out equally momentous reforms in domestic, not foreign, policy. Taiwanese leaders carefully studied the mistakes of the Republican era to develop strategies for agricultural and economic development. This set Taiwan on a path to rapid industrialization and a high standard of living. In contrast to China, Taiwan emphasized light industry, consumer products, international trade, and connection with the outside world two decades before the economic reforms under Deng Xiaoping. These reforms produced a GNP over 40 percent the size of China's. Such comparative statistics constituted an indictment of the economic policies of the CCP.

Therefore, Deng Xiaoping matched Mao's reorientation of foreign policy with a reorientation of domestic policy. The Four Modernizations constituted an abandonment of Mao's emphasis on ideology, replacing it with an emphasis on economic performance and professional expertise. Deng's highly successful reforms created a level of prosperity and stability unmatched since the early Qing dynasty. Despite the about-face in foreign and domestic policy, not only did the CCP maintain its mandate of heaven, but Deng Xiaoping's economic reforms set the Communists on the path to dynastic restoration. Prosperity and stability remain the hallmarks of legitimate rule. Deng strengthened both. Neither Taiwan under Chiang Kai-shek nor China under Deng Xiaoping, however, embraced far-reaching political reforms.

The economic reforms took on a life of their own. As markets appeared, the *hukou* system of internal passports no longer excluded the rural population from China's cities. They no longer needed ration coupons to eat while in cities, but could now buy food on the open market. By 1993 the urban ration coupons had largely been abolished. However, the absence of a city *hukou* deprived such rural migrants of many urban services, effectively making second-class citizens out of those who independently sought work in cities. Because of the reforms, the CCP greatly reduced its control over the countryside, over prices and wages, and over population migration.

Deng's economic program of opening up to the West was soon nicknamed the Open Door Policy, a name filled with unintended irony: The originator and great promoter of the original Open Door Policy had been the United States, which orthodox Communist hagiography vilified as an "imperial power." This epithet, in turn, was even more ironic, because the United States, unlike China, had actually once been a colony, won a war of national liberation against Great Britain, and then moved on, whereas many Chinese continued to view their own history through the prism of their victimization by others. But outsiders had nothing to do with the mayhem of the Great Leap Forward, the Great Famine, or the Cultural Revolution. These were Han Chinese policies inflicted on Han and non-Han Chinese alike. Much the same can be said about the Tiananmen Massacre.

BIBLIOGRAPHY

Barnett, A. Doak and Ralph N. Clough, eds. *Modernizing China: Post-Mao Reform and Development.* Boulder, CO: Westview Press, 1986.

Bonavia, David. *Verdict in Peking: The Trial of the Gang of Four.* New York: Putnam, 1984.

Chang, Pao-min. *Kampuchea between China and Vietnam.* Singapore: Singapore University Press, 1985.

Chen, King C. *China's War with Vietnam, 1979.* Stanford, CA: Hoover Institutions Press, 1987.

Copper, John F. *Taiwan: Nation-State or Province?* 4th ed. Boulder, CO: Westview Press, 2003.

Duiker, William J. *China and Vietnam: The Roots of Conflict.* Berkeley: University of California Press, 1986.

Gilks, Anne. *The Breakdown of the Sino-Vietnamese Alliance, 1970–1979.* Berkeley: University of California Press, 1992.

Gong, Ting. *The Politics of Corruption in Contemporary China: An Analysis of Policy Outcomes.* Westport, CT: Praeger, 1994.

Ho, Samuel P. S. *Economic Development of Taiwan, 1860–1970.* New Haven, CT: Yale University Press, 1978.

Khan, Azizur Rahman and Carl Riskin. *Inequality and Poverty in China in the Age of Globalization.* Oxford: Oxford University Press, 2001.

Kleinberg, Robert. *China's "Opening" to the Outside World: The Experiment with Foreign Capitalism.* Boulder, CO: Westview Press, 1990.

Knight, John and Lina Song. *The Rural–Urban Divide: Economic Disparities and Interactions in China.* Oxford: Oxford University Press, 1999.

Lardy, Nicholas R. *Foreign Trade and Economic Reform in China, 1978–1990.* Cambridge: Cambridge University Press, 1991.

Lü, Xiaobo. *Cadres and Corruption: The Organizational Involution of the Chinese Communist Party.* Stanford, CA: Stanford University Press, 2000.

Marti, Michael E. *China and the Legacy of Deng Xiaoping: From Communist Revolution to Capitalist Evolution.* Washington, DC: Brassey's, 2002.

Meisner, Maurice. *The Deng Xiaoping Era: An Inquiry into the Fate of Chinese Socialism, 1978–1994.* New York: Hill & Wang, 1996.

Ross, Robert S. *The Indochina Tangle.* New York: Columbia University Press, 1988.

Rubinstein, Murray A., ed. *Taiwan: A New History.* Armonk, NY: M. E. Sharpe, 1999.

Taylor, Jay. *The Generalissimo's Son: Chiang Ching-kuo and the Revolutions in China and Taiwan.* Cambridge, MA: Harvard University Press, 2000.

Teiwes, Frederick C. and Warren Sun. *The Tragedy of Lin Biao: Riding the Tiger during the Cultural Revolution 1966–1971.* London: Hurst, 1996.

Terrill, Ross. *White-boned Demon: A Biography of Madame Mao Zedong.* Rev. ed. Stanford, CA: Stanford University Press, 1999.

Tien, Hung-mao. *The Great Transition: Political and Social Change in the Republic of China.* Stanford, CA: Stanford University Press, 1987.

Thaku, Ramesh and Carlyle Thayer. *Soviet Relations with India and Vietnam.* New York: St. Martin's Press, 1992.

Unger, Jonathan. *The Transformation of Rural China.* Armonk, NY: M. E. Sharpe, 2002.

Vogel, Ezra. *The Four Little Dragons: The Spread of Industrialization in Asia.* Cambridge, MA: Harvard University Press, 1991.

Witke, Roxane. *Comrade Chiang Ch'ing.* Boston: Little, Brown, 1977.

Wu, Tien-wei. *Lin Biao and the Gang of Four: Contra-Confucianism in Historical and Intellectual Perspective.* Carbondale: Southern Illinois University Press, 1983.

NOTE

1. Cited in Roderick MacFarquhar, "The Succession to Mao and the end of Maoism," in *The Politics of China: The Eras of Mao and Deng,* 2nd ed., Roderick MacFarquhar, ed. (Cambridge: Cambridge University Press, 1997), 302–3.

Chronology

19 December 1984	Anglo-Chinese declaration on the return of Hong Kong
11 March 1985	Mikhail Gorbachev comes to power
5 December 1986	Pro-democracy student movement begins, becomes nationwide
16–22 January 1987	Zhao Ziyang replaces the popular Hu Yaobang
13 April 1987	Sino-Portuguese agreement on the return of Macao
26 October 1988	Chinese foreign minister visits Soviet Union after a thirty-two-year hiatus
15 April 1989	Hu Yaobang dies
15–18 April 1989	Gorbachev visits China; normalization of Sino-USSR relations
17 April 1989	Pro-democracy demonstration at Tiananmen Square
17 May 1989	Huge pro-democracy demonstration in Tiananmen Square
19 May 1989	Zhao Ziyang removed from power
20 May 1989	Martial law proclaimed in Beijing
31 May 1989	Large sympathy demonstration in Taipei
4 June 1989	Second Tiananmen Incident (the first occurred at Zhou Enlai's funeral in 1976)
23–4 June 1989	Jiang Zemin replaces Zhao Ziyang
3 September 1989	Normalization of Sino-Vietnamese relations
11 October 1989	Chinese official visit to India after a nineteen-year hiatus
6–9 November 1989	Jiang Zemin replaces Deng Xiaoping as chairman of the Central Military Commission
8 December 1991	Soviet Union dissolved
18 Jan.–21 Feb. 1992	Deng's southern tour to promote reform program
25 February 1992	Territorial Waters and Contiguous Areas Act
19 February 1997	Deng Xiaoping dies
1 July 1997	Return of Hong Kong to Chinese sovereignty
20 December 1999	Return of Macao to Chinese sovereignty
1 April 2001	Downing of the U.S. EP-3 plane on Hainan Island
15 March 2003	Hu Jintao assumes presidency

27   Tiananmen

China, a father who has killed his own children
This very night is molesting his own daughter China China

. . .

It's a country crawling with peasants
It's a country crawling with petty citizens
It's a country crawling with bureaucrats

They haven't achieved salvation through endless wars
In thousands of years throughout history and time
At death's turning point At one with the structures of
earth
They move from slavery to slavery[1]

Anonymously published in a
Hong Kong monthly on 15 June 1989

Deng Xiaoping returned China to the world stage after three decades of diplomatic isolation, internal chaos, and warfare, restoring peace and real prosperity for the first time since the mid-Qing dynasty. During the 1980s, the economy boomed, foreign tourists arrived in droves, and Chinese citizens, particularly students, had a chance to travel and study abroad. China focused on economic reforms, eschewing the political changes emphasized in Taiwan and the Soviet Union. In the 1980s, Mikhail Gorbachev sought to rescue the USSR's underperforming economy through political and then economic reform. From 1989 to 1991, Gorbachev allowed the Eastern European countries to regain their independence. Ordinary Chinese citizens watched events in the first Communist country with great interest. Many hoped that their government would also engage in political liberalization. China's educated youth became particularly outspoken. In 1989 they massed on the streets of Beijing and in particular in Tiananmen Square, where so many popular demonstrations had taken place. Instead of political liberalization, the demonstrations triggered a bloody crackdown, as Deng released the PLA on the youth of Beijing. Deng created an international symbol of brutality encapsulated by the term "Tiananmen Massacre," brought live to the world by foreign reporters in Beijing to report on Gorbachev's state visit.

I. The Dissolution of the Soviet Union

As the Long March generation dominating Chinese politics aged, generational succession loomed on the horizon. Events in the Soviet Union provided Chinese leaders and citizenry with a glimpse of the possibilities facing China. Mikhail Gorbachev (1931–) came to power in 1985 upon a succession of deaths of his immediate and aging predecessors: Leonid Brezhnev in 1982, Yuri Andropov in 1984, and Konstantin Chernenko in 1986. As in China, communism had brought political unification, economic integration, and a universal basic standard of living, but the long postwar economic surge of the West, Japan, South Korea, and Taiwan produced a yawning income gap between them and Russia. China also faced a widening income gap.

Gorbachev focused on political reform as a prerequisite for economic reform. When he eased press censorship and overseas travel restrictions, however, discussion soon focused on Stalin's atrocities. As in China's Hundred Flowers Movement, popular criticism rapidly extended to the Communist Party. Gorbachev, as party chairman, could not adequately distance himself from Stalin's crimes. Press coverage of the discovery of mass graves containing tens of thousands of victims, the 1986 Chernobyl nuclear power plant disaster in which radioactive contamination was spewed as far afield as

Scandinavia, the stalemated Soviet war in Afghanistan (1979–88), and nationalist uprisings in the three Baltic states all proved highly corrosive to the legitimacy of Communist parties throughout the Soviet empire. As the unrest spread, consumer goods disappeared from the shelves, exacerbating popular dissatisfaction.

The reform movement rapidly moved in unintended directions: In 1989 the Berlin Wall fell; in a domino effect, a cascade of Communist governments in Eastern Europe broke with Moscow and soon were out of office; and in 1991 the Soviet Union itself disintegrated, leaving a Russian rump state composed of only half of the Soviet population. In the 1990s the Russian economy collapsed, the Communist Party fell from power, and the Cold War ended––on Western, not Soviet, terms. Gorbachev's reforms had not shored up but rather had fatally compromised Communist rule. Events of the Gorbachev period profoundly influenced China's leadership and its educated urban population.

Although strategically China benefited from the implosion of the Soviet empire, the collapse of the first Communist state had implications for the longevity of Communist rule in China. The popular reaction to the airing of Stalin's crimes suggested that an open discussion of the Maoist period might prove equally lethal for the CCP. While China's urban youth latched on to the political ferment in Russia and Eastern Europe that promised political change, China's leaders fixated on the dangers of political anarchy and a return to *luan* (chaos) that would serve no one's long-term interests.

In the 1980s, however, the ultimate consequences of Gorbachev's reforms were still far from clear to many Soviet citizens, let alone to those Chinese youth infatuated with Gorbachev's persona. In the spring of 1989, Chinese university students organized what became a nationwide movement to pressure their government to democratize. Hu Yaobang's death on 15 April 1989 became the catalyst. Hu had joined the Long March as a child of thirteen and later became part of Deng Xiaoping's *guanxi* network. He suffered during the Cultural Revolution. Upon his restoration to power in 1980 as party general secretary, he promoted greater freedom of expression, tacitly supporting the Democracy Wall Movement. He strove for greater government accountability and greater popular representation. In 1987 he was blamed for the growing student unrest in support of his program and was sacked. Yet, Hu remained tremendously popular for his rehabilitation of those who had suffered during the Anti-Rightist Movement following the Hundred Flowers Movement and during the Cultural Revolution.

Upon his death, thousands of ordinary citizens gathered in Tiananmen Square to honor the man and to demand the realization of his dreams. They called for greater democracy, elimination of corruption, and a dialogue with their government. Students concentrated their criticism on Premier Li Peng, the adopted son of Zhou Enlai. After studying in the Soviet Union, Li had survived the Great Leap Forward and the Cultural Revolution unscathed, rising to membership of the exclusive Standing Committee on the Politburo. In contrast to Hu Yaobang, whose personality attracted popular support, Li Peng's lack of charisma and reliance on Communist phraseology repelled it.

Deng's preceding decade of economic reforms had given citizens a wide variety of freedoms in economic life but no corresponding freedoms in political life. The dramatic rise in the standard of living for many had been accompanied by an equally dramatic rise in inflation for all. The increasing freedom of employment had been matched by a commensurate rise in corruption. Inflation and corruption were both hallmarks of the discredited Republican era. Students, starting in Beijing, spearheaded demonstrations throughout China. In the manner of Confucian scholar-officials, they sought their government's attention to solve problems in its administration. As idealistic young people, they did so without fully anticipating the possible consequences of their actions.

Soon the students were joined by workers hurt by inflation, by entrepreneurs who desired political rights commensurate with their economic power, and by intellectuals who no longer believed it possible to work for change within the CCP. While the students' calls for democracy were vague, the workers organized. For the first time since the Communist Revolution, they established an independent workers' organization, the Federation of Autonomous Workers. The organizers of the pro-democracy movement did not look to the United States as their model but rather to the USSR, which at that time seemed to have found the way to move from communism to a more open political system. It is true that U.S. democratic models may have served as an ultimate goal for some, as indicated in the symbolism of the Goddess of Liberty—closely resembling heroic imagery of the French Revolution or the later French-made U.S. Statue of Liberty—erected in Tiananmen Square, but the route to this ultimate goal seemed to be provided by the new Russia.

II. Tiananmen Demonstrations

The pro-democracy movement lasted for fifty-four days—just one day less than the fifty-five-day foreign seige during the 1900 Boxer Uprising—from the death of Hu Yaobang on 15 April to its bloody suppression on 4 June 1989. At its height, in late April, over a million people gathered in Tiananmen Square (see the feature on page 432). Events paralleled those of the 1976 Tiananmen Incident, when thousands of Chinese had also converged on Tiananmen Square to mourn the death of Premier Zhou Enlai, who, like Hu Yaobang, was also perceived to be a great reformer. Even though the student leaders employed nonviolent tactics, the government characterized the movement in late April as a conspiracy. In the midst of the growing protests, Gorbachev was scheduled to arrive in Beijing on 15 May 1989 for an historic reconciliation to end the Sino-Soviet split. Deng Xiaoping intended the reconciliation to be one of the crowning achievements of his rule. A Soviet leader was coming to Beijing, in the manner of tributary states of the past, to express friendship with China. Instead, the presence of the famous Soviet reformer electrified the student protesters.

Inflation, corruption, unrest, and the moral indictment of China's most educated youth suggested a dynasty in decline. In the previous generation, student demonstrations had accompanied the collapse of Nationalist power on the mainland, and student unrest a generation earlier still had led to the May Fourth Movement that had sent shock waves throughout the country. In China, at an individual level, public criticism causes a loss of face. At a government level, in the absences of regularly scheduled elections, widespread public criticism endangers its mandate to rule. Protests are not as destabilizing in the West because Western governments are based fundamentally on laws, institutions, and regular elections, not on individuals and their interlocking *guanxi* networks. Institutions survive individuals, while *guanxi* does not. Thus, student unrest in China potentially had far greater ramifications than were possible in the West.

The Chinese government fully appreciated the implications of the protests for the survival of Communist rule. Unlike Gorbachev, Deng Xiaoping had already been a political leader at the time of Khrushchev's Secret Speech denouncing Stalin. Deng had even been in Moscow at that time to observe the reaction. He clearly understood the connection between demystifying the party helmsman and undermining Communist rule both at home and in the empire. Bringing attention to the failings of the CCP would undermine its authority. The Chinese students did not concern themselves with the possible ramifications of their demands vis-à-vis the retention of the lands of the former Qing empire. Their focus was on creating a more participatory form of government. Beijing, however, understood the

implications on both the national and imperial levels. It responded accordingly.

Hu Yaobang's funeral meant that citizens could assemble legally to mourn his passing. Beginning on 17 April 1989, pro-democracy demonstrators congregated around the Monument to the Martyrs in Tiananmen Square. Some affixed wall posters lauding Hu as a people's hero, while others were highly critical of the Communists, making such comments as "Seventy years have passed since the May Fourth Movement and still we have no freedom and democracy!"[2] Students also presented a seven-point petition to the National People's Congress demanding greater press freedom, the freedom to protest, and a renunciation of political campaigns to repress political dissidents. On 19 April and the morning of 20 April, the first hint of violence appeared. Some 20,000 demonstrators gathered outside the compound where Premier Li Peng and the other major Communist leaders lived to demand that he personally address them. Under the guidance of Wuer Kaixi, a young education student of Uighur descent from Xinjiang, the crowd remained peaceful. Government spokesmen accused the demonstrators of being reactionaries. Soon, policemen appeared and began to beat the students. Those arrested became martyrs and the movement quickly grew in size.

During the late evening of 21 April, thousands gathered in Tiananmen Square in preparation for Hu Yaobang's funeral the following day. As the ceremony was taking place in the Great Hall of the People, crowds outside again called for Premier Li Peng to come outside to receive their petition. In a gesture reminiscent of imperial times, three student representatives knelt before the doors, while one held a scroll intended for the "emperor." The government leaders declined to accept the petition but could not escape the highly unfavorable symbolism of the moment. On 26 April the *People's Daily* attacked the students, hinting that military force might be necessary. The next day students protested the editorial, while 150,000 demonstrators converged on Tiananmen Square. Deng Xiaoping responded by visiting the regional military commanders and ordering their units to deploy to Beijing. The PLA was in position by 18 May.

On 13 May, about 400 students began an unprecedented hunger strike that lasted for seven days until 19 May. Historically, China has been a country of terrible famines. Therefore, food deprivation has enormous symbolism. The last great famine had been caused by Mao's policies during the Great Leap Forward. The hunger strike implied the moral bankruptcy of Communist rule. Deng Xiaoping and Zhao Ziyang, who had been intimately involved in ending the Great Famine, could not have missed this message.

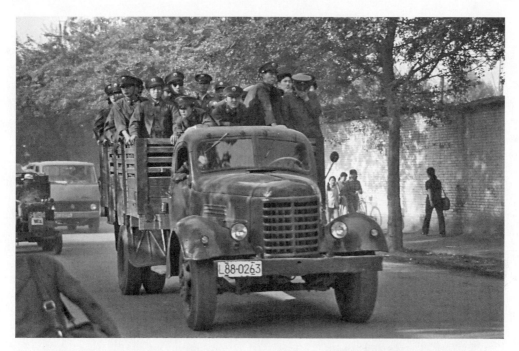

The end of the Cold War was applauded by the PRC, but the collapse of the USSR, which implied the bankruptcy of the Communist system, was not so welcome. During the Tiananmen Square demonstrations, PLA troops repeatedly refused to obey orders to shoot at student protestors. Reportedly, the troops who massacred the students on 4 June 1989 were not from Beijing but from rural areas far from the city, and many did not even speak Mandarin.

III. The Beijing Massacre

President Gorbachev's arrival in China on 15 May delayed military action against the pro-democracy activists. Not until after his 18 May departure did the government order the PLA to intervene. Many foreign correspondents originally sent to cover the Gorbachev visit lingered in Beijing to continue reporting on the growing student demonstrations. By that time, over a million demonstrators were estimated to be in Tiananmen Square. On 19 May, Li Peng visited hospitalized hunger strikers in an attempt to convince the students to return home, but to no avail. Later that night he announced that the PLA would be deployed in Beijing, and the next day martial law was declared.

During late May, PLA troops tried but failed to enter the capital. Local residents surrounded their trucks, refusing to let them pass. These soldiers did not want to fire on fellow citizens; they turned back instead. At 10:30 P.M. on the night of 3 June, PLA troops were loaded into trucks and provided with live ammunition. A total of 25,000 troops converged on Tiananmen Square, while another 75,000 troops waited in reserve outside the city. PLA tanks slowly rolled into the square, crushing all in

their path. By 3:00 A.M. on 4 June, PLA troops and tanks approached the remaining demonstrators, who gathered around the statue of the Goddess of Democracy; thirty minutes later, the square was empty. According to Beijing, no one died. Unofficial early estimates reported 4,000 dead and 6,500 wounded, while Russian sources reported 10,000 deaths.

In the aftermath of the massacre, Beijing labeled the pro-democracy demonstrators as counterrevolutionaries; it described the massacre as a restoration of public order; and it arrested and imprisoned the leaders of the movement. Yet, many of the main instigators made the long overland journey from Beijing to Hong Kong and from there to exile. Even though they were recognized throughout the country, their fellow citizens not only failed to turn them in, but some aided their escape. On 9 June, Deng Xiaoping came out of retirement to hail the PLA as "a truly Great Wall of iron and steel around the Party and country."[3] From his point of view, the bloodshed was minor in comparison to that of the Cultural Revolution, whereas inexperienced youths in command of political movements were truly dangerous; the youthful Red Guards had brought political and economic chaos. Two generations earlier,

CHINA'S CHANGING URBAN LANDSCAPE

The 4 June 1989 massacre took place directly outside the Forbidden City's Gateway of Heavenly Peace. The government's decision to send tanks against unarmed students shows how fearful certain CCP leaders were of losing power. Although the PRC has denied that any students were killed, Soviet reporters (with extensive experience in how Communist dictatorships quell social unrest) have estimated that approximately 10,000 people were killed.

The reopening of China has brought with it the revitalization of much of the urban landscape that suffered from decades of inattention and the addition of Stalinist wedding-cake architecture. The Communists neglected China's pre-1949 architectural heritage to build poured-concrete structures on monolithic Soviet models. Neither the Soviet-style structures nor their aesthetics have aged well. Since the 1990s, a profusion of ultra-modern skyscrapers designed by Chinese and foreign architects have transformed the skyline, with dazzling new buildings in China's coastal cities and capital.

The events of Tiananmen took place in a very historic part of downtown Beijing. The Ming dynasty built the Gateway of Heavenly Peace (Tiananmen) in 1417, called in those days the Great Ming Gate. The Qing renamed it the Great Qing Gate, while the Republican-period governments of China called it the Gate of China. During the imperial period, only the emperor crossed its threshold. The Boxer Uprising heavily damaged the ministry buildings in front of the gate, which were then razed to create a moderate-sized square. From 1950 to 1972, the Communists destroyed not only the neighborhoods in the vicinity of the gate to create a vast plaza for mass rallies, but also the historic outer and inner city walls, and reused the materials to build the subway and sewage systems. In 1979 the government ordered the preservation of the remaining wall and moat fragments and two surviving watchtowers.

Since the time of the Ming dynasty, the Gateway of Heavenly Peace has symbolized the nation. Hence, demonstrators chose it as the site for the initial rallies of the May Fourth Movement in 1919, those following the death of Zhou Enlai in 1976, the pro-democracy rallies in 1989, and the site of the attempted self-immolation of seven alleged Falun Gong members in 2001.

Until the Communists assumed power, Beijing had numerous neighborhoods of well-preserved Ming and Qing dynasty buildings, gateways, and stunning temples. The Qing had inherited a rich architectural heritage from the Ming dynasty that they adapted and greatly expanded upon, particularly during the first half of their dynasty. Rather than focusing on the structural elegance of the Ming, the Qing emphasized the interrelationship of architectural and decorative elements to produce more complicated and interlocking buildings than the square form favored by the Ming. The great wealth of the Qing coupled with a highly developed handicraft industry allowed the inclusion of elaborately carved screen walls, banisters, gates, window frames, and other ornamentation. Qing architects played with the forms of walls, entryways, halls, roofs, and eaves, and largely abandoned the thick pillars and dominating eaves favored by the Ming. Placement of buildings followed the rules of *fengshui* or geomancy in order to promote good luck and keep ghosts at bay. Because of the shortage of timber, an incipient sign of environmental stress, Qing architects relied increasingly on brick, stucco, and tile construction for walls and roofs.

The Qing maintained the north-south axis of Beijing, the capital of both dynasties, but extensively rebuilt the Ming administrative and imperial districts and expanded the suburbs to create an exclusively Manchu inner city and a Han and minority group outer city, both within the greater city walls. The Qing retained most of the buildings of the Forbidden City, the residence of the ruling dynasty and the location of key government offices. The Qing also built elaborate tomb complexes. They developed their two main post–Ming conquest burial sites in Hebei province, where all Qing emperors from Shunzhi on were interred.

The wealth of the Qing financed a vast building program of temples, monasteries (especially the lamasaries of Lama Buddhism), aristocratic homes, and particularly gardens, which reached the height of their development during the reigns of the Qianlong and Jiaqing emperors. Gardens followed asymmetrical plans to reflect nature but included common elements: a pond and a stream to represent lakes and rivers or the *ying* elements in nature, and rocks to represent mountains or the *yang* elements. Gardens also often included pavilions for relaxation, bridges, covered arcades, verandahs, and studies for reading, while plants considered auspicious, such as bamboo, maple, orchids, chrysanthemum, peony, and lotus flowers, were cultivated. ·

Although there were at least forty architectural styles for residences, the most common was the courtyard-style house, with four sides enclosing each courtyard, a type favored especially in North China. The architectural focus of such housing was the courtyard, the center of activity. While courtyard designs differed, in general all main buildings opened onto a courtyard, often linked by roofed arcades that defined the courtyard's perimeter. Windows opened onto the courtyard, while blank walls faced the street. In large establishments, there were many interlocking courtyards. For example, in a three-courtyard complex, the main entertainment and residential building might have two subsidiary courtyard-building complexes, one on either side. Even larger establishments might have an additional axis of buildings as well as a garden. Each room had a function. These included reception rooms, accounting rooms, sleeping chambers, doorman's chambers, and servants' residences—the last usually near the entry to the first courtyard. Housing was allocated by seniority so that the oldest generation resided in the main hall, flanking by their eldest children's families, while more junior family members and more distant cousins had proportionately more distant residences. An exterior wall enclosed the entire housing complex. Neighborhoods composed of such buildings were called *hutong*, literally "lane" or "alley," referring to the labyrinth of narrow, winding alleys that characterized them. Beijing was particularly famous for its meandering neighborhoods of *hutongs*, where it was easy for visitors to get lost.

With the rapid modernization of China since Deng Xiaoping's death, such neighborhoods are rapidly disappearing. There has been little organized effort to preserve China's stunning architectural heritage. In fact, the reverse has been the case. The Cultural Revolution brought the systematic destruction of China's artistic heritage. When an inventory of Beijing's architectural treasures was made during the early part of the Deng Xiaoping Restoration, fewer than 100 remained and most of these had been heavily damaged during the Cultural Revolution.

the student demonstrations of the May Fourth Movement of 1919 had caused political turmoil and a reorientation of Chinese foreign policy toward Soviet political and economic models. Under Gorbachev, political openness had not brought prosperity to Russia either. From Deng's point of view, more than anything else, China needed a prolonged period of stability. He would not allow reckless youths to threaten this. Yet, he underestimated the impact of the foreign press coverage. Where tear gas would have sufficed to empty Tiananmen Square, Deng authorized the use of live ammunition and tanks. In doing so, he failed the moral litmus test of the West and the Confucian litmus test of his people.

The Beijing Massacre undermined the rose-tinted versions of China then popular in intellectual circles abroad.

Such views emphasized the positive achievements of Communist rule—barefoot doctors serving rural communities and growing literacy—with little consideration for the costs. Western intellectuals had remained largely silent during the Great Leap Forward and the Cultural Revolution. Some denied the mayhem for lack of proof, while the Great Famine went largely unreported. Television footage of the bloodshed at Tiananmen, however, meant that certain pro-Communist positions were no longer tenable. Although the numbers killed or wounded were but a fraction of those who perished in the earlier political campaigns, the stark images stood for the millions of deaths under CCP rule. The Beijing Massacre occurred at the same time that Russians were reexamining their own Communist past and for the first time publishing accurate figures on the number of those who perished under Stalin. Events in both countries suggested that the reality of Communist rule, in contrast to the official propaganda, was one of Naziesque brutality. (See Table 27.1.)

The psychological impact of the massacre on the Chinese people was profound. Their government had turned the army on their children in the plaza of the people in the nation's capital. The victims included some of the country's finest students, those who had managed to secure admission to the best institutions of higher education, largely located in Beijing. China's elite was stunned; these were their children, often only children due to China's one-child policy. In a Confucian society, the thought of turning soldiers, the lowest tier of society, on scholars, the highest tier, flew in the face of all norms of propriety. This act compromised the moral basis for the Communist mandate of heaven.

Soldiers of the PLA had initially resisted their deployment to Beijing. On 21 May, seven retired high-ranking PLA officers, including a former minister of defense as well as the for-

mer head of the PLA General Staff, warned Deng not to deploy the PLA. Rumors circulated that those chosen to go into Tiananmen were mainly uneducated peasants, reportedly brought in from Inner Mongolia, who believed that they were fighting counterrevolutionaries and did not even understand Mandarin, the official dialect. The student demonstrators had probably expected arrest and a rough-up, not gunfire and tanks. Prior to Tiananmen, the PLA had reserved live ammunition mostly for the ethnic minorities of Tibet and Xinjiang, not unarmed children of the Han elite. Although there had been much bloodshed during the Cultural Revolution, the lines had never been so clearly drawn between the PLA and the people. Growing numbers of Han perceived the PLA not as a liberator but as an occupying force. China's cyclical view of history helps explain the CCP's disproportionate response to the student demonstrations. China's leaders had deployed the PLA and tanks because they perceived their mandate of heaven to be under attack. Their response both indicated their assessment of the threat and vindicated the student critique.

Table 27.1   Human Costs of Communist Rule

Years	Campaign	Deaths
1945–9	Chinese civil war	6,168,000
	Combatant deaths	1,200,000
	Communist killing of noncombatants	2,645,000
	Nationalist killing of noncombatants	2,323,000
1949–53	Land reform	4,500,000
1949–52	Suppression of counterrevolutionaries	3,000,000
1952	Three- and Five-Antis Campaigns	100,000
1949–53	Other political movements	1,425,000
1954–8	Collectivization and the Great Leap Forward	5,550,000
1959–63	Great Famine and Retrenchment	30,000,000*
1965–75	Cultural Revolution	1,613,000
	Total	52,356,000

*Jasper Becker, *Hungry Ghosts: Mao's Secret Famine* (New York: Free Press, 1996), 274. Better statistics for the Great Famine became available after the publication of Rummel's book.

Source: R. J. Rummel, *China's Bloody Century: Genocide and Mass Murder Since 1900* (New Brunswick, NJ: Transaction, 1991), 26, 275–95.

Comparative International Data

1914–18	World War I	15,000,000
1917–22	Russian Civil War	9,000,000
1937–45	World War II	55,000,000
1945–75	China	52,356,000

Source: http:users.erols.com/mwhite28/warstat1.htm, "Source List and Detailed Death Tolls for the Twentieth Century Hemoclysm."

IV. Governance without a Preeminent Leader

Tiananmen drew virtually the universal censure of the Western democracies. The World Bank suspended loans for a time. The United States, in particular, halted many types of exchanges. Thereafter, diplomatic relations remained tense. China's economy suffered as foreign tourists stopped coming and foreign companies were hesitant to invest. Comparisons of political freedoms in Taiwan versus the PRC had become increasingly unflattering. The positive phase of the Deng Xiaoping Restoration ended. In response to this growing diplomatic isolation, the Chinese government sought to reduce tensions along its borders. In September 1989, it normalized relations with Vietnam after a ten-year hiatus following the Sino-Vietnamese War. Then in October, the Chinese vice-foreign minister visited India after a nineteen-year hiatus following the Sino-Indian War.

Leadership changes followed in the wake of the Tiananmen unrest. Zhao Ziyang, China's former premier and head of the CCP, fell from power after he visited the students in Tiananmen Square on 19 May, urging them to go home before it was too late. The next day, Zhao opposed martial law and the use of troops. His reward was long-term house arrest and permanent surveillance until his death on 17 January 2005.

Although Deng had officially retired from all official appointments by November 1989, he increasingly feared that a conservative backlash within the party leadership in response to the recent unrest would reverse his economic reforms. Like Mao, who ignored the central government to start the Cultural Revolution in Shanghai in order to preserve his revolution, Deng also avoided the center by reaching out to provincial leaders who had greatly benefited from his reforms. In both cases, the solution bypassed Chinese institutions of government.

Behind the scenes, Deng negotiated a grand compromise that preserved his reforms.[4] The central government would continue to promote economic reform. In return, provincial leaders would continue to funnel to the central government the tax revenues necessary to sustain the reforms and a growing military budget. The central government would generously fund the continued modernization of the PLA. In return, the PLA would support the reforms and accept party leadership. This arrangement met the most essential desires of three key constituencies: the military, the central government, and the provincial governments. It prevented the Soviet faction from restoring centralized economic management. Like Mao, Deng hoped that an extrainstitutional arrangement would endure beyond his death to make his changes permanent. Deng believed that China had a fifty-year window of opportunity to transform itself into a great power. The window opened in 1991 with the collapse of the Soviet Union and it would close when Russia rose again.

Jiang Zemin replaced the fallen Zhao Ziyang. Born in 1926, Jiang is considered part of the so-called third generation of Chinese leaders following Mao and Deng. In 1989, Jiang was relatively unknown, having served as the mayor of Shanghai. During May 1989, he suppressed the student movement there without resorting to military force. Untouched by the loss of face from the massacre that afflicted many of the CCP's top leaders, Jiang was initially put in charge as a stopgap measure. In November 1989, following Deng's retirement, he became chairman of the Central Military Commission.

Through this appointment, for the first time civilians controlled the military, but it was unclear whether the military would always obey. While Mao had emphasized CCP control over the military, all previous chairmen of the Central Military Commission had actually served in the military. Jiang, with his exclusively civilian service, represented a departure from previous norms. (See Table 27.2.) Deng helped Jiang stave off his main political opponent, Premier Li Peng, who had inherited the *guanxi* network of Zhou Enlai. Thereafter, it took several years for Jiang to consolidate power, finally ousting in 1993 the octogenarian President Yang Shangkun, who had been instrumental in modernizing the PLA after its poor showing in the 1979 border war with Vietnam and in deploying the army for the Beijing Massacre. Meanwhile, in 1992, Deng, in a return to an imperial tradition resurrected by Mao, made a tour through southern China in the manner of the Qianlong emperor. Deng called for a faster pace of reform. At the Fourteenth Party Congress, Jiang adopted the policy of a "socialist market economy."

In 1997, Deng Xiaoping died. He was the last major Chinese leader of the Long March generation that brought the CCP to power. The next generation, having missed the heroic era of Communist hagiography, had no one of equal prestige. The Long March generation shared strong civil and military affiliations because they were all military leaders during the civil war. They had been responsible for creating both China's civil and military institutions. The successor generation had higher levels of education and more orthodox career paths, but the expertise of each member had a narrower scope and rarely crossed civil–military boundaries.

Jiang attempted to emphasize the centrality of party rule. According to his Three Represents platform, first introduced in a speech in February 2000 and then formally proclaimed on 1 July 2001 on the eightieth anniversary of the

Table 27.2 Leaders of the CCP and the Chinese Government

Communist Party

Chairman of the CCP*	From	To
Mao Zedong	8 Jan. 1935	9 Sept. 1976
Hua Guofeng	7 Oct. 1976	29 June 1981
Hu Yaobang	29 June 1981	11 Sept. 1982

General Secretary*		
Deng Xiaoping	27 Sept. 1956	1957
Hu Yaobang	29 Feb. 1980	16 Jan. 1987
Zhao Ziyang	16 Jan. 1987	24 June 1989
Jiang Zimin	24 June 1989	15 Nov. 2002
Hu Jintao	15 Nov. 2002	

Chairman of the Central Military Commission†		
Deng Xiaoping	29 June 1981	9 Nov. 1989
Jiang Zemin	9 Nov. 1989	19 Sept. 2004
Hu Jintao	19 Sep. 2004	

Chinese Government (Evolution of the Position of Chief Executive)

Chairman of the Central People's Government		
Mao Zedong	1 Oct. 1949	27 Sept. 1954

Chairman (President)		
Mao Zedong	27 Sept. 1954	27 Apr. 1959
Liu Shaoqi	27 Apr. 1959	31 Oct. 1968‡

Chairman of the Standing Committee of the National People's Congress		
Zhu De	17 Jan. 1975	6 July 1976
Ye Jianying	5 Mar. 1978	18 June 1983

President of the Republic		
Li Xiannian	18 June 1983	8 Apr. 1988
Yang Shangkun	8 Apr. 1988	27 Mar. 1993
Jiang Zemin	27 Mar. 1993	15 Mar. 2003
Hu Jintao	15 Mar. 2003	

*When the position of chairman was abolished in 1982, general secretary became the CCP's top position.

†The National People's Congress also has a Central Military Commission, but it is far less powerful than the CCP's Central Military Commission. The commission was created under the 1982 Constitution.

‡The position was abolished in 1975. From 1968 to 1975, vice-chairmen acted in the chairman's stead.

Source: http:www.terra.es/personal2/monolith/china.htm; Colin Mackerras, *The New Cambridge Handbook of Contemporary China* (Cambridge: Cambridge University Press, 2001), 20, 35; http://www.chinadaily.com.en/english/doc/2004-09/19/content_375772.htm.

Pictured is PRC President Hu Jintao inspecting the PLA garrison in Hong Kong on the tenth anniversary of the city's return to China. As China's revolutionary leaders have passed from the scene, the new Communist rulers of China must retain sufficient authority to control the military. This is especially important with regard to the Chinese Navy, which mutinied to support antigovernment revolutionaries in both 1911 and 1949. Even though China's military is modernizing, therefore, loyalty to the CCP remains paramount.

founding of the Communist Party, the party achieved and retained power because it had consistently represented the requirements for economic development, progress in Chinese civilization, and the fundamental interests of the overwhelming majority of the population. Jiang attempted to use the Three Represents to establish his legacy as a great leader alongside Mao Zedong and Deng Xiaoping. His formal announcement of the slogan anticipated his scheduled retirement as party general secretary in 2002, president of the PRC in 2003, and chairman of the Central Military Commission in 2004.

Members of the Long March generation ruled into their eighties and nineties, which kept the next generation out of power until it was also on the verge of retirement age. They functioned much like the genro of Meiji Japan, whose influence lay in their personal connections more than in their institutional office. In China, the successor generation (with the exception of Deng Xiaoping) comprised junior members of the Long March and/or the Chinese civil war. Lacking the prestige of their elders, they were not allowed to rule from their deathbed. The grandchildren of the Long March generation, the so-called Fourth Generation (after Mao, Deng, and Jiang), began to assume key leadership positions with the election of Hu Jintao (1942–) as president of the PRC on 15 March 2003. Hu also became general secretary of the CCP Central Committee and vice-chairman of the Central Military Commission. Jiang retained the presidency of the Central Military Commission until September 2004, when Hu assumed full control, but Jiang relinquished his final post as chairman of the State Central Military Commission only in March 2005.

V. Rising Nationalism

To help overcome the political damage from Tiananmen, the CCP actively promoted nationalism to legitimate its continued one-party rule in the manner of such World War II–era governments as those of fascist Germany, Imperial Japan, and Nationalist China. The CCP cultivated antiforeign movements to direct attention away from domestic problems, playing on traditional Han xenophobia and the widely shared Han sense of aggrievement vis-à-vis the West and Japan. According to this reasoning, the West, not internal factors, constitutes the primary impediment to restoring China's greatness. Nationalism, once fueled, however, can take on a life of its own, as Japan learned in the 1930s, when it discovered that wars are easy to start but hard to end. China's minority populations were less enthusiastic about a nationalism that seemed more Great Hanism than an equally shared sense of nation across the ethnic spectrum.

Nationalism has been expressed in public support for the continuing Sinification of Xinjiang and the suppression of the growing Muslim unrest. (See Table 27.3.) Instability in Xinjiang has been a continuous fact of life ever since the Qianlong emperor overextended the empire in the eighteenth century. In the 1980s, there were various demonstrations and acts of infrastructure sabotage. Part of the Deng Xiaoping Restoration entailed the reopening of mosques and allowing the circulation of Islamic literature. Unrest degenerated into riots in April 1990 among the Kyrgyz of southern Xinjiang. In June 1993 a bomb damaged government buildings in Kashgar. There were other rumored bomb incidents, while mass strikes erupted in the Ili region

Table 27.3   Distribution of the Muslim Population

Minority	Location	Language	1990 Census	2000 Census
Hui	All China, esp. Ningxia, Gansu, Henan, Xinjiang, Qinghai, Yunnan, Hebei, Shandong	Sino-Tibetan	8,602,978	9,816,805
Uigur	Xinjiang	Altaic (Turkic)	7,214,431	8,399,393
Kazak	Xinjiang, Gansu, Qinghai	Altaic (Turkic)	1,111,718	1,250,458
Dongxiang	Gansu, Xinjiang	Altaic (Turkic)	373,873	513,805
Kirghiz	Xinjiang, Heilongjiang	Altaic (Turkic)	141,549	160,823
Salar	Qinghai, Gansu	Altaic (Turkic)	87,697	104,503
Tadjik	Xinjiang	Indo-European	33,538	41,028
Uzbek	Xinjiang	Altaic (Turkic)	14,503	12,370
Baoan	Gansu	Altaic (Mongolian)	12,212	16,505
Tatar	Xinjiang	Altaic (Turkic)	4,873	4,890
		Total	**17,597,370**	**20,320,580**

Source: Dru C. Gladney, *Muslim Chinese: Ethnic Nationalism in the People's Republic* (Cambridge, MA: Harvard University Press, 1991), 20; People's Republic of China, National Bureau of Statistics of China, *China Statistical Yearbook 2004* (Beijing: China Statistics Press, 2004), 46.

in April 1995. The Chinese government responded to these incidents with massive force in the Strike Hard Campaign initiated over the summer of 1996; the demonstrations were short, the arrests were many, but peace remained elusive. There is enormous resentment among the native population of continued Han immigration and exploitation of local resources for Han use. Whereas only 6 percent of the population of Xinjiang was Han in 1948, by 1991 they accounted for 30 percent. Unrest resumed in 2008–2009. The Tibetans have also unsuccessfully resisted Sinification and sought independence. While the Han population in Tibet remains small, a new railway line threatens to change this situation. There is a powerful Han consensus to retain all of the former lands of the Qing empire even though their retention has been very costly economically, requiring large government expenditures. (See Table 27.4.)

The return of Hong Kong and Macao to Chinese sovereignty served as occasions for a vast outpouring of Han nationalism. The day before the scheduled celebration of the return of Hong Kong to China, an estimated 1 million Chinese flooded into Tiananmen Square in a show of patriotism. Macao reverted to China in 1999. The Chinese government has used these occasions to focus on grievances from the treaty port era and other lingering territorial issues.

In 1992 the Chinese government promulgated the Territorial Waters and Contiguous Areas Act, which claims as Chinese territory not only Taiwan but also the Pescadore, Diaoyu, Pratas, Paracel, and Spratly islands and the Macclesfield Bank. The Spratly Islands (Nansha in Chinese) consist of more than 200 small islands, half-submerged rocks, and reefs scattered over a vast area surrounded by the Philippines, Malaysia, Brunei, Vietnam, Indonesia, Thailand, and China,

Table 27.4   Burdens of Empire

	Ratio of State Expenditures to Revenues (percentage)[*]				State Revenues Minus Expenditures Per Capita (in yuan)[†]			
	1982	1983	1984	1985	1982	1983	1984	1985
Whole PRC	79	82	89	90	29	25	18	20
Inner Mongolia	178	171	200	170	−76	−77	−124	−109
Xinjiang	192	173	183	211	−36	−59	−101	−142
Tibet	4,600	2,800	5,900	1,800	−520	−610	−560	−520

[*]Percentage > 100 = deficit. Percentage < 100 = surplus.

[†]Positive number = surplus revenues. Negative number = central government subsidies.

Source: Lynn T. White III, *Unstately Power: Local Causes of China's Economic Reforms,* vol. 1 (Armonk, NY: M. E. Sharpe, 1998), 199–200.

On 1 July 1997, the United Kingdom officially returned Hong Kong to the PRC. Although the island of Hong Kong had been ceded to Britain in perpetuity in 1842, the New Territories, obtained for ninety-nine years in 1898, included the business center of Kowloon and virtually all of Hong Kong's freshwater sources, which made retaining Hong Kong island on its own impossible. To many Chinese, the reversion of Hong Kong in 1997, followed by the return of tiny Macao in 1999, appeared to end Western interference in Chinese affairs, while to other Chinese it merely made reunifying with Taiwan even more important.

all of which have made claims to all or part of these waters. (See Map 27.1.) Estimates of natural gas and oil reserves range into the tens of billions of barrels, closely linking the issues of sovereignty and future economic growth. Key shipping routes of East Asia traverse the South China Sea, so that sovereignty over the many disputed islands also will determine whether these sea lanes traverse international or national waters, with security implications for all. In particular, Chinese, Japanese, South Korean, and Taiwanese energy supplies all use this route.

Since the 1990s, China, to make good its territorial claims, has invested heavily in naval ships, often bought from Russia. This will transform the PLA Navy from a coastal defense force to a blue-water navy potentially capable of projecting power and influencing events far from China's shores. Disputed territory includes the Diaoyutai Islands (Senkaku in Japanese), the islands of the South China Sea, and Taiwan.

Since 1894, Japan has had de facto control over the Diaoyutai Islands, uninhabited rocks projecting out of the sea. They were long considered worthless. In July 1996 this dispute reignited when Japan included these islands within its Exclusive Economic Zone, meaning that Japan claimed the right to exploit any surrounding resources such as gas, oil, and fish. The PRC immediately protested, sponsoring mass demonstrations aimed at Japan. Ever since, PRC activists have regularly slipped through Japanese coast guard patrols to land on these islands in a bid for Chinese sovereignty.

In June 1996, the book *China Can Still Say No* appeared on PRC bookshelves. It laid claim to all these disputed territories, blamed the United States for organizing the rest of Asia against China, and portrayed China as the victim. It ignored the competing interests of the many other countries involved. The authors asserted that China should reclaim all the territories lost since 1662, the year after the Ming loyalists retook Taiwan from the Dutch. During the breakup of Yugoslavia, the accidental U.S. bombing of the Chinese embassy in Belgrade, Serbia, on 7 May 1999 triggered mass protests two days later in the embassy district in Beijing. The Chinese public considered the bombing deliberate, not accidental, despite an immediate U.S. apology, while Western journalists reported official sponsorship of the demonstrations.

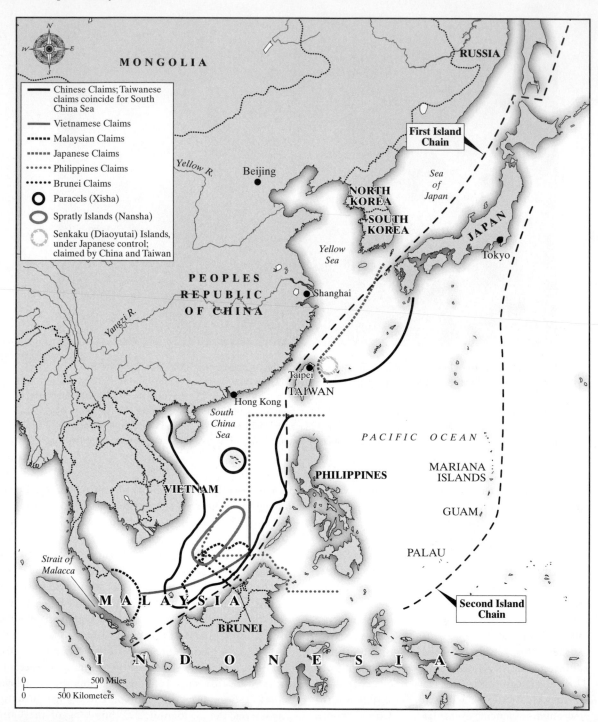

Map 27.1   Chinese Territorial Claims

In 2001, tensions flared when a Chinese fighter bumped a U.S. EP-3 plane monitoring Chinese naval activities. The Chinese pilot died, and the U.S. plane barely managed to land safely on China's Hainan Island; ten days of tense negotiations followed before the PRC agreed to release the crew. Much later, it returned the plane in pieces, thoroughly studied. Domestically, there was an outpouring of anti-U.S. sentiment.

The most important outstanding territorial issue remains, as always, Taiwan. Nationalists in the PRC accuse Washington of manipulating Taiwanese politics to prevent reunification. In particular, they condemn the U.S. arms sales mandated by the 1979 Taiwan Relations Act. There is widespread popular agreement in the PRC that Taiwan should rejoin the motherland. There also seems to be widespread public support for a coercive solution if Taiwan refuses. No consideration is given in the PRC to the fact that many Taiwanese reject reunification.

Since the 1960s, China has resolved or attempted to resolve numerous border issues with many of its fourteen neighbors, including Burma, Nepal, Mongolia, Pakistan, North Korea, Laos, Russia, Kazakhstan, India, and Vietnam. Some of the disputed areas are small but others are enormous, including China's age-old claim against Russia for millions of square miles of territory in Siberia, Outer Mongolia, and Tannu Tuva. The Indians, in particular, remain bitter about the 1962 war. Therefore, China's many border issues remain tinder for ultranationalists.

The Chinese government has not created, but it has attempted to manipulate, Chinese nationalism. A sense of nation and a pride in national accomplishments are natural outcomes in a rapidly modernizing country with numerous recent successes against a backdrop of terrible past tragedies. Nationalism, however, is volatile, easy to release but hard to control.

China's expenditure of enormous sums on the new athletic facilities and on the Olympic ceremonies was linked with rising nationalism. China lobbied hard to secure the 2008 Olympics. It was a matter of national prestige, and was intended as a celebration of the country's enormous economic achievements and recent return to the world stage as a great power. China's leaders hoped that the Olympics would provide an opportunity for the CCP to strengthen its mandate of heaven by hosting the nations of the world on a scale dwarfing the tributary missions of the past. The Olympics would also become a forum for Chinese nationalism, an essential glue cementing Communist rule. The troubled global Olympic torch relay, however, became a public relations nightmare when nationalistic Chinese scuffled with demostrators protesting China's 2008 crackdown on Tibet in country after country along the torch's route. But the stunning opening and closing ceremonies had their desired effect at home and abroad by showcasing China at the center.

Conclusions

The breakup of the USSR had an enormous impact on China. Domestically, it helped foment a pro-democracy movement and also created doubts about the long-term survival of communism anywhere. Internationally, it greatly reduced security concerns on the Sino-Russian border, allowing China to focus instead on reunification with Taiwan (discussed in Chapter 28). The Beijing Massacre had equally far-reaching consequences. Domestically, the PLA's brutality called into question the legitimacy of the government, and internationally it disillusioned would-be supporters of the PRC. While Deng Xiaoping offered the prospect of a dynastic restoration, Tiananmen suggested continuing dynastic decline. Like the successor generations to the early Manchu leaders, who had both led their armies and ruled their empire, the post–Long March generation of Chinese leaders lacked the prestige, authority, and combined civil-military expertise of their predecessors. The Western solution to this problem has been to create strong civil and military institutions ruled by laws that set both jurisdictions and rules for appointment and retirement. As a result, Western institutions are generally not so heavily reliant on personalities and supreme leaders as has typically been the case in China.

At Tiananmen, the PLA showed itself to be the power behind the throne. Like the Manchus before them, the Communists continued to rely on the military to remain in control. Mao depended on the PLA to win the civil war, to fight the Korean War, to requisition grain during the Great Leap Forward, to control the Cultural Revolution, and to eliminate both Liu Shaoqi and Lin Biao. Deng then used the PLA to rise to power by imprisoning the Gang of Four and to eliminate the student movement of the 1980s. During the Chinese civil war, both Mao and Deng had commanded forces. They were first and foremost military leaders. While the PRC has the appearance of civil rule under the CCP, the reality has been military dominance over the civilian population. The immense size of the PLA indicates its internal garrisoning responsibilities.

The Communists have consistently employed coercive measures to take and retain power. The Beijing Massacre is just the most recent, and visible, of such events. According to Table 27.1 over 52 million people died in the Chinese civil war and ensuing political campaigns and Great Famine. Another estimate of the number of Chinese who died of either state-induced famine, war, or state repression between 1949 and 1987 totals almost 75 million.[5]

Such figures are highly impressionistic since there are no reliable data, only estimates, but by any measure the numbers are enormous. For comparison, the Boston Massacre during the American Revolution resulted in five deaths and the Kent State Massacre that occurred during the height of the anti–Vietnam War movement caused the deaths of four students. While hundreds of thousands died during the U.S. Civil War, at war's end only the commandant of the southern POW camp at Andersonville, Georgia and the assassins of President Abraham Lincoln were executed, while the commander of the Confederate forces, General Robert E. Lee, remained a free man. Many Chinese continue to portray their history as Han victimization by foreigners, when the reality has overwhelmingly been a case of Chinese brutalizing other Chinese. Successive Chinese governments have made disastrous choices for their countrymen. In the communist era, only under Deng Xiaoping, the Beijing Massacre notwithstanding, has there been a major improvement in the choices made in the area of economic policy.

BIBLIOGRAPHY

Barmé, Geremie R. *Shades of Mao: The Posthumous Cult of the Great Leader.* Armonk, NY: M. E. Sharpe, 1996.

Bramall, Chris. *Sources of Chinese Economic Growth, 1978–1996.* Oxford: Oxford University Press, 2001.

Chang, Maria Hsia. *Return of the Dragon: China's Wounded Nationalism.* Boulder, CO: Westview Press, 2001.

Cheng, Siwei. *Studies on Economic Reforms and Development in China.* Oxford: Oxford University Press, 2001.

Dillon, Michael, *Xinjiang - China's Muslim Far Northwest.* London: Routledge Curzon, 2004.

Fu Xinian et al. *Chinese Architecture.* New Haven, CT: Yale University Press, 2002.

Graff, David A. *A Military History of China.* Boulder, CO: Westview Press, 2002.

Gregor, A. James. *A Place in the Sun: Marxism and Fascism in China's Long Revolution.* Boulder, CO: Westview Press, 2000.

Gries, Peter Hays. *China's New Nationalism: Price, Politics, and Diplomacy.* Berkeley: University of California Press, 2004.

Hansen, Mette Halskov. *Frontier People: Han Settlers in Minority Areas of China.* Vancouver: University of British Columbia Press, 2005.

Hutchings, Graham. *Modern China: A Guide to a Century of Change.* Cambridge, MA: Harvard University Press, 2001.

Marti, Michael E. *China and the Legacy of Deng Xiaoping: From Communist Revolution to Capitalist Evolution.* Washington, DC: Brassey's, 2002.

Nathan, Andrew and Bruce Gilley. *China's New Rulers: The Secret Files.* 2nd rev. ed. New York: New York Review of Books, 2003.

Saich, Tony. *Governance and Politics of China.* Basingstoke, England: Palgrave, 2001.

Sneath, David. *Changing Inner Mongolia: Pastoral Mongolian Society and the Chinese State.* Oxford: Oxford University Press, 2000.

Starr, S. Frederick, ed. *Xinjiang, China's Muslim Borderland.* Armonk, NY: M. E. Sharpe, 2004.

Yang, Dali L. *Remaking the Leviathan: Market Transition and the Politics of Governance.* Stanford, CA: Stanford University Press, 2004.

NOTES

1. Anonymous, "Mad Woman," in *The Columbia Anthology of Modern Chinese Literature,* Joseph S. M. Lau and Howard Goldblatt, eds. (New York: Columbia University Press, 1995), 582–3.
2. Bruce A. Elleman, *Modern Chinese Warfare, 1795–1989* (London: Routledge, 2001), 303. Citing Orville Schell, *Mandate of Heaven: A New Generation of Entrepreneurs, Dissidents, Bohemians, and Technocrats Lays Claim to China's Future* (New York: Simon & Schuster, 1994), 46–7.
3. Cited in Orville Schell, *Mandate of Heaven* (New York: Simon & Schuster, 1994), 167.
4. Michael E. Marti, *China and the Legacy of Deng Xiaoping* (Washington, DC: Brassey's, 2002), ix.
5. R. J. Rummel, *China's Bloody Century: Genocide and Mass Murder since 1900* (New Brunswick, NJ: Transaction, 1991), 12.

Chronology

1 January 1979	United States changed its official recognition from Taiwan to the PRC
26 April 1979	Taiwan Relations Act providing U.S. military support
10 December 1979	Kaohsiung Incident
28 September 1986	End of the Nationalist one-party monopoly in Taiwan
15 July 1987	End of martial law in Taiwan after thirty-eight years
2 November 1987	Taiwan allows citizens to visit relatives on the mainland
13 January 1988	Chiang Ching-kuo dies; replaced by Lee Teng-hui
20 January 1989	Law on Civic Organizations permits the creation of new political parties in Taiwan
26 January 1989	Taiwan law on retirement of senior parliamentarians
10 June 1989	Direct phone links opened between China and Taiwan
4 July 1990	Conference concluded in Taiwan on government reforms
30 April 1991	Lee Teng-hui recognizes the PRC government
21 December 1991	National Assembly elections in Taiwan
19 December 1992	Legislative Yuan elections in Taiwan
21 July 1995	PRC begins test-firing missiles off Taiwan
8 March 1996	PRC begins test-firing missiles off Taiwan
12 March 1996	PRC begins military exercises off Jinmen Island
18 March 1996	PRC begins joint war games off Taiwan
23 March 1996	Presidential elections in Taiwan, reelecting Lee Teng-hui
30 June 1998	Bill Clinton's Three No's Policy
21 February 2000	PRC issues a white paper on Taiwan
18 March 2000	Cheng Shiu-bian of the Democratic Progressive Party wins the Taiwan presidency
14 March 2005	PRC Anti-Secession Law
22 March 2008	Ma Ying-jeou of the Nationalist Party wins the Taiwan presidency

28   The Mandate of Heaven

Nostalgia

When I was young,
Nostalgia was a tiny, tiny stamp,
Me on this side,
Mother on the other side.

When I grew up,
Nostalgia was a narrow boat ticket,
Me on this side,
My bride on the other side.

But later on,
Nostalgia was a lowly grave,
Me on the outside,
Mother on the inside.

And at present,
Nostalgia becomes a shallow strait,
Me on this side,
Mainland on the other side.[1]

Zhou Mengdie (1920–   ) poet
in 1949 fled with Nationalists to Taiwan, 1972

Historically the mandate of heaven has rested on three pillars: prosperity, righteousness, and, most importantly, territorial unity. Its opposite is chaos or *luan,* which destroys all three pillars. In the Great Leap Forward, the CCP created a nationwide famine. In the Cultural Revolution, the CCP brought China perilously close to chaos. The tremendous human toll of the Communist period, capped off with the Beijing Massacre, has compromised the moral basis for continued CCP rule. Without righteousness, this has left the Communist mandate of heaven dependent on the twin pillars of economic performance and Han nationalism, the first of which requires a fast-paced 6–8 percent annual industrial expansion simply to maintain, let alone improve, the general standard of living. Deng Xiaoping focused on the most obvious and easy-to-remedy inefficiencies of Maoist economic management. As a result, never before in Chinese history have so many Chinese lived so well, yet potential bottlenecks to future economic growth remain, including population management, the money-losing state-owned sector of the economy, bad loans threatening the banking system, environmental degradation, water shortages, and affordable energy supplies. Recent political reforms on Taiwan have exacerbated the legitimacy problem for the CCP, since the ruling party in Taiwan now acquires legitimacy not by fiat but through elections. The issue of Taiwan is intimately connected with the third pillar of the mandate of heaven, namely, territorial integrity. The Communists have very successfully rallied Han nationalism around the issue of reunification. However, they have not been able to generate support from the ethnic minorities of Tibet and Xinjiang. Therefore, Chinese nationalism remains Han nationalism, which simultaneously alienates the non-Han peoples of the empire and invigorates the Han majority to retain control over them. Rising expectations, a rapidly growing middle class, and unprecedented links with the outside pose challenges to the CCP's continued monopoly over political power.

I. Population and Prosperity

In an attempt to limit families to one child, population bureaus were established throughout China in 1979, followed by a succession of regulations to enforce the limit. This was belated recognition of the demographic disaster caused by Mao's encouragement of large families: According to China's 1982 census, the population had surpassed 1 billion, almost doubling since the 1953 census. (See Tables 28.1 and 28.2.) The debate in China over population growth goes back more than two millennia, with most seeing advantages in a large population and problems from underpopulation. Sun Yat-sen believed that China had grown too slowly, equating a large population with state power. Mao concurred and thought that large families were a confirmation of the superiority of communism, China's best defense against nuclear war, and the basis for great wealth. In November 1957, Mao told an appalled Khrushchev: "We shouldn't be afraid of atomic missiles. No matter what kind of war breaks out—conventional or thermonuclear—we'll win. As for China, if the imperialists unleash war on us, we may lose more than three hundred million people. So what? War is war. The years will pass and we'll get to work producing more babies than ever before."[2] Mao's government-sponsored health care polices, in combination with the end of the civil war, dramatically decreased mortality rates. Birthrates skyrocketed, particularly in the 1950s and 1960s.

From the Great Leap Forward through the end of the Cultural Revolution, the CCP suppressed warnings of the dangers of overpopulation. Fertility rates, meaning the number of children born to each woman, remained high for the duration of Mao's rule, typically five to six per family. Some in the government did not share Mao's views. There were efforts to moderate population growth after the Great Famine, but a real decline in the birthrate did not happen until the late 1970s when it fell,

remaining below three children per family. Deng Xiaoping believed that overpopulation constituted a major impediment to prosperity. Although the one-child policy clearly moderated the growth rate, the huge number of women born under Mao's policies meant a large cohort of women of childbearing age, the standard statistical measure used to predict future growth.

With the increasing availability of amniocentesis, abortions have been used to ensure the delivery of sons. This has resulted in a highly skewed sex ratio among the younger generation. Barring a major war, there will be a shortage of wives in the coming decades. In the past, social stability depended on the interlocking obligation of older and younger siblings, while the *guanxi* system relied on extended family networks. Single-child families may prove extremely corrosive to both Confucianism and *guanxi*. The prevalence of single children has given rise to the expression "little emperors" referring to these adored but pampered offspring. The rapid change in fertility rates will also mean a rapid aging of the Chinese population. Between 1975 and 2000, its median age rose from slightly more than twenty years to about thirty and is projected to reach forty by 2025. The West and Japan also face aging problems, but they are wealthier than China will be when it has to support a large elderly population.

There have also been repeated attempts to redistribute China's vast population. During the Cultural Revolution, Mao sent many urban residents to the countryside, often as a means of border defense and sinification of minority areas. Under the Qing, such policies had resulted in the sinification of Manchuria so that today the Manchu population is thor-

Table 28.1 Population Growth

Year	Population	Rate of Increase
1949	541,670,000	16.00
1950	551,960,000	19.00
1955	614,650,000	20.32
1960	662,070,000	−4.57
1965	725,380,000	28.38
1970	829,920,000	25.83
1975	924,200,000	15.69
1980	987,050,000	11.87
1985	1,058,510,000	14.26
1990	1,143,330,000	14.39
1995	1,211,210,000	10.55
2000	1,267,430,000	7.58
2005	1,307,560,000	3.17

Sources: Gabe T. Wang, *China's Population: Problems, Thoughts and Policies* (Aldershot, England: Ashgate, 1999), 56–7; Tian Congming, ed., *People's Republic of China Yearbook 2004* (Beijing: PRC Yearbook, 2004), 802; Li Xiaochao, ed. *China Statistical Yearbook—2008* (Beijing: China Statistical Press, 2008), 87.

Table 28.2   Chinese Population as a Percentage of Global Population (in millions)

Year	World Population	Chinese Population	% of World Population
1650	550	123	22.4
1750	725	260	35.8
1850	1,175	412	35.1
1950	2,556	552	21.6
1980	4,458	987	22.1
2000	6,085	1,267	20.82

Source: Gabe T. Wang, *China's Population: Problems, Thoughts and Policies* (Aldershot, England: Ashgate, 1999), 6; *The World Almanac and Book of Facts 2005* (New York: World Almanac Books, 2005), 849; Tian Congming, ed., *People's Republic of China Yearbook 2004*, vol. 24 (Beijing: PRC Yearbook, 2004), 802.

oughly integrated into the Han population and constitutes no separatist threat. The Communists applied similar policies to Inner Mongolia so that the Han immigrant population soon overwhelmed the local Mongols, ending any effective separatist movement there. Xinjiang and Tibet have been more difficult. They remain the main minority areas where the Han population is not in the majority despite long-standing Han efforts to tip the ethnic balance. Mao actively promoted the creation of state farms run by Han immigrants in Xinjiang. In 2006, China completed the first rail link to Tibet, which will permit a more rapid influx of Han migrants. In 1996, 97.1 percent of the population of Tibet remained Tibetan and 61.9 percent of the Xinjiang Uighur Autonomous Region was non-Han, although Han Chinese dominate the main cities. A large enough native population remains in Xinjiang and Tibet to rebel with predictable regularity.

Conversely, the Communist government has sought to limit the migration of the rural population to the cities. Through its internal passport system instituted in 1953 and strengthened in 1958, public schooling, medical care, and other social services are denied to those living outside of their official place of residence without permission. The household registration system, or *hukou,* specifies a person's place of residence, usually the place of birth. Babies generally inherit from their mothers their status of agricultural or nonagricultural laborer. This status is extremely difficult to change and constitutes enforced discrimination against rural Chinese because urban status means better educational opportunities, job prospects, medical care, and other social services.

To maintain strict control over the urban population, the CCP introduced the work unit (*danwei*) and personal dossier (*dang'an*) systems. Each organization maintains its own *danwei,* which provides not only employment for the members of a factory, school, government office, and so on, but also housing, medical care, schools, and recreation. The government also maintains a file on each of its urban residents recording their political background, education, skills,

work status, and so on, and constantly updates these files. Those blacklisted have no recourse. Together the *hukou, danwei,* and *dang'an* give the government great control over its citizenry. The absence of *danwei* in the countryside helps account for the great disparity in rural and urban standards of living, since urban residents receive enormous subsidies from their *danwei* in the form of housing, medical care, and education that rural residents must pay for out of pocket and are of generally inferior quality. In recent years, these controls have been weakening through relaxed enforcement of the laws, growth of the private sector, and legal reforms giving people more mobility. Reshuffling the population, however, does not eliminate overpopulation problems. In 1995 it was estimated that 15–20 percent of China's urban population was underemployed. Other estimates allude to a floating population of over 100 million in pursuit of employment. Another study estimated that in 2000, 20 percent of the rural labor force sought employment away from their villages.

The unemployment problem becomes even more severe when considered in combination with the Maoist legacy of money-losing state enterprises. Closing them down would unleash a vast number of unemployed persons on an already saturated labor market. So far, the central government has continued to extend credit to allow these enterprises to limp along, but this is a stopgap measure. The country has about 300,000 state-run enterprises, whose associated *danwei* provide the coveted amenities of an urban *hukou* status. The PRC Constitution provides legal protection to the continuing existence of these companies, describing them as central to the economy, so that there is no legal basis to dismantle them. Yet, their inefficiency threatens the solvency of the banking system through accumulating nonperforming debts that have little likelihood of ever being repaid. In 2005 it was estimated that $500 billion in bad loans burdened the Chinese banking system. Although the Chinese government initiated banking reform so that loans are issued on the basis of profitability, old patterns of throwing a lifeline to rust-belt industries and to long-time friends have proven highly resistant to change. *Guanxi* remains alive and well in China. Entry into the World Trade Organization will put unprofitable state-run enterprises and banks under far greater scrutiny, yet there is no painless way to transfer employees to other occupations.

In addition to absolute numbers, another way to measure overpopulation is in relation to the available arable land. From 1959 to 1977, China lost 72 million acres (29 million hectares) of farmland despite the reclamation of 42 million acres (17 million hectares). From 1957 to 1980, it suffered an average annual net loss of cultivated land of 1.3 million acres (545,000 hectares). This translated into a 56 percent decline of the per capita land under cultivation from 1950 to 1995. Some of this loss resulted from the urbanization that accompanies industrialization. The continuing efforts under Mao, Deng, and their successors to develop small towns to disperse the population more evenly has also entailed a loss of farmland because buildings take up land. Finally, overpopulation has also left a huge amount of environmental degradation in the form of deforestation and desertification.

II. Environmental Challenges

Anyone traveling to China is struck by the scarcity of wildlife, trees, and even grass. Extreme population pressures caused massive environmental degradation, particularly from the mid-Qing dynasty on. Warfare—civil and foreign—then greatly magnified the damage. After the Communists came to power they focused on industrialization, which has been extremely hard on the environment the world over, from the suffocating smoke described in the novels of Charles Dickens in the nineteenth century to the warnings in *Silent Spring* outlined by the American environmentalist Rachel Carson in the 1960s. China is just now entering this dirty phase of industrial development. It does so not with a pristine preindustrial environment, but with one already severely stressed from centuries of overpopulation. Even under the best circumstances, China suffers from severe weather patterns: torrential rains in the South and terrible droughts in the North. Overpopulation and environmental degradation magnify their impact. (See Table 28.3.)

Mao chose policies that further damaged the environment. Within a decade, he silenced the scientific community during the Anti-Rightist Campaign in 1957. Mao was a believer in the ability of willpower to overcome material limitations and scientific laws. Such mind-over-matter thinking lay at the root of his disastrous Great Leap Forward, which called for backyard furnaces to create steel production throughout the countryside. The peasantry rallied to the call, cutting down trees to fuel the furnaces and destroying 10 percent of

China's forests as a result. Wood, however, burns at too low a temperature to smelt steel; hence, the backyard furnaces produced useless metal output, so that the nationwide deforestation was for naught. This was only one of three major periods of deforestation in the Communist period. The so-called Three Great Cuttings took place during the Great Leap Forward, the Cultural Revolution, and after Deng Xiaoping's decollectivization. Whereas in 1949 13 percent of China had been forested, in the late 1980s this forest land had been reduced to only 8 percent. This constituted a 38 percent decline in forests. In 1979, China ranked 120th in the world in terms of forest cover.

During the Cultural Revolution trees were cut to create farmland; the remaining forests grew largely on land unsuitable for agriculture. In Hunan, deforested sandy soils resulted in flooding and topsoil loss, leaving the land less suitable for forests or food. Deforested hills yielded similar results. In the South, forests were cut to grow rubber trees. Whereas 60 percent of Yunnan had been forested in the 1950s, only 30 percent remained so in the 1970s, resulting in a climate change affecting temperatures and rainfall. Yunnan rubber, however, was not competitive with that grown in the more suitable southerly climate of Southeast Asia. In Inner Mongolia and Ningxia, attempts to cultivate the dry grasslands formerly used only for grazing herds caused topsoil loss. Afterward, not even grass would grow, causing desertification. Filling in the lakes and wetlands of Hubei for farmland led to widespread flooding of the Yangzi River in 1995, 1998, and 1999, while reclaimed wetlands in Heilongjiang decimated the salmon population. As a result of desertification, the number of sandstorms, primarily in North China, has greatly increased, from an annual average of five in the 1960s to twenty-four in the 1990s, while deserts are growing at the rate of nearly 10,000 square kilometers per year.

Soil erosion, sedimentation, desertification, damming, and deforestation have compromised the biodiversity in China. Mao's Four Pests Campaign of the Great Leap Forward destroyed the bird population. Large mammals are virtually nonexistent, having long ago been eaten in times of famine or ground up into Chinese medicine. In ancient times, China had large elephant, rhinoceros, and tiger populations throughout much of the South. According to the *Xinhua* news agency, since the 1960s, one-third of the sixteen original aquatic species of the Yellow River have become extinct. This is the second largest river system in China. Industrial pollution is to blame, with 4.2 billion cubic meters of pollutants dumped into the river each year, double the rate in the 1980s. Other Chinese rivers face the same problem. The available water supplies in China are becoming increasingly polluted at levels unknown in the West.

Table 28.3   Natural Disasters (1985–2004)
(Natural Disasters Affecting over 10 Million Persons)

Year	Flood	Drought	Storm/ Typhoon	Affected Population	Affected Area
1988	✓			22,000,200	Zhejiang, Heilongjiang
1988		✓		49,000,000	Hubei, Jiangsu, Henan, Anhui, Shandong, Zhejiang
1989			✓	30,007,500	Sichuan
1989	✓			100,010,000	Anhui, Hebei, Hubei, Jiangsu, Jiangxi, Jilin, Sichuan, Zhejiang
1990	✓			26,130,805	Hunan
1990	✓			16,000,000	Shandong
1991	✓			210,232,227	Anhui, Jiangsu, Henan
1992		✓		12,000,000	North and Central China
1994	✓			78,974,440	Guangdong, Guangxi, Hunan, Jiangxi, Zhejiang, Fujian
1994	✓			30,547,665	Guangdong, Hunan, Fujian, Guangxi
1994			✓	11,001,800	Fujian, Zhejiang, Jiangsu
1995	✓			114,470,249	Hunan, Jiangxi, Guizhou, Hubei, Sichuan, Zhejiang, Fujian, Anhui, Guangdong, Guangxi
1995	✓			11,100,162	Liaoning, Jilin
1996	✓			154,634,000	Anhui, Guizhou, Hebei, Henan, Hubei, Hunan, Zhejiang, Jiangxi, Shandong, Shanxi, Fujian, Xinjiang
1996			✓	15,005,000	Guangdong, Guangxi
1998	✓			238,973,000	Hubei, Hunan, Sichuan, Jiangxi, Fujian, Guangxi
1998			✓	11,000,038	Hubei, Sichuan
1999		✓		19,000,000	North China
1999	✓			101,024,000	Anhui, Zhejiang, Jiangxi, Jiangsu, Hubei, Hunan, Guizhou, Sichuan, Yunnan
2000		✓		150,000,000	Jilin, Jiangxi, Anhui
2001		✓		16,000,000	Sichuan, Yunnan
2001			✓	14,998,298	Guangdong, Guangxi
2001		✓		15,800,000	Shandong, Henan, Hebei
2002			✓	100,000,000	North China
2002	✓			20,000,000	Hunan
2002	✓			190,035,257	Shanxi, Sichuan, Hubei, Guizhou, Fujian, Jiangxi, Hunan, Guangxi,
2003		✓		48,000,000	Inner Mongolia
2003	✓			150,146,000	Zhejiang, Jiangsu, Shaanxi, Guangxi, Guizhou, Gansu, Sichuan, Hunan, Jiangxi, Hubei
2004	✓			33,652,026	Shandong, Henan, Hunan, Hubei, Guangxi, Sichuan, Yunnan

Note: Under Deng Xiaoping, reporting of natural disasters became more accurate. Hence this table begins in 1985.

Source: EM-DAT: The OFDA/CRED International Disaster Database, www.em-dat.net - Université Catholique de Louvain - Brussels - Belgium.

The problem is not just the quality of the water but also its quantity and distribution. North China has historically received inadequate rainfall, and the water table around Beijing is allegedly falling, making water consumption rates unsustainable in the long term. Even in the Yangzi River valley, which traditionally has had ample water supplies, fifty-nine cities suffered water shortages in 2002. Since 1985, the Yellow River, long known as "China's sorrow" for its frequent and devastating flooding, has periodically run dry. Yet, China's population and industrialization are both increasing, implying greater water consumption demands. Meanwhile, more than 70 percent of the water in five of China's seven main river systems is so bad that humans should not be in contact with it, much less drink it. In the sixth major system, the Yangzi, nearly half of the flow falls into this category. Only the Pearl River system in South China has water suitable for human contact. In November 2005, a factory explosion caused 100 tons of the carcinogen benzene to pour into the Songhua River in Manchuria in probably the largest spill of its kind. The city of Harbin (Haerbin), population 3.8 million, had to shut down its entire water system for several days, and the severe environmental damage extended to Russia and the Amur River system.

Currently, China's fresh water per capita is one-quarter of the global average. The planned South-North Water Transfer Project is an attempt to remedy this problem by redirecting water from the Yangzi River. It will flow along three routes to the industrial centers of North China. The two running through Shandong are scheduled for completion after 2010 but they have reportedly encountered delays. A third will traverse mountains near Tibet to link up with the headwaters of the Yellow River to prevent it from running dry. This third route is not scheduled for completion until 2050. The environmental implications of this gargantuan project are the subject of heated debate, as are those of the Three Gorges Dam, completed in 2006, but scheduled to become fully operational only in 2011. After years of controversy the PRC decided to dam the Yangzi River, destroying its most beautiful and famous parts, in order to prevent flooding and to produce hydroelectric power. The holding pool behind the dam, however, will permanently remove arable land from cultivation, and sewage and silting problems may be hard to manage.

Air pollution is also a problem. Currently, coal generates 70 percent of China's energy supply and only 5 percent of its power plants have emissions controls, making for acid rain. China generates most of its electricity from high-sulfur coal, which individuals also burn in their stoves and heaters. High-sulfur coal produces large amounts of pollutants per BTU of energy. Rapidly growing car ownership is also contributing to air pollution. Particulate and sulfur dioxide emissions in China are among the highest in the world. According to the World Health Organization, China has seven of the world's ten most polluted cities. This, combined with extraordinarily widespread smoking, means that cancer rates will increase. In the past, poverty limited cigarette consumption, but since the Deng Xiaoping Restoration, those who want to smoke can now afford to do so. In studies conducted in 2000–1, 20 percent of the children in Beijing, 50 percent of those in Shanghai, 60 percent of those in the Special Economic Zone of Shenzhen, and 80 percent of those in Guangzhou had lead in their bloodstream above the World Health Organization's safe levels. Lead poisoning diminishes intelligence and causes other serious health effects.

Taiwan also went through this dirty phase of industrialization. In the 1980s, air pollution was so bad in Taipei that many children suffered permanent lung damage and high rates of nose cancer. In that decade, Taiwan started to implement regulations mandating unleaded fuel for cars, prohibiting the burning in Taipei of PCB-laden wire casings to salvage the copper, and so on. The air quality has improved. Unlike Taiwan, the PRC is far from turning this corner, although environmental concerns have recently begun to appear on its political agenda.

III. Energy and Industrial Growth

In order for the Chinese to improve their standard of living, they must continue to industrialize. This implies ever higher levels of energy consumption. In the 1990s, China's electrical capacity fell 10 percent short of demand, while 72 million people lacked any electricity. Although China is the third largest producer of energy after the United States and Russia, it is also the third largest consumer. On a per capita basis, it has low supplies of coal, oil, gas, and hydroelectric potential. In 1993, for the first time, it became a net oil importer, importing 6.4 percent of its oil. This rose to 31 percent in 2002 and to 45 percent in 2005. (See Table 28.4.) From 2002 to 2004, its energy consumption grew at twice the rate of its gross national product, at 65 percent and 30 percent, respectively. From 2000 to 2004, while U.S. coal consumption remained stable, China's more than doubled. Even so, electricity supplies have been unable to keep up with demand, resulting in blackouts. In response, factories have purchased diesel generators, adding to the demand for oil. In 2004 China accounted for 12.1 percent of global energy consumption, second to the U.S. 24 percent share, but its inefficient factories must consume three times the global energy average to produce one dollar of gross national product.

Table 28.4   Per Capita Crude Oil Consumption

Year	Crude Oil Consumption (10,000 tons)	Per Capita Crude Oil Consumption (10,000 tons)
1980	9,205	.09
1985	9,509	.09
1990	11,762	.10
1995	14,886	.12
2000	21,232	.17
2002	22,541	.17

Note: Between 1990 and 2000, per capita crude oil consumption increased by 70 percent.

Source: Tian Congming comp., *People's Republic of China Yearbook 2004* (Beijing: PRC Yearbook, 2004), 802; National Bureau of Statistics of China, comp., *China Statistical Yearbook* (Beijing: China Statistics Press, 1987–2004).

Per Capita Energy Consumption in International Perspective

	Per Capita Residential Energy Use for 1999 (kilograms of oil equivalent per person)	Per Capita Electricity Consumption for 1999 (kilograms of oil equivalent per person)
China	233	65
Japan	391	639
United Kingdom	716	465
United States	906	1,023

Source: http://earthtrends.wri.org/datatables/index.cfm?theme6, "Energy Consumption by Source 2003." The statistics are based on information from the International Energy Agency.

Given China's huge population and the enormous standard-of-living gap that it hopes to close as it becomes a developed country, its energy demands will skyrocket. The alternative is for the majority of its population to remain in poverty. Its per capita energy consumption remains minuscule compared to that of developed countries. This situation will surely change. Who supplies this energy and at what price will have a significant impact on Chinese growth rates. For instance, high world energy prices in 2004 were attributed to China's and India's growing energy consumption. Energy consumption levels will also have an impact on China's continuing environmental degradation.

After 1949, China began to develop its own oil resources, particularly the oil fields of north-central Manchuria. The widespread use of coal, the scarcity of automobiles, and the emphasis on railways made internal supplies of energy appear adequate. With Deng Xiaoping's reforms many of the imported industrial plants run on oil, not the low-grade coal that China produces in abundance. Prosperity has brought burgeoning private automobile ownership, while rapid urbanization and the desire to use cleaner-burning fuels have combined to increase the Chinese demand for petroleum.

Acquiring sufficient sources of energy is a government priority. New oil fields in Manchuria, Inner Mongolia, and Xinjiang will help meet the demand. There has been major new construction of hydroelectric dams. The Three Gorges Dam should produce 17 million kilowatts, or 84 billion kilowatt-hours every year, equal to 40 to 50 million tons of coal. Although this will equal 10 percent of China's total power production in 1990 of 130 million kilowatts, it will be less than 3 percent of the estimated demand of 600 million kilowatts in 2015. China will need to increase its power production by 8 percent per year just to keep up with the expected growth in demand.

Many of the most promising locations for new energy deposits are offshore, in particular near the Paracel Islands (Xisha in Chinese) south and southeast of Guangdong province, and in the vicinity of the Spratly Islands (Nansha in Chinese) between Vietnam and Brunei. Oil and gas fields may soon be found in the East China Sea. All of the surrounding nations also claim parts of these fields. Japan and Taiwan have claims in the East China Sea, and a much larger group of nations have competing claims in the

South China Sea, including Malaysia, Indonesia, Brunei, and Vietnam. (See Map 27.1.) The economic development of these countries also depends on possession of these energy supplies. At the turn of the millennium, over 15 millions barrels of oil traveled every year from the Middle East into the Strait of Malacca, through the Spratly and Paracel Islands, and on to East Asia. Much of this oil was headed for the PRC and Taiwan. This adds a national security dimension to possession of the disputed island chains, since they could become choke points for enemies seeking to interdict Chinese energy supplies. Proponents of a strong Chinese Navy argue that the PRC must claim maritime dominance all the way to the Strait of Malacca in order to secure Chinese energy supplies or build a pipeline through Burma to Yunnan province. All of this creates fertile ground for conflict.

Other potential oil and gas supplies may come from Russia and Central Asia. (Map 28.1.) In 2006, Kazakhstan opened an oil pipeline to China. In recent years, the Chinese government has signed oil contracts with the Russian firm Yukos to build a pipeline through Siberia and south into Manchuria. It would travel along the route of the Trans-Siberian Railway to provide China with millions of barrels of Russian oil. Japan, however, appears to have outbid China, proposing instead a much longer pipeline all the way to the Pacific Ocean that would deliver fuel mainly to Japan, not China. Tensions over the two pipelines remain high because Russia lacks the capacity to supply both markets. The Putin government in Russia took control of Yukos and put its head behind bars, so the pipeline route remains unresolved.

In the near to medium term, most of China's oil imports will continue to come from the Middle East. This has kept Chinese criticism of U.S. policies in Iraq muted because China and the United States have a mutual interest in keeping Middle Eastern oil flowing to East Asia. In addition, the Chinese occupation of Xinjiang makes the northwest a potential target for Muslim extremist terrorism. Some of those arrested as terrorists during the post-9/11 war in Afghanistan were Xinjiang natives getting terrorist training from the Taliban. In 2008 unrest in Xinjiang reignited. Because continued economic growth is essential to the Communist mandate of heaven, securing stable and affordable oil supplies will remain a key priority.

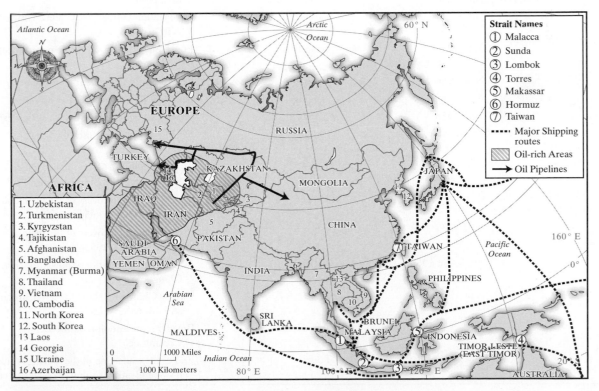

Map 28.1   Potential Energy Routes

IV. Democracy in Taiwan

Chiang Kai-shek died in 1975, a year before Mao. Taiwan followed the imperial model for succession, with Chiang's son, Chiang Ching-kuo, assuming the presidency. Although Chiang Kai-shek's final years of rule had been marked by extensive economic reforms and a rapid rise in the general standard of living, there had been little political reform. Taiwan remained a police state. Dissent led to persecution, jail sentences, and even death. Printed materials were censored. Taiwan had an active secret police, and corruption continued to mar Nationalist-business relations. Only the Nationalist Party could legally compete in elections. The National Assembly, with representatives from all of the mainland provinces, was frozen in time, barring a highly unlikely conquest of the mainland and the resumption of elections there. Thus, its seats amounted to life terms, while the Nationalist Party remained stuck in its Soviet mold. (Table 28.5 shows the changing Nationalist platform, while Table 28.6 provides a timeline comparing Taiwanese and Chinese leadership changes.)

Chiang Ching-kuo charted a new course for Taiwan. He had been born to Chiang Kai-shek's first wife of three when his father was a relatively unknown twenty-three-year-old military student. In 1925, at the early age of fifteen, Chiang Ching-kuo had been sent to Moscow to be trained at the Sun Yat-sen University, where after his father's purge of the Communists in 1927, he became a hostage. As a student in Moscow, Chiang Ching-kuo became a devoted Trotskyite, meaning that he favored prioritizing a global Communist revolution over revolution in any particular country, and he denounced his father. He also became a good friend of fellow student Deng Xiaoping. The Soviets did not allow him to return home until 1937, after the formation of the Second United Front. During these years, Chiang married a Russian woman and they had several children. Because of this mixed and especially Soviet heritage, the children appear to have been excluded from politics in virulently anti-Communist Taiwan. This chance circumstance may help explain Chiang Ching-kuo's willingness to forego creating a dynasty to promote democracy instead. After fleeing with his father to Taiwan

Table 28.5 Major Party Congresses of the Nationalist Party

Congress Number	Date	Location	Party Line
1st	Jan. 1924	Guangzhou	United Front
2nd	Jan. 1926	Guangzhou	Cooperation with Soviet Union, censure of Nationalist right wing
3rd	Mar. 1929	Nanjing	Enormous dissent over future government structure
4th	Nov. 1930	Nanjing	Reorganization of government and army
5th	Nov. 1935	Nanjing	Chiang Kai-shek consolidates power
Extraordinary	Mar. 1938	Wuhan	Strategy of National Resistance against Japan
6th	May 1945	Chongqing	Chiang courts allies for civil war against Communists
7th	Oct. 1952	Taipei	Opposition to the Communists, resistance to Russia; Three People's Principles
8th	Oct. 1957	Taipei	Reconstruction, recovery of the mainland, Three People's Principles
9th	Nov. 1963	Taipei	Reconstruction, recovery of the mainland, Three People's Principles
10th	Mar.–Apr. 1969	Taipei	Acceleration of transfer of power to Chiang Ching-kuo
11th	Nov. 1976	Taipei	Chiang Ching-kuo elected party chairman after his father's death
12th	Mar.–Apr. 1981	Taipei	Broader representation on the Central Committee
13th	July 1988	Taipei	End of the leadership of the Chiang family 65% of Central Committee newly elected

Source: R. Keith Schoppa, *The Columbia Guide to Modern Chinese History* (New York: Columbia University Press, 2000), 311–13. Copyright © 2000, Columbia University Press. Reprinted with permission of the publisher.

Table 28.6 Nationalist-Communist Timeline

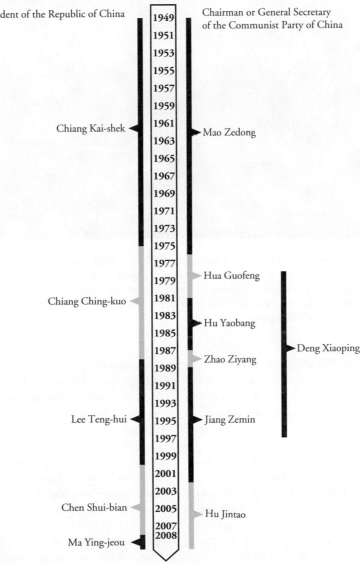

1912
Creation of the Republic of China
1926–8
Northern Expedition and Reunification of China
1949
Creation of the Republic of China on Taiwan and the People's Republic of China

President of the Republic of China

Chairman or General Secretary
of the Communist Party of China

President of the Republic of China	Year	Chairman/General Secretary
	1949	
	1951	
	1953	
	1955	
	1957	
	1959	
Chiang Kai-shek	1961	Mao Zedong
	1963	
	1965	
	1967	
	1969	
	1971	
	1973	
	1975	
	1977	
	1979	Hua Guofeng
Chiang Ching-kuo	1981	
	1983	Hu Yaobang
	1985	
	1987	Zhao Ziyang
	1989	Deng Xiaoping
	1991	
	1993	
Lee Teng-hui	1995	Jiang Zemin
	1997	
	1999	
	2001	
	2003	
Chen Shui-bian	2005	Hu Jintao
	2007	
Ma Ying-jeou	2008	

in 1949, he held a variety of government positions, including minister of national defense, prime minister, and interim president following his father's death. In 1978, Chiang Ching-kuo became president for a six-year term, which was renewed in 1984 and ended only with his own death in 1988.

Meanwhile, as Taiwan became increasingly prosperous, more Taiwanese demanded political rights. Many, including the first democratically elected president of Taiwan, Chen Shuibian, and his running mate, Annette Lu, suffered persecution in this period. Chen Shui-bian's

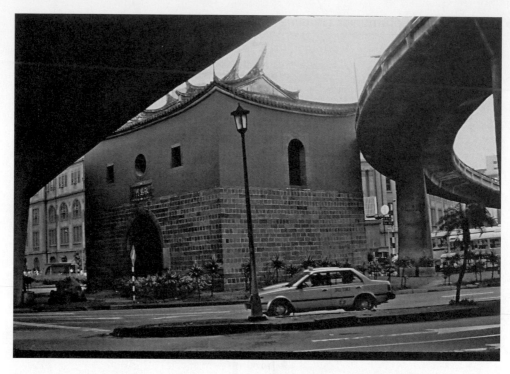

Huge economic growth rates in Taiwan during the 1970s and 1980s were accompanied by massive infrastructure projects. Here, a former Qing-era city gate in Taipei is now almost completely surrounded by concrete elevated highways. Modernization projects in the PRC are taking a similarly steep toll, as many traditional houses—and even entire neighborhoods—are bulldozed and destroyed to make way for new buildings.

wife remains paralyzed from the waist down from an attempt, probably by Nationalist sympathizers, to run her over with a truck, and Chen spent several months in prison for criticizing the regime. Annette Lu served a five-and-a-half-year prison term as a result of the political protests in 1979 that became violent and are known as the Kaohsiung Incident. A combination of pressure from below and leadership from above pushed Taiwan in the direction of democratization. In the mid-1970s, Chiang Ching-kuo embarked on anticorruption campaigns in the government and tried to bring more Taiwanese-born politicians into the Nationalist Party. A key beneficiary was his successor, Lee Teng-hui, a Cornell-educated Ph.D. who became vice president in 1984.

The end of the Vietnam War and the development of the Sino-Soviet split marginalized Taiwan in U.S. security calculations. Vietnam had been important as a means to prosecute the Cold War until the Sino-Soviet split opened a far more promising avenue for victory: The United States and China would improve relations to pursue the common goal of bringing down the USSR. Taiwan was no longer a convenient supply base to wage the war in Vietnam. Nor was the containment of China a high priority. The 1979 Sino-Vietnamese border war had made it clear that Vietnam would resist Chinese domination. Instead, the United States wanted to minimize friction with the PRC over Taiwan so that China would keep the pressure on Moscow in anticipation of the growing overextension of both the Soviet military and economy from the costs of militarizing the long Sino-Soviet border. Taiwan could only interrupt, not help, these plans.

The U.S. recognition of the PRC and derecognition of Taiwan in 1979 created a radically different security environment. It left Taiwan in international limbo. Although the Taiwan Relations Act passed by the U.S. Congress urged that the two-China problem be solved peacefully, it promised to provide Taiwan military aid in the meantime and potentially includes U.S. protection in the event of a war, embargo, or boycott even though Taiwan lacks the status of a nation-state. Yet, it engaged in all of the activities of one, while its nearest neighbor had a foreign policy agenda that included invading and overturning its government. Taiwan had very few options given the enormous asymmetries of a small island defending its independence against the vast Chinese empire. During the Maoist era, China had been a cooperative adversary: It had pursued domestic policies that had kept its population poor and preoccupied either with domestic matters or with problems along its land borders. Under Deng Xiaoping, this situation changed. (See Table 28.7.)

Chiang Ching-kuo supported democratization. During 1979 and early 1980 there were public debates in Taiwan on promulgating new election rules. In November 1980, electoral campaigning was introduced. While the election resulted in a landslide Nationalist Party victory, this was but the first of many incremental reforms. In the national elections in 1983, those opposing the Nationalist Party called themselves the *dangwai,* meaning "outside the party," but could only agree on the most general principles. Opposition parties remained illegal. In 1986, when Chiang allowed opposition parties to organize and compete in local elections, some *dangwai* members banded together to establish the Democratic Progressive Party (DPP) to create a two-party election. Ironically, the DPP modeled its organization on the Leninist structure used by the Nationalists, including party congresses and a central committee. Chiang Ching-kuo also took steps toward implementing a truly parliamentary system of government. For the first time, the Nationalist Party faced genuine competition from other political parties.

In 1987, the government lifted martial law, which had been a fixture of Nationalist rule. Martial law had given the government broad authority to arrest, imprison, and squelch dissent. For the first time, the government also allowed the general population to travel to China via the British colony of Hong Kong. The Taiwanese were overjoyed at the opportunity to visit long-lost relatives but were appalled when they saw the enormous disparity in living standards—many times greater than the disparity between East and West German living standards prior to their unification. Many Taiwanese began to question the wisdom of their government's one-China policy that previously had been a matter of unquestioned orthodoxy. Reunification under the best circumstances would bring an implosion of Taiwanese living standards. Many Taiwanese also noted the hostility of family members who had survived Mao's many campaigns and believed that their far richer Taiwanese relatives owed them recompense for their suffering.

In 1989 the Beijing Massacre caused a marked improvement in Taiwan's international standing. The international trade sanctions applied to China meant that investment moneys flowed into Taiwan instead. As a result, Taiwan's economy boomed. Taking advantage of Western squeamishness, Taiwanese investment into the PRC helped fill the vacuum, with billions of dollars of capital flowing from Taiwan to the mainland. The Tiananmen Incident also opened the door for greater Taiwanese political independence. Taiwan's growing democratization put it in the ranks of the developed countries, now in political as well as economic terms. The stark contrast between the political freedoms of Taiwan and the massacre in Beijing generated much international sympathy for Taipei.

With Chiang Ching-kuo's death in 1988, the presidency had gone not to another politician with recent roots in mainland China, but to Lee Teng-hui, whose family had lived in Taiwan for generations. In 1989 a Law on Civic Organizations permitted the creation of new political parties, and the 1936 constitution was amended to phase out the old parliamentary incumbents in the National Assembly originally elected on the mainland. By 1991 all of them were fully retired in time for the first general elections since 1949, held on 21 December 1991. Legislative Yuan elections were then held in 1992 and thereafter the functions of the National Assembly were reduced. In 1996, Taiwan held its first direct presidential election, which resulted in the reelection of President Lee. (See the feature on the next page.)

The CCP observed this democratization with horror because it believed that a democratic Taiwan would be more likely to declare independence. In 1995 and 1996, the PRC attempted to influence the Taiwanese presidential election by

Table 28.7 Taiwan's GDP as a Percentage of China's GDP

Year	Percentage
1970	32.73%
1975	35.06
1980	42.31
1985	35.20
1990	37.31
1995	26.60
2000	25.69
2005	18.97

Note: Since 1980, the relative size of the Taiwanese economy has declined in the face of the extraordinarily rapid growth of the PRC economy.

Source: http://151.121.68.30/Data/macoeconomics/Data/ HistoricalRealGDPValues.xls. Based on World Bank World Development Indicators, compiled by Mathew Shane at the U.S. Department of Agriculture. Shane provides calculations for the real GDP of both the ROC and the PRC in billions of constant 2000 dollars. We have calculated the ROC's real GDP as a percentage of the PRC's real GDP.

TAIWANESE GOVERNMENT

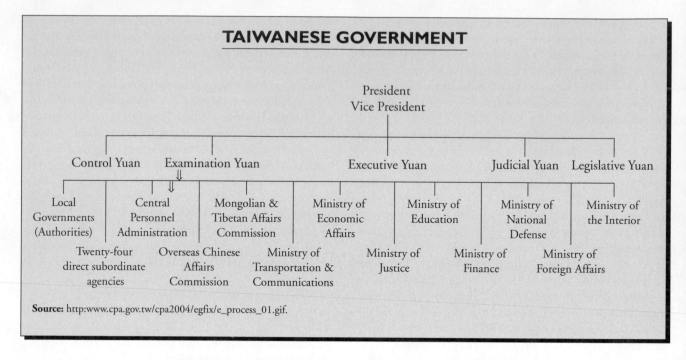

President
Vice President

Control Yuan   Examination Yuan   Executive Yuan   Judicial Yuan   Legislative Yuan

| Local Governments (Authorities) | Central Personnel Administration | Mongolian & Tibetan Affairs Commission | Ministry of Economic Affairs | Ministry of Education | Ministry of National Defense | Ministry of the Interior |

| Twenty-four direct subordinate agencies | Overseas Chinese Affairs Commission | Ministry of Transportation & Communications | Ministry of Justice | Ministry of Finance | Ministry of Foreign Affairs |

Source: http:www.cpa.gov.tw/cpa2004/egfix/e_process_01.gif.

firing missiles in the vicinity of the island: On 21 July 1995, it began eight days of test firing of surface-to-surface missiles off Taiwan's northern coast. The timing corresponded with the fiftieth anniversary of the World War II Potsdam Declaration mandating the return of Japanese colonies, including Taiwan. On 8 March 1996, China began another eight days of test-firing off of Taiwan's major northeastern and southwestern ports; on 12 March it began nine days of naval and air exercises off of Jinmen Island (Quemoy) and the Penghu (Pescadore) Islands; and on 18 March it began eight days of joint war games also off Taiwan. While the missiles were not armed, the flurry of military activities sent the message that the PRC would use deadly force to prevent a formal Taiwanese declaration of independence.

The PRC strategy backfired. PRC belligerency cut short public protests on the Japanese island of Okinawa pressuring Washington to remove its major military base there; the PRC had offered a compelling reason why the bases were necessary. It had also opened a long-dormant debate in Japan over whether or not to remilitarize. The United States increased its support for Taiwan, deploying two aircraft carrier battle groups, including one led by the aircraft carrier *USS Independence.* The name of the aircraft carrier undoubtedly jarred PRC sensibilities. The fall of the USSR and the end of the Cold War in 1991 had greatly reduced the geostrategic importance of mainland China to the United States. Formerly, China had been the essential pressure point on the Soviet empire. That empire was no more. This change allowed the

United States to follow bedrock instincts to support democracy in the face of a hostile dictatorship. Although Washington continued to recognize the PRC diplomatically, it backed Taiwan militarily.

In Taiwan, the pro-independence candidate, Chen Shuibian, almost won the 1996 presidential election; he and his Democratic Progressive Party, composed mainly of those whose families had lived in Taiwan for generations, won the following election in 2000 when the Nationalist Party peacefully relinquished the office that its representatives had monopolized since the 1920s. This was the first peaceful and fully democratic change of power in Taiwan or mainland China. President Chen Shui-bian was outspoken in his opposition to reunification. The PRC had offered indisputable proof to many voters why independence was not a luxury but an imperative. From Beijing's point of view, the Nationalist Party of Lee Teng-hui was an enemy, but an enemy that accepted the general terms of engagement, meaning one China. Under Chen's DPP, Taiwan-Chinese relations moved into uncharted waters. (See Table 28.8.) After Chen served his two full terms in office, the 2008 presidential elections restored the Nationalists to power with the victory of Ma Ying-jeou.

A key motivation for democratization under Chiang Ching-kuo and Lee Teng-hui was national security. Under Deng Xiaoping, the PRC had imitated the Taiwanese economic miracle. This meant that it would eventually overtake Taiwan economically. It was already channeling some of this

Table 28.8 Elections on Taiwan

Elections	GMD	DPP	NP	PFP	TSU	Other
Legislative Yuan Members						
1989	60.10	28.20	—	—	—	11.70
1992	61.67	36.09	—	—	—	2.24
1995	46.07	33.17	12.59	—	—	8.17
1998	46.43	29.56	7.06	—	—	16.95
2001	31.28	36.57	2.86	20.34	8.50	0.45
2004*	32.83	35.72	—	13.90	7.79	9.73
2008*	53.48	38.65	3.95	—	3.53	0.40
Presidential Elections						
1996	54.00	21.13	12.59	—	—	24.87
2000	23.10	39.30	0.13	—	—	37.47
2004*	49.89	50.11	—	—	—	—
2008**	58.45	41.55	—	—	—	—

GMD   Nationalist Party

DPP   Democratic Progressive Party

NP   New Party. This is an offshoot of the GMD formed in 1993 in support of better ties with the PRC.

PFP   People First Party. James Soong formed the PFP after the 2000 presidential election over former President Lee Teng-hui's failure to provide full support for Soong's presidential candidacy.

TSU   Taiwan Solidarity Party. When the GMD expelled Lee Teng-hui after the 2000 presidential elections, his supporters founded the TSU.

*Election Study Center, National Chengchi University, On-line Categories and Results of Elections in Taiwan, http://vote.nccu.edu.tw/engcec/vote4.asp

**Taiwan Central Electoral Commission (www.cec.gov.tw) at http://www.210.69.23.140/vote3.asp?pass1=A2008A0000000000aaa.

Source: Ko-lin Chin, *Heijin: Organized Crime, Business, and Politics in Taiwan* (Armonk, NY: M.E. Sharpe, 2003), 129; John F. Copper, *Taiwan: Nation-State or Province?* 4th ed. (Boulder, CO: Westview, 2003), 58–9, 138–43.

wealth into military modernization programs that would soon make possible a cross-Strait invasion. This drove Taiwan into a corner. It did not have international recognition, let alone a seat at the UN. It could not defeat the PRC militarily. In the recent past it had surpassed the mainland economically, but this situation was changing. Taiwan's new strategy was to defeat the PRC politically. Democratic changes had strengthened the legitimacy of the Taiwanese government, which had done very well by its citizens in comparison to the Communist government of China. The growing popular support in Taiwan for formal independence put the PRC in an awkward position. Reunification would require a bloody invasion, an open act of aggression. At best, this would trigger short-term trade sanctions that would subvert domestic economic development, a key pillar of the CCP mandate of heaven. At worst, it would trigger military intervention by the United States, Japan, and other countries. The international response to Iraq's invasion of Kuwait in 1991 provided a cautionary tale for China of the potential costs of an invasion.

There was also an economic element to the Taiwanese strategy. If foreign countries had investments throughout Taiwan and East Asia in general, and if Taiwan had significant investments in China from which China derived great economic benefits, an invasion would come at an enormous economic cost to the PRC. War would undermine the economy of Asia in general, which would grab the attention of the United States and Japan, raising the possibility of allies. Undoubtedly, many Taiwanese hoped that such potential costs might be sufficient to deter a PRC invasion.

V. The Two-China Problem

Until 1987, when the Taiwanese could travel to the mainland, their government openly and incessantly claimed to be the legitimate government of China. After the Taiwanese saw for themselves the gap in living standards, their demand for reunification fell silent, replaced by calls for official independence and repeated applications for UN membership. The stunning disparity in wealth, differing political outlooks, divergent economic preferences, and virulent PRC nationalism made many Taiwanese conclude that they had everything to lose and nothing to gain from reunification. In the seven-year period from late 1987 to mid-1994, when cross-Strait tensions were low, the Chinese government still threatened at least sixty times to employ coercion against Taiwan. Not wishing to test the PRC, a plurality of Taiwanese preferred the ambiguous status quo rather than risk a war. Deng Xiaoping had hoped to arrange a Third United Front with his erstwhile schoolmate, Chiang Ching-kuo, in order to reunite Taiwan; Deng publicly lamented Chiang's death in 1988.

Beginning in 1991, Taiwan began to act more like an independent country. In particular, President Lee Teng-hui rejected the PRC's One Country, Two Systems doctrine by announcing that there was a People's Republic of China on the mainland and a Republic of China on Taiwan. On 30 April 1991 he formally renounced Taiwan's claim to sovereignty over mainland China and recognized the government of the PRC. He advocated that the two governments recognize each other as equals to work toward the goal of reunification. He noted that Taiwan would never submit to a Communist government. This suggested that democracy and capitalism on the mainland would be prerequisites for reunification. Beijing, however, in line with Han traditions, accepts no peers. In the aftermath of the Beijing Massacre, Taiwan rapidly expanded its defensive capabilities with major arms purchases from Europe and especially the United States. In 1992, the ROC's Ministry of Defense issued its first white paper on national defense, and in that same year, the Ministry of Foreign Affairs issued its first foreign policy white paper.

The PRC responded to this growing Taiwanese separatism with threats that it would regard a formal declaration of independence as grounds for war. Its booming economy was rapidly putting it in a position to realize the dream of reunification. Invasion would require an extremely difficult amphibious landing, given the breadth of the Taiwan Strait. Even Adolf Hitler had been unable to launch a cross-channel invasion of England during World War II; the English Channel is but 21 miles wide at the Strait of Dover, its narrowest point, while the Strait of Taiwan is about 105 miles wide at its narrowest point. In the 1990s, the Chinese started buying from Russia the ships and naval technology necessary to launch such an invasion. They also began installing medium-range missiles along the Fujian coastline capable of bombarding Taiwan. From Russia's point of view, naval sales to China not only provided much needed cash but, more importantly, they deflected Beijing's attention far

to the south of their mutual border, much of which still remained under dispute in the 1990s.

By 1993, Jiang Zemin had consolidated his authority over the three main organs of power in China: the party, the military, and the government. That same year, reunification talks opened between China and Taiwan. During most of the 1990s, negotiations on political differences made no progress. Talks concerning cross-strait trade were more productive. In 1990 Taiwan had created the Straits Exchange Foundation (SEF), while the PRC had established the Association for Relations Across the Taiwan Straits (ARATS). A huge indirect trade developed through Hong Kong and limited direct trade routed through the offshore island of Jinmen.

In the 1990s, both governmental and personal contacts increased. The lifting of travel restrictions in both the PRC and Taiwan has enabled Taiwanese to open businesses on the mainland, but Taiwan has limited visitors from China for fear of an invasion via tourist visas. This has increased their island's mystique. For many mainland Chinese, especially the young, Taiwan is a symbol of prosperity and a source of popular music, television shows, and movies. Taiwan has also provided one concrete answer to the question, first posed in 1919 during the May Fourth Movement, concerning how to modernize and develop China along combined Confucian, Meiji, and Western lines. It has also disproved the myth, long espoused by Westerners and Chinese alike, that there is an inherent incompatibility between Han culture and Western democracy.

The Taiwanese have preserved much of the culture that the Communists blamed for China's backwardness. This applies not only to language, where the Taiwanese have retained the traditional complicated characters, but also to art, literature, and education. The Taiwanese have preserved the Han traditions, customs, and artistic heritage far more consistently than the PRC, which tried to eradicate them in the Cultural Revolution. During the Communist period, little survived the destruction of artwork, temples, historic buildings, and even rare books. The finest examples of Chinese paintings, ceramics, and jade carvings are not to be found in the PRC museums, but in the Palace Museum in Taipei. Yet Taiwan, not the PRC, has created the first modern Han nation-state.

The combination of democracy and prosperity in Taiwan presents a compelling political and economic model for mainland China. Taiwan demonstrates what is possible, but it also demonstrates what PRC leaders may fear the most: a prospering Han democracy. Democracy in the PRC would entail competing political parties and the likelihood of the removal of the CCP from power. This would implode some of the most well-connected *guanxi* networks in the nation. As in other de-

Chinese shipping firms already dominate Asian trade lanes and are rapidly expanding worldwide. Container ships, like this one in Keelung (Jilong), Taiwan, have made global shipping by sea both cheap and dependable. If tensions over Taiwan were ever to erupt, then one of the main casualties would be global trade, since the Taiwan Strait is one of the world's most important sea lines of communication.

Communized nations, democracy would open the possibility of punishment for those implicated in the deaths of so many millions. Democracy could also result in the implosion of empire. Empires have not fared well in the age of nationalism. When subject peoples have had a choice, as demonstrated by the disintegration of the Soviet empire in 1991, they have overwhelmingly chosen independence. Taiwan constitutes an enormous mandate of heaven problem for Beijing, which is why Taiwan's very existence is a threat and also why a military invasion of Taiwan remains under discussion in the PRC.

On 21 February 2000, the Chinese government released a white paper entitled "The One-China Principle and the Taiwan Issue," justifying military intervention in Taiwan under three circumstances: (1) attempted independence, (2) a foreign invasion of Taiwan, or (3) a refusal by the Taiwanese government to continue negotiating the island's reunification with the mainland. U.S. policy on Taiwan continues to vacillate. In 1998, President Bill Clinton announced the Three No's Policy while visiting China, meaning a no for (1) two Chinas, (2) one China, one Taiwan, or (3) ROC membership as a nation-state in international organizations. His successor, President George W. Bush, alternately implied that the United States would defend Taiwan against a PRC invasion and pressured the Taiwanese government not to inflame passions by declaring in-

dependence. Without the implied U.S. security guarantee, China would have invaded Taiwan in 1950. On 14 March 2005, the Chinese government issued an Anti-Secession Law that also mandated military intervention in Taiwan if the "possibilities for a peaceful unification should be completely exhausted," a determination that it reserved the right to make.

Conclusions

Ever since 1949, Taiwan's independence from the PRC has been real, even though neither country has officially stated the obvious. To do so would acknowledge that there is not just one China. The physical separation provided by the Taiwan Strait allowed Taiwan to adopt economic and political reforms while both retaining much of traditional Han culture and claiming to adhere to a one-China policy. Yet, the rapid economic development of the PRC may soon provide the military means to overcome the physical barrier. Cross-strait relations remain tense, as the one-China principle coexists with a two-country reality.

Both the Japanese in the late nineteenth century and the Chinese in the late twentieth century desired to modernize, meaning to acquire, produce, and ultimately create the full array of state-of-the-art technology that distinguishes developed countries from the rest. They intended modernization to transform their countries into world-class powers and to provide their citizenry with a world-class standard of living. The Japanese concluded that this was possible only with a significant degree of westernization of their educational, political, legal, economic, and military institutions.

At that time there was just one genus of westernization, the liberal democratic variant. World War I, however, brought to life two powerful Western critiques of westernization—fascism and communism—while the Great Depression produced an environment in which these two critiques thrived. In the twentieth century China gravitated toward these alternatives, with the Communists favoring the Soviet model and the Nationalists initially favoring a Leninist-fascist hybrid. Only the Communists followed the Soviet economic model, but both adopted a Leninist party organization.

Since 1949, the Taiwanese have gradually jettisoned the Leninist-fascist hybrid for a liberal democracy. They have

done so as a strategy for survival in a hostile regional environment. During the years of the Taiwanese economic miracle, the Nationalist government focused on becoming prosperous, the economic pillar of state legitimacy, while China remained mired in Mao's political campaigns, most notably the Great Leap Forward and the Cultural Revolution. During the Deng Xiaoping Restoration, when China threatened to match Taiwanese wealth, the Nationalist government responded with democratization and Taiwanization, the ethical pillar of state legitimacy. The 2000 presidential vote constituted the first electoral transition of power between opposing parties in Han history. The growing prominence and power of native Taiwanese and their increasingly vocal insistence on a separate ethnic and national identity from the citizens of China together create a powerful ethical and empirical argument not for two Chinas, but for one China and one Taiwan.

Meanwhile, the PRC has had difficulty settling on a constitution, let alone permitting free elections. (See Table 28.9.)

Table 28.9 Constitutions and Free Elections in the PRC and ROC

ROC			PRC		
Year	Constitution	First Free Elections	Year	Constitution	First Free Elections
1912	Provisional Constitution (1912–31)*				
1931	Provisional Constitution of the Political Tutelage Period				
1936	draft constitution				
1947	Constitution; under martial law (1947–87)				
1948	Temporary provisions during . Communist rebellion (1948–91)				
			1954	First constitution (1954–75)	
			1975	Second constitution (1975–8)	
			1978	Third constitution (1978–82)	
			1982	Fourth constitution (1982–present)	
1986		Local			
			1988	Amendments	
1991	First revision				
1992	Second revision	Legislative			
			1993	Amendments	
1994	Amendments				
1996		Presidential			
1997	Amendments				
1999	Amendments		1999	Amendments	
2000	Amendments				
			2004	Amendments	
2005	Amendments				

Note: *Temporarily superseded by Constitutional Compact (1914–16)
The lighter the shading, the more democratic and open the political system.

Whereas wealth in Taiwan is remarkably evenly distributed, income in China remains low and has become skewed. In 2007 China had the second most unequal income distribution in Asia, following Nepal. The prosperity and freedoms of Taiwan call into question the wisdom of many CCP policies and, by implication, threaten its mandate of heaven. This helps explain the intense PRC rhetoric concerning reunification and the expensive military purchases from Russia to make reunification possible.

Either emulating or defying the Taiwanese political model could result in the CCP's overthrow. For the Nationalists, the price of liberalization was initial electoral defeat. For the Soviet Union, it was electoral defeat as well as the loss of empire and great powerhood. The CCP has chosen a path of economic, not political, reform, banking on growth for its political survival. It is an open question whether or not any political party or government can survive a political legacy that has entailed the violent deaths of tens of millions of its citizens. The fate of communism in Eastern Europe and the Soviet Union is not encouraging for the CCP.

The Deng Xiaoping Restoration focused on the easiest and most obvious economic reforms: decollectivization and the restoration of a degree of free enterprise. The next phase requires coming to grips with extremely difficult problems including overpopulation, environmental degradation, water shortages, rising energy costs, unequal income distribution, and corruption. Future growth will rely increasingly on foreign sources of energy, meaning that China will be paying market prices. Increasing energy consumption will also mean more pollution in a highly degraded environment. Industry also requires water, which is in short supply. It remains to be seen whether China will be able to grow at the same high rates under these conditions.

If growth falters, the CCP will be left with only one last pillar supporting its mandate of heaven: nationalism. Han nationalism requires a clear target, and Taiwan has been the habitual target. Despite the enormous achievements of the Deng Xiaoping Restoration and of Deng's successors, who have continued the economic reform program, China still faces many hard choices.

BIBLIOGRAPHY

Alagappa, Muthiah, ed. *Taiwan's Presidential Politics: Democratization and Cross-Strait Relations in the Twenty-first Century.* Armonk, NY: M. E. Sharpe, 2001.

"Asia's Great Oil Hunt." *Business Week Online.* 15 November 2004. http://www.businessweek.com/magazine/content/04_46/b3908044.htm.

Brown, Melissa J. *Is Taiwan Chinese?: The Impact of Culture, Power, and Migration on Changing Identities.* Berkeley: University of California Press, 2004.

Chang, Maria Hsia. *Return of the Dragon: China's Wounded Nationalism.* Boulder, CO: Westview Press, 2001.

Cheung, Tai Ming. *China's Entrepreneurial Army.* Oxford: Oxford University Press, 2001.

Chin, Ko-lin. *Heijin: Organized Crime, Business, and Politics in Taiwan.* Armonk, NY: M. E. Sharpe, 2003.

Copper, J. F. *Taiwan.* 4th ed. Boulder, CO: Westview Press, 2003.

Diamond, Larry and Ramon H. Myers. *Elections and Democracy in Greater China.* Oxford: Oxford University Press, 2001.

Dickson, Bruce J. and Chien-min Chao, eds. *Assessing the Lee Teng-hui Legacy in Taiwan's Politics.* Armonk, NY: M. E. Sharpe, 2002.

Eberstadt, Nicholas. "Four Surprises in Global Demography." *Foreign Policy Research Institute* 5, no. 5 (July 2004), http://www.fpri.org.

Economy, Elizabeth C. *The River Runs Black: The Environmental Challenge to China's Future.* Ithaca, NY: Cornell University Press, 2004.

Elvin, Mark. *The Retreat of the Elephants: An Environmental History of China.* New Haven, CT: Yale University Press, 2004.

Feigenbaum, Eva. *China's Techno-Warriors: National Security and Strategic Competition from the Nuclear to the Information Age.* Stanford, CA: Stanford University Press, 2003.

French, Howard W. "'Green Walls' Campaign Scrutinized in China: Billions of Trees Fail to Contain Desert." *International Herald Tribune.* 12 April 2004, 6.

Garnaut, Ross and Yiping Huang. *Growth without Miracles: Readings on the Chinese Economy in the Era of Reform.* Oxford Oxford University Press, 2001.

Gerth, Karl. *China Made: Consumer Culture and the Creation of a Nation.* Cambridge, MA: Harvard University Press, 2003.

Gong, Ting. *The Politics of Corruption in Contemporary China: An Analysis of Policy Outcomes.* Westport, CT: Praeger, 1994.

Guldin, Gregory Eliyu. *What's a Peasant to Do?: Village Becoming Town in Southern China.* Boulder, CO: Westview Press, 2003.

Han Minzhu, ed. *Cries for Democracy: Writings and Speeches from the 1989 Chinese Democracy Movement.* Princeton, NJ: Princeton University Press, 1990.

Hutchings, Graham. *Modern China: A Guide to a Century of Change.* Cambridge, MA: Harvard University Press, 2001.

Jun Jing. *Feeding China's Little Emperors: Food, Children, and Social Change.* Stanford, CA: Stanford University Press, 2000.

"Kazakh Oil Pours into China through Pipeline." *Asia Times Online.* 27 May 2006.

Khan, Azizur Rahman and Carl Riskin. *Inequality and Poverty in China in the Age of Globalization.* Oxford: Oxford University Press, 2001.

Kriz, Margaret. "Fueling the Dragon." *National Journal* 37, no. 32, (6 August 2005): 2510–2513.

Lampton, David M. *The Making of Chinese Foreign and Security Policy in the Era of Reform, 1978–2000.* Stanford, CA: Stanford University Press, 2001.

Lee, James Z. et al. *One Quarter of Humanity: Malthusian Mythology and Chinese Realities, 1700–2000.* Cambridge, MA: Harvard University Press, 1999.

Lewis, John Wilson and Xue Litai. *Imagined Enemies: China Prepares for Uncertain War.* Stanford, CA: Stanford University Press, 2006.

Lü, Xiaobo. *Cadres and Corruption: The Organizational Involution of the Chinese Communist Party.* Stanford, CA: Stanford University Press, 2000.

————and Elizabeth J. Perry, eds. *Danwei: The Changing Chinese Workplace in Historical and Comparative Perspective.* Armonk, NY: M. E. Sharpe, 1997.

McDonald, Joe. "Harbin," *ABC News International.* 26 November 2005.

Mulvenon, James. *Soldiers of Fortune: The Rise and Fall of the Chinese Military-Business Complex, 1978–1998.* Armonk, NY: M. E. Sharpe, 2001.

Rubinstein, Murray A., ed. *Taiwan: A New History.* Armonk, NY: M. E. Sharpe, 1999.

Rummel, R. J. *China's Bloody Century: Genocide and Mass Murder since 1900.* New Brunswick, NJ: Transaction, 1991.

Schapiro, Judith. *Mao's War against Nature: Politics and the Environment in Revolutionary China.* Cambridge: Cambridge University Press, 2001.

Scharping, Thomas. *Birth Control in China 1949–2000: Population Policy and Demographic Development.* London: Routledge, 2003.

Seymour, James D. and Richard Anderson. *New Ghosts Old Ghosts: Prisons and Labor Reform in China.* Armonk, NY: M. E. Sharpe, 1998.

Smil, Vaclav. *China's Environmental Crisis: An Inquiry into the Limits of National Development.* Armonk, NY: M. E. Sharpe, 1993.

Taylor, Jay. *The Generalissimo's Son: Chiang Ching-kuo and the Revolutions in China and Taiwan.* Cambridge, MA: Harvard University Press, 2000.

Wang, Gabe T. *China's Population: Problems, Thoughts and Policies.* Aldershot, England: Ashgate, 1999.

Wang, Hui, Theodore Huters, and Rebecca E. Karl. *China's New Order: Society, Politics, and Economy in Transition.* Cambridge, MA: Harvard University Press, 2003.

Wu, Harry. *Laogai: The Chinese Gulag.* Boulder, CO: Westview Press, 1992.

————*Bitter Winds: A Memoir of My Years in China's Gulag.* New York: Wiley, 1994.

Zhang, Li. *Strangers in the City: Reconfigurations of Space, Power, and Social Networks within China's Floating Population.* Stanford, CA: Stanford University Press, 2001.

Zhong, Yang. *Local Government and Politics in China: Challenges from Below.* Armonk, NY: M. E. Sharpe, 2003.

NOTES

1. Zhou Mengdie, "Nostalgia," in *The Columbia Anthology of Modern Chinese Literature,* Joseph S. M. Lau and Howard Goldblatt, eds. (New York: Columbia University Press, 1995), 538.
2. Cited in Judith Schapiro, *Mao's War against Nature: Politics and the Environment in Revolutionary China* (Cambridge: Cambridge University Press, 2001), 32.

Conclusion

China in Transition

March of the Volunteers

Arise ye who refuse to be slaves;
With our very flesh and blood
Let us build our new Great Wall!
The peoples of China are at their most critical time,
Everybody must roar defiance.
Arise! Arise! Arise!
Millions of hearts with one mind,
Brave the enemy's gunfire,
March on!
Brave the enemy's gun fire,
March on!
March on! March on! March on, on![1]

Reinstated as the PRC national anthem in the 2004 Constitution; lyrics written in 1935 by poet and playwright Tian Han (1898–1968), who died in prison during the Cultural Revolution

History is the study of choices against a backdrop of constraints. People respond to challenges by choosing from among alternatives. We live in a world shaped by the choices of preceding generations, just as we shape the future by our own choices. Since the fall of the Ming dynasty, external forces have decisively influenced the course of Chinese history. The Manchus, the West, Russia, Japan, and Taiwan have in turn challenged China in unprecedented ways, compelling successive Chinese generations to respond by making difficult choices. External challenges that have forced pivotal choices in Chinese history include the Manchu invasion, the Industrial Revolution and the wars it precipitated, the Bolshevik Revolution, the Japanese invasion, and the democratization of Taiwan.

The Manchu invasion compelled the Han Chinese to choose between resistance and cooperation. After military defeat, the Han population ultimately chose to cooperate with the Manchus—despite the small numbers of the invaders—and accept that the mandate of heaven had passed from the Ming to the Qing dynasty. The Manchus then grafted their highly effective military organization, the banner system, onto the Han state Confucian tradition of civil rule. This civil-military structure allowed the Manchus to incorporate the nomad lands of Inner Asia, creating a vast empire under their minority rule. In doing so, they changed the way the Han defined China: Instead of consisting of just the core Han provinces, China became a multiethnic empire. What would China look like today if the Han had never cooperated with the Manchus? Would China as we know it still include these non-Han lands? Would modern China be an empire?

In the nineteenth century, the Industrial Revolution overturned the international balance of power, first in Europe and then gradually throughout the globe. Instead of choosing to accept this change, like the Japanese, who systematically westernized a whole array of domestic institutions, the Manchus chose to resist. Although the Chinese desired Western armaments and technology, they rejected the liberal-democratic Western institutional environment that had produced these products. They also rejected international trade under Western legal institutions, meaning international law, but demanded instead that trade continue under the tributary system. What if the Chinese had embraced rather than rejected the Western trading regime and invested the profits in infrastructure development? Would China long ago have merged with the global trade network even then being established? What if the Manchus had decided not just to modernize but also to westernize? Would Japan have ever been able to defeat China? Would China have remained the dominant power of Asia?

Trade disagreements with the West and political dis-agreements with Japan soon translated into military defeats, entailing increasingly onerous treaty settlements including the 1842 Treaty of Nanjing, the 1860 Treaty of Beijing, the 1895 Treaty of Shimonoseki, and the 1901 Boxer Protocol. All weakened the ruling dynasty and further discredited Confucianism. China became not more but less capable of closing the technological gap. When the Qing dynasty finally decided to westernize, it was a case of too little too late. The newly modernized Han military forces mutinied in the 1911 Wuchang Uprising and brought down the dy-nasty. What if the Manchus had not fought and, therefore, never lost these wars? Would Confucianism or the Manchus have become so discredited? Would the Han have felt compelled to overthrow the Manchus? Would the Chinese have searched for an alternative to both westernization and Confucianism, and perhaps adopted something other than communism and fascism?

The Bolshevik Revolution in 1917 offered communism as an alternative to the liberal-democratic variant of western-ization. This ideology appeared to provide a viable explana-tion for China's predicament: Foreign imperialists working hand in hand with corrupt Chinese politicians were at the root of China's problems. Outsiders had victimized China. This ideology also promised a solution: expulsion of the hated foreigner, instant gratification through confiscation of the wealth of the rich, and a workers' paradise to follow. The results of the 1919 Versailles Peace Conference, which were inaccurately reported by the international press to an already embittered Chinese public, seemed to confirm the Bolshevik view. But what if China's delegates to Versailles had not op-posed but cooperated with Japan? What if, instead of protest-ing, they had applauded the U.S. compromise solution for the Shandong question? Would success in China have encouraged the United States to join the League of Nations to make that organization more effective? Would Chinese intellectuals ever have felt the urgency to study communism? Would Japan and China have gone to war?

The Japanese invaded Manchuria in the 1930s to halt Soviet expansionism. What if the Nationalists had rejected the Manchu definition of China as the lands of the multiethnic Qing empire to focus on unification and economic develop-ment of the core Han lands that had traditionally defined China? What if the Nationalists had chosen to cooperate with the Japanese by rejecting communism and tolerating Japanese colonization of Manchuria instead of choosing resistance? With-out a Japanese army of occupation, would Mao have been able to develop a rural insurgency? If the Nationalists had chosen not to fight Japan, would the Communists have won the civil war?

In our own day, changes in Taiwan indicate an im-pending round of portentous choices. Unflattering compar-isons between Taiwan and the PRC used to be confined to

China's highly successful Olympics began on 8 August 2008 or 8/8/2008 (note the multi-ple use of "8," signifying prosperity in China). Although to many this sporting event sym-bolized China's reentry on the world stage as a great power, the sheer cost—estimated to exceed $44 billion—was almost double that of the Three Gorges Dam project.

economic performance. Recently, they have broadened to include political freedoms. Within a generation of losing the civil war, little Taiwan produced a standard of living that became an indictment of Communist economic policies on the mainland. The Taiwanese economic miracle precipitated the Deng Xiaoping Restoration, which entailed the westernization of many economic but not political institutions. The Taiwanese government continued in the footsteps of Japan to complete a westernization program for a broad array of economic, political, legal, educational, and social institutions. This culminated in full democratization in 2000. How, if at all, will the CCP respond to these political changes?

If external factors have forced the need to choose, what internal factors have helped shape the choices made?

I. Top-down Characteristics: Civil-Military-Ideological Underpinnings of Power

Manchu rule rested on a combination of civil rule based on state Confucianism and a fusion of the banner system with Sunzi's military doctrine, and an ideology of Sinification. These top-down cultural elements formed the civil-military-ideological core of Manchu rule. After the Republican interregnum, the Communists replaced Confucianism with communism while retaining the severe Legalist traditions to maintain party rule. In keeping with Legalism, the needs of the state justified policy choices. Mao Zedong incorporated Sunzi's military doctrine into his own theory of people's war and tried to replace the ideology of Sinification with Mao Zedong Thought. The Deng Xiaoping Restoration retained the Leninist party structure for civil rule while introducing a variety of westernized economic reforms. This entailed discarding Mao Zedong Thought and updating Sinification with Han nationalism.

Historians of China generally emphasize its civil traditions, but from the fall of the Ming dynasty to the present, the reality has been one of nearly constant warfare. In the seventeenth and eighteenth centuries, these were wars of conquest against Ming remnants and the peoples of Inner Asia. The former include the defeat of the Three Feudatories, the Southern Ming, and Taiwan, while the latter include the conquest of the Mongols, the Tibetans, and the peoples of Xinjiang. Civil wars and secession movements consumed the nineteenth century. While the White Lotus, the Eight Trigrams, the Nian, and the Taipings all attempted to overthrow the dynasty, the Miao, the Panthay, the Donggan, and the Muslims

of Xinjiang all attempted to secede. As the nineteenth century progressed, foreign wars overlaid these domestic conflicts. The Opium, Arrow, Sino-French, and Sino-Japanese wars and then the Boxer Uprising all followed in rapid succession.

The interregnum between the fall of the Qing dynasty and the Communist victory in the Chinese civil war was one long period of constant warfare. The major wars included the Anhui-Zhili War, the First and Second Fengtian-Zhili wars, the Northern Expedition, the Sino-Soviet railway war, the Central Plains War, Chiang Kai-shek's five encirclement campaigns, the Manchurian Incident, the North China War, the Second Sino-Japanese War, and the Chinese civil war. As with the Manchus, a victory by conventional military forces brought the Communists to power. Their rule was no more peaceful than their predecessors'. The Korean War; the Three Antis, the Five Antis, and the Anti-Rightist Campaigns; the government-induced famine of the Great Leap Forward; the Cultural Revolution; and the Sino-Indian, Sino-Soviet, and Sino-Vietnamese wars together cost millions of Chinese their lives. The political campaigns were part of Mao's concept of people's war.

In wartime, Sunzi argued, military, not civil, leaders should make key decisions. While this is the Han tradition, it is not the modern Western tradition, where militaries operate under civilian control. Chinese governments have gained, retained, and lost power through warfare followed by military occupations. Those who lacked military backing lost: Sun Yat-sen, the Gang of Four, and the students at Tiananmen Square all succumbed to superior force. In contrast, the Wuchang Uprising succeeded because it was a mutiny of conventional forces. Will the military remain the final arbiter of Chinese politics?

Successions have been problematic from the Qing dynasty to the present. The succession of the Yongzheng emperor, the failing years of the Qianlong emperor, and the intrigues of the Empress Dowager Cixi come immediately to mind for the Qing dynasty. One way to characterize the entire Republican period would be as the period of disputed successions. The Communists have not been any more adept at regularizing succession. They have consistently failed to apply the rules either of the constitution or of the CCP, but have relied instead either on *guanxi* (in the case of Deng Xiaoping's desire for Hu Jintao to replace Jiang Zemin) or on some other power play (such as the post-Mao infighting that removed Mao's designated successor), or on the crisis produced by the Beijing Massacre (which left Zhao Ziyang out of a job and under house arrest). In contrast to the image of Confucian placidity and institutional regularity, the reality has been quite different.

Out of fears of mutiny and popular unrest, modern Chinese governments have relied on Legalist traditions to retain power. The *baojia* system of collective responsibility, which the Qing employed to fund the state and maintain local control, has Legalistic roots. The Japanese re-created that system in their Manchurian puppet state in the 1930s and 1940s. Afterward, the Communists employed their modern variant, the *danwei* system, as another method of local control and collective responsibility. These legal institutions protected the interests of the state, and particularly those of the supreme leader, not those of the citizenry or the individual.

Likewise, Chinese economic development is intended to further state, not individual, interests. The Qing controlled vital monopolies, directed or hindered economic development, and tried to control trade. The Communists evolved in the direction of a Soviet-style command economy, whose primary purpose was to create a strong military. Communist rule has entailed a massive transfer of wealth from rural to urban China. Urban Chinese live well at the expense of their far more numerous fellow citizens whose passports confine them to rural China.

Legalism has been brutal but effective, certainly at silencing unarmed dissent. In China, dissent indicates the breakdown of authority. When central authority is strong, dissent is not tolerated but eliminated. This has been true for the Manchus, the warlords, the Nationalists, and the Communists alike. It has changed only on Taiwan and there only very recently. What will be the impact of China's increasing contacts with the outside world on these Legalist traditions?

China routinely executes hundreds, if not thousands, of its own citizens each year. Tax evasion can be a capital crime.

Proceedings are not open to the public, to outsiders punishments seem arbitrary, and death sentences are carried out with unusual dispatch in a society not known for great efficiency. (See Table C.1.) In 2004, Anhui province's former vice-governor sent a message prior to his execution for corruption: "[A]s I am guilty and I must die; but it is also unreasonable for me to die because of having no powerful backing. Please bring my message to the central authorities: no more than 20 percent of cadres at the provincial level are not guilty of practicing corruption."[2] In other words, he would pay with his life, while others, who had committed the same crimes but who had allies, would remain in power.

Inequality before the law and *guanxi* have a long history in China. So far, China has not applied these laws to foreigners. In the nineteenth century, draconian punishments mandated by the Chinese legal system were the origin of extraterritoriality. In 1980, early in the Deng Xiaoping Restoration, Provisional Regulations for Lawyers were issued, 1986 saw the first national bar examination, and a full-fledged Lawyers Law went into effect in 1996. Whereas in 1981 China had fewer than 6,000 lawyers, two decades later it had over 110,000; in 1996 alone, over 120,000 people took the bar exam. What will happen when individuals attempt to force the state to adhere to its own laws?

While Legalism is alive and well in China, Confucianism has survived only in part. Its failure to parry the Western challenge in the nineteenth and twentieth centuries left the Chinese with an ideological void that they have yet to fill. In the late Qing period, westernization and Meiji Japan competed

Table C.1   Executions (1995–2005)

Year	Death Sentences in China	Executions in China
1995	3,110	2,190
1996	6,100	4,367
1997	3,152	1,876
1998	2,701	1,769
1999	2,088	1,263
2000	1,939	1,356
2001	4,015	2,468
2002	1,921	1,060
2003	1,639	726
2004	6,000+	3,400
2005	3,970	1,770

Note: Amnesty International's statistics include only those death sentences and executions it can document. It estimates the real number of executions in China to be far higher since many, if not most, executions are not publicly reported.

Source: Amnesty International annual reports for China (1996–2006) located at http://web.amnesty.org/library/.

to fill this void. In the Republican period, communism and fascism, two Western critiques of the liberal-democratic version of westernization, also competed. Although communism won, its economic, political, and human track records forced the CCP to abandon the Communist economic principles that in Marx's writings formed the basis for his ideas. Although Mao attempted to eliminate Confucianism, in reality he relied on certain Confucian principles, such as his emphasis on reeducation of political opponents and on social hierarchy (his based on class, not education). His attempt to substitute party loyalty for Confucian family loyalties was unsuccessful. Since Mao's death, there has been a resurgent interest in Confucianism and the roots of Han civilization.

In the traditional Confucian social hierarchy, the state mirrored the family, with the emperor as patriarch of the state. Until the death of Deng Xiaoping in 1997, China was ruled by a supreme leader whose authority no other leader could match. Mao, despite his persecution of Confucianism and his destruction of Confucian temples and burial sites, was an emperor in all but name, and his servitors mirrored the old literati. As in the past, when the imperial examination system vetted a lettered elite to run Chinese civil institutions, under the Communists, first party files and later the highly competitive university entrance examination became a Communist examination system whose control was more comprehensive than the imperial system because the party controlled all educational opportunities and assigned students to jobs. The content of that education has increasingly gravitated toward technical and westernized subjects.

Frustrated scholars have been a continuing source of instability, including the Taiping leader Hong Xiuquan; the founding father of both the PRC and Taiwan, Sun Yat-sen; the founder of the CCP, Chen Duxiu; and the Great Helmsman, Mao Zedong himself. Many scholars who died during the Beijing Massacre sacrificed their lives to change the political system. Meanwhile, the living standard of peasants, who made the Communist victory possible, stagnated at a low level under Mao. Only during the early period of Deng Xiaoping's reforms did their relative standard of living improve. As business acumen has increasingly become linked with China's prosperity, merchants' status has also risen. Urban standards of living, however, have consistently outpaced those of rural areas. Can such unequal growth continue or does it threaten social stability?

Historically, the Chinese have relied on the ideology of Sinification in order to extend and consolidate their rule. In the past, China was militarily, technologically, economically, politically, and culturally dominant. When push came to shove, it forced its neighbors to adopt Chinese ways. East Asian countries, with few exceptions, adopted or—at least in

diplomatic settings—conformed to Confucian norms of conduct. The Industrial Revolution undermined a key basis of Sinification: Han technological and military superiority. Meanwhile, the combined onslaught of westernization, Meiji Japan, fascism, and communism eroded Confucianism, another key aspect of Sinification.

During the nineteenth and twentieth centuries, for the first time, Westerners—many of them Christian missionaries—came to East Asia in increasing numbers. What they had to offer beyond religion included the scientific method of analysis, British industry and technology, international law, and Western democratic institutions. These models ultimately proved to be more attractive to many East Asian countries than the Chinese alternatives, whether Confucian or Communist. Japan made its choice in the nineteenth century and rapidly westernized; many other countries, such as Japan's former colonies of Taiwan and South Korea, did so in the twentieth century. Sinification lost its power when local populations were no longer convinced of Chinese superiority. This applied equally inside and outside the empire. From the time of the Qianlong emperor, China has consistently resisted westernizing reforms. The Chinese have sought the material benefits, and their governments the military hardware, provided by an industrialized economy. However, many remain skeptical concerning the necessity, let alone the desirability, of adopting the institutional systems that originally produced these items. Will China choose to converge with international norms or, as in the past, resist them?

In the Republican era, both the Nationalists and the Communists attempted to harness Han nationalism instead of Sinification to reunite the lands of the former Qing empire. Particularly after the Japanese invasion in the 1930s, nationalism became increasingly effective for rallying the population of the core Han provinces, but the Tibetans, the Muslims of Xinjiang, and the Mongols answered their own separate and secessionist calls for nationalism. Although nationalism invigorated the Han to recapture the empire, it steeled the non-Han to resist. Since the 1980s, the Han have expressed nationalism in increasingly racial terms emphasizing the common descent of the Chinese people from the long-lived Yellow Emperor (r. 2697–2597 BC), who is credited with the invention of Chinese writing, astrology, alchemy, the calendar, coinage, the compass, the wheel, and various armaments, and also with the expulsion of the Miao people from the Yellow River valley. Given the divergent views concerning nationalism of the Han and non-Han citizens of China, the Han have attempted to overcome this underlying fracture line in the empire by overwhelming the restive minority areas with Han immigration. This was highly effective in Inner Mongolia and Manchuria. In Tibet and Xinjiang, this population shift is ongoing. What will be the outcome?

Rising nationalism in China concerns not only China's minority peoples but also its neighbors. There have long been irredentist claims, under Mao to territory lost to Russia in the nineteenth century, and in recent years to the many island chains of the South and East China seas, which the Chinese government has defined as integral parts of its *shengcun kongjian* or vital living space. *Shengcun kongjian* is also the Chinese translation for the German word *Lebensraum*, a concept used to justify German expansion during World War II. The Chinese government has proclaimed the resources of the East and South China seas to be vital for its future prosperity. Will irredentism continue to color Chinese nationalism?

Although the particular civil-military-ideological components of Chinese rule continue to evolve, their underlying purpose remains the maintenance of a top-down structure of rule to defend the territorial integrity of China. Historically, the Chinese have favored overarching ideological systems—Confucianism and then communism—and authoritarian rule. As China continues to grow economically and to develop an increasingly well-educated and middle-class work force, will one-party rule continue? In keeping with these hierarchical traditions, will promotion continue to be made by age, seniority, and ideological correctness or will it shift to merit and professional expertise?

II. Radial Characteristics: Relations with the Outside

The ideograph for China, *zhongguo* (see the Subject Index for the character) or Middle Kingdom, puts China at the center of the world, surrounded by lands of increasing barbarity in proportion to their distance from Han China. Sinocentrism did not set the precise boundaries demanded by the Western construct of the nation-state, just China's centrality, from the first character, *zhong*. Yet, the ancient ideograph implies boundaries, a population, and a military, because these are the three radicals making up the second character, *guo*, often translated as "kingdom" or "country." Traditionally, the Chinese thought of themselves not primarily in terms of geographic boundaries, race, or language, but in terms of civilized life. This gives rise to the question: What is China? The civilization? The empire? The core provinces? The lands largely populated by the Han people? The lands where Mandarin is the primary language? The limited vocabulary for these things implies a correspondence since the term "China," unlike the word for other nations, can embrace them all.

Until the fall of the Qing dynasty, the fluidity of tributary ties entailed a corresponding fluidity in the extent of the Chinese empire. Dynasties ruled over territories of widely different geographic extent. Territory shifted among provinces, colonies, and tributary states without necessarily affecting the core areas of the empire. This situation changed with the territorial penetration of the Russians from the north and west; the Portuguese, Dutch, British, French, and Germans from the south and east; and finally the Japanese from the north and east. These nations rejected the fluid sense of territory of the Chinese. They demanded permanent surveyed boundaries. In the absence of formal boundaries, they competed for spheres of influence.

Over the last two centuries, there have been wild gyrations in Chinese control over the frontier areas of Manchuria, Mongolia, the Tarim and Junggar basins, Tibet, and Taiwan. Together these territories constituted over three-fifths of the lands of the former Qing empire. Although Manchuria was a tributary of the Ming dynasty, an enormous influx of Han immigrants gradually changed its ethnic composition so that it became incorporated into the provincial system during the late Qing period. The Japanese invasion transformed the region into the puppet state of Manchukuo. Only defeat in World War II forced the return of Manchuria to China.

Likewise, Mongolia shifted among frontier, tributary, colony, province, and independence. The Mongols invaded China during the thirteenth century to found the Yuan dynasty. When the Ming defeated the Yuan, tributary relations resumed with the Mongols. Under the Manchus, however, what began as a tributary relationship gradually changed, and Mongolia divided into Inner and Outer Mongolia. The former, mainly through Han Chinese emigration, eventually became a Chinese colony and then a province. The latter broke away with the assistance of the Soviet Union to become fully independent of China in 1946 and free from Russia as well in 1991.

Similarly, Tibet was divided into Inner Tibet and Outer Tibet, and at one time encompassed Qinghai and Western Sichuan, the latter becoming the separate province of Xikang under the Nationalists during the 1930s and 1940s. As in the case of Mongolia, a foreign power, this time Britain, competed for control over the region. From the fall of the Qing dynasty until the reconquest by the PLA in 1951, Tibet was virtually independent. The Tarim and Junggar basins also broke away from central Chinese rule after the fall of the Qing dynasty. The Soviet Union came to dominate the area until Mao Zedong reunified these territories. As in Tibet, the Communists have not been able to eliminate native resistance to Han rule. Finally, Taiwan moved from frontier to province in 1885, to Japanese colony in 1895, to Chinese frontier in 1945, to de facto independence after the Nationalists' retreat in 1949.

Mao attempted to restore China's position at the center through the development of Mao Zedong Thought and leadership of the international Communist movement. While Marx had written about the most advanced industrial economies and Lenin had adapted Marxism to the proletariat of a less industrialized country, Mao adapted Leninism to the rural environment of an impoverished, largely preindustrial country. His modifications, he believed, were far more relevant to the developing countries of the twentieth century than anachronistic versions of communism predicated on a highly developed industrial base.

The problem was that his economic development strategy did not work in practice—neither did Marxism or Leninism. The despised West continued to produce the high standard of living and technological by-products that had compelled the Chinese to react in the nineteenth century. Although Maoism has been largely abandoned, there is little indication that Sinocentrism has been jettisoned. Indeed, trading patterns indicate just the opposite. While China is happy to take advantage of the liberal trading rules of foreign countries, it has pegged its own currency to the dollar in order to raise a barrier to imports. Recently, both North and South Koreans have been outraged by Chinese historians claiming an ancient Korean dynasty as Chinese and, by implication, Korea as well. Beijing has also claimed the entire South China Sea. Trade with its small immediate neighbors has rapidly increased, while China has tried to dilute U.S. influence by creating regional organizations—like the Shanghai Cooperation Organization that includes Russia and the former Central Asian states—and forums that specifically exclude the United States. Will China create an alternate set of regional institutions in East Asia or will it treat its neighbors as subsidiaries, as it did in the past? Will Sinocentrism be expressed in the future through virulent nationalism, and perhaps a restoration of Chinese influence over its former tributaries, or will Sinocentrism be abandoned altogether?

The ancient Han strategy of barbarian management remains very much in use today. *Yi yi zhi yi,* or playing off one barbarian against another, has a long history of success. The Kangxi emperor played off the Russians against the Zunghar Mongols to extend his rule into Mongolia, and the Manchus played off the Westerners against the Taiping and Nian rebels to defeat the internal rebellions with Western help. The strategy worked to a certain extent against the Japanese in the First Sino-Japanese War, when the Triple Intervention forced Japan to moderate its peace settlement demands.

In the twentieth century, however, more often than not, this strategy proved counterproductive. The Manchus tried to repeat past successes, this time pitting the Boxers against the foreigners. The foreigners defeated the Boxers, but at the cost of a huge indemnity. The Beijing government then played off Soviet Russia against the West. When the West backed down on certain issues, this weakened the Western counterbalance to the growing Soviet influence. Chiang Kai-shek's attempt to play off the Soviet Union against the West, then the Soviet Union against Japan, and finally Japan against the United States brought personal disaster because, in the end, he alienated all three. Mao was more successful at playing off the United States against the Soviet Union, as well as Vietnam against the Soviet Union. His choices contributed to the demise of the Soviet empire but at an unanticipated cost: Communism's failure in Russia has cast doubt on its survival in China.

Barbarian management had the xenophobic goal of expelling foreign influence. The Manchus attempted to quarantine foreigners on the imperial periphery to minimize their cultural impact. In the eighteenth century, they kept the Russians at bay in distant continental treaty ports set up under the Treaty of Kiakhta. Under the unequal treaties of the second half of the mid-nineteenth century, they set up a similar but more extensive trading regime for the maritime powers at an expanding list of treaty ports. When the foreigners rejected the tributary system, the Chinese periodically attempted to expel their influence altogether with the Opium Wars, the Boxer Uprising, and the Communist Revolution. All proved unsuccessful. Hermetically sealing off China from the outside world did not address the growing post–Industrial Revolution asymmetry between Western and Chinese economic development. In an attempt to use Western technology to catch up while limiting Western cultural influence, Deng Xiaoping created Special Economic Zones that, in many ways, paralleled the treaty port system as areas under a separate legal regime more conducive to economic development.

Since the Deng Xiaoping Restoration, modern technology has made foreign influence pervasive. Modernization requires westernized education in a wide variety of technical subjects. It also requires familiarity with law, which is an administrative, not a scientific, discipline. Law cannot be relegated to a highly specialized intellectual sphere since it is the cornerstone of government rule. Modernization has entailed intrusive contacts with outsiders, precisely the kinds of contacts generations of Chinese rulers rejected. Currently, admission to the World Trade Organization is requiring China to revamp its internal legal system governing enterprises, not just in a few ports, as in the nineteenth century, but throughout China. In order to fit into a global world, China has obligated itself to follow not selected parts of international law, but international law in general. This is an about-face from the Qing rejection of international law and international trade in the mid-nineteenth century. In the past, the Chinese rejected foreign norms of conduct. Will this attitude persist? How will China respond when its obligations under international law and customary political practices conflict? What are the implications for continued one-party rule?

China has always faced the centrifugal pull of local authorities against the centripetal tug of central control. The Qing did quite well for a time, as did the Nationalists with the Northern Expedition and the Communists with their reunification of the empire. However, the Communists failed to reclaim Outer Mongolia and Taiwan. While China retains the provincial system of the Qing dynasty in the sense that many of the provincial names remain the same, the provinces have been subsumed under overarching military districts; this means that the civil and military lines of authority do not have jurisdiction over the exact same territory. Dynastic and Communist traditions of rule all emphasize central authority, not local autonomy or freedom of action. In the core provinces, as many as 150 million citizens have left their homes for work in the cities and the government has lost track of their whereabouts. Modernization has required a loosening of central control over the economy. This loosening of control has entailed increasing unrest, with growing numbers of urban and rural strikes. Cell phones, text messages, and the Internet have spread the word in a way that was totally unimaginable a decade ago. What are the implications for maintaining order in a country of China's size and diversity, with its history of endemic warfare?

With the spread of private enterprise, the CCP's ability to micromanage the economy is decreasing, especially in South China, which has long been the most prosperous part of the empire. Recent economic growth rates have increased the difference in regional incomes both between North and South China and between the coast and the interior. By 1995, China had among the highest levels of inequality of any developing country in Asia. Will the government continue to favor urban over rural China? As economic growth rates continue to diverge, will North China allow South China more autonomy or will it attempt to recentralize? More generally, will the government continue to try to homogenize the country under central control or will it permit a more federalized system? If there is a loosening of control over the provinces, what are the likely consequences for the longevity of the Chinese empire?

III. Bottom-up Characteristics: Education, Globalization, and Han Nationalism

In the past, Daoism and Buddhism were the bottom-up forces that influenced much of China. Daoist and Buddhist beliefs have endured to the present despite the Maoist destruction of most of the country's Daoist and Buddhist temples. During the Cultural Revolution, virtually all temples, regardless of sect, were vandalized. As recently as the 1980s, the Chinese were still deconstructing temple furnishings to sell carved panels at rock-bottom prices to foreign tourists in Hong Kong souvenir shops. Recently, there has been revived appreciation of China's artistic heritage, with Chinese buyers starting to dominate the international market for their country's artistic treasures.

Today, the Falun Gong reflects the bottom-up dynamic. It began as a group promoting an exercise regime hearkening back to such Han traditions as Tai Chi, but it then grew into an apolitical mass movement that the CCP considered worthy of a full-scale crackdown, apparently out of fear of any nationwide organization independent of its own control. In the past, unrest preceding dynastic change often began in heterodox sects and secret societies, such as the Taipings, who nearly overthrew the Qing dynasty. Not surprisingly, Falun Gong members became increasingly critical of the government as the crackdown proceeded. Persecution of this million-member movement in the late 1990s forced it underground.

In the Republican period, a middle class started to emerge, only to be decimated during the civil wars, Japanese invasion, and Communist political campaigns. With the recent economic reforms, there has been a proliferation of family businesses so that a flourishing middle class has reemerged. This group is defined not by profession, as in the old Confucian order, but by standard of living. China's growing middle class is using poetry—often in song lyrics—and other cultural media like film to advocate political change from below. In addition to a growing entertainment industry of aspiring lyricists, China has a booming movie industry, whose films have won international acclaim for their vivid portrayals of the Great Leap Forward and the Cultural Revolution—hardly flattering topics for the CCP. Will the government tolerate a popular culture increasingly outside of its control? Will the CCP allow the middle class to flourish or constrain it as a rival source of power? What are the implications for continuing economic growth, political stability, and centralized rule?

The key bottom-up factors influencing China today are the spread of universal westernized education, a mass media and communication system increasingly beyond government control, and rising Han nationalism. On the one hand, modernization requires a highly educated citizenry in touch with the outside world. On the other hand, the Western analytical tradition emphasizes free thought—including political criticism—while the foreign media cover a wide variety of political and social agendas, some highly critical of communism. Movies, recordings, and the Internet have given average Chinese unprecedented connections with the outside world. Their influence on people's thinking is anyone's guess. Beijing's decision to require the Google Internet search engine to censor Chinese searches indicates the government's fear of its own population.

The Chinese are acutely conscious of the rapidity of the changes taking place in their country, and are justifiably proud of their recent economic accomplishments and ancient cultural achievements. This is often expressed in an outspoken Han nationalism. The Chinese increasingly see their security in terms of island chains, defining the Asian Pacific in the same way that Japan did during the height of Japanese nationalism in the 1930s and 1940s. Recently, China has acquired foreign port facility rights, which have been likened to "a string of pearls." (See Map 27.1 and Map C.1.) In the past, the leaders of many of China's neighbors willingly adopted Confucianism because it supported their own rule. For similar reasons, many later found communism attractive. The current ideological replacement for Confucianism and communism is Han nationalism. What will be the reaction of China's many small neighbors and minority peoples to Han nationalism?

Unlike the Qing period or most of the Communist era, record numbers of Chinese are now traveling or studying abroad. Under the Qing, foreign travel was a career killer, with returned students sidelined and ignored. Only very late in the dynasty was a very small number of students encouraged to go abroad, but many returned not with science but with revolution on their minds. In the Republican period, many more Chinese went abroad to bring back new modes of political and military organization: Democracy, communism, and fascism all proved politically destabilizing until the Communist victory cut off contact with the West. The first post–civil war generation of Communists went to the USSR to study. This proved insufficient for modernization. During Deng's Restoration, China sent its equivalent of the Meiji generation to study in the West.

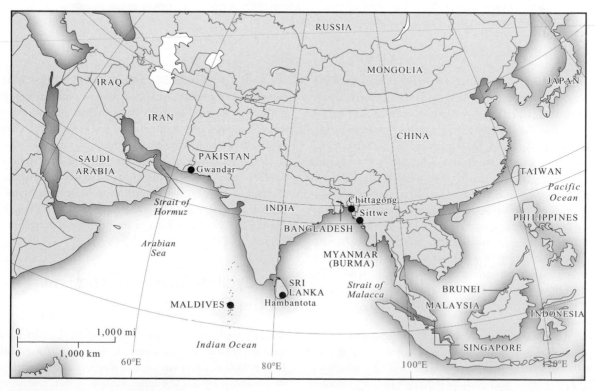

Map C.1　String of Pearls Port Access.

Today, Chinese and Taiwanese enjoy unprecedented prosperity. While many Chinese are critical of the way China was brought into the world community, very few would criticize the benefits of this transition. Today, more Chinese than ever live and work in cities, own cars, and enjoy all the benefits and perks of middle-class life. In a photograph from the mid-1980s, a typical Taiwanese family, including three young daughters, enjoys a visit to the Taipei zoo.

As in the late Qing period, however, foreign ideas threatened revolution at home. Just as the late Qing reforms ended in the Wuchang Uprising, the Deng Xiaoping Restoration ended with the Tiananmen democracy movement and the ensuing Beijing Massacre. Yet, Deng and his successors have continued to encourage study and travel abroad as essential for modernization. Gone are the days when a Mao-like emperor can seal off the country from Western contacts. Instead, a much more cosmopolitan younger generation stands poised to exert increasing influence. It is a generation influenced by the youth of Taiwan, Japan, and the West. At what point and to what degree will its impact be felt? Will this younger generation gravitate more toward Han nationalism or toward globalization? How heavily does the emotional baggage of their country's tragic modern history weigh on their shoulders?

While the CCP continues to try to promote Han nationalism and Sinification from the top down, growing contacts with foreigners via trade, business dealings, education abroad, the Internet, and popular culture have all promoted globalization from the bottom up. China's economic growth has been truly impressive. From 1979 to 1995, China's per capita GNP quadrupled. The Chinese produce top-quality consumer goods that stock store shelves around the globe. There is a sense that China is on the verge of reclaiming its historical position. How will China define this position? Will it seek great power status in the conventional terms of regional or even global dominance and demand an overhaul of the international order according to its specifications? This has been the way of Western great powers since the time of the Greeks. Or will China chart an original course that will surprise us all?

IV. Cyclical Elements: The End of the Dynastic Cycle?

Yin and *yang,* the dynastic cycle, and notions of historical continuity have not disappeared. Western technical subjects have provided alternate methodologies to the cosmic forces of *yin* and *yang,* yet the latter remain in use, particularly in areas such as Chinese medicine, exercise, and diet. The dynastic cycle and its underlying cyclical view of history remain a relevant analytical framework for understanding Chinese history, because history is influenced by human beliefs. Human beliefs can inspire human actions that transform the beliefs into self-fulfilling prophecies, not so much because the beliefs are objectively correct but because enough people believe them to be correct and so act accordingly. To a degree, outcomes follow beliefs. As long as enough Chinese believe that political regimes follow a Buddhist life cycle of birth, flowering, and decay, and shift their allegiances accordingly, the dynastic cycle paradigm will hold true.

The Chinese have written about their own history as a succession of dynasties following a prescribed cycle of upswing and flowering, stagnation and decline, and fall and interregnum. The strength of a dynasty's mandate of heaven positioned it on this cycle. Historically, the pillars supporting the mandate of heaven have been prosperity, ethical rule, and territorial integrity. These features characterized the early Qing and early Communist periods. With the Northern Expedition, the Nationalists seemed to be heading toward dynastic consolidation, but internal unrest and the Japanese invasion cut them short. Instead the Communists seized the mandate of heaven; Mao reunited the lands of the former Qing empire; extended Chinese influence into two key former tributaries, North Korea and Vietnam; and began to improve China's living standards.

Then, in the manner of all living things, decay set in. Signs of stagnation emerged in the late Qianlong period, the Nanjing decade, and during Mao's declining years. Signs of dynastic decline have generally included increasingly visible corruption, internal unrest, natural disasters, and foreign invasion. In the Qing period, when comets appeared in 1811, the imperial Court quickly proclaimed them to be a good omen, but planners of the Eight Trigrams Rebellion saw portents of dynastic change and launched their rebellion accordingly. Thirty years later, many Chinese construed the loss of the Opium War (1839–42) as an indication of an impending change in dynasties. The leaders of the ensuing Taiping Rebellion (1850–64) used this analysis to gain almost enough adherents to topple the dynasty. Devastating flooding of the Yellow River precipitated the Nian Rebellion (1851–68), while a succession of Muslim secession movements coincided with these Han attempts to overthrow Manchu rule. Famine then followed in the wake of civil war, and over 10 million died in the North China famine of 1876–9. Foreign wars with France and Japan soon ensued. By the end of the Qing dynasty, China had become synonymous with corruption for foreign observers and domestic dissidents alike. The long Republican period interregnum was likewise a time of unmitigated man-made and natural disasters. Under communism, the self-destructive political campaigns were signs of dynastic decline. The Great Famine followed the Great Leap Forward. The CCP then turned on itself in the decade-long Cultural Revolution.

Dynastic legitimacy has been closely associated with rural prosperity. Peasant rebellions nearly toppled the Qing dynasty, and peasant loyalties tipped the balance in the Chinese civil war. The reforms of the Deng Xiaoping Restoration greatly benefited the peasantry but, in the long run, they also greatly increased rural–urban inequality. (See the feature on the next page.) Although the Deng Xiaoping Restoration brought prosperity to many, corruption and internal unrest have become increasingly visible. Student demonstrations, workers' strikes, ethnic tensions, and peasant protests have all increased in recent years. In 2006, over 90 percent of the 3,200 Chinese with assets exceeding 100 million yen were relatives of high party or government officials, while senior officers of the PLA were disproportionately drawn from descendants of former senior PLA cadres. How will the CCP reconcile its ideology emphasizing equality with the reality of growing inequality?

Historically, the periods of dynastic decline have been long and tragic. The Qing dynasty spent a century in decline, the terrible interregnum lasted another half century, and the Communist decline set in even before Mao Zedong, the founding emperor, had died. Yet, when the Chinese have perceived the mandate of heaven to be irretrievably lost, their allegiances have shifted with breathtaking rapidity. The Ming general Wu Sangui declined to defend the capital but instead allowed the invading Manchu armies to pass through the Great Wall at the Shanhai pass. Thereafter, many Ming civil servants remained at their posts to serve the new Qing dynasty, while the former Ming army became the Qing Army of the Green Standard. Their allegiance followed the mandate of heaven. Two and a half centuries later, at the collapse of the Qing dynasty, the organized armed forces of the dynasty evaporated, later to coalesce in a kaleidoscopic array of warlord armies, while the Manchus themselves disappeared from the political history of China. They seem to have just blended into the general population. During the final year of the Chinese civil war, when the Nationalists displayed all the hallmarks of a government with no mandate of heaven—rampant corruption, brutality, poverty, and instability—Nationalist commanders defected with vast armies so that the Communists took all of South China in less than a year. What is the primary basis for loyalty to the CCP today?

RURAL–URBAN INEQUALITY

During the Maoist era, the state determined the flow of investment and the flow went to urban industries. Agriculture was expected to provide surplus income to help fund this flow through the agricultural tax, averaging 15 percent of the value of the crop paid to the central government and another 13 to 15 percent paid to the local government, meaning almost one-third of agricultural income. In addition, the state, which set agricultural prices, made these prices artificially low, creating a second avenue for revenue extraction from rural China. (See the graph "Urban Consumer Subsidies at the Expense of the Peasantry" to understand the full financial impact of China's below market prices on agricultural production.)

Urban Consumer Subsidies at the Expense of the Peasantry

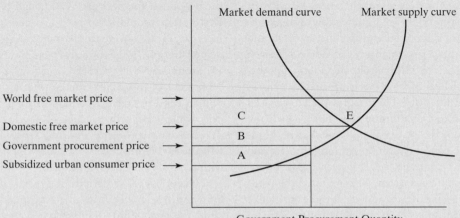

Rectangle A   = urban consumer subsidy borne by government
Rectangle B   = urban consumer subsidy borne by peasants
Areas of C + E = further losses borne by peasants forced
                 to sell below world market prices

Source: John Knight and Lina Song, *The Rural–Urban Divide: Economic Disparities and Interactions in China* (Oxford: Oxford University Press, 1999), 246.

   To prevent peasants from seeking a higher standard of living in the cities, the government forcibly kept them on the land through the internal passport (*hukou*) system that deprived them of food rations in the cities. With no new land available for farming and with a growing population, this has meant a growing supply of surplus labor legally stuck in the countryside. From 1952 to 1995, the arable land per rural worker fell by nearly one-half. Prior to the liberalization under Deng Xiaoping, there were no private markets to find food. This prevented any unregulated population migration and further urbanization. In effect, the Communists enserfed the rural population. With the liberalization under Deng Xiaoping, the rural population can migrate to cities but they are not eligible for any of the urban subsidies or services. Migrants can apply for only the most undesirable jobs, are typically scorned by China's privileged urban *hukou* holders, have no hope of getting such internal passports themselves, and so remain second-class citizens. This migrant population has grown to over 100 million.

   Urban workers receive numerous nonmonetary subsidies, the most important being food coupons, housing subsidies, and lower electricity rates. Nearly 40 percent of urban income comes from such subsidies. In contrast, those in rural areas make a net payment of 2 percent of their income to the government (subsidies minus taxes). The total per capita urban subsidy is equivalent to 90 percent of the per capita rural income. Urban residents also have far better educational opportunities and medical care, as well as preferential treatment on the university entrance examinations. Rural health schemes had been part of the commune system, but they disappeared with the liberalizing reforms under Deng Xiaoping. This meant that the rural population participating in health coverage programs dropped from 82 percent in 1978 to 5 percent in 1986. Most urban workers remain covered by such programs.

Even though China has undergone enormous change in past decades, which has increased the opportunities and choices for hundreds of millions of Chinese citizens, there are still many Chinese peasants who have been denied the fruits of modernization. Estimates of China's migrant worker population range well above 100 million.

As a result of these factors, urban income per capita in China is nearly three times higher than rural income per capita, and the urban consumption rate is nearly three and a half times the rural consumption rate per capita. In Taiwan the comparable statistics are 1.32 and 1.43, respectively. Unlike Taiwan, most of China's population remains in the countryside. In 2000, 74 percent of China's population held a rural *hukou*. Thus, the peasants of China have paid a high price for their fellow citizens to live comparatively well in the cities. In essence, the *hukou* system makes rural *hukou* holders foreigners in their own land, and legally excluded from many of the benefits of China's recent prosperity. The *hukou* system is the legal reason behind China's increasingly uneven economic development and unequal income distribution. Rural *hukou* holders constitute a disproportionate percentage of China's unemployed and underemployed population, and also suffer disproportionately from the country's lack of a social security program.

In the period under consideration, outside contacts fatally undermined two belief systems that for a time organized Chinese life: first Confucianism, then communism. The Industrial Revolution and westernization undermined Confucianism as an effective political system—whether it remains a relevant ethical system today is a separate matter. The inability of the Manchus to adapt Confucianism to parry the Western threat and their last-resort shift to westernization contributed to their loss of the mandate of heaven. Likewise, since the Deng Xiaoping Restoration, the CCP has abandoned the economic foundations on which Communist the-

ory and politics were based. Can the political superstructure survive without the original foundations? What pace of economic growth is necessary to satisfy China's citizenry? If victory in the Chinese civil war and the Korean War legitimated Communist rule for the first generation after 1949, what will be the primary sources of legitimacy in the future? Will the human costs of the CCP's numerous political campaigns come back to haunt it in the future? Can the CCP find an ethical basis for its one-party monopoly?

This leaves the third pillar of the mandate of heaven, territorial integrity, which, in the case of China, means empire.

Empire is an expensive proposition. The Western powers concluded that in the age of nationalism it was no longer a money-making one and gave up their colonies in the twentieth century. The Qing never had to deal with competing nationalisms of the peoples of Inner Asia. China remains the world's last major continental empire. Nationalism has destroyed all the other empires surviving into modern times, including, most recently, the Soviet empire. Can China break with the trend to retain its empire indefinitely? Or will the dynasty continue to the next stage of the cycle, to lose sections of its extended empire in the manner of decolonization in the West?

The dynastic cycle paradigm implies life within prescribed limits, whereas the linear Western model presents life as an unbounded progression. Economic growth implies a bigger pie potentially with bigger slices for all. Under this model, life is not a zero-sum game; there are win-win possibilities because a growing pie means extra servings to go around. In the West, the dynastic cycle is a fiction, because life does not follow prescribed patterns. U.S. politics do not turn on whether or not Puerto Rico chooses independence. In Puerto Rico's most recent referendum on the subject, it chose to retain its special relationship with the United States.

Taiwan has already moved on. Whereas the Communists chose a centrally planned economy based on heavy industry in order to create a strong military and have retained one-party rule, Taiwan chose a free market emphasizing consumer goods and the Nationalists allowed free elections even though they lost power in the process. While China continues to limit its contacts with the outside world, Taiwan has embraced the global order. Taiwan, understanding that its very survival is at stake given the PRC's foreign policy goal of reunification, has also minimized the particularistic tradition of *guanxi* to embrace universalistic laws. Taiwan has had no choice but to glue itself to the West as the only hope for its continued political survival. In doing so, it has rejected the dynastic cycle, Legalism, and empire and has attempted to rewrite its fate. The purpose of its government is to promote internal prosperity. The Chinese government faces no such extreme compulsion to embrace political reforms. Will China ever abandon the dynastic cycle? If it does, would this make reunification with Taiwan a nonissue? Logically, why should Chinese politics turn on Taiwan?

V. Retrospective Elements: Fatalism or Choice?

Retrospective elements include fate and the sources of knowledge. To a significant degree, an acceptance of fate seems to have set the parameters of Chinese existence. It helps account for the passivity of most people during mass movements, as well as mass defections during periods of dynastic change. The parameters of human knowledge, however, have broadened immeasurably since the days of the imperial examination system, the tumultuous years of civil war, and the period of Mao's *Little Red Book*. Thousands of China's most promising students have been sent abroad to receive a Western education and to bring back this knowledge to China. Many more are hooked into the global exchange of ideas via the Internet.

Belief in fate, and divination as a means to discover it, have been tenacious even among China's educated elite. The famous Han reformer Kang Youwei (1858–1927) remained a firm believer in omens, physiognomy, and geomancy. He spent his life advocating constitutional government for China and an educational system based on Western science and technology. Yet, in 1923, he recommended that the entire city of Jinan, Shandong, be moved because its location violated the rules of *fengshui*. The Communists sought to upend many divination practices. They focused on the destruction of grave sites, apparently in an attempt to undermine the old order in the eyes of *fengshui* believers. Severing their ties with the dead meant that the dead could no longer mediate between heaven and earth. Yet, the Communists were unable to eliminate divination. Care is still usually taken to schedule weddings on auspicious days, while the rules of *fengshui* determine the placement even of Hong Kong high-rises.

In the future, will the Chinese emphasize fatalism or choice? Will they continue to present their history primarily in terms of their victimization by others or will they see the role that their own choices have played? How is it possible that the Western powers single-handedly destroyed China in the nineteenth century? Given China's enormous population, limited infrastructure in the countryside, and the tyranny of distance, how could the West have caused China's numerous internal problems? These problems endured during the Communist period, when there was no Western influence. Will the Chinese government continue to use anti-Americanism to stir nationalist passions?

The hallmark of the civil side of Communist governments is central planning and economic management. Control over money translates into control over the nation. China has a long and vibrant tradition of commerce. In the Confucian order, because those engaged in commerce occupied the lowest rungs of society, governments did not try to direct their activities but only taxed their trade. Commerce thrived in Imperial China precisely because the government did not deign to become involved. This is no longer the case. Ever since the Industrial Revolution, the economic basis of national power has become increasingly evident. This has motivated Communist governments to engage in highly intrusive, although not necessarily effective, economic policies. As China moves away from Marxism and toward a more rational economy, will Beijing turn over primary responsibility for the economy to free markets? Or will it continue to promote some kind of mixed system combining limited markets with central control?

In recent years, the Chinese government has dramatically widened the scope of economic choices. It has also broadened access to information. In the past, the sources of knowledge were the Classics, originally the Confucian Classics, and later the Maoist classics. In today's world, the potential sources of knowledge are global. Will the Chinese government continue to try to control the flow of information? For example, during summer 2007, when a number of Chinese miners were trapped underground, all of China's major newspapers had the identical front page. Although Beijing cannot monopolize information as in the past, will it continue to limit Internet searches or will it give its citizens free and unhindered access to the world?

Will the Chinese government also broaden the scope of its citizens' political choices? Are political institutions totally unrelated to economic performance? Do free peoples or dictatorships create a higher standard of living? The richest countries in the world are also the most democratic: Is this mere coincidence? What does all this mean for China? In the nineteenth century, the leaders of Meiji Japan concluded that modernization and westernization were a package deal. One could not be had without the other. What will China conclude? Undoubtedly, the rapid disintegration of the Soviet empire serves as a powerful negative example for Chinese leaders. Will these fears preclude political reform? Will China ever become democratic?

Final Words

Guanxi and face have been the social glue binding the Chinese social and political systems. Chinese society, in contrast to Western societies, has been based on a social hierarchy cemented by the personal bonds of *guanxi,* not on the universalistic structures of law that have increasingly organized Western societies since Roman times. To fail in China has ramifications far beyond those in the West. Failure means a loss of face and an erosion of *guanxi,* which are both far more difficult to restore than to create in the first place. Chinese reliance on *guanxi* makes political institutions and political successions difficult to fathom for foreigners and nationals alike. This is because, unlike in the West, where politics operates within a public framework of law, in China much of the important decision making occurs within the framework of each policymaker's personal and highly secretive *guanxi* network. This makes succession particularly traumatic, with the decapitation of the passing leader's *guanxi* network leading to a free-for-all among his successors to absorb as much as possible of his imploding *guanxi* network into their own. Any transition to a Western-style legal system would be extremely difficult since the Chinese have historically organized society on the basis of particularistic connections, not universal rules of conduct applying to all equally. Their rules take into account relative status to consider the individual in the context of the whole.

The coming years and decades will undoubtedly bring many critical foreign and domestic challenges. The Chinese economist Cheng Siwei admonished his fellow citizens to "absorb Western culture selectively and inherit Chinese cultural critically."[3] The Chinese government has already abandoned the Communist economic model, but the fate of the Communist political model remains unclear. Will political power remain based on *guanxi*? Can China fully exploit technological modernization without embracing political westernization, meaning a free and open society based on the rule of law, a free press, and open and fair elections?

BIBLIOGRAPHY

Chang, Maria Hsia. *Return of the Dragon: China's Wounded Nationalism.* Boulder, CO: Westview Press, 2001.

Cheng, Siwei. *Studies on Economic Reforms and Development in China.* Oxford: Oxford University Press, 2001.

Goodman, Peter S. "China's Unyielding Banking Crisis." *Washington Post Foreign Service.* 6 June 2005, A01.

Gregor, A. James. *A Place in the Sun: Marxism and Fascism in China's Long Revolution.* Boulder, CO: Westview Press, 2000.

Khan, Azizur Rahman and Carl Riskin. *Inequality and Poverty in China in the Age of Globalization.* Oxford: Oxford University Press, 2001.

Knight, John and Lina Song. *The Rural–Urban Divide: Economic Disparities in China.* Oxford: Oxford University Press, 1999.

Kuehner, Trudy. "Understanding China" *Newsletter of the Foreign Policy Research Institute* vol. 12 no. 1 (March 2007).

Office of the Secretary of Defense. *Annual Report to Congress: Military Power of the People's Republic of China 2006.* Washington, DC: U.S. Department of Defense 2006.

Peerenboom, Randall P. *Lawyers in China: Obstacles to Independence and the Defense of Rights.* New York: Lawyers Committee for Human Rights, 1998.

Tanner, Murray Scot. "China Rethinks Unrest." *The Washington Quarterly* 27, no. 3 (Summer 2004): 137–56.

Waldron, Arthur. "Mao Lives." *Commentary* (Oct. 2005): 31–8.

Yu Zeyuan. "Analyst: Hu Jintao Consolidates His Military Power by Promoting 10 Generals." *Singapore Lianhe Zaobao* 19 July 2006.

NOTES

1. http://english.peoplesdaily.com.cn/china/anthem.html
2. Ha Yuan, "Anhui Vice Governor's Message before Execution," *Hong Kong Cheng Ming*, 1 March 2004, no. 317, 18. Translated by *FBIS*.
3. Siwei Cheng, *Studies on Economic Reforms and Development in China* (Oxford: Oxford University Press, 2001), 2.

Appendix A

Geographical Names by Transliteration System

Pinyin	Traditional Spelling	Wade-Giles*	Pinyin	Traditional Spelling	Wade-Giles*
Aihun	Aigun	Ai-hun	Heilongjiang	Heilungkiang	Hei-lung-chiang
Andong	Antung	An-tung	Hekou	Hokow	Ho-k'ou
Aomen	Macau	Ao-men	Henan	Honan	He-nan
Anhui	Anhwei	An-hui	Hubei	Hupeh	Hu-pei
Baicaogou		Pai-ts'ao-kou	Hunan	Hunan	Hu-nan
Beihai	Pakhoi	Pei-hai	Jiangmen	Kongmoon	Chiang-men
Beijing	Peking	Pei-ching	Jiangsu	Kiangsu	Chiang-su
Changchun	Changchun	Ch'ang-ch'un	Jiangxi	Kiangsi	Chiang-hsi
Chongqing	Chungking	Ch'ung-ch'ing	Jiangzi	Gyangtse	Chiang-tzu
Dadonggou	Tatungkow	Ta-tung-kou	Jiaozhou	Kiaochow	Chiao-chou
Dalian	Dairen	Ta-lien	Jiayuguan	Suchow	Chia-yü-kuan
Faku	Fukumen	Fa-k'u-men	Jilin	Kirin	Chi-lin
Fenghuangcheng	Fenghwang	Feng-huang-ch'eng	Jinzhou	Kinchow	Chin-chou
			Jiujiang	Kiukiang	Chiu-chiang
Fengtian	Shengking	Feng-t'ien	Juzijie		Chü-tzu-chieh
Fujian	Fukien	Fu-chien	Kashi	Kashgar	K'a-shih-ka-erh
Fuzhou	Foochow	Fu-chou	Kebuduo	Kobdo	K'e-pu-to
Gansu	Kansu	Kan-su	Kulun	Urga	K'u-lun
Gedake	Gartok	Ke-ta-k'e			(modern
Gongbei		Kung-pei			Ulaanbaator)
Guangdong	Kwantung	Kuang-tung	Liaoyang	Liaoyang	Liao-yang
Guangxi	Kwangsi	Kuang-hsi	Liaoning	Liaoning	Liao-ning
Guangzhou	Canton	Kuang-chou	Lüshun	Port Arthur	Lü-shun
Gucheng	Kucheng	Ku-ch'eng	Longjingcun		Lung-ching-ts'un
Guizhou	Kweichow	Kui-chou			
Haerbin	Harbin	Ha-erh-pin	Longzhou	Lungchow	Lung-chou
Hailaer	Hailar	Hai-la-erh	Manzhouli	Manchouli	Man-chou-li
Hainan	Hainan	Hai-nan	Menggu	Mongolia	Meng-ku
Hami	Hami	Ha-mi	Mengzi	Mengtsz	Meng-tzu
Hangzhou	Hangchow	Hang-chou	Nanjing	Nanking	Nan-ching
Hangkou	Hangkow	Hang-k'ou	Neimenggu	Inner Mongolia	Nei-meng-ku
Hankou	Hankow	Han-k'ou	Ningbo	Ningpo	Ning-po
Hebei	Hopeh	Ho-pei	Ningguta	Ninguta	Ning-ku-t'a

Pinyin	Traditional Spelling	Wade-Giles*	Pinyin	Traditional Spelling	Wade-Giles*
Ningxia	Ningsia	Ning-hsia	Wenzhou	Wenchow	Wen-chou
Qingdao	Tsingtao	Ch'ing-tao	Wuzhou	Wuchow	Wu-chou
Qinghai	Koko Nor	Ch'ing-hai	Wuliasutai	Uliassutai	Wu-li-ya-su-t'ai
Qiongzhou	Kiungchow	Ch'iung-chou	Wulumuqi	Urumchi	Wu-lu-mu-ch'i
Qiqihaer	Tsitsihar	Ch'i-ch'i-ha-erh	Xiamen	Amoy	Hsia-men
Sanshui	Samshui	San-shui	Xi'an	Sian	Hsi-an
Sanxing	Sansing	San-hsing	Xianggang	Hong Kong	Hsiang-kang
Shanxi	Shansi	Shan-hsi	Xigang	Sikang	Hsi-kang
Shaanxi	Shensi	Shan-hsi	Xinjiang	Sinkiang	Hsin-chiang
Shanghai	Shanghai	Shang-hai	Xinmintun	Sinmin	Hsin-min-t'un
Shashi	Shasi	Sha-shih	Xizang	Tibet	Hsi-tsang
Shenyang	Mukden	Shen-yang	Xuzhou	Hsuchow	Hsü-chou
Sichuan	Szechwan	Si-ch'uan	Yadong	Yatung	Ya-tung
Simao	Szemao	Szu-mao	Yan'an	Yenan	Yen-an
Suzhou	Soochow	Su-chou	Yantai	Chefoo	Yan-t'ai
Shantou	Swatow	Shan-t'ou	Yichang	Ichang	I-ch'ang
Tacheng	Tarbagatai	T'a-erh-pa-ha-t'ai	Yili	Ili	I-li
Tengyue	Tengyueh	T'eng-yüeh	Yingkou	Newchwang	Ying-k'ou
Tianjin	Tientsin	T'ien-chin	Yining	Kuldja	I-ning
Tieling	Tiehling	T'ieh-ling	Yunnan	Yunnan	Yun-nan
Tongjiangzi	Tungkiang	T'ung-chiang-tzu	Zhangjiakou	Kalgan	Chang-chia-k'ou
Toudaogou		T'ou-tao-kou	Zhejiang	Chekiang	Che-chiang
Tulufan	Turfan	T'u-lu-fan	Zhenjiang	Chinkiang	Chen-chiang

*Even those who use the Wade-Giles system often rely on the traditional spellings for place names. Blanks in the Traditional Spelling column indicate places for which we were unable to locate an alternate spelling. Sources for the traditional spellings: H. C. Tien, Ronald Hsia, and Peter Penn, *Gazetteer of China* (Hong Kong: Oriental Book Co., 1961); U.S. Department of the Interior, Board of Geographic Names, "Guide to Geographical Names in China," Special Publication No. 24 (Washington, DC: U.S. Government Printing Office, 1944); U.S. Department of Defense, Geographic Names Division, *Mainland China Official Standard Names,* 2 vols. (Washington, DC: U.S. Government Printing Office, 1968).

Appendix B

Pinyin Wade–Giles Conversion Table

Pinyin	Wade–Giles	*Pinyin*	Wade–Giles	*Pinyin*	Wade–Giles	*Pinyin*	Wade–Giles	*Pinyin*	Wade–Giles
a	a	che	ch'e	die	tieh	gu	ku	jing	ching
ai	ai	chen	ch'en	ding	ting	gua	kua	jiong	chiung
an	an	cheng	ch'eng	diu	tiu	guai	kuai	jiu	chiu
ang	ang	chi	ch'ih	dong	tung	guan	kuan	ju	chü
ao	ao	chong	ch'ung	dou	tou	guang	kuang	juan	chüan
ba	pa	chou	ch'ou	du	tu	gui	kuei	jue	chüeh
bai	pai	chu	ch'u	duan	tuan	gun	kun	jun	chün
ban	pan	chua	ch'ua	dui	tui	guo	kuo	ka	k'a
bang	pang	chuai	ch'uai	dun	tun	ha	ha	kai	k'ai
bao	pao	chuan	ch'uan	duo	to	hai	hai	kan	k'an
bei	pei	chuang	ch'uang	e	o, e	han	han	kang	k'ang
ben	pen	chui	ch'ui	e	eh	hang	hang	kao	k'ao
beng	peng	chun	ch'un	en	en	hao	hao	ke	k'o
bi	pi	chuo	ch'o	er	erh	he	ho	kei	k'o
bian	pien	ci	tz'u	fa	fa	hei	hei	ken	k'en
biao	piao	cong	ts'ung	fan	fan	hen	hen	keng	k'eng
bie	pieh	cou	ts'ou	fang	fang	heng	heng	kong	k'ung
bin	pin	cu	ts'u	fei	fei	hong	hung	kou	k'ou
bing	ping	cuan	ts'uan	fen	fen	hou	hou	ku	k'u
bo	po	cui	ts'ui	feng	feng	hu	hu	kua	k'ua
bu	pu	cun	ts'un	fo	fo	hua	hua	kuai	k'uai
ca	ts'a	cuo	ts'o	fou	fou	huai	huai	kuan	k'uan
cai	ts'ai	da	ta	fu	fu	huan	huan	kuang	k'uang
can	ts'an	dai	tai	ga	ka	huang	huang	kui	k'uei
cang	ts'ang	dan	tan	gai	kai	hui	hui	kun	k'un
cao	ts'ao	dang	tang	gan	kan	hun	hun	kuo	k'uo
ce	ts'e	dao	tao	gang	kang	huo	huo	la	la
cen	ts'en	de	te	gao	kao	ji	chi	lai	lai
ceng	ts'eng	dei	tci	ge	ko	jia	chia	lan	lan
cha	ch'a	den	tun	gei	kei	jian	chien	lang	lang
chai	ch'ai	deng	teng	gen	ken	jiang	chiang	lao	lao
chan	ch'an	di	ti	geng	keng	jiao	chiao	le	le
chang	ch'ang	dian	tien	gong	kung	jie	chieh	lei	lei
chao	ch'ao	diao	tiao	gou	kou	jin	chin	leng	leng

B-1

Pinyin	Wade–Giles	Pinyin	Wade–Giles	Pinyin	Wade–Giles	Pinyin	Wade–Giles	Pinyin	Wade–Giles
li	li	niang	niang	rao	jao	tai	t'ai	yi	i
lia	lia	niao	niao	re	je	tan	t'an	yin	yin
lian	lien	nie	nieh	ren	jen	tang	t'ang	ying	ying
liang	liang	nin	nin	reng	jeng	tao	t'ao	yo	yo
liao	liao	ning	ning	ri	jih	te	t'e	yong	yung
lie	lieh	niu	niu	rong	jung	tei	t'ai	you	yu
lin	lin	nong	nung	rou	jou	teng	t'eng	yu	yü
ling	ling	nou	nou	ru	ju	ti	t'i	yuan	yüan
liu	liu	nu	nu	ruan	juan	tian	t'ien	yue	yüeh
lo	lo	nü	nü	rui	jui	tiao	t'iao	yun	yün
long	lung	nuan	nuan	run	jun	tie	t'ieh	za	tsa
lou	lou	nüe	nüeh	ruo	jo	ting	t'ing	zai	tsai
lu	lu	nuo	no	sa	sa	tong	t'ung	zan	tsan
lü	lü	o	o	sai	sai	tou	t'ou	zang	tsang
luan	luan	ou	ou	san	san	tu	t'u	zao	tsao
lüe	lüeh	pa	p'a	sang	sang	tuan	t'uan	ze	tse
lun	lun	pai	p'ai	sao	sao	tui	t'ui	zei	tsei
luo	lo	pan	p'an	se	se	tun	t'un	zen	tsen
ma	ma	pang	p'ang	sen	sen	tuo	t'o	zeng	tseng
mai	mai	pao	p'ao	seng	seng	wa	wa	zha	cha
man	man	pei	p'ei	sha	sha	wai	wai	zhai	chai
mang	mang	pen	p'en	shai	shai	wan	wan	zhan	chan
mao	mao	peng	p'eng	shan	shan	wang	wang	zhang	chang
me	me	pi	P'i	shang	shang	wei	wei	zhao	chao
mei	mei	pian	p'ien	shao	shao	wen	wen	zhe	che
men	men	piao	p'iao	she	she	weng	weng	zhei	chei
meng	meng	pie	p'ieh	shei	shei	wo	wo	zhen	chen
mi	mi	pin	p'in	shen	shen	wu	wu	zheng	cheng
mian	mien	ping	p'ing	sheng	sheng	xi	hsi	zhi	chih
miao	miao	po	p'o	shi	shih	xia	hsia	zhong	chung
mie	mieh	pou	p'ou	shou	shou	xian	hsien	zhou	chou
min	min	pu	p'u	shu	shu	xiang	hsiang	zhu	chu
ming	ming	qi	ch'i	shua	shua	xiao	hsiao	zhua	chua
miu	miu	qia	ch'ia	shuai	shuai	xie	hsieh	zhuai	chuai
mo	mo	qian	ch'ien	shuan	shuan	xin	hsin	zhuan	chuan
mou	mou	qiang	ch'iang	shuang	shuang	xing	hsing	zhuang	chuang
mu	mu	qiao	ch'iao	shui	shui	xiong	hsiung	zhui	chui
na	na	qie	ch'ieh	shun	shun	xiu	hsiu	zhun	chun
nai	nai	qin	ch'in	shuo	shuo	xu	hsü	zhuo	cho
nan	nan	qing	ch'ing	si	ssu	xuan	hsüan	zi	tzu
nang	nang	qiong	ch'iung	song	sung	xue	hsüeh	zong	tsung
nao	nao	qiu	ch'iu	sou	sou	xun	hsün	zou	tsou
ne	ne	qu	ch'ü	su	su	ya	ya	zu	tsu
nei	nei	quan	ch'üan	suan	suan	yai	yai	zuan	tsuan
nen	nen	que	ch'üeh	sui	sui	yan	yen	zui	tsui
neng	neng	qun	ch'ün	sun	sun	yang	yang	zun	tsun
ni	ni	ran	jan	suo	so	yao	yao	zuo	tso
nian	nien	rang	jang	ta	t'a	ye	yeh		

Teaching References

I. General

The Cambridge History of China, in fifteen volumes, provides an excellent and extensive survey of Chinese history from 221 BC to 1982. Volume 8 pertains to the late Ming dynasty, volumes 9 to 11 to the Qing dynasty, volumes 12 and 13 to the Republican period (John K. Fairbank et al., eds.), and volumes 14 and 15 to the Communist period up to 1982 (Roderick MacFarquhar et al., eds.). Each volume is composed of focused essays on key topics in Chinese history.

Cohen, Myron L., *Asia: Case Studies in the Social Sciences* (Armonk, NY: M. E. Sharpe, 1992) provides essays on anthropology, economics, political science, and sociology concerning China, India, Indonesia, Korea, Taiwan, Pakistan, the Philippines, and Thailand. Useful for comparative purposes.

Embree, Ainslee T. and Carol Gluck, eds., *Columbia Project on Asia in the Core Curriculum: Asia in Western and World History: A Guide for Teaching* (Armonk, NY: M. E. Sharpe, 1997) provides a wide variety of essays by experts concerning Asia in Western and world history and themes in Asian history. Many essays focus on China specifically. Others focus on the other countries of Asia.

National Bureau of Statistics, *China Statistical Yearbook* (Beijing: China Statistics Press, published annually) provides comprehensive statistics compiled by the Chinese government. The volume is bilingual.

Schoppa, R. Keith. *The Columbia Guide to Modern Chinese History* (New York: Columbia University Press, 2000). Excellent general reference divided into four parts entitled "Historical Narrative," "Compendium of Key Events, Terms, Institutions, and Figures," "Resource Guide," and "Chrono-logical, Documentary and Statistical Appendices." The Resource Guide provides an extensive annotated bibliography of books, movies, and electronic resources.

II. Historical Dictionaries and Encyclopedias

Embree, Ainslie T., ed., *Encyclopedia of Asian History,* 5 vols. (New York: Charles Scribner's Sons, 1988) has entries on numerous important topics in Asian history.

Hutchings, Graham, *Modern China: A Guide to a Century of Change* (Cambridge, MA: Harvard University Press, 2001) provides numerous topical entries focusing on society, politics, and regions.

Leung, Edwin Pak-wah, ed., *Historical Dictionary of Revolutionary China, 1839–1976* (New York: Greenwood Press, 1992) provides fewer but longer entries than O'Neill (below).

Mackerras, Colin, *Modern China: A Chronology from 1842 to the Present* (San Francisco: W. H. Freeman, 1982) provides a 600-page chronology of China from 1842 to 1980 covering economics, official appointments, culture, publications, births and deaths, natural disasters, and politics.

———, *The New Cambridge Handbook of Contemporary China* (Cambridge: Cambridge University Press, 2001) comprises sections on chronology (1950–2000), politics and law, eminent contemporary figures, bibliography, foreign relations, economy, population, gazetteer, minorities, and education.

O'Neill, Hugh B., *Companion to Chinese History* (New York: Facts on File Publications, 1987) is a convenient historical dictionary.

Perkins, Dorothy, *Encyclopedia of China: The Essential Reference to China, Its History and Culture* (New York: Checkmark Books, 1999) is an excellent reference book covering a comprehensive range of topics.

Pong, David, ed. *Encyclopedia of Modern China,* 4 vols (Detroit: Gale, 2009) focuses on China since 1800 and especially since 1949.

III. Biographical Information

General: Chün-tu Hsüeh, ed., *Revolutionary Leaders of Modern China* (New York: Oxford University Press, 1971) provides short, assignable, biographic articles of key leaders of the Taiping Rebellion, the 1911 Revolution, and the Communist movement.

Choy, Lee Khoon, *Pioneers of Modern China: Understanding Inscrutable Chinese* (River Edge, New Jersey: World Scientific, 2005). Choy, a Singaporian parliamentarian, provides chapter-length biographies of key historical figures emphasizing their provincial origins. Figures include Lin Zexu, Sun Yat-sen, Chiang Kai-shek, Mao Zedong, Lin Biao, Deng Xiaoping, Jiang Zemin, Zhao Ziyang, Hu Yaobang, and Hu Jintao, among others.

Willis, John E., Jr., *Mountain of Fame: Portraits in Chinese History* (Princeton, NJ: Princeton University Press, 1994) likewise provides short biographies of Confucius, Zheng Chenggong (Koxinga), the Qianlong emperor, Hong Xiuquan the leader of the Taipings, the reformer Liang Qichao, and Mao Zedong.

For major biographical dictionaries, however, see the following:

Qing Period: Hummel, Arthur W., ed., *Eminent Chinese of the Ch'ing Period (1644–1912),* Library of Congress (Washington, DC: U.S. Government Printing Office, 1943) provides a superb biographical dictionary covering numerous important figures of the Qing dynasty. It contains over 1,000 oversized pages of entries and a thorough index.

Republican Period: Boorman, Howard L., ed., *Biographical Dictionary of Republican China,* 5 vols. (New York: Columbia University Press, 1967–70).

Communist Period: Klein, Donald W. and Anne B. Clark, eds., *Biographic Dictionary of Chinese Communism 1921–1965,* 2 vols. (Cambridge, MA: Harvard University Press, 1971).

Leung, Edwin Pak-wah, ed., *Political Leaders of Modern China: A Biographical Dictionary* (Westport, CT: Greenwood, Press, 2002), a more up-to-date but less comprehensive work than Klein and Clark's dictionary above.

IV. Supplemental Readings

Compact Readings: Cohen, Warren I., *America's Response to China: A History of Sino-American Relations,* 4th ed. (New York: Columbia University Press, 2000) starts with the treaty port system and continues through the 1990s.

————, *East Asia at the Center: Four Thousand Years of Engagement with the World* (New York: Columbia University Press, 2000) provides a comprehensive overview of the relations among China, Korea, Japan, and Southeast Asia.

Dernberger, Robert F. et al., eds., *The Chinese: Adapting the Past and Facing the Future* (Ann Arbor: University of Michigan Press, 1991) reprints short articles by numerous authors organized by such subjects as geography, ethnicity, politics, family, community, social divisions, agriculture, industry, trade, literature, and technology.

Dudden, Arthur Power, *The American Pacific: From the Old China Trade to the Present* (New York: Oxford University Press, 1992) gives an overview of U.S.-Asian relations.

Elman, Benjamin A., *A Cultural History of Modern Science in China* (Cambridge, MA: Harvard University Press, 2006) has sections on the Jesuits, the Classics, manufacturing, missionary science teachers, science textbooks, and arsenals.

Koller, John M., *Asian Philosophies,* 4th ed. (Upper Saddle River, NJ: Prentice Hall, 2002) presents concise chapters on the major Indian, Buddhist, and Chinese philosophies.

Lee Siow, Mong, *Spectrum of Chinese Culture* (Selangor Darul Ehsan, Malaysia: Pelanduk Publications, 1986) as of 2006 was in its fourth printing. It is a lavishly illustrated and wide-ranging book on Chinese culture with chapters on the family, rites of passage, mythology, festivals, the home, the arts, music, the performing arts, religion, and philosophy.

Richardson, Philip, *Economic Change in China, c. 1800–1950* (Cambridge: Cambridge University Press, 1999) offers a short economic history of China.

Smith, Richard J., *China's Cultural Heritage: The Qing Dynasty, 1644–1912* (Boulder, CO: Westview Press, 1994) includes chapters on the Qing political order, social and economic institutions, language, thought, religion, art, literature, and social life.

Stuart-Fox, Martin, *A Short History of China and Southeast Asia: Tribute, Trade, and Influence* (Crows Nest, Australia: Allen & Unwin, 2003) has chapters on China's early relations with Southeast Asia, the Mongol expansion, the tributary system, the arrival of the Europeans, World War II, the Cold War, and contemporary relations.

Fabulous Reads: Chang, Jung, *Wild Swans: Three Daughters of China* (New York: Doubleday, 1991). This autobiography is a gripping account of Chinese history from the warlord period through the early 1980s. It describes this period through the eyes of three generations of women in one family: the grandmother, who was married off as a concubine to a warlord; the mother, who joined the Communist underground as a teenager; and the daughter, who was sent to the countryside during the Cultural Revolution but managed to study in Britain afterward and write a book about it. This book is particularly good at explaining the overarching political events and showing their devastating impact on individual lives.

Anthologies of Literature and Documents: Atwill, David G. and Yurong Y. Atwill, *Sources in Chinese History: Diverse Perspectives from 1644 to the Present* (Upper Saddle Rivers, New Jersey: Prentice Hall, 2010) is an anthology of short primary documents.

Berninghausen, John and Ted Huters, eds., *Revolutionary Literature in China: An Anthology* (Armonk, NY: M. E. Sharpe, 1976) provides essays and short stories written between 1914 and 1966.

Best Chinese Stories (1949–1989) (Beijing: Panda Books, 1989) is an anthology of short stories.

Birch, Cyril, ed., *Anthology of Chinese Literature: From the Fourteenth Century to the Present Day,* vol. 2. (New York: Grove Press, 1972) provides a wide variety of short selections.

Chang, Kang-I and Haun Saussy, eds., *Women Writers of Traditional China: An Anthology of Poetry and Criticism* (Stanford, CA: Stanford University Press, 1999) includes a broad selection of the work of Qing and early-twentieth-century poetesses.

Clubb, O. Edmund, ed., *The Great Contemporary Issues: China,* The New York Times (New York: Arno Press, 1972) provides facsimiles of *New York Times* articles covering China from the 1900 Boxer Uprising through President Nixon's visit to China in 1972.

Dooling, Amy and Kristina M. Torgeson, eds., *Writing Women in Modern China: An Anthology of Women's Literature from the Early Twentieth Century* (New York: Columbia University Press, 1998) is a collection of short stories.

Ebrey, Patricia Buckley, *Chinese Civilization: A Sourcebook,* 2nd ed. (New York: Free Press, 1981) provides not only literature but a wide variety of primary sources emphasizing everyday life in China.

Hinton, Harold C., ed., *The People's Republic of China: A Documentary Survey* (Wilmington, DE: Scholarly Resources, 1980–6). Hinton compiled five massive volumes covering 1949–79 and a second series of two massive volumes covering 1979–84. They focus on government domestic, foreign, and economic policies.

Huang, Harry J., ed., *An Anthology of Chinese Short Stories* (Beijing: Foreign Languages Press, 2005) has stories categorized under the following sections: teasing in life, human harmony, loving parents, caring children, sweet romances, love in the air, missing the heart, broken strings, love bubbles, wits at risk, humans and animals, and ancient stories.

Hsu, Kai-yu and Ting Wang, eds., *Literature of the People's Republic of China* (Bloomington: Indiana University Press, 1980) is a chronologically organized anthology divided as follows: Yan'an to Beijing (1942–55), the Hundred Flowers Movement and the Anti-Rightist Campaign (1956–8), the Great Leap Forward (1959–61), the Socialist Education of the People (1962–4), the Cultural Revolution (1964–70), and the Fall of the Gang of Four (1971–).

Lau, Joseph S. M. and Howard Goldblatt, eds., *The Columbia Anthology of Modern Chinese Literature* (New York: Columbia University Press, 1995) provides a wide selection of poetry, fiction, and essays written from 1918 to 1991. (For the volume on the ancient period see Mair below.)

Lawrance, Alan, *China Since 1919—Revolution and Reform* (London: Routledge, 2004) reprints a wide variety of short documents covering the period from 1915 to 2000.

Leung, Laifong, *Morning Sun: Interviews with Chinese Writers of the Lost Generation* (Armonk, NY: M. E. Sharpe, 1994) is an anthology of interviews of the generation of the Cultural Revolution.

Mair, Victor, ed., *The Columbia Anthology of Traditional China Literature* (New York: Columbia University Press, 1994) provides a comprehensive selection of philosophy, verse, prose, and fiction from the earliest period of Chinese history through the end of the Qing dynasty. (For the volume on the modern period, see Lau above.)

Mair, Victor H., Nancy S. Steinhardt, and Paul R. Goldin, *Hawai'i Reader in Traditional Chinese Culture* (Honolulu: University of Hawai'i Press, 2005) is an anthology of articles and literary works on such topics as heaven's mandate, the various Classics, filial piety, mourning, alchemy, Gu Yanwu's phonology, the Miao albums, the Qing poet Yuan Mei, biographies of exemplary women, the revolutionary Kang Youwei, and the author Lu Xun. The last 125 pages out of nearly 700 are devoted to the Qing dynasty.

Martin, Helmut and Jeffrey Kinkley, eds., *Modern Chinese Writers: Self-Portrayals* (Armonk, NY: M. E. Sharpe, 1992) contains selections from numerous famous PRC authors on topics such as historical blunders, political victims in the 1980s, rural realities, political protest, and entertainment fiction, as well as selections from the Republican era.

Miller, Barbara Stoler, ed., *Masterworks of Asian Literature in Comparative Perspective: A Guide for Teaching* (Armonk, NY: M. E. Sharpe, 1993) gives an overview of Chinese, Indian, and Japanese literature as well guidance for choosing texts, themes, and points of comparison for Asian literature.

Owen, Stephen, ed. and trans., *An Anthology of Chinese Literature: Beginnings to 1911* (New York: W. W. Norton, 1996) has a long section consisting of literary selections from the Qing period.

Saich, Tony, ed., *The Rise to Power of the Chinese Communist Party: Documents and Analysis* (Armonk, NY: M. E. Sharpe, 1996) is a 1,504-page volume of documents covering the CCP from 1920 to 1949.

Shieh, Milton J. T., *The Kuomintang: Selected Historical Documents, 1894–1969* (Jamaica, NY: St. Johns University Press, 1970) contains a broad selection of Nationalist Party documents.

Siu, Helen F., ed., *Furrows: Peasants, Intellectuals, and the State: Stories and Histories from Modern China* (Stanford, CA: Stanford University Press, 1990) contains essays on the frailty of power, the force of dogma, and critique and ambivalence.

Wang, Jing, ed., *China's Avant-garde Fiction: An Anthology* (Durham, NC: Duke University Press, 1998) reprints multiple short stories by seven authors.

Yeh, Michelle, ed., *Anthology of Modern Chinese Poetry* (New Haven, CT: Yale University Press, 1992) offers selections from poets born from 1893 to 1963, beginning with Hu Shi.

V. Movies

The PRC currently produces beautifully filmed movies focusing particularly on the twentieth century. Search video and DVD Web sites by directors' names. In particular, look for the director Zhang Yimou, whose movie *Red Sorghum* is set dur-

ing the Sino-Japanese War of 1937–45; *To Live,* set during the period from the Great Leap Forward through the Cultural Revolution; and *Not One Less,* set during the reform period under Deng Xiaoping, depicting the impact of the reforms on the countryside. He directed the 2008 Olympic opening and closing ceremonies, which are also available on DVD.

See also the director Tian Zhuangzhuang, whose *The Blue Kite* starts in 1953 and continues through the Cultural Revolution period.

Other directors include Yin Li and Chen Kaige. See also Hou Xiaoxian of Taiwan.

VI. Web Sites

The U.S. Library of Congress maintains a comprehensive Web site at *www.loc.gov.* For a list of Web sites related to China, go to *http://www.loc.gov/rr/international/asian/china/china.html.* For a country study with encyclopedic information on China, go to *http://lcweb2.loc.gov/frd/cs/cntoc.html.* The Library of Congress also maintains an extensive collection of digitized historical photographs at *http://www.loc.gov/library/libarch-digital.html.*

http://www.princeton.edu/~classbib/ Benjamin A. Elman, professor of East Asian studies and history, maintains an excellent Web site that includes topical bibliography for books on Qing history as well as a comprehensive list of electronic resources for Chinese studies.

http://hua.umf.maine.edu/China/bibtxt2.html The University of Maine provides an extensive "Chinese Bibliography and Collections of Resources." The bibliography lists sources on a wide variety of topics and dynasties.

http://www.worldstatesmen.org/China.html provides the flags, anthems, leaders, and twentieth-century chronologies for China and its breakaway republics of Manchukuo, Inner Mongolia, East Turkestan, and Tibet.

http://www.teacheroz.com/Non_Western.htm maintains a large Web site on non-Western cultures. The section on China provides numerous maps, timelines, historical topics by dynasty, and information on current events.

http://www.asiasource.org/ is maintained by the Asia Society. Under the link entitled Country Profiles, it provides basic comparative statistics for all Asian countries.

http://www.maps-of-china.net/index.html provides maps of China by province and city.

Photo Credits

Name Index

Note: Page numbers in italics refer to tables. Page numbers in bold refer to maps. Words are alphabetized by English orthography, not by Chinese characters. Entries for Chinese persons are listed first in *pinyin*, then in complicated characters and in simplified characters if different from the complex, then in Wade-Giles. Occasionally other common spellings are listed. *Pinyin* and Wade-Giles are not provided for Korean names. Japanese names are written first in Japanese characters, and then in complicated and simplified Chinese characters when they differ from the Japanese. When people are commonly known by the non-*pinyin* spelling of their name, the pinyin is provided last. When dates of both birth and death are unknown, the century is listed.

Subject Index

Note: Page numbers in italics refer to tables. Page numbers in bold refer to maps. Words are alphabetized by English orthography, not by Chinese characters. Romanizations are always provided in *pinyin*. Wade-Giles is also provided for dynasties, kingdoms, Classical Chinese book titles, and commonly used historical terms. Chinese terms are followed by the characters, first complicated and then simplified if different, and then by the English translation.

Order *Modern China: Continuity and Change 1644 to the Present* with

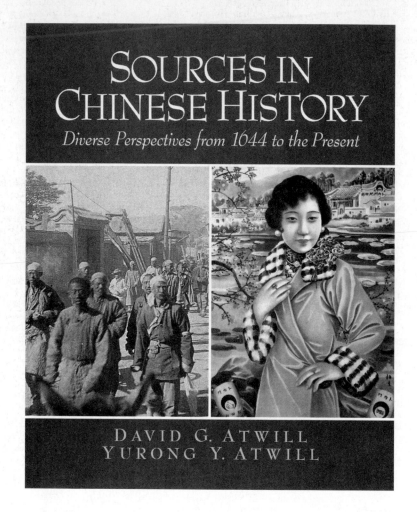

and receive a significant discount when the two titles are packaged together.

Please use ISBN 0-205-71703-9 when placing your book order.

Please contact your Pearson representative for details or go to www.pearsonhighered.com for more information.